High-Assurance Design

High-Assurance Design

Architecting Secure and Reliable Enterprise Applications

Clifford J. Berg

Addison-Wesley

Upper Saddle River, NJ • Boston• Indianapolis • San Francisco
New York • Toronto • Montreal • London • Munich • Paris • Madrid
Capetown • Sydney • Tokyo • Singapore • Mexico City

The publisher offers excellent discounts on this book when ordered in quantity for bulk purchases or special sales, which may include electronic versions and/or custom covers and content particular to your business, training goals, marketing focus, and branding interests. For more information, please contact:

U. S. Corporate and Government Sales
(800) 382-3419
corpsales@pearsontechgroup.com

For sales outside the U. S., please contact:

International Sales
international@pearsoned.com

Visit us on the Web: www.awprofessional.com

Library of Congress Cataloging-in-Publication Data:

Berg, Clifford J.

High-assurance design: architecting secure and reliable enterprise applications / Cliff Berg.

p. cm.

ISBN 0-321-37577-7

1. System design. 2. Computer architecture. I. Title.

QA76.9.S88B46 2005

004.2'2–dc22

2005018459

Pearson Education, Inc.
Rights and Contracts Department
One Lake Street
Upper Saddle River, NJ 07458

ISBN 0-321-37577-7
Text printed in the United States on recycled paper at R.R. Donnelley and Sons in Crawfordsville, Indiana.
First printing, October 2005

CONTENTS

Foreword

Security and reliability are attributes that are very difficult to attain with any nontrivial assurance. Achieving both at the same time is even more difficult.

A frequent adage is that security or reliability is only as strong as its weakest link. However, what we have today is often merely a large assortment of poorly designed and badly implemented weak links: that is, weakness in depth rather than strength in depth. As a consequence, attackers and accidental causes have a major advantage over the defenders: exploits or malfunctions of only a few weak links (or, in some cases, only one) can result in chaos, whereas the defenders typically would need to ameliorate most of the serious weak links to prevent bad effects.

There is a long history of efforts devoted to the formulation of principles, adherence to which would tend to greatly increase the security, reliability, and trustworthiness of the resulting systems. Such principles go back at least as far as the Multics development that began in 1965, which led to my 1969 paper on "The Role of Motherhood in the Pop Art of System Programming," and the fundamental 1975 paper by Jerry Saltzer and Mike Schroeder, "The Protection of Information in Computer Systems."

This book is another significant step forward in that direction. Security and reliability are both emergent properties of an entire system, network of systems, or indeed an entire enterprise. Thus, it is absolutely essential that these critical attributes be considered in the large and that system developments seek to adhere to the best principles and to consciously strive to avoid bad experiences of past efforts. We must always remember that there are no easy answers when it comes to ensuring the trustworthiness of our systems and computer-based enterprises, especially in the presence of fallible or malicious people, flawed software, and faulty hardware. Eternal vigilance is the characteristic watchword, but following the good counsel found in this book can help significantly.

Peter G. Neumann

Principal Scientist in the Principled Systems Group of the Computer Science Laboratory at SRI International

Author of *Computer-Related Risks* (Addison-Wesley), and Moderator of the ACM Risks Forum

Menlo Park, California, USA, June 2005

Acknowledgments

I am indebted to these individuals for their help in this effort: Peter Neumann (SRI International), for his generous feedback, encouragement, and deep insight. Hany Ammar (West Virginia University), for his invaluable ideas and comments on the manuscript. Elfriede Dustin (Symantec), for her helpful review of the verification and testing material. Li Gong (Sun Microsystems), for helpful feedback related to Java security. Gary Ellison (Sun Microsystems), for helpful responses to questions related to the Java security implementation, in particular the DomainCombiner. John Hughes (Entegrity) for his interest and feedback. Ronald Monzillo (Sun Microsystems) for his help in providing early access to JACC. Patrick McGowen (Microsoft) for his dialog regarding the Microsoft security model. Christopher Losa, for his ideas and valuable dialog. Eric Trautman, for his ideas and valuable dialog. Vincent Giusto, for his ideas and valuable dialog.

I am also indebted to my family, including Jacqueline and Roxanne, for their enduring support throughout this project.

About the Author

Cliff Berg has been a pioneer in the use of Internet technologies and software development methodologies to build scalable and reliable enterprise systems. Cliff was co-founder and CTO of Digital Focus,[1] a company that specializes in the use of Agile methods for developing enterprise-class systems, profitably executes most projects on a fixed-price basis, and which was voted the eighth fastest-growing company in the Washington DC metropolitan area based on five years of revenue growth. Cliff was also a member of the team that developed the feature-driven design (FDD) approach including Peter Coad,[2] Jeff DeLuca,[3] and David Anderson[4] in Singapore during the 1997-1999 period. Today Cliff is president and founder of Assured By Design, which helps enterprises incorporate assurance into their software creation processes and systems—without sacrificing agility.

In addition to assurance-based agile and FDD methodologies, Cliff is an expert in architectural quality audits and assessments in the areas of design integrity and scalability, and is a world-renowned expert on J2EE technologies. Cliff was the sole author of *Advanced Java Development for Enterprise Applications*, published by Prentice Hall and translated into Japanese, and the very first book to cover Java enterprise application architecture issues in an in-depth manner. Cliff also authored the 800-page second edition, *Advanced Java 2 Development for Enterprise Applications*, which was published under Sun Microsystems' official Java series. Cliff has written numerous articles in various magazines, and founded the Java Q&A Column in *Dr. Dobbs Journal*, which was the most popular Java technology column during the two years that Cliff wrote the column. Earlier in his career, Cliff was involved in the development of the VHDL design and simulation language, and wrote compilers for that language.

---

1 For more information on Digital Focus, see their web site at `http://www.digitalfocus.com/`.

2 For more information on Peter Coad, see `http://www.pcoad.com/`.

3 For more information on Jeff De Luca, see `http://www.nebulon.com/`.

4 For more information on David Anderson, see `http://www.agilemanagement.net/`.

PREFACE

The state of affairs in the world of custom application development is nothing short of a crisis. Consider these facts:

- The average programmer is woefully untrained in basic principles related to reliability and security.
- The tools available to programmers are woefully inadequate to expect that the average programmer can produce reliable and secure applications.
- Organizations that procure applications are woefully unaware of this state of affairs, and take far too much for granted with regard to security and reliability.

This book attempts to bring awareness of these issues to the mainstream software development community, and tries to provide developers with basic principles and techniques that can be applied to the development of business applications. Today's dynamic development environment—driven by a desire for agility, responsiveness, and low cost—can adopt these techniques to improve their processes.

Indeed, there is a substantial disconnect between the security and reliability communities and application developers. I discuss this problematic situation somewhat in the introductory chapter. Blame resides on both sides: developers do not take security and reliability seriously; and experts in security and reliability have not tried to talk in the language of developers. For example, the very term "security policy" has a significant turn-off effect on developers, as it sounds bureaucratic, lethargic, and removed from the ground-level struggles that developers face. I would propose eradicating that term and replacing it with a set of more tactical terms such as security principle, decision, rule, goal, and design. But in this book I am not going to belabor terminology.

This book is somewhat timely because the frequency of high-profile security breaches affecting the public seems to be on the increase. At the same time, companies are increasingly accountable for lapses in security and diligence.

Who This Book Is For

This is not a programming book. It has little code in it, and the patterns are abstractly expressed. It is also not a book about hacking. Hacking is inherently technology specific. This book is about fundamentals, and its intent is to help lay a foundation from which the reader can begin the journey of understanding how reliable and secure applications can be designed and implemented.

This book is written for the practicing software application architect who works in a business application design and programming environment. It is also written for lead designers and technical managers in such an environment, as well as those who manage IT organizations and are somewhat technically inclined. This book is not intended to be useful to pattern gurus, reliability experts, or security experts, because it does not meet their standards of formality.

Prerequisites

The reader is expected to have basic knowledge of the software development lifecycle as well as knowledge of software core concepts and techniques such as object-oriented design, authentication, and software testing. The book draws examples from a variety of technologies, but familiarity with the basic syntax and security models of Java and .NET will facilitate understanding of some examples.

A Crossover Book

This book addresses several topics that are traditionally treated distinctly. As a "crossover" book, it receives the scrutiny of experts in each of the various specialized areas, even though it is not written for them. It will be compared with specialized books in those fields, and found to be very different—but the differences are for good reason.

This book does not focus on one particular technical area. This is deliberate. In my work I have found that problems related to reliability and security tend to fall all over a range of issues of different kinds. Application software architects do not have time to become experts in each area. This book attempts to draw attention to those areas that I have found to be problematic in many applications. Thus, this book is highly cross-disciplinary by its very nature. Because of this book's intended audience, and because of the integrative nature of the content of this book, coverage of topics is not "canonical" in a traditional sense; rather, coverage is concise so as to not overburden the intended type of reader—who tends to be a very busy deadline-driven and results-oriented person—and coverage attempts to reveal the synergy between the topics that are covered.

The result is a kind of "handbook" format, tailored to the vocabulary and knowledge of the typical software project architect. Those wanting a more formal or complete treatment should refer to specialized texts in the separate subjects of reliability and security. The purpose of this book is therefore not to teach one how to design an arbitrarily reliable or secure system; rather, it is to help architects of critical business applications learn how to make their applications meet the reliability and security needs of business. Those who need to build the very most reliable or secure systems such as spacecraft, operating systems, nuclear systems, etc., must have expert level knowledge and the budget to go with it, and those communities need to employ experts in the various areas and utilize very deliberate methodologies that include detailed modeling, simulation, and comprehensive quality control. Most business application projects—even enterprise-level projects—do not have the budget or time for such an approach.

The design principles and patterns in this book are based on actual usage, and no attempt has been made to distill them into an abstract minimal subset. Thus, while the principles are not necessarily orthogonal, and the patterns are not necessarily minimally composed, they are nevertheless practical and represent real-world situations. Indeed, all of the patterns in this book have been used in real-world business applications.

The patterns shown here are not always structural, but more frequently are temporal and focus on activities and relationships. Thus, *structural issues that impact reusability, such as inheritance, are not my primary concern.* In this book, I am more concerned with accessibility, closure, and completeness of function.

Diagram Syntax

The diagrams in the book use Universal Modeling Language (UML) syntax. However, in many cases UML syntax is "bent" or extended in order to be able to combine information of different kinds on a single diagram, or to represent new concepts. Thus, expect some informality in the diagrams. Despite this informality, an effort was made to achieve precision and clarity. One type of extension is noteworthy: In order to be able to represent invocation (from which there is a return) and serial flow of control (from which there is no return) within a single diagram, solid-headed arrows are used for the former, and open-headed arrows are used for the latter.

What Is Not Covered

This book discusses methodological principles related to security and reliability, but it does not present a methodology. The assumption is that most businesses choose application development methodologies for other reasons, and merely need guidance about how to tweak those methodologies so that their applications can be more reliable and more secure. The book does not discuss scalability and performance, because while these are assurance topics, there are ample sources on these topics. The book also does not discuss infrastructure: this is a book about application design, and there are many sources that discuss infrastructure.

Cliff Berg

CHAPTER 1

INTRODUCTION

"Everything is broken." –Bob Dylan

Since the mid-1990s, the author of this book has provided design review and consulting to a wide range of companies that build Web and object-oriented technology systems. Much of the demand for that work has resulted from situations in which existing systems went awry, failed a security audit, or became less reliable over time instead of more reliable, and the builders or procurers of those systems wanted to know why. Other aspects of the author's work have involved design review of the planned architecture of systems that were in the early stages of design. The author's work, therefore, has focused largely on providing technical quality auditing, either for existing systems that had problems or for contemplated systems in order to prevent problems.

This work has provided the author with a broad awareness of the regrettably poor state of affairs with the design of the majority of systems that use Web or object-oriented technology. All of us have experienced strange or suspect behavior when using Web sites. One generally trusts that the main functions of a Web site work well, but it is often the case that if you do something a little bit out of the norm, something will go wrong—sometimes terribly wrong. And surely one does not have to make the point that the software products industry has shown itself incapable of producing secure software, and custom-built software is in an even worse state. As a whole, the software built by most organizations for their own use is both insecure and fragile.

As a whole, the software built by most organizations for their own use is both insecure and fragile.

End users often assume that an unreliable system results from either operator errors or application logic "bugs." However, that perception is very skewed. Table 1.1 shows the historical breakdown of the causes of failure of one fairly typical system that was examined.

Table 1.1 Causes of Application Software Failure

Cause of Failure	% of All Causes
Corrupt or late data from external sources	32
Technical "glitches" (explained below)	41
Business rule errors	9
Data entry, configuration, or other operational error	18

As can be seen from the table, most failures in this system resulted from various and sundry technical "glitches"—situations where the software designer might have said, "That is unlikely to happen," and the support staff later said, "We'll never be able to reproduce that." This category also includes those errors that cannot be explained by the technical staff.

External sources and systems were another major source of problems, and this can be especially problematic because one usually has little control over such external components. Human error was another major source of problems—either at an operator level or at a user level. Finally, business rule errors—errors of application logic—accounted for only 9% of all failures—*yet this is the area in which requirements analysts generally focus most of their attention!* In my experience, this breakdown is more or less typical, depending on the kind of system.

> "Unlikely things happen all the time. Every time a hand of poker is dealt out, the exact constitution of the hands involved is extremely unlikely. The exact position of the molecules in this room at the present time is an astronomically unlikely arrangement."
> —Robert Koons, Associate Professor of Philosophy, University of Texas, Austin

Users will even tolerate unreliable systems, to a point, if they understand the sources of unreliability or if they feel that the problems are transparent and can be worked around. Users become most anxious when the cause of a problem is unknown and must always be figured out by technical experts, and chronic problems eventually lead the users to conclude that the "experts" are incompetent. Further, in a business setting, an unresolved situation quickly becomes a crisis that escalates to upper management. Therefore, *problem transparency is as important as reliability.* Unfortunately, system requirements rarely specify this crucial aspect (i.e., the manner or detail of diagnostic response when something goes wrong). Thus, because there are no *requirements* for what information should be captured when the system fails, error reporting gets little attention by programmers who are almost always in a great hurry to meet a deadline, leading to poorly worded error messages that give no information about what really went wrong or what the user should do; and because the error response requirements are not specified, they are not included in a test plan. The result is a system that causes users tremendous frustration when the inevitable happens: Something goes wrong.

> Problem transparency is as important as reliability.

1.1 The Technical Problem Areas

One problem with today's technologies is that they rely on the interconnection of many interoperating components, such as Web servers, application servers, databases, security policy servers, user directories, mainframes, custom applications, Web services, and so on. Each of these is deployed independently and therefore has its own configuration and deployment mechanism—and its own maintenance schedule. Thus, even if each component is fairly reliable, when you put all these together, the chance that *something* will go wrong on any given day is fairly high. In this kind of environment, applications need to be *resilient* to failure, because periodic failure is normal.

Applications built in-house tend to be anything but resilient. It has been the author's experience that the great majority of custom-developed applications have problems in many of these areas:

Sound Transactions

- The architecture is usually inadequately transaction-centric. A transaction-centric architecture is important if the system is to be scalable, robust, and secure. It does not take long to uncover transactional integrity errors in most multi-user applications—problems that manifest themselves infrequently but result in incorrect database data or anomalous behavior.
- Interfaces to non-database external systems, such as third-party application servers, LDAP, and Web services, are seldom transactionally sound.

Security

- The security features are seldom adequate for anything but a limited non-malicious user community.
- Authorization rules are very typically interspersed throughout business logic. That makes it impossible for the authorization rules to be audited and validated or to provide assurance that all required authorization rules are actually implemented (and implemented correctly).
- Systems are typically devoid of strongly enforced security layer concepts and therefore are vulnerable to security holes resulting from potential programmer errors at any level.
- Systems typically employ a very large number (often ten or more) of internal credentials for accessing back-end or host resources, including Web server PKI keys, application server connection and process owner

passwords, database passwords, and administrator passwords for the application, directory store, policy server, and host operating systems and various keystores. In spite of this, there is often no plan for managing and securing these aside from trusting it all to a single set of individuals.

Sound Web Applications

- Request dispatching and session management frameworks are often more complex than what is needed, especially if they are home-grown. This can impact scalability, performance, and maintainability.
- Web applications are often designed in such a way that if a user performs more than one task at a time (for example, in different browser windows), incorrect results can occur. This is a surprisingly common design flaw that is rarely tested.

Sound GUI Applications

- Graphic user interfaces (GUIs) are almost never designed correctly. Many designs attempt to follow a "model-view-controller" design, but in fact depart substantially from a core requirement of that design pattern—namely that there be a single source (the "model") for all GUI updates. This can result in GUIs that show the wrong data if multiple users access the same data in a database or if the same data appears on multiple parts of the GUI.
- Custom-built GUIs (and many product-based GUIs) often implement database interaction incorrectly. Established design patterns such as "optimistic concurrency control" are necessary but are often not used due to the inexperience of local programming teams.

Consideration of Failure Modes

- The required behavior of the system when things go wrong is rarely specified, so failure logic is rarely designed and is almost never tested for. Yet, testing under failure conditions is extremely important to avoid crisis-level problems during operation.

Sound Database Integration

- Most systems have a persistence (database access) layer, and this layer continues to present a substantial design and maintainability problem. Relational databases mate very poorly to object-oriented applications, so programmers have great difficulty building a quality persistence layer. There are tools to assist the process, but they often can map in only one direction, or cannot handle complex schema. The result is that many persistence layers have internal problems that go undetected.

These are critical areas. One would expect that organizations that use technology to perform mission-critical functions would ensure that those systems are designed and built without problems such as those listed previously. Yet this is not true at all. Rather, it is the case that most organizations expect that these technologies are inherently safe to use, and little attention is given to vetting the design against these potential problem areas until problems actually arise—when fixes are costly or impossible. Jack Ganssle, author of *The Art of Designing Embedded Systems*, has said,

> *"I collect software disasters and have files bulging with examples that all show similar patterns. Inadequate testing, uninspected code, short-cutting the design phase, lousy exception handlers, and insane schedules are probably responsible for 80% of the crashes. We all know these things, yet seem unable to benefit from this knowledge."*[1]

As a result, organizations expend a huge amount (1) employing workarounds to deal with the various sources of unreliability, (2) maintaining systems that are expensive to maintain due to their many workarounds and design flaws, and (3) employing a cadre of irreplaceable "guru" staff that understands the design flaws and workarounds.

The only organizations that rise above this are those that have huge resources, have gone through many lifecycles of pain and have learned the hard way, and for which reliability is core to their business and shows up in a measurable way against the bottom line.

1.2 It's the Process

The core of the problem is that the predominant software development methodologies do not provide guidance with regard to *where an organization should expend its efforts*. Business information technology applications cannot be built using the sure and methodical processes used to build spacecraft, nuclear reactors, operating systems, and communications systems. Business applications need to be built quickly and cheaply. It is, therefore, not practical to use a thorough and canonical process for every system and every component in a system. Yet, these applications also need to be reasonably reliable and secure. A smart organization figures out how to *focus its efforts where it matters*. In practical terms, this means that part of the planning and design of a system needs to include identifying which components are critical and need to be thoroughly designed and tested and which others can be implemented in a more lax manner. *Different processes* and *different levels of expertise* might need to be used for these different components. It has also been argued that the very personalities of the programmers who work on architecture-intensive infrastructure components should be different from those who work on business logic. [2]

Therefore, the problem has to do with methodology more than it has to do with technology. However, the problems manifest themselves in terms of technology. For example, a design flaw may result in inconsistent transactions, so the cause appears to be that a correct transaction design pattern was not used. Yet the root causes might be that there is no clearly delineated transactional core for the system, that a DBA was not employed to review the design of that core, and that the core was not thoroughly tested under various concurrent usage conditions. Another problem is that the skill level to design correct

A smart organization figures out how to focus its efforts where it matters.

multi-user applications is significantly higher than the experience and training level of most programmers, yet this distinction is not recognized in most application programming environments, and nowadays most organizations do little to train their programmers in multi-user application design.[1]

The educational system also needs to be more proactive. For example, developers almost always lack training in software security, and many still emerge from their academic careers with a hacker mentality. Developers need to consider security and reliability as *integral aspects* of object-oriented design—not as added features—and this requires training that should occur before developers enter the workforce. The academic and research communities have done an excellent job of providing the required technical knowledge base but have done a poor job of integrating that information with development methodologies or of disseminating that information to the practitioner community: e.g., most security books for programmers focus on what *not to do* (in effect, "anti-patterns"), instead of *what to do* (i.e., patterns). In Bertrand Meyer's terminology, such negative advice often has the characteristics of "advisory principles," which, in his words, "are fraught with the risk of uselessness." [3]

Security and reliability can—and should—be addressed as part of the normal design of real-world application software.

1.3 Design Assurance

As it turns out, the characteristics an application needs in order to be secure are largely the same as those needed in order to be reliable [4], so security and reliability can—and should—be addressed as part of the normal design of real-world application software.

This book makes an attempt to integrate the concepts of secure design with concepts for reliable design and present that information in a form that is accessible to mainstream business application architects, technical leads, and project managers. Comprehensive assurance with regard to an application's design

1 As part of its Secure Computing initiative, Microsoft has given every Windows developer and tester training in secure design and test practices, including the use of fault injection and threat analysis.

for reliability, security, and performance is referred to as *design assurance*. [5, 6] Toward that end, this book interprets many design principles that have been developed by the security community (for example, [7, 8, 9, 10, 11, 12]) into a form that is more understandable to and usable by mainstream software architects. Principles for reliable design are provided and are related back to the security principles. This is done with the recognition that agility is key during business application development, and business application developers are not afforded the time to develop detailed plans and analyses for much of their work. Performance and scalability are not covered in this book because there is so much developer-focused literature already on those subjects.

Integrating these areas is not easy, because application design, reliability design, and security design are traditionally very disjointed subject areas. It was also a goal to keep the text as concise as possible, so as to facilitate the use of this book as a "handbook" rather than a comprehensive text. For the reader who is interested in an in-depth treatment of any of the separate areas of reliability, security, or application architecture, ample references are provided.

This book does not champion a particular methodology. Methodological requirements for high-assurance are addressed, but a prescriptive approach for meeting those methodological requirements is not provided. Thus, the material here applies to a variety of projects, from agile development projects to projects that utilize formal methods.

The processing patterns that are defined in this book are described as abstractly as possible, primarily using Universal Modeling Language (UML) [13] activity diagrams (sometimes a hybrid diagram is used for conciseness). This is done with the hope of making the patterns more directly usable for mapping them to existing designs. The pattern descriptions are as succinct as possible and are written using layman's terminology to make them more accessible to readers who are not pattern aficionados.

Finally, this book is about software design. It does not address infrastructure, disaster recovery, platforms, or technologies. There are many sources of information about designing and deploying reliable, secure, and scalable infrastructure using ever-changing technologies, so the focus here is strictly on fundamental patterns and principles related to application design.

1.4 Roadmap

This book is focused primarily on design. It is not a programming book, but programmer-related issues are covered, especially because the line between programming and design is blurry today. Process issues are also discussed, including methodological issues.

The instructional material is centered around a set of design principles. These principles form the backbone of the book. The principles are augmented by logical design patterns that provide guidance to designers for incorporating the principles into their designs. The principles, design patterns, and other material roughly fall into the categories of requirements specification, design specification and verification, design, and methodology.

The instructional material is accompanied by exercises at the end of each chapter to help the reader test his or her understanding of the material. At the end of the instructional material, several case studies are presented. These were chosen because of their representative character.

Figure 1.1 shows how this book's material can be applied during a software development project. In Figure 1.1, the book's content is depicted on the left, broken down into four categories. Requirements analysts may use this book to help them identify the kinds of assurance requirements that are relevant to their project. Designers and architects may use this book as a source of design principles to remind them of important issues with respect to assurance. The design patterns can be used as a basis for solving some of the harder design problems in a robust way that includes considerations for security and reliability. Programmers may use this book to check that their implementation adheres to the intended principles and patterns. Project managers can use this book to help them identify risks, and to help them in their discussions with project architects and in developing assurance-related requirements. Project managers can also use this book to help them fine-tune their project's methodology in order to provide a more assurance-conscious process. Quality assurance and testing professionals can use this book to help them understand assurance requirements.

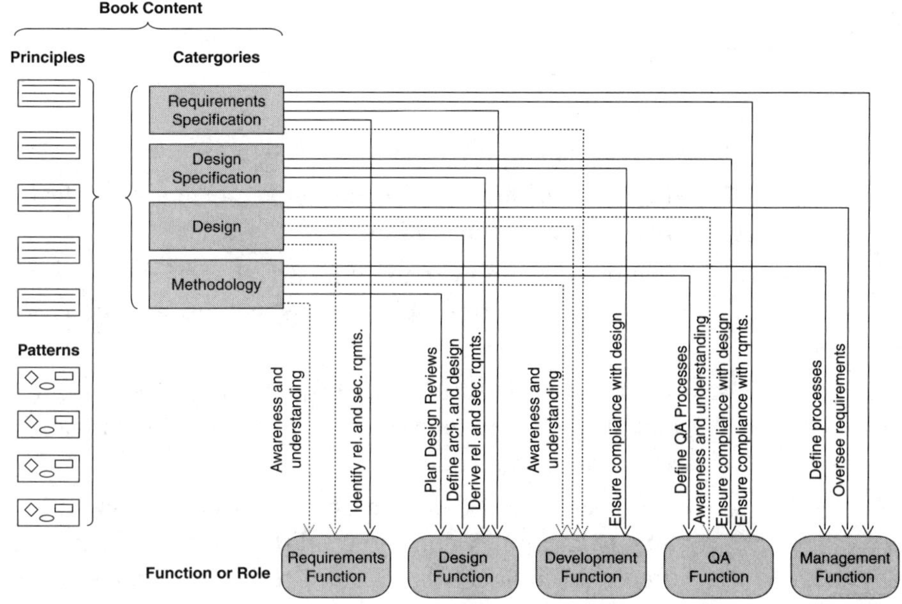

Figure 1.1
Roadmap.

1.5 Summary

Software errors in complex applications manifest as a variety of technical problems that are often difficult to reproduce. Because modern applications are often constructed by the assembly of components across multiple computers and networks, applications must be designed to be resilient to failure and unavailability.

Today's software developers are often untrained in developing applications that need to be secure and reliable. Too little attention is paid to these aspects, when these are, in fact, important areas for most business applications.

The software development processes used in most organizations do not adequately address assurance. Organizations need to differentiate different software components based on risk, and focus their quality efforts where it matters. Only then can sufficient resources be made available to meet the assurance goals of businesses in a competitive environment.

1.6 Exercises

1. List and explain the aspects of design assurance.
2. What kind of testing is important to prevent crisis-level problems during operation?
3. If an organization cannot exhaustively test every component, where should it focus its most strenuous efforts?
4. True of false: Business logic errors tend to account for most of the operational failures that occur in complex multi-user applications?
5. Interfaces to non-database external systems, such as third-party application servers, LDAP, and Web services, often tend to have what kind of technical problem?
6. Explain why problem transparency to the end user is important when a failure occurs.
7. Identify at least one reason why modern computing applications operating in complex organizational environments might be especially prone to occasional system failure compared to older systems.

Answers and hints for these exercises can be found at `http://www.assuredbydesign.com/haa/`.

CHAPTER 2

ASSURANCE REQUIREMENTS

"...don't ask me no questions now baby, and I, I won't tell you no lies."–from "Ask Me No Questions" by B.B. King and Leon Russell

In a design meeting some years back, the author of this book was considering the security vulnerabilities in a design that was being presented and mentally took a step back and asked the project architect, "If the client had told you that this system needs to be secure against malicious outside users, would you design it differently?" He thought for a moment, and one could see him redesigning the entire system in his head. He then sketched out an entirely different design that was based on layers of resources.

The point is that the client had not articulated a requirement for security, but the requirement was there. The client did not understand security, and it was clear that our requirements team had not done a sufficiently thorough job of extracting the requirements out of them. Further, the client viewed security as part of the plumbing, and expected it to exist as by default.

The same is true of other kinds of reliability, performance, and "failure-response" requirements, which collectively are also often referred to as "non-functional requirements." That term "functional requirement" is somewhat misleading because every requirement is functional from someone's perspective, whether it is the end user or the system operator. The term "assurance requirement" speaks more truthfully to the goal of assuring that business objectives are met over the range of things that can happen or "mishappen." In addition, one must be cognizant of who is accountable for losses when a failure occurs. Table 2.1 summarizes these four aspects of system assurance.

Table 2.1 Assurance Categories

Assurance Category	Description
Reliability	Technical assurance that the system will faithfully provide access to correct business functionality, and not lose data, inhibit access, permit inappropriate access, perform functions incorrectly, or otherwise fail.
Performance	Technical assurance that the system will operate reliably and responsively and with sufficient throughput over the required range of load.
Failure Response	Technical assurance that the overall system will respond in an appropriate manner when a component failure of any kind occurs, to enable: ■ Recovery and continued operation to the extent possible ■ Containment ■ Immediate or early identification of the failure and traceability to its source and cause ■ Notification of response personnel ■ Informative response to the user
Accountability	Contractual, legal, or regulatory responsibility for costs or losses incurred by a failure.

Reliability requirements specify the range of conditions over which failures of specific kinds should not occur—*including failures related to security*. For example, a failure due to a software virus[1] is still a reliability failure. [1] Security is so important in its own right, however, that it is usually identified separately, and this book often refers to "reliability and security" even though reliability encompasses security. Hopefully the context always makes the usage clear.

Performance requirements specify the range of scaling over which the system should meet specified throughput and response time criteria, and this also includes security considerations because scaling and performance limits can affect security. Failure-response requirements specify the desired system behavior when failures *do* occur—again, including security, but from the perspective of how the system responds when a security-related failure occurs.

Failure-response requirements specify the desired system behavior when failures occur.

The issue of accountability is not a technical issue, but it must be understood by the technical team because it can be an important consideration in deciding whether particular technical assurance mechanisms are needed: For example, there might be no need to incorporate user-level authorization for partner organizations if each organization assumes full responsibility for all actions of its users. In that case, authorization at the organization level might be sufficient. Thus, understanding accountability might eliminate some technical requirements. Performance and reliability accountability, as well as who must respond to a failure, is often spelled out in a service-level agreement (SLA). Accountability for security failures is often left unaddressed, but should also be included.

Understanding accountability might eliminate some technical requirements.

Non-technical users and inexperienced procurers of systems usually assume that reliability, performance, and failure-response requirements are implicit, but if these requirements are not written down at some point, they will not be accounted for in the design, and they will not be tested for. Therefore, it is critical

---

[1] A *virus* is a trojan horse program that is distributed via the distribution of a corrupted host program. Trojan horse programs are discussed in Section 5.1.21, "Embedded Attack."

that the design team assist the requirements team in documenting all reliability, performance, and failure-response requirements.

Non-technical users and inexperienced procurers of systems usually assume that reliability, performance, and failure-response requirements are implicit.

This book concentrates on the reliability and failure-response aspects of system assurance, and only as it pertains to software design. There are many sources that provide methodologies and technical guidance for building in the required performance, and there is also a great deal of information available about fault-tolerant clustering and hardware. The issue of accountability is chiefly non-technical and this is a technical book, so accountability issues are not covered.

2.1 Security Requirements

From a user's perspective, security requirements can generally be grouped into the following two categories: (1) requirements that *limit* what users can *do*, and (2) requirements that specify what the system should *do* or provide certain things that users can *do*. User-limiting requirements include things such as specifying that a user without a password cannot log into the system or that a user without a certain role cannot perform a certain business function. These limiting requirements can be considered reliability requirements because they require that one can rely on the system to protect itself and disallow certain kinds of threats and security mishaps.

A security requirement is either *user-enabling* or *user-limiting*.

Requirements that specify things that the system or users can do, such as the ability to delegate a function to another user, or the ability to log all transactions, can generally be thought of as security "features." These include failure-response requirements related to security because they specify what the system should do *if a security failure occurs*. For example, there might be a requirement that a security administrator is paged whenever a security risk event occurs. Such a feature must, of course, have its own reliability requirements.

Security requirements generally pertain to the generic aspects listed in Table 2.2.

Table 2.2 Generic Security Aspects

Confidentiality or anonymity	A communication cannot be observed, deciphered, or a participant identified, or any combination of these. Taken together, these are aspects of privacy.
Authentication	A participant, asserted identity, or some value is unambiguously proved to be true or valid.
Proof of action	An action can be shown to have occurred, in some manner or at some time. This is commonly referred to as *non-repudiation*.
Protection against modification	A computing base, set of information, or infrastructure is protected against malicious (or accidental) modification or intrusion. This is commonly referred to as *integrity*.
Detection and response	A security failure will be detected and responded to. This is commonly referred to as *intrusion detection*.
Management	Security aspects of an application will have certain manageability characteristics.

Security requirements of any kind are traditionally very hard to financially justify in application development budgets. Most users think of security as a necessary evil and try to get along without it as long as they can. Business users also tend to view security as an infrastructure requirement that should not burden their application.

Security does affect business plans, however—often too late. A security audit can reveal that an application's internal design is fundamentally insecure, requiring a large expense to retroactively repair the structural weaknesses. A result such as that can cause pending financing or merger plans to fall through if the technology is strategic.

Some courts and regulators have recently decided that system providers *may be liable for losses due to security vulnerabilities*. For example, in April 2004, the company that operates the

Web site for music retailer Tower Records settled complaints by Federal Trade Commission (FTC) regulators that the company allowed hackers in 2002 to steal personal information about thousands of Tower's online customers. The agreement reached with FTC regulators stated that a company must maintain a "reasonably designed" system to assure the security of customers to the Web site and employ outside consultants every two years over ten years to test the site's security. Howard Beales, director of the FTC's Bureau of Consumer Protection, was also quoted as saying, "Companies must have reasonable procedures in place to make sure that *changes do not create new vulnerabilities*" (italics added).

The last part is especially significant. If this legal theory prevails, it means that a user of a software system has the right to expect that the provider of the system has processes in place to ensure the *continued* security of its technology whenever changes have been made to the system.

On top of this rising tide of legal liability, the U.S. Sarbanes-Oxley[2] bill increases the expectations of technical diligence and accountability for U.S. corporations. American companies are now expected to have full control, security, accuracy, and auditability of their information—or be in violation of the law, with potential criminal penalties for executives who have to sign off on the existence of appropriate internal controls.

> FTC regulators have ruled that users of a software system have a right to expect that there are processes in place to ensure the *continued* security of the system, whenever upgrades have been made to the system by its provider.

The ramification of all this for system builders is that their software development and maintenance processes must include security in their requirements and perform *continual verification of security requirements as new versions of the system are released*—or be liable for losses.

2 The text of the law can be found online at `http://frwebgate.access.gpo.gov/cgi-bin/getdoc.cgi?dbname=107_cong_bills&docid=f:h3763enr.tst.pdf`. See also Section 3.3, "Defining and Verifying Architectural Rules."

This means that there must be an appropriately complete security test plan that is exercised with each release. To make this feasible, automation must be employed to the extent possible. For example, the regression test suite should include tests that verify that all access control rules are upheld. To not have such a test suite is to risk hugely costly or embarrassing failures, due to the action of a single programmer, as a result of routine maintenance. Widely reported examples of this include Barclays Bank [2] and the Cahoot online banking system. [3] ♦

♦ See also Section 3.3, "Defining and Verifying Architectural Rules."

Aside from expressing authorization rules, users find it hard to define their expectations with regard to security because they do not understand the issues, and even those who understand security find it hard to quantify risk and assign an expected dollar value to it. There are risk-evaluation methodologies, for example, DREAD [4], but they are seldom used by builders of custom applications because of lack of training and also because users must be educated about security, and forcing a methodology on them requiring that they produce estimates of the value of organizational assets is probably too much to expect of them in today's fast-paced world.

Despite these challenges, it is important that security goals are not over-simplified, for example, by saying that "the system should be secure." No system can be completely "secure": Security is relative. One must define a level of security to strive for and find a way to be specific about deciding if that "level" is being maintained. That way, the technical team will be able to define concrete objectives and work toward those.

One way to define a security level is to specify a set of procedures that evaluate security by assessing compliance with a standard or set of criteria. For example, a project may require a security audit or assessment by an independent group or company. That is generally a good approach for a typical organization that wants to make sure that its systems are secure. Note that the assessment can be based on static criteria (such as what features the application has), or it can be based on a dynamic process, such as security penetration attempts.

> One way to define a security level is to specify a set of procedures that assess security compliance.

Some industries promote security certification (certification testing is discussed in Section 3.2.2, "Testing"), which provides a well-defined, tiered level of assurance based on analysis and possibly testing by an independent party according to standard criteria. For example, the banking industry supports the BITS [5] certification process, the accounting industry supports the WebTrust system [6], and many security products have undergone various levels of Common Criteria [7] certification. See also [8], [9] and [10], although the last is a little dated. See [11] (p. 424 ff.) for a discussion of reliability certification.

An important advantage of certification or any kind of formal assessment is that you find out up front what the criteria are. That gives the development team a list of technical requirements that they can build to and strive for. Even if you do not plan to undergo certification, it is useful to look at the certification criteria that are used by various certification standards. The BITS criteria can be found on the BITS Web site (`http://www.bitsinfo.org`). For most business applications, it is not feasible to take the formal approach that a certification organization would take, but it is important to identify security requirements that you feel might be overlooked if they are not spelled out, and formal certification criteria can serve as a guide and starting point for this thought process.

As an example, a project developing an externally-facing Web application might specify the security requirements shown in Table 2.3. It is up to the technical project manager and application architect to find ways to implement these requirements.

Table 2.3 Sample Security Requirements for an Externally Facing Web Application

Adhere to *accepted* "best practices" for security

- Adhere to standard best practices with regard to HTTP services, including input validation and scanning for scripts or URLs embedded in input, not trusting hidden tags, and so on.[3]

3 The Open Web Application Security Project (OWASP) can be found at http://www.owasp.org/. Their "top ten" list can be found there under /documentation/topten.

Auditable and testable authorization rules

- Ensure that all authorization rules specifying business policy with regard to who is allowed to do what within the application are clearly identifiable within the application and can be easily and automatically tabulated in an understandable format that the requirements team (or a security auditor) can review and validate on a regular basis.

Proof that as-built = as-designed

- Provide a process for verifying that code enhancements and maintenance do not compromise the intended and documented design of the application, especially with regard to design aspects on which security depends.

Will pass annual audit

- The security auditor must understand the level of security that is desired—i.e., what is a "reasonable level" for the application. Audit techniques can be adjusted accordingly. This audit criteria must be provided during this project's design phase.

Will have low administrative costs

- The application should not impose a large and growing burden on system operators to maintain business rules, security policy, application-level access rights, and other elements that should be borne by the application and the application call center.

Will not require trust to be concentrated in a single administrator

- The roles of system administrator and application security administrator should be distinct, and the system administrator should not be capable of accessing the contents of sensitive user data.
- Sensitive functions, such as user creation and changes in user access rights, should require a series of actions by different individuals, and the system administrator or security administrator should not be capable of bypassing these and other safeguards without the cooperation or knowledge of others.

Will not require all developers and support programmers to understand security

- Aspects of the system design that relate to security should be separated from the business application code into distinct layers or component types so that most maintenance programmers do not have to understand all aspects in order to perform maintenance.
- Portions of the code that implement security-related aspects of the system design should be maintained by and only be modifiable by a smaller group of programmers who are trained in the security design.

These requirements provide the technical design team with some objectives that they can use to assess whether their design accomplishes the security expectations of the users and the business as a whole.

2.1.1 Methodology-Based Requirements

Methodology-based requirements are those which are difficult to explain to a non-technical requirements team but are nevertheless judged by the technical team to be important for achieving the business objectives, and they are reusable–i.e., they would apply to any similar project.

For example, a requirement that technical design documents are kept in sync with the as-built system would be a methodology-based requirement. Such a requirement may be important for making it possible to achieve security objectives, but the business value of updating a document is hard to explain to end users–especially when it competes with demands for more functionality.

Requirements of this kind *need to be incorporated into the development methodology* so that they become part of the development process. That is the only way to ensure that they are not traded for business features. It is then up to the project manager and system architect to decide what methodology-based requirements to enforce, based on their understanding of the complete business and technical issues and their mutual desire to deliver the business objectives.

2.2 Writing Reliability Requirements

Software reliability requirements need to be authored by the requirements team, but in doing so they can be expected to lean heavily on the technical design team. This is because reliability requirements must be expressed as service levels for various aspects of the system–some technical, and some in terms of the net effect on business services. For example, reliability can specify that the system will operate correctly 99% of the time, but "correctly" must be defined, and correct operation might include tasks that do not complete due to certain technical circumstances, such as incorrect input data. Thus, it is not a trivial matter to codify service-level requirements, and a collaborative effort between the requirements team and the technical design team is usually required.

2.2.1 Start with Business Objectives

Requirements are nothing more than detailed business objectives. It is useful to group business objectives according their timeframe for realization. For example, objectives could be divided into short-term, mid-term, and long-term objectives. This somewhat decouples the planning of tasks or features associated with each timeframe.

THE PROBLEM WITH PRIORITY-BASED TASK SCHEDULING

After requirements have been defined, the design team can develop a design and a task list for implementing the design or feature set. The tasks can then be scheduled based on priorities and task dependencies. When performing this priority-based scheduling, *it is important to resist mixing tasks associated with objectives of different timeframes.* For example, a mid-term objective might require the completion of *many* interdependent tasks before it provides tangible value, so it is not feasible to prioritize those tasks individually along with short-term tasks because each mid-term task does not have business value by itself and will always be at the lowest priority when compared with any given short-term task that provides immediate incremental business value.

Short-term tasks are normally each associated with a single tactical business objective, although several tasks could share an objective. For example, a pair of bug fix tasks could together remedy a single operational issue that has been a problem for the business. Longer-term objectives normally require multiple tasks because longer-range objectives are normally more complex and require broader changes. Aspects of a design that affect reliability and security often require a set of long-term objectives.

When the set of objectives has been defined, these can be broken into finer detail, yielding a hierarchical list of requirements. The requirements can then be prioritized according to the specific issues that they address.

2.2.2 Reliability Categories

Software reliability objectives generally fall into the categories discussed here:

Correct core processing—Correct identification and implementation of business rules. For example, updates to the database are consistent with the user interface display and with business rules.

System availability—Operation without catastrophic software failures that make important application(s) unavailable.

Fault tolerance—The ability to continue performing unrelated functions when failures in certain application areas occur.

A *recoverable error* is one for which a workaround or repair is found within an acceptable period of time. For example, reliability for core processing, availability, and fault tolerance could be expressed as follows:[4]

If a recoverable error is one for which a workaround is found within two hours, there must be:

- No *recoverable* errors in 95% of all days within a one-year period.
- No *unrecoverable* errors during the same period.

The reliability requirements should specify the assumptions about the system's usage and service levels, such as the average and peak numbers of users, average and peak request rates, other concurrent applications running on the system, time of day, and so on. For example:

4 A comprehensive methodology for defining availability is provided in [12], page 217.

- Up to 200 users can access, use, and enter data via the user interface concurrently, working according to the usage profile developed by the requirements team and included in the appendix to these requirements.
- The application will operate with the operating system and hardware requirements specified in the system configuration design, or better.
- The application will have exclusive use of the application server and share the database with only two other applications, namely....
- The application will be tested and developed according to the procedures defined in the Quality Assurance and Testing Guide.
- The application will be deployed according to the procedures defined by the Deployment Guide.
- The computing systems will be operated according to the procedures defined in the Operations Guide.

2.2.3 Adding Derived Requirements That Affect Reliability

Table 2.4 summarizes the most common causes of unreliability in the design of business applications, along with the resulting business impact.

Table 2.4 Deficiencies That Reduce Reliability

Deficiency	Business Impact
System does not faithfully adhere to correct design patterns.	The system is unreliable and difficult to maintain, secure, and enhance.
A security audit found the system to be moderately secure at the Web interface level, yet we require it to be very secure throughout.	The system cannot be confidently opened up to a large user community with the associated high visibility.
System has many independently configured components in a multi-application environment.	Operation is error-prone unless (1) the deployment and configuration processes are well-designed, (2) system management tools are used, and (3) the application incorporates features that indicate its status and dynamic resource requirements.

Table 2.4 Deficiencies That Reduce Reliability continued

Deficiency	Business Impact
System is not thoroughly stress tested for concurrency and varied conditions.	Mysterious errors occur that are labeled as "bugs" when, in fact, there might be design flaws that were not discovered during integration testing. The result is that maintenance programmers are unable to fix the problems, and the system is generally unreliable, especially whenever usage patterns change.
System does not incorporate sufficient features to enable it to be managed effectively.	Operators are not able to foresee problems before they occur, or the application is so complex to manage that operators constantly make mistakes. Either outcome results in more system down time.
System is hard to maintain.	Maintenance staff introduces errors and corrupts the core design, making the system even harder to maintain and more fragile and dependent on a small group of programmers who are aware of all the workarounds and temporary fixes.

> The business requirements should include not only what the system should do when everything goes well, but also what features will be needed to prevent problems and what should happen when something goes wrong.

These business impact areas should be discussed with the application stakeholders in order to develop a complete set of requirements that encompass not only business functionality, but also the security, reliability, manageability, and maintainability characteristics of the application. Thus, the final set of business requirements should include not only what the system should do when everything goes well, but also the *assurance objectives* for the application: what features will be needed to prevent problems, what the application should do when something inevitably goes wrong, who will respond to problems, and what features they will need in order to do so. This final requirements list should be expressed in layman's terms so that all stakeholders can understand it.

After the stakeholder-expressed assurance requirements are obtained, these requirements must be translated into technical architectural requirements. This translation process requires the collaboration of the project architect and the project manager because it involves tradeoffs in terms of cost and value. The resulting technical requirements are known as *derived requirements.* See Chapter 19, "Methodological Considerations," for more discussion of this process and how it can be used with agile methodologies.

Table 2.5 lists some very important assurance-related objectives and provides examples of how those can be expressed as derived technical requirements for an application. Note that the derived technical requirements incorporate architectural strategies for how the assurance requirements will be achieved.

Table 2.5 Examples of Derived Technical Requirements

Assurance Objective	Derived Requirements
System Design Must Be Verifiable	The system's as-built design should be well-documented. The primary layers and tiers of the system should be testable using test programs with minimal human interaction. Each tier should be testable without the availability of any other tier. This may require the development of test "stubs" to simulate tiers on which the tier being tested depends.
System Must Be Deployable	Deployment should involve a minimum of manual configuration. All actions and configurations required to deploy the application should be specified completely and unambiguously in a deployment guide. The deployment process should be identical for each environment, including the development, test, user acceptance, and staging environments. All dependencies on external components, libraries, and services should be specified in the application release notes, including those with which the application is expected to be compatible and those with which it has been tested.

Table 2.5 Examples of Derived Technical Requirements continued

Assurance Objective	Derived Requirements
System Must Be Scalable	Based on the concurrent user requirements (200), and based on the usage profiles developed by the requirements team, it is estimated that the application must support up to 10 application server actions per second, with a latency that averages under two seconds during peak usage hours.
System Must Be Manageable	The user should be able to determine the status of any user-initiated task or action at any time and be able to safely abort those tasks and actions. The operator should be able to determine at any time the status of any and all application services, user requests or tasks, and resources, and be able to safely abort any of those.
System Must Be Maintainable	The application components should be sufficiently documented so that a programmer who is unfamiliar with the application can maintain the application without the assistance of those who are experienced with it. For this project, this means that (1) all code will be liberally commented, including comments regarding the *purpose* and *expected usage* of each section of code and that (2) design documents will be maintained and *contain all important design decisions*.
System Must Be Securable	The system's design should be validated from a security perspective. The as-built design should be accurately documented. There should be a process for ensuring that programmer modifications do not inadvertently alter the design or compromise the principles intended by the system's architects, for example, by bypassing a security layer.

Many of the derived requirements listed are very technical and might be hard to justify to business users who do not understand the linkage between their articulated requirements and the derived requirements. It is important to express business assurance objectives in terms of derived requirements, however, because assurance objectives are too vague and are usually not concrete. Derived requirements can be made very concrete so that designers and programmers can work from them.

Derived requirements are usually hard to explain to end-users, but they are important for programmers.

It is appropriate to consider which of the derived requirements can be addressed through methodological requirements. For example, the very first derived requirement, "The system's as-built design should be well-documented," could easily be made part of the development methodology. This removes it from scrutiny. The project manager must be involved in this decision because it involves tradeoffs with regard to the overhead and cost of development and the ability to meet the requirements.

2.3 Writing Failure-Response Requirements

Failure-response requirements should be authored by the requirements team, with heavy reliance on the technical design team. This collaboration is necessary because failure-response requirements consider what the system should do when various kinds of *system-level events* occur. In order to create a list of these potential events, one must have a deep knowledge of the systems involved.

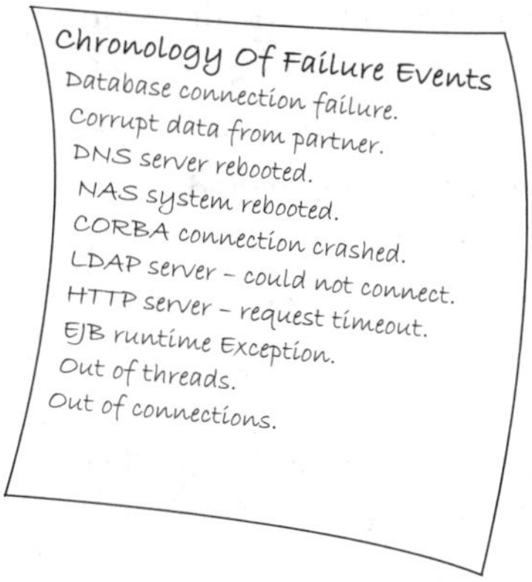

Figure 2.1
A list of failure causes and events should be maintained beyond the design and deployment of a system.

A list of failure conditions and events should be maintained beyond the design and deployment of a system and should grow over time. This results in an ever-better understanding of the factors that affect system reliability. The list can be maintained as documentation of the test suite, as long as it is readable by non-programmers, such as members of the requirements and QA teams.

System component failures are detected by application software in one of two ways: (1) an expected condition does not exist or occur, such as a value is null when it should not be, an assertion fails, and so on, or (2) a failure is detected at a lower or internal level and results in a program exception, signal, or error return code. Application-level failure response, therefore, amounts to what the program does when a failure is detected by either of these two means.

In general, users would like to see things such as:

- *Detection* of error conditions as soon as possible. This includes detection of invalid input.
- *Transparency* of problems: Users would like to know what the *true* cause of a problem is when it occurs.
- *Actionable* error messages: Users would like to know what they can do to resolve a problem.

A programmer's idea of a reasonable error response is usually very far from a user's idea of what reasonable is.

Operators of applications need the above, but to a greater degree because they are servicing many users. Thus, operators generally require:

- Monitorability: The ability to observe the application's state of health at any time, as well as immediate notification of a problem.
- Transparency of problems: Accurate information about the true cause of any problem that is detected, as well as the ability to diagnose problems.
- Actionability and recoverability: Operators need to know precisely what to do when something goes wrong, so that they can (1) enable response teams to diagnose and address the problem, and (2) restore the application to an operational state when required.

Unless programmers are told otherwise, they will usually design software that falls woefully short in the listed areas. This is no fault of theirs—they are merely doing what they are told to do, and if failure response is not spelled out, they will do what they feel is "reasonable"—and a programmer's idea of a reasonable error response is often very far from what a user's idea of what reasonable is.

The table in Appendix B provides a starting point from which you can write your own list of failure-response requirements. The list is generic, with a slant toward Java 2 Enterprise Edition (J2EE) applications, and should be customized to be specific to the kind of system that you have.

2.4 Summary

This chapter has presented concepts related to the specification of stakeholder-expressed requirements for application reliability and security and for the development of assurance-related derived requirements based on the stakeholder-expressed requirements. As a project assembles a set of stakeholder-expressed and derived requirements, an application can be designed that meets those requirements.

Be proactive in obtaining requirements from *all stakeholders*. Assurance considerations include reliability, performance, failure response, and accountability. Failure-response requirements specify the desired system behavior when failures occur. Security requirements either specify limitations on what users can do or specify what features should be provided. Categories for security requirements include the following:

1. Confidentiality
2. Authentication
3. Non-repudiation
4. Integrity
5. Detection and response
6. Manageability

Reliability requirements may include correctness of business processing, availability, and fault tolerance.

Some recent U.S. regulatory decisions have held that companies may be liable for losses due to neglectful security vulnerabilities and that technology providers have a responsibility to continually test for security as an application is enhanced and maintained.

Security certification is a process for assessing a system's security according to well-defined criteria and then granting a certification level based on the assessment.

The next chapter discusses techniques for defining assurance-related architectural features and rules and for verifying that an application's design or implementation complies with design-level decisions or rules.

2.5 Exercises

1. Explain what an assurance requirement is.
2. Explain why security is fundamentally a reliability requirement.
3. What can a development team do in order to ensure that tasks critical to achieving assurance objectives are not skipped in favor of adding functionality?
4. List three characteristics that are important to users with regard to information messages received from an application.
5. Explain how a derived requirement is different from a user-specified requirement.
6. Who should be involved in the definition of requirements for a high-assurance application?
7. List three categories of objectives for software reliability.

Answers and hints for these exercises can be found at `http://www.assuredbydesign.com/haa/`.

CHAPTER 3

DESIGN SPECIFICATION AND VERIFICATION

"Trust me, that module has not changed during this iteration."—A typical response of a software developer when asked unexpectedly if a particular piece of code has changed. More often than not, the module has indeed changed, or something that it depends on has changed.

Obtaining assurance-related requirements is a significant milestone: At that point, success has been defined. However, there still remain the challenges of (1) *designing* an application system that meets those requirements, (2) *ensuring or verifying* that the design satisfies the requirements, (3) *implementing* the design, and (4) *ensuring or verifying* that the implementation conforms to the intended design and meets the specified requirements.

Different software development methodologies apply different levels of concurrency to these distinct processes: for example, agile methodologies unify the design and development processes and enable requirements gathering and testing to occur almost concurrently with design and development. Regardless of the level of concurrency, *the four processes must all occur in order to achieve high assurance.*

Methodology and process issues are discussed in depth in Chapter 19, "Methodological Considerations."

Design consists of the elaboration of a requirements specification into another specification that is expressed in terms of implementable technology. The term *elaborate* means to translate or expand into a more complete and detailed form.

When created, a design's conformance to requirements must be verified. This can be achieved in a number of ways, including human inspection, testing through simulation, the building of a prototype, and the proof of conformance using mathematical or assertion logic techniques. It can also be achieved through construction: by using reusable parts or patterns that are predefined and that have known features so that a design composed of those parts or patterns will also have the same features. In that case, the design need not be verified: It is known a-priori to satisfy certain requirements because of the way in which it is created. Thus, compliance with requirements can be achieved through verification or through construction. Either way, the process ensures that the design meets the requirements.

After a correct design has been created, it must be elaborated again into an implementation. This final elaboration can be performed automatically or through a creative human "coding" process. Again, the implementation must be shown to meet the requirements. If the design is known to satisfy the requirements, verification of the implementation can be achieved to a large degree by demonstrating that the implementation conforms to the design. This is sometimes achievable through the use of a validated high-level compiler that translates a design into an implementation.

Compliance of an implementation with requirements can also be demonstrated through testing. Testing is an *a posteriori* verification technique—it acts upon an implementation that has already been created. [1]

Even if an implementation is shown to comply with all requirements, it is still important to ensure that the implementation conforms to the design. Otherwise, the two are potentially out of sync, and future programmers might not have the benefit of the original architect's guidance and the concepts for reliability and security that are built into the system may degrade over time. Further, the design expresses the intent of the designer and contains many implied objectives and decisions that are likely of value for the longevity of the application.

A design must account for all eventualities and events. As stated so sublimely in [2]:

> *"The most important principle is that all effects observable at any level be included in the specifications. The design can then be proven secure. This principle is, of course, applicable to all areas of system design, not only recovery."*

Implementations often stray from a design unintentionally. Design verification studies have shown this. For example, [3] documents an effort to test the efficacy of several different design verification approaches, and it was found that different verification methods uncovered different kinds of errors.

Most of this book is devoted to design principles that help the designer create a design for a reliable software application. This chapter discusses ways in which a design can be validated or verified: (1) ensuring or verifying that a design meets requirements and (2) ensuring or verifying that an implementation complies with a design and with requirements.[1] The latter is, strictly speaking, an aspect of "implementation verification,"

1 The terms "verification" and "validation" are used interchangeably in this book.

but the line between design and implementation is often sufficiently blurry that it is not helpful to distinguish between design verification and implementation verification. This book, therefore, uses the single term *design verification* to refer to both and to consider that there may be rules or constraints that must remain satisfied and that may be added to or refined as an application progresses from requirements through design and finally implementation.

When applying design principles to the design of an application, it is therefore important to simultaneously give thought to how those design principles can be verified or enforced as the design is implemented and as the system undergoes maintenance cycles, upgrades, and other lifecycle changes.

Software testing is an important tool for the verification of designs and implementations. However, this chapter does not attempt to provide detailed coverage of software testing. There are many sources that cover the subject of testing in detail, for example [4]. The focus here is on design verification. Toward this end, there are many techniques available, and this chapter focuses on the techniques that are practical for business applications, particularly with respect to verifications of compliance with requirements and design features that affect reliability and security.

Design verification has two principle aspects: (1) verifying that a design meets requirements, and (2) verifying that an implementation complies with a design.

Design verification has historically received more attention in the hardware design world because errors are so costly to correct after a system is put into manufacturing or in placed the field. As a result, the techniques used by the hardware design world for design verification are much more sophisticated and comprehensive than those used by software designers. Testing plays the predominate large role, as does reuse, and these are legitimate techniques that contribute to the goal of design verification.

Common approaches to software testing are often inadequate. A recent study [5] commissioned by the National Institute of Standards and Technology (NIST) found that:

"Software bugs, or errors, are so prevalent and so detrimental that they cost the U.S. economy an estimated $59.5 billion annually, or about 0.6 percent of the gross domestic product...over half of the costs are borne by software users and the remainder by software developers/vendors...more than a third of these costs, or an estimated $22.2 billion, could be eliminated by an improved testing infrastructure that enables earlier and more effective identification and removal of software defects. These are the savings associated with finding an increased percentage (but not 100 percent) of errors closer to the development stages in which they are introduced. Currently, over half of all errors are not found until "downstream" in the development process or during post-sale software use."

The hardware design field makes heavy use of the concept of "design for testability," which is a design principle that says that systems should include features that make it easier to test them. This is an important principle in software testing as well, although it is seldom adhered to. [6] However, there are compelling arguments that while comprehensive testing is critically important, is not sufficient–that software must be designed for reliability rather than merely tested to death.[2] Design assurance, therefore, should include a focus on ensuring that designs are correct and not merely that sufficient testing is performed.

Design assurance should include a focus on ensuring that designs are correct, and not merely that sufficient testing is performed.

Much work has been done in the field of software design verification and testability, but little of it has come into use for various reasons. As a result, this book merely articulates a simple principle of "design for verifiability."

See the principle "Employ Security Design Patterns That Are Verifiable" in Section 4.2, "Designing for Verifiability."

Even though the cost of making post-deployment design changes to software is far less than making comparable changes to hardware, design verification is still critically important for high-assurance systems. The reason is that software tools give a programmer complete freedom to design a system in any manner possible, and only the selection and application of correct principles during the architecture and design process ensures

2 For example, see Parasoft's white paper on design rule verification [7].

that the system's design is reliable and secure. If the as-built system deviates from these chosen principles, however, the system's design has been compromised and it might have unknown weaknesses. Verification of *compliance with the design*—as well as with requirements—is therefore critical.

If the as-built system deviates from the design's principles, the system's design has been compromised and it might have unknown weaknesses. Verification of compliance with the design—as well as with requirements—is therefore critical.

Part of the problem is that the most widely used programming languages in professional settings tend to be those that achieve widespread popularity among programmers, and programmers tend to choose those languages that have the most empowering features. For example, it can be argued that features such as inheritance do more to enable reuse and leverage existing assets than they do to enhance reliability and security, and the various forms of inheritance seem to be a central topic of differentiation among popular languages.

Verification, enforcement, and perpetuation of design principles can be achieved using manually intensive methods, for example, by design reviews or through automation (such as by using code generation tools that generate code that adheres to design patterns that have been verified). There are other approaches as well. In fact, there are actually a great many options for design principle enforcement. In practice, you will need a combination of these because a comprehensive secure application design and development platform does not exist.

Fundamentally, any form of verification relies on redundancy. For example, the required redundancy can take the form of a design and an implementation that are shown to match; an implementation and a test suite that are shown to agree; two independent verifications of the same design; or two independent implementations. In any case, human error must be accounted for, by providing some form of redundancy in the work product and comparing.

3.1 Design Specification

Design specification consists of writing down or encoding a design; but what is a design? The distinction between what is a design and what is an implementation is very nebulous and has more to do with the tools that are available than with any inherent difference between a design and an implementation.

One might be tempted to say that an implementation differs from a design in that an implementation is executable, but that is not normally the case: Program code is usually considered to represent an implementation, but program code is not directly executable because it must first be compiled. Further, some designs are directly executable.

The difference between a design and an implementation is, therefore, more conceptual. An implementation is generally recognized to represent the lowest level of design, such that after the implementation has been created, all remaining steps are largely automatic. In contrast, a design is generally considered to be a step that occurs before implementation but that occurs after requirements have been captured.

A design can contain structural definitions, and it can also contain behavioral definitions. Behavioral definitions specify what the application must do, whereas structural definitions specify what computational structures will exist to perform the application's functions. A design can also contain rules or constraints that define the intended relationships between design features or the external environment. Such rules or constraints can be expressed formally or informally, depending on the power of the design language.

After a design is defined, it must be elaborated into a lower-level design or an implementation. This elaboration step consists of translating the design into increasingly concrete constructs, working toward an executable system. This process can be automated to varying degrees, or it can be entirely manual.

It should be noted that there is a difference between a *design* and a *design specification*. A design specification is the documentation of a design, whereas a design consists of the structural features combined with the conceptual intent of those features. The intent is important, because it guides developers when they attempt to add new features or structures.

The issue of design versus design specification is important to proponents of "evolutionary design," who claim that a design emerges from a robust implementation process. Without getting into the middle of this debate, it is clearly true that design does emerge in the course of refactoring code, and design can exist in the heads of software developers even if it is not written down. However, if it is not written down, then there is no means of proving or claiming that the design meets any properties that are not directly testable, and properties related to assurance often fall into this category (this issue is discussed in Section 3.3, "Defining and Verifying Architectural Rules"). Thus, for assurance purposes, it is necessary to document intent, and so the terms "design" and "design specification" become essentially synonymous, as do "architecture" and "architecture specification," even if the design or architecture "document" is manifest as code comments or as a set of statements written on a napkin. When speaking of a design specification or architecture specification, this book will often merely use the terms "design" or "architecture," respectively.

3.1.1 Modeling Languages

A *modeling language* is a language that is *intended to be* used to express an aspect of a design, but not necessarily to be the basis of design verification or automated elaboration into an implementation. Modeling languages often lack the completeness needed to render an implementation from the design model. For example, models often abstract aspects of a system, such as by representing direct communication between elements that, in an actual design, would not communicate directly. This makes direct elaboration difficult. The intent of a modeling language is to provide a tool for creating artifacts that can be used to analyze a design or system concept. The analysis serves as a conceptual basis from which an actual design or implementation is created.

When a modeling language is used as the basis of a design, verification and elaboration is performed manually or with the aid of additional tools. That is, the design must be validated using either manual inspection, simulation, or reduction techniques; and the design must be elaborated through at least partially manual coding of the implementation. Comparison of the final implementation with the design and verification of the satisfaction of requirements is also manual.

This is not to say that a language that is intended only for modeling a design cannot be used to perform design verification or elaboration into an implementation. Rather, a modeling language is one that was specifically created only for the purpose of modeling a design, without a vision of full verification or implementation elaboration.

There are a vast number of modeling languages, each with its own preferred domain of usage, strengths, and weaknesses. Modeling languages exist that are graphical or textual, that express structure or behavior, that are functional or procedural, that aid simulation, and that aid in implementation generation.

For enterprise application development, the most widespread modeling language in use presently is the Universal Modeling Language (UML) [8]. UML provides a graphical notation that allows a designer to define an application using a large variety of paradigms, including activities and states, type structure (classes and inheritance), instance structure and cardinality, and event sequence and messages. Powerful methodologies also exist to guide the designer in the creation of a robust and complete application design. An example of such a methodology is the Pattern-Oriented Analysis and Design (POAD) methodology [9].

The semantics of UML notation are now defined with sufficient precision that code generation *is feasible* directly from a sufficiently complete UML application definition, so UML is a modeling language that can sometimes be the basis of elaboration. Many such code generation tools have come into use. There is also a standard textual syntax for the export of a UML application definition, to facilitate exchange between design tools.

There have been efforts to employ UML as a basis for expressing assurance-related design intent, e.g., [10, 11] for expressing security constraints and [12] for expressing fault-tolerance.

The next section presents techniques for design verification and elaboration. Approaches are discussed for the case of modeling languages and for more sophisticated languages that support some level of design verification or elaboration.

3.2 Design Verification and Elaboration

The discussion here will use a very broad definition of the term "design verification" to mean any technique that helps to ensure that either a design or an as-built application adheres to a chosen set of design principles, patterns, designs, rules, or requirements. Thus, design verification is really a matter of verifying the integrity of the elaboration of a specification into a more detailed specification or implementation.

Design verification is really a matter of verifying the integrity of the elaboration of a specification into a more detailed specification or implementation.

Design serves no purpose in its own right: It is merely a tool for the creation and maintenance of an implementation. However, if a design cannot be verified, it is useless for creating or maintaining a high-assurance implementation. Further, from an assurance perspective, elaboration of a design is only of interest to the extent that the elaboration process can be shown to accurately reflect the design—which has been validated and therefore can be trusted—and produce a correct and robust implementation.

Thus, when one distills what is of interest for assurance, we are actually interested only in design, design verification, and faithful elaboration—the process of elaboration is important in its own right, but from an assurance perspective, it is secondary to the consideration of its faithfulness in reflecting the design. *This book is not about software development, except for those aspects that affect assurance.*

Methods of design verification include testing, run-time tools that perform various kinds of checks (for example, related to security boundary or scope rules), design tools, and build tools: thus, all phases of development can utilize techniques to achieve design verification.

The emphasis here is on techniques that have found their way into tools used by developers of enterprise applications. Regrettably, many viable academic techniques still remain untapped in this domain because of lack of awareness on the part of developers and also because of lack of support by developer-centric tools. A listing of widely used general techniques by category follows.

3.2.1 Human Intervention

Human intervention can occur during design verification or elaboration. Intervention during verification involves demonstrating that a design–if implemented–meets assurance objectives. Note that implementation is key–a design is not an objective in itself.

Human intervention during elaboration occurs if the implementation cannot be automatically generated. This is, of course, normally the case in most application domains, and the elaboration process is widely referred to as "coding." It is nevertheless conceivable that the practice of coding can someday be eliminated, given suitably powerful design tools.

Design Reviews, Code Reviews

Design reviews performed during a design phase involve inspection of the design. Design reviews performed during an implementation phase involve comparison of the implementation (usually code) against the design, as well as review of design and implementation issues.

Code reviews involve inspection of the code, and these reviews are more-often-than-not focused on compliance with low-level coding standards. Code reviews, therefore, have limited value from a design verification perspective; yet it is surprising how many developers view a code review as if it were a design review. Nevertheless, problems discovered in a code review sometimes do indicate a design flaw, requiring a re-examination of the design.

Some disadvantages of reviews are that (1) the process is manual, and (2) reviews require many different areas of expertise as well as understanding of the application design by those experts.

Traditional design or code reviews focus on the examination of artifacts for the purpose of finding errors. In contrast, an alternative is to focus on demonstrating through deductive or inductive argument or proof that a design or implementation is correct—that is, that it satisfies requirements or intent. One methodology that uses this approach is the "cleanroom software engineering" methodology [13]. Proponents of this approach claim that it entirely obviates writing unit tests.

Threat modeling is a special kind of design review that attempts to uncover vulnerabilities by challenging developers and security experts to think of ways to subvert the application. This technique can be applied to reliability analysis as well, by making any kind of application failure the focus of the analysis.

Reuse

Reuse of previously built components is one of the most commonly used methods in business application settings for ensuring design correctness. The theory is that if the component has been used before successfully, it is very likely that it adheres fairly well to its specification and is fairly error-free. Thus, prior use serves as a form of real-world testing. Reuse can be at a component level, package level, or class level.

Reuse can introduce some peril, however, if the component's implementation depends on assumptions about its earlier usage. Reuse without verifying design assumptions led to the crash of an Ariane 5 rocket. [14] Intention-based methods address this concern by explicitly defining the domain over which inputs to any function are considered valid. This enables maintainers or future users of the code to know precisely what assumptions were made.

3.2.2 Testing

Testing involves exercising the application and comparing its behavior against predicted behavior. Testing is an important technique for verifying compliance of a design or implementation with requirements, as well as verifying compliance of an implementation with a design.

A critical aspect of testing is the method of assuring that the test suite provides sufficient "coverage." A test suite's *coverage* is the extent to which the suite completely exercises the breadth and depth of the application. This can be measured in terms of the application's requirements, or it can be measured in terms of the application's structural features—or both. Coverage of structural features is extremely important for testing hardware, but it can be used for software as well to ensure that all logic paths are traversed.

The most common form of testing performed for business applications is based on the functional requirements expressed by the end user. In business settings, assessing test coverage based on functionality is usually more practical than alternatives, even for critical applications, due to the maintainability of the test suite and due to greater compatibility with current development methodologies.

TYPES OF TESTING

Behavioral—Verifies conformance to functional requirements.

Structural—Utilizes knowledge of the internal design of the system under test (SUT).

Path, Branch—Are based on knowledge of the paths or branches of control within the SUT.

Unit—Verifies the operation of a single component (unit) of the SUT.

Regression, N+1—Techniques for repeating tests and measuring progress by comparing successive runs.

Smoke, Sanity—Very cursory tests that merely verify that the SUT is operational.

Stress—Any form of testing that forces the system to perform at or beyond the boundaries of its expected operational envelope.

Performance—Assesses the performance of the SUT, usually including its responsiveness under varying degrees of load.

Scalability—Assesses the ability of the SUT to have adequate responsiveness or performance under specified levels of load.

Soak, Volume—Drive the SUT to high load levels for operational periods that are long in duration, to detect memory leaks, space exhaustion, and other forms of duration-induced failure.

Load—Any form of testing that drives the SUT's load to a high level.

Compatibility—Tests the interoperability of the SUT with other components in the operational environment.

Acceptance—Performed by the users or stakeholders to determine acceptability and fulfillment of requirements.

Ad-hoc—Exercises the system in unpredictable ways to assess the SUT's robustness when inputs are varied and unexpected.

Certification—Exercises the SUT according to predefined criteria, but with inputs that are not known to the SUT's builders prior to the testing.

Agile—The practice employing test-driven development, in which tests are written before the implementation code is written.

QA—Performed by an independent party to provide an independent and thorough assessment with respect to comprehensive project requirements.

White box—Utilizes knowledge of the implementation of the SUT.

Black box—Utilizes no knowledge of the implementation of the SUT: Only the requirements are used to design the tests.

Beta—Is performed against a preliminary ("beta") release by a group of end users.

Integration, System—Attempts to assess the interoperation of all components of the SUT.

End-To-End—Tests the entire SUT, with all operational components and external systems in place.

Workflow—Tests the system according to expected scenarios or use cases.

Boundary Condition—Attempts to assess the behavior of the SUT when "edge conditions" are reached or crossed.

Bottom-up—Tests subcomponents first, followed by testing the entire SUT.

Top-down—Tests the SUT without testing subcomponents—e.g., by replacing subcomponents with "test stubs."

Concurrency—Assesses the behavior of the SUT when multiple users or multiple requests are serviced.

Data-Driven—Utilizes test cases composed of different data sets, as opposed to different test programs.

Failure, Recovery—Tests the ability of the SUT to recover appropriately when errors occur.

Negative—Attempts to force the SUT to fail.

Ramp—Progressively increases the stress on the SUT to see at which point it will fail.

Static—Assesses the correctness of the SUT without actually executing the SUT.

Usability—Assesses the ability of the SUT's users to actually use the SUT.

Therefore, a suite of tests is usually based on the need to test that all requirements are satisfied. For this purpose, test data is almost always required in order to provide input to the tests. It is highly preferable to construct this data based on the requirements and test objectives, rather than to use actual data. (The problems of using production data for testing are discussed in more detail in Section 19.5.4, "Release Testing.")

Testing can be performed at various levels, from a class or module level to the subsystem level to the entire application. (The various levels of testing are described in Section 3.5, "Levels of Verification.") When performed above the module level, it is known as "integration testing." When performed on an ongoing basis so that results can be compared over time, it is known as "regression testing."

Behavioral Test Specifications and Regression Testing

In a behavioral approach to testing, test analysts write test specifications and test programmers write accompanying tests. The tests are based primarily on functional requirements and test that the behavior of the application satisfies the functional requirements expressed by the users and other stakeholders, as well as any other behavior aspects that the designers deem to be important.

Behavioral test coverage can be assessed in a variety of ways, such as by simple coverage of functionality or by "path analysis," which seeks to ensure that every *logical* path or combination of functionality is tried. Behavioral approaches to testing are nearly universal in business application settings.

See Section 2.2.3, "Adding Derived Requirements That Affect Reliability."

Behavioral testing is generally a necessary part of development, but in practice it is not often done in a comprehensive manner because implicit requirements and design features that affect reliability, security, and other non-functional aspects will escape testing if those requirements are not fully articulated. This can be corrected by using the techniques in this book.

Test-Driven Development

In test-driven development (TDD), programmers write tests for a module before they begin coding—or even designing—the module. The test is limited to the module, and is therefore a "unit test." The practice of test-driven development is often referred to as "test-first design" because the existence of the tests guides the design.

TDD is espoused by agile development methodologies. It provides a high level of assurance that a module meets the articulated requirements and that requirements are well-understood. However, it cannot replace independently written behavioral or integration tests.

A disadvantage of test-driven development is that it tends to obviate design artifacts because the tests themselves become the design specification. Tests are inherently incomplete as a design specification because they omit meta aspects, such as intent—aspects that are critical for expressing non-functional requirements. Design artifacts are not precluded by TDD, but in practice they are often discouraged, and so the probability that the as-built implementation deviates from the intended architecture (if there even is one) is increased. This can be easily remedied by ensuring that other forms of testing and design verification are performed as well.

FAILURE-RESPONSE TESTING AND STRESS TESTING

Failure-response testing observes how an application behaves when failures of various kinds occur and compares the application's behavior under those conditions with the desired behavior. Failure-response testing, which will be referred to here as *failure testing*, is often called *recovery testing* because its objective is typically to verify that the application recovers as required when errors occur. The term "failure-response testing" is more general because recovery is not always possible or required: In many cases, it is sufficient that the application does not fail catastrophically.

Failure-response tests should address the following behaviors, in response to the range of conceivable failures:

- **Recovery** (consistency and sufficient completeness after recovery from failure)
- **Atomicity** (all-or-nothing)
- **Failover** (uninterrupted or automatically recovered operation across a failure)
- **Concurrency** (no loss of data consistency during resource contention)

Stress testing is similar to failure testing, except that stress testing does not necessarily push the application to a point of failure, but rather assesses how the application behaves just short of failure or under stressful conditions. Thus, performance testing (not addressed in this book) is a particular form of stress testing. Failure testing and stress testing serve to validate that a design or implementation satisfies assurance requirements. The simulated conditions can involve incorrect inputs, component failures, or high levels of load. For load testing, the complete implementation must be tested, and special load generation tools are often used in a special load-testing environment.

Failure-response testing and stress testing are different from most other forms of testing because they require the simulation of failure or near failure conditions. This generally requires a high level of technical expertise and often requires a special test environment.

Any high-assurance application should undergo recovery testing to assess the application's ability to be returned to an acceptable operational state after a failure occurs. Recovery testing should include checks for atomicity: that the application did not "half-complete" actions that were in progress when a failure occurs, such that the application state cannot be returned to a sufficiently complete and consistent state.

A high-availability application that incorporates redundancy in order to continue operation when a failure occurs should be tested under conditions that cause its failover components to take over. The purpose of this form of failure testing, which can be referred to as *failover testing*, is to assess the sufficiency and integrity of the failover system. Multi-user or multi-task applications should include tests for concurrency by simulating or creating actual contention for shared objects or data, to assess the application's ability to separate concurrent activities so that they do not interfere with each other and to verify that the application recovers properly from situations in which contention forces the system to abort or retry some activities.

Testing under deliberately-created concurrency is known as *concurrency testing*. Concurrency testing should observe the behavior of the application as the number of simultaneous activities *increases*. This should be done from the perspective of correct operation, as well as the ability to handle concurrent load without incurring unexpectedly high contention or frequent deadlock for resources.

Concurrency is discussed in Section 12.2.8, "Concurrency Testing and Validation," and Chapter 12, "Concurrency."

Failure-response testing should include the range of types of failures that are considered to be of sufficient risk to warrant consideration. This normally includes tests for *resource exhaustion*. Resource exhaustion tests typically include a series of long-duration runs to observe the behavior of resource usage over time. Some of the long-duration runs should be performed at high load levels—so-called "soak tests"—in order to see if unexpected behavior occurs in prolonged high-usage conditions. Conditions that may occur during this kind of testing include out-of-memory, out-of-threads, out-of-connections, and out-of-disk-space.

Resource allocation is discussed in Section 11.2, "Object Allocation and Deallocation."

Failure testing can also be performed that assesses the application's response when there is data inconsistency. For example, incorrect or inconsistent data can be presented at a subsystem interface, or inconsistent data can be returned from a subsystem. This kind of testing serves to verify an interface's ability to deal with unexpected inputs or outputs, and is especially important when interfacing to untrusted components.

Other classes of failure to be tested may include the following:

- Loss of transactions, data, or messages
- Loss of session
- Loss of connection between one element and another
- Insufficient resources
- Timeout

Additional testing considerations are discussed in Section 3.5, "Levels of Verification."

CERTIFICATION

So-called "certification testing" is a form of acceptance testing that is used to assess whether an application meets the requirements for the granting of a certification. The certification provides assurance to users and others who will need to trust that the application meets a certain level of quality and assurance as defined by the certification.

Certification testing often includes some amount of static analysis as well as negative testing that attempts to make the application fail. The negative testing typically involves subjecting an application to randomly selected stresses or inputs according to a test plan or strategy.[3]

3 In the security field, the term "certification" merely means the assignment of a designation indicating that a component has passed a particular kind of certification test. In the field of software reliability, however, the term "certification testing" implies the use of random inputs to achieve a required (certified) level of reliability (see for example, [15] p. 424). In security work, the vernacular use of the term "certification testing" has come to imply the performance of tests by an independent party with particular inputs that are unknown to the developer of the component, followed by certification if the tests are passed.

Even though certification testing may (but won't necessarily) involve randomness and applying unexpected inputs, the procedures and success criteria should be well-defined ahead of time. The test results should also be well documented so that analysts can see what actual inputs were used and what the results were. Otherwise, there is no evidence that the tests were done diligently or fairly.

The disadvantage of certification testing is that it is expensive and takes a lot of time to perform.

3.2.3 Dynamic Verification

Dynamic design verification techniques include all methods that are available for monitoring the runtime actions of an application to ensure that it adheres to design rules.

DESIGN-BY-CONTRACT

So-called "design-by-contract" technologies [16, 17] provide means of specifying required behavior. Tools can be used to instrument the code or to watch the code execute using debugger techniques. Eifel is the predominant example of a design-by-contract language, but there is a variety of other technologies that provide the ability to specify expected behavior, from Java assertions to JML [18]. (JML can also be used for static analysis.) Languages that provide pre- and post-conditions (for example, many aspect-oriented languages) also fall into this category.

Design-by-contract approaches provide great assurance value when used to encode assumptions made by methods and components. However, this alone falls short of the need for expressing patterns or intended function. Design rules that have introspective access to program structure can be used to create capable rules, but such rules tend to be very complex to develop and maintain.

ASPECTS AND SEPARATION OF CONCERNS

Aspect-oriented programming (AOP) languages attempt to allow programmers to separate the design of various aspects of a program so that a programmer does not have to envision every aspect when a module is designed. A programmer can separately design aspects related to particular concerns, such as authorization or error handling. For example, see [19]. This decoupling of different "aspects" simplifies design and programming.

Aspects can be added that implement verification rules that are invoked at different points in a program's execution. These verification aspects are in effect interposed wherever required, and do not affect the existing design—*as long as the aspects are truly independent.* This qualification is important, and therefore the use of aspects is no "silver bullet": The designer must still consider the global effects.

The AspectJ (see [20]) and HyperJ (IBM Alphaworks) languages are important contenders in AOP.

3.2.4 Static Analysis

Static analysis involves specifying design rules or patterns and verifying compliance by analyzing the implementation—i.e., the code.

EXTERNALLY-EXPRESSED STATIC DESIGN ASSERTIONS OR RULES. STRUCTURAL (STATIC) VERIFICATION SCRIPTS AND PROGRAMS

There are many code analysis tools that perform different kinds of design-rule verification in which the design rules are expressed by the designer in a separate specification using some form of design-rule language. Many such rules are very low-level, such as rules related to the use of certain language constructs.

Some tools analyze code complexity or attempt to identify security vulnerabilities based on a standard set of rules, but the value of such tools is a subject of controversy.

The use of an external specification allows the consolidation of design rules for a single purpose (aspect). For example, all design rules that are related to security design patterns can then be consolidated into a single rule file.

Examples of simple static analysis tools include macker [21] and Parasoft Jtest. A more sophisticated example is MOPS [22].

FORMAL ASSERTION LANGUAGES, INTENTIONAL LANGUAGES, AND CORRECTNESS PROOFS

If a very disciplined methodology is employed to develop an application, it may be possible to logically prove the correctness of the application—i.e., the validity of formally expressed assertions regarding its security and reliability. This is not constrained to small applications; by hierarchically decomposing an application into tractable pieces, the entire system can be proven correct. A seminal example of the use of this approach is the use of the Hierarchical Development Methodology (HDM) to design the Provably Secure Operating System (PSOS) [23]. More recent work includes the Prototype Verification System (PVS) [24].

This approach requires a fairly high level of computer science, so at the present time it is primarily used in very high-security products and specialized settings.[4] As examples, the Secure Computing *Sidewinder* firewall appliance is based on the PSOS work, [25] and there has been success in the area of developing verifiers that prove the integrity of generated Java bytecode. [26] Formal approaches have proven their viability, so it is hoped that they will gain more attention and that more software practitioners will undertake to become proficient in the fundamentals required for these techniques.

So-called *intentional programming* approaches, which seek to define programs as hierarchical specifications of intent, also fall into this category.

3.2.5 Design-Oriented Programming

Design-oriented programming languages allow an application designer to become the application programmer: The line between design and programming vanishes, and the design becomes the program.

Languages That Provide Advanced Pattern Representation Techniques

There are many languages that allow the programmer to embed design rules, patterns, or intentions directly within the program. This allows the close association and concurrent maintenance of program source and associated design rules. The JML language falls into this category. One could argue that intentional programming approaches also fall into this category.

An especially significant design-oriented language, from a reliability and security perspective, is the ArchJava language (see [27]). ArchJava provides intrinsic representation of patterns

4 The introductory document to HDM's successor, EHDM, states, "As a minimum, therefore, you should be familiar with first-order predicate calculus and its model-theoretic semantics."

related to closure. This language is discussed later in this book (see the pattern "Component and Port" in Section 7.18.1, "Component-Oriented Design").

ELABORATION FROM DESIGN LANGUAGES

A design language allows a designer to create an abstract design that is then used to automatically generate an implementation that can execute on the target platform—or at least to simulate the actual intended design (as opposed to a highly-abstract model). Such a language is often referred to as an architecture description language (ADL). An example of such a language is Acme [28], although many exist.

Reliability can be derived from the fact that code matches design (if the code is automatically generated) and design patterns are easily reused by maintaining libraries of designs. Reliability can also be derived from the encoding of verifiable architectural rules that guard the intended relationships within the design.

TEMPLATE DEFINITION LANGUAGES

Template-based languages allow a designer to define a design pattern as a reusable specification. The template contains variable sections or expressions that are replaced with actual values when the template is instantiated into a design.

Template-based approaches have the disadvantage that they are not amenable to overlapping concerns. (This is discussed more in Section 3.4, "Code Generation.")

Examples of template-based approaches include most Model-Driven Architecture (MDA) compilers and most design-oriented code generation tools.

EXTENSIBLE-GRAMMAR LANGUAGES, DOMAIN-SPECIFIC LANGUAGES

Extensible-grammar languages are programming languages that allow their very syntax and semantics to be extended to fit different problem domains. This approach is also known as "language-driven development." This allows the programmer to embed design patterns within the language itself. For example, a loop construct is merely a design pattern that is embedded in most languages; for example, via a "for," "loop," "while," or "repeat" construct. Examples of extensible languages include maya [29], JSE [30], OpenJava [31], and TXL [32].

FUNCTIONAL LANGUAGES

Functional languages represent a non-procedural programming paradigm. They deserve mention here because their adherents claim them to be more resistant to specification errors. Examples include Lisp, Scheme, Standard ML, and Mercury.

Functional language programs are especially amenable to functional analysis, a method pioneered by Harlan Mills. [33]

3.3 Defining and Verifying Architectural Rules

The greatest risk of deviation from design exists within business application code and user interface code because these are often coded by programmers whose main focus is on business requirements and who are the least likely to be familiar with the details of the system's technical architecture. Critical architectural components are usually maintained by the most experienced developers on a team, and they are most likely to be aware of architectural concepts.

Security architecture rules or principles can either be *existence and completeness* or *prohibitive*. Table 3.1 lists some common types of security architecture rules that are of the prohibitive kind: i.e., they prohibit certain practices within the code. For each type of rule, the table lists some techniques for verifying that the code complies with the rule. This table is presented here in order to provide the reader with an understanding of how design rules and verification strategies can be expressed. Secure design principles are introduced in Chapter 4, "Planning for an Assurable Design."

Table 3.1 Common Types of Architecture Rules Related to Verification or Enforcement of Prohibition

Architectural Rule Violation	Possible Verification or Enforcement Techniques
1. Acceptance of unvalidated or unbounded data.	Type-safe language. Run-time stack-checking tools. Object-oriented approach to construction of input objects. Static checking for required use of validation logic. Lint-like code quality analysis tools.
2. Inappropriate access to resource objects across layers.	Scoping of resource objects and their methods. Scoping can be implemented by: -Language-based scoping. -Platform-based security scoping; for example, via a security manager. -Resource lookup scoping; for example, by scoping the lookup methods. -Static checking of inappropriate direct instantiations. -Manually encoded method pre-condition checks.
3. Inappropriate access to internal objects and their methods.	Scoping of internal objects and methods. For example: Comparison of public resource methods against the list of permitted transactions. Automatic generation of resource interfaces. Static checking of inappropriate direct access.
4. Inappropriate placement or absence of authorization checks in certain components.	Scoping of access to context and context attributes, such as user identity and role(s). For example: Scoping of access to security databases, such as user access rights or roles. Static checking of inappropriate direct access.

Architectural Rule Violation	Possible Verification or Enforcement Techniques
5. Inappropriate transactional inconsistency.	Instrumenting the application's thread context to detect if a single user request is serviced by multiple transactions. Static checking of design patterns within transaction clients.

Prohibition-related features are very hard to test because they specify that someone *should not be able to do something.* Prohibition-related features can be verified by static analysis, as well as by negative testing—e.g., by performing penetration analysis. [34] Usually a combination of techniques is warranted.

Table 3.2 lists some common types of security architecture rules that are of the *existence and completeness* kind; that is, each rule requires that the code includes certain actions and that those actions are performed to a certain level of completeness of coverage.

Table 3.2 Common Types of Architecture Rules Related to Verification or Enforcement of Existence and Completeness

Architectural Rule Requirement	Possible Verification or Enforcement Techniques
1. Completeness of coverage of business-mandated authorization rules.	Encapsulation of authorization rules as pre-conditions.
2. Completeness of coverage of all possible error conditions.	Language-supported error trapping. Lint-like code quality analysis tools.

A project should develop a list of its own like Table 3.1 and 3.2. That list should include all the architectural rules for the application. The developers of the application should be made aware of these rules and understand that the integrity of the system depends on them.

There are many code analysis tools that can be applied to the task of verifying code against architecture rules. The most powerful tools utilize formal methods such as predicate calculus to prove program attributes. Many tools exist that automatically scan existing code and find vulnerabilities or flaws, but the most effective method is to formally express assertions or logical functions for modules as they are designed and developed, and then utilize theorem proving tools to prove those assertions. Formal techniques are not the subject of this book, however, so the discussion here will consider tools that do not require formal methods or predicate calculus.

One such tool that requires only basic computer programming knowledge is Jtest, which is widely used for testing of Java applications for compliance with design rules. Jtest can implement both static and dynamic design rules. Tools change from year to year, so Jtest is presented here only in order to illustrate the concept of a tool that enables the specification of verifiable design rules.

Jtest has a set of built-in rules that embody a collection of Java "best practices." In recognition of the fact that what might be a best practice for one project is a limitation for another, Jtest allows you to choose which rules to apply. It also allows you to design your own rules, wherein lies the power for the purpose of implementing architectural (for example, security-related) design rules.

At this writing, Jtest's rule specification language is a graphical language without a textual equivalent. That makes it difficult to exchange design rules between teams or to print them out and review and maintain them. However, the tools' power makes this disadvantage worth accepting.

Let's consider an example of the use of Jtest for verification of compliance with a security rule. Suppose you have specified the following rule:

Example architecture rule:

Methods that are declared in layer2 can be called only from layer2.

Jtest allows you to specify this rule with its graphical language and then apply the rule to your code, on a class-by-class basis if necessary. In order to express this rule in the Jtest language, let's re-word the rule as follows:

Example architecture rule, reworded:

For each method call, if the called method is declared in layer2, and if the call is not made from layer2, then generate a rule violation.

The rule, as expressed in the second form, is shown in Figure 3.1 using Jtest's graphical rule language.

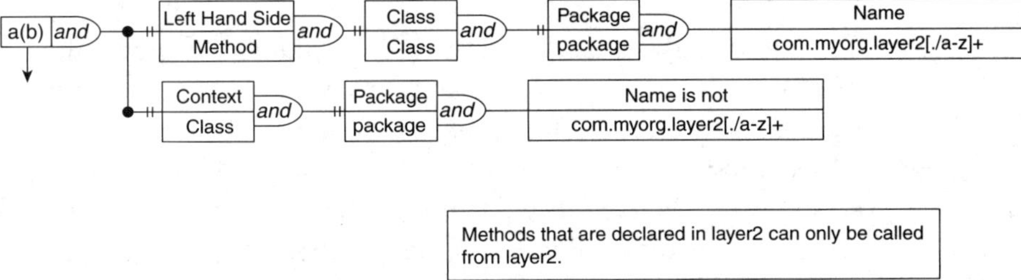

Figure 3.1 Expressing a design rule using Jtest.

The syntax shown in the figure expresses that any method call to package com.myorg.layer2 (or a sub-package) must be made from that same package—otherwise, a design rule error will be detected by the Jtest static analysis tool.

Another simple tool that is available at this writing for analyzing Java code is the "Macker" [35] tool. Macker is an open-source tool that allows you to specify rules in XML and then analyzes Java class files for compliance. The kinds of rules that it allows you to specify include rules related to which classes can call other classes. The powerful pattern-matching features of Macker make this tool viable for verifying code for static compliance with a wide variety of architectural rules. For example, this author has used it to implement checks for rule types 1-4 in Table 3.1.

Because Macker is rule-driven, it is limited by the kinds of rules that its rule language allows you to specify. A more flexible approach is to use a tool that parses a program and then allows you to hand-code your own analysis routines. An example of such a tool is the commercial tool "PMD" [36]. Tools of this kind can be used to verify existence and completeness rules that a rule-based tool might not be able to handle. Semantic analysis tools, such as PMD, require you to actually write procedural code to implement your own rule checks, whereas rule-based tools simply require you to compose rules in a rule language. For a general discussion of static analysis with regard to Java, see [37].

If you intend to use static analysis, you should restrict the use of any APIs or constructs that would defeat the analysis tools.

Static analysis has limitations. For example, if the implementation language supports an interface style that uses runtime method binding (for example, the Java reflection API, which allows a class and method to be specified at runtime by a string-valued name), it might not be possible for a static analysis tool to verify some rules in places where that API is used. Therefore, if you intend to use static analysis, you should restrict the use of any reflection-like APIs except for specific modules: Indeed, you could write static analysis rules to detect and flag the disallowed use of such APIs.

Another weakness of static analysis is that it cannot verify the presence or absence of namespaces when those namespaces are not statically bound. For example, the Jtest rule presented earlier is effective only if the layer2 method definition is "final"—i.e., the method cannot be overridden by a subclass. Otherwise, the type in which it is defined could be extended by another namespace (for example, another package), and the extended version could be called from other layers without violating the above rule—but defeating its intent. In order to prevent this, there need to be rules or mechanisms (such as using final) to prevent the layer from being extended.

An alternative to static analysis is to use a run-time scoping enforcement technique, such as a security manager, that enforces policy with regard to which code objects are allowed to call each other. This is important for security in any case, especially in a multi-application environment.

Both static analysis tools and run-time scoping tools have difficulty enforcing rules across run-time boundaries. For example, a remote object invocation originates in one run-time environment and executes in another. In that case, it is not possible for the execution environment to determine any more about the call environment than can be conveyed to it through security attributes. Thus, it would not be possible to verify that a certain client object was of a certain kind, unless there was a trusted security attribute that specified that, or unless the client runtime environment is also trusted.

This is discussed further under the principle "A Trusted Context Should Always Include the Code Context" in Section 7.17.3, "Code Context."

You may need to create additional architectural structures in order to facilitate static analysis.

Finally, you may need to create architectural structures in order to facilitate verification. For example, if you desire to check that a certain tier does not access certain methods in a second tier, but the first tier is allowed to access *other* methods in the second tier—depending on how your static analysis tool works—you may have to ensure that the restricted methods are encapsulated in a set of classes that you can restrict access to. Otherwise, you would need to restrict access on a method-by-method basis, which some tools might not be able to do. At this writing, Macker is limited to class-level analysis, but the plan is to extend it to be able to perform method-level analysis. The point is that you should expect to have to adjust your system architecture a little here and there to facilitate design rule verification.

Remember, the discussion here is about the expression and enforcement of design rules, not about security or access control. The purpose of static analysis tools is to help ensure that programmers adhere to the intended design patterns—not to prevent rogue code from doing inappropriate things.

3.4 Code Generation

3.4.1 What Is Code Generation?

Code generation involves the generation of an implementation from a higher-level design specification or model. Design details are automatically filled in by a compiler, with consideration of the target environment. Code generation from a high-level model is exemplified by tools that support Model Driven Architecture (MDA) [38], spearheaded by the Object Management Group (OMG).

Any compiler is a code generator.

Technically, any compiler is a code generator.[5] A compiler takes input in the form of a source-language program and generates output in the form of a target-language program. The target language is typically the instruction set of a computer. Source languages can range from simple low-level languages, such as the original C language, to very advanced functional and structural languages, such as Ada, VHDL, and Java 5.

The target language of a compiler can often be varied. For example, the GNU C++ compiler allows the programmer to specify the target machine. Target machines can be high level or low level. In the late eighties, this author wrote a research compiler for the VHDL language, a very complex Ada-like language used for hardware design. The compiler had the ability to input an algorithmic specification and generate a complete implementation of a microcoded hardware chip that would perform the algorithm, using the maximum concurrency of the hardware resources. Thus, the target language could not go any lower: It was the very electronic building blocks of a circuit. At the opposite end of the spectrum, the target of a high-level-language compiler need not be a computer, but could be a computing platform, such as a J2EE application server. In that case the target "language" consists of Java together with the various J2EE APIs.

5 A compiler designer would prefer to say, "Any compiler has a code generator." However, for our purposes, that is splitting hairs.

> The target of a high-level language need not be a computer, but could be a computing platform, such as a J2EE application server.

3.4.2 The Role of Templates in Code Generation

Compilers that must generate code for multiple target environments often utilize templates of some kind to facilitate the specification of the form and content of the generated code. This is a very powerful approach. However, it has a weakness: If different compilers are used to generate different modules, the generated code might be incompatible or might violate design rules. This is because each compiler uses different templates.

The hardware world is very familiar with this problem. In the hardware world, there has long been a concept of template libraries. Templates are instantiated and "elaborated" into a design in order to match them to the design requirements, such as bus width, word length, and so on. However, it is well-known that templates must be written in such a way that a set of separate templates work together. Hence there is a concept of design "families" consisting of compatible templates. This is because templates represent in effect *parameterized building blocks of a particular meta design.* That is, a template includes design choices, such as whether to employ microcode versus combinatorial logic, bus architecture, and so on. Fundamental design patterns, such as whether to employ parallelism in an algorithm, often apply regardless of design choices and regardless of what kinds of design structures are used. However, a template library requires that the choices be consistent. That is because a template is a low-level component, and is described in terms of structures instead of *concepts such as states and events.*

3.4.3 Patterns Versus Templates

In contrast, a design "pattern" can either be concrete or conceptual, but ideally should be as abstract and generic as possible.[6] A pattern often contains classes and specifies details, but only to the extent necessary to express the pattern's intent. Pattern definitions typically contain verbal explanation of the concepts and decision criteria in order to enable programmers to understand them and their intended usage. A formal (i.e., machine-readable) pattern library would have to augment the verbal explanations with formal semantic definitions, possibly using state definitions, event definitions, and formally expressed relationships between these.

Design patterns are important because they are generalizations of a concept and can be applied to many different design domains. They are a concept distilled to its essence. A pattern embeds an intent, and if there is a way to express the pattern in a design and ensure that the pattern is retained as the design evolves, there is a basis for ensuring that design intent is retained—with all the benefits to reliability and security that result from maintaining design integrity.

It is worth noting that patterns can exist at many levels. The most basic patterns used in design, including fundamental concepts such as the Singleton pattern and the Facade pattern, are often termed "foundation patterns" [39]. Intermediate level patterns that still represent localized functions have been referred to as "scaffolding patterns." Finally, the term "framework pattern" has been used to refer to those patterns that describe the highest levels of abstraction within a system.

In order to preserve patterns across multiple design tools or if the code is manually edited, there needs to be a mapping between the design patterns that are chosen and the templates or design features that a software architect wishes to apply to implement the patterns. The existence of this mapping is often referred to as *traceability*, [40] and the task of reconciling traceability errors has been referred to as synchronization. [41]

6 One definition of "pattern" from Merriam-Webster's online dictionary is "A discernible coherent system based on the intended interrelationship of component parts."

Design patterns embed design relationships and rules, and these relationships and rules must be verified to ensure that the intent of the design is preserved as the design evolves. Further, *multiple design patterns may be employed in a single design, and can overlap in terms of the components that they influence.* In contrast, the designs produced by the expansion of multiple design templates cannot overlap, but rather must be joined together.[7]

> There needs to be a mapping between the design patterns that are chosen and the design features that a software architect wishes to apply to implement the patterns.

Unfortunately, at this writing, the field of code generation for application platforms, such as J2EE, is relatively new and immature, and tools that preserve end-to-end traceability between patterns, designs, and implementations are few.

3.5 Levels of Verification

Design verification needs to occur at multiple levels of an application's hierarchy. Ideally it should be performed at each level, from the lowest to the highest. In practice, this is not always feasible.

The lowest level of verification is typically the function or method level. Testing that is performed at this level is known as *unit testing*. Unit testing is not the only means of function-level verification, however: other techniques are possible, including automatic code generation from specifications and correctness proofs.

Unit-level verification can be performed at several levels of hierarchy. Once the outermost level of a subsystem or system is reached, verification will need to focus on testing, even if at lower levels non-test techniques such as code generation are used to ensure implementation integrity. This is because the accumulated uncertainty in the correctness of the constituent components mandates comprehensive testing of the aggregate subsystem or system. The discussion in the remainder of this

7 In [42], Yacoub and Ammar refer to these paradigms as "overlapping" versus "stringing."

section will therefore focus on levels of testing as a method of verification; and because this is a book about assurance, the focus will be on assurance testing.

Just as the requirements team relies on the technical design team to help write assurance requirements, the test team should author the assurance requirements tests, but with heavy support from the technical design team because technical knowledge is needed to compose practical scenarios for simulating or creating system level failures in a test setting. For this reason, assurance testing cannot be done purely by user interface level "testers," but must be a collaborative effort between test *programmers* and application testers.

> Assurance testing cannot be done purely by application testers, but must be a collaborative effort between test programmers and application testers.

Most application software development methodologies define different "levels" of testing that are done at the various points in a quality assurance flow. These "levels" usually correspond to different test environments, different scope, are designed to satisfy different stakeholders, and have different objectives. The most common levels of testing are described in Table 3.3.

Table 3.3 The Most Common Levels of Testing

Unit testing

- Tests are written and performed by programmers on an ongoing basis in their development environments. Test data is constructed by the programmer, and is for the specific use of the unit tests.
- Execution and result reporting should be fully automated.
- Should be performed using resources (for example, database tables) that are owned by each programmer. If that cannot be achieved, the application should be developed in such a way that either (1) resource access can be compartmentalized so that programmer unit testing does not conflict, or (2) test bench "stubs" are used in place of actual resources.
- Ideally, utilizes repeatable test data that is created dynamically or restored as part of the setup of each test or group of tests.
- Scripts for building a component should be tested as well and treated as part of the component.
- **Should include unit-level reliability and failure response requirements that can be tested by simulating failures programmatically.**

Integration testing

- Tests the collective operation of multiple components—possibly an entire release.
- Utilizes test programs to test each major independent layer of the component or system being tested, executed by testers. Test data is constructed by the test programmers and is for the specific use of the integration tests.
- Should utilize a methodology that ensures sufficient functional coverage of the requirements of each portion of the system that has a specification. This generally requires that the test specifications are written by a party other than the developers of the components being tested.
- Utilizes test cases that verify correct end-to-end operation of the components.
- **Should include all reliability and failure response requirements that can be tested by simulating failures programmatically.**
- Should utilize a release build process and then a deployment process to an independent environment—not just the copying of development files. This ensures that the release build and deployment processes themselves are tested as part of integration testing.
- Should not require special (e.g. licensed) testing tools that are available only to testing staff; programmers should be able to execute local copies of integration tests within their development environments.
- Execution and result reporting should be fully automated so that the tests can be run quickly and frequently.
- Normally includes execution of the unit test suite as well, to provide maximal coverage.
- Should be performed using resources that are owned by and modifiable only by the testing team. Ideally, should be performed in an isolated environment that shares no configurations or resources with the development environment, and that is not even accessible via LAN access from any of the other environments. (Ref. [43] page 245.)

Failure and stress testing

- Should test a complete release.
- Utilizes tests that are designed and performed by the testing team, with technical assistance as required from the development team. Test data is constructed by the testing team, and is for the specific use of the failure and stress tests.

Table 3.3 The Most Common Levels of Testing continued

- Should be performed in a separate test environment that can be configured as needed to create the required test conditions. Normal access to this environment is on a scheduled time-window basis.
- **Should include the creation of all conditions and failures that are required to test the reliability and failure response requirements. These should automated *to the extent possible* and driven by test programs rather than specialized testing tools.**
- Should include scalability and performance testing, driven by specialized (e.g. licensed) load testing tools if necessary.
- The test environment and application should be configured so that they are as similar to the intended deployment as is necessary to ensure that the results can be considered to be indicative of what would occur for the deployed application.

Acceptance testing

- Should test a complete release.
- Should be designed and performed by all of the requirements stakeholders, with the assistance of the testing team, for the purpose of acceptance of the delivered system. Test data is normally constructed by the stakeholders, and is for the specific use of the acceptance tests and no other purpose.
- Should be performed in a separate controlled acceptance testing environment that is highly similar to the target operating environment, and that is agreeable to all parties.
- Must have well-defined criteria for what success is.
- *Does not pertain* to any preliminary or informal user testing that is done during development for the purpose of requirements definition or elaboration.
- Typically allows for acceptance that is often conditional on a "warrantee."
- Should utilize a permanent environment that later can be used to reproduce (or help disprove) problems that are uncovered in production. In many cases, the environment can be the stress test environment.
- **Should demonstrate that all reliability and security requirements are satisfied. This may include certification-style testing.**
- See also "User Acceptance" in Section 19.5.5.

Post Acceptance

Staging area testing

- Should test a completely deployed release.
- Does not serve the purpose of testing the application's correctness: The purpose is to *test the deployment configuration* and to verify that the intended actual deployment configuration does not adversely affect the application's operation.
- Should be designed by the development team or deployment team. Performed by the deployment team or operator. Test data should be constructed by the deployment team or development team, and is for the specific use of the staging area testing. An *approved subset* of actual production data should be tested against as well.
- Should be performed in a staging environment that mirrors the operational environment's equipment and configuration. If a staging environment does not exist, this testing must be done in another test environment and then in the actual operational environment.
- **All assurance tests that do not require the creation of failure conditions should be run to verify that environmental factors have not introduced weaknesses. Some limited failure testing should be performed to identify possible environmental problems.**

Production area testing

- Should test a completely deployed release.
- Serves the purpose of "checking out" the application in the live environment, to verify the configuration. Consists essentially of "spot-checking" against a list of critical aspects and tests, and verifying that execution indicators are what they should be.
- Typically designed by the development team or deployment team. Performed by the deployment team or operator. An approved subset of the production data should be tested against.
- **All assurance tests that do not require the creation of failure conditions should be run to verify that environmental factors have not introduced weaknesses. Some limited failure testing should be performed during low-usage periods to identify possible environmental problems. These tests should access only a "test subset" of the production data.**
- Requires that a rollback plan must be in place; otherwise, nothing can be done if the configuration is found to be flawed and unrecoverable.

Deployment to each environment should be from an unmodified release module rather than a migration from one environment to the next.

Failure-response requirements should ideally be tested at all levels, just as for any other kind of requirement. However, many failure-response requirements require the creation or simulation of conditions that are difficult. For example, showing that the system fails gracefully under high load requires the generation of high load. As another example, showing that a certain error message occurs when a connection fails requires that the connection be caused to fail.

> Failure-response requirements should ideally be tested at all levels.

For this reason, accurate and comprehensive failure testing must eventually be performed in an isolated environment, and each failure-response test requires a detailed plan or strategy. These strategies should be mapped out by the test team, with heavy assistance from the technical design team. In most cases, special test programs need to be written that drive the tests and that facilitate the simulation of failure conditions.

It is often highly worthwhile to write modules that simulate resources so that failure conditions can be simulated instead of actually creating those failures. These "simulators" can be used in development and during integration to perform preliminary verification against failure requirements.

Acceptance testing by the user should include some level of "certification style" testing to verify that the application is as robust and secure as claimed. Most user organizations do not have the expertise to do this, however, so they can rely either on an independent third party, or if the relationship with the application developer is good enough and there is a strong "warrantee" in place, acceptance testing can be done collaboratively. This approach is discouraged, however, if the application is a high-risk application.

Assurance testing should also be performed in the staging environment and even in the production environment. However, these environments present challenges. A staging area does not normally lend itself to the creation of failure conditions, and one certainly does not want to cause visible or risky failures in a production environment! Some failure testing must be done, though, in order to verify that failures are handled properly. The right approach is to perform some limited failure testing in each environment—just enough to provide some assurance that environmental factors have not compromised the application in an unexpected way. In the production environment, this kind of testing must be done in a very controlled and planned manner, preferably during a low usage period, and with a rollback plan in place.

3.6 Writing Test Plans for Reliability and Failure-Response Requirements

Writing a test plan involves specifying how test objectives will be met. It is useful to attack this at two levels: overall testing strategy, and detailed test plans. Overall testing strategy addresses the testing approach in the aggregate and specifies how the prevalent challenges will be met, overall procedures, technical approaches for groups of tests, environments, responsibilities, checkpoints, and so on. Detailed test plans implement these strategies on a test-by-test basis and define the specific procedure to be followed for each test that is to be constructed and performed.

3.6.1 Technical Testing Strategies

Some of the more prevalent technical strategies for implementing and performing tests include:

Manual testing, in which human testers perform the functions that users would perform in actual usage.

"Robot" testing, in which specialized tools are used to simulate the actions of human testers.

Protocol-based testing, in which specialized tools are used to generate requests to a server application from simulated remote clients.

Programmatic testing, in which custom-written test programs automatically invoke functions within the application.

Manual testing is extremely costly, time-consuming, and error-prone. Manual testing is only justified (1) when user acceptance testing is performed, (2) for initial testing performed to help define or construct automated tests, or (3) when an automated testing method is not feasible. Manual testing has the extreme disadvantage that tests cannot be run frequently or whenever changes are made to the code, because testing requires people to perform all of the tests manually, which can often require weeks to do.

Manual testing has the extreme disadvantage that tests cannot be run whenever changes are made to the code.

Robot testing is an effective method for testing an application at the user interface level. It has the disadvantages, however, that (1) it is fragile with respect to small—even cosmetic—changes in the user interface, [44] and (2) it does not replace the need to test the system at a transaction level, using protocol-based testing or programmatic testing. Robot testing is sometimes referred to as "analog" testing, [45] because it works based on the positions of GUI elements instead of identifying them as logical components or objects.

Robot testing does not replace the need to test the system at a transaction level.

Protocol-based testing is often used for performance testing, to observe the system's response to load. Tools that are used for this purpose typically work by employing a load generation tool to generate simulated client requests from multiple clients to a server application and then using a separate server-based tool to listen to the responses.

Programmatic testing is the most powerful technique and is the method that programmers normally use to write unit tests. It has the advantage that the tests can utilize the language features of the application's programming language, including type safety, to verify that certain types of exceptions are thrown, instead of having to parse response messages. This technique often employs testing frameworks in order to ensure uniformity in the way that the tests are written and run.

Programmatic testing is a highly suitable method for developing a test suite for reliability and failure-response tests. This is because a great deal of technical expertise is required to actually specify what a test of this kind should do, and the best place to specify that is in the program that implements it. A test program also provides the programmatic control that is needed to establish precise failure conditions. However, it is often necessary for a failure-response test plan to have manual steps that are required to set up test conditions or to observe a response. In that case, those conditions should be documented in the test plan.

For programmatic tests, the system architect should develop test program guidelines that specify the commenting requirements, what tools and frameworks are to be used, what test bench and simulation components are to be used, how results are to be determined and reported, and so on. Instead of writing all this into a document, a more agile approach is to write a few sample test programs to illustrate the approach, with comments that spell out the guidelines. Test programmers should then write test programs that are well-commented and document the test objectives according to the test program guidelines.

> Programmatic testing is often the most suitable method for developing a test suite for reliability and failure-response tests.

It is generally a waste of time to write a separate test specification document for each individual programmatic test unless there are manual steps that are involved. However, there should be an overall test plan that lists and describes each programmatic assurance test, its objective, and how it is to be achieved.

> There should be an overall test plan that lists and describes each programmatic assurance test, its objective, and the strategy for how it is to be achieved.

For robot and protocol-based tests, the testing team should author detailed test procedures with assistance from members of the performance testing team who are expert at using those tools. Any scripts that are written by test programmers should be well-commented and reference or incorporate the test objective for each test.

The testing strategy should specify what kinds of testing approach should be used for each category of system components. This is a decision that the testing team should make in collaboration with the technical design team. When developing the test strategy, the testing team and design team should make notes of design features that will be needed to allow the test plan to be implemented. This includes the development of test benches, test stubs, and design rules, such as specifying that certain methods that test drivers need to access should be public. This approach is generally known as "design for testability." The required testability features should be incorporated into the list of technical derived requirements.

When developing the test strategy, the testing team and design team should make notes of design features that will be needed to allow the test plan to be implemented.

3.6.2 Writing Detailed Test Plans for Reliability and Failure-Response

There should be a specific test plan for each component. The plan needs to be tailored to the component because the plan needs to consider the criticality of the component, its unique position within the application, and its technical characteristics and testability.

When a test plan is developed for a component, the project architect needs to review it from a cost feasibility perspective. In most applications, no component can be tested as thoroughly as it should. The architect needs to consider the tradeoffs and select the tests that provide the most coverage and that focus on the highest risk areas.

Even if a comprehensive suite cannot be built right off the bat, it might be possible to accumulate a high coverage test suite over time, as the application is maintained and more features are added. For this reason, failure tests should be maintained in a test suite and treated as a cumulative regression test suite.

3.7 Summary

This chapter has provided a foundation that is needed for the chapters that follow by laying out the tools that are available for defining and verifying compliance with design rules and decisions that affect assurance. These included languages intended only for design, as well as languages and techniques that can be used to verify an implementation against a design. Testing was discussed as a form of design verification. Failure-response testing was discussed as a means of verifying compliance with recovery and reliability requirements. The importance for assurance of verifying compliance with design rules was discussed. Design patterns were compared with design templates, and pattern traceability was discussed. Finally, methods were presented for designing assurance tests. Much of the remainder of this book consists of design principles and patterns that help a designer to design a high-assurance application. Later in the book, methodological issues are explored.

3.8 Exercises

1. Explain why software testing is a form of design verification.
2. Explain the difference between a pattern and a template.
3. What is the central difficulty in using code generation templates to implement design patterns in applications that cannot be entirely generated automatically?
4. List and briefly explain six levels of software testing.
5. Which member of a project must consider the tradeoffs with regard to which failure tests should be performed?
6. What is an architectural rule, and what are the advantages of specifying architectural rules?
7. What are the two primary kinds of security architectural rules?

8. What is the main requirement for aspect-oriented design rules?
9. List four technical strategies for implementing and performing tests.
10. Explain the difference between a design and an implementation.
11. What are the two principal aspects of design verification?

Answers and hints for these exercises can be found at `http://www.assuredbydesign.com/haa/`.

Chapter 4

Planning for an Assurable Design

World-renowned computer security expert Peter Neumann, Principal Scientist at the Computer Science Laboratory of SRI International, said recently [1],

"Good system and network architecture is perhaps the most fundamental aspect of any efforts to develop trustworthy systems, irrespective of the particular set of requirements whose satisfaction is necessary."

The point that Dr. Neumann is trying to make in this statement is that security cannot be merely added on after the fact: It must be designed in [2]. It is, therefore, necessary that the development of a high-assurance system take security into account when designing the overall system architecture and not relegate security to a side aspect. Secure design principles must be adhered to by all parts of the system and affect the system's design throughout. The expectations and requirements for security must also be well-understood because security is not an absolute (see Section 2.1, "Security Requirements").

The previous statements carry the implication that a design *must exist* and *the actual system must match the design*—otherwise, there is no hope of claiming that the design is secure!

PRINCIPLE: A SYSTEM CANNOT BE SAID TO BE SECURE IF THE DESIGN OF THE ACTUAL SYSTEM CANNOT BE ARTICULATED.

Security and reliability are not easy to achieve in a complex, evolving application. There is no "silver bullet" for designing a reliable and secure enterprise system. As explained earlier, reliability and security are mostly a result of the process that is used to build a system and are not purely technical issues. That said, design patterns and approaches that consider reliability and security are a necessary condition for a system that must be reliable and secure.

Applications that represent extremely high financial or life-threatening risk warrant high levels of *redundancy*, exhaustive consideration of *all contingencies*, methodical procedures for *validating the design* and any *design change*, and highly rigorous testing and possibly certification. Examples of such applications include control systems for nuclear power plants, spacecraft, and aircraft. Other examples include operating system kernels and software embedded in mass-produced hardware on which a large number of products or systems depend.

"Each door is held in the open position by a suitable friction clutch, which can be instantly released by means of a powerful electro-magnet controlled from the captain's bridge, so that in the event of accident, or at any time when it may be considered advisable, the captain can, by simply moving an electric switch, instantly close the doors throughout and make the vessel practically unsinkable." —from an article describing the Titanic, *Shipbuilder* magazine, 1911.

Rigorous reliability processes add significantly to development time and cost and reduce agility. Further, the mindset of reliability must permeate the organization. In the words of Ron Hughes, a reliability consultant, trainer, and certified nuclear instructor with Reliability Center, Inc.:

"Reliability is ... a state of mind. For Reliability to thrive in any organization we must change our way of thinking to remove the business as usual attitude that is so prevalent. A proactive approach to Reliability must be developed and implemented." [3]

> Rigorous reliability processes add significantly to development time and cost and reduce agility.

There exist software design techniques that are used to achieve high operational reliability through redundancy. These include "N-Version Programming" [4] and "Recovery Blocks" [5]. These techniques utilize *independently designed and implemented* redundant implementations to handle situations in which an algorithm fails but the application absolutely must recover.

> Our focus here is on business applications.

For most business applications—even high-availability ones—the cost of these design techniques and the cost of a highly rigorous process cannot usually be supported. A middle ground approach is, therefore, needed for business applications, which provides a high level of assurance but also allows the organization to retain the agility and economic efficiency that is needed for success in the marketplace. The principles and patterns in this book are intended to be applied to business applications.

> Most business applications—even high-availability ones—cannot afford the cost of the high-assurance techniques that are used to design extremely high-risk or life-protecting systems.

It is true, however, that even a middle-ground approach requires a change in mindset of the organization to a certain degree. The process changes and changes in design approach that are needed to improve reliability need to be broadly perceived as critical for success.

> A middle-ground approach is needed for business applications, which provides a high level of assurance but allows the organization to retain the agility and economic efficiency that is needed for success in the marketplace.

4.1 Applying Effort Where It Matters Most

If all the design principles outlined in this book were rigorously adhered to, it is likely that the system would be too expensive to build, unless it is known up front that the system must be highly reliable and secure. The application of assurance principles requires extremely informed and acute judgment. The critical parameter is risk: Effort must be applied where the risks are greatest. This is an established doctrine in security [6], as well as quality assurance and reliability [7]. Further, risk must take into account both the likelihood of a failure and the full cost of that failure as a percentage of the size or ability of the organization to bear unexpected costs. This means that most effort should be focused on the components that are most accessible or vulnerable and those that protect or represent the highest value assets. [8]

PRINCIPLE: MATCH DILIGENCE TO RISK.

If all the design principles outlined in this book were rigorously adhered to, it is likely that the system would be too expensive to build.

In this context, "diligence" refers to getting the requirements, design, and implementation right.

4.1.1 Security-Related Risk

High-risk applications generally require stronger authentication than low-risk ones; therefore, a high-risk application should invest more in the authentication infrastructure and procedures than a low-risk application, as well as the inconvenience of multiple authentication factors. High-risk applications justify the inconvenience of narrower user roles and multiple levels of authorization, and possibly the elimination of some single sign-on features. High-risk applications justify the severe compartmentalization of various administrative functions, such as system-log administration, whereas low-risk applications may be reasonably safe with a single administrator who performs all these functions.

Within a system, various functions represent different risks. For example, administrative functions present greater risk than most user functions. Therefore, risk must be considered on a function-by-function basis, as well as a role-by-role basis, and security principles applied based on the level of risk.

The most sensitive components in a system should be the focus of the most attention. These components present the greatest risk, because if they are compromised, they can lead to the broad compromise of the rest of the application. Examples of such sensitive components include authentication systems, password stores, and so on. These kinds of components should be built with a higher level of quality assurance than the rest of the system in order to bring them up to a level of trustworthiness that is required for components that protect the horizontal breadth of the application.

PRINCIPLE: APPLY STRINGENT QUALITY CRITERIA TO HIGH-RISK COMPONENTS.

In this context, "high risk" refers to those components that are complex and, therefore, hard to verify the security integrity of, and whose failure would represent a potentially costly security vulnerability.

It also follows that if there is a limited capacity to provide stringent quality control, and if attention must be primarily focused on the most sensitive components, minimizing the number of sensitive components or simplifying them will increase the amount of quality that can be applied to each component.

PRINCIPLE: MINIMIZE THE NUMBER, SIZE, AND COMPLEXITY OF HIGH-RISK COMPONENTS.

This principle is sometimes referred to as "minimizing the trusted computing base," or "minimization of what must be trustworthy" [9].[1]♦

♦ See also the principle "Identify and Assess All Context Bindings," Section 7.17.1.

1 In the original "Orange Book" [10] definition of "trusted computing base," it was asserted that "a TCB should be as simple as possible consistent with the functions it has to perform."

> "Talent does what it can; genius does what it must."
> —Edward George Bulwer-Litton

This is sometimes the hardest principle to enforce. It is, unfortunately, the case that the most talented software developers often have a tendency to design complex infrastructure that is often not really needed by the business.[2] Such "home-grown" over-designed components can become a liability with regard to security and maintainability, especially as their designers move on to other roles in the organization.

4.1.2 Reliability-Related Risk

The complexity of an application's components often falls along a spectrum, with some components being much more complex than others. The most complex are often "infrastructure" components that provide a framework for business rules, authorization, workflow, or for information flow. Such components should be implemented according to clear design patterns to ensure that their design does not contain hidden flaws that are uncovered only as a result of unlikely circumstances—circumstances that *will eventually crop up during operation.*

Adherence to well-vetted design patterns helps to protect against unforeseen flaws, so it is important to ensure that complex components adhere to a design pattern that has been thought through abstractly instead of coded in an ad-hoc manner.

> ***PRINCIPLE: RELIABLE COMPONENTS SHOULD ADHERE TO A CAREFULLY CRAFTED OR APPLIED DESIGN PATTERN.***

This principle is analogous to the security principle "Employ Security Design Patterns That Are Verifiable" in Section 4.2, "Designing for Verifiability."

This level of design care cannot be afforded to all the components in a business application because to do so would slow down the entire project. It is, therefore, critical that the project have a process for differentiating complex or high-risk components from other components and have more stringent quality assurance processes for the former.

2 The notion of "Parkinson's Law" theorizes that people will fill the available time they have with inessential work. Proposed by Prof. Cyril Northcote Parkinson, University of Malaya, 1955.

As a result of the close connection between security and reliability, the design principles discussed in Section 4.1.1, "Security-Related Risk," in the context of security apply to reliable design as well. These are:

- Apply Stringent Quality Criteria to High-Risk Components
- Minimize the Number, Size, and Complexity of High-Risk Components

In a reliability context, "high risk" refers to components that are complex and, therefore, hard to verify, and whose failure would represent a potentially costly system or business failure. To make this possible, there must be a process for identifying those components that are high risk. The term "diligence" refers to the effort expended to validate the reliability of a component.

4.1.3 Risk Assessment

If factors external to an application, such as the level of threat and the competence of the technical team, are ignored, risk can be considered to be represented by the following formula: [11]

risk ~ cost of failure (severity) • complexity

Cost of failure is related to the value of the assets or activities that are at risk, and it can be considered in terms of worst-case scenarios or expected loss. Complexity is related to the technical difficulty involved in implementing the mechanisms in question.

For business-level analysis, external factors must be added. The threat that is present is largely subjective and depends on the visibility and attractiveness of the target. The greater the threat, the greater the risk, and so the threat level is a factor. The competence of a technical team is related to experience, knowledge, diligence, and resources. The greater the diligence, the lower the risk, and so risk varies inversely with diligence.

Thus,

absolute risk ~ (complexity • cost of failure (severity)) • (threat / competence)

relative risk = absolute risk ÷ total investment

Complexity has historically been evaluated based on subjective assessments from prior experience with similar applications or on numeric predictions of the number of features or structures of various kinds. An interesting approach that assesses complexity based on an application's UML design has been developed by researchers at the University of West Virginia [12]. In this approach, a tool is used to interpret UML state diagrams and compute the dynamic complexity (using a cyclomatic complexity approach), and sequence diagrams are scanned to compute the degree of coupling between components. Risk is then estimated based on the computed dynamic complexity, degree of coupling, and severity of failure. This analysis can be done in a hierarchical fashion, traversing the various layers of an application. Total system risk is computed based on the component interactions that occur according to each use case for the application.

A UML-based risk analysis tool is powerful because risk can be assessed early in the design process when it is still possible to consider alternative designs.

4.2 Designing for Verifiability

Chapter 3 discussed the concept of "design for testability" (DFT). This is an especially important concept in systems engineering for high-reliability systems; for example, the design of microchips, in which an error that makes it to production can have enormous financial consequences.

The basic idea is that if you constrain what you can design and how you design it, you can make it possible to test the system using automated means.

This concept applies to the design of high-assurance software in that it is possible to design software such that it can be *automatically* examined and verified for compliance with architectural requirements that promote security or reliability. This does not guarantee that the software is completely secure or reliable, but it goes a very long way toward that end.

> If you constrain what you can design, and how you design it, you can make it possible to test the system using automated means.

PRINCIPLE: EMPLOY SECURITY DESIGN PATTERNS THAT ARE VERIFIABLE.

The basic premise is fundamental: If engineers can design and build something in any way that they choose, there is no hope of verifying it; but if constraints are established, the challenge of verification goes from being intractable to highly practical. Note that the term "verify" does not necessarily imply the use of mathematical techniques: it merely means that appropriate verification procedures have been used, in order to attain the level of assurance judged to be sufficient for the application.

The first step in defining such constraints is to establish a system architecture that provides the required assurance. Again, the term "assurance" *is relative*–there can be no guarantees, especially when human factors are considered–but a system that is acceptably secure and reliable by design has a conceptual framework that has been analyzed and is therefore highly robust compared to a system that has no such framework. This book attempts to define the principles that can be applied for the purpose of designing such a framework for an important business application.

When a suitable architecture has been defined, the next step is to identify ways to constrain the implementation so that deviations from the architecture can be detected in some manner, such as by running a code analysis tool or by triggering a "tripwire" at runtime. That way, mechanisms can be designed to "keep the programmers honest." This is very important because one of the greatest challenges is keeping the architecture pure. Computing languages provide only a minimal computing

Manual or automated mechanisms should be designed to detect deviations from the architecture.

framework—they leave architecture completely up to the programmer. Also, most programmers are not familiar with many secure design concepts. Therefore, a means is needed to ensure that the software is actually implemented in the way that is intended by the architect (and maintained that way). In short, verification tools are of great value for this purpose.

4.2.1 Constraining the Implementation

The methods that you can use to constrain an implementation depend on what tools, platforms, and languages you use to build your software. For example, suppose the language has the ability to define preconditions on methods. You could then implement all your resource method authorization checks as method preconditions and build a tool that scans the source code (or intermediate form) and extracts all the preconditions and presents them in a list that you could manually verify against the known authorization rules.

The previous is an example that checks that something *has been done*—that the required authorization rules have been implemented. A rule that requires that something has been done is both an *existence* and a *completeness* rule: The required action has been performed, and performed in its entirety. What about checking or enforcing that something *has not been done*? For example, how do you check that a programmer has not encoded a direct call to an object that is internal to a resource, thereby bypassing the protected resource interface? This is a *prohibition* rule. Recall the discussion in Section 2.1, "Security Requirements," that security requirements are either user-enabling or user-limiting. See also Section 3.3, "Defining and Verifying Architectural Rules."

It takes work on the part of project management to constrain an implementation.

It takes work on the part of project management to constrain an implementation. In most commercial custom software development efforts, all programmers have access to all components, and quality assurance processes—if they exist at all—usually focus on testing; the development process itself is commonly left up to the developers and the technical leads. If a higher-assurance level must be applied to particular sensitive components, this requires that (1) the system architecture *is partitioned so as to minimize and isolate sensitive or critical components,* (2) those components are identified in the first place, and (3) special configuration control processes are applied to ensure that those components are *accessible to only those who are qualified to work on them.*

PRINCIPLE: *MINIMIZE THE ACCESSIBILITY OF SENSITIVE COMPONENTS.*

Thus, the project manager must ensure that the development processes achieve these things by defining separate categories of components based on risk, criticality, or sensitivity, defining a process for categorizing individual components, and defining a small set of developer qualification tiers to separate who can work on what—or at least who is required to supervise whom when certain components are worked on.

This principle is primarily a development-time principle but also applies to a deployment, to ensure that only appropriate personnel are able to "patch" components on which the security of the entire application depends.

4.2.2 Build Versus Buy

In general, home-grown security mechanisms are less reliable than commercial security components. For example, the primary functions of an authentication product, such as Netegrity Siteminder are to authenticate, authorize, and create a reliable and secure context: Siteminder authenticates the user, using an established credential verification mechanism, and then sets the user's identity in the HTTP request context, as a POST parameter. The value is reliably set by Siteminder with each HTTP request for as long as the Siteminder session is maintained. This is a highly reliable mechanism because the value proposition of the product depends on it being so. Thus, when commercial security products are available, they are usually more reliable than mechanisms that are created in-house.

PRINCIPLE: *PREFER HIGHLY RELIABLE COMPONENTS FOR SENSITIVE FUNCTIONS.*

Home-grown password management, cryptographic, or random number-generation functions should be avoided as well.

4.3 Think in Terms of Survivability

Survivability-oriented thinking is very pessimistic. It is like always thinking in terms of the worst case. In life it pays to be somewhat optimistic, but when designing high-assurance systems, this optimism must be tempered by the realization that eventually everything that can go wrong will, and so planning for the worst is merely prudent and natural.

Survivability-orientation with respect to security has been referred to as *intrusion-aware design.* It begins by presuming that an application will be compromised, and proceeds by designing responses that allow the organization to contain an intrusion and survive from it. According to Moore and Ellision [13]:

"Fundamental to the goal of survivability is the existence of recovery plans for those attacks that we cannot effectively prevent."

For example, it is inevitable that most, if not all, highly visible public Web sites or some of their users will eventually be compromised in some way—either through a direct attack, through phishing[3] scams, through denial-of-service attacks, or through some other means. Therefore, planning for this eventuality is as prudent as it is prudent to plan for occasional transaction errors in a database application.

An intrusion-aware design should define containment and recovery approaches for each type of identified threat that cannot be prevented in the long term by the design or by operational procedures. For this to be possible, the threats to the application must be identified. This is an important justification for performing ongoing threat analysis as part of the design process.

> An intrusion-aware design should define containment and recovery approaches for each type of identified threat that cannot be prevented in the long term by the design or by operational procedures.

As with any derived requirement or design constraint, survivability features must be tracked so that they are retained as the design evolves. It might not be possible to incorporate such

3 A phishing attack uses both social engineering and technical subterfuge to steal a consumer's personal identity data and financial account credentials. For example, a web page made to look like the consumer's bank web page may ask the user to log in, and in that manner obtain the user's banking credentials.

features into a test suite and, in such cases, the features must be preserved in the same way that design features are preserved, as discussed in Section 3.3.

4.4 Think in Terms of Incremental Processing

How can an algorithm be designed so that if the inputs change, a revised output can be computed *based on the change alone*—rather than re-running the entire algorithm from the beginning on all inputs?

An algorithm that operates in this manner, which is referred to here as an "incremental" (or "delta") algorithm, has the tremendous advantages that processing is more rapid and therefore is less vulnerable to system failures and that delta-analysis can be performed on input to gauge the effect of changes if the results appear suspect. The advantages have a significant impact on general reliability and robustness because problems can be diagnosed more quickly and easily.

As an example, consider a securities portfolio hedging analysis for a large trading portfolio. Now imagine that a user of the results detects that they do not look quite right—yet the results are not so far off that one could definitively say that they are wrong. Meanwhile, securities traders are anxiously waiting for the data. In examining the inputs, it is discovered that the inputs for one of the trading instruments are wrong. Instead of running the entire process from the beginning for the entire portfolio, it would be beneficial if the change could be input and the result computed based on the change. This would most likely require a completely different algorithm, but the advantage would be quick response to problems, and there would also be side benefits to the business in the kinds of elasticity analysis it could perform.

4.5 Think in Terms of Concurrency

How can an algorithm be designed so that if some portion of its input is corrupt, the algorithm *can continue*, and the corrupt portions can be processed later after they have been fixed?

An algorithm that can be partitioned this way has multiple outputs that are independent of each other. This lends itself to concurrency because separate portions of the inputs can be processed independently—even at the same time. Computations that have this natural form of concurrency can usually be slightly modified so that they can operate concurrently even if they were not designed to do so from the beginning.

This kind of concurrency—multiple independent but identical algorithm computations—has a positive impact on reliability because it compartmentalizes the effect of a failure.

4.6 Think in Terms of Recovery

When designing a multi-stage algorithm, always think in terms of what the operator or user should do if something goes wrong and how your application can assist the user in recovering as much of their work and effort as possible so that they do not have to start all over.

There are two basic approaches to recovery: (1) checkpoints and (2) redundancy. A checkpoint is a saved intermediate state: Recovery involves restoring that state and resuming work from there. All work that was done after the most recent checkpoint is lost, but at least one does not have to start from the very beginning.

Redundancy provides for recovery in that it allows for a failing component to "fail over" to a redundant component. When failover occurs, some amount of state might be lost, which is usually limited to the current transaction or the current session. A highly reliable system incorporates a checkpoint approach to save the current session or transaction state so that even those are not lost during a failover.

> A highly reliable system incorporates a checkpoint approach to save the current session or transaction state, so even those are not lost during a failover.

Most home-grown applications do not pay enough attention to recovery, even though checkpoint-based recovery is often easy to add. Some level of failover redundancy is usually provided by application server clusters, and database backups are the usual mechanism for ensuring that database data is not lost. Database replication is a common method of ensuring that a failover database exists, and with todays's highspeed networks, a failover database instance need not even be co-located.

The cost of a failure should influence the choice between a checkpoint-based approach and a redundancy-based approach, with redundancy preferred to reduce loss to a minimum level. As an extreme example, an airplane has a very high cost of failure, so redundancy is crucial, and indeed aircraft employ high levels of redundancy for all critical systems. Spacecraft have a very high cost of failure, so critical systems are redundant when possible; for example, spacecraft computer systems are often highly redundant. Spacecraft mechanical systems are usually not redundant due to weight, but increasingly a failover capability is being engineered into designs; for example, single-stage-to-orbit spacecraft designs have considered the ability to continue to operate after losing a main engine. [14]

4.7 Summary

Building a high-assurance application requires selecting overall approaches that will enable a reliable and secure application to be designed and implemented: Reliability cannot be added on any more than security can be added on. Processes for design and implementation must also reflect the requirement for reliability rather than trying to add reliability back in through extensive testing and patching.

This chapter discussed risk assessment, and the importance of matching effort to risk. Fundamental design paradigms were discussed along with their relationship to assurance, including incremental processing, concurrency, and recovery.

The chapters that follow provide design principles and patterns to assist the reader in developing reliable and secure enterprise applications. The topics that are covered are those that tend to arise during the design of the majority of applications built within companies for their own use.

4.8 Exercises

1. What is the most fundamental aspect of any effort to develop a trustworthy application?
2. What are the two basic approaches to recovery?
3. In what situation(s) does concurrency benefit reliability?
4. Why should organizations avoid building their own cryptographic functions?
5. Name a highly effective means of checking that circumscribed programming practices are avoided.
6. Explain what "minimize the trusted computing base" means.
7. What are the factors that affect risk?
8. List three things that are required in order to apply a higher assurance level to particular components of an application compared to the rest of the application.

Answers and hints for these exercises can be found at `http://www.assuredbydesign.com/haa/`.

CHAPTER 5

METHODS OF ATTACK

"To an extent, it was through magic that I discovered the enjoyment in fooling people."–Kevin Mitnick [1]

This chapter will present some of the common attack techniques that are used to compromise computer systems. Attacks often exploit security design flaws, but not always. For example, a "denial of service" attack that interrupts or overwhelms an application can be successful in putting an impregnable system out of service. In general, attacks exploit any form of technical or human weakness. Technical weaknesses can include design flaws, implementation flaws, inadequate protection features, and environmental changes or weaknesses. Human weaknesses can include poor usage practices, inexperienced or inadequately trained users, and poor physical security.

The discussion here focuses first on attacks against technical weaknesses, which are referred to here as technical attacks. The discussion then turns to the methods used against humans in order to obtain computer access. The latter is often referred to as "social engineering."

5.1 Technical Attacks

The enumeration of attack patterns provided in this section is not exhaustive, as the patterns that are possible are limited only by the ingenuity of attackers. It is important to understand these basic patterns as a precursor to examining the software design principles presented afterwards, so that the purpose and motivation of those principles can be appreciated. The attack patterns presented here are not intended to be mutually exclusive or orthogonal. In fact, many of them overlap or are related, and real attacks often fall into more than one pattern or use multiple techniques in combination.

The attack patterns presented here are based primarily on the work of others (for example, [2, 3, 4, 5, 6, 7, 8, 9, 10, 11, 12]). The categories here are arranged in a way that is, hopefully, relevant to the way that most software developers think. This book's Web site[1] contains references to sources and other work related to vulnerability and attack taxonomies.

1 This book's Web site can be found at `http://assuredbydesign.com/haa`.

TECHNICAL ATTACKS, BY SECTION

Interception	5.1.1
Related: Sniffing. Covert channel.	
Man-in-the-Middle	5.1.2
Replay	5.1.3
Modification in Place or in Transit	5.1.4
Related: File manipulation. MiM.	
Interruption	5.1.5
Saturation and Delay	5.1.6
Related: Denial-of-service	
Exploitation of Non-Atomicity	5.1.7
Related: TOCTTOU	
Coordination Interference	5.1.8
Forced Crash and Retrieval of Crash Artifacts	5.1.9
Forced Restart, Forced Re-Install	5.1.10
Environmental Interference	5.1.11
Spoofing	5.1.12
Hijacking	5.1.13
Circumvention	5.1.14
Trap Door	5.1.15
Exploit of Incomplete Traceability	5.1.16
Related: Non-repudiation	
Exploit of Incomplete Validation	5.1.17
Related: Buffer overflow	
Exploit of Incomplete Authentication or Authorization	5.1.18
Exploit of Exposure of Internal State	5.1.19
Exploit of Residual Artifacts	5.1.20
Related: "Dumpster diving" or "trashing"	
Embedded Attack	5.1.21
Related: Planting. Trojan horse. Time bomb. Logic bomb.	
Pattern Matching and Brute Force Guessing	5.1.22
Related: Exhaustive search	
Namespace Attack	5.1.23
Weak Link as Gateway	5.1.24
Trusted Resource Attack	5.1.25
Scope Attack	5.1.26
Related: Domain errors	

5.1.1 Interception

Attacks that involve any form of subversive *interception* of information can be categorized as either "eavesdropping" or "sniffing." The term "sniffing" usually refers specifically to non-intrusive and often undetectable interception, such as by reading information that is broadcast or by attaching a passive listener to a communication channel. The term "eavesdropping" is a less technical term and applies more broadly and loosely.

This category of attacks often involves the use of a "covert channel." A *covert channel* is any communication pathway that exists but was not intended by the designers of the system and thereby violates the system's security policy. [13] A covert channel need not be an actual mechanism intended for *any* form of communication at all; for example, the technique of varying the load on a CPU has been used as a covert channel for the binary encoded signaling of sensitive information to another process in an undetected manner.

Notorious examples of eavesdropping or sniffing attacks include:

1. Sending ICMP packets in order to re-direct packets to flow through an attacker's system, thereby allowing the attacker to read the data in the packets.
2. Reading the mailbox message files in a POP server.
3. Installing a keyboard handler that silently listens to keystrokes.
4. Reading someone's screen on an X-Windows system or on a Windows system via a program such as RealVNC.

When an application reads the information stored by another application, this is often also referred to as "interference," especially if that information is then acted upon in a subversive manner or is used to interfere with the operation of the other application.

5.1.2 Man-in-the-Middle

When a party succeeds in interposing itself between two endpoints and is thereby able to intercept and possibly modify the communication without either party being aware, this is referred to as a "man-in-the-middle" (MiM) attack.

MiM is related to interception, but requires that the interception occurs as the result of the interposition of a listener rather than strictly passive eavesdropping.

5.1.3 Replay

Replay involves the interception of information intended for a target system, followed by sending that information–possibly with additional information inserted–to the target system for the purpose of attacking the system.[2] Replay is a form of MiM attack in which the intercepted message is not modified, although it may be augmented.

Replay often (but not always) involves the use of an intercepted bearer credential of some kind, such as a password or session credential. If an attacker intercepts information that is used to access a resource, such as credentials, the attacker might be able to impersonate a trusted party and thereby access the resource. In this scenario, the attacker "replays" the intercepted information, leading the receiver to believe that the attacker is a trusted party. An example of this kind of replay is intercepting someone's browser session cookie or authentication header and using it to masquerade as the user's session.

Replay may be coupled with a timing attack (see Section 5.1.6, "Saturation and Delay") against a credential-validation server to thwart the detection of credential expiration.

5.1.4 Modification in Place or in Transit

Many attacks rely on the ability to modify data in a persistent store or while it is in transit. A credential store or password file is an obvious target for an attack, as is a password on its way to an end user.

In business computing environments, it is far more common that persistent data sources are attacked rather than data in transit because the latter requires network-level penetration, a higher level of sophistication, and constitutes a MiM attack. Attacks against persistent stores have been categorized by others as "File Manipulation" attacks [15].

---

2 See [14] for a taxonomy of variations of the replay attack.

The practice of modifying hidden tags in a Web form can be considered to be modification in transit and is not a MiM attack because the client is usually the attacker.

5.1.5 Interruption

If a system's security depends on the completion of certain precursor processes, and those processes can be interrupted such that the system assumes that they completed, it might be possible to put the system into an insecure state by interrupting the precursor processes. For example, overwhelming a logging service such that it fails might be used to prevent a trace of intrusion activity from being recorded. This is often considered to be a denial of service, but often there is no service involved–merely an interconnected process–and so the term "interruption" seems more appropriate. Denial of service also can be caused by overwhelming an application, rather than by interrupting it. See the next attack description.

5.1.6 Saturation and Delay

In some systems, security relies on the existence of a service that will detect intrusion. In that case, all that is needed is to delay the response of the intrusion detection system long enough to allow an attack to complete or to force the service request to time out so that the requester uses cached data. This can often be accomplished by overwhelming the service or intrusion detection system. This is a type of attack that is commonly referred to as a denial of service, but the actual technique is a saturation technique; denial of service is the immediate effect [16] on the service or intrusion detection system, and there is then a security consequence as a result of the failure of the system to detect intrusion.

The intrusion detection system might not be specifically designed as an intrusion detection system per se, but might merely be, for example, a normal service that is designed to shut down if any anomalous behavior is detected; for example, if packets with the same sequence number are received.

Delay is a powerful technique because it takes time to identify an intruder, and if delay can be achieved, the attacker has time to cover their tracks and leave–and possibly enter through another means or mount an attack from a different compromised host location.

Besides their use as a means of penetrating a system, saturation and delay can be attack objectives in their own right. Saturation or delay perpetrated *for the purpose of making a system inaccessible or unusable* (i.e., making it "unavailable") is properly known as a *denial of service* attack. However, note that denial of service can be achieved in other ways; for example, by interfering with any process that is critical to an application.

5.1.7 Exploitation of Non-Atomicity

If a software process or thread of execution accesses objects or resources that can be accessed by other processes or threads, or by other activities of the same thread, there is a possibility that logically concurrent access by more than one process, thread, or activity might interfere and make it possible to compromise the state of the system.♦

> ♦ Non-atomicity is the *underlying cause* of a great many kinds of security vulnerabilities. This is a result of the very design of the von Neumann computing model that performs one computation at a time, instruction by instruction. As a result of this processing paradigm, any form of non-hardware-supported authorization check must be performed at discrete predetermined points in time instead of continuously, whereas security attacks can be launched at unexpected points in time.

Some languages, such as Java, provide low-level primitives for controlling concurrent access to language objects. Databases provide locking mechanisms for serializing concurrent access to file-based data. A proper design for a concurrent system usually employs these mechanisms to ensure that interference does not occur. This often means designing software routines that access shared resources in such a way that the accesses are "atomic"—that is, that their effect is all-or-nothing, and intermediate states are unobservable.

If there is non-atomicity in the system, it is sometimes possible to force the system to perform steps out of sequence, thereby putting it into a state that was not anticipated by its designers. This is often referred to as a "race condition."

A special case of this is when the interference is purposefully performed after a resource access rule is checked but before the resource is accessed: During that interval, a change is made to a critical context value, such as a user identity, causing the system to perform a function in a different context than the context that was authorized. This is referred to as a "time of check to time of use" (TOCTTOU) attack.

Attacks based on non-atomicity are often coupled with a denial of service attack that slows a system down and thereby "opens a window of vulnerability."

5.1.8 Coordination Interference

Non-atomicity and delay pretty much cover attacks related to synchronization, but a related class of attacks deserves its own consideration for systems that are inherently asynchronous or independent and that depend on presumed event sequences, timing, or timestamps. Independent systems that cooperate are sometimes assumed to perform actions in a certain sequence or with certain effects, and interference with one of these systems can result in inconsistent effects that cause a failure in a different system.

Delay is often used to achieve this type of interference, for example, by interfering with or spoofing a timing service. Interference with a messaging service can result in certain events not being registered that are relied upon.

5.1.9 Forced Crash and Retrieval of Crash Artifacts

When systems fail, they often leave traces of their internal operation or leave resources in an inconsistent and potentially unprotected or insecure (for example, unencrypted) state. Access to protected information can, therefore, sometimes be achieved by forcing a system to crash and then examining the artifacts that remain.

A crash can sometimes be achieved by exploitation of incomplete validation of inputs or exposure of internal objects that can be modified during an attack to force the system into a state that causes failure.

The most common type of artifact left behind is a file containing an image of the process. Such an image often contains sensitive data, such as unencrypted credentials or the details and relative addresses of stack variables and program code.

5.1.10 Forced Restart, Forced Re-Install

One way of inserting malicious software into a system is by compromising a system's bootup or installation configuration. If the system is then caused to crash or become unusable so that it will have to be re-started, or corrupt so that it will have to be re-installed (with a compromised installation), the compromised configuration will be started or installed, respectively.

This is an extremely powerful and subtle technique. It is unfortunately true that "backup" resources are usually much less protected than primary resources. Thus, by silently implanting a trojan horse (see Section 5.1.21, "Embedded Attack") in a backup resource (or in an emergency response tool) and then merely forcing the primary resource to crash or be crippled, the compromised backup resource will be installed.[3]

This technique is closely related to the "Trusted Resource Attack" (discussed in Section 5.1.25).

5.1.11 Environmental Interference

The normal operation of programs usually presumes the availability of resources, such as memory, threads, sockets, and file space. Software designers often do not anticipate the failure conditions that can occur when these resources are unavailable or are exhausted. This can result in certain functions not completing that are expected to complete. If the system's security depends on these functions (for example, a system log) it might be possible to attack a system without traceability or without intrusion detection completing.

5.1.12 Spoofing

Spoofing involves forging or corrupting (destroying the *integrity* of) a resource or artifact for the purpose of pretending to be—i.e., for the purpose of *masquerading as*—something or someone else. There are many variations on spoofing, and it can be done at any level of a system, from the network level through the application level. Some examples are:

- Forging IP packet source addresses.
- Forging ARP packets to fool a router into thinking that your machine has someone else's IP address.
- Creating misleading Web pages that fool a user into thinking that they are at a different site [17].

3 Tools exist that protect bootup configurations by using encryption.

- Sending a name resolution request to a DNS server, forcing it to forward the request to a more authoritative server, and then immediately sending a forged response—causing the first DNS server to cache the forged response and supply that address to its clients. (Attacks that use this technique as a method of tricking users into accessing sites that mimick trusted sites, for the purpose of obtaining user credentials or other personal identity information, are often referred to as "pharming".)
- Replacing a trusted file or program with a file or program that mimics the original one but that contains malicious data or code. This is also a kind of "trusted resource attack" (see Section 5.1.25).
- Forging or constructing an application object through abnormal means in order to instantiate an illegitimate instance that appears to be legitimate.

> Spoofing of domain names may be made easier by the fact that names expressed in international character sets might be allowed. It used to be the case that a domain name had to consist of 7-bit ASCII characters. Unicode is now being considered for domain names. Because many Unicode glyphs have the same appearance, it is possible to have two domain names that look identical, but are actually composed of different Unicode characters. For example, the character glyph "a" represents the Unicode 16-bit hexadecimal value x0061 from the Basic Latin set, but it also represents the value x0430 from the Cyrillic set. This means that if you receive an email containing a link to "abc.com," you can no longer be sure where the link might take you. This horribly regrettable situation will hopefully be remedied by new browser and email program security features that call attention to the use of links containing mixed or different character sets. A Web site can also help by enabling the browser to authenticate it using SSL, but that requires users to type "https" instead of "http."

Spoofing often exploits an unsophisticated end user. For example, many Web users do not adequately understand or manage their browser security policies. Common ways of exploiting weakly secured browsers to spoof users include creating hidden windows from which attacks on other windows are launched, as well as manipulating the appearance and contents of the window to make it appear as if it were another kind of window, and modifying other windows that show legitimate content.

Spoofing is especially effective when coupled with delay or interruption because many spoofing schemes involve preventing a legitimate service from responding before an illegitimate one does. It is also powerful in combination with a forced restart or forced re-install or any kind of interference requiring an operator emergency response. This is because diagnostic tools or incident response tools can often be attacked more easily than the system itself. When users are in a crisis, they usually do not question the integrity of tools they invoke to help them respond to their crisis. Thus, the combination of attacking poorly-protected tools or configurations, followed by an attack that forces the system to fail and the tools to be used, is extremely powerful. This is in fact the very technique used by the thieves in the movie *Ocean's Eleven*: The thieves accomplish the removal of the bank's assets by carrying them away in the equipment bags of a spoofed SWAT team, having compromised the 911 channel and thereby enabling the spoof SWAT team to respond to the robbery. See also "Distraction and Diversity," discussed later in this chapter.

5.1.13 Hijacking

The term "hijacking" is usually used to refer to an attack that involves disconnecting a server resource in some manner from a resource channel and replacing it with a different server resource. Thus, the channel is "hijacked."

This is a variation of spoofing because users of the channel think that they are accessing the intended resource, via the channel, but are "spoofed" by the replacement resource.

5.1.14 Circumvention

This book shall define "circumvention"' as any method by which an attacker bypasses intended controls, access checks, or system pathways in order to gain access to or control of protected resources. Circumvention can involve a covert channel or it can involve incompletely protected resources. Many of the attacks discussed here represent variations of circumvention.

5.1.15 Trap Door

A *trap door* is a mechanism embedded within a system that allows the normal access paths or access checks of a system to be bypassed. This often takes the form of a special password that is hard-coded into the software. It can also take the form of a special diagnostic interface.

5.1.16 Exploit of Incomplete Traceability

If the *system's design* is such that it fails to record the actions of users, this can lead to a situation in which either appropriate or inappropriate actions are later untraceable or unprovable. It is important to emphasize that this is a result of the system's design—not a result of an attack directed against its logging mechanism. (An attack directed against the logging mechanism would most likely be a trusted resource attack, which is discussed later.)

The ability of a party to deny having performed *appropriate* actions or aspects of those actions (for example, the time at which they were performed) is known as *repudiation*. For example, a user might deny that she performed a particular transaction such as a purchase, and if there is no record that conclusively links her to the transaction, her denial might be successful. Another example would be denial that a message was received when in fact it was. The term *non-repudiation* refers to the ability of a system to defeat repudiation attempts, for example, by recording authenticated records (logs) of all transactions and by using communication mechanisms that provide secure acknowledgment at both endpoints.

Incomplete logs can also enable an intruder to perform *inappropriate* actions without traceability. For example, if an attacker's modification of sensitive files is not recorded in a manner that identifies the attacker's identity, the attack cannot be traced to its source. A failure to log actions in a traceable manner, therefore, represents a significant vulnerability.

5.1.17 Exploit of Incomplete Validation

If a software module does not fully check that its inputs fall within expected ranges, it might be possible to invoke the module with inputs outside of those ranges and thereby cause the program to do things that were not intended by the software designer. This might enable an attacker to circumvent normal system pathways or checks.

The infamous "buffer overflow" attack is a variation of incomplete validation, although in a buffer overflow the validation failure can be considered to be within the application framework (for example, language itself) rather than in the application design because a secure application framework should prevent buffer overflow as well as any other kind of type failure or range failure.

5.1.18 Exploit of Incomplete Authentication or Authorization

The design or configuration of a system might intentionally or unintentionally *omit* certain checks, enabling an attacker to "slip through" access control or authentication mechanisms and thereby obtain unauthorized access or control. This is most likely to be possible if authorization decisions are interspersed throughout the application code.

5.1.19 Exploit of Exposure of Internal State

Circumvention can also occur if resources expose their internal state, thereby allowing a client module to read or modify the resource's internal state in unintended ways.

Inappropriate *reading* of a resource's internal state is a breach of confidentiality because information that is intended to be private to the resource is revealed to an unintended party. This is known as a *containment failure.*♦

♦ See Section 7.1, "Secure Resource Containers," for more discussion of containment.

Inappropriate *writing* of internal state is a breach of integrity. For example, if a resource's interface returns references ("aliases") for internal objects instead of returning separate copies of those objects, any client of the resource might be able to modify the internal objects because they can obtain direct references to them. This kind of failure has been categorized by some as an "integrity failure" resulting from an "aliasing error." [18]

This form of attack is the motivation behind the security model embedded in many browsers. In this model, often referred to as the "same origin" policy, Web pages can only affect their own contents. However, there are loopholes in the policy. For example, scripts can embed executable objects that do not adhere to the security policy, but rather adhere to a different (possibly looser) security policy.

5.1.20 Exploit of Residual Artifacts

If objects are re-used and contain artifacts of prior use, an attacker might be able to use those artifacts to obtain secret information or to obtain references to protected objects. This is analogous to an intruder searching through your trash can, a practice sometimes referred to as "dumpster-diving" or "trashing." [19]

5.1.21 Embedded Attack

This book uses the term "embedded attack" to refer to all attacks that rely on the placement of attack software within a trusted software system. The act of setting up an embedded attack is commonly referred to as *planting*, [20] because a subversive component is "planted" on the target system. Planting can be achieved using other techniques, such as social engineering (discussed in Section 5.2, "Social Engineering") or technical means.

A very common form of embedded attack is known as a "trojan horse" attack. A *trojan horse* is a trusted component that is imported or installed (somehow) into the system but which contains a secret mechanism to facilitate a subsequent attack. Generally the user has rights that the program's author (i.e., the attacker) does not, so the attacker obtains the user's rights by "hiding" inside a trusted component. This implies that the attacker has access to the trusted component, has convinced the user that the component can be trusted, or has lured the user into installing or enabling it.

A trojan horse program can be installed (planted) as a result of a computer virus. An example of this delivery method is the "Troj/BankAsh" virus (2005), which attempts to disable anti-virus software and then monitors the user's Internet access for banking Web sites, such as Barclays, Cahoot, Halifax, and others. If a banking Web site is accessed, the program silently monitors the user's keystrokes in order to capture a login ID and password and other account information and then FTPs this information to a remote site.

So-called "script injection" attacks are a special case of a trojan horse attack in which a script (i.e., a program) is input in lieu of data and is then later inadvertently interpreted (executed) by the application. A trojan horse can also be used to execute a MiM attack by intercepting internal information "from the inside" and using it maliciously.

An embedded attack is sometimes implemented as a "bomb." A *time bomb* is a subversive mechanism secretly embedded within a trusted system for the purpose of initiating an attack at a later point in time. A *logic bomb* is similar to a time bomb except that it is triggered by a sequence of program events rather than by the passage of time.

Embedded attacks are especially effective when coupled with a forced crash. An example is the compromise of a repair tool or boot script followed by causing the system to fail so that it will have to be repaired or rebooted using the compromised tool or script. This is particularly effective because "build-time" components, such as tools and scripts, are often less stringently protected than runtime systems.

5.1.22 Pattern Matching and Brute Force Guessing

Attacks that utilize sophisticated knowledge to derive or anticipate the state of a system or credentials used for authentication are often referred to as "oracle" attacks. These include deciphering, discovery of exploitable patterns, non-randomness or predictable pseudo-randomness, and exploitation of algorithmic weaknesses. A notorious example is the cracking of Netscape's implementation of SSL by taking advantage of a weakness in its random number generation.

Attacks that merely try every possibility until they succeed are known as "brute force" or "exhaustive search" attacks. Encryption algorithms that are not sufficiently strong or that use relatively short keys can often be cracked using brute force: This is a result of the ever-decreasing cost of computing power.

5.1.23 Namespace Attack

Many attacks exploit weaknesses in the name resolution process used to identify resources. These include the insertion of rogue components in a name-resolution path as well as the insertion of components with similar names that are equivalent. It is often the case that abbreviated names are used to identify resources, and a failure to canonicalize a resource name can enable an attacker to substitute other resources with the same abbreviated name but a different canonical name.

5.1.24 Weak Link as Gateway

Attackers often reach their goal by following a circuitous path: entering a weak point and then using that point as a point of trust from which to reach other points.[4]

Human resources Web sites are famous examples of this. Those sites are often poorly protected, but because they have the same domain as other organization sites, they can be used as a launching point when compromised.

4 See the discussion of "transitive confinement" in [21], page 441.

Virtual private networks (VPNs) represent another consideration. For example, if a network is linked to a partner via a VPN and the partner's network has a known weakness, the partner's network can first be penetrated and then used as a gateway to the target network.

5.1.25 Trusted Resource Attack

An application can often be penetrated by attacking a resource on which the application relies. Examples of this include:

- Attacking a DNS server's zone files.
- Attacking an object lookup service, for example, by covertly embedding a trojan horse within its code.
- Modifying the system time. (Some taxonomies identify this kind of attack as a category in its own right.)
- Modifying files that are used by an application but that have insufficient protection.
- Attacking log files that are used to record the actions of users.
- Attacking *other* programs that are poorly protected and that access (and ideally modify) the same resources on which the application of interest relies.[5] Thus, this approach is *transitive* in that it involves attacking a trusted resource, in order to attack another target that uses the trusted resource. This particular pattern is an example of a "Weak Link as Gateway" attack.

This is how source code to Cisco Systems routers was stolen in 2004—by planting a compromised version of the trusted SSH program on Cisco's network to act as a trojan horse by sending users' passwords to the attacker. [23]

> An effective way to attack a protected resource is to subvert resources used by those resources—with many levels of transitivity in between.

5 See [22] for a discussion of how users can be lured into installing tools such as compilers that contain malicious code.

This technique has easy parallels in the non-computer world. There was a movie in the 1960s called *Kaleidoscope* in which a professional card player stealthily entered the factory of a playing card manufacturer and modified the very dies used to print a popular brand of playing cards. He alone knew of the tiny modifications and was able to play poker and win. This is an example of a two-level transitive attack: He attacked a resource (the factory) used to produce the resources used by the casinos (the cards). Thus, an effective way to attack a protected resource is to subvert resources used by those resources. This includes emergency response resources. (See the "Forced Restart, Forced Re-Install" attack.)

5.1.26 Scope Attack

Weaknesses in scoping mechanisms, such as a runtime container, a language-defined scoping boundary, or any other security policy domain or mechanism designed to keep objects from communicating, can be used to access objects or resources outside of their intended scope or boundary. Weaknesses that make this kind of attack possible have been described as "domain errors" [24].

A security domain or access scope can sometimes be circumvented by employing a circumvention technique such as a covert channel (discussed previously). Another kind of scoping attack is to exploit the inadvertent exposure of a resource's internal structure (see the "Exploit of Exposure of Internal State" attack in Section 5.1.19).

5.2 Social Engineering

Malicious actions performed against *people*, including deception or the physical theft of sensitive information such as credentials, represent highly effective avenues of attack against computers. In these cases, the errors or failures are human, and for this reason approaches that utilize human failings are known as *social engineering* attacks.

> "I became absorbed in everything about telephones—not only the electronics, switches, and computers, but also the corporate organization, the procedures, and the terminology. After a while, I probably knew more about the phone system than any single employee. And I had developed my social engineering skills to the point that, at seventeen years old, I was able to talk most Telco employees into almost anything, whether I was speaking with them in person or by telephone."
> —Kevin Mitnick

Deception perpetrated for the purpose of theft or subversion, known as *fraud*, usually involves misplaced confidence in the perpetrator, and for this reason fraud schemes are often referred to as confidence schemes, or "con games." More direct attacks against humans involving the theft of information through surveillance or the actual theft of information or assets of value are also common, such as the theft of volumes of customer information.

Social engineering attacks are as old as civilization. What is new is their application to obtain computer access. Most social engineering computer attacks utilize one or more of the techniques discussed next. For those who are interested, comparable "con schemes" used by non-computer crooks are listed in the sidebars.

SOCIAL ENGINEERING METHODS, BY SECTION

Physical Theft	5.2.1
Emotional Pressure	5.2.2
Haste	5.2.3
Reliance on Inadequate Protection	5.2.4
Instilling Undeserved Trust	5.2.5
Breaking Prior Trust	5.2.6
Trusted Resource Attack	5.2.7

5.2.1 Physical Theft

Physical theft of computer assets or documents that contain computer-related information can be used to compromise a system. An example is the theft of a computer or storage media containing information of value. Another example is the theft (or reclamation) of discarded assets from which computer-related information can be retrieved—so-called "dumpster-diving" (see "Exploit of Residual Artifacts").

5.2.2 Emotional Pressure

Most social engineering techniques utilize some form of emotional pressure in order to induce the target to accept something that is unvalidated or to make a decision based on unvalidated information. This is usually done in conjunction with a technique to instill trust in the perpetrator. The emotional pressure usually takes one of these forms:

1. **Emotional investment**: Example: Claim to need help with something, but then in the middle of the effort, request help with something else that would require authorization–and explain that it would be very helpful to bypass procedure in order to expedite things.
2. **Intimidation**: Example: Telling an administrator that if they do not expedite a request by circumventing a security procedure, the company's profit might be at risk, and hence their job.
3. **Pride**: Example: Challenging an administrator to do something that requires broad-ranging privileges.
4. **Inconvenience** (for example, inconvenience of checking something out): Example: Presenting proof of validity that is unusual and appears legitimate but that would take time and effort to verify.
5. **Enticement** (perhaps sufficient to induce you to avoid safeguards): Example: Promising an insider that they will participate in a lucrative fraud scheme, when in fact the only objective is to get them to perform an act of subversion, such as allowing use of their computer account.
6. **Crisis**: Create a crisis that needs a solution and offer the solution (target accepts inadequate validation from the responder). Example: Send advertisement for a service professing to identify hackers and then slightly hack the target's computer; if contacted, induce the target to provide full and direct access to their system.

TRADITIONAL EXAMPLES OF ENTICEMENT SCHEMES

Scheme Name	Method
Nigerian Letter	Letter recipient is enticed into participating in a lucrative scheme—for a fee that is later revealed.
Pigeon Drop	Target is enticed into sharing in a valuable treasure find, provided the target puts up "good faith money." The treasure is either worthless or taken away.
Pump-and-Dump	False rumors are generated to cause a stock price to inflate. This is an enticement scheme because the rumors are not substantiated.
Spanish Prisoner	Purported ex-prisoner entices target into sharing a stolen fortune, as long as target provides funds to get to it.
Rocks-in-the-Box	Target is enticed into buying purportedly valuable but shady merchandise for cash, only to find that the merchandise is worthless.
Country Boy	Target is enticed into defrauding an apparently naïve person, provided that the target provides "good faith money."
Contest Winner	Target is enticed into sending money to claim a supposedly large prize.
3-Card Monte	Target is enticed into playing a rigged card game based on a controlled demonstration that it is easy to win.
Truck load scam	Target is enticed into buying shady merchandise and pays up front only to find the truck has left.
Bankruptcy fraud	Naïve creditors are enticed into accepting an early unconditional settlement of a debt when told that a bankruptcy is imminent for the debtor, but the bankruptcy application is then rescinded.

5.2.3 Haste

Most schemes to deceive involve a sense of haste or urgency. The perpetrator requires haste in order to prevent detection, because given time, credentials can be validated, and a story double-checked. Also, given time, intrusion detection processes and notification processes complete.

The most common way to induce haste in a victim is to create a form of pressure that is time-based; the time aspect may be real (verifiable) or artificial (would fail verification, but the time pressure makes verification inconvenient or seemingly risky). For example, the perpetrator might ask that things be done quickly in order to make some form of deadline.

TRADITIONAL EXAMPLES OF CRISIS-BASED PRESSURE

Scheme Name	Method
Bail bond scheme	Target is contacted and urged to provide bail money for a relative who is known to be presently inaccessible. The target is under pressure to provide the money immediately without confirming that their relative is indeed in jail.
Phony COD delivery	Target is approached at home by a legitimate-looking delivery person asking for a COD fee. In the pressure of the moment, the target pays the fee.

5.2.4 Reliance on Inadequate Protection

Software applications protect assets of value: information and transactions. If the protection mechanisms have loopholes or are inadequate, an attacker merely needs to discover those sources of inadequacy.

Inadequate protection can result from merely not having enough resources to respond to an emergency of large magnitude or to multiple emergencies concurrently. Many of the attacks in this category rely on overwhelming a response system. The techniques include:

1. **Diversion**: Cause an *unexpected* crisis that *overwhelms response resources*. Example: Attack a system that is not of interest but that is easy to attack so that security administrators are focusing their attention there; then attack the actual target. Another example is to cause a different kind of crisis, such as a fire.
2. **Decoys**: Overwhelm response resources, by creating a storm of false events that prevent the responders from identifying the real events.[6] An example of the use of decoys would be a storm of packets from many compromised "decoy" systems preventing security administrators from tracking the true source of the attack.

6 An interesting example of the use of decoys was in the movie *The Thomas Crown Affair* (1999), in which the thief was expected to appear at a certain time and place where police were waiting, but when he appeared he had also arranged for a great many other men to appear, dressed in the same way and in such a manner that these men could not be distinguished from the thief himself—overwhelming the police to check each man and allowing the thief to escape.

3. **Distraction:** Create innocent confusion that disrupts thought processes or safeguards. Example: Ask an administrator for help that requires that he access sensitive information in your presence and have someone else interrupt him several times.
4. **Reliance on naiveté:** Identify a new and inexperienced administrator.
5. **Reliance on ineffectiveness:** Rely on incompetence, lack of diligence, or an inability to contain or identify an attacker. Example: Falsifying fulfillment transactions that are less well protected. All technical security weaknesses also fall into this category because they represent an ineffective system.
6. **Attack the responders (or compromise them):** Example: Implant a trojan horse in a recovery image.

TRADITIONAL EXAMPLES OF RELIANCE ON INEFFECTIVENESS

Scheme Name	Method
False Claims	Reliance on the inability of a claim processing system to validate claims of expenses.
Kiting	Reliance on the inability of a clearing operation to reconcile related transactions in real time.
Shorting	Delivering less than promised and relying on the inability of the recipient to verify the amount or quality.

Distraction and diversion are classic human behavior techniques that rely on the limited ability of people to deal with multiple situations at the same time as well as the inability of people to think through unusual situations in a timely manner. For example, if an intrusion detection system is repeatedly triggered in some manner that is identified as a "false alarm," the response staff might temporarily disable it until it can be examined. This opens a window of vulnerability.

Distraction can be caused by any abnormal situation that diverts the attention of staff. Diversion involves deliberately triggering an alarm so that response staff will then not notice *other alarms* because they are responding to the first.

Attacking emergency responders is a very powerful technique because when they are not "on-guard" they are usually poorly protected compared with the assets that they protect.

5.2.5 Instilling Undeserved Trust

In order to convince someone to perform an action that you request, you must get them to trust you. Therefore, most social engineering schemes include a method of instilling trust and then exploiting that trust such as inducing the target to perform an unprotected action (especially when you are desperate and your guard is down).

The common methods of instilling undeserved trust are:

1. **Stolen credentials** (or any validation information): Example: "Shoulder surfing" to obtain someone's logon, and then using it. Another example: Enrollment through fraudulent representation. Another example: Using the customer service pathway; for example, calling to change your address and then having sensitive information mailed to you.
2. **Counterfeit credentials**: By presenting counterfeit credentials or evidence of legitimacy. Example: Posing as a system administrator and demonstrating knowledge to buttress the claim, and asking a user to provide sensitive information. This is a variation of the so-called "bank examiner" fraud in which a perpetrator poses as a bank official and tells a customer to turn over funds from their account under false pretenses. Another example: Similar domain names. Another example: Imitation PayPal link schemes, or clicking on any legitimate-looking link in an email from an unvalidated source.
3. **Juxtaposition with something legitimate**: By association or juxtaposition with something legitimate. Example: Links to the Web page of legitimate services.

4. **Successful interactions:** Through legitimate or seemingly legitimate interactions. Example: Free services that build trust and eventually solicit sensitive information.

TRADITIONAL EXAMPLES OF INSTILLING UNDESERVED TRUST THROUGH SUCCESSFUL INTERACTIONS

Scheme Name	Method
Ponzi scheme	Targets invest more and more, based on what they perceive to be good experiences. Their money is eventually taken.
Big store	Target witnesses lots of apparently successful transactions, and uses that as a basis for trust.
Salting the gold mine	Target trusts an investment based on the initial discovery of valuable resources or gains that were actually planted.
Sweetheart swindle	Trust is developed through courtship.

5. **Peer collusion:** Through interactions with a third party that is secretly collusive. Example: Relationships with other seemingly legitimate companies, that are actually "fronts."
6. **Interactions with trustworthy entities:** Through interactions with an entity trusted by the target. Example: Evidence that services were obtained from a trusted security company.

5.2.6 Breaking Prior Trust

Rather than instill trust, it is often possible for a perpetrator to persuade a party that is already trusted to act in collusion with them. This is usually achieved through some form of incentive, such as bribery or mutual gain. The forms of collusion include:

1. **Collusion with an insider:** Often a result of a conflict of interest, or when roles are not sufficiently separated. Examples: An administrator altering a transaction log; a back door inserted by a trusted programmer; causing a financially favorable error in the account of an employee who has high authority to see if they report the error; transactions recorded as discounted when they are not.

2. **Collusion with outsiders:** Example: A collusive security monitoring service.

Indeed the members of the notorious DrinkorDie Web piracy group *often relied on moles in large corporations* and cracked security codes for Norton Antivirus, Microsoft's Word and Excel products, pirated games and design programs, and posted the entire Windows 95 operating system on the Internet two weeks before it was released. [25]

TRADITIONAL EXAMPLES OF INSIDER COLLUSION

Scheme Name	Method
Embezzlement, or "Cooking the Books"	An employee modifies accounting records in order to conceal unauthorized transactions.
Kickback	An insider grants a contract based on the expectation that the contractor will secretly provide a gift.
Salami	An unnoticeable portion ("slice") of proceeds is taken on an ongoing basis.
Under-Ring	A transaction is entered for less than the actual amount charged, and the difference is pocketed.
Employee Account Fraud	The insider has both a work relationship and a business relationship with the organization, and uses employee access to business records to modify the account.
Fictitious Refunds, Fictitious Sales, Negative Invoicing	False refunds, sales, and invoices are submitted by an outsider and facilitated by the insider.
"Ghost" employees	A managerial employee budgets for staff who do not exist, and pockets their payroll checks.
"Salting Cash"	Insiders who would be willing to compromise their organization are identified by causing errors in their favor and observing if they report the error.

5.2.7 Trusted Resource Attack

This form of attack has already been discussed in the context of technical attacks. It is included here because it can be used to attack non-computing assets, and also because of its tremendous power and importance.

Example: Compromise the tools used by emergency response personnel.

5.3 Summary

The methods of attack that are available are broad-ranging and insidious, yet many of them are available to even amateur hackers through the use of tools widely available on the Internet. For this reason, securing applications today is no small challenge. The principles presented in the chapters that follow help to guide the design of applications that are resistant to attack.

This chapter discussed the various kinds of attack, including categories and examples of social engineering attacks. The next chapter presents concepts for trust, which is an important foundation for understanding Chapter 7, "Access Control Containers," in which authorization and containment are discussed at length.

5.4 Exercises

1. Which type of data is attacked more frequently: persistent data, or data in transit?
2. An attack that involves disconnecting a server resource in some manner from a resource channel and replacing it with a different server resource is known as what kind of attack?
3. What type of subversive action must be completed before a trojan horse attack can be performed?
4. Explain what non-repudiation is.
5. What type of system deficiency does a buffer overflow attack exploit?
6. What type of organizational deficiency does a diversion rely on?
7. Varying CPU load to secretly signal internal sensitive information to an external listening process is an example of what kind of mechanism?

8. What type of system deficiency does a race condition exploit?
9. Inserting a rogue reference into a path variable exploits what kind of system weakness?

Answers and hints for these exercises can be found at `http://www.assuredbydesign.com/haa/`.

CHAPTER 6

REALMS OF TRUST

"If any man shall offer to run away, or keep any Secret from the Company, he shall be marroon'd with one Bottle of Powder, one Bottle of Water, one small Arm and shot."
–Article 2 of the pirate's code of John Philips

6.1 Understanding Trust and Authorization

An authorization decision for access to a protected resource can be broken into two parts:

1. Trust in the requesting party.
2. Appropriateness for access.

Trust has to do with the strength of your beliefs about a party's competence, honesty (intent), security, and dependability. [1] Thus, trust is a form of confidence—an estimation of the probability of success when you contemplate dealing with an entity. It does not have anything to do with that entity's appropriateness for performing a particular function—for example, the entity's "need to know"—nor does it have anything to do with the risk or value of the transaction.

PRINCIPLE: AUTHORIZATION SHOULD BE BASED ON TRUSTWORTHINESS AND APPROPRIATENESS.

Trust must be evaluated within the context of a relationship; for example, a gangster might be trustworthy (in terms of intent and sincerity) to members of his family, but not to those outside his family. In terms of competence, you might trust your lawyer to give you reliable legal advice, but not to diagnose an illness. In a computing context, the trust relationship includes the kinds of transactions that you intend to perform. For example, you might consider an online user to be trustworthy for small dollar amounts, but not with large dollar amounts.

Many software applications do not differentiate between levels of trust. That is, it is assumed that if an entity authenticates using a pre-arranged mechanism, their identity is fully trusted, and that identity is then used to make authorization decisions.

Applications that allow the dynamic and automated enrollment of users and partner organizations should allow an administrator to define criteria by which partner organizations attain particular levels of trust.

There are collaborative applications where a simple model of undifferentiated trust is not sufficient. The PGP model [2] is an example of a dynamic system in which the entire set of users is not known ahead of time, so a flexible model is needed for assessing trust. In this model, users "introduce" other users, and they in turn introduce others, leading to a "web of trust."[1] This approach seems to work well for email, but weakness related to the creation (for example, by a virus) of multiple false identities has been claimed. [4]

1 See [3] Section 3.4, "Code Generation," for a discussion of transitive trust in distributed systems.

A key factor in considering how important it is to factor out trust is the degree to which the application is *dynamic with regard to the enrollment of users* and, even more importantly, the *enrollment of partner organizations.* Will organizations be enrolling their own partners? Will those partners enroll their partners in turn? *How much will you trust* your partners' partners, if your partners decide to delegate functions to their partners?

In a dynamic situation, it is not feasible to define specific trust relationships a-priori because the participants change dynamically. Instead, a framework is needed that allows participants to add new participants, in a manner that does not compromise the policies of the leading organization. The framework should allow a realm administrator to define criteria by which partner organizations attain levels of trust, what methods of authentication are required for each level, and what levels or kinds of trust are needed by each role.♦

> ♦ Applications that support collaborative decision making need to consider trust.

Collaborative applications often rely on information that is provided by multiple parties during a transaction, and a method is needed to assess the trustworthiness of the information. For this purpose, "entitlements" provide a useful mechanism. An *entitlement* ♦ is an unforgeable assertion by a trusted party that another party has authorization to perform a particular transaction or assume a particular role. Digital signatures are usually used to provide unforgeability.[2, 3]

> ♦ The use of entitlements is discussed more fully in Section 7.1.9, "Entitlements."

As an example of multiparty collaboration, suppose party A provides you with a signed entitlement object, signed by party B, that states that party C should be granted access to data originally given to you by party B, and that that data should be used in a transaction that you would like to perform. Can you trust the signature? Can you trust the entitlement object? Can you trust party A? Can you trust party B? Can you trust party C? Such situations are actually not uncommon, but because

2 Entitlements are an example of data origin authentication. See [5], p. 121.

3 So-called "attribute certificates" implement the concept of an entitlement using PKI technology.

there is no protocol for handling such complex situations, they are custom-programmed or handled manually using pre-arranged methods for setting up the required trust relationships, usually backed by contractual instruments laboriously executed between each and every party. Applications that are built this way quickly reach a saturation point in terms of number of organizations or number of users beyond which the administrative burden becomes oppressive.

Applications built with hard-coded relationship logic quickly reach a saturation point in terms of the number of organizations or number of users beyond which the administrative burden becomes oppressive.

In order to begin to handle complex trust relationships, it is necessary to clearly distinguish between trust and authorization. Just because someone authenticates does not mean that you trust them or that you even fully trust their identity. Depending on the level of trust, however, you might be willing to engage in certain transactions with them. By encoding the rules for what you would be willing to do, depending on the trust in the party to the transaction, you will have a more flexible framework for adding more partners and kinds of transaction.

For example, if an authorization decision is based on whether a particular participant is initially "trusted" at a certain level, and if the participant later becomes more trusted, their access rights need not be re-visited in entirety; they merely move into a different category and the appropriate rules then apply.

By encoding the rules for what you would be willing to do, depending on the trust in the party to the transaction, you will have a more flexible framework for adding more partners and kinds of transaction.

PRINCIPLE: DISTINGUISH BETWEEN TRUST AND AUTHORIZATION.

6.1.1 Modeling Trust

There are many approaches to defining trust [6, 7, 8, 9, 10, 11, 12, 13, 14, 15, 16, 17]. The right model to use depends on the application requirements, of course. One broadly applicable approach is presented here, for illustration.

> Applications that allow the dynamic and automated enrollment of users and partner organizations have the strongest need to separate trust and authorization concepts in their security model.

A flexible framework should allow the specification of rules for computing (inferring) trust based on other trust relationships; for example, if you trust entity A and entity A trusts entity B, what is *your* trust in entity B? (Such transitivity should not be assumed.) The framework should allow administrators to define such patterns in order to provide the kind of dynamism that is needed.

Even if your application does not require a sophisticated trust model, it is still good practice to define trust explicitly, either as a design assumption or as an enumeration type attribute, and not intertwine it with authorization. Making trust explicit raises its visibility so that the conditions on which that trust depends can be tracked and trust re-evaluated if the situation changes. Assume that all systems are insecure for which trust has not been explicitly defined.

The pattern defined next provides an approach for decoupling trust determination, appropriateness, and authorization.

DESIGN PATTERN: APPROVAL-BASED TRUST

Related Patterns
Used by the "Role-Based Permissions" pattern presented in Section 7.1.6, "Role-Based Access Control."

Context
An authorization system needs to accommodate many different classes of users from a growing number of different organizations.

Problem
It is burdensome to maintain access control lists for lots of users or for complex networks of users. Business scenarios that require the automation of the assignment of roles to users, groups, or partner organizations can be more easily addressed if the decision criteria for the assignment of roles are specified up front and decoupled from the assignment of permissions.

Solution
This pattern incorporates a concept of trust as an aspect of a user's authentication. This can be used to decouple the determinations of trustworthiness and appropriateness from the determination of the permissions that a user has. (The latter is addressed with a separate pattern, "Role-Based Permissions.")

This pattern models the granting of trust to a user based on (1) the strength of authentication used by the user to log on and (2) approval criteria, which may be application-specific. For the discussion of this pattern, refer to Figure 6.1.

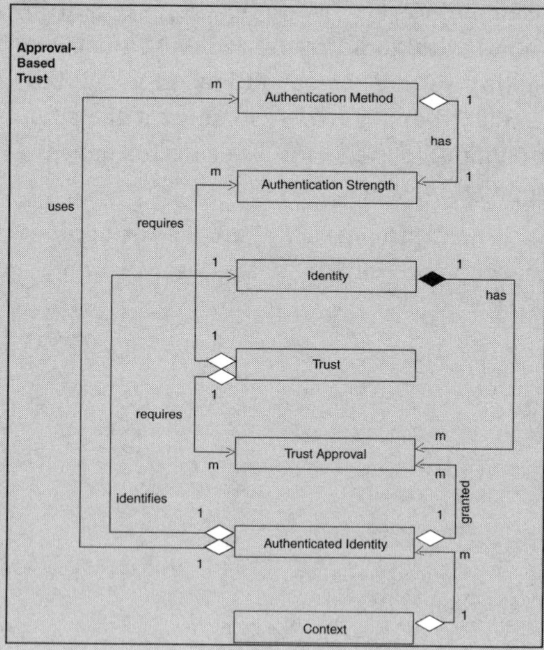

Figure 6.1
Structure.

A user logs on, using an authentication method that is of a preconceived strength. For example, users who log on with a password might be assigned a strength of 1 (the lowest), and users who log on with a biometric identifier might be assigned a strength of 2. A user might also log on using more than one authentication method; for example, via password and biometric. In that case, the user has a single authenticated identity, but that identity is proven using two different authentication methods, each with a different strength.

The objective of logging on is to associate the user's session context with a particular identity that is known to the system. The session context is the only transient object in this model: The session context exists only for the duration of the user's session. This pattern distinguishes between an *authenticated identity* and a *known identity*. An authenticated identity is an identity asserted by the user based on one or more authentication methods. The process of a successful logon results in the association of an authenticated identity with a known identity. The latter is merely referred to as the "identity," for brevity. The known identity is what exists in the application's directory of known (enrolled) users.

The ultimate objective of the user is to have one or more *roles* associated with the user's session context so that he or she can perform some functions that those roles have permission to perform. In this model, *a role requires a pre-configured type of trust*. Thus, trust is not blanket: It is tied to the actions that the user is intending to perform. In order to obtain the role, the user must attain the level and type of trust that the role requires.

Trust is broken down into two components: (a) strength in the user's identity—that is, their strength of authentication—and (b) judgment that the user is "inherently trustworthy" in that role.

The criteria for approval are application specific, so approval is only shown here generically as a box labeled "Approval." As an example of approval, the application might require that the user have a Dunn-and-Bradstreet number and present a letter of credit from a bank.

After approval has been determined, it is associated with the user's identity as a persistent but derived relationship. Note that a link between the approval and the authenticated identity is maintained in case the authenticated identity is later found to be invalid and all approvals granted to it must be reversed.

After the user's session context has the trust required for a particular role, the user can be granted that role. Any attempts to access resources are then authorized based on the user's context meeting the authorization rules for the resource.

Consequences

An authorization system can use the trust that is assigned to an authentication context as a basis for assigning permissions to that context. The decoupling of trust from authentication makes it possible to make role assignment contingent on a level of trust and appropriateness. Users do not need to be manually assigned roles by an administrator; rather, the process of role assignment can be automated and dynamic. This makes the process of user enrollment much more scalable for complex multi-organizational applications.

Issues related to the management of trust data are discussed next in Section 6.2, "Managing Trust."

6.2 Managing Trust

Section 6.1, "Understanding Trust and Authorization," discussed the importance of distinguishing between trust and authorization. To recap that discussion, trust represents the confidence you have in a party's intentions, affiliations, and identity, whereas authorization represents the appropriateness of that party to access certain functions or information.

It is often possible to group external entities according to similar trust characteristics, even if those entities have no relationship with each other. For example, you might decide to trust all "external" (for example, Internet) domains a certain way, and "internal" (for example, those within your organization) a different way. This is the "zone" concept: Different policies are applied for different client locations (for example, inside versus outside).

6.2.1 Realms of Trust

To facilitate the discussion that follows, it is necessary to define a general term, *security realm*, or "realm" for short, to mean any container that manages security policies for a set of protected entities–including objects such as identities, credentials, or access rights for resources–on behalf of or as an integrated function of a resource container.

A security realm is any container that manages security policies for a set of protected entities.

The term "domain" is often used to mean the same thing as "realm," but the term "domain" is a more general term, so this book uses "realm" to mean the narrower concept described here.

Real-life examples of realms include a file system, an application server, a Web server, a Kerberos realm, and a Web policy server. Each of these container-like systems provides logical compartments for resources (files, application objects, and Web resources) and implements trust relationships with the outside world. Each of these different kinds of realms has significant differences from the other kinds, and some offer a more flexible and extensible model than others. Some containers can contain multiple independent realms. Depending on the technology, realms may include items such as informational or transactional resources, users, roles, groups, and attributes related to other realms.

Realms are important for managing trust (familiarity or believability) relationships between sets of resources and the outside world. For example, a backend application server might allow a particular Web application server to authenticate to it, but no other client. As another example, a Windows "domain" can be configured to trust (i.e., believe) another domain's user identities, if a trust relationship is set up between them.

As another example, the Kerberos key distribution protocol is designed to permit federated operation via a trust network. A hierarchy (or network) of independent key distribution points (i.e., realms) can set up trust relationships between themselves and thereby allow a client to obtain credentials to access a service in a remote realm by authenticating to its own realm and then progressively obtaining credentials for intermediate realms. The destination realm can elect to trust the client by virtue of the fact that it was authenticated by a realm that is trusted by a realm that is trusted by a realm that is—and so on—trusted by the service's own realm. (The trust relationship is for authentication purposes only.) Because the path is preserved by the protocol, the destination can examine the authentication path and elect to trust or not trust a realm in the path, and thereby decide to trust or not to trust the identity of the client.

Trust *does not* imply authorization, however. The identities recognized by a realm do not necessarily all have the same access rights to the realm's resources, as that would violate the principles of *least privilege* and "need to know." ♦

> ♦ See also the principles"Compartmentalize Roles" in Section 8.1.1, "Role Separation," and "Segment Data and Resources According to Risk or Sensitivity," also in Chapter 8.

A realm can be a useful mechanism to prevent "interference" between resources from different sources. For example, a realm can grant access to one of its resources by clients of another realm contingent upon a level of trust of the other realm and also contingent upon appropriate authorization for the client; both attributes (the trust and the authorization) can be set and managed by the realm that owns the resource.

Because the administrator of a realm has the power to set access rights for the items within the realm, the owner of those items must fully trust the realm's administrator. For many realms, the administrator will have technical ownership of the realm.

A realm can be a useful mechanism to prevent "interference" between resources from different sources.

6.2.2 Hierarchies of Trust

Realms may contain other realms, in a hierarchical fashion, thereby providing a mechanism for decentralization and solving the single administrator problem. Hierarchy is an important feature for any class of resources that must be managed. For a security realm, hierarchy can provide these advantages:

- The items in the realm (resources, users, and so on) can be aggregated into sub-groups ("sub-realms") for administrative convenience.
- Sub-realms can be defined that share specific trust relationships with the outside world.
- The administration of sub-groups of resources, users, and so on, can be delegated and narrowed so that one administrator is not burdened with administering so many granular things.
- Assuming that the global identification of the items in a realm is tied to the identification of the enclosing realm, sub-realms permit the partitioning of the namespace of realms—and therefore the items that they contain—which makes administration and naming of large numbers of resources more tractable.
- Operations can be done on an entire sub-realm as a unit, such as applying a new policy to all members of the sub-realm.
- Policies can be defined that are automatically inherited by sub-realms. Ideally, these policies can be implemented (at the realm administrator's option) in a manner such that they cannot be overridden by a sub-realm.

The last item, policy inheritance, is valuable for environments that need to ensure that certain policies that are critical to the security of the organization's infrastructure or business policies are not compromised by participating organizations that use that infrastructure and that administer their own realms within it. For example, if an organization has a trusted set of partners and wishes that those partners do not *delegate certain processes* (for example, realm administration) to their respective partners, the organization realm administrator could define a policy that prevents any sub-realm administrator from delegating their administrative function. This ensures that unknown partners (of unknown trustworthiness) will not be involved in performing sensitive administrative functions.

> A realm administrator can define a policy that prevents any sub-realm administrator from delegating their administrative function.

The ability to define such mandatory inherited policies, of course, presumes that the realm technology implements a policy inheritance feature. This is not the case with all kinds of realms.

PRINCIPLE: CONSIDER HIERARCHICAL REALMS AND INHERITED SECURITY POLICIES WHEN POSSIBLE.

The ability to delegate the administration of sub-realms to sub-realm administrators makes a hierarchical realm structure inherently decentralized. Delegation of administration is an important feature because most security administrators do not want to centrally administer all of the organization's security policies. When you ask them if they want centralized management, the answer is usually "yes," but when it comes time to deal with all the policy rules that applications crank out, it quickly becomes apparent that that model is not scalable. In actuality, administrators want to manage *global* policy and leave application-specific authorization models to the groups that develop and maintain those applications. That is how it should be.

> Most security administrators do not want to centrally administer all of the organization's security policies.

PRINCIPLE: PROVIDE FOR DECENTRALIZED ADMINISTRATION OF APPLICATION SECURITY POLICY.

It is important that a parent realm does not have mandatory permission to modify the access rights of items contained within a child realm. The parent only needs permission to set policies that apply to sub-realms and to perform operations on the sub-realms themselves, possibly including deleting sub-realms and their contents. (Delete ability would depend on the overall realm administration policy.)

Some kinds of realms are more naturally hierarchical than others. For example, file systems and Web resource containers serve objects that natively form a hierarchical namespace because most file systems are hierarchical and most Web resource containers can authorize and serve objects based on a relative file system path. The objects served by an Enterprise JavaBeans application server container can also map to a hierarchical "JNDI" namespace.

◆ Ownership and composition are discussed in Chapter 11, "Compositional Integrity."

When defining a resource hierarchy, it is important to clearly define the *nature of the hierarchical relationship*. For example, does the hierarchy represent ownership? ◆ Does it represent a policy hierarchy, such that policy is assumed to propagate down the tree? Or is the hierarchy merely a namespace hierarchy?[4] Also, does a hierarchy imply independence among the sub-portions of the hierarchy? That is, can you create a larger system by connecting various components together or will that result in conflict between them or some kind of emergent behavior?

When considering a hierarchical structure, it is important to first understand if the hierarchy represents *composition* or *control* because these are typically the two distinct kinds of hierarchy in resource hierarchies.

Composition is an extremely important abstract concept in computing. "Composition" (discussed in detail in Chapter 11) is the concept that an object is composed of its parts, just as a family is composed of its family members. Thus, a compositional hierarchy is a representation of which objects are composed of which other objects. Compositions are always hierarchical.

Collections of objects can also be grouped together in ways that do not imply composition. For example, control ownership implies that an object controls and is responsible for its parts, just as a parent is individually responsible for the children of the family. A parent is not *composed of* its children, however.

4 See [18] for a discussion of hierarchy in the context of program languages.

Note that because there can be two parents in a biological family, the structure of the relationships between parents and children is not hierarchical: there are actually two hierarchies, one for each parent, and each child belongs to both hierarchies.

These distinctions are important because the access rights that should be granted for access to a resource tree as a whole may be different than the access rights that should be granted to a particular item in the tree. The relationships between the items in the resource hierarchy need to be clearly defined so that policy errors do not occur as a result of confusion over the way in which access rights propagate down a hierarchy.

For example, in a file system, file access permissions are sometimes set up so that the permissions of a directory propagate to the files and sub-directories below the directory. On the other hand, there might need to be specific sub-directories with different access rights.

> **PRINCIPLE: CLEARLY DEFINE THE MEANING OF HIERARCHICAL RELATIONSHIPS.**

6.3 Summary

This chapter explained the critical role that trust plays in online interactions and the importance of understanding where trust is being applied. Key concepts were presented with respect to the representation and management of trust in an authorization system. The concepts of realm and domain were explained, along with issues related to realm design, such as hierarchy, decentralization of administration, and delegation. The next chapter continues with a discussion of authorization and containment systems for protecting access to sensitive resources.

6.4 Exercises

1. What is another term for "realm"?
2. What are the two parts of any authorization decision?

3. Which of the following is *not* an advantage of hierarchical security realms?
   a. Policies can be overridden by sub-realms.
   b. The administration of sub-groups of resources can be delegated.
   c. The administration and naming of resources is more manageable.
   d. Policy changes can be effected for an entire sub-realm as a unit.
4. By encoding the level of trust in the rules for a transaction, what kind of flexibility is derived?
5. Realms are important for managing what kinds of relationships?
6. For what kinds of applications is it especially important to explicitly represent trust in transaction rules?

Answers and hints for these exercises can be found at `http://www.assuredbydesign.com/haa/`.

CHAPTER 7

ACCESS CONTROL CONTAINERS

"I built the Trojans the wall about their city, so wide and fair that it might be impregnable..." –Neptune talking to Apollo, from Book XXI of the Iliad

The principles presented here lay a consistent foundation for the technical elements and features of a software system that controls access to and by a set of resources.[1] In this parlance, a protected resource is any computing asset that needs to be protected via an access control mechanism. For brevity, this book often simply uses the term "resource." A protected resource should have an authorization mechanism (policy enforcement point) that cannot be bypassed (is "non-bypassable"); its execution environment must provide sufficient security context with known or determinable trust characteristics (i.e., how believable the context is); and the authorization mechanism must be sufficiently flexible to permit the expression of appropriate authorization rules.

1 See [1] for a comparison of access control and information flow authorization models.

Besides protecting a secure resource from access by those who should not have access to it, an environment that hosts a resource needs to be protected against an errant or malicious resource. An errant or malicious resource might allow or cause sensitive data to leave the resource container. The problem of protecting such leakage is known as the "confinement problem" [2], [3]. An errant or malicious resource can also operate incorrectly and produce incorrect results, or it might even damage or compromise its environment.

7.1 Secure Resource Containers

In this book, the term resource container—or merely "container" for short—describes a framework or platform for hosting resources. Thus, in this usage, the term "container" includes the framework used to manage the contained resources. This usage is consistent with contemporary usage of the term by application programmers.

A container ordinarily provides APIs or methods for the container's resources to access services that are provided or managed by the container. A container may also provide a means for clients of the resources to locate and access the resources. For example, an "EJB container" is an infrastructure that not only contains Enterprise JavaBeans, but also adheres to the EJB container specifications and, as such, provides certain APIs and management facilities.

A *secure resource container* is a framework or platform for accessing resources in such a way that (1) the runtime and other resources in other security domains of the overall system are protected from an errant resource (i.e., are compartmentalized), and (2) the resources are protected from *inappropriate* or *untrusted* access—i.e., access is controlled or authorized.

In order to achieve these purposes, a resource container not only manages the resources that it contains and the level of exposure of those resources to the outside world, but it also manages the trust relationships between its resources and other resource containers and provides contextual parameters that can be used to make authorization decisions for access to the contained resources as well as managing authorization policies and rules.

A properly designed resource container does not ever allow its resources to pass information to the outside world without the knowledge and coordination of the container. This is referred to as the "containment" or "confinement" requirement. Inadvertent failure of containment is discussed in detail in Section 7.13, "Resource Interface Design," when we consider the design of resource interfaces.

A corollary concept is that the internals of a container's resources should never be exposed to the outside world. This is the information hiding principle articulated by Parnas [4].

The containment requirement includes objects produced or exposed by the resources. For example, if a resource method returns a value, that value may not expose references to any compartment objects, except those that are part of the intentionally exposed interface. There are various ways of enforcing such a policy, including static analysis, design rule verification, and utilizing a design language that provides these features, or deploying with a runtime that provides a resource gateway framework.

Whatever mechanism is used for protecting access to resources, it is important to verify that any possible means of bypassing the authorization mechanism are prevented. For example, if an authorization layer implements a gateway pattern, and the gateway in turn calls business resources, can those resources be called directly by a client, thereby bypassing the authorization gateway? If the business resources access a database, can the database be accessed directly? Are there any attack patterns that could be used to obtain direct access to the protected resources; for example, by hijacking a communication pathway?

PRINCIPLE: ENSURE THAT AN AUTHORIZATION MECHANISM CANNOT BE BYPASSED.

Non-Bypassability

There are many models for implementing secure resource containers. Most are similar in that they rely on some kind of security policy mechanism that interposes itself between a resource and parts of the resource's environment—including clients—that interact with the resource. The interposition mechanism is most commonly implemented either as a "reference monitor" or as a "gateway." These are both described next, along with some other important related models.

7.1.1 The Reference Monitor Model

A *reference monitor* is a component that interposes itself between a client of a resource and the resource by monitoring, intercepting, or otherwise controlling all references to the resource.[5] Usually, this requires support at the level at which resource references are dispensed and "dereferenced"—i.e., at the hardware or virtual machine level. After a resource reference is intercepted, authorization rules can be applied.

To be effective, a reference monitor must have these properties:

1. It is always invoked; i.e., there is no way to bypass it.
2. It is tamper-proof.[2]
3. It is small enough to be verifiable, so that the correctness of its decision process can be proven with reasonable confidence.

A reference monitor is, therefore, a reliable interposition mechanism, *by definition.* The means by which interposition is achieved varies with the implementation of the monitor technology.

One of the more interesting implementations of a reference monitor is the Kava system [6]. In the Kava system, permission check calls are inserted into the compiled code before the code is allowed to run, thereby achieving the monitoring of all resource accesses. This makes it impossible for Kava-compiled applications to bypass the permission checks.[3] The security checks are also transparent to the application code.

---

2 Tamper-proof is unrealistic: The best that can be achieved in practice is tamper-resistant.

3 This is assuming that the Kava system itself or a lower layer of the runtime environment has not been compromised.

DESIGN PATTERN: REFERENCE MONITOR

Context

Sensitive resources must be protected so that they can be accessed only by those who are authorized.

Problem

On most application platforms, applications merely need a reference to a resource in order to be able to access it. Because references can be copied, stored, and passed to other security domains, this makes it possible for applications to purposefully or inadvertently enable other unauthorized applications to access resources.

Solution

The Reference Monitor pattern is a fundamental pattern [7] for access control.

The pattern relies on the fact that most runtime platforms utilize some form of indirection to address resources, so any resource access by an application relies on the dereferencing of a reference to the resource. For example, in a C++ language program, a resource (for example, an object) cannot be accessed unless a pointer to the object is first dereferenced by the runtime. Dereferencing involves translating a reference value held by an application into a value that can be used by the runtime to transfer control to, read, or modify a resource. In the process of dereferencing a reference value, access control logic can be applied. Thus, *the access control mechanism must be built into the dereferencing mechanism.*

For a reference monitor to be reliable, there must be no alternative means of accessing the object—i.e., the dereferencing mechanism cannot be bypassable. The reference monitoring mechanism can be implemented as part of the runtime itself, or it can be achieved by any reliable process that inserts calls at all points of dereference within the application code.

The essential concept is shown in Figure 7.1.

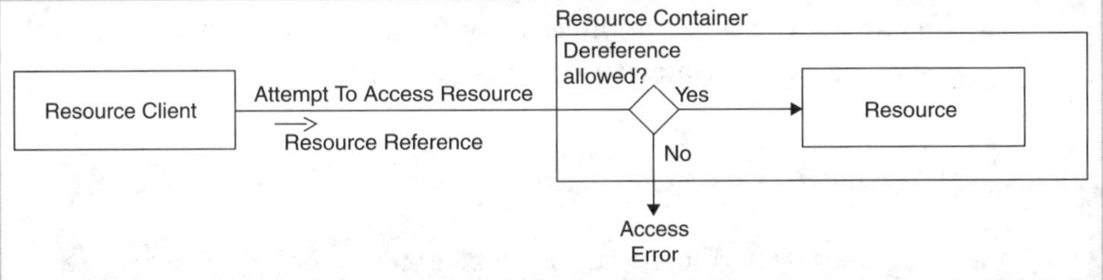

Figure 7.1 The reference monitoring activity.

As can be seen in the figure, any application that attempts to access a resource must provide a reference for the resource to the resource container (runtime). The container interprets the nature of the access (for example, a read access, write access, or execution access), and if the access is allowable, the container translates the reference value into the actual address of the resource and passes control to the runtime to perform the access.

Because all resource references used by applications are infallibly interpreted by the reference monitor before they can be used to access a resource, it is not possible to accidentally pass a direct address to a resource that would allow it to bypass the reference monitor.

Consequences
Resources can be securely guarded by the reference monitor. However, this does not prevent resources from revealing sensitive or inappropriate information when they are accessed by authorized applications.

A reference monitor is a generic mechanism, so it is economical to implement if the platform's dereferencing mechanism is open enough to make the insertion of a reference monitor possible.

7.1.2 Gateway Models

A gateway is a component that is interposed between a resource and clients of the resource. Clients of the resource access the gateway, which in turn accesses the resource on their behalf. If the gateway is constructed so as to mimic the resource's interaction, it is known as a "proxy."

The term "gateway" is widely used in product literature and in Internet specifications. The term "guard" is a related but somewhat obscure term: A guard *protects* access to a sensitive resource.♦ The term "gateway" is also sometimes used more loosely to mean simply a guard.

♦ See also the discussion of wrappers in Section 7.20.6, "Native Resources."

Gateways are commonly used in the Internet. For example, a firewall is a kind of gateway. Gateway models have been applied to application security frameworks as well, such as the Java Wallet Gateway Security Model [8].

DESIGN PATTERN: RESOURCE PROXY GATEWAY

Context
Sensitive resources must be protected so that they can be accessed only by those who are authorized.

Problem
(Same as for the "Reference Monitor" pattern.)

Solution
The concept of a resource "gateway" is described in the body of Section 7.1.2, "Gateway Models." In this resource protection design pattern, a resource client accesses a resource through a gate-way object, which guards the resource. A client never has possession of the address of the actual resource object, and therefore is not able to ever access the resource directly: The client has access only to the gateway object. The gateway object itself exists

within a protected environment and cannot be modified by the resource client. The gateway object incorporates calls to the authorization mechanism to check whether the client has permission to access the resource.

Resources often return references to other resources and sometimes (perhaps erroneously) return references to objects contained within their internal state. A resource gateway has to intercept such returned references and translate them into resource gateway references or disallow them and raise an exception to ensure that real resource references and internal state are never returned to a resource client.

A resource gateway that mimics the interface of the resource that it protects is a "proxy gateway." This is the most practical form of gateway because of its economy of interface definitions. The resource proxy gateway concept is shown in Figure 7.2.

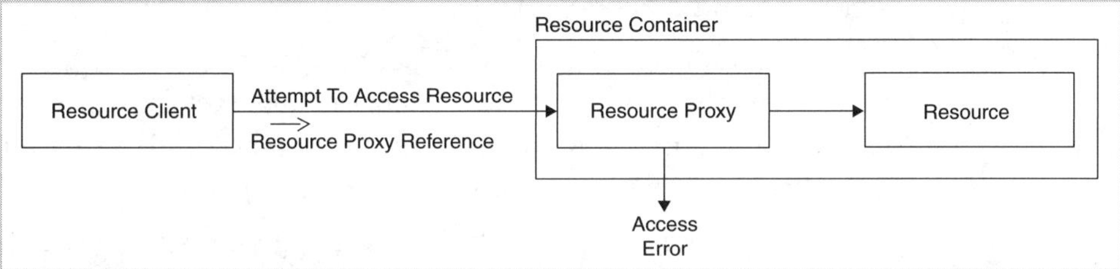

Figure 7.2 Activities of a resource proxy.

Consequences
Resources can be securely guarded by a resource gateway. If properly designed, the gateway can prevent the revelation of inappropriate information. This is because the gateway must be aware of all the information elements conveyed by the resource's interface, so it is in a position to discern the appropriateness of the values of those elements.

7.1.3 The Capability Model

A capability-based resource container maintains a list of "capabilities" for each resource client. [9] In this model, a *capability* is an *unforgeable* permission set within a resource container, specifying the *client's access rights* with respect to *a particular resource*. The client may identify the resource only by referencing the capability, so a capability provides a layer of indirection for accessing a particular resource.

Thus, there exists one capability for each resource that the client may access, and the capability specifies the ways in which the client may access the resource. This is depicted in Figure 7.3. Thus, a capability list is in effect a set of permissions, logically or physically associated with each resource. A capability list may change during the client's session with the resource.

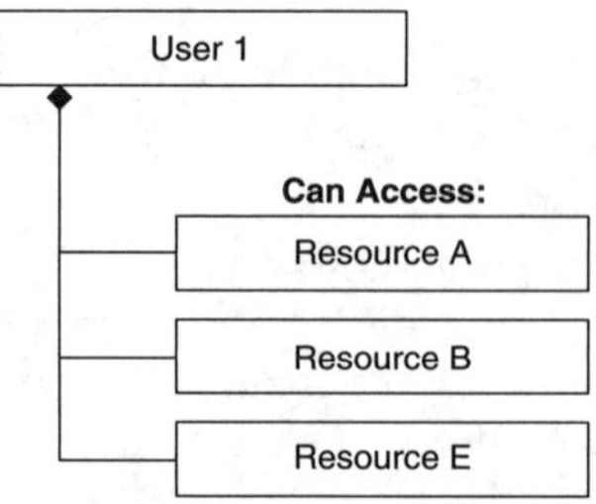

Figure 7.3
A user's capability list identifies the resources that the user can access and how the user may access them (i.e., which methods can be accessed).

A capability permission may specify access for a single resource method, or a permission may be abstract with a many-to-many relationship between resource methods and the permissions that each method requires for access.

Some systems treat capabilities as permissions or entitlements, with a looser requirement with regard to the cardinality between capabilities and resources.[4, 5]

Some implementations of capabilities utilize a gateway to provide indirection between a resource client and a resource and also to provide an interface to the resource.

The set of capabilities that a user has for accessing a resource defines a "sphere of protection" around the resource. This is because the user cannot bypass the container's enforcement of the resource's capability requirements. The capability set, in effect, becomes the user's "sandbox" for accessing the resource.

7.1.4 Access Control Lists

An access control list (ACL) is a *list of users* who are allowed to access a resource.[6] An ACL is associated (bound to) a resource, and the resource's authorization mechanism checks the ACL

4 For example, the Kerberos security protocol specification (IETF RFC 1510) defines the term "capability" to mean more or less what we defined in Chapter 6, "Realms of Trust," as an entitlement.

5 See [10] for an early (1997) discussion of capabilities and code source in Java, which were subsequently implemented in the Java platform.

6 For a seminal paper on access control lists, see [11].

whenever a user attempts to access the resource. The ACL approach can be used by a reference monitor or by other models of resource access control.

An ACL is the logical inverse of a capability set because an ACL is bound to (applies to) a particular resource and lists users, whereas a capability set applies to a particular user and lists resources (capabilities). This is depicted in Figure 7.4.

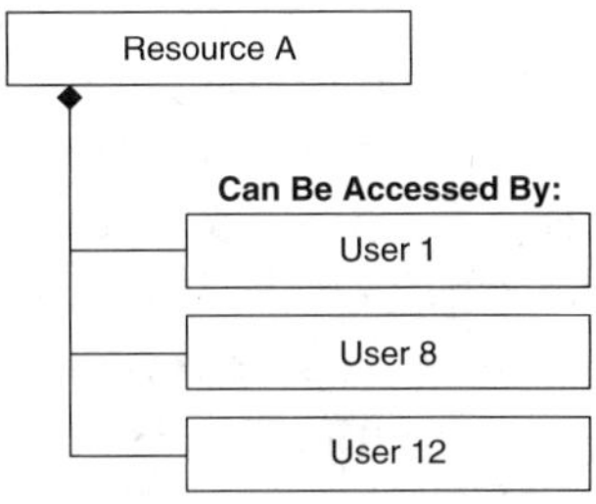

Figure 7.4
A resource's access control list identifies which users can access the resource, and how.

7.1.5 The Sandbox Model

The "Sandbox Model" was greatly popularized by early versions of the Java language (versions prior to 2).[7] In a sandbox model, an application (resource client) has very limited access to system resources and effectively operates within a limited and relatively safe environment, often referred to as a sandbox or "jail." A widely used sandbox is the "chroot jail" on Unix systems.[8]

In the Java sandbox model, the runtime's security manager decides whether an application is trusted or not and, therefore, whether it should be run within a sandbox. In this implementation, security checks are embedded within each resource: A resource is responsible for making an explicit call to a security manager to see if the user context should be allowed to proceed. The combination of the security manager and the embedded resource checks constitutes the sandbox. The Java sandbox implementation, therefore, lacks a reference monitor in that there is no means by which the Security Manager can guarantee that it will always be called, because a Java resource must explicitly make calls to the security manager.

7 See [12] under "1.1 The Original Sandbox Model."

8 See `http://olivier.sessink.nl/jailkit/`. See also [13] for a discussion of FMAC, a file-system sandbox.

The Java 2 security mechanism has been substantially enhanced compared to earlier versions and is no longer a "sandbox" model, but the current model still requires resources to make explicit calls in order to verify access.[9] Also, the Java 2 Micro Edition for small devices such as cell phones still uses the sandbox model.

7.1.6 Role-Based Access Control

Role-based access control implements security policy by defining a set of roles and the permissions or capabilities that each of those roles has. Users are then assigned roles based on the trust and responsibilities of each user. Role-based access control is a *non-discretionary* access control technique because the access rights of users are predefined based on a user's roles and are not specified for each user.

The Role-Based Access Control (RBAC) model has been promoted by the National Institutes of Standards and Technologies (NIST) [14]. It defines a methodology for defining roles that can be associated with user identities for the purpose of access control. In the RBAC model, a "role" is a set of permissions to perform operations. This allows *application access rules to be defined in terms of roles*, and users can be granted roles as required for various functions. There are disadvantages to defining access rules in terms of roles, which are discussed in Section 7.10, "Dynamic Conditions," but nevertheless, the role-based model is very powerful.

This book defines a *role* as a named set of permissions. In the RBAC model, a role can be a set of permissions to perform *operations* (as opposed to permissions to access certain *data*), where each permission maps to a particular operation. In contrast, this book's definition of permission is looser because it does not require a one-to-one mapping between a permission and an operation. (Section 7.7, "Permissions," explains permissions in more detail; for the discussion here, simply consider a permission to be a right to perform a given operation.)

9 This leads to a need for some framework components that would allow a resource designer to define a permission model for a resource and to ensure that the required security check calls are always made.

The use of roles based on permissions as an authorization paradigm does not obviate the need to take trust into account. The trustworthiness of the user must be considered when deciding whether to assign them a role. When assigned, though, a role should have a predetermined trust associated with it. Thus, the ability of a user to take on a role should depend on that user's assumed trustworthiness as well as the strength of their authentication. See Section 6.1, "Understanding Trust and Authorization," for more discussion of the assignment of roles based on trust.

Trust is, therefore, a characteristic of a role. It must be, because a role implies permissions, and permissions cannot be implied without a given level of trust.

The use of role-based permissions to perform authorization is illustrated by the following design pattern.

DESIGN PATTERN: ROLE-BASED PERMISSIONS

Related Patterns

This pattern expands on the "Approval-Based Trust" pattern in Section 6.1.1, "Modeling Trust."

Context

A resource requires that any context that accesses it must have a certain set of permissions.

Problem

A role-based model is very convenient administratively, and a permission-based model is very convenient for resource development. However, the role model and permission model are often disjointed. For example, role-based access control systems often utilize an access control list that associates users with roles.

Solution

This pattern provides an approach for defining a resource's authorization requirements in terms of permissions. With this pattern, users can be granted access to roles based on criteria related to trustworthiness and appropriateness (need to know), and those roles convey certain permissions, depending on the role. Users who have the required permissions—as a result of having one or more roles—can access a resource.

This pattern is based on the "Approval-Based Trust" pattern. A role has a certain set of permissions associated with it—that is, possession of the role conveys those permissions. The role also requires a certain level of trust for it to be granted to a user, where trust is modeled according to the "Approval-Based Trust" pattern. The pattern is shown in Figure 7.5.

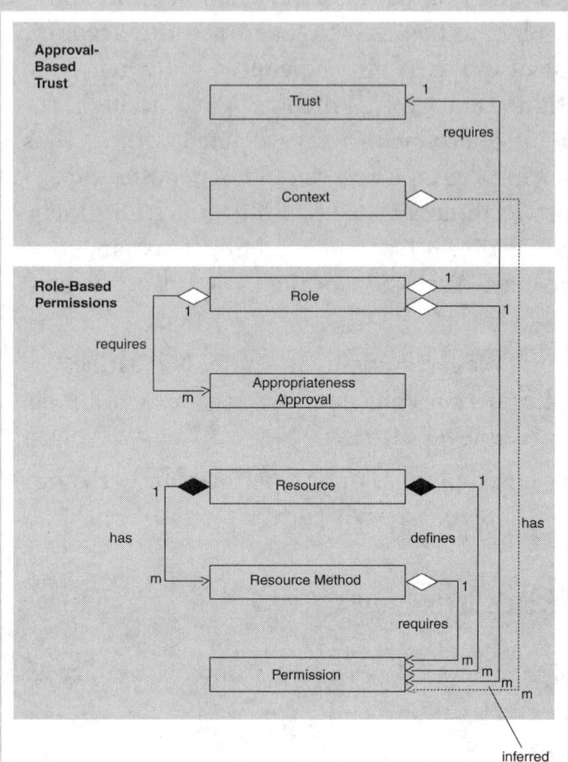

Figure 7.5
Structure.

In addition to inherent trustworthiness, the user must be judged to be *appropriate for the role*—their "need to know." Thus, a role requires one or more "appropriateness approvals."

After the user's session context has the trust required for a particular role and the user had been approved for the role, the user session's permission set can be calculated by querying which permissions the user's role is defined to have and conveying those permissions to the user's session context. *This inferred permission set exists at most for the duration of the user's session.* Permission sets are a powerful approach to determining authorization and are discussed further in the pattern "Parameterized Permissions" in Section 7.8.

Note that this pattern makes it easy to independently tweak the authentication methods required for a particular role, the criteria that are used to grant access to a role, and the permissions that are possessed by a role.

Consequences

Role assignment to users and permission requirements for a resource are decoupled, allowing for each to be specified and maintained separately.

7.1.7 Rule-Based Access Control

This model utilizes a repository of access rules for the purpose of making access control decisions. The assumption is that there is a reference monitor of some kind that interposes the evaluation of authorization rules prior to any resource access. This model is very flexible, and the rules can be designed to reflect actual business conditions.

Rule-based access control is a *discretionary* access control technique because it provides the flexibility to customize permissions for each user—at the discretion of an administrator and perhaps even at the discretion of the user (within the domain of objects owned or installed by the user). Discretionary techniques are generally more vulnerable than non-discretionary techniques because of this flexibility and decentralization of control, and protection against trojan horse attacks may require some form of monitor that alerts the user when an application accesses a resource not explicitly requested by the user or allowed by an administrator for that application.[15]

Rule-based access control is especially effective when used to augment role-based permissions. For example, authorization can be based on the user having a required set of permissions, in addition to a set of authorization rules being satisfied. The permissions can be inferred from the roles that the user currently has. This provides the maximum flexibility and allows issues of trust to be resolved at the time that the user's roles are granted while retaining the ability to layer on additional authorization rules that reflect changing conditions.

7.1.8 Evidence-Based Authorization

Evidence-based authorization emphasizes the use of trusted attributes to make authorization decisions. It is the model implemented by the Microsoft .NET security framework.

The essential concept of evidence-based authorization is that authorization policy decisions are made based on "evidence" assembled about an execution context. The trustworthiness of the evidence is taken into account by the policy evaluation mechanism.

7.1.9 Entitlements

In this model, the user's context bears a set of entitlements (already discussed in Section 6.1, "Understanding Trust and Authorization") for the duration and purview of the context. An entitlement is a set of verifiable permissions for a particular identity to access particular resources.[10] The context must request a resource and the presence of the required entitlement in the context will allow the context to obtain the resource.

The entitlement model also allows "negative entitlements"—denials—to be associated with a context. This is a risky practice, however, because it introduces the possibility that a failure to resolve or interpret a negative entitlement might result in allowing the context to access something that they should not. Therefore, any failure of that kind should usually result in a reduction to a least-permission state.

7.2 Resource Types and Layers

A *resource* is anything that is used by a program and that is managed in some way by the platform on which the program runs. The "platform" is any layer or interface that logically sits underneath the program, either immediately underneath or several layers underneath. Platform layers include any third-party APIs used to talk to external resources that exist on other platforms. A platform "manages" a resource if the platform keeps track of the resource's usage and maintains it in some manner.

Things that meet this definition of a resource include files, network connections, database connections and tables, Web applications, Web services, and application server objects.

Each of these things is a very different kind of entity. For example, a file is a very different animal than an application server object: Their usage is very different, and their APIs are very different. One important similarity is that a resource of any

10 See [16], Part 6, for more information on the use of entitlements in policy servers.

of these kinds can have more than one way of accessing it. For example, a file can be read, written, or deleted. Similarly, a Web application can include multiple URLs for access, and a Web service can include multiple SOAP methods, each providing a different service.[11] The various SOAP methods constitute distinct "access methods" for the SOAP resource, and the various Web application URLs constitute distinct "access methods" for the Web service. Thus, an *access method* is a way of accessing a resource: It is a service exposed by the resource. This book refers to a resource access method merely as a "method," for brevity.

7.2.1 Relying on the Natives

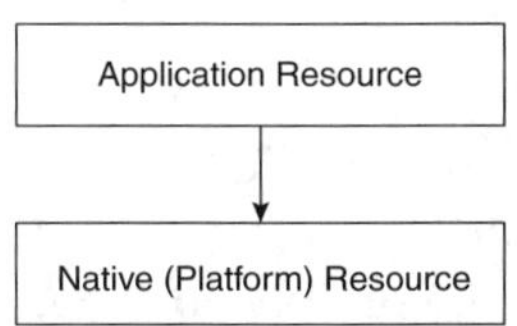

Figure 7.6
Access to platform resources.

The term "native resource" is often used to refer to operating system methods or APIs that sit just above the hardware level. However, the term "native" is relative. In general, a resource is "native" if it exists at a "lower" API level than the calling resource. (See Figure 7.6.) All applications run on a platform of some kind, and the platform constitutes the native resource level. For example, a business application that runs in an application server treats the application server's API set as the native resource API. Thus, if the application accesses a database or a file, it does so (normally) through the application server's APIs. The application server in turn considers the operating system's resources to be "native," so its API set consists of the OS-level APIs or whatever APIs the application server uses to access those resources, such as the Java runtime APIs. The point here is merely to clarify the term "native" so that there is no misunderstanding: *"Native" is relative to the layer of processing that accesses a resource.*

11 Simple Object Access Protocol. See `http://www.w3.org/TR/soap/`.

7.2.2 The Resource Definition Layer

The term "native" is relative to the layer of processing that accesses a resource.

An entity is native to a layer if it is defined in that layer.

Often in this book there is discussion that encompasses the interaction of multiple layers within an application. When an object is said to be *native to a particular layer*, it means that the object is defined in that layer. Similarly, if a type (for example, a class) is said to be native to a particular layer, it means that the type is defined in that layer.

This book uses the term *resource definition layer* to refer to the layer in which an application's resources are defined. Of course, applications can have multiple such layers, but in the discussions and design patterns in this book, there is usually only one such layer involved in order to convey a concept or define a pattern.

Consider Figure 7.7. If it is said that an exception thrown by a resource should be defined in the resource's definition layer, it means that the exception should be defined in such as way that it is considered to be part of the layer in which the resource belongs. This layering might be implemented by packaging, and so on, but that depends on the language and deployment mechanisms.

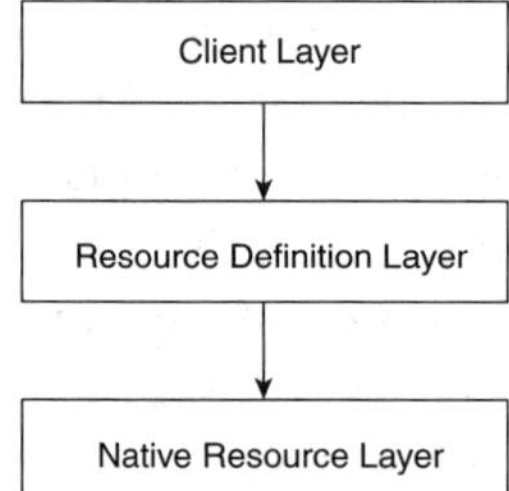

Figure 7.7
A resource layer and the layers above and below.

Layers and layer dependencies are discussed again in later chapters.

7.3 Diversity

Diversity in the technology of your infrastructure and software applications is important for the same reason that diversity is important in the biological world. In nature, there are always individuals who are resistant to a virus or bacterial agent, so an entire population is usually not wiped out when an infection spreads.

PRINCIPLE: EMPLOY MODERATE DIVERSITY.

Diversity is a two-edged sword. On the one hand, the chance that you are vulnerable increases with the more technologies you have. On the other hand, if your technologies are all the same kind and one of your systems is compromised, it is possible that all your systems will share the same vulnerability and will be compromised in one fell swoop. Diversity is, therefore, not a strategy to reduce exposure; it is a strategy to reduce the *scope* of your risk. It is a strategy to keep you from losing all your assets if and when your security systems are penetrated.

Diversity is extremely important for any infrastructure that cannot be strenuously monitored and that will inevitably experience some number of failures—either of a security nature or reliability nature. The reason is that if a single type of component is broadly deployed and a vulnerability is discovered, all deployed instances are affected, resulting in a potentially broad failure. This is the natural selection principle from Evolution Theory: Failures will eventually occur, and only diversity enables a population to survive.

Diversity is extremely important for any infrastructure that cannot be strenuously monitored and that will inevitably experience some number of failures.

A widely publicized example of this is the ubiquity of Windows workstations. Windows is the operating system used by more than 80% of the personal computers in existence. As a result, it is the target of virus writers and spyware, and every time a security flaw is found in the Windows platform, hundreds of millions of users are immediately at risk. According to Bruce Schneier:

> *"The problem is not specific to Microsoft; it's a general problem of monocultures. The security risks would be no different if the country standardized on Macintosh System 10 or Linux. The security risks were the same in 1989, when the Morris worm*[12] *propagated freely in an Internet that standardized on Unix."*[13]

---

12 A computer "worm" is a program that distributes copies of itself to other machines.

13 From *Computerworld*, November 24, 2003. Available online at `http://www.computerworld.com/securitytopics/security/story/0,10801,87470,00.html`.

Diversity is especially important for the resource containers that you employ. Thus, if an attacker finds a way to compromise one type of container, he will still be stopped by the others, and the attack will be (hopefully) somewhat contained. In concrete terms, this translates into having a few different brands of operating system, application server, database, and security policy repository. It also implies having applications that are well-compartmentalized across those resource containers, so that, for example, compromising one database system by guessing the administrator's account password does not provide access to all the databases and therefore all the data used by all applications.

Compartmentalization is discussed in Chapter 8, "Compartmentalization and Classification."

Diversity adds cost because it introduces operational heterogeneity, hinders maintainability, and generally adds complexity. This cost is the price of insurance against loss. For example, it is often taken for granted that the operators of the application containers are intimately familiar with procedures for safe operation; however, it is equally important that the designers of applications that will run within those containers have current knowledge of the specific vulnerabilities that are known for each kind of container, application language, and all technologies that are being employed.♦ Diversity increases this cost because it results in more technologies that designers need to learn about. (For a discussion of vulnerabilities and best practices specific to the Java platform, see [17].)

♦ See the principle "Maintain Awareness of Vulnerabilities in Components" in Section 10.7, "Maintainability."

Having diversity does not require that interoperability be sacrificed. For example, different kinds of email systems may share the same protocols and therefore have a high degree of interoperability in their use, but if the systems are of different brands they will have different kinds of configuration files, their credentials may be stored in different places, and so on. These are the kinds of things that are often attacked, rather than the core application protocol itself.

7.4 Auditability of Policy Coverage

It is important to ensure that the authorization rules that are implemented for a system are "transparent." That is, the authorization rules should be *auditable*: A business analyst should be able to easily locate the rules, understand them (without advanced technical expertise), map their correspondence to business resources, and thereby correlate the rules in the code with authorization rules that are expressed in business use cases. Use cases that specify what a user should not be able to do are sometimes referred to as "misuse cases" [18].

> ***PRINCIPLE: AUTHORIZATION RULES SHOULD BE AUDITABLE.***

An auditable implementation has these advantages:

- The business level managers in the organization gain confidence in the system.
- The authorization rules can be shown to have "100% coverage" in terms of the rules expressed by the business side. This helps to prevent "loopholes" from existing in the authorization rules. (See "Exploit of Incomplete Authentication or Authorization" in Section 5.1.18.)
- The inputs to the authorization rules can be easily identified, which helps to determine the vulnerabilities in the system (more on that later).
- The authorization rules are maintainable so that when code changes are made, the appropriate updates can be made to the authorization rules in a transparent and auditable manner.

Auditability usually leads to consolidation: In order to achieve auditability, the authorization rules must be separable from the business logic, or at least identifiable, and that usually means that they are aggregated or distinguishable in some manner. The importance of this separation has been expressed as "Separation of policy and mechanism" [19].

A side effect of this separation is that because all the rules can be easily identified, they are easier to reuse if the application takes on another method of access. For example, a Web application's authorization rules can be reused for a Web service, rather than duplicating them. This leads to reduced cost as well as greater security.

PRINCIPLE: AVOID DUPLICATION OF ACCESS RULES.

7.5 Perimeters

A set of resources should have multiple perimeters of protection so that if one perimeter is penetrated, the resources are still protected. By analogy, if you keep valuables in your home, you want to have more than just secure locks on your doors: you might want to have locked cabinets for valuables and possibly even a safe for items of great value. Even if a thief gets past your outer door locks, the thief must still spend time inside the house cracking the safe, during which time he or she risks detection.

The balance between security and convenience is an ever-present tradeoff. Ideally, you would like to eliminate all unintentional entry paths and be diligent about securing known entry paths. For example, if you are confident that every door and every window in your home is locked, you can focus on making sure that you do not lose track of your house key. In any complex system, however, people make mistakes, and so it is quite possible that a window will be left open. The inner perimeter—the safe—is there to protect against such oversights and unintended vulnerabilities in the outer perimeter. Perimeters are often breached by looking for oversights rather than by brute force attacks on the securing technology.[14]

PRINCIPLE: USE MULTI-TIER ("DEEP") AUTHORIZATION PERIMETERS.[15]

The perimeter concept is related to the layered security model [22, 23] in which a system is composed of independent layers that each rely only on the next layer inward. Layer dependency is revisited in Section 7.19.1, "Layers."

Each perimeter, ideally, should rely on different practices and be independent in an administrative sense so that if an oversight is made that creates a hole in one perimeter, the same hole is not simultaneously created in another perimeter. For example, credentials for one perimeter should not be managed in the same way as credentials for another perimeter.

This policy seems to go against the trend toward single sign-on and centralized security administration. However, it does not necessarily. For example, access to a backend database is usually performed using different credentials than those of the user. That said, single sign-on does represent a risk.♦

> ♦ This is discussed further under the principle "Prefer to Employ Different Credentials for Each Role" in Section 8.1.3, "Convenience Versus Safety."

A perimeter should adhere to the principle of "Least Privilege." This principle is widely espoused by security experts and states that a user should be given the least privileges that they need in order to accomplish a task.♦ The rationale is that giving users more privileges introduces the risk that they will accidentally or intentionally "go where they should not go" or open a door that they should not open, and possibly leave it open, metaphorically speaking.

> ♦ See the principle "Compartmentalize Roles" in Section 8.1.1, "Role Separation."

"Least Privilege" implies that privileges are defined with enough granularity to enable users to have narrow permissions so that they do not need to be given widely scoped permission in order to accomplish isolated tasks.

---

14 The limitations of perimeter-based approaches are discussed in [20].

15 See the related principle "Layered and Distributed Protection" in [21].

PRINCIPLE: FINE-GRAINED AUTHORIZATION (LEAST PRIVILEGE) AT EACH PERIMETER.

The concept of least privilege should be central in the design of roles for an application. Overlap of privileges should be minimized, and sensitive operations should require multiple roles to complete.

7.6 Levels of Processes within an Organization

Regardless of security considerations, a well-designed business application environment should distinguish between these classes of resources (refer to Figure 7.8):

Workflow programs: These perform user workflow processes that invoke business transactions. These processes represent the workflow of the organization at any point in time and often change significantly during an application's lifetime.

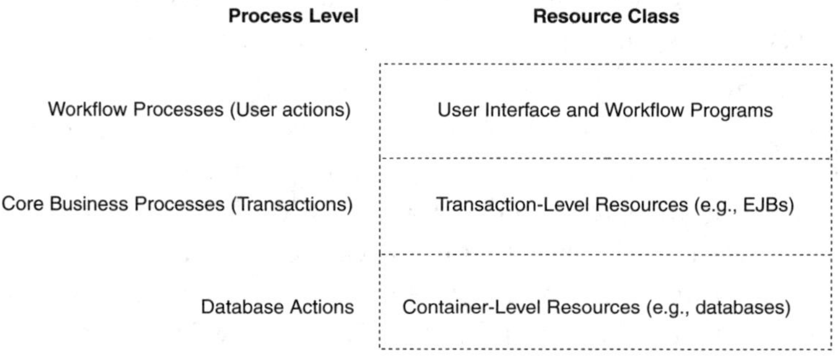

Figure 7.8
Layers of process.

Transaction-level resources: Core business processes or repositories that provide business transactions. These are usually considered to be critical reusable components. Examples include mainframe transactions, EJBs, and JMS transaction messages. SOAP methods might be included here if they are known to be transactional. Transactional resources tend to be a stable but growing set over a period of years.

Container-level resources: Native system or application container resources that have no significance in the business operational model. From the perspective of the business operational processes, container-level resources are "plumbing." Examples include a database, a file system, and any APIs that provide the application with access to those kinds of resources.

Use-case analysis typically defines a set of business-level processes that are decomposed by software designers into workflow processes built on top of transaction-level resources that in turn access container-level resources, such as databases.[16] The distinction between these levels is extremely important from a system architecture standpoint: Transactions provided by transaction-level resources are atomic functions that are self-contained. These transactions can be safely aggregated within the scope of a transactional container. In contrast, workflow processes consist of non-atomic aggregations of transactions because they execute outside a transactional container, and the user is cognizant of the status of each step in the workflow. This includes so-called "business process integration" processes. When a workflow process invokes multiple transactions, it must keep track of which transactions complete and which do not and report this information to the user because the workflow process is not assumed to be atomic or transactional as a whole.

The concept that workflow processes (which are typically manifest as user interface-level processes; see Figure 7.9) use transaction-level resources is an important one. The purposes for which the transactions are used may change over time. Ideally, one would like the transactions to be a reliable foundation that remains stable but grows as client processes change and grow. This stability has served many organizations well, as many organizations today successfully leverage legacy mainframe-based transactions that were created literally decades before but have been repurposed for new workflows by connecting to them via Web technology. The confidence in the transactional foundation is generally so high that businesses treat them as the most critical component of their infrastructure.

16 Note that in this text, the term "container" includes the framework for managing the contained resources. See the definition of "container" in Section 7.1, "Secure Resource Containers."

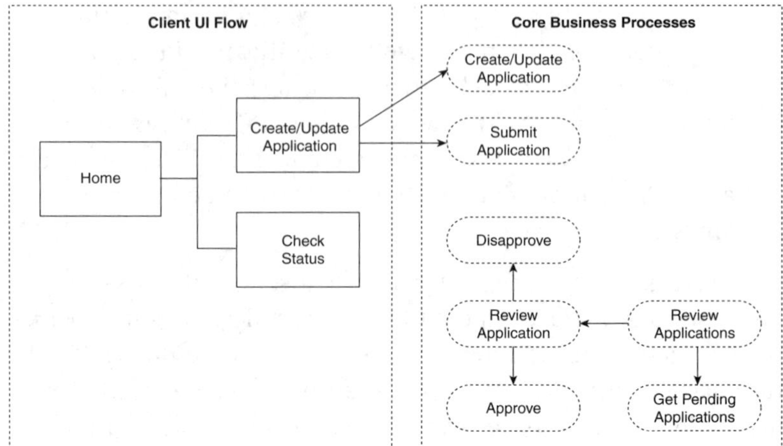

Figure 7.9
Distinguish between workflow and core business processes.

Workflow processes tend to be very dynamic by comparison. For example, a role that defines the participation of a partner may need to be divided into sub-roles when the partner introduces additional partners of its own. Workflow processes are, therefore, typically defined in terms of roles (user case "actors"), but those role definitions should not be exposed to (known to) the underlying transactions, in order to shield the transactions from the relative instability of the workflow processes.

To put it another way, we should attempt to define transactions in such a way that they represent core business processes and can be *repurposed over time* as roles and workflows change. This requires a resource-oriented view of business transactions such that the resource protection rules do not change as the ways that the resources are used change.

PRINCIPLE: DISTINGUISH BETWEEN WORKFLOW AND CORE BUSINESS PROCESSES.

This approach, therefore, requires that authorization rules be factored into separate strata according to the class of resource that they protect. In particular, we should distinguish between:

- Container-level resource authorization rules
- Transaction-level resource authorization rules
- Workflow process rules and policies

Workflow process authorization rules, if any exist, do not protect resources. Rather, they enforce client workflow policies. In contrast, transaction-level resource authorization rules specifically protect the transactional business resources. Those rules should not be expressed in terms of roles, but rather should have no knowledge of roles or how the resource is being applied. To encode knowledge of roles in the transaction authorization rules makes it impossible to repurpose the transactional resources without recoding their authorization rules.

This is often used as an argument for factoring all authorization rules out into a centralized policy store. However, administrators seldom want to deal with resource-level authorization rules. In fact, they usually do not understand the application rules at that level and are incapable of administering them. It would be like asking the Federal Government to establish and maintain all the rules for your community's schools.

> Workflow process authorization rules should not protect resources. Rather, they should enforce client workflow policies.

Transaction authorization rules should be absolute and represent the authoritative word for what is required to be allowed to access a resource. For example, it should not be possible to compromise a resource by bypassing a client process workflow rule: The transaction resource's authorization rules should keep an unauthorized user out. Thus, oversights in client process rules should still leave the core transactional resources intact, as long as the decision context data used by the transaction authorization rules is not compromised.

> It should not be possible to compromise a resource by bypassing a client process workflow rule.

The workflow and transactional domains can cross. This occurs predominantly in use cases related to the assignment or modification of user roles. Such processes require transactions that set user roles in order to be able to perform their functions. Thus, by their nature, such processes use core transactions that may change as often as the overall workflow changes.

This means that the transaction resources that modify user roles represent a special case and might appear to be an exception to the rule that roles should not be encoded in the transactional resources. However, the rule is that roles should not be encoded in the *authorization rules* for access to a transactional resource. Transactions that modify roles encode role references in their business logic—not in their authorization logic. Such transactions should be protected in the same way as any transactional resource, and roles should not be explicitly encoded in their authorization rules.

There are often workflow rules that have enduring meaning to a business.

The term "workflow" was used previously in the context of client processes, but there are often workflow rules that have enduring meaning to a business. For example, a status indicating whether a request has been approved by a senior executive represents a workflow element, but if that status event is part of the core business model, it deserves to be represented at a transactional level. For example, the status might indicate the approval of a loan application by a VP-level authority, which may have legal significance to the business. This is illustrated in Figure 7.10.

It is, therefore, not true that everything that is "workflow" in nature should be excluded from the transactional resource level. *It depends on whether the process has meaning to the core business model,* as opposed to the way the model is implemented with current user interfaces and methods of doing business.

PRINCIPLE: DISTINGUISH BETWEEN CLIENT WORKFLOW AND BUSINESS WORKFLOW.

Core business workflow rules should generally be incorporated into the business transactional resources and enforced at that level. The user interface or business process integration layer should not be relied upon as an enforcement mechanism for this category of workflow rules.

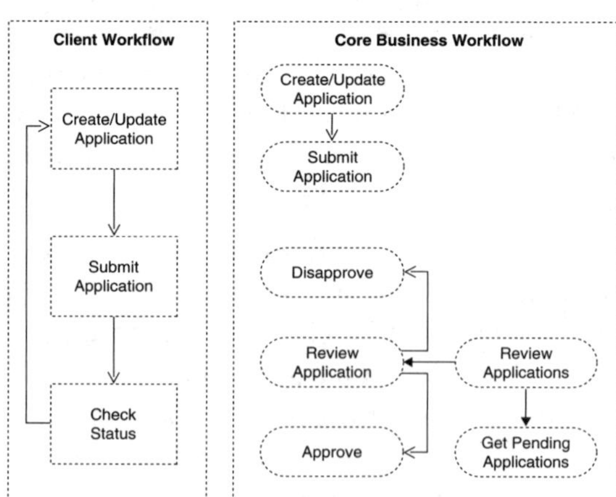

Figure 7.10
Distinguish between client workflow and core business workflow.

In contrast, most workflow rules relate to the user interface model and have no actual business relevance in terms of business transactions. These kinds of rules can be implemented by the user interface, although the wisdom of *coercing* users to use a particular interface workflow when that workflow has no actual business significance is questionable. Users often like to change the intended user interface workflow in order to improve their own productivity. For example, it is common for users to bookmark internal pages in a Web site so that they can go to them directly, and it is also common for users to work in more than one browser window at a time. If the user interface or Web security tier actively prevents either of these modes of use, or if the Web tier design precludes it (most often by being stateful), the user's productivity is likely to be impacted adversely—perhaps to a severe degree. These design considerations are out of the scope of the present security discussion except to say that you should not use the user interface to impose policy that has business significance, and you should question the value of policy that does not have business significance.

The traditional view of server application product vendors is that the products' security configuration occurs offline and is performed by a single or small group of administrators. This assumption is increasingly false as organizations allow partners and users to participate in the configuration of the services that they use. For example, a partner of yours might be permitted to enroll its users in your application. This means that the user enrollment and configuration functions need to be real-time transactional functions, just as any business function. The assumptions that configuration occurs offline or by a single administrator does not hold.

> Beware of non-transactional (non-atomic) administrative functions that are accessible to multiple application or user administrators.

> Beware of non-transactional resources, such as LDAP.

In order to be able to accommodate complex collaborative or partner-based user administration functions, it is necessary to treat those functions as any other business process and design them using use cases and the same design process that is used for business transactions. User administration should not be treated separately or as an after-thought.

PRINCIPLE: TREAT ADMINISTRATIVE PROCESSES AS BUSINESS PROCESSES.

◆ This is discussed further under the principle "Enforce Separation Duties" in Section 8.1.1.

When designing such administrative processes, one should ensure that processes that affect the security configuration of an identity, role, resource, or compartment should be limited to an administrative role that requires mutual exclusion with regard to other roles.◆

◆ Categorization of information is discussed further in Chapter 8.

Two implications of this principle are that information about administrative processes, techniques, and configurations should be categorized according to their sensitivity, and only appropriate user roles should be allowed access to that information.[24] For example, information about any intrusion detection systems that are in place should not be publicized or made available except to the user roles that need to know about them and that have appropriate trustworthiness.◆ That is, persons having that role should not also have other sensitive roles.

7.6.1 The Gray Line Between Business Rules and Security Rules

The line between which rules are in the security domain and which are in the application domain is a gray line.

It is sometimes hard to distinguish what constitutes a security-related authorization rule and what is simply an application-level rule. For example, is a verification of a loan officer's loan limit a security check? Or is it an application check that has nothing to do with security? The answer depends on the perspective of the organization and can change over time. The line between which rules are in the security domain and which are in the application domain is a gray line, and that is an argument for keeping security authorization rules closely bound to the definition of the resource that they protect. This allows authorization rules to be easily migrated from the application domain to the security domain over time as required and to facilitate the maintenance of the resource's authorization model.

7.7 Permissions

Authorization models are ways of specifying and organizing authorization decisions. Authorization can be complicated. For example, it might consider the time of day (perhaps you do not want users to log on after hours); it might consider someone's job role; it might consider how well a user is authenticated (perhaps you do not want them to access the most sensitive functions when they log on from home); it might consider how much you trust a particular user (perhaps they belong to a partner organization rather than your own); it might consider aspects of the transaction that they want to perform (perhaps they are allowed to approve purchases up to a certain dollar amount, but not beyond), and so on. In short, authorization can be based on any business information, so the complexity of authorization is determined by how complex your business rules are. In light of this, if your business rules are complex, it is valuable to look for ways to simplify the authorization rules by refactoring them into common categories.

A *permission* represents a right that a context or user has been granted. In a permission-based approach to authorization, the set of permissions that is required for access to a resource method is *defined by the designer of the resource.* Consider, for example, a system-level resource, such as a file system. The designer of the file system decides what operations one can perform on the file system and provides methods to perform those. The methods do not necessarily map one-to-one to the set of things one can do. For example, there may be convenience methods that perform multiple operations, or there may be methods that perform an operation in a particular mode. As a concrete example, consider that the set of permissions for a file system, for operations related to files, might be { create, modify, delete }. Consider that there might be methods { create, seek, write, rewrite, erase, delete }. It may be that the write, rewrite, and erase operations require the caller to have the permission to modify. Whether this is true depends on the intent and semantics of the permission model defined by the file system architect. The authorization rules must faithfully adhere to those definitions when performing checks against the permissions that a caller has been granted.

PRINCIPLE: MODEL AUTHORIZATION IN TERMS OF PERMISSIONS.

An effort should be made to define a resource's required permissions so that they are as independent of each other as possible; i.e., they should be *orthogonal.* This independence makes it easier to write clear and unambiguous authorization expressions. It means that one permission does not "imply" another; for example, "Write" permission does not necessarily imply "Erase," and vice-versa, depending on the intended resource access model.

PRINCIPLE: PERMISSIONS FOR A RESOURCE SHOULD BE DEFINED TO BE ORTHOGONAL.

Permissions often are context-specific. For example, a user might have the permission to write to a file—but only a particular file. Thus, the user has write permission in the context of a particular file. More on that in a moment.

Even if permissions are contextual, there still may need to be authorization rules that cannot easily be expressed as a statically granted permission. For example, a user's right to access an object might depend on other data, such as a credit analysis result. Such data is potentially dynamic, so the decision should reflect the current state of the data in the system. Expressing this as a permission is not a good fit from a system architecture perspective.

7.8 Permission Parameterization

Permissions are very often parametric. Let's consider a business-oriented example. Suppose a loan origination application provides an "Approve" operation that loan officers use to approve loans. Most likely, the loan officer would be authorized to approve loans only up to a certain dollar limit, beyond which higher-level approval might be needed. The approve operation, therefore, needs to invoke a rule that decides if the requested approval can be authorized. The rule might take the form, expressed in English, as "*Requester must have Approve permission.*" The requester's Approve permission might have a parameter: the approval limit. Thus, any given loan officer can be given Approve permission, subject to a limit.

A permission parameter can be thought of as a policy setting because it can be designed to be set administratively, if the resource architect so chooses. The rule itself is not considered to be part of administrative policy because the rule is bound to the resource as part of the authorization model for the resource. On the other hand, if there are any rules that are defined administratively, such as client workflow rules, those might be considered to be policy rules.

Principle: Distinguish Between Policy and Resource Authorization Models.

Policy attributes should be scoped to the security realm in which they are defined: the realm that owns the resources that are being protected. That realm administers those policy attributes. The term "realm" here—and in the remainder of this book—is used to mean a domain of trust. (See Section 6.2.1, "Realms of Trust," for a complete explanation of the realm concept.)

Policy attributes (and rules, when they exist) should not require understanding of the resource's internal function. Administrators do not want to have a deep understanding of the resources they administer, because nowadays they have so many things to administer. They need policy attributes to be simple and to define concepts that map conceptually to the business. *Administrators do not want to define and maintain application-specific rules.* To require them to do so is to give them a huge and costly administrative burden, and inevitably the rules will get out of sync with the code and security holes will result. This cannot be stressed enough, as the author has seen this outcome many times.

> Administrators do not want to maintain application-specific policy rules.

It is, therefore, preferable that any "policy" configuration that is to be maintained by administrators who are a step or more removed from those who define policy should involve no resource-level *rules*, but rather involve primarily simple attributes that are easy to administer. Attributes are also easier to distribute and cache than rules. Centralized rules are not as easy to make scalable.

Client workflow processes are a different matter. Many firms have achieved great flexibility by composing business workflows using business process modeling (BPM) tools.

Processes defined at this level are created and maintained by business analysts rather than by programmers. Such processes are best limited to role assignments, notification of events, initiation of transactions, and distribution of information. Core business resources, such as scheduling functions and order transactions, are best created with the precision of professional programming, and implemented as secure resources. Advanced BPM users might be trusted to use the BPM tools to define new transactional resources if they are proficient in security policies with regard to the design, auditing, and deployment of resources.

In summary, define parameters as part of a resource permission model, and treat these parameters as policy settings when administratively assigning permissions to users or to roles.

DESIGN PATTERN: PARAMETERIZED PERMISSIONS

Context

An application defines a set of resources and a set of permissions for accessing those resources. The authorization rules for accessing each resource are to be defined in terms of the permissions.

Problem

The rules for accessing a resource are complex, so permissions must be qualified in some manner; for example, having "file access" permission is too broad—permission must be narrowed.

Solution

This pattern presents an approach for defining permissions that can be qualified—i.e., parameterized, so that access rules can be written in terms of those permissions and the allowed actual parameter values.

For each resource to be protected, define an orthogonal set of permissions that represent the entire functional space of the resource, for the purpose of authorization. These permissions may have parameter definitions ("formal parameters") to cover situations in which a permission is qualified (scoped) in some way; for example, a "file read" permission might be granted for files only within a specified directory.

For each resource method, define a logical expression specifying the required combination of permissions in order to be granted access to the method. The expression may use any permission parameter, as well as any implicit or explicit context parameters that are passed when invoking a method on the resource, including method arguments and policy parameter settings for the context.

Refer to Figure 7.11.

In Figure 7.11, a resource definition ❶ includes several method definitions ❹. For example, if the resource is a Web service, each method might be a SOAP method. Each method definition includes several parameter definitions ❺.

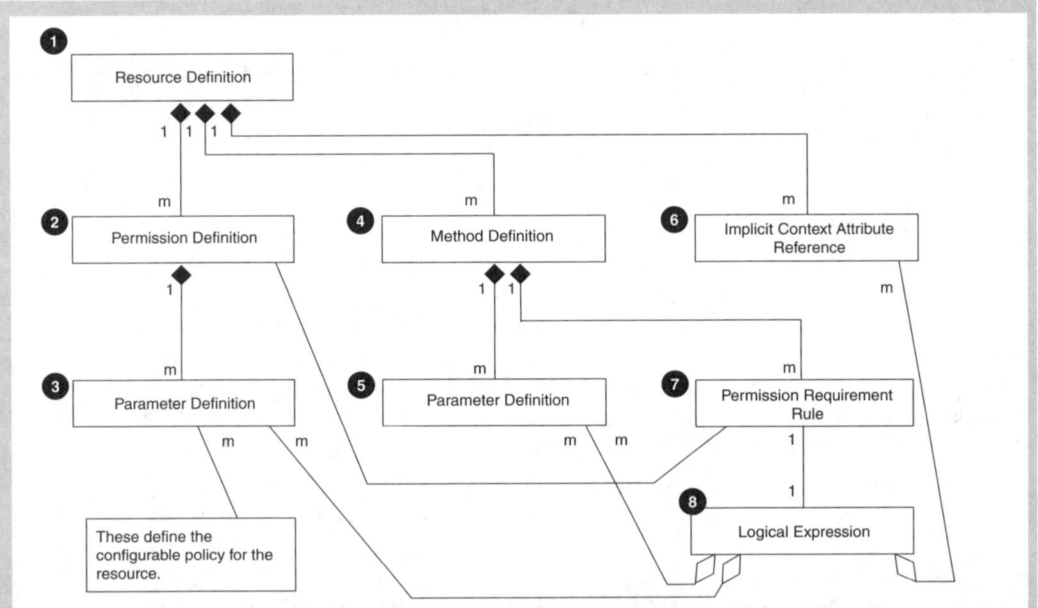

Figure 7.11 Structure.

In addition to method definitions, the resource defines a set of permissions ❷. Each permission may define a set of parameters ❸. This allows the permission to be qualified.

The container in which the resource is hosted and executed must associate permissions with the context that accompanies the invocation of a resource method ❻. It must be possible for the resource method to test the actual values of any permission parameters.

In addition, the runtime container may associate other attributes with the invocation context. A typical example would be the caller identity. Such attributes can also be referenced in an authorization rule.

Therefore, rules ❼ for access to a resource method may include references to any of the method actual parameters, permission actual parameters, or context attributes. The access rule definition ❼ is associated with the resource method ❹, and the access rule definition includes a logical expression ❽ that may reference any of the aforementioned actual values or attributes.

To illustrate the use of this, consider Table 7.1. As can be seen, the business has defined a resource called "LoanApplication." This resource might be an Enterprise JavaBean (EJB), or it might be a Web service, or any other kind of business resource. In this example, the resource has to do with the processing of an application for a monetary loan.

As shown in the table, the business has also defined a permission, "CanUpdateRegion," which is used to define access rules for this resource's methods. In addition, this permission is parameterized: its region parameter indicates that if a user has CanUpdateRegion permission, that permission is qualified so that it applies only to a particular geographic servicing region.

Table 7.1 Resource Method for LoanApplication

Defines Methods	Method Authorization Rules	Reference (Use Cases)
ModifyApplicantData	Requester Must Have: (1) LoanApplication. CanUpdateRegion(<loan region>) (2) LoanApplication. ModifySensitiveData	2.1.4 Applicant Modifies Loan Data

The previous example deals with a particular method of the LoanApplication resource: the "ModifyApplicantData" method. This method could be an EJB method or a Web service SOAP request. The table defines an authorization rule for the method. This rule specifies that the caller must have "LoanApplicant.CanUpdateRegion" permission and must also have "LoanApplicant.ModifySensitiveData" permission. The first permission is qualified: The user's permission must be for the region associated with the loan application.

When implementing this rule, the application designer must decide how to supply the <loan region> value. One approach would be to obtain it directly from the LoanApplication object instance that is being invoked. Thus,

```
Region r = getRegion();
if (! SecurityPolicy.contextHasPermission(CanUpdateRegion.class, r)) {
        throw new CannotUpdateRegionException();
}
```

In this code snippet, the application has a home-grown security policy manager that is accessed by the reference "SecurityPolicy." This policy manager provides a method to check if the current context has a specified permission. The method takes a permission class type, followed by a variable number of arguments that serve to qualify the permission. (This makes use of Java 5's varargs feature.) The actual permission argument supplied in this example is the LoanApplication's region, obtained by querying a method on the LoanApplication instance. Note that the region *should not be included in the exception that is thrown if access is denied* because it represents information obtained as part of the function of the method that the user is attempting to access.

Some permission class implementations contain the resource-level authorization rules for the resource, which evaluate a permission class (with actual parameters) possessed by the caller's context. (This approach is used by the Java runtime.) When this approach is taken, the permission classes must be protected by the platform to ensure that the contained authorization model is not modified.

Consequences

Permission can be granted on a qualified (scoped) basis and still managed independently of the application's resources.

The policy manager must be accessible to the application.

7.9 Role Parameterization

Because it is possible to parameterize permissions, roles may be parameterized, if the permissions they contain are parameterized. For example, if the role "RegionalBuyer" is composed of the permissions "CanBuyForRegion(Region)" and "CanAuthorizeAmount(Amount)," the role RegionalBuyer is effectively parameterized accordingly, with the parameters Region and Amount. Specification of these parameters can be done by a policy administrator for the realm that defines the role, which presumably includes the users who participate in that role. This allows the realm's administrator to set *policy parameters* for the realm based on the permission models exposed by the realm's resources.

PRINCIPLE: FACTOR OUT ROLE PARAMETERS AS CONFIGURABLE POLICY.

The author's opinion is that roles should not be used to define authorization rules. This is contrary to widespread practice, but this opinion is based on years of seeing the difficulties that result. Embedding roles within authorization rules results in a loss of flexibility at the workflow level. Instead, roles should have permissions, and the authorization rules should be expressed in terms of the permissions—not the roles. Keeping roles out of the authorization rules allows the resources to be designed independently of the current vision of how the resources will be used. Over time, roles change and often are divided into more granular roles. It is desirable if the users of the resources have the freedom to re-map roles to permissions and be able to repurpose the business transactional resources without having to alter their code.

Do not use roles to define authorization rules. Use permissions instead.

7.10 Dynamic Conditions

As we saw previously, contextual roles can change, depending on data. If the data that determines the role is relatively dynamic, it is usually better to treat the role as a dynamically evaluated condition rather than a role. For example, consider the following role definition:

Role	Permissions
RegionalBuyer	CanBuyForRegion(Region)
	CanAuthorizeAmount(Amount)

The RegionalBuyer role consists of two permissions, but the permissions are contextual: They apply only over a limited range. If the range is relatively static, there is no problem. That is, if the region that a particular regional buyer is authorized for changes only infrequently, there will be little confusion about the role: a buyer will know "their region." If, however, the permission range is relatively dynamic, there may be confusion about the role: for example, if the amount that the buyer can authorize changes weekly, the "role" will be unclear. In that case, the role should be re-cast as a dynamic *condition.*

This book therefore reserves the term "role" to refer to relatively static roles that are assigned to users by administrators or other authoritative parties or processes. Thus, for this discussion, the term "role" is always limited to static roles that are not contextual or that have a relatively static contextual range and are a (relatively) constant attribute of the user context, unless otherwise noted.

PRINCIPLE: DISTINGUISH BETWEEN ROLES AND CONDITIONS.

Permission-based access rules are very powerful but are often insufficient to express the complete set of authorization rules for a resource.

Permission-based access rules are very powerful but are often insufficient to express the complete set of authorization rules for a resource. The access rule requirements for a resource method may need to be augmented with expressions that access dynamic conditions in order to fully implement business rules related to authorization. This book refers to this approach as the "Dynamic Condition Set" pattern.[17] In this design pattern, dynamic authorization conditions are factored into a collection of "sets" such that the user's membership in a set can be tested by evaluating the expression that defines the set. The dynamic authorization rules can then be reduced to a series of set membership tests. All of dynamic logic is encapsulated in the expressions that define the sets.

17 The author owes his awareness of this pattern to a colleague, Vincent Giusto.

This is a powerful technique because it turns out that most business authorization rules tend to be of an inclusive or exclusive nature. For example, an authorization rule for the CheckStatus transaction of a loan application might specify that:

> The user must have CheckStatus permission **AND**
>
> (The user must be a member of the set of applicants for this loan **OR**
>
> The user must be a member of the set of loan officers for this loan).

The first condition is a permission requirement, and that permission might be granted as a baseline permission for all roles that authenticate (i.e., are not anonymous). The second and third conditions identify membership in one or both of two dynamic sets. The first set consists of the applicants of the loan in question, and membership in that set can be computed dynamically using an expression that may include a SQL call to a database or a query to a Java Entity Bean. The second set consists of the loan officers handling this particular loan, and this can also be computed dynamically based on data stored in a database.

Note that the sets "applicants for this loan" and "loan officers for this loan" have intuitive meaning, so their intent can be verified with business analysts to ensure that the authorization rules are correct. In other words, the casting of the authorization rules in terms of dynamic set memberships provides an intuitive model that can even be incorporated back into the business rules developed by the business analysts.

It is also reasonable to define conditional permissions such that a user has a permission if and only if a given condition is satisfied. Such a permission has a condition rule associated with it. Condition rules of this kind may be parameterized so that the condition depends on inputs from the request context or other data.

DESIGN PATTERN: DYNAMIC CONDITION SET

Context

A resource's access rules depend on data that is relatively dynamic within the application.

Problem

Managing dynamic access rules is difficult without a framework for organizing and categorizing the rules.

Solution

In this pattern, all authorization rules that depend on dynamic business conditions are factored into a set of dynamically computed sets, such that all dynamic authorization rules can be evaluated by an equivalent series of dynamic set membership tests.

After the set of resource-level authorization rules has been assembled as shown in the previous sample table, we have accomplished our objective of defining resource level authorization rules. However, our rule set is still somewhat cumbersome because it will turn out that many of the rules will be repeated in the rule sets for different methods. It will also turn out that most of the rules will be such that they can be re-cast as tests of whether the user belongs to a particular set of users, where the set membership is based on dynamic conditions. For example, if the user is a loan "primary applicant" or a "secondary applicant," and if many rules need to test whether the user is one of these, it might make sense to define a concept of an "applicant" consisting of the set of primary and secondary applicants for a loan. A helper method can then be created that tests if the user is a member of this dynamically computed set. Note that: (1) the set is based on data that can change at any time; and (2) the set membership is unique for each loan—i.e., it is based on a particular data object, rather than being global or system-wide, such as a role is.

First, define the dynamic set memberships. The example in Table 7.2 illustrates this.

Table 7.2 Dynamic Set Memberships

Set Name Description	Contextual Parameters	Other Decision Data	Defining Expression (i.e., where the set is used)
		e.g., database columns that are used by any queries that define the set.	May contain references to native resources; e.g., database queries.
Example:			
SetOfLoanApplicants Requester is one of the applicants for the specified loan.	Loan, Requester		Requester= Loan.primaryApplicant OR Requester IN Loan. getSecondaryApplicants

◆ This is discussed in the principle "Identify and Assess All Context Bindings" in Section 7.17.1.

The middle two columns are "sensitive attributes," and their integrity must be assessed.◆

Next, re-express authorization rules in terms of capabilities and dynamic set memberships. The example in Table 7.3 illustrates this.

Table 7.3 Use of a Dynamic Set Membership Rule

Resource	Defines Methods (may have parameters)	Authorization Rules (Expressed in terms of capabilities, capabilities parameters, and dynamic set relationships)	Reference (Use Cases)
LoanApplication	ModifyApplicantData	In terms of required capabilities and dynamic set memberships. Example: Requester Must Have: LoanApplication.CanUpdateRegion(<reg>) LoanApplication.ModifySensitiveData And Requester Must Belong To: SetOfLoanApplicants	2.1.4 Applicant Modifies Loan Data

Now that a maintainable set of authorization rules has been defined, the problem is how to enforce them. Should you hard-code them using a design pattern? Should you put them in a rule repository? Should you cache them?

There are various models for implementing the authorization check. All that this pattern specifies is that the authorization rules should be written in terms of dynamic condition sets.

How and when those rules are evaluated depends on the design of the resource container. However, let's consider an example, based on a very simple approach, which defines a security manager that is called (somehow) whenever an attempt is made to invoke a method on a protected resource. See Figure 7.12.

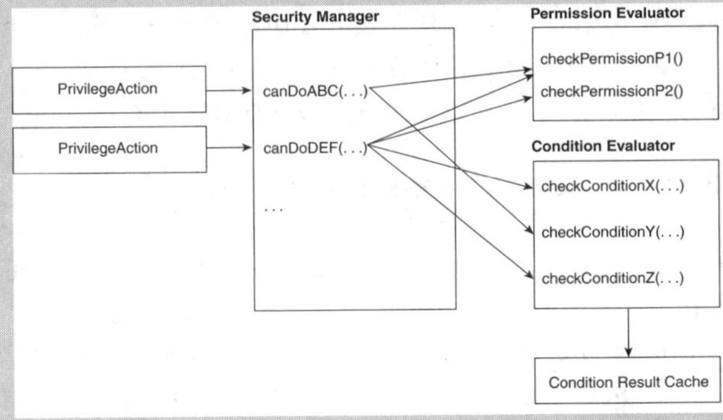

Figure 7.12 Example of a security manager that evaluates dynamic conditions.

In this example, the resource method is referred to as a "privileged action." The security manager gates each privileged action by (1) checking that the caller has the required permissions, and (2) performing one or more dynamic condition checks. If these tests pass, the privileged action is allowed to proceed. Dynamic condition evaluations can be cached, if necessary, depending on the volatility of the condition—this is determined by the technical approach of the condition evaluator and its degree of configurability.

Again, this is only an example to illustrate the use of dynamic authorization rules expressed in terms of dynamic conditions.

Consequences

Almost any business condition that affects authorization can be cast as a dynamic condition set. These sets tend to make intuitive sense to analysts and, therefore, make the maintenance of the authorization rules easier.

7.11 Default Policies

A well-established security principle is that an application must have "secure defaults" [25].[18] What this means is that if the application's authorization mechanism somehow fails to discern the appropriate policy to apply for a request, a default policy should be automatically and infallibly used that is secure. An inadequate default policy in a Web server can allow attacks such as "forceful browsing" in which internal site URLs are directly entered by a client or directory traversal of Web sites. It can also enable attacks that crash application-level protection mechanisms. Thus, inadequately secure default policy might be the result of a failure of the policy mechanism's logic or mechanism, a misconfiguration, or a forced re-initialization or restart of the authorization mechanism.

It is, therefore, important to use an authorization mechanism that defaults to the most secure mode if anything unexpected occurs or if an error occurs.[28] If the authorization mechanism needs to access a policy configuration or policy resources and cannot, it should always default to the most restrictive policy.

PRINCIPLE: DEFAULT TO THE MOST SECURE (LEAST PERMISSION) LEVEL. [29]

This principle is actually an old technique that predates computers. For example, it is more secure to rely on something *not happening* as a means of notification that something is wrong than to rely on something *happening* as notification that all is well. This is why better security alarms detect a *loss of a connection* and why a spy should provide instructions that "if you *don't* hear from me, assume that I have been compromised."

18 See also [26], "Fail secure (FPT_FLS)" and the principle articulated in [27] that "A system should be able to come up in a recognizably secure state."

The secure default principle presents an argument for not using "denials"—negative permissions that specify what a user *cannot* do instead of what the user *can* do (see Section 7.1.9, "Entitlements"): If the applicable policy configuration cannot be identified, the denial (which is stored in the policy configuration) is not retrieved and the user might be able to access the resource when they should not be allowed to. If denials are used, design the system so that full denial is assumed if the policy configuration cannot be accessed.

Configure resource methods so that they either do nothing or fail securely (do nothing that is potentially insecure) if a method cannot recognize or interpret a request, or if the request contains an error. For example, when you make a request to an external system, always validate the result that is returned; do not assume that a return result will be valid or well-formed. This applies even if you trust the external system because that system might be compromised: External systems are often used as a "launch point" into a system that is targeted.

Authorization services often use policy repositories as input to authorization decisions. Authentication systems often use remote credential stores to validate credentials. Remote accesses are slower than local accesses, so policy and credential data can be cached locally in order to improve performance. When credentials have been compromised, a common form of attack is to "take down" the authentication or authorization repositories so that out-of-date cached data will be used.

It is, therefore, good practice to refuse to use cached data if the authoritative source of that data is not reachable. Such sources often use a "forward cache" design that forces updates to cached copies, thereby ensuring synchronization. A denial of service attack against one of those sources might prevent this update from occurring.

PRINCIPLE: IF A CRITICAL AUTHORIZATION OR TRUST SERVICE IS UNREACHABLE, DO NOT USE A CACHED VALUE.

A practical problem is that networks and servers are sometimes unreliable, so it might be necessary to use cached security data in order to be able to access a system if the network is not available. A compromise strategy is to allow access to *local* data or less sensitive data based on cached credentials, but not allow access to remote data. Thus, if the authentication server is down but authentication can be performed based on locally stored credential data, the user might be granted access to local data but not data on other servers even though they might be reachable through the network.

When the application is prepared for distribution to points of deployment, pre-configure the application using secure settings according to what is customary or expected for that kind of application. Rather than providing a convenient default configuration that has relaxed security, require the user to explicitly and knowingly change settings in order to relax security.

PRINCIPLE: DEPLOY WITH A SECURE DEFAULT CONFIGURATION.

Do not reconfigure security-related application settings unexpectedly or without notice to the user. This includes during upgrades and other lifecycle configuration changes. Do not automatically re-enable features that the user has turned off, disable features that the user has enabled, or change settings that they have set without providing notification to the user that this has occurred.

7.12 Association of a Resource and Its Authorization Model

As a practical matter, an auditable implementation almost always results in an encapsulation of the authorization rules. Rather than dispersing authorization rules throughout the application and its many tiers, as is commonly the case in custom-coded business applications, the rules are encoded in a well-defined layer so that they can be located. By “encapsulated,” it is not meant that they are all crammed into a single component or database; rather, they are stratified so that all business transactions invoke their respective authorization rules in the same manner and at the same logical stage in their processing.

Authorization rules should be encoded according to a design pattern, layer, or mechanism that separates them from ordinary business logic. That way, the authorization rules are easily identifiable and therefore auditable.

However, it is important that resource-level authorization rules not be completely "detached" from the resource that they protect. The authorization model for a resource consists of business logic, but of a special kind: logic related to authorization. It closely relies on the permission model of the resource, defined by the resource's designer. The authorization rules are, therefore, understood best by the resource's designer and should be maintained according to the same maintenance cycle. The person who maintains a resource should not have to look far to find the authorization model for that resource. In addition, rules execute most efficiently if they are co-located with the resources that they protect.

A resource's authorization model is best understood by the resource's designer, and should be maintained according to the same maintenance cycle.

PRINCIPLE: DEFINE AUTHORIZATION MODELS ALONGSIDE THE RESOURCES THEY PROTECT.

The recommended approach is, therefore, to *separate but juxtapose* a resource and its authorization model. This ensures that the designer of the resource considers the authorization model and that it is not merely added on after the fact.[19]

As a simple example, a design pattern can be employed such that all authorization rules are encoded at the beginning of each resource method, as a "precondition," and delineated with comments.

In general, keep authorization models with the resources that they protect.[20] Maintain them together, if at all possible. Doing so also ensures auditability.

19 See the description of "Separation of policy and mechanism" in [30].

20 See the discussion of assertion of privilege in [31], p. 354.

◆ See the principle "Factor Out Role Parameters as Configurable Policy" in Section 7.9, "Role Parameterization."

◆ This important issue is discussed more in Section 7.17.1, "Identifying Decision Context."

It is useful to allow authorization *parameters* to be specified at an administrative policy level.◆ This allows the authorization model to be designed by the designer of the resource, but provides a mechanism to allow an administrator to fine-tune access to the resource, using pre-defined parameters that are explicitly exposed by the resource.

It is useful for analysis purposes to keep a table of the context attributes (for example, user identity, user role, and so on) that are used by resource authorization rules. However, while such a table is important for many reasons that are discussed next,◆ this information is far more useful to developers if it is also documented right in the code. Therefore, any context attributes used to authorize access to a resource method should be documented where the authorization rules are defined—particularly those context attributes that are propagated implicitly and therefore do not appear in the resource method's argument list. This helps to ensure that the context attributes and authorization rules are maintained in sync with the resource as they undergo maintenance cycles.

PRINCIPLE: TIGHTLY ASSOCIATE RESOURCE AUTHORIZATION RULES WITH THE DEFINITION OF THE INPUT CONTEXT THEY REQUIRE.

7.13 Resource Interface Design

Recall from the discussion of resource containers that a resource should never return or transmit information that reveals anything about its internal operation. For example, a resource method should not return internal references that might allow the caller to manipulate the internals of the object directly. Objects that are returned should be independent lightweight value objects with no direct ties back to the inside of the resource. An exception is if an internal object is immutable and all objects that it references are also immutable, and therefore none can be manipulated. Even this situation presents some risks, however, as an immutable object's structure might be used to infer information about the internals of the resource.

PRINCIPLE: DO NOT EXPOSE INTERNAL OBJECTS OR ATTRIBUTES.

Be careful when returning value copies ("clones") of objects. If the cloning technique makes a deep copy, it might include sensitive information. This is discussed further in Section 11.1.3, "Cloning Risks."

Along the same lines, a resource should not return references to other resources in a manner that compromises their protection. For example, in a gateway proxy protection model (see Section 7.1.2, "Gateway Models"), a resource should not return another resource reference directly as a return value. Instead, if it needs to return a resource reference, it should return a reference to a proxy for the resource such that the proxy implements a resource gateway. In that way, the returned resource is not actually exposed outside the container, but instead its gateway object acts on its behalf. The risks of exposing internal objects to an untrusted caller are illustrated in Figure 7.13.

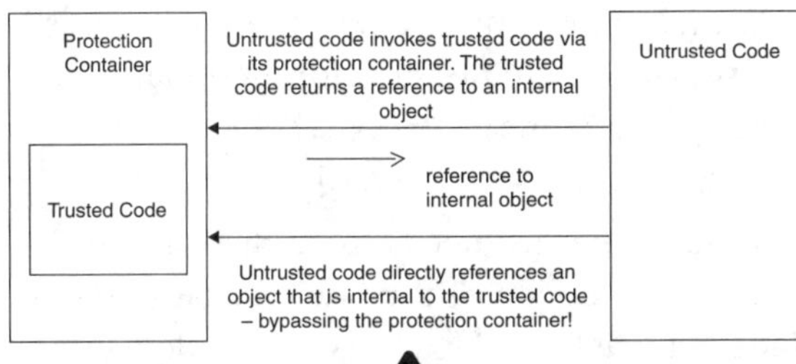

Figure 7.13
A trusted resource should not expose its internal objects or structure to untrusted callers.

This concept applies to network attributes as well; for example, IP addresses, which should not be revealed outside of a private network. Do not embed internal LAN IP addresses in application messages that leave the application's environment. Pay special attention to protocols that reveal internal information, such as network IP addresses (HTTP, RMI, and IIOP). Such protocols should be proxied and the internal addresses translated, if possible.

Be especially careful in situations in which a resource method returns a collection. Many collections are implemented as shallow copies, so their members are actual internal objects instead of copies. Such return values are sometimes referred to as collections that are "backed" by the internal objects because changes to the collection objects immediately affect the internal objects—possibly because they are one and the same. In contrast, a collection can be a "value copy" such that any change to any of its members cannot affect the actual objects within the resource. The latter should always be the case at the interface of any protected resource: Resources should never return "backed collections" unless those objects in the backed collection are themselves protected in some way, such as by a gateway.

PRINCIPLE: DO NOT EXPOSE INTERNAL OBJECTS VIA COLLECTIONS.

Be especially careful in situations in which a resource method returns a collection.

Object-oriented design often leads to the separation of an interface into multiple related object interfaces instead of a single monolithic interface. For example, a software function is sometimes visualized as a "layer" that is actually defined by multiple object interfaces. Components within the layer may need to communicate among themselves, so those components need to expose an interface *to each other*. An internal interface that is used for that kind of intra-layer communication is sometimes referred to as a "collaboration" interface. (See the "Layer Interface" pattern presented in Section 7.19.1.)

A layer's collaboration interface needs to be distinct from the interface that is exposed outside of the layer, because the collaboration interface may well—in fact, most likely does—expose functions and types that should not be available externally.

A layer's internal inter-component interface needs to be distinct from the interface that is exposed outside of the layer.

If a layer exposes multiple behavioral components as part of its public interface, it is important to also have an internal collaboration interface that allows the layer's components to access each other without using the public interface. The public interface might impose security functions or other externalization functions that internal components should not have to bear when communicating among themselves.

PRINCIPLE: EMPLOY A COLLABORATION PATTERN FOR INTRA-LAYER COMMUNICATION.

In order to be able to define a secure collaboration interface, it is necessary to have a secure mechanism for scoping access to the interface. In particular, it must be possible to prevent external components from accessing the internal interface. This can be achieved by the language-scoping mechanism if the components execute within a secure runtime.

7.13.1 Type Safety

By far, the most notorious type of security vulnerability is the "buffer overflow" scenario, in which a malicious client sends more data than a resource expects and causes a fixed-size data buffer to overflow and thereby cause data to be written outside of the bounds of the buffer. If the client can predict what lies beyond the buffer, the client can arrange the input so that data, or program code, are written in a way to cause a predictable effect. such as allowing the client to bypass security safeguards.

The buffer overflow vulnerability receives too much attention. Instead, the failure of the programming language to prevent buffer overflow should receive the attention. The C programming language is commonly used to implement server software, and C has no language-defined built-in mechanisms to prevent or detect buffer overflow (although the C language does not preclude such a mechanism as long as certain practices, such as variable-length argument lists, are not used). In contrast, even a moderately type-safe language, such as Java, prevents buffer overflow at a method interface because the runtime ensures that no data can be written outside of the object that contains it. Because an array is an object, the bounds of data written to the object are checked at run-time. Buffer overflows, therefore, cannot occur in Java, although they can occur in native extensions or interfaces to a Java program if the extensions or interfaces are not implemented using a typesafe language or framework. Others have also observed that security problems such as buffer overflows tend to be fewer when higher-level languages (compared to C) are used—strongly typed or otherwise.[32]

The buffer overflow vulnerability receives too much attention. Instead, the failure of the programming language to prevent buffer overflow should receive the attention.

(Note: This discussion does not consider the issue of whether compiled code can be corrupted or whether "invalid" compiled code can be generated. That issue is discussed under the principles "A Trusted Context Should Always Include the Code Context" in Section 7.17.3, "Code Context," and "Deploy Securely" in Section 10.1, "Designing for Secure Deployment." The discussion here is over whether a protected code base can be caused, via un-protected inputs or other means, to violate the constraints of the language model, possibly even causing the context switching mechanism—i.e., the stack—to fail.)

It is, therefore, strongly recommended that a reasonably type-safe language, such as Java, should be used for processing all interactions with untrusted clients, whenever possible. If the language is not fully type-safe, use a language or tool that has features that help trap known problem areas. For example, newer C/C++ compilers have built-in stack protection ("canaries") to help protect against stack overflow.[21]

PRINCIPLE: EMPLOY A STRONGLY TYPED LANGUAGE AND DESIGN APPROACH FOR THE INTERFACE.

◆ See the principle "Validate Anything Received from Untrusted Sources" in Section 7.17.4, "Validation of Context Data."

In addition, program code should make extensive use of assertions and pre- and post-conditions to detect unexpected violations of required conditions.◆ This does not protect against stack overflow, but can protect code constructs that depend on assumptions such as the size of data objects.

Type conversions are a potent source of bugs and vulnerabilities because a type conversion operation subverts the type-safety of a language. Type conversions are sometimes necessary, however, such as when it is necessary to derive a value from another value based on knowledge of the context.

The main problem with a type conversion is that information might be lost. A common example is the conversion of an integer value to a character value.

21 Some operating systems also have runtime protections against buffer overflow. For example, Windows XP's Data Execution Prevention (DEP) traps attempts to execute data as code.

Another problem is that the conversion might be incomplete or inaccurate (non-canonical). For example, consider the case in which a character value is compared with the numeric values of 'a' and 'z' to determine if it is a lowercase character. That works for ASCII characters, but not for UTF-8/Unicode characters, because it is possible to have lowercase characters from other language sets.

For these reasons, any potentially risky conversions and comparisons should employ a thoroughly tested format converter or comparator that detects and traps all possible conversion errors.

PRINCIPLE: SECURELY TRANSFORM AND COMPARE VALUES.

Safe conversion is important for reliability as well. See the related principle "Safely Transform and Compare Types and Values" in Section 18.2.1, "Ensuring That All Situations Are Handled."

7.13.2 Simplicity

Avoid adding unnecessary methods to a resource. If a method has not been scrutinized and verified to be secure, remove it or scope it so that it is inaccessible outside of the resource.

PRINCIPLE: EXPOSE AS FEW PATHWAYS AND INTERFACES AS POSSIBLE.

This principle is sometimes described as "reducing the attack surface". [33]

This does not necessarily mean that you should consolidate methods. Aggregating a large set of simple methods into a smaller set of complex methods defeats the intention of this principle. The point is to remove unnecessary functions from the interface–functions that the callers do not really need. Thus, keep the call interface simple–that is the real goal.

7.14 Ensuring Atomic Access to Resources

A non-atomic entry allows an intruder to slip in.

The methods exposed by a protected resource should be designed in such a way that all security-sensitive aspects of their effect are all-or-nothing. That is, if a resource method is interrupted during processing and is not able to complete, the state of any and all databases, objects, or processes affected by the resource should be the way they were before the resource method was invoked.

In addition, it should not be possible to observe the effects of a resource method before the resource method completes. In database parlance, this is to say that the resource method executes in "isolation."

These characteristics make a resource method "atomic": a resource method behaves as a primitive system operation, such that it completes as if it were a single native operation of the system. Intermediate states do not exist as far as external callers of the resource are concerned. The concept of atomicity is discussed in detail in Chapter 12, "Concurrency" and further in Chapter 13, "Transactional Integrity."

It is important for a secure resource to expose only methods that are atomic. This is because a common method of attack discussed earlier—exploitation of race conditions—is difficult or impossible if a resource's methods are atomic.

PRINCIPLE: DESIGN SECURE RESOURCE INTERFACES TO BE "ATOMIC."

Atomicity can be a concern in transactional applications as well as multi-threaded applications. A transactional application—for example, one that accesses a database—needs to ensure that all the operations performed by a resource method occur within a single database transaction. Otherwise, it might be possible to overwhelm the system with requests in order to create a race condition or to interrupt the resource before it completes the request, potentially leaving data in an incorrect or vulnerable state.

Similar approaches can be used to attack a multi-threaded resource that does not behave in an atomic manner. In order to protect against interference between separate concurrent requests, many application platforms enforce a single-thread-per-request model and do not allow a resource object to service a new request until the current request thread has completed. In such systems, high concurrency is nevertheless achieved by having multiple resource instances, each able to service one request at a time. This allows each resource instance to operate in an atomic manner.

Make sure that all timeout conditions and other timing-related or sequence-related behavior in the system are completely analyzed and accounted for. This may require the creation of a state diagram. In the author's experience, it is often extremely difficult to get programmers to create a state diagram, even for a system that has lots of asynchronous behavior. For example, a messaging application often needs to account for many different states, defined by the sequence of arrival of different kinds of messages. It is important to make sure that you know exactly what the system will do if, for example, a message that cancels an order is received just before or just after a transfer of funds is initiated; or if an authentication session times out before a servlet session times out. A state diagram is often the only way to decompose these kinds of problems and analyze the problem repeatedly until you are sure that all situations are covered.

7.15 Secure Error Handling

As we have seen, many methods of attack involve causing an application to produce an error condition that the programmer either did not anticipate or that the runtime system does not protect against, causing the system to crash and leave behind artifacts that can be targeted, or to expose an internal state. A methodology, therefore, should be used to carefully identify all possible error conditions and to make sure that all are adequately covered so that they do not result in a vulnerability.

PRINCIPLE: CAREFUL DESIGN-TIME CONSIDERATION OF ERROR CONDITIONS.

Avoid using return codes to signal errors.

If possible, use a language (such as Java, C#, or C++) that facilitates error handling and propagation. Use the language mechanism instead of application-defined mechanisms. For example, avoid using return codes to signal errors, as a calling routine might neglect to check a return value, allowing an error condition to propagate into code that expects that everything is OK.

◆ Use an "exception firewall" for each application thread.

Make sure that the application executes within an "exception firewall." That is, ensure that the runtime catches any and all error conditions that the application might possibly generate, even if the condition represents an un-anticipated programming error. Many application platforms (for example, EJB servers) provide an outer exception handling layer that catches runtime exceptions and prevents the application from crashing. If the runtime does not provide such a protection layer, write one, and make sure that all application threads run under such a mechanism.◆

The exception firewall concept is discussed again under the principle "Coordinate Error Response Across All Independent Paths of Control" in Section 12.2.2, "Coordination of Error Response," and in more detail in Section 18.2, "Effective Error Handling."

◆ The issue of ill-formed inputs was explained under the principle "Employ a Strongly Typed Language and Design Approach for the Interface" in Section 7.13.1, "Type Safety."

Do not assume that inputs to a resource are well-formed, even if the client is an automatically-generated component. If the request stream is unprotected, pay special attention to the possibility of corrupted or ill-formed ("hacked") inputs.◆

Use assertions liberally to check expected conditions. For example, if a method returns a collection and should never return null, assert that the return value is not null. If the assertion fails, throw an exception. However, the exception should not reveal information that the caller is unauthorized to receive (this is discussed more in the following sections).

7.15.1 Code That Performs Authorization

When checking whether a required condition is satisfied before proceeding to the next processing step, make access to the next step contingent upon the condition being met; do not make denial of access to the next step contingent upon a criteria being met. In other words, access to the next step should be denied by default and granted only if a narrow condition is true.♦ Writing code in this way helps to detect logic omissions. This does not apply to assertions, however, because assertions, by their nature, are coded based on an assumption of success; for example, "assert x is not null." For this reason (and others), assertions should be used as an adjunct to application logic and should not substitute for condition checking that is required by the application.

♦ See the principle "Default to the Most Secure (Least Permission) Level" in Section 7.11, "Default Policies."

> Write authorization code such that access to the next step is denied by default and granted only if a narrow condition is true.

Special attention should be paid to any code that establishes or protects any security-sensitive context. For example, if a user's role is stored in the user's session, make sure that the code that sets this attribute is completely covered with regard to its error handling. Special attention should also be paid to code that interposes authorization rules.

When you deny access, do not provide information that might be useful to an attacker. For example, if a user is denied access to a resource object, do not report to the user the system-dependent name, location, or any other information pertaining to the resource object. Such information can potentially be used to make a more direct attack against the system or allow the user to infer something about the naming conventions used for internal objects.

> ***PRINCIPLE: PROVIDE NO DENIAL INFORMATION THAT COULD BE USEFUL TO AN ATTACKER.***

This policy needs to be balanced against the need for "friendliness" in normal user access. For example, if a user's password has expired, it is OK to let them know that that is the reason that they are being denied access, because this fact does not reveal internal information.

7.15.2 Propagation of Unauthorized Information

◆ This issue was explained under the principle "Do Not Expose Internal Objects or Attributes" in Section 7.13.

◆ See the principle "Objects Returned to Higher Layers May Be Translated" in Section 7.19.1.

Do not allow internal error messages or stack traces to propagate directly to the user, as they can reveal too much about the internal working of the application and might even contain sensitive runtime information.♦ Exception information should always be translated into a form that is suitable for the clients of the layer that handles the exception.♦ In doing so, ensure that clients do not receive inappropriate information—either via exceptions or otherwise.[34]

The job posting Web site widely used by IT industry professionals, dice.com, displayed the following error dump (truncated here) across a Web page:

```
Error 500—Internal Server Error
java.lang.NoClassDefFoundError: com/dic
at com.dice.DiceProfile.cookProfileQuer
at com.dice.navigation.NavigationProces
at com.dice.navigation.NavigationProces
at com.dice.SeekerMan.doPost(Ljavax.ser
at com.dice.SeekerMan.doGet(Ljavax.serv
at javax.servlet.http.HttpServlet.servi
at javax.servlet.http.HttpServlet.servi
at weblogic.servlet.internal.ServletStu
at weblogic.servlet.internal.ServletStu
at weblogic.servlet.internal.ServletStu
at weblogic.servlet.internal.WebAppServ
at weblogic.security.acl.internal.Authe
at weblogic.security.service.SecurityMa
at weblogic.servlet.internal.WebAppServ
at weblogic.servlet.internal.ServletReq
at weblogic.kernel.ExecuteThread.execut
at weblogic.kernel.ExecuteThread.run()V
at java.lang.Thread.startThreadFromVM(L
```

This information reveals the internal classes of the application, which would allow an attacker to attempt to obtain these classes and look for security vulnerabilities in them.

PRINCIPLE: *FILTER SENSITIVE DATA FROM EXCEPTIONS.*

As a practical matter, it must be possible to recognize what information is included in an exception in order to filter it. If the exception information is expressed only as a human-readable message (which might change undetected across a maintenance cycle), a caller of the method that throws the exception will not be able to ascertain what information is included and will not be able to effectively and selectively filter it.

The need to filter data from exceptions poses a dilemma: Exceptions are most useful if they contain internal information for diagnostic purposes,♦ yet this information should not be exposed to a client. The solution is to split the path of the exception information so that it is not lost: appropriate information is allowed to remain in any propagated exception, and inappropriate information (information that the caller is not authorized to have) is logged to a secure logging service that is accessible to error response personnel.

◆ This is discussed in the principle "Never Discard Exception Information" in Section 18.2.6, "Providing Sufficient Information."

PRINCIPLE: SECURELY LOG SENSITIVE DATA RATHER THAN DISCARD IT.

The following design pattern incorporates the preceding two principles.

DESIGN PATTERN: EXCEPTION FILTER

Related Patterns

See also the "Use Checked Exceptions for All Lifecycle Errors" pattern in Section 18.2.1, which deals with the need to translate many unchecked conditions into checked conditions to force upper layers of software to handle the condition.

Context

A method internally receives an exception from operations that it has attempted. The exception is either known to contain information that the method's caller might not be authorized to receive or there is the possibility that it does. The application is operating in a production (non-debug) mode.

The assumption is that the exception can be trapped. Otherwise, there is no way to intercept it and filter its data.

Problem

Exceptions provide useful information for problem diagnosis, but they can also reveal inappropriate information.

Solution

This pattern provides an approach for filtering data from an exception that the caller of a method might not be authorized to receive. The logic is encapsulated in an exception handler that this pattern will call a "transformation handler" because it does not truly handle the exception, but rather merely translates it into another exception in a manner that preserves certain information and removes other information.

The first action that should be taken is to log the exception, as it is, in a secure log. This preserves the information for the ultimate post-mortem response: digging through the log.

After the exception event has been logged, the next action should be to perform any required cleanup to restore the application to a consistent state. In a transactional application, this might merely require setting the transaction for rollback.

After cleanup has been completed, a new exception object should be constructed and populated with information from the original exception—but including only information that the caller is known to have permission for. The new exception need not be the same kind of exception: It can be a different exception—one that is meaningful to the caller and that is defined in the current layer. The new exception is then raised and returned to the caller via the exception path.

◆ See the principle "Use Checked Exceptions for All Lifecycle Errors" in Section 18.2.1.

If the original exception is known to be possible but is undeclared by the method ("unchecked"), and there is no compelling reason to trap it,◆ there is still a risk that it would propagate unauthorized information to outer layers. Therefore, even undeclared exceptions should be trapped and filtered as described here.

The pattern is illustrated in Figure 7.15.

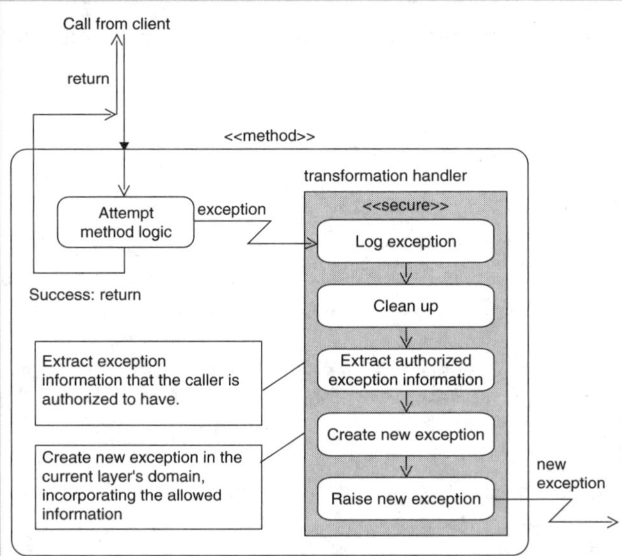

Figure 7.14 Activities.

Consequences

A clear methodology can be applied by programmers to assess what exception information should be propagated and how.

As an example of the use of this pattern, consider the following Java code:

```
public class AccountEJB implements SessionBean
{
	public void deductMonthlyProcessingFee()
	throws
		ProcessingFeeException,
		TimeoutException,
		IOException
		SQLException
		AuthorizationException
	// Permissions reqiuired to call this:                     ❶
	//	CanInitiateStandardCalculations permission.
	{
		SecurityPolicy.checkPermission(getContext(),   ❷
			new Permission[]
			{ new CanInitiateStandardCalculations() });

		try {
			deduct(Fees.getMonthlyProcessingFee());
				// Note: It is believed this can also throw        ❸
				// ArithmeticException under some circumstances.
		}
		catch (AccountComputationException acex) {
			SecureLogger.logException(acex);               ❹

			// Extract information that the caller is allowed to see.
			// Do not propagate the prior balance in the
			// exception: the caller might not be authorized
			// to receive that.
			AccountNumber anum = acex.getAccountNumber();
			Date transactionDate = acex.getTxDate();

			// Clean up.
			getContext().setRollbackOnly();

			// Construct new exception, containing only authorized   ❺
			// information.
			AccountComputationException eFiltered =
				new AccountComputationException(
				acex.getAccountNumber(), acex.getTxDate());

			// Throw the new exception, in place of the old one.   ❻
			throw new ProcessingFeeException(
				"While deducting monthly fee", eFiltered);
		}
		catch (SQLException sqex) {
			SecureLogger.logException(sqex);

			getContext().setRollbackOnly();
```

```
                    // Check for timeout.
                    if (sqex....) { throw new TimeoutException(); }
                    else { throw new SQLException(); }
            }
            catch (IOException ioex) {
                    SecureLogger.logException(ioex);

                    getContext().setRollbackOnly();

                    throw new IOException("Account " + getAccountNumber());
            }
            catch (ArithmeticException aex) {                                  ❼
                    // This exception is unchecked, but we catch it anyway,
                    // because we know that it can be thrown here.
                    SecureLogger.logException(aex);

                    getContext().setRollbackOnly();

                    throw new ArithmeticException(
                            "While deducting monthly fee for "
                                    + getAccountNumber());
            }
    }

    protected void deduct(DollarAmount amt)
    throws AccountComputationException, SQLException, IOException { ... }
    protected EJBContext getContext() { ... }

    protected AccountNumber getAccountNumber() { ... }
}   ...EJB lifecycle methods...

public class AccountComputationException extends Exception
{
    public AccountComputationException(AccountNumber acctNum,
            Date d, DollarAmount priorBal) {
            ...
    }

    public AccountComputationException(AccountNumber acctNum, Date d) {
            this(acctNum, d, null);
    }

    public AccountNumber getAccountNumber() { ... }
    public Date getTxDate() { ... }
    public DollarAmount getPriorBalance() // requires CanViewAccount permission
    { ... }
}

public class ProcessingFeeException extends Exception
{
    public ProcessingFeeException(String msg, Throwable cause)
    { super(msg, cause); }
}
```

This example shows an Enterprise JavaBean (EJB) that provides a deductMonthlyProcessingFee() method as part of its interface. We consider this EJB to be a protected resource for the purpose of this example. This is very typical because EJBs are usually important transactional resources.

Assume that a data modeling effort has classified the organization's data according to the permissions that are required to access each data item and defined roles that encompass those permissions. Assume that this effort decided that an account balance requires CanViewAccount permission.

The comment at ❶ specifies the permissions that are required for the deductMonthlyProcessingFee() method call.[22]♦ The line at ❷ checks security policy. This line merely performs an authorization check, using a home-grown security framework called "SecurityPolicy," passing the current EJB context and the permission set that is required for the current method.

> ♦ This is in accordance with the principle "Define Authorization Models Alongside the Resources That They Protect" presented in Section 7.12, "Association of a Resource and Its Authorization Model."

The comment at ❸ indicates that the method immediately above it—Fees.getMonthlyProcessingFee()—is known to throw ArithmeticException in some circumstances. That exception is not declared in the definition of Fees.getMonthlyProcessingFee() because it is a RuntimeException (in Java, a RuntimeException does not have to be declared), and it apparently occurs only in unusual circumstances. Regardless, the getMonthlyProcessingFee() code documents that the exception can occur. Thus, we will need to catch it at ❼.♦

> ♦ See the principle "Use Checked Exceptions for All Lifecycle Errors" in Section 18.2.1.

At ❹, we log the exception to a secure logger so that its full information is not lost. This is potentially important for diagnostic purposes. The logger must be highly secure because this log will contain potentially any data logged by any part of the application.

At ❺, the AccountComputationException is caught and a new exception is constructed that contains *only information that the caller is authorized to receive.* We know that the caller has CanInitiateStandardCalculations permission—or the method would have aborted at line ❷, but that is all we know about the caller. However, the data modeling effort had decided that a user must have CanViewAccount permission in order to receive the account balance. Therefore, we had best not include the account balance in the exception that is returned, even though it is included in the AccountComputationException.

22 The EJB authorization model is based on roles. This book discourages the expression of authorization rules in terms of roles and prefers permissions.

At ❻, we throw the new exception that replaces the original one that was thrown and caught.

7.15.3 Backup Systems

Organizations often take shortcuts on backup systems. This is understandable because they do not expect to use those systems that often, and only then for a short while.

For security-sensitive activities, however, backup systems are critical because some of the most successful forms of attack involve backup systems. The attack technique known as a *transitive* attack (see "Trusted Resource Attack" in Section 5.1.25) involves attacking a resource used by the primary target: by compromising the resource, the actual target can then be compromised. A backup system is a trusted resource, and it is easy to cause a system to fail over to a backup system: simply cause some kind of physical catastrophe to cause the main system to fail—bringing the backup system into use.

Emergency response systems, disaster recovery systems, and any tools used to respond to an emergency are all potential high-value targets.[23] For this reason, backup environments should be as secure as the primary environment, and include only trusted and frequently validated tools and components. Emergency service providers should also be validated, especially if they are new on the scene.

7.16 Secure Logging

One cannot overstate how important it is to log activity that occurs in relation to sensitive resources. Logs give you protection against fraud: if someone assumes your identity, a log can often reveal the point at which your identity credentials were obtained. This presumes that the log itself cannot be attacked.

Logs are a two-edged sword. A log preserves traceability to help trace the source of unauthorized activity, but a log also

23 In March 2005, Time Warner lost an offsite disaster recovery tape while in transit, containing the names and social security numbers of 600,000 current and former employees. The tape was not encrypted, resulting in the need to reassure its millions of subscribers—21.7 million on AOL alone—that only employee information was in the missing tapes, and also resulted in broad embarrassment from reports in the news. [35]

represents a very attractive point of attack. The problem with the very concept of a log is that it violates the most important concept in security: compartmentalization. A log is generally a flat structure, and if the log is encrypted or protected at all, access to it is often either all-or-nothing. Logs themselves, therefore, need to be both very reliable and very secure and designed carefully so that they do not unnecessarily include sensitive information.

Logs are a two-edged sword. A log preserves traceability to help trace the source of unauthorized activity, but a log also represents a point of attack.

7.16.1 Log Requirements

A log should be *unalterable*: It should not be possible for an attacker to access a log and erase or replace what the log contains. For example, the log could be written at brief intervals to a write-once-read-many (WORM) device (for example, a CD-ROM) that is not erasable.

The log should be *fail-safe*. The application should be written so that it cannot operate unless the log is operating). This may mean that the application makes "test reads" of the log at intervals to ensure that it is actually being written to.

The fail-safe requirement also means that the log should not be able to lose information, even if the message rate is high; and it means that the log messages are guaranteed to arrive at the log and not be diverted, and that fallacious log messages cannot be inserted.

Log access should be *compartmentalized*. For a high-value application, a single administrator should not have access to both the application infrastructure and the log. To do so puts too much trust in a single individual role and violates the concept of "separation of duties."♦ On many systems, system administrators automatically have access to logs. Thus, it is good practice if *application administrators do not have access to the logs* and if *system administrators do not have access to the applications and their resources*.

♦ See the principle "Enforce Separation of Duties" in Section 8.1.1.

A log should be recoverable so that if there is a system failure, or a password or key is lost, the contents of the log can be retrieved and read (even decrypted) by using alternate but secure means.

7.16.2 Log Design

Because access to a log normally requires an administrative level of privilege, and a rogue administrator is a very dangerous threat, this implies that privilege alone should not be used to protect a log. The log access mechanisms should be specially designed so that normal mechanisms cannot be used to access them. For example, a cryptographic key might be required to access portions of a log that are sensitive and are therefore encrypted, and the system administrator should not have this key.

Highly secure logs should be redundant. It may be justifiable to create duplicate logs and store them in different locations that require different credentials to have access to. This protects against after-the-fact modification or destruction of the log.

Logs should be physically secure and stored separately from the application. An administrator who has access to an application's deployment configuration should not also have access to the logs. This is the "Ensure that Traceability Functions Such as Logging and Monitoring Are Independent of Other Application Operation Functions" principle that is discussed later in Section 8.1.1. This may require an application architecture or platform architecture that allows this separation of duties, which is not often the case, unfortunately.

Logs are, therefore, often digitally signed and also encrypted using a secret key or private key. There are many public domain tools for doing this; it is not "overkill;" and many commercial security products provide this level of logging security. Remember that a log is an auditing mechanism, and it is critical to protect it. *A party who wants to perform an "inside job" will certainly first think about how to attack the logs, to either obtain information or to erase all trace of their actions.*

An encrypted log needs to be recoverable in the event that the encryption key is lost. This is problematic because the need to be recoverable works against the need to be secure. Solutions to this include "key escrow" systems.[24]

An application logging system should be monitored, so that if the logging system fails or is compromised in any way an

24 Microsoft's Encrypting File System (EFS) provides for secure "recovery agents" that in effect provide an alternate means of decrypting the encrypted content.

alert will be generated. Of course, the alert mechanism needs to be secure and should go to several parties. It should not be possible for any user to silently disable security-related logging when the system is operating in "production" mode or for the logging system to go down without responders immediately being made aware of it.

The information stored in a log is often sensitive, and so the contents of a log should be secret. *It is very bad practice to store credentials of any kind in a log.* Alternative authentication information (information used to authenticate a user if they forget their password) should also be excluded from logs or encrypted. Logs often contain personal data or other information that is compartmentalized within the application but laid out in a completely flat and un-compartmentalized manner within the log. It is preferable that logs contain primarily events and any data that is important to provide for non-repudiation, but without any sensitive application data.

> It is preferable that logs contain primarily events, without any sensitive application data.

If a log is not designed to be secure, it becomes an ideal place for an attacker to find sensitive information, and may be easier to penetrate than the application itself. Database transaction logs contain every single update that is ever made to the database, and these should be maintained and tracked using secure operating procedures and not stored over time.♦ Application logs should preferably contain information about events and diagnostic information, but not actual sensitive application data.

♦ Backups are also a vulnerability. See "Deciding What to Encrypt" in Section 9.1.1.

PRINCIPLE: ENSURE THAT LOGS ARE SECURE, UNALTERABLE, AND RELIABLE.

Logs perform an important function for "forensic analysis"—that is, investigating an attack after it has occurred. For this purpose, each entry to a log should generally include the identity of the user who performed each access. However, forensic analysis should not require the analyst to possess any user authentication credentials. Thus, any encryption within the log should be performed using keys specifically for encrypting the log data—not a user key.

Security-related logs should not be automatically recycled.

It is common practice to recycle (write over) logs after a period to economize on disk space or media. Security-related logs should not be automatically recycled. They should be maintained for as log as is necessary to fulfill their function as an auditable mechanism for what users did.

In real systems, it is often not possible to achieve all of these goals for a logging system. A log can still be made sufficiently secure however if many of the principles outlined previously are implemented.

DESIGN PATTERN: MONITORED LOG WRITING SYSTEM

Context

An application requires a secure logging system that presents an API for the application to call. There is a strong preference for an open source solution. Further, the cost of a sophisticated logging system cannot be justified in an early phase of the project, yet the logging API needs to be chosen now.

Problem

The logging solutions provided by open source tools usually do not provide the level of security and reliability that is needed. However, many of those tools provide for extensibility.

Solution

The goal of this pattern is to develop a robust solution that meets our requirements for secure logging and that decouples the logging mechanism from the API. This is so that a simple solution can be used during development and testing and the more robust mechanism substituted at a later point in time. The more robust mechanism provides for unalterability, fail-safe operation, and separation of duties.

Figure 7.16 shows the logical subcomponent structure of the system; an actual implementation might have a different physical structure.

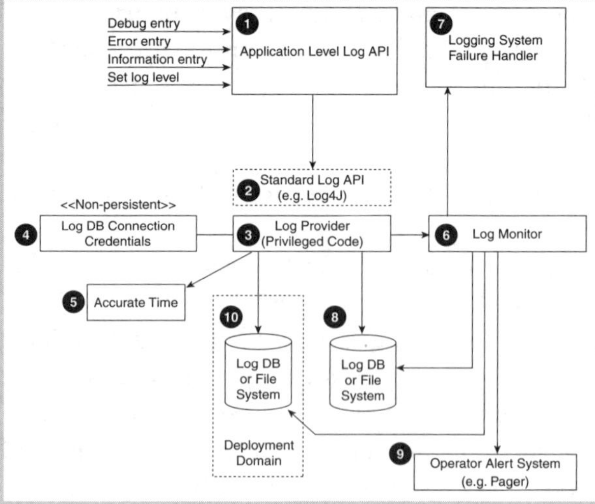

Figure 7.15
Structure.

Solution Layers

The logging system has four layers. These are:

(1) An application-level API layer ❶.

(2) A standardized logging system API layer ❷.

(3) A logging system provider layer ❸.

(4) The actual log(s), such as a database, file system, or logging server ❽ ❿.

These layers are typical in logging system implementations. The first layer is what the application actually calls. In addition to these layers, the solution includes a Log Monitor ❻ and a Logging System Failure Handler ❼. These are discussed next.

The first layer adds features that the third-party package does not provide, such as translating context into standard format to be logged. Calls to this layer carry a thread context. These calls should be synchronous and at least guarded re-entrant, to ensure that different application threads can invoke the logging system concurrently without problems. However, logging calls should return quickly. Therefore, in low-latency applications, the first layer should employ a device-driver-like design in which the incoming calls merely queue their arguments in a first-in, first-out manner. (A design approach is provided in the "Requester/Servicer" pattern in Section 12.2.3, "Multithreading Design Patterns.") The queued log data is then written asynchronously, but in the order received. Thus, the application thread does not need to wait for the logging action to complete.

The second layer represents a logging API obtained from a third party. An example within the Java domain is the well-known Log4J package or the native Java logging API. Calls to the second layer must be serialized in terms of their original order of receipt at layer 1, to ensure that they complete in the same order in which the client performed the log call.

The third layer is a provider interface. Third-party APIs often provide a "provider interface" that serves to adapt a variety of log implementations to meet the needs of the application. For example, Log4J comes with a file system provider and a database provider. A provider layer is represented by the third layer, and this layer should be developed according to the guidelines here, possibly by customizing an out-of-the-box implementation.

The Log Monitor ❻ can be designed to be synchronous or asynchronous, or both. A synchronous Log Monitor would merely receive notification from the Log Provider when failure events occur. It might also perform read-backs, by reading what has been written and verifying that it matches. An asynchronous Log Monitor would initiate independent application actions that are known to cause information to be logged, and verifying that the log action actually occurs. An asynchronous Log Monitor can also actively monitor the status of all resources used by the logging system.

Fail-Safe Operation

The Log Monitor should *ensure that log entries are never lost*. For example, if the log message rate becomes too high, the Log Monitor should either throttle the application or stop it altogether. Any messages that cannot be accepted by the log database should be stored locally.

The Log Monitor has two independent paths of action when a log failure occurs. One path is to notify responders, such as the operator or administrator. Another path is to invoke an application-defined handler that performs application actions that are appropriate when a logging failure occurs. Such actions might include shut down of the application, throttling of the application, or whatever is necessary to reduce security exposure while attention is simultaneously brought to the problem (i.e., the application does not need to wait for an administrator to respond to a logging failure: the response is automatic and immediate).

The fourth layer—the actual logs—may be either a database, a file system, or a logging server. A database is preferred because it can be used to perform incident analysis—perhaps even real time intrusion detection. However, the database must be configured and accesses designed for sufficient throughput to handle the application's peak logging load, and this can be a significant effort.

Communication with the fourth layer should be connection-oriented and authenticated, in contrast to the approach used in many standard logs, such as Unix system logs.

Unalterable

For maximum security, the logs should be replicated. Ideally, each log instance should be in a separate physical location, managed by a separate individual or team, and the credentials used to access each log should be distinct.

Separation of Duties

In order to achieve some level of separation of duties with regard to the logging system and the application, the logging system and the application are deployed independently, by different administrative roles, and secured mutually by each of those roles.[25] Thus, there is an application deployment administrator, and a logging system administrator. (See the listing of roles in the table to the right.)

The application deployment administrator, which this pattern will call the "deployment administrator" for short, is responsible for deploying and configuring the application—but excluding the deployable components associated with the logging system.

Likewise, the logging system administrator, which this pattern will call the "log administrator" for short, is responsible for deploying and configuring the logging-related components.

The deployment administrator is also responsible for validating the accurate and secure deployment of the logging system and creates an unforgeable snapshot (for example, a digital signature of a digest) of both the logging system and the application, including all code and configuration files. In an analogous manner, the log administrator must validate the accurate and security of the deployed application, and creates snapshot of both the application components and the logging system. These snapshots should be computed in a location-independent manner so that they produce the same result regardless of where in a directory tree the components are located.

When the application is started, the operator must provide the runtime credentials to be used by the logging system. These credentials *are not written to any persistent location within the operational or deployment environment*. The credentials should be changed at frequent intervals (for example, daily) and saved in a secure location under the control of the operator.

---

25 This approach is referred to as a "dual-control" approach.

Protecting Sensitive Information

Encryption may be used to ensure privacy for sensitive information that is logged. If this is deemed necessary, all the log contents (except for timestamps, error names or codes, and other non-sensitive standard log entry keys) should be encrypted rather than only specific portions because the log cannot foresee what data the application will need to log, so the logging system is not in a position to differentiate what should be encrypted or not. Encryption may use a key escrow technology.

Setting Log Level

The application-level logging API includes methods for making log entries that represent program errors, entries that are informational in nature only, and debug-only entries (that are written only when in debug mode).

The application should be deployed so that the *logging level can be set to "debug" mode only by starting it in that mode*. Other-wise, there is a risk that malicious code could force the application into a debug mode, causing it to log inappropriate levels of information.◆

Consequences

High-assurance applications can be provided with a relatively secure log that can be managed with basic procedures that are acceptable to most organizations. In addition, security features are confined to a "back end" provider layer that can be plug-replaced at different stages of development, allowing the costs and complexities of the security features to be postponed.

Role: Deployment administrator

Deploys and configures application and verifies its integrity.

Creates credentials for deployment environment access.

Verifies integrity of log.

Signs application and log code and configuration.

Deployer creates this role within the application and its credentials.

Permissions: Update access to deployment environment.

Role: Log administrator, security administrator

Deploys and configures log.

Verifies integrity of application.

Signs application and log code and configuration.

Deployer creates this role and can assign it only once.

No functions can be performed before the assignee changes credentials, and after this happens, the role cannot be re-assigned without re-deploying.

Permissions: Update access to log environment.

Role: Operator, super user

Provides additional runtime credentials to be used to encrypt the most sensitive application data and the most sensitive log data and to encrypt any stored credentials.

Monitors application, from a computing resource, scheduling, and event perspective.

Permissions: Start application. Stop application.

Role: Application administrator, customer service

Enrolls and assists ordinary users.

Permissions: Restricted to a particular resource subset (for example, "all users accounts in Virginia), or to limited changes to the resources.

Role: Ordinary user

Role can be authenticated using an infrastructure identity.

◆ See the principle "Secure All Caches" in Section 7.20.7, "Caches and Artifacts."

7.17 Scope, Session, and Context

When a resource receives a request, the request usually has some information that is implicitly associated with it that describes the requester or the environment. For example, the resource might be able to query the requester's identity. Another common attribute that is often associated with a resource request in a server-based application is the transaction that the request is executing within.

Such attributes are not explicitly set by the requester each time a request is made. For example, in a Web application, the user does not enter the password every time they click Submit. Rather, the typical sequence of events is that a cookie is passed between the Web browser and the server, and that is used to identify a session in which the user's identity is stored. Thus, the caller's identity is remembered by the server and mapped to each request based on the cookie provided by the requesting application—the browser, in this case.

The *context* of an operation is the set of conditions that exists when the operation is performed. The context of an operation normally includes things such as the call chain (i.e., the call stack), the identity of the process owner, environment variables, and so on, and in a server environment usually includes the requester identity, data pertaining to the requester's session, the request's transaction, and so on.

Unless otherwise noted, it is assumed in this text that an operation's context is visible to (readable or detectable by) the operation; otherwise, it is not accessible and cannot be acted upon by the operation.

Context may be maintained in a bi-directional ("peer-to-peer") manner, or it may essentially be one-sided ("client-server"). For example, two communicating peers can each maintain context information about the other. Web browsers, while essentially one-directional clients in their usage, use a two-sided model in which the server may maintain context about the client such as the client's identity and SSL security context if any, and the client maintains context information about the server such as URL of the current page, the SSL security context if any, and a token (a cookie) used to identify the current session. A small amount of context information (for example, a session token) is always needed at each endpoint in order to be able to maintain a session.

Context—The interrelated conditions or data values that exist during which an operation is performed.
Visible Context—Contextual data that is visible to (detectable or readable by) an operation.
Session—A distributed context.
Explicit context— Context that is passed as an argument.
Implicit context—Any context that is not passed explicitly.
Context binding—Process of securely associating a context attribute with the context.
Authentication—The process of establishing the veracity of a context attribute.

A *session* is a set of (usually two) independently managed contexts or entities that maintain at least one shared context attribute, thereby creating a collective context. The independent contexts are usually the endpoints of a communication channel, and the shared attributes usually include a session identifier. For example, a browser and server maintain a session if both the browser and server maintain a shared session identifier (maintained in the browser by a session cookie) so that each can identify the session when a request is made and a response is given. In a sense, a session is a distributed context.

A session endpoint can also be a non-computer entity—i.e., a human user—and in that case, the shared session attributes are represented on the user's side by the user's mental recollection of the data entered during and purpose of the session.

Context can be propagated explicitly or implicitly. *Explicit context* is context that is passed as an argument or application-specified parameter when calling another object or layer. *Implicit context* is any context that is not passed explicitly; for example, a security identity available as part of a thread, session, or process context. (See also the design pattern "Implicit Context and Explicit Context" in Section 18.2.5, "Providing Context.")

Context binding is the process of associating a context attribute with the context. For example, setting a user identity attribute within a session binds the user identity to the session. A binding can be achieved by maintaining the bound attribute within a secure session. A secure binding can also be achieved by digitally signing the attribute value in combination with the identity of the context that it describes. For example, a digitally signed user name and permission can be used to verify that the user has the specified permission—i.e., it binds the permission to the user's context.

When a program reads a context attribute, the program might use the attribute immediately, or it might choose to store the attribute in a session. If the program stores the attribute, it needs to be cognizant of the scope over which the session applies; for example, the request, a session maintained by the application, and so on. It is important not to store data within a scope that exceeds the scope of the context to which the attribute applies or, when doing so, at least be cognizant that the data may no longer be valid.

PRINCIPLE: DO NOT TRUST CONTEXT DATA BEYOND THE SCOPE OF THE CONTEXT TO WHICH THE DATA APPLIES.

Authentication is the process of establishing the veracity of a context attribute. The attribute is most commonly the user identity, but it can be any attribute. Authentication can be achieved via a password, verification of a digital signature, exchange of a shared secret, biometric authentication, or other means.

PRINCIPLE: DO NOT TRUST AN UNAUTHENTICATED CONTEXT.

The requirement for authentication extends beyond user identity. Any implicit or explicit aspects (attributes) that are presented to a resource, are used to make an authorization decision, or are used as input to a process that might represent a target for attack should be authenticated. Authentication can be achieved by establishing a secure context and a secure channel of communication, using any of the technologies described earlier.

Vulnerabilities are often introduced by methods that make assumptions about "preconditions." Be wary of any such preconditions that you assume to be true. Always verify any assumed preconditions using data obtained securely.

7.17.1 Identifying Decision Context

Let's assume that the authorization model of each resource is defined as a set of rules for each resource method, expressed in terms of:

- The permissions or capabilities possessed by the caller's implicit context.
- The input arguments to the resource method call or request.
- Any other attributes or values that are accessible to the resource method or request handler.

The inputs to all authorization decisions are known at this point. This is an extremely important outcome. The ramification is that assuming that the authorization model has been audited and shown to have 100% coverage of all authorization rules, the trustworthiness of the authorization mechanism is equal to the trustworthiness of the mechanisms used to set the inputs, combined with the trustworthiness of the overall containing infrastructure. In other words, we can now break down the problem of risk management and have a tool for assessing how vulnerable our system is—at least with regard to its authorization mechanism.

To make this possible, the inputs to all the resource authorization rules should be tabulated. This table then defines the complete *authorization decision context* for the resource set. It may contain attributes from the implicit context of resources (for example, Web session attributes) and also contain attributes from explicit context: values obtained from explicit call parameters. Together, these represent the full decision context.

In order to determine the vulnerability of the decision context, the mechanisms used to set and protect each value must be traced and analyzed.[26] For example, if an input argument to a resource method is used by an authorization rule that protects that method, we must discover how that argument's value is set prior to being passed into the method. In some cases, the value will be set as a result of a remote call to the

26 See the discussion of "tainted variables" in the section "Privileged Code Guidelines" in [36].

Trace how securely each authorization decision variable is set and maintained.

resource. In that case, the security of the entire path of the remote call must be traced. In other words, we must look at the trustworthiness of the binding of the context value: What mechanism is used to set and secure the value? This is sometimes referred to as a "trusted path."

PRINCIPLE: IDENTIFY AND ASSESS ALL CONTEXT BINDINGS.

More colloquially, trace how securely each authorization decision variable is set and maintained.[27]

◆ See also the principle "Apply Stringent Quality Criteria to High-Risk Components" in Section 4.1.1, "Security-Related Risk."

This has also been expressed by others as the principle of "Constrained dependency" [38]. It relates to an early security concept: that security depends on identifying the "security-relevant" portions of a system. [39]◆

To assess the trustworthiness of the authorization mechanism, assess the trustworthiness of each input to an authorization decision. How is each input set (bound to its value) in the application? In the pattern "Dynamic Condition Set," discussed in Section 7.10, a table of "dynamic set memberships" is developed (reproduced here as Table 7.4). The two middle columns of that table, "Contextual Parameters" and "Other Decision Data," identify the sensitive attributes that are used to compose a dynamic condition set. The trustworthiness of these attributes, therefore, must be assessed, based on the security of the mechanisms used to set them, and the trustworthiness of their ultimate source–i.e., who provided them. (See Section 6.1, "Understanding Trust and Authorization.")

27 There is a PKI analog to this principle; namely, a certificate's policy defines the applications that the certificate is deemed to be sufficiently trustworthy for, based on the robustness of the methods used to validate the certificate owner when the certificate was created. See [37] p. 264.

Table 7.4 Dynamic Set Memberships Table, from the "Dynamic Conditions Set" in Section 7.10

Set Name Description	Contextual Parameters	Other Decision Data	Defining Expression (i.e., where the set is used)
		e.g., database columns that are used by any queries that define the set.	May contain references to native resources; e.g., database queries.
Example:			
SetOfLoan Applicants	Loan, Requester Requester is one of the applicants for the specified loan.		Requester= Loan.primaryApplicant OR Requester IN Loan. getSecondaryApplicants

To assess the trustworthiness of a sensitive attribute, break down its source into the various paths that have had an opportunity to modify it, ending with the container-based components that handle it. The result should be a table consisting of a column that identifies the data item and a column for each domain that handled the data along its path to the authorization system. Each of the domain columns should contain a numeric or qualitative (possibly rule-based) estimation of the trustworthiness of the data item. A final column should contain an aggregate estimate of the trustworthiness of the data item, based on the other columns. An example of such a table is shown in Table 7.5.[28]

28 Some researchers have applied "aspect-oriented programming" concepts to the problem of identification of sensitive data and bindings. For example, see [40]. In this approach, a grammar is used to declare which components are sensitive and to specify conditions that must be satisfied before a sensitive data item can be accessed.

Table 7.5 Example of Addressing the Trustworthiness of a Context Attribute

Attribute	Immediate Source Realm	Intermediate Source Realms	Original Source Realm	Trust in the Attribute
User Identity	Our Authentication Server: 90% because it is currently operated by an ISP that we would like to change.	Partner A's SAML assertion server: We trust it 100% because they take full responsibility for any misuse of their infrastructure.	Partner A's B2B application: We trust it 100% because they take full responsibility for any misuse of their system.	90% x 100% x 100% = **90%**
...				

It is important to recognize that the aggregate assessment is not necessarily a multiplication of the various trust factors because it might be based on conditions or even on the combination of parties involved in a transaction. (For example, you might trust A to do X if A is working with B, but you would not trust A if they are working with C—possibly because C is known to leave all its doors unlocked. See also the discussion of collusion under "Instilling Undeserved Trust" in Section 5.2.5, "Instilling Undeserved Trust.") In most cases, however, a simple set of rules yielding a yes or no, or a multiplication to yield an aggregate trust factor, is sufficient. Also, trust might be determined based on legal or liability considerations that have *nothing to do with actual technical security*, and the rules in that case might be complex and based on who the participants are or other factors such as liability limits.[29]

> Trust is often based on legal or liability considerations that have nothing to do with actual technical security.

The real goal here is to allow us to identify potential weaknesses. By examining the trustworthiness of each decision variable, we can identify potential points of attack.

29 See [41], p. 225-226 and Chapters 9, "Transport and Storage of Secrets," and 10, "Design Considerations for Secure Operation," for a discussion of risk and liability in the event of a private key compromise. The reader should also be cognizant of local laws regarding liability.

7.17.2 Identity Context

A trusted decision context should always contain an identity attribute. The user identity attribute represents a level of trust of the end user, and that level of trust can be used to assign permissions as well as to assign group membership for that user. Users who are not authenticated are not trusted and should, of course, be granted very limited access rights.

> ***PRINCIPLE: A TRUSTED CONTEXT SHOULD INCLUDE A PROVEN IDENTITY.***

7.17.3 Code Context

The user identity is usually not sufficient for authorizing access to application and system resources in an open computing environment serving multiple communities or realms. Do not allow *untrusted code* to execute, even if the user context is trusted.[42] To do so allows the untrusted code to do something in the name of the user.

> ***PRINCIPLE: A TRUSTED CONTEXT SHOULD ALWAYS INCLUDE THE CODE CONTEXT.***

This seems like an obvious principle, but surprisingly it is often ignored. In fact, the entire legacy of Microsoft Windows applications through Windows ME ignored this principle because those Windows platforms did not have a code protection mechanism. This is the primary reason that that platform has been such a pronounced target for viruses. Even today there are great practical challenges to building and deploying applications that utilize the code context as a security attribute. This is discussed further in Section 7.17.11, "Writing Privileged Code on Method Policy Platforms."

The lack of a security policy that considers code context is behind many exploits. For example, a trusted resource attack relies on the fact that a trojan horse can be planted because the trusted resource is not verifiable.[30]

---

30 See [43] for a discussion of the vulnerabilities introduced by models that do not adequately constrain applications that are installed at a user's discretion.

◆ This is a special case of the risks discussed under the principle "Do Not Expose Internal Objects or Attributes" in Section 7.13.

Callbacks from a trusted server into an untrusted client also have peril for the server in that a callback is performed from trusted code, but invokes untrusted code (the client), so it is easy for a programmer to unintentionally be lured into passing internal objects that normally would be passed only to trusted code. For example, if trusted code exposes a method that accepts a callback object as an argument, it is possible for an attacker to provide a malicious object to be used as a callback, luring the trusted code into passing an internal object. This is depicted in the next figure.♦

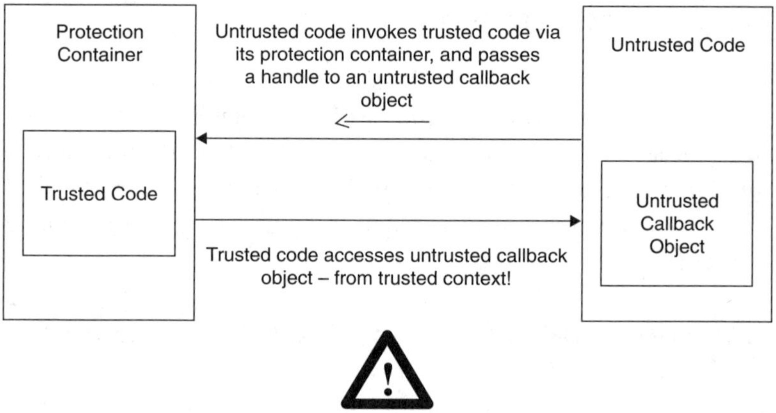

Protection Container

Untrusted code invokes trusted code via its protection container, and passes a handle to an untrusted callback object

Untrusted Code

Trusted Code

Untrusted Callback Object

Trusted code accesses untrusted callback object – from trusted context!

Figure 7.16
Callbacks to an untrusted client are perilous and can enable the client to impersonate you.

In general, callbacks into untrusted code are risky, *especially if they inherit the context of the server* or *pass references to internal structures—even though the code performing the callback is trusted.* Never allow an untrusted domain to impersonate you or lure you into exposing internal objects.[31]

Callbacks are not the only way to fool an application into executing untrusted code within the application's context. Another way is to input the code as data in such a way that it will inadvertently be interpreted. This is how the well-known attack technique of "script injection" works: A script such as SQL, Javascript, or ASP code is input to a Web form, in a form field that is expected to contain data. Later, a server component parses the form data, and a server-side engine sees the script and executes it—*in the context of the server application and, therefore, with the server application's privileges.* This is why server applications should never be deployed to run under a root or

31 See [44], p. 287.

administrator privilege and should run under a special user ID created for only that server application, with the minimum privileges needed for the application. (This is discussed further in Chapter 8.)

> Callbacks from your server into an untrusted client have peril in that a callback is performed from trusted code but invokes untrusted code.

In general, scripting is something to watch out for. Because scripted programs can be loaded at runtime, they present an opportunity to inject malicious code at any time that ends up being executed in a server or trusted user context. The mere existence of a scripting engine on a server presents a point from which an attack can be performed if the attacker merely finds a clever way to introduce a script to the script engine.

> Because scripted programs can be loaded at runtime, they present an opportunity to inject malicious code at any time that ends up being executed in a server or trusted user context.

A third mechanism that can be used to cause untrusted code to execute is to input data that is expected to be transferred to another environment later and interpreted there. A typical example of this is posting an executable file in a newsgroup or attaching it to an email so that users who later download or receive the file will inadvertently execute it in their environment (i.e., on their workstation).

So called "mobile code" provides a fourth mechanism. Mobile code is code, such as a Java applet, Javascript, ActiveX, or Flash, that is automatically downloaded from a Web site into the client's environment and executed there.

Spyware is yet another mechanism. Spyware is software that executes on a compromised machine and "spies" by monitoring or inspecting the machine and reporting back to the attacker. Spyware is often downloaded and installed by a user unintentionally, perhaps as part of another application; thus, the user is unaware of the installation because it piggybacks on the installation of some other program that the user has requested.

Most modern computing platforms provide mechanisms for assessing the trustworthiness of code. For example, the Java Security Manager and Access Controller components verify the signature of signed code and apply configured security policy based on the code's identity. The Microsoft Common Language Runtime provides a similar mechanism. However, neither of these mechanisms is yet widely used by applications, partially because users are unaware of them and configuration is not simple,[32] and also because programmers do not know how to use the language constructs to define permission models.[33]

7.17.4 Validation of Context Data

Any data that is input to a resource should always be validated in terms of its conformance to the allowed range and characteristics of the data.[34] Data validation is a standard "best practice" with all software systems, but it is especially important for reasons of security. Validation is an important aspect of "defensive programming."

Validation of resource input has two phases: prior to resource invocation and during resource invocation. The former must be done by the resource activation framework and is done prior to when context is switched to the resource. For example, an EJB method cannot be called until the dispatching mechanism has received well-formed input from the request stream. The inputs are therefore guaranteed to conform to proper language types and ranges.♦

> ◆ See the principle "Employ a Strongly Typed Language and Design Approach for the Interface" in Section 7.13.1.

Validation during invocation must be done by the resource itself or by a precondition evaluation mechanism. This level of validation goes beyond language type validation and is defined by the application. It addresses conformance to application-defined data ranges or formats, assumptions about input values, and so on.

Validation is even more important if the input is received form a partially trusted context, such as a public user input screen. Even though the user might be authenticated, a user

---

32 Most J2EE application server installations are, in fact, deployed without a security manager.

33 See this book's Web site for guidance on defining Java permission models.

34 See [45], p. 262.

who is using a guessed password might be attempting to elevate their privileges or causing the system to do something that it is not designed to do by "breaking" the system, and invalid data is a common way of accomplishing that.

Validate all data from partially trusted or untrusted sources, including user screen input, messages, serialized objects, and so on. While such data might not be used to make an authorization decision, it might be used in unanticipated ways that could represent a trojan horse. For example, data, such as a user's address that is input by a user, might be stored in the database and later displayed on a Web page, and if it contains HTML tags that point to another Web site, or a script that would be interpreted by the server application, the result could be an "cross-site script" or "script injection" breach, respectively.[35]

PRINCIPLE: VALIDATE ANYTHING RECEIVED FROM UNTRUSTED SOURCES.

The responsibility to validate also applies to the client application and client application user—including the user of a browser. For example, when visiting a Web site that you do not fully trust, you should validate (check the target of) any link before clicking on it. That is, make sure that the link's address and parameters are what you would expect them to be. Otherwise, you could fall prey to a cross-site script. This is a severe risk to the user, because a cross-site script—by virtue of the fact that it is executed within a trusted context—has the power to read your browser cookies, install a keystroke sniffer (if your browser's configuration treats the target site of the URL as a trusted site), or virtually anything that is allowed by the user's security configuration for a trusted context.

Note that validation is not the same as authentication. Authentication of a user or of data involves verifying the veracity of the user identity or data, respectively. Validation has nothing to do with veracity, but rather verifies that the input falls within allowed ranges and conforms to any required formats.

35 The PERL language feature known as "taint checking" can be used to help prevent script injection attacks in PERL programs. It can be used by executing PERL with the -T option.

Validation also includes verifying any *assumptions about sequence*. For example, if there is an implicit assumption that another resource method has been performed prior to the current one, this should be verified if the caller is not internal and therefore not fully trusted.

Validation includes verification that values are within allowed ranges, conform to required formats, and verification of any assumptions about sequence.

7.17.5 Validation for Non-Repudiation Purposes

So far, we have discussed validation as a requirement for achieving trust in some form, either for establishing data integrity or authenticity. However, validation also has another important usage: non-repudiation—that is, proving that a transaction took place.

If the client provides some form of signature associated with the data, and the signature can be validated, the signature becomes a means of proving the authenticity of the data and the client's involvement in producing it. A digital signature can be used for this purpose. For example, if a set of data is digitally signed by a client, later validation of the signature (and the client's certificate) is sufficient to prove that the client signed the data.

So-called signed objects can be created using a variety of mechanisms, including XML signatures and PKCS #7 format signatures. The appropriate format depends on the predominant technology that is used by the application.

7.17.6 Contextual Scope

The characteristics of the user's client environment should be considered when designing a mechanism for containing the user's session. In particular, what is the scope of control that the user has over the session? If the session is used as a basis for storing a security context, the user must be known to have full control over the session—that is, that the session cannot be co-opted by someone else.

For example, if the user uses a shared workstation, do other users have access to the user's session data when the user is not present? Are session artifacts left on the system by the client software? An especially worrisome scenario is a public access terminal. If a user accesses her bank account using a public-access computer in an airport and leaves to catch a plane, forgetting to close all browser windows, her session will continue to exist until it times out. Therefore, applications that are accessed using public access terminals should have a much shorter timeout than applications that are exclusively accessed from an office environment.

PRINCIPLE: SET SESSION AND CREDENTIAL SCOPE APPROPRIATELY.

The author personally uses his own bank's Web site for paying all his bills and has found it very frustrating that a user session times out after only five minutes, which is sometimes not long enough to print a summary and answer an unexpected and ill-timed phone call. The bank's CTO has explained that the short timeout is because many people access the system from public access systems. He is right to have the short timeout. However, one feature suggested to him was to have a persistent session so that the security session times out quickly, but the user's data session continues to persist for a longer period, so that if the security session times out, the user can log back on and get back to "where they were." This can represent a huge usability improvement for users.[36]

Credentials and user privileges should not have an unlimited lifetime either. Whenever a user is enrolled in an application or is given privileges to access it, those privileges and credentials should be configured to have a lifetime that is *less than the expected* time through which the user will need them. This is to help ensure that the user will not retain access rights beyond the user's needs. The time period should also be frequent enough to keep the user's passwords from becoming "well-known," because passwords often become known to other users as a result of daily usage.♦

◆ See also the principle "Periodically Replace Secrets" in Section 9.2, "Credential Management."

36 Unfortunately, the author does not have enough in his bank account to convince the bank to implement the suggested improvement.

PRINCIPLE: PROVIDE FOR TIMELY REVOCATION OF PRIVILEGES.

In the event that a user's credentials or access rights are revoked ahead of schedule, it may be necessary to ensure that the user's current sessions are terminated. This is known as "global logout." For example, suppose the user is suspected of being engaged in malicious activity, and the system administrator has been instructed to shut off the user's access to all systems. If the user currently is engaged in several Web sessions with different applications, this might be hard to do unless the login mechanism utilizes a central authorization system and authorization is enforced for each request–not just for login.

7.17.7 Context Propagation

There are many computing frameworks that allow an application to dynamically create new independent contexts of execution. For example, Unix systems provide process forking and threading. In the forking model, a process executes a fork() operation, which causes it to make a copy of itself (including its entire runtime execution state), resulting in two processes. The only difference between them is that a process can determine if it is the copy and make different decisions based on that fact. In the threading model, a program can create a new runtime object called a "thread," which runs independently of the main program thread of execution. Threads share process memory space and can therefore access the same heap memory data objects, whereas forked processes each have their own process data heap.

Whenever a new execution context such as a spawned process or thread is created, it is important that the security context associated with the originating execution thread or process propagate to the new execution thread or process. It should not be possible for an application to forge a weaker (for example, unauthenticated) security context and then create a new execution thread or process with the forged context but with the original context's priveleges or level of trust. In a similar vein, a default security context should never be applied to a spawned execution environment unless it can be assured that all the permissions of the default context will be lower than those of the creating environment. More simply, the new environment (process or thread) should reflect the context that created it; or it should be guaranteed to reflect the most pessimistic (mistrustful) view of its originating environment. (An exception to this rule is when the code is a highly trusted module that has permission to create an execution context.)◆

◆ See the principle "Define Privileged Context Boundaries" in Section 7.17.9, "Encapsulation of Privelege."

PRINCIPLE: PROPAGATE CONTEXT ACCURATELY OR PESSIMISTICALLY.

This principle also applies to an execution thread or process that is created in response to a request. For example, when a remote request is received by a server, an execution context is created to handle the request. That context should possess security attributes that accurately reflect the environment of origin, to the extent possible. If the environment is not completely trusted, trust attributes should be associated with any context attributes that are propagated from the client environment. For example, if the application has two methods of logon–single password and dual password–contexts (i.e., sessions) that log on with one password should be identifiable as such and trusted less.

7.17.8 Contexts of Control

Suppose an authentication context contains more than one user. Should all users be required to have permission in order to be able to access a resource, or at least one user?

This might seem like a bizarre scenario, but it is not. For example, suppose that an operation requires permissions P1 and P2. Organization A has permission P1, and organization B has permission P2. Organization A authenticates itself and sends a request to perform the operation, providing an entitlement object that asserts P1, and organization B authenticates itself and also sends a request to perform the operation, providing an entitlement object that asserts P2. Should the union of these permissions be taken? Or should both A and B each have both permissions?

This is analogous to the two users each turning a key: Each performs a role, and each must execute the key turn at the same time–as part of the same request to perform a single action.

Conceptually, each user is authenticated to the same session that is invoking the requested action. Even if each user logged on independently, the context that invokes the requested action contains the authenticated identity of each required role, and the full set of permissions required for the action must be present in the union of those roles.

This book uses the terms "execution context" and "control context" to refer to the context that accesses the protected resource in an execution sense. These terms will be used somewhat interchangeably, although the term "execution context" refers more narrowly to computer-based control whereas "control context" could include a human or mechanical element.

Normally, the control context would be the context of the execution thread and the entire context that is accessible to that thread at the point of attempted resource access. This context must have all the permissions required to invoke the requested action or access the resource.

There are other circumstances, however, in which all participants should individually have all required permissions. This would be true, for example, when viewing sensitive information. In that scenario, each participant represents his own individual context of control, and for that type of application, contexts should not be combined for making authorization decisions.

PRINCIPLE: REQUIRE EVERY EXECUTION CONTEXT TO HAVE PERMISSION.

7.17.9 Encapsulation of Privilege

It is often the case that an object needs permission to access a resource, but it would be inappropriate to expect the object's clients to also have that permission.♦

> ♦ See the "Fine-Grained Authorization (Least Privilege) at Each Perimeter" principle in Section 7.5, "Perimeters."

For example, suppose that a purchasing object P provides a purchase function purchase(), and that purchase() calls a method debitAccount() on resource Account. While one would expect that callers of the purchase() function would be required to have permission to access it, one would not expect those callers to have explicit permission to access the debitAccount() function. That permission is needed only by the purchase() function. In effect, we would expect that purchase() would take responsibility for its actions so that none of its functions can compromise the consistency or integrity of the Account resource. Therefore, assuming that purchase() is properly designed, the Account resource is protected, and users only need to have permission to call purchase() in order to make purchases.

The debitAccount() function is what is known as a *transitive resource*,[37] from the perspective of the purchase() caller. The debitAccount() function is not directly accessed by the purchase() caller, but it is used behind the scenes to satisfy the request.

The boundary provided by the purchase() function is what this text will refer to as a *privileged context boundary*. The boundary defines a scope outside of which a calling context does not need to have the permissions that are required by the inner context, which consists of "privileged code."[38]

PRINCIPLE: DEFINE PRIVILEGED CONTEXT BOUNDARIES.

The privileged boundary concept is defined in the design pattern that follows.

DESIGN PATTERN: PRIVILEGED CONTEXT BOUNDARY

Context

A resource needs to access other protected resources to perform its operation, requiring specialized permission to access those protected resources.

Problem

It is often unreasonable to expect the users of a resource to have the low-level permissions that the resource requires to perform its function.

Solution

This pattern provides a basic template for encapsulating privileged operations. In this pattern, a resource, A, is accessed by one or more clients (not shown). Those clients only need permission to access A.

Resource A in turn needs to access some privileged operations that the clients cannot be expected to have permission for. Resource A therefore switches its context to a context that has permission. Resource A must have permission to perform this context switch at this point. (Different approaches for performing the context switch are discussed later in this section.)

---

37 See [46] p. 54.

38 The term "privileged section" is often used to describe privileged code. For our discussion, the boundary between privileged code and regular code is more pertinent, so this text will use the term privileged context boundary for this boundary implementation, which is often system-dependent.

When the privileged code has been executed, the original context is restored in a manner that is reliable regardless of whether an error occurs while executing the privileged code.

This pattern is depicted in Figure 7.17.

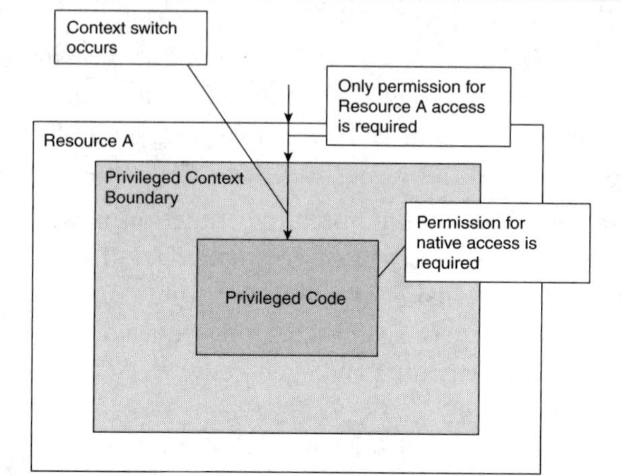

Figure 7.17
Structure.

Consequences

Trusted applications can access protected resources without requiring the user to have permission for those resources.

It is good practice to define a privileged context boundary in order to encapsulate the permissions needed by a secure resource. Doing so narrows the permissions that are needed by roles that access resources.

Only define a privileged context boundary at or within a secure resource.

A privileged context boundary is also often used for the purpose of limiting access to native resources. If it is possible to configure security policy such that only the priveleged code can access the native resources, the application can have greater confidence that those resources will be accessed only by users who are granted permission to access the boundary that encapsulates the priveleged code.

7.17.10 Privilege Encapsulation Approaches

There are at least two different approaches to defining a privileged context boundary. These are:

1. An application temporarily *modifies* (elevates or augments) the privilege that the current control context (e.g., the current thread) has.

2. A separate trusted context (e.g., an object or code module) *assumes responsibility for* the security of the action, in lieu of the user having permission.

Privilege Modification Approach

The first approach is often achieved by temporarily changing the context to a more privileged context. For example, Unix programmers are familiar with the concept of context switching in the form of the setuid() system call, which allows a process to take on an alternate (preconfigured) privileged identity to perform an operation that requires privilege. Unfortunately, the rules for using setuid() are confusing and differ from one version of Unix to another [48]. It also represents a procedural approach rather than a structural or declarative approach, and therefore is prone to being used incorrectly.

The first approach can be unreliable if the programmer does not ensure that the prior privilege level will be reliably restored when the privileged code is exited. This can be achieved by using language scoping mechanisms that provide a reliable exit path, such as a Java try block with a finally clause: The finally clause can be used to restore privilege.[39]

When a privileged context boundary is achieved by modifying the context, it is often the case that the attributes of the originating environment (for example, including the caller identity) are not propagated through the call, and entirely newly authenticated or chosen attributes are applied for the purpose of the privileged operation (perhaps based on a configuration of the server).[40] This context switch is actually a form of "impersonation" but is done in a controlled manner and only by trusted code.[41] For example, this is how the "runAs()" method works in J2EE application servers.

The Java runtime uses the second approach mentioned. It is a scope-based mechanism that uses the scope of a method call to enforce restoration of normal privilege state. Its "doPrivileged(PrivilegedAction)" effectively places a boundary

39 For an explanation of try blocks and how they are implemented on the Windows platform, see the excellent article [47].

40 See the discussion of hiding of call context in [49] on p. 129.

41 Impersonation is sometimes confused with "delegation." True delegation retains the context of the originating request but appends a new context that the requester requests be used in order to handle the request. The request handler can always refuse to accept the delegator, but this is only possible if the handler knows the identity (i.e., context) of the original request. Impersonation, on the other hand, does not preserve the context of the requester, but substitutes an entirely new context.

Assumption of Responsibility Approach

around the privileged action that is performed. From that point and below on the call stack, the thread context must have permission; but beyond (above) that point permission is *not needed.*[42] The module that invokes doPrivileged(...) effectively assumes responsibility for the safety of the privileged operations, even though they are invoked by users who do not have those permissions.

In order to assume responsibility in lieu of the user, a module must have all required permissions.

The "PrivilegedAction" is an object that encapsulates the operation that is to be performed that requires privilege; that is, the doPrivileged(...) method runs the run() method of the PrivilegedAction argument.

In order to call doPrivileged(...) the calling *module*—rather than the user—must have all required permissions. The module's permission set is configured by the security policy of the deployed code module. In this way, only certain protected and secure modules are allowed to invoke doPrivileged(...), to assume responsibility for the call and relieve the caller from being required to have low-level privileges. Thus, privilege for the user is replaced by privilege for the code. In effect, the writer of the module is saying, "The client of my code does not need low-level permissions to safely do this function as long as it is done through my code—just give *my code* those permissions and everything will be ok."

Because privileged code executes with more privilege than the caller, but at the caller's request—i.e., under the caller's indirect control—it offers a malicious user an opportunity to attack the application or its environment by attacking the privileged code. This is a type of Trusted Resource Attack. Thus, if the privileged code has any vulnerabilities (for example, reliance on any insecure system files), configuration files, initialization files, or other resources, the privileged section can be co-opted and thereby the application that uses it can be used as a pathway to initiate malicious actions. (See the principles "Securely Connect to All Resources," "Secure Native Resources," and "Securely Identify All

42 The details of the doPrivileged mechanism are described in more detail on this book's Web site.

Resources" in Sections 7.20.4, 7.20.5, and 7.20.6, respectively.)[43] For this reason, a privileged context boundary should only be defined by very secure code. Such code should access as few external resources as possible and be made as small as possible so that the privileged operations are well isolated and of short duration.[51] This facilitates analysis of the component to ensure that the design is sound and cannot be compromised.

Privileged code should be highly secure.

PRINCIPLE: TIGHTLY ENCAPSULATE PRIVILEGED OPERATIONS.

7.17.11 Writing Privileged Code on Method Policy Platforms

Many application server frameworks make it very difficult to use code policy mechanisms. For example, the J2EE resource authorization models are based on role access control lists for resource methods; there is no provision for defining access rights based on the module origin, even though that capability exists natively in the core Java virtual machine.

Some Java application servers provide proprietary tools for configuring the security policy of an application based on the sources of its constituent components. For example, BEA Weblogic provides the <security-permission-spec> for granting permissions to EJBs. However, this feature is little used, and most programmers would not know how to use it even if they were aware of its existence and were inclined to use a proprietary mechanism.

For server-based applications, it is often most practical to define security policy at a transaction method (for example, EJB and/or Web service) level. In this situation, the call interface at which policy is enforceable necessarily becomes a privileged context boundary.

Consider Figure 7.18, which shows the use of an EJB container to define a privileged context boundary around some privileged code. If you compare this figure with the figure from the "Privileged Context Boundary" pattern in Section 7.17.9, you will see that the privileged context boundary is implemented by the EJB container and that the sensitive code that requires privilege is encapsulated in Local EJB B. So-called "local" EJBs

43 See the discussion of injection points in [50] on pp. 153 ff.

An EJB Example

are EJBs that are accessible only from within the same Java virtual machine. A call to a local EJB does not have the overhead of a remote call. This discussion will refer to Local EJB B as "EJB B" for short.

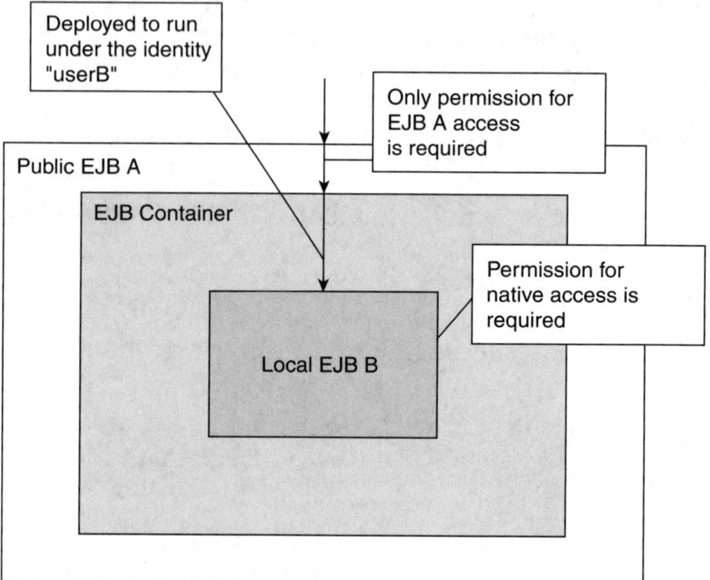

Figure 7.18
Example of defining a privileged context boundary using a local EJB.

Notice that EJB B is deployed so that it runs under the identity "user B" instead of the identity of its caller (the identity under which Public EJB A runs).[44] User B can be granted access to EJB B and also to any native resources that EJB B needs to access. EJB A does not need to have these access rights: It only needs to be able to call EJB B.

In this way, it is possible to greatly limit the access rights that are granted to the application. Code that needs access to sensitive resources (for example, database connection pools) can be encapsulated in local EJBs and run under a special identity that has the rights required to access the sensitive resources.

Classes that come from the same source should be grouped based on the capabilities that they need in order to define sets of classes that have the same origin (trust) and the same capability

44 This automatic context switch is a feature of the J2EE platform. It allows a server component to be "run as" an administratively defined identity.

requirements. Those that have the same origin and same capability requirements should be packaged together and run under an identity that has only the required capabilities—an no more.

This is an application of the principle of least privilege.♦ This has the effect of creating a policy domain for each set of classes, delineated by their package.

♦ See the principle "Fine-Grained Authorization (Least Privilege) at Each Perimeter" in Section 7.5.

PRINCIPLE: PACKAGE RESOURCES OF EQUAL TRUST AND EQUAL CAPABILITY REQUIREMENTS TOGETHER.

7.17.12 Objects Obtained Via Elevated Privilege

Consideration should be given to objects held or transferred by a privileged boundary resource.♦ *If an object required permission to obtain it, do not give that object to others outside the context that has the permission.* The term "object" is meant to refer to any potentially shared structure, usually represented by a reference, alias, handle, or pointer.♦

♦ This is the principle already discussed, "Do Not Expose Internal Objects or Attributes."

♦ This is discussed further under the principle "Tightly Control Access to Resource References" in Section 7.20.3, "Vulnerable References."

7.18 Controlling Communication Pathways

The concept of encapsulation of function is extremely important for building reliable systems, under the theory that if you reduce the number of ways that external components access the internal state of a component, there is a combinatorial reduction in the number of circumstances that are unanticipated and can cause an error.

The essence of encapsulation is to reduce the paths of communication into and out of a component and make those pathways visible and typesafe so that a programmer must explicitly deal with the entire set of values that travel in and out of the component. Unfortunately, the encapsulation mechanisms that are provided by languages and platforms do not always match what is required by an architectural pattern.

The encapsulation mechanisms that are provided by languages and platforms do not always match what is required by an architectural pattern.

◆ Closure is explained more fully under the principle "Interference and Closure" in Section 7.20.

Closure refers to the ability to define and control all communication pathways, and is therefore a stronger concept.[45]◆ Closure is an important concept for reliability for preventing unintended interference between components and also for security for preventing "covert channels" (see "Interception" in Section 5.1.1) and many other forms of attack.

In the Java language, encapsulation and closure are achievable using the various scope control mechanisms that are built into the Java language and platform. These mechanisms are summarized in Table 7.6.

Table 7.6 The Scoping Boundaries Provided by Java

Scope	Scoped (Protected) Items
VM	Threads
	Stack data
	Class loaders
	Root class loader
	System properties
Class Loader	Static class data (data = "intrinsic type data", incl. obj. refs.
	Property resources
Package	Static class data
	Instance data
	Classes
	Property resources
Class	Static class data
	Instance data
	Nested classes (but implementations violate this)
Method	Method (stack) data
	Nested classes (but implementations violate this)
	Method parameters
Code Block	Local variables
Code Source	Resources requiring permission (i.e., that perform checkPermission)

45 In this book, the term "closure" is not to be confused with a language feature known as a "closure" in languages such as Ruby.

Notice that Java does not provide an *object-level* scoping mechanism of any kind. Also, the package-level scoping is all-or-nothing: elements of a package are either publicly visible or they are private to the package—there is no way to specify the scope of a package *with respect to a particular other package*—so-called "friend" relationships.[46] Finally, there is no scoping mechanism that deals with different classes of information or object attributes—for example, security levels—that could be defined and checked at runtime. All these limitations make it hard to design reusable components that are secure and that can guarantee that other components do not interfere with their internal operation.

Java does not provide an *object-level* scoping mechanism of any kind.

7.18.1 Component-Oriented Design

Object-level scoping is often found in "component"-oriented languages. The component-oriented paradigm generally contains these concepts:

- Objects are treated as opaque, and can share information only through explicitly defined "ports"—communication structures defined by the programmer.
- Objects that are interconnected at a port level are generally considered to be compatible if their port methods have compatible signatures: ports do not have to implement identical interfaces.

Some authors distinguish between *design-time* components and *assembly-time* (or deployment-time) components: Design-time components are not opaque because their internal features must still be elaborated into final implementation constructs and assigned to physical components.[47] Nevertheless, components are opaque *with respect to other components* because they are expected to have well-defined interfaces and communicate only through those interfaces.

The hardware design community is component-focused and, therefore, has had solutions to the object-level scoping problem for decades. For example, the VHDL language (see [53]), which

46 Friend relationships are being considered for a future version of Java.
47 For example, see [52], p. 50.

is a universal standard for the design of electronic integrated circuits, incorporates ports. The intent of a VHDL port is to model a physical communication port on a device; however, it can be used to model any abstract information conduit. Some business application design frameworks also employ the concept of ports; for example, Microsoft's BizTalk.

The concept of a port is generally useful only if it can be assumed that components can communicate *only* through explicit structures, such as ports or explicitly defined shared structures–i.e., that all implicit communication mechanisms are blocked. This book, therefore, refers to this approach as a "structural domain." A structural domain is an approach to satisfying the "Law of Demeter" principle [54], which is a loosely defined concept that requires that a component should communicate directly only with other components that are immediate neighbors in some sense and therefore trusted.

The structural domain concept is very relevant to secure software design because one of the central problems in secure design is to ensure that communication does not occur through unanticipated pathways (for example, covert channels; see Section 5.1.1). If all pathways are explicitly defined and connected, covert channels and interference are very unlikely to exist.

Unfortunately, there is very little collaboration between the software design community and the hardware design community, so hardware-oriented languages such as VHDL have not appreciably impacted software design languages, and component-oriented software development has had trouble defining itself. However, this book defines the term *component*, for the purpose of the discussion here, to mean a system that employs an outer structural domain–that is, a system that communicates only through explicitly defined pathways. This can be achieved either through a language- and platform-enforced mechanism or through very rigorous design and development processes that ensure that no unrecognized "back doors" exist.[48]

48 See [55] for a proposal for adding a "module" concept to Java.

Design Patterns: Component and Port

Context

A component is instantiated within an application. The component contains internal objects and data that may not be visible outside the object. Yet, the component must communicate with other components.

Problem

The reliability and security of a component is closely tied to the degree to which the components internal state can be accessed by other components or by the environment. There is therefore a need to define approaches for limiting access.

Solution

This pattern provides a way of defining components within a software system. It defines for each component a structural domain that can communicate only with other component domains or their environment via explicitly defined ports. No other communication is allowed. See Figure 7.19.

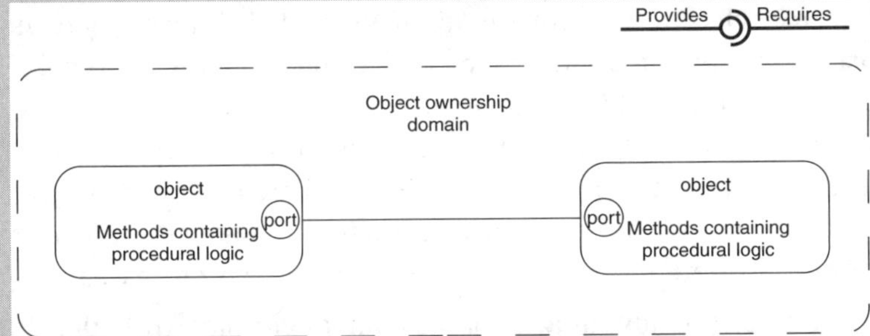

Figure 7.19 Domains connected by ports.

In order to ensure that passed object references cannot introduce a "back door" into a component, the concept of object reference ("alias") uniqueness must be provided for objects that are passed from one component to another: Object references can either be passed through a port in such a way that they are no longer referenceable by the original component, or they must be passed by value.

A structural domain is very hard to achieve using most object-oriented languages such as Java, C++, and C#. This is because these languages do not provide the required kinds of scope control that are needed for structural domains. Newer languages, such as ArchJava [56], provide direct language support for structural domains. However, even ArchJava slightly breaks the component paradigm because objects can still communicate via their environment through global properties.

Just because a language provides ways to circumvent the encapsulation of a domain does not mean that a well-closed structural domain cannot be created. The use of encapsulation-breaking constructs must be scanned for and disallowed. For example, a code module can be statically scanned for references to classes that the design defines to be outside the domain of the module.

Consequences

Components can be separated from other components with reduced risk of unintended communication or interference.

An innovative language that incorporates the port concept is the ArchJava language [57]. ArchJava requires a programmer to explicitly define all communication pathways (it even uses the term "port").

> The port paradigm separates software design into distinct behavioral and structural aspects.

A consequence of the port paradigm is that it separates software design into distinct *behavioral* and *structural* aspects. Components are connected together structurally and allowed to communicate in explicitly defined ways. The internals of the interconnected components may be defined using either behavior (employing an algorithmic or formulaic definition) or structural definitions, but at the lowest level components are either defined behaviorally or their behavior is intrinsic to the design language.

In ArchJava, components implement their internal behavior using standard Java language syntax and semantics, but subject to the enhanced object instance scoping rules provided by the ArchJava language. The language also enforces compositional integrity of ownership and uniqueness, thereby eliminating communication that can occur through the inadvertent sharing of object internal state when objects are copied or passed.

One of the advantages of the component pattern is that it allows the creation of reusable building blocks as a result of the fact that systems that have limited and well-defined inputs and outputs tend to be easily composable into larger aggregate systems. Composability is discussed in Section 7.20.1, "Composability."

Another advantage of the component pattern is that it allows the easy data flow decomposition of program units and facilitates concurrency analysis. This makes it possible to deploy the program units on concurrent computing systems such as clusters.

The embedding of structural decomposition and information flow control mechanisms within software languages is long overdue, but nothing short of revolutionary—as long as the software community recognizes the advantages and makes use of these new languages.

7.19 Domain Integrity

The term "domain" is used in many different ways (for example, as a synonym for "realm"), but the discussion here will use a definition that is most useful for describing software security design patterns: A *domain* is a set of objects that can be treated as the same policies with regard to their trustworthiness, or which share a single set of policies with regard to their trust of objects outside the domain, or both. The "separation of domains" principle [58] allows for the compartmentalization and trust of resources according to where the resources reside and are managed from.

A Java codesource is a domain. This is because classes (which are effectively static lifetime objects in their own right) that are from the same codesource (same origin and same author) are treated as a single entity when defining Java VM security policy. However, the Java codesource domain concept is not useful for application design because too much overhead is required to define a domain, so it is not a feature that is used to define domains *within* applications. A Java codesource also is defined in terms of classes, so it cannot be used to create domains of class *instances*.

Domains are an important tool for implementing "separation of concerns" between different aspects of an application (see Section 11.3, "Component Roles and Contracts"). For example, business logic should not be intermixed with infrastructure logic or other non-business logic, because to do so makes it hard to maintain each of these aspects, and also tends to complicate and obfuscate the logic—leading to unreliability and unauditability.

> ***PRINCIPLE: DO NOT INTERMIX BUSINESS LOGIC WITH INFRASTRUCTURE OR OTHER NON-BUSINESS LOGIC, UNLESS THE SEPARATION IS SIMPLE AND CLEAR.***

Thus, access to APIs that represent lifecycle methods, security APIs, session management (but not access) or persistent management (but not access) should be handled in a separate set of modules that are factored out from the business logic modules. Such modules are often implemented as software "layers," which are discussed next.

7.19.1 Layers

Layer concepts have already been introduced (see "Resource Types and Layers" in Section 7.2). Most programmers recognize the concept that a layer is a strata within a system, and many recognize that code within a particular layer should depend only on code that is in lower layers of the code strata. This interpretation is valid, but we need to add a little more precision to it. We can now do so by interpreting it in terms of the domain concept that we have just discussed.

A *layer* is a component domain (in terms of objects or classes) within a stratified tier of domains such that components within the layer can depend only on or *directly* access components in "lower" domains. The term *level* is also used in computing literature to represent this concept, but current application development parlance seems to prefer the term "layer," so this book uses that term.[49]

The one-directional dependency rule for a layer implies that upper layers may call only lower layers. However, that is not necessarily true. If an upper layer passes a callback object to a lower layer, the lower layer may use it to call back to the upper layer. (See for example, the "Separated Interface" pattern in [60].) By and large, however, upper layers call only lower layers. A layer can also depend on external non-layered components or utilities that are shared by multiple layers.

The rationale for utilizing a layered design is based on the concept that the business model is the core and enduring part of the system and that each successive outer layer is dependent on that model and on layers that are closer to the model. This assumes that the closer you are to the core model, the more stable the software layer is likely to be. It therefore makes sense that dependencies should flow only inward toward the central model.

PRINCIPLE: APPLICATION-SPECIFIC DEPENDENCIES SHOULD FLOW ONLY TOWARD THE BUSINESS MODEL.

49 For example, the seminal work [59] by Neumann, et al. on multilevel security and PSOS uses the term "level."

The inward flow of dependency has important advantages for security [60] because it allows for the decomposition of security into separate domains, represented by each layer with a set of security policies. If a layer is shown to be secure, and the next layer depends only on the secure layer, there is reason to believe that the outer layer is secure as well, as long as it adheres to secure principles.[50]

Another justification for a layered design is that layers often implement policies with regard to access control, synchronization, error handling, and data transformation. For example, the system architecture might specify that a certain layer is responsible for responding to and logging errors. If an outer layer bypasses an inner layer, the policies that are implemented by the bypassed layer can be circumvented.

PRINCIPLE: LAYERS SHOULD NOT BE BYPASSED.

When a layer accesses a lower layer, any objects that are returned should be of types that are defined in a lower layer or are defined in a non-layered component or utility. Again, this rule can be broken in the situation when an upper layer provides a factory to a lower layer, thereby allowing the lower layer to create an object whose concrete type is defined in an upper layer–but without the lower layer being compilation-dependent on the upper layer. This practice (passing a factory to a lower layer) should only be allowed, however, if the lower layer trusts the upper layer, or if the callback can be executed in a "sandbox".

PRINCIPLE: OBJECTS PASSED TO LOWER LAYERS SHOULD BE EXPRESSED IN THE TYPES DEFINED IN THOSE LAYERS.

Exceptions that are returned by a lower layer and that should be propagated on to higher layers should first be mapped to the current layer's domain so that they make sense in that domain. (See the Convert Exceptions pattern in [63].) For example, an exception thrown by a resource should preferably be defined in the resource definition layer. (See the design pattern "Authorization as a Precondition" in Section 7.21, "Home-Grown Authorization.")

50 See [62], pp. 11 ff.

If an object to be returned to the caller is an exception, make sure that any unauthorized information is filtered and logged in a secure manner.

Exception information should never be lost when an exception is translated into (i.e., replaced by) another exception.♦ Typically, exceptions should be chained rather than replaced. If some exception information must be removed because exposing it to higher layers or clients *would pose a security risk*,♦ the removed information should not be discarded but should be logged to the logger that is trusted by the current security domain.♦

♦ See the principle "Securely Log Sensitive Data Rather Than Discard It" in Section 7.15.2, and the pattern "Exception Filter." Later, this is discussed again in the reliability principle "Never Discard Exception Information" in Section 7.15.2.

♦ See the principle "Filter Sensitive Data from Exceptions" in Section 7.15.2.

♦ See the principle "Securely Log Sensitive Data Rather Than Discard It" in Section 7.15.2.

Principle: Objects Returned to Higher Layers May Be Translated by Each Layer into Types That Are Meaningful in That Layer.

A layer represents a logical strata of processing within an application. It, therefore, defines a structure for calls between layers. However, internal calls within a layer should not use methods that are part of the layer's public interface. To do so is to make it impossible for the layer's internal design to differentiate between external (upper) calls and internal calls. It is of great value to differentiate between external calls and internal calls because internal methods can then have a different approach for error handling, security, object sharing, and so on. None of these optimizations are possible if internal calls are made to publicly accessible methods.

For this reason, it is useful to specifically define a logical "interface" for a layer. The logical interface represents what upper layers see. The rest of the layer is internal. Methods that are defined in the logical interface should not directly or indirectly invoke other methods that are also defined in the logical interface; similarly, internal methods should not invoke methods that are defined in the logical interface. This pattern is described next.

PRINCIPLE: A SOFTWARE LAYER SHOULD DEFINE AN "INTERFACE" FOR USE BY UPPER LAYERS ONLY.

DESIGN PATTERN: LAYER INTERFACE

Context

A layer represents an interface to the layers that exist below it.

Problem

A layer itself needs to present an interface yet also have internal methods that are not exposed to the outside. Cross-calls between methods that are exposed to the outside can present problems because the behavior required when called by an outside client or upper layer may be different than that required for a call that is from another component within the same layer.

Solution

This pattern provides an approach for differentiating between the external and internal aspects of a layer. The pattern's structure is depicted in Figure 7.20.

A *layer interface* is the logical interface exposed by the components of a layer to components of a higher layer. Depending on the language, it can consist of abstract and concrete classes, interface definitions (for example, Java interfaces, IDL, WSDL, and so on), and any other artifact needed by a client of the layer to communicate with it.

To the extent possible, artifacts that do not belong to the logical layer interface should be made private to the layer. This can be achieved using any mechanism available, including class- or object-level scoping, package scoping, or security domain.

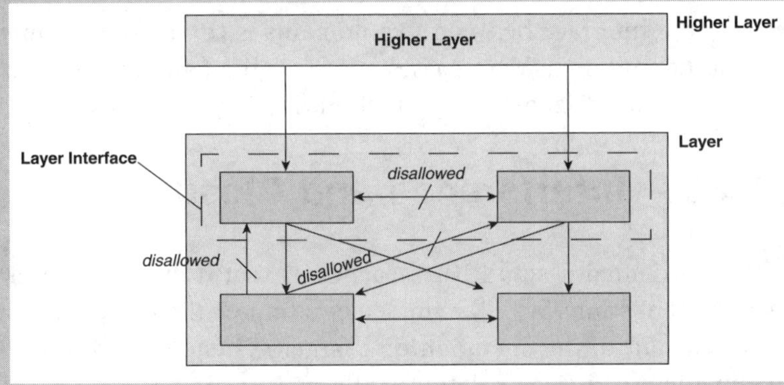

Figure 7.20
Structure.

Consequences

Internal and external interfaces are clearly differentiated, simplifying decisions about what functions to perform in each.

7.19.2 Information Sharing Across Domains

Do not share *data* possessed by a domain with other domains unless the sharing is performed via an interface that is designed to interconnect the domains. The intent here is to ensure that there is a well-considered protocol for information exchange between domains, and that information sharing across domains should not be ad-hoc.

Some domain interfaces may require authorization, while some might not. For example, the exchange of information from one layer to another within an application might not require authorization even though each layer is a kind of domain. On the other hand, an EJB layer might require authorization in order for a client layer to access it. In both cases, the layer domains should interact via the interface of each layer and not be bypassed.

◆ This principle is related to the principle "Require Every Execution Context to Have Permission" discussed in Section 7.17.8, "Contexts of Control."

PRINCIPLE: TRANSFER OF INFORMATION FROM ONE DOMAIN TO ANOTHER SHOULD ALWAYS BE THROUGH AN INTERFACE THAT CONSIDERS THE TRUSTWORTHINESS AND AUTHORIZATION OF EACH DOMAIN.◆

If the interface between two domains is trivial and requires no authorization as data passes across it, the two domains can be said to be "friends" and "collaborative."

7.20 Interference and Closure

Object-oriented design (OOD) teaches us that if one specifies a component's interface, the implementation of the component is not relevant to the operation of a larger system as long as each component satisfies its defined interface.

This is incorrect. The problem with interfaces in most contemporary computing languages is that they omit information. That information might be of no interest to other inter-operating components, but it is of interest to the system as a whole. A component's implementation—its "underbelly"—defines what internal elements are exposed by the component to the rest of the system.

From a security perspective, it is also important to be able to define what a component should *not* do. For example, we need to be able to specify things like, "Component C implements specification S, and *nothing more*."

From a security perspective, it is important to be able to define what a component should *not* do, for example, "Component C implements specification S, and nothing more."

It is, therefore, important to have a mechanism for constraining, or at least declaring, what those exposures are. A specification of a component's *closure* is the delineation of the complete scope of its exposure: what is accessible, through any means.[51]

Interfaces should not only specify functional behavior but should also delineate side effects, collaboration, and internal visibility. This includes specifying whether methods return objects by value or by reference and whether the returned values are mutable (can be modified).

PRINCIPLE: SPECIFY CLOSURE.

After an application has been completed, the scope of all declared names (for example, class, method, and variable declarations) should be examined to determine if the scope and mutability of any names can be further constrained based on which components actually need access to those names. Those that can be reduced in scope should be, preferably with an annotation made as to what the original scope was. There are likely to be a large number of names that will need to have their scopes reduced.

Closure is important for preventing Scope Attacks.

PRINCIPLE: IMPLEMENT CLOSURE.

51 The term "closure" comes from Group Theory, which defines a closed group as one for which a or b belongs to the group, where a and b are any members of the group, and op is an operation that belongs to the group. In this book, the term "closure" is used more loosely to mean that the act of combining components does not introduce additional unintended communication paths between those components or with the outside. Thus, a collection of components that has closure retains that closure when it is combined into a larger, more complex system.

7.20.1 Composability

Given a collection of components that each have a set of required properties, the components are *composable* if the act of assembling the components into a larger system preserves the required properties for the individual components and for the system as a whole. For example, if all a component's operations are required to be atomic, and if assembling two instances of the component together produce a combined system with operations that are all still atomic, the component is composable. Composability makes it easier to design systems that are reliable and secure.

The term *compositional* implies that the act of combining multiple components into a larger whole results in additional behavior or properties that are not present (or at least not observable) in the individual components. Compositional behavior can result from structure present in the arrangement of the constituent parts. For example, the human brain exhibits compositional behavior as a result of the structure inherent in the arrangement of the individual neurons. Compositional behavior within a system of software components is a normal expectation of application designers: An application achieves the property of fulfilling its purpose only when its components are assembled.

The assembly of secure components can produce compositional behavior that involves a loss of security. If this is possible, the components are not composably secure. Thus, composability is not a trivial property, and must consider any emergent behavior that might result from assembly. For example, the interactions of components of a system can sometimes be used to infer information about the constituent components, even if the components are individually secure.[52] This is called the *inference problem.*

7.20.2 Reusable Components

Some components might be designed to be reusable, so those may need to liberally expose a public interface and be designed to be extended. Reusable components therefore present a special

52 An example of this phenomenon is the ability to infer the contents of a database by observing statistics about the database. See [64].

risk in that they can serve as an unintended conduit, or as a weak link for accessing other components.

A reusable component should, therefore, be encapsulated by the applications that use it, and the encapsulating components (for example, package or class) should be implemented with the most restrictive scoping. The rest of the application should then reference only the encapsulation component in lieu of the encapsulated reusable components.

Even if the reusable component is encapsulated, any internal extensibility of the component might still represent a risk. For example, less-trusted code might instantiate the component elsewhere within the application and directly call internal (for example, "protected") methods within it. Therefore, *if possible*, security policy (for example, Java codesource security policy[53] or .NET CodeGroup policy[54]) should be configured to allow only the encapsulation component to directly access the actual reusable component. This effectively turns the encapsulation layer into a gateway that restricts access to the actual component.

Another consideration when encapsulating a component is where action responses are handled. Actions should always be handled within and by a secure codebase. Therefore, *a message should not provide its own handler unless the message codebase can be validated*, but that is conceptually unusual because messages are usually thought to originate from the outside, and validating complex messages (for example, messages with behavior) is costly and complex (for example, requires ensuring that deserialization is secure and binds to the correct trusted class). Note that a rogue message could be used as a trojan horse to compromise the message handler infrastructure.

> A rogue message can be used as a trojan horse to compromise the message handler infrastructure, for example, by materializing a rogue object via deserialization.

Closure can also be violated if sensitive code declares global variables or class-scope variables, because these can potentially be accessed by less trusted code that is able to access the scope of the variables.

53 See [65] under Permissions and Security Policy, and [66].

54 See the discussion of System.Security.Policy in [67], at http://msdn.microsoft.com/library/en-us/cpref/html/frlrfsystemsecuritypolicy.asp.

DESIGN PATTERN: CLOSURE OF REUSABLE COMPONENTS

Related Patterns

See the Adapter (aka "Wrapper") pattern in [68].

Context

A component is designed to be reusable but performs sensitive functions within an application.

Problem

A component that performs sensitive functions or contains sensitive data or objects must have no unanticipated or uncontrollable communication pathways in and out of it. Most computing languages do not provide constructs that ensure closure of a component.

Solution

This pattern provides a technique for limiting access to a component that was not designed in such a way that access can be easily restricted or controlled. Native components and third-party components often fall into this category. The pattern's structure is depicted in Figure 7.21.

The basic approach is to wrap the reusable component in an encapsulation layer that becomes the only layer that is allowed to directly access the reusable component. The encapsulation layer in effect becomes a gateway to the component.

For this to work, there needs to be *some* mechanism that can be used to control communication pathways to the reusable component, even if the application language does not provide that ability. As long as there is some mechanism that can be used, access to the reusable component can be limited to the gateway component.

For example, both the Java and Microsoft CLR platforms provide a means of controlling which code sources can access a component, as long as the component makes a security check. If the component does not make a security check, these mechanisms are ineffective, and another approach must be used. One possible approach is to instrument the compiled code using a tool such as Kava, in order to insert security checks. Another approach is to use a tool to scan all the code in the application to ensure that no part of the application accesses the reusable component except for the encapsulation layer. This approach is effective only if the entire codebase is controlled and there is no possibility of dynamically inserted code (for example, through deserialization or dynamic deployment) that has not been scanned for conformance with design rules.

> For this technique to work, there needs to be some mechanism that can be used to control communication pathways to the reusable component.

The encapsulation layer permits the reusable component to retain its existing interface and design. The encapsulation layer exposes only those methods that are needed by the application. This pattern is similar to the "Privileged Context Boundary" pattern presented in Section 7.17.9.

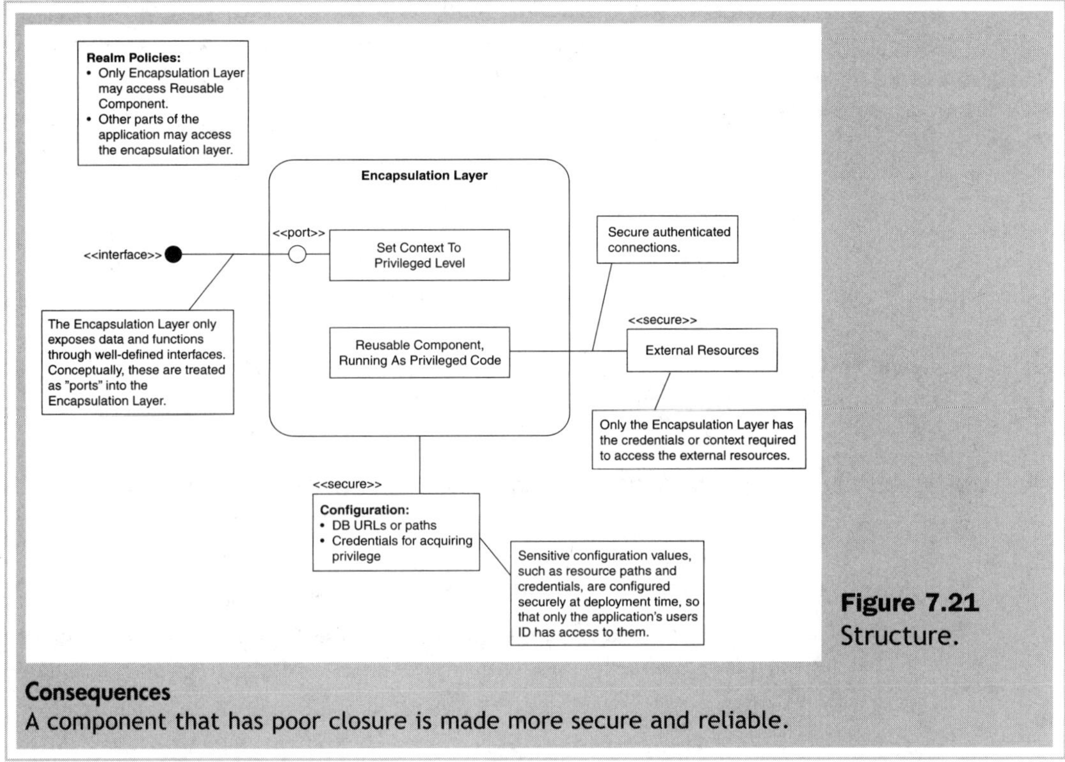

Figure 7.21 Structure.

Consequences

A component that has poor closure is made more secure and reliable.

If a component is self-contained, or a set of components is self-contained, identify that fact in the component's documentation and establish it as part of the component's specification. If practical, add tests to the set of design verification tests (see Section 3.3, "Defining and Verifying Architectural Rules") to verify—at least partially—that the component does not violate being self-contained in obvious ways, such as by reading external static values. Conversely, if internal aspects of a component are accessible to other components, identify those exposures in the component's documentation. All this may seem like a lot of trouble, but to achieve the goal of reusability in a reliable and trustworthy way, the effort is necessary.

The goal is to make it clear when components or groups of components can be assembled, and the resulting assembly has behavior that is essentially the "sum of the parts"—i.e., the resulting behavior of the assembled components is easily predicted from the behavior (and specification) of the individual components.

This has important implications for security because it means that if a component is considered to be secure, then it is useful to know if a system made up of several such components is also secure, or if the act of assembly introduces conflicts that could potentially be exploited. A system that can be assembled from multiple components without introducing unexpected conflict of behavior is sometimes referred to as a *composable* system. (See Chapter 11, "Compositional Integrity," for a discussion of composition, which is a related concept.)

> If a component is considered to be secure, then it is useful to know if a system made up of several such components is also secure.

PRINCIPLE: CLEARLY DELINEATE WHICH COMPONENTS SHARE INTERNAL DEPENDENCIES.

The ability to create a composable system hinges primarily on the ability to create closure for the sub-components: that is, to be able to enumerate all of their cross-dependencies and be sure that there are no dependencies or potential access points that violate the scope of the controlled application and platform.

7.20.3 Vulnerable References

Be especially careful with any form of reference to a resource, such as file system links, resource "handles," scripted references to resources by name, and aliases. Resource handles can be especially problematic, because they can often be serialized or stored independently of the resource that they reference. First of all, make a clear distinction whether access to the handle implies access to the object that it references. That is, does possession of the handle infer permission to access? Second, a handle is a kind of resource in its own right that needs to be protected, and it should be treated as such. For example, consider a system in which access to a handle requires different access rights than access to the actual resource (that is normally the case). If a resource is specified in a script by referencing the path of the handle, changing the *handle* might allow someone to substitute a different resource, thereby hijacking the path to the resource. Of course, changing the script would have the same effect, but perhaps would be easier to detect.

> Changing a reference or handle to a resource might allow someone to substitute a different resource, thereby hijacking the resource.

PRINCIPLE: TIGHTLY CONTROL ACCESS TO RESOURCE REFERENCES.

Note that any form of reference to a resource, including a resource path embedded in a script, represents the same form of potential vulnerability: an indirect reference that can be attacked in lieu of the actual resource. Thus, the risk described here applies to any form of indirection artifacts such as handles, "soft links" or "shortcuts" that are provided in some operating systems. If the artifact containing the indirect reference (for example, a script, link, or handle) is modified by an attacker, and if that artifact will later be executed by a more privileged user, the attacker has succeeded in substituting a different resource as a result of modifying the indirect reference to the resource.

In order to safeguard against resource hijacking as a result of malicious modification of a resource reference, make sure that all trusted references to resources of any kind have the same or more stringent access rights compared to the configuration settings of the resources that are referenced.

> Any form of reference to a resource, including a resource path embedded in a script, represents a potential vulnerability.

There are other means of attacking resource references, including resolution path attacks. This is discussed further under the principle "Canonicalize All Security-Sensitive Names."

Section 7.18, "Controlling Communication Pathways," discussed the scoping mechanisms provided by the Java platform. Operating systems also provide scoping mechanisms such as processes and name resolution paths. Utilize the available scoping mechanisms to your best advantage to limit visibility and communication between resources to those that need it.

> All trusted references to resources of any kind should have the same or more stringent access rights compared to the configuration settings of the resources that are referenced.

PRINCIPLE: TIGHTLY SCOPE ALL RESOURCES.

After a resource reference is obtained, either by resolving it or by explicitly specifying its address, a secure connection to the resource must be established and maintained.

7.20.4 Resource Connections

In general, a secure connection is achieved using a stateful authenticated encrypted connection. However, if the connection exists within a trusted environment, connection-level security may not be needed. For example, there is no need to maintain an authenticated session between two C functions that call each other because at runtime they will exist within the same process, and the process is (in most circumstances) considered to be a trusted environment. As another example, if a closed network is fully trusted, there may be no need to use authenticated connections between servers within that network, although in general this is recommended.

However, the flaw in this thinking is often that if the network is secure, all the resources on it are secure. If all systems on the network are very tightly controlled, this might be true; however, more often than not there are at least a few less carefully watched systems, and these can serve as attack launching points if they are compromised. For this reason, it is good practice to secure each and every connection in any environment in which less than 100% of all resources are fully protected.

PRINCIPLE: SECURELY CONNECT TO ALL RESOURCES.

If possible, configure resources such that they *require* secure connections. (Some kinds of resources, for example, message queues and HTTP servers, allow un-authenticated connections.)

Secure connections should be maintained, if possible, for communication with:

- Lookup services.
- Business logic (transactional) resources.
- Data resources.
- Configuration resources.

- Any service that communicates sensitive data or data that could be used as a first point of guessing or attack on sensitive data.

A common rule of thumb in network security is to disallow connections *from* an untrusted environment *into* a protected environment, and instead always initiate a connection in the other direction. The rationale is that by eliminating untrusted connection requests, you effectively filter out all those who are motivated to connect to you, which probably includes many parties with ill intentions. Instead, you initiate all connections to those who have a need to communicate with you.

PRINCIPLE: PREFER TO INITIATE CONNECTIONS FROM A POINT OF TRUST.

You might think that if you used this approach you would be precluding traffic from the public, because Web browser requests from the public arrive at random and you would not be able to initiate the connections: The Web browser must initiate the connection to your server. However, this is not actually true. The key is the *level of protocol at which we are talking.* For example, it is possible to use a proxy to transport an inbound request on an outbound connection. In that scenario, which is commonly used in DMZs for communication with backend resources, an HTTP proxy receives inbound TCP connection requests. The proxy maintains a pool of connections between itself and the backend servers. Those connections are initiated from the backend servers. Each of those connections sits in a pool, waiting for a response. When the proxy needs a backend connection, it takes one from the pool and sends the data to the backend as a response. In effect, a request is sent as a response. This design pattern is known as the "blocked registrant." The blocked registrant pattern is presented in detail in Section 15.1.1 after the "Requester Responder" pattern has been discussed.

In the blocked registrant pattern, the application level request still flows logically from requester to server, but at a communication protocol level (for example, both TCP and HTTP in this case) the request data is sent as a response. Thus, direction is a matter of perception, and depends on the protocol level we are focusing on.

The increased security in this scenario derives from the fact that DMZ routers can be configured to disallow inbound connection requests to backend servers. That prevents attacks that are based on a compromised DMZ server (bastion host) because those attacks commonly use a compromised host as a launch point for attacks against the internal network and need to make inbound connections in order to succeed. Thus, the protection actually derives from knowing in advance what connections are needed and preventing all others.

Inbound requests are not always the source of problems, however. In fact, *outbound* requests are as worrisome. This is counter-intuitive because the presumption is that threats come from the outside. A trojan horse usually does its work by sending data out from the network that it has compromised to a remote source that is waiting for the data. This is increasingly the main problem with threats that exist for desktop computers.

The main defense against rogue outbound requests is to require credentials for outbound connections at the firewall, as well as pre-configuring to the extent possible the set of known outbound addresses and ports that are allowed.[55] It is, therefore, important to design an application so that it accommodates proxy authentication for outbound requests.

Outbound requests can be used to impersonate you.

Outbound requests can also be used to impersonate you. This risk of callbacks was discussed in Section 7.17.3. For example, suppose you are notified that a client requires a service, and you act on that by innocently making your own outbound callback connection to the client. It may later turn out that the original notification of the service request was fraudulent. A callback request can be a mechanism to get your system to do someone's dirty work, thereby removing traceability to them and making you look like the culprit.

◆ See separate discussion on this under the principle "A Trusted Context Should Always Include the Code Context" in Section 7.17.3.

This problem can occur only if your callback service blindly makes a callback without verifying and approving the callback destination. A callback should, therefore, be controlled by security policy, based on its destination.

Do not agree to make callbacks unless you really know what you are calling.♦

55 Preventing untrusted applications from being installed in the first place is the best defense.

PRINCIPLE: DO NOT MAKE BLIND CALLBACKS.

Prefer stateful (connection-oriented) protocols rather than stateless protocols. Stateful protocols are harder to penetrate successfully because an intruder must feign a legitimate state.

PRINCIPLE: PREFER STATEFUL PROTOCOLS.

On the other hand, a stateful protocol introduces the possibility of a design error, such that the application trusts a request based on the existence of an apparently legitimate stateful value. For example, sending an RPC context object might be considered to be evidence that the communication comes from a legitimate source, because presumably the source would have had to legitimately obtain the context object. However, it is well known that an RPC context object is not secure and can be forged. (This is an example of "juxtaposition with something legitimate." See the fraud technique of "Instilling Undeserved Trust" in Section 5.2.5.) Thus, while statefulness can make it harder to penetrate a protocol, this is true only if the application is designed properly and does not mistakenly assign trust to unauthenticated context values.

7.20.5 Resource Resolution and Configuration

Resource containers rely on native scoping mechanisms to prevent an unauthorized entity from accessing a resource. This not only includes the authorization container for application-level resources, but also any internal or native authorization container on which security depends. Examples of scoping mechanisms include:

- Resource runtime containers, for both application level resources and native resources.
- Scope boundaries between resources that are enforced by languages or other mechanisms.

As an example of the second bullet, a language syntactic method scoping mechanism separates method resources from classes or packages that are outside scope and are, therefore, not authorized (based on a statically defined policy) to access certain methods. A scoping mechanism that is vulnerable and cannot be protected should not be relied on.

PRINCIPLE: RELY ON SECURE SCOPING MECHANISMS.

◆ See Section 5.1.12, "Spoofing."

Resource spoofing (and hijacking) is a common form of attack in distributed applications. In such attacks, an application is fooled into accessing a rogue resource when it thinks it is accessing the intended resource. Some of the methods of achieving this are discussed in preceding sections.◆

In order to protect against resource spoofing and hijacking, all resource lookup/resolution (and thereby access) should be authenticated to the extent possible.[56]

PRINCIPLE: SECURELY IDENTIFY ALL RESOURCES.

Do not deploy untrusted applications on a common platform or within a common container environment if doing so might allow one application to override or hide classes of other applications in that container or platform. For example, Enterprise Java-Beans (EJBs) that are deployed within the same J2EE "Enterprise Application" can override resources (classes and property files) of other EJB and Web applications that are co-deployed within the same Enterprise Application. Similarly, on many EJB and Web platforms, it is possible to override the classes that are used by other applications by simply deploying replacement classes in the right place, so that they are within the Java "class path" of the Java runtime used by the application server's process. A common attack tactic is to place a substitute version of a resource ahead of the real resource in an unprotected search path.

Specify absolute paths for resource locations.

Always bind resources explicitly by fully specifying their full namespace path, unless you are sure that any name resolution path used by the name resolution or resource lookup mechanism is secure. For example, do not rely on the process' "path" environment variable (or any environment variable, for that matter) unless you are sure that you have full control of it.

56 See [69] for a proposal for securing the way that Java resolves (links to) classes at runtime.

This applies to hardware resources as well. Bind every network adapter (IP address) explicitly, rather than merely specifying a TCP or UDP port. Network adapters that are not bound explicitly are vulnerable because the application that most precisely specifies the adapter wins, so another application could hijack the adapter that your server application is using. If that application has sufficient privilege, it can receive traffic that previously had been going to you on your port. It is also a good idea to make adapter selection (as well as port selection) configurable by an administrator so that the administrator can explicitly separate the resources used by different applications.

Be careful about the trust that you put in resource name resolution processes. In particular, you should mistrust any unauthenticated name resolution services and any resource addresses or references that were resolved using an unauthenticated service. The Domain Name Service (DNS) used by most IP applications is a notorious example. Local domain names are resolved by a local DNS server, and this also applies to remote hosts that have their own domain and DNS server. For example, suppose you need to resolve abc.somewhere.com. The domain "somewhere.com" will likely be resolved by an ISP DNS server, but in all likelihood the address of abc.somewhere.com will be resolved by the DNS server that serves the somewhere.com network: It is likely to be a "split DNS" server that sits on the perimeter of somewhere.com's network, serving remote name resolution requests. Thus, if the somewhere.com DNS server is compromised (DNS servers are compromised a lot), it is a simple matter to compromise all the name resolution requests for hosts within the somewhere.com domain and send those clients elsewhere without any indication to them.

Resources that are resolved by name are vulnerable to a variety of tricks based on the complexity of parsing and recognizing valid names for those resources. This applies not only to server resource names, but also includes the names of anything that needs to be "looked up" by an application and that needs to be trusted, including authentication context attributes (for example, user name), assertion names and values, resource names or paths, and so on.

> Include name resolution or lookup services in the threat analysis.

As a particularly menacing example, some embedded attack programs rely on the ability to hide based on differences in how names are parsed by different low-level system components: e.g., low-level "raw" system APIs might ignore the presence of null characters in a name, whereas higher-level APIs might interpret a null character to signify the end of a name. This difference can be used to allow the full name of a trojan horse program to go undetected by security scans that utilize the higher-level APIs. Embedded attack programs that are able to hide from operating system scans are called "root kits." To protect against this kind of weakness in your application design, low-level APIs or layers should be directly executable only by trusted components.♦

◆ See the principle "A Trusted Context Should Always Include the Code Context" in Section 7.17.3.

In general, always "canonicalize" names that are input by users and that must be resolved, translated into a resource handle, or used to identify something.[57] The term "canonicalize" means to convert the name into a standard and unambiguous form. For example, in a computer system that uses file names that are not case-sensitive, you might construct all file names in upper case in order to make it possible to unambiguously compare file names. Whatever rules you define for the canonicalized form, it should result in names that uniquely identify whatever resource they refer to. Canonicalization prevents many kinds of script injection attacks.

PRINCIPLE: CANONICALIZE ALL SECURITY-SENSITIVE NAMES.

Canonicalization effects are listed in Table 7.7.

In general, if there are any equivalences, always canonicalize them, so that the resulting name deterministically uses one and only one of the equivalences. For example, if both "file:" URLs and file paths are allowed, define a canonicalization rule so that only one of these two equivalent forms is used in the canonicalized name.

57 See also [70], p. 211 ff.

Table 7.7 Canonicalization Effects

Character set conversion (for example, converting Unicode characters to 7-bit ASCII).
Character conversion (for example, converting forward slash to back-slash).
Encoded character (escaped) translation.
Truncation.
Character deletion (for example, trailing slash).
Implicit value insertion (for example, inserting an drive letter).
Elaboration (for example, expansion of ./ and regular expressions).
Searching or name resolution (for example, searching a path).
Upper/lowercase conversion.
Safe removal or conversion of delimiters such as quotes.
Character range filtering (for example, not allowing foreign language characters in a URL).

Always canonicalize a name *before* using it—especially before making an authorization decision based on the name. The canonicalization logic should be consolidated so that it is not duplicated, in order to prevent the possibility that it is performed differently in different places in the code. A widely reported bug in Microsoft's IIS product was the result of different and inconsistent implementations of resource path canonicalization.[58]

Make sure that the canonicalization process does not rely on anything that could be changed by an attacker. This applies especially to implicit value insertion or any kind of name resolution. For example, if the operating system is Windows, can an attacker re-map a drive letter? If the platform is Unix, can NFS be attacked and used to re-mount a file system somewhere else? If so, you cannot fully trust a file path, even if it is fully and unambiguously specified, and these possibilities need to be included in the threat analysis.

It may sometimes be necessary to preserve the original name that was input, for example, for the purpose of re-displaying it to the user for confirmation. Still, always use the canonicalized version for all decisions and identifications.

58 See [71] page 75.

It may sometimes be necessary to preserve the original name that was input, for example, for the purpose of re-displaying it to the user for confirmation.

Point-to-point dedicated connections that are statically configured are generally more secure than dynamic connections. This is true at all layers of a system, from the hardware level to the application level. Examples of connections that could be considered to be "point-to-point" include: (1) a private digital line between two hardware endpoints; (2) a logical connection between two server TCP ports, enforced by a router such that only the intended servers can communicate on the intended ports; (3) an encrypted channel between two authenticated endpoints; for example, using SSL. The last example is different from the others because SSL dynamically establishes the connection, whereas the other kinds are most commonly statically configured by an administrator.

PRINCIPLE: PREFER STATIC RESOURCE PATHS.

Dynamic connection establishment has such enormous benefits that it should not be discarded out of hand unless the security concerns are severe and it is the best solution. Dynamic configuration is what distinguishes today's interoperable networks and applications from those of the early days of computing, in which every link between every application had to be anticipated ahead of time and planned out by administrators and application designers. Nowadays, connectivity is largely automated at many levels. There is a security cost to this, however.

It is common practice to use routers within DMZs and back-end networks to restrict the set of connections that is possible; in effect, locking down the systems to a preconceived set of connections. This removes some of the unneeded dynamism of the network, and this is appropriate for a secure environment that has a predetermined purpose and for which the exact configuration can be planned.

Applications should enable an administrator to explicitly specify all resource bindings such as adapters and client-side port numbers, rather than allowing the system to make the choice.

From the perspective of greatest security, one should remove as much dynamism as possible, and anticipate and control all connections. For example, when designing a DMZ or backend network, one should decide what traffic will be occurring on which ports and which network adapters, and configure routers and switches to allow only that. At an application level, one should make provisions so that an administrator can explicitly specify resource bindings that are normally chosen by the system, such as network adapters and client-side TCP port numbers when there is a small fixed number of clients, as well as the "working directory" of the application.

A form of trojan horse attack is to attack the objects that are used to build, configure, deploy, or initialize a system, thereby resulting in a system with an embedded weakness constructed by the attacker and unknowingly deployed by the administrator. (See the attack pattern "Trusted Resource Attack" in Section 5.1.25.) To prevent this, the systems used for development, configuration, and deployment should be secured in order to ensure that they are not compromised and a trojan horse inserted.

PRINCIPLE: SECURE NON-RUN-TIME RESOURCES.

Property files or initialization files that are used during deployment or system initialization are extreme points of vulnerability because they are easily interpreted by an attacker and a small change can introduce a severe security vulnerability that might go unnoticed for days or weeks–long enough to allow an attack to occur and for all trace of it to be removed. Configuration data that affects security, such as user-chosen security level options, should also be stored in a secure manner.

Unfortunately, securing all points of configuration is not a small task. For example, Windows provides a plethora of points at which a reference to a malicious program can be inserted so that it launches automatically. When a Windows program or the operating system starts, the Windows Registry is checked in a myriad of places to see if there are programs that should be started. Thus, write access to the registry represents an immense risk because it enables a malicious application to insert commands into these registry locations—and when the inserted programs are launched, they will execute with the user's or operating system's identity.[59]

The method of the attack pattern "Forced Restart, Forced Re-Install" discussed in Section 5.1.10 is to modify configuration data, then cause a crash, and wait for the system to be restarted and re-initialized with the compromised configuration.

PRINCIPLE: SECURE CONFIGURATION DATA.

◆ See also the principle "Deploy Securely" in Section 10.1, "Designing for Secure Deployment."

Some systems approach this by placing the configuration on a non-writable medium.[60] Of course, never hard-code credentials into code. Code can be disassembled.◆

There are two different schools of thought with regard to securing highly sensitive configuration data and credentials. One is to centralize the data, such as in a centralized property file or credential store. The advantage of this approach is that the centralized store can be hardened and watched very closely. The disadvantage is that it represents a high-value and, therefore, high-risk asset. The alternative approach is to de-centralize this kind of information. The advantage of decentralization is that there is no single point of attack for obtaining all a system's credentials, but the disadvantage is that it is hard to administer many decentralized pieces of sensitive data—and that increases risk.

There are two different schools of thought with regard to the centralized storage of highly sensitive configuration data and credentials.

Administrative components that are used to monitor, configure, or repair the system should be protected as securely as the most sensitive resources that they are used to administer. These components should generally exist in the same subnet as the administered components.

PRINCIPLE: SECURE ADMINISTRATIVE RESOURCES.

59 See the Web site `http://www.silentrunners.org/sr_launchpoints.html` for a list of startup points.

60 For example, the LOCKSS system uses non-writable media for both the operating system and its configuration. See `http://www.lockss.org/`.

7.20.6 Native Resources

Never assume that resources that exist within a protected network are secure and therefore do not need to require authentication and confidentiality. One of the primary ways of attacking a secured application is to attack the resources on which it depends.[61] For example, an application that accesses a database can be compromised by compromising the database. This is an example of what we have referred to as a "Trusted Resource Attack."♦

♦ See Section 5.1.25.

PRINCIPLE: SECURE NATIVE RESOURCES.

This applies especially to services that are used to look up resources, because the compromise of a lookup service exposes the user to a potential for being "spoofed" into using a different resource–one installed by an attacker.

Resources that are installed by an application should be secured by using a native mechanism to protect the resource so that only the intended application can access it. For example, if an application installs a small database or properties file, it is preferable to take advantage of native access controls, such as database permissions and file permissions, to ensure that only the application can access the data. This might not be critical if the data is merely user profile data, but it can be very critical when sensitive data is involved. This is the issue of "non-interference" between resources that come from different sources.

An application should always wrap native resource lookup calls.[62] (Refer to the definition of a *native resource* in Section 7.2 "Resource Types and Layers.") This enables the application to interpose a layer between itself and native resource accesses that enforce certain practices, including argument canonicalization, argument validation, and error handling. See the pattern "Closure of Reusable Components" in Section 7.20.2, "Reusable Components": A native resource can be treated as a reusable component.

61 See [72], p. 152.
62 See also the discussion of wrappers in [73] and secure composition in [74].

One should always ensure that all requested native resource names and call arguments are valid before executing the call, to the extent possible, and anticipate all native error conditions. Wrapping native resource access allows such checks and handling to be centralized and thereby provides a way to ensure that it is consistent and that appropriate handling is not overlooked somewhere.

PRINCIPLE: ENCAPSULATE NATIVE RESOURCE ACCESS.

7.20.7 Caches and Artifacts

Applications often cache data that is obtained from resources in order to improve efficiency. If the data is sensitive in any way, the cache represents a possible point of attack.[63]

When designing a cache, carefully consider its points of vulnerability. Can the cache be read from another process or a different context? Will its contents be exposed if the application crashes? Note that a common attack strategy is to force a crash, and then read the artifacts that result from the crash; will cached data be present in such artifacts? Another attack technique is to force the application into a debug mode, and then read the process' data space, which contains the cached values. Note that finding credentials in a core dump is easy, as it is possible to filter based on the unique and random properties that credentials tend to have.

PRINCIPLE: SECURE ALL CACHES.

Never cache permanent user credentials.

It is preferable to send a presented credential to a secure authentication service rather than comparing values in memory. Credential values should be cached only if there is high confidence that the cache is secure, and in all cases only *session* credentials should be cached—*never cache permanent user credentials.*

Persistent caches are especially vulnerable and should be protected as resources in their own right. Persistent caches can be violated by reading their contents or by inserting false values

63 See [75], p. 60.

into them to cause the application to do things that it would not normally do, such as access a different location, thereby achieving a spoof of a resource.

> "Should you, or any member of your I.M. force, be caught, or killed, the secretary will disavow all knowledge of your actions. This tape will self-destruct in five seconds."
> —from *Mission Impossible*

It is good practice to physically erase any sensitive data (and in particular, credentials), immediately after it is used or as soon as it is no longer needed, in order to preclude any possibility of covert use of the data before it is eventually erased or reused by the system.[64] For example, if a layer of the application verifies a session credential before proceeding with normal request processing, that layer should immediately write over the credential value used for that verification.

PRINCIPLE: ERASE SENSITIVE DATA IMMEDIATELY AFTER USE.

Sensitive data that is deleted should be physically erased from any persistent storage system that contains it. Thus, for highly sensitive data, you should use mutable (erasable) structures or objects and explicitly clear them after use before disposing of them.[65]

PRINCIPLE: DISPOSE OF SENSITIVE DATA SECURELY.

When persistent storage is involved, this is sometimes hard to achieve; writing over the data is not always guaranteed to actually purge it from storage: (1) there might be a time lag for data to be written through; (2) overwrites might be implemented by replacement, merely returning replaced segments to unallocated storage; or (3) the storage may be a technology (such as so-called "WORM" storage) that does not support actual erasure. In many applications it is sufficient to provide for physical security of mass storage during operation, to perform a low-level format of any drive that is removed for repurposing, and

---

64 See [76] Section 2.1.

65 See "Clear Sensitive Information" in [77].

to physically and permanently destroy the contents of any device that is to be discarded.

The same guidelines apply to temporary files. There have been many attacks based on reading files in the /tmp directory on Unix. If you create temporary files that contain sensitive data, make sure that they are secure and remain appropriately secured even if the system crashes.

File permissions for the process current directory should be severely restricted.

In general, it is a good practice to make sure that artifacts, such as core dumps, error logs, and so on, occur at a highly secure location so that an attacker would not be able to access them. For example, file permissions for the process current directory should be such that only the application process user and restricted application support staff can read any files in that directory, and only the application process can write to it.

Principle: Provide Secure Locations for Failure Artifacts.

7.20.8 Build-Time Closure

Closure and compartmentalization are not merely runtime considerations. Any tool that touches a secure resource, either directly or transitively, is part of the trusted computing base and must also be examined for the ways that it can possibility affect that resource and for the need to secure the tool. For example, a compiler is a strong candidate for attack, because it is used to generate the runtime code for applications, and it therefore could be used to insert a trojan horse in every single application built by an organization—and tools such as compilers are almost never suspect![66] Other tools present the same opportunity and are even easier to hack; for example, the popular Java "ant" tool is written in Java and is used to invoke the Java compiler, so it is almost a simple matter to modify ant so that it inserts a back door into every application for which it calls the Java compiler.

Any tool that touches a secure resource, either directly or transitively, is part of the trusted computing base.

66 See [78] Section 3.2.4.

It is generally not feasible to fully protect and control a business application development environment, but it is feasible to control a build environment. For example, source code that is created in a development environment and is checked into a source code repository can be extracted into a secure build environment and used to build a release for either testing or deployment. The tools and file systems in the secure build environment should be tightly controlled, with their origin verified, and routinely verified against MACs (secure hashcodes) that are stored separately to ensure that they have not been replaced. In addition, build scripts should employ explicit paths for tools instead of relying on a path resolution mechanism, such as a PATH variable that includes a series of directory locations, to ensure that the intended tool is used for each step and not a replacement.

7.21 Home-Grown Authorization

In the absence of a suitable authorization framework, application builders have to write custom code to implement the authorization rules that are required by the application. The choices are generally one of the following or some variation of these:

1. Build a complete authorization mechanism that acts as either a reference monitor or as a gateway.
2. Hard-code authorization rules explicitly within each method.
3. Hard-code calls to an authorization framework within each resource method.
4. Use a code generation tool to insert authorization calls.

Approach (1) is generally inadvisable because of its complexity.♦ If approach (1) is followed, it should be designed by the team's best designers and thoroughly vetted using threat modeling or some other verification technique. Approach (2) sounds inadvisable because "hard-coding" smacks of poorly-designed code, but actually it is reasonable if the authorization rules are well-demarcated and adhere to a well-defined design pattern (see the pattern "Authorization as a Precondition,," later

♦ See the principle "Minimize the Number, Size, and Complexity of High-Risk Components" in Section 4.1.1.

in the section). Approach (3) is also reasonable and has the advantage that authorization rules can be factored into a capability model or a dynamic condition set model as discussed previously (see Section 7.10). Approach (4) is also reasonable, but requires that the team's programmers obtain and learn a code generation tool. Approach (4) has the disadvantage that the authorization rules would then have to be defined externally in files that are input to the code generation tool. This might be acceptable if the rule definition file is kept with the code—allowing easy access and maintenance by programmers. The rules would be precisely defined and clearly identify which method each rule applies to. Thus, the principle "Define Authorization Models Alongside the Resources that They Protect" would be satisfied.

Regardless which approach is used (or even if another approach is used), it is important that authorization is performed before the resource method performs any functions. Thus, authorization checks should be inserted at the beginning of each resource method instead of scattering them around in a disorganized fashion, which would defeat auditability.♦ The rules then become a pre-condition for execution of the rest of the resource method, and the resource designer can be sure that the authorization rules cannot be bypassed.

♦ See the principle "Authorization Rules Should Be Auditable" in Section 7.4, "Auditability of Policy Coverage."

PRINCIPLE: AUTHORIZATION SHOULD BE A PRECONDITION FOR EXECUTION OF ANY AND ALL BUSINESS LOGIC WITHIN A FUNCTION OR METHOD.

When writing authorization preconditions, it is important to ensure that the act of executing an authorization rule does not itself introduce a vulnerability. An unexpected failure can occur in four ways:

1. A type range failure (such as a buffer overflow) can cause the resource to fail.
2. An input is out of range of the values that are legitimate with respect to business rules.

3. An access to a resource used by an authorization rule fails.
4. A logic error in an authorization rule.

The fourth kind of failure represents a program "bug" and cannot be anticipated; therefore, it should be trapped at an outer later that traps all unexpected internal non-lifecycle failures (this is discussed further in Section 18.2.1. If any of the other kinds of failure are not protected against, unexpected behavior might occur.

A type range failure can be protected against by ensuring that the mechanism that invokes a resource method is type-safe.♦ An input range failure can be protected against by validating the input with respect to business rules.♦ A resource access failure can be protected against by trapping all lifecycle failures that might occur during the resource call. This issue is discussed in detail later;♦ but for now, just consider that it is desirable to trap any kind of resource failure that might occur when accessing an external resource, even if the access occurs within an authorization check and not in the actual business logic.

The result is a design pattern that safely performs authorization checks at the beginning of each method call. Those checks can be encapsulated in a security component call, or they can be implemented inline, or even by a precondition if the programming language supports the definition of preconditions. Regardless, they must occur before business logic is performed and be completely safe.

◆ The importance of type-safe inputs was discussed under the principle "Employ a Strongly Typed Language and Design Approach for the Interface" in Section 7.13.1.

◆ Input validation was discussed under the principle "Validate Anything Received from Untrusted Sources" in Section 7.17.4.

◆ See the principle "Use Checked Expressions for All Lifecycle Errors" in Section 18.2.1.

DESIGN PATTERN: AUTHORIZATION AS A PRECONDITION

Context

A resource method must be protected against unauthorized access, but there are no existing authorization mechanisms available that meet all the requirements.

Problem

The application must develop its own authorization mechanisms in order to meet the requirements.

Forces

Authorization rules are often more complex than what is supported by ready-made frameworks. Platform-based frameworks often cannot be accessed in a manner that allows programmers to easily maintain an authorization model. Platform-based frameworks often do not allow the consolidation of policy management in a manner that is convenient for the operators of the application, especially when all applications are considered.

Solution

This pattern provides an approach for embedding authorization checks within an application-defined resource method. In this pattern, each resource method is broken down into four logical processes that occur in sequence. These are depicted in Figure 7.22.

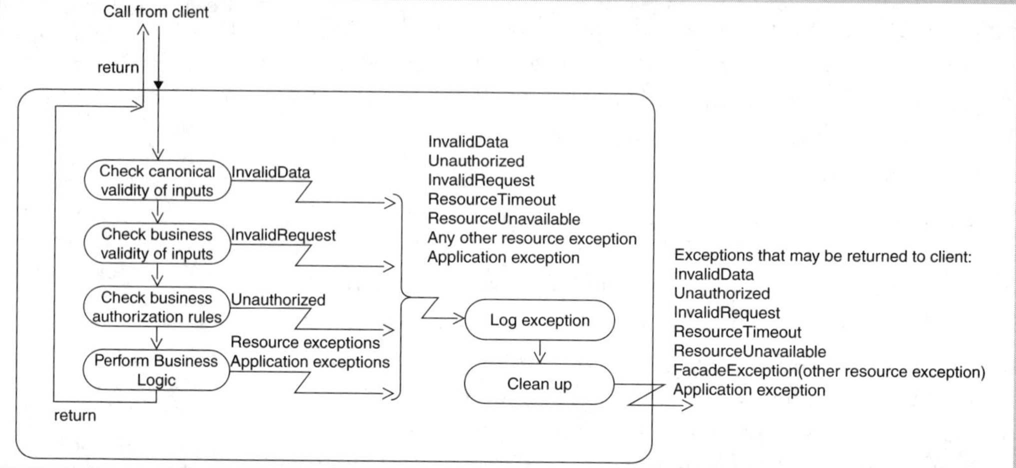

Figure 7.22 Activities.

As can be seen, entry to the method begins with verification that the inputs (any arguments or context values used by the method or its authorization rules) conform to the value constraints defined by their type. This would include, for example, a *safe* verification of array sizes, value ranges, and so on. Any deviations would produce an exception condition, represented in the diagram as "InvalidData." Note that if a type-safe language is used for the resource interface, this step is performed automatically by the language.

After inputs are verified to meet type-based value constraints, they need to be checked for business validity. Business validity checking consists of checking data range constraints to make sure that all input values "make sense" in terms of their meaning to the business. For example, checking that a dollar amount is not negative might be such a rule: it might be allowed by the data type used to represent dollar values but disallowed by the meaning of the data field.

Checks for business validity do not include checks that values are being used correctly in combination: that should be discovered as part of the business processing. For example, checking that a dollar range is within a limit allowed for a certain user should not be considered to be a business validity check.

Any deviations from business validity rules should result in an exception, represented previously as a "InvalidRequest" exception.

After business input validity rules have been satisfied, authorization rules for accessing the resource should be checked. The authorization rules should be able to assume that all their inputs are valid and well-formed. If any authorization rules are not satisfied, an exception should be raised that indicates unambiguously that authorization failed and why. *The exception should not reveal sensitive information other than what was provided by the caller.*

If authorization succeeds, the core business logic is invoked. This is normally through a delegation pattern, but it can be encoded inline.

Any native-level exceptions that occur are trapped and translated into (wrapped by) a higher-level exception that indicates one of the conditions discussed previously: (1) invalid data, (2) invalid request (i.e., the data does not make sense), (3) the request is not authorized, or (4) an error while performing business logic. When any of these conditions occur, the error event is logged, cleanup is performed, and the method returns via an exception path. The exception type should be defined in the resource definition layer (see Section 7.2.2, "The Resource Definition Layer").

The business authorization rule check can be implemented using either hard-coded authorization rules or hard-coded calls to an authorization framework that contains the authorization rules.

Consequences
The home-grown authorization mechanism adheres to a standard pattern that facilitates the design of protected resources and the maintenance of authorization rules.

The design pattern "Transaction Facade" in Section 13.9, "Layer Access Rules for Transactions," applies this pattern in a transactional context, for defining a robust layout for transactional resource methods that incorporates input validation, authorization, and failure handling.

7.21.1 Caching of Authorization Data

Authorization mechanisms can have a lot of latency if they must access policy rules stored in a remote system. In order to improve performance in that situation, caches are often used. Designing such a cache is complex and is generally not advisable for a system that is developed in-house. However, with an experienced team it can be done correctly and greatly improve performance.

An important consideration when designing such caches is the extent to which updates need to be synchronous. For example, if policy is changed, do the access rights of *in-progress* user sessions need to be re-evaluated? Similarly, if a user's access rights are removed, should that user be immediately logged off of all systems he no longer has the required access rights for? If data that was used in an authorization decision is changed, should all sessions that were granted access based on that data be re-evaluated for access? Often, the answer to questions like these is no, and that has a big impact on the design of the caching mechanism. It also has an effect on the application architecture because it might determine the extent to which changes in application data must trigger other events that propagate to the security system.

7.22 Summary

This chapter addressed the very complex and multi-faceted problem of the authorization and containment of sensitive resources. Models for containment and authorization were presented. The importance of auditability of authorization rules was discussed, followed by a discussion of multi-level security. A model for separating an organization's security policy into separate strata based on its granularity and relationships to core processes and workflow was presented. Permissions, access control lists, and roles were discussed, along with permission parameterization and role parameterization. A model was then presented for casting access control rules in terms of dynamic conditions. The issue of secure defaults was explained. A case was made for keeping a resource's authorization scheme alongside the resource's definition. Issues related to the design of resource interfaces were examined, including type safety, simplicity, atomicity, and error handling. Logging was discussed, in the context of security and the need for separation of duties with regard to log administration and application administration and operation. Authorization context was discussed, and issues and models related to privilege elevation were discussed. Communication between resources was discussed from a domain perspective. Composability and configuration were discussed.

The next chapter presents the concepts of compartmentalization and classification and their relationship to data and to users.

7.23 Exercises

1. Is it advisable to hard-code authorization rules into a resource method? Explain.
2. Explain at least one technique for obtaining sensitive data that is cached in memory by an application.
3. Explain what a “root kit” is.
4. Explain why server-to-server connections on a LAN should generally use authentication.
5. Explain the difference between “composable” and “compositional.”
6. Select one: Layer dependencies should flow (a) toward the business model, (b) away from the business model, (c) only within a layer.
7. What are two predominate concepts that distinguish component-oriented design from object-oriented design?
8. Explain two approaches for encapsulating a privileged action.
9. Input validation should include verification that values are within allowed ranges, that they conform to required formats, and what else?
10. List and explain two important elements of execution context.
11. An authorization decision involves assessing the balance in the user’s account: If the amount is above a predetermined level, the user will be authorized for access to special services. Should the authorization decision be modeled using roles? Explain.
12. What are the advantages of ensuring that an application’s authorization rules are auditable?
13. What are the three properties that are required of a reference monitor?
14. Which types of access control techniques are generally more vulnerable: discretionary or non-discretionary, and why?

15. What properties must a capability have?
16. A programmer is provided with a utility API for accessing a file system's low-level API. Which API is "native," and why?
17. A public method of a protected resource returns a collection. What properties should the collection have?
18. Compare and contrast object-level scoping with class-level scoping.

Answers and hints for these exercises can be found at `http://www.assuredbydesign.com/haa/`.

CHAPTER 8

COMPARTMENTALIZATION AND CLASSIFICATION

In the information security profession, a "compartment" is meant to represent a domain of information that a small group of people need access to in order to perform a specific function. People have access to compartments based on a need-to-know basis as well as sufficient clearance level. A compartment limits the scope of exposure if there is a security break. The idea is to spread risk across multiple compartments so that the risk or cost to the organization if one compartment is compromised is no greater than if any other compartment is compromised, and there are enough compartments so that that risk is dispersed to an acceptable level. Another motivation behind the "need-to-know" strategy is to ensure that people only have access to what they need to have access to—and no more. This helps to minimize the risk of unintended access.◆

◆ See the "Fine-Grained Authorization (Least Privilege) at Each Perimeter" principle in Section 7.5, "Perimeters."

Clearance level represents a kind of "strength of authentication" in the sense that higher clearance levels provide higher assurance that the participant has been securely researched in terms of their trustworthiness.[1]

Many secure operating systems—both commercial and custom-built—provide these kind of compartmentalization features. (Examples include Trusted Solaris, GEMSOS,[2] and PitBull.[3] See also [2] and [3] for research systems.) However, mainstream commercial application platforms (operating systems, application servers, and so on) do not implement a full compartment concept because computer systems vendors claim that such an approach is too cumbersome for most users. According to Paul Karger and Roger Schell, who worked on the original Multics system:

> *"...most of the vendors would claim that the marketplace is not prepared to pay for a high assurance of security. And customers have said they have never been offered mainstream commercial products that give them such a choice, so they are left with several ineffective solutions collected under marketing titles like 'defense in depth'."* [4]

Mainstream commercial platforms, such as Unix and Windows, nevertheless do provide simplified compartments of a sort. In commercial computing, it is useful to think of standard information boundaries, such as directories, realms, and databases, as candidates for compartments. In this view, a compartment is conceptually a realm of trust such that the items within a compartment share a common concept of who they trust outside of the compartment, in terms of which users and which other realms are allowed to interact with the compartment.

1 See [1] for a theoretical model.

2 GEMSOS is now supported and marketed by aeSec Corporation; see `http://aesec.com/`.

3 See `http://www.argus-systems.com`.

Compartmentalization should be thought of in the design of any important workflow process, application, and information asset. For example, you do not want a single administrator to have access to all the organization's data and processes, nor do you want to make it possible for a single hacker to stop a critical application's entire function.

A central question is whether users have direct access to data, such as for ad-hoc queries that go directly to the database and bypass applications. If they do not, the compartmentalization task should be focused on the processes that use the data and designing the various user groups that have a need to access to those processes. Care should be taken that actual users do not belong to more than one group except where necessary.

A central question is whether users have direct access to data.

If, on the other hand, the users do have direct access to data, the compartmentalization task should be focused on *data classification*; that is, rating the various data elements in terms of their sensitivity and designating different user groups that need access to them (based on their "need to know"). If both direct- and application-based access to data are supported, usually the data is separated in terms of "warehouse" and "production" tiers, and a different approach can be used for each of these tiers.

The concept of compartmentalizing data and resources can be expressed by the following principle.

PRINCIPLE: SEGMENT DATA AND RESOURCES ACCORDING TO RISK OR SENSITIVITY.

This principle is pregnant with implications and issues, such as how to ascertain risk or sensitivity. Such issues are outside the scope of this book, so the discussion here will take a more pragmatic approach by examining related issues and models that typically arise in business application development, such as the need to provide for separation of duties and to reduce risk by reducing the amount of data to which users have access.

The issues of how to determine need-to-know and clearance level are also not addressed here; instead, the discussion will address issues related to user roles as they pertain to authorization and separation of duties.

8.1 Role Separation

A previous section discussed the advantages of decentralization of realms, so that detailed resource-level security administration can be performed by administrative roles in small groups that are closely associated with the resources that they maintain. It is often the case that application roles are defined in terms of global groups defined in user directories. This approach is unwieldy because it places a burden on the central administrator to maintain those groups and their definition, whereas the roles that those groups represent are defined by applications that may operate at a departmental level.

It is better if the group that maintains the application also maintains the definition of the user groups who use the application. For that to occur, the groups are best defined in a context that is scoped below the organization level, so they can be administered by the group that maintains the application. Of course, it is always possible to delegate administration of organization-level groups to a particular department, but it is better practice to allow a department to define its own groups and administer them.

8.1.1 Role Separation

It is sometimes also advantageous to "sub-class" user roles so that, for example, a "Buyer" role can be used as a basis for defining a "Regional Buyer" role and a "National Buyer" role. These sub-classed roles could be defined in a realm scope that is unique to the department but based on an organization-wide role that is defined in a realm scope that is owned by the organization's administrator.

Remember that roles are merely named aggregations of permissions. When defining a role sub-class, it is good practice to define the sub-classed role relationship such that a sub-class of a role automatically and implicitly inherits all the permissions of the parent role. This is because a common operation with roles is a test for the role; for example, "Is user A in role R?" If user A participates in a sub-role of R, the test will return true, and it is likely that any code performing that test will infer permissions or attributes for the role based on the test. Therefore, sub-roles should implement only an additive permission model, not a subtractive model, in order to safely be able to be used in role participation tests.

Sub-roles should only implement an additive permission model, not a subtractive model, in order to safely be able to be used in role participation tests.

Constraints that apply to roles should be inherited as well. Thus, if an administrator sets a policy that prevents a particular role from performing certain functions, that policy should apply to derived roles as well, in order to prevent the policy from being circumvented merely by defining a sub-role. This allows global policies to be defined for roles and prevents those policies from being overridden by realms that do their work in the context of sub-roles. However, it is important to ensure that the constraints cannot be made less restrictive by declaring a sub-role and redefining any variables that are referenced in an inherited constraint. Thus, inheritable constraints should not reference any variables or methods that can be overridden.

DESIGN PATTERNS: EXTENSIBLE ROLE AND DERIVED ROLE

Related Patterns
See the pattern "Parameterized Permissions" in Section 7.8, "Permission Parameterization."

Context
A security realm manages a set of security roles for the resources that the realm contains. New roles need to be defined based on existing role definitions, but with narrower specialization.

Problem
Roles are aggregations of permissions, so a methodology must be decided upon for the way in which permissions are inherited by subclassed roles.

Solution
This pattern provides a way to "subclass" roles—to derive new (private) roles based on globally defined roles. A role consists of a set of permission assignments, referred to in the model here as "permission instances." Because a permission can be defined to have parameters (see the pattern "Parameterized Permissions"), values must be assigned to these arguments (if any) when a role is assigned permissions. The structure is shown in Figure 8.1.

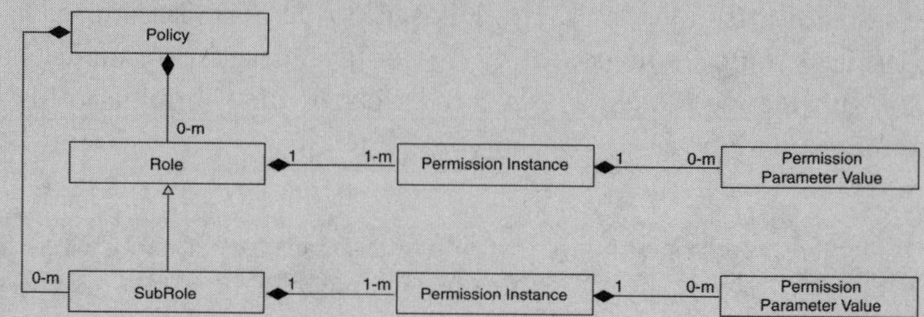

Figure 8.1
Structure.

A role can be subclassed by extending the role definition such that the extended role inherits all the permissions and policy constraints of the parent role. Sub-roles can add additional constraints and permissions, but these apply only to the sub-role, and the constraints of the parent role must not be violated.

This model requires that the sub-role belong to the same policy realm as the parent role. If the parent role belongs to a parent policy realm, the parent realm might impose limitations on the extent to which a derived role in a child realm can add permissions. (See Section 6.2.2, "Hierarchies of Trust.")

A role is part of a realm's policy, but it is possible to define roles ahead of time, by parameterizing them so that they can be instantiated in a realm. A role's parameters are merely the parameters of the role's constituent permissions.

Consequences
Roles can be subclassed in order to define new roles that carry the same, and possibly additional, permissions and constraints. Roles that can be subclassed in this way can be described as "extensible roles." Roles that subclass other roles can be described as "derived roles."

Roles should be narrowly defined so that a single role does not have permission for many different functions, at least not without secure traceability. The CTO of a Fortune 100 financial services company once bragged to me over dinner that if he wanted to, he had the ability to secretly divert a billion dollars from his firm, erase all traces of his actions, and disappear before it was discovered. Clearly, the principles of separation of duties and compartmentalization were not being practiced within his organization. Similarly, in one of the largest cases of identity theft to date [5], a low-level employee of Teledata Inc. had access to the database containing information about customers that it handled and sold information about 30,000 of those customers. In an even larger case [6], an AOL employee sold 93 million of the company's email addresses, as well as telephone numbers, ZIP codes, and the types of credit cards customers use to pay AOL bills. He did this by stealing the user ID of another employee. (This is an example of collusion with an insider. See "Breaking Prior Trust," Section 5.2.6.)

Even seemingly small events can have severe consequences that go far beyond the immediate value of the information that is compromised if the events are newsworthy. For example, an April 2005 Forrester Research report warned that what appears to be a single minor theft from a single corporation might reduce the entire Indian Business Process Outsourcing (BPO) industry's growth by 30 percent. The report was referring to the alleged theft of $350,000 from Citibank customers by three former employees of MphasiS BFL's outsourcing operation Msource in Pune, India. The employees allegedly acquired the passwords to customer accounts and transferred the money to their own accounts opened under fictitious names. [7] This is why it is important for service and administrative roles to not have access to user passwords.

Require very sensitive or potentially damaging operations to be safely bounded (limited in their extent) so that only small changes can be made during a certain period, accompanied by notification. This amounts to treating a role's scope of control as a "compartment" and adjusting the compartment size (role's scope) so that the risk is acceptable.

> Two individuals should be required to each "turn their key" for any sensitive operation.

An alternative way of limiting the damage that a role can inflict is by requiring multiple roles to perform sensitive actions. Create a workflow that requires that two roles be required to complete any sensitive function. This is analogous to having two people who have to each "turn their key" to do something critical. Of course, this works only if the two roles are not performed by the same individual.

PRINCIPLE: COMPARTMENTALIZE ROLES.

The principles of role compartmentalization and independence of auditing specify the need to scope roles according to the resource on which they operate and to keep certain administrative and auditing roles separate from application roles, respectively. The need for separation of roles is broader, however. In general, applications should be designed according to a principle of "separation of duties" (sometimes referred to as "separation of privilege") such that roles do not overlap unnecessarily.

There is a methodology known as "mutual exclusion of roles" [8] that attempts to define criteria for separating roles according to different areas of risk (i.e., compartments) and mandating that role permissions do not overlap. However, while this concept is a useful one, it is probably impossible to establish a "cookbook" guideline for defining roles. The natural workflows of an application will be the major factor in the design of the roles for the application, mainly because business analysts typically define roles, and it is hard to tell business analysts what functions a role that they define should be allowed to perform. However, the system's designers should undertake to ensure that multiple roles do not have unnecessary direct (authorized for their identity) access to resources in multiple "compartments" (for example, tiers and business areas). The use of "privileged context boundaries" (see the principle "Define Privileged Context Boundaries" in Section 7.17.9, "Encapsulation of Privelege) is useful in order to reduce the number of "compartments" that a user needs authorized direct access to.

PRINCIPLE: ENFORCE SEPARATION OF DUTIES.

Particular attention should be applied to roles that perform functions such as the assignment of roles, or that assign permissions to roles. These critical administrative functions should be analyzed as any other, using the principles defined here, and the role-assignment and permission assignment (policy administration) functions should be treated as resources.♦ In general, administrative functions related to system and application configuration should be performed by an administrative role, and operational functions such as log file administration and application operation should be handled by other roles, and segmented so that there is oversight and compartmentalization of each function that must be secure. [9]

♦ See the principle "Treat Administrative Processes as Business Processes" in Section 7.6, "Levels of Processes Within an Organization."

The application administrator who assigns roles or permissions to roles is in a position to assign those roles or permissions to herself. This person, therefore, needs to be trusted with all the application resource assets that they administer.

PRINCIPLE: ROLES THAT GRANT ACCESS RIGHTS MUST HAVE THOSE SAME RIGHTS. [4]

The administration of the traceability mechanisms, such as logs, intrusion detection alerts, signing mechanisms, and the credentials associated with these should require different privileges that are not owned by the roles that perform the functions that are being monitored.

PRINCIPLE: ENSURE THAT TRACEABILITY FUNCTIONS SUCH AS LOGGING AND MONITORING ARE INDEPENDENT OF OTHER APPLICATION OPERATION FUNCTIONS.

This is a very general principle. It is surprisingly difficult to accomplish, mainly because the assumption made by most product vendors is that the system administrator is not only trusted to deploy the product but also is trusted to monitor it. As a result, it often requires a lot of work to create the independence that is desirable—often more work and cost than is merited by the risk. It may be more practical to simply hire a trustworthy administrator. The right decision depends on the level of risk involved.

4 This is sometimes referred to as the principle of "attenuation of privilege". See [10], page 43.

8.1.2 Secure Communication in Multi-Role Operations

If two roles are required to cooperate to complete a sensitive task, as described previously (two "keys to turn"), the event that causes each role to be notified should not rely on the credentials that authenticate the other role. Otherwise, there is, in effect, only one role initiating and authorizing the action: that would be analogous to one of the key turners saying to the other, "You should turn your key—the boss said so." In other words, each "key turner" (each role that must cooperate to complete a sensitive operation) should receive its instructions through independent and secure means.

> Beware when someone tells you to do something.

> ***PRINCIPLE: IF TWO ROLES ARE REQUIRED TO BE INDEPENDENT, THEIR COMMUNICATION CHANNELS SHOULD ALSO BE INDEPENDENT.***

A more mundane example would be that an administrator receives an email from another administrator saying, "We need to both do our thing to authorize Larry." The email originates from the other "key turner," using their email address. How does the administrator know that the sender of the email is the other administrator? Even if the email is signed, that might prove only that the sender was able to log on to the other administrator's account; and if the "key turn" operation uses the same credential, it would be necessary only for an attacker to steal that one credential (the log on password) to send the email and "turn the other administrator's key"—thereby defeating the requirement for two separate roles to perform the operation. See also the discussion of the social engineering attack technique of "Instilling Undeserved Trust" in Section 5.2.5.

8.1.3 Convenience Versus Safety

For sensitive operations, it is a good idea to design the user interface so that the user can do only one thing at a time. Users who are busy may become distracted and make a mistake during a critical operation. Confusing an operator while the operator is performing a requested action is indeed a social engineering technique (see Section 5.2.4, "Reliance on Inadequate Protection").

PRINCIPLE: FOR SENSITIVE OPERATIONS, ENFORCE ONE ACTION AT A TIME.

Highly sensitive actions should have a delayed effect rather than being real-time. The delay allows for time to pass during which an intrusion might be detected. Delay always works against an attacker. This is why "timed vaults" are effective. Thus, customer service functions that affect privileges, move large dollar amounts, or reveal sensitive information should all be examined to see if they can be modified to take affect after a slight delay of say, one hour or ideally long enough to notify the affected user through alternate means.

> Highly sensitive actions should have a delayed effect rather than being real-time.

PRINCIPLE: DELAY THE AFFECT OF SENSITIVE OPERATIONS.

Users enjoy having a "single sign-on" system in which they log on once to a single user identity and, based on the roles that their single identity has been associated with, they are able to access any function that their roles are authorized to perform, across all their job roles.

Convenience weighs in favor of "single sign-on." This should not be ruled out for common business applications and the normal user roles in those applications. However, for administrative roles, it is discouraged. It is more secure to allocate one narrow role per identity when the role performs sensitive functions.

> A single sign-on identity should not be usable for performing sensitive functions across multiple applications or systems.

PRINCIPLE: IMPLEMENT SINGLE SIGN-ON SPARINGLY.

The role and associated identity should be unique on each application or system that must be maintained. This ensures that different credentials are used to authenticate the user's identity for access to each of those roles. That way, a user who manages to compromise an identity's credentials can at most perform the functions associated with the single role owned by that identity on a single system or application.

PRINCIPLE: *PREFER TO EMPLOY DIFFERENT CREDENTIALS FOR EACH ROLE.*

Having different identities or different credentials for each sensitive role can present a great inconvenience—sometimes too much so. For example, users might have to remember multiple passwords. If strong authentication is used, the user might have to have multiple digital certificates (for example, multiple smartcards)—one for each sensitive role. The user might also have multiple user profiles—one for each identity—unless there is a way to link the profiles. Still, for a highly sensitive role, these inconveniences may be justified. The decision needs to be evaluated in terms of the risk.◆

◆ See the principle "Match Diligence to Risk" in Section 4.1.

8.1.4 Server Roles

In general, server applications should always be executed with a special user identity or role that has limited permission—only the permissions needed to perform its function. Access to the files that the server needs should be restricted to the server's role (or identity). This restricts what the server can do and thereby helps to prevent attacks that insert malicious code or otherwise co-opt a server into performing unintended actions: If the server is executing with an administrative ID, it is capable of accessing any resource in the system.

PRINCIPLE: *CREATE UNIQUE ROLES OR USER IDENTITIES FOR EACH SERVER APPLICATION, WITH ONLY THE PERMISSIONS THAT ARE REQUIRED.*

After a unique role or identity has been created for a server application's exclusive use, it is then possible to prevent access by any role except for the unique role or identity created for the server's use. Administrative ownership of the resource should remain with a narrowly defined administrative role, however, in order to prevent the server role from having the ability to expand its access rights.

PRINCIPLE: PROVIDE A SERVER'S EXECUTION ROLE OR USER IDENTITY WITH EXCLUSIVE ACCESS TO THE RESOURCES THAT THE SERVER OWNS.

In applications that access back-end servers, such as databases, it is advisable to utilize a separate connection pool and server connection role for each user-level role. Even though the database access is performed using server user IDs instead of actual user IDs, dividing up the accesses according to the user role model helps to implement a least-privilege policy with regard to the database connections.

PRINCIPLE: COMPARTMENTALIZE SERVER CONNECTIONS.

8.2 Summary

This chapter discussed the use and separation of user roles within applications. As a prelude to that discussion, the concepts of compartmentalization and classification of data and resources were presented.

The next chapter discusses issues pertaining to the secure storage, transport, and management of highly sensitive data, such as credentials and any validation data used in lieu of credentials.

8.3 Exercises

1. A loan approval process in use at a bank requires a lending officer to indicate preliminary approval by sending a completed loan application to the loan processing department via a secure email containing an indication of approval. If a loan is for more than a certain amount, the lending supervisor must indicate approval as well by also emailing a notice of approval of the loan application. What principle is violated in this scenario?

2. A multi-user application accesses a database. The application is configured such that database connections are opened using a special identity created only for that purpose. The special identity also owns the database (e.g., it owns the dataset or tables). Explain the flaw in this scheme.
3. A multi-user application administrator is considered to be the must trusted user of the application. Should the administrator have access to the data stored within the application? What principle(s) apply here?
4. The administrator of a multi-user application manages all application functions, including databases, logging, and application server functions. Explain the risks and vulnerabilities of this arrangement.
5. A customer service function used by a call center enables a customer service representative to perform updates to user accounts, including the correction of account balances. The customer service function's hallmark is that it can immediately address problems in order to help users. What safeguard(s) should be employed in order to reduce risk to the organization and users?
6. A workflow application requires the existence of three roles: (a) user administrator, (b) manager, and (c) ordinary user. A manager has all the rights as an ordinary user but can also create new activities. A user administrator has all the rights of an ordinary user but can also create and enroll new users. Access rights are based on the group to which a user belongs. Create a UML structural (class) model of the roles and permissions for this application.

Answers and hints for these exercises can be found at `http://www.assuredbydesign.com/haa/`.

CHAPTER 9

TRANSPORT AND STORAGE OF SECRETS

"I believe that the scroll is a treasure map, setting out an ancient code that offers vital clues in the greatest quest that mankind has ever known—the search for the Holy Grail." —from The Secret Scroll, *by Andrew Sinclair, Churchill College, Cambridge*

Even those of us who are not secretive by nature but who use computers have lots of secrets. A password is a secret, as is a session key between two endpoints in an SSL session—not to mention the transmitted encrypted data itself. Secrets tend to be one of the following:

1. Sensitive information.
2. Credentials or data that *enable* the secure exchange or storage of sensitive information.

When sending sensitive data from one point to another, do not rely on obscurity for security. Just because no one except the recipient knows that you are sending the data does not mean it will not be intercepted. Consider the case of the hacker who during 2004-2005 hacked into email servers at wireless giant T-Mobile and monitored U.S. Secret Service email pertaining to the very investigation of his activities![1]

9.1 Basic Vulnerabilities

Transport systems often leave "artifacts" of what they transport. For example, email systems are normally backed up, especially given today's environment in which traceability is more of a concern for national security reasons, and laws require that information be retained.[1] It is often possible to divert transported traffic as well, causing it to pass through a rogue system for the purpose of silently intercepting the traffic. It is then a simple matter to run programs or scripts that scan for passwords and other sensitive information.

PRINCIPLE: TRANSPORT SENSITIVE DATA SECURELY.

To transport data securely, the endpoints must be secure, and the channel of communication must be secure.

The requirement for secure transport is not limited to network-based transport. In general, care should be taken to secure any transport of secure data between two endpoints. For example, do you know if the data that you enter into your keyboard is transported securely to the applications that you run? There are keyboard-sniffing programs that are widely available that can be installed by a virus.

It is important to never store insecure (for example, unencrypted) data in a location that is also used to store secure (for example, encrypted) data [2]. A very common form of attack is to infer information based on unsecured data that is stored in a location that is normally secure.

1 For example, the U.S. Congress Sarbanes-Oxley Act of 2002, Section 802, establishes penalties of up to 20 years in prison for altering or deleting documents relevant to financial auditing disclosure.

PRINCIPLE: DO NOT STORE UNSECURED DATA IN A SECURE LOCATION.

For example, suppose a file contains an unencrypted value and that value is later encrypted and used to replace the unencrypted value. If an intruder had access to the file, the intruder now has two versions of a datum: an unencrypted version and an encrypted version. These two versions can potentially be used to infer something about the encryption algorithm. For example, if a stream cipher is used, the encrypted value will re-appear at each point in the file where the value repeats, enabling the attacker to observe how often and where the value occurs in the file.

It is sometimes possible to exploit a race condition to observe a buffer before and after a store operation completes. The race condition might be forced to occur by an attack or by repeated attacks. If the buffer is used to first contain the unencrypted value and is then re-written with the encrypted value, the intruder obtains a powerful type of information. Thus, it is good practice to never do anything that might allow an intruder to correlate an encrypted and unencrypted value. This applies in particular to re-using a buffer for the dual-purpose of storing an unencrypted and encrypted value. It might even be possible to create a condition such that the buffer remains in an insecure state while the application thinks that it is in "secure mode."

In general, do not use a secure location, such as a buffer, file, or table, for other purposes, and do not alternate between secured and insecure states. Doing so might allow an attacker to create a condition that causes the system to stay in an insecure state or allow the possibility of correlating secure and insecure data.

A seemingly obvious principle is to never store secrets in an insecure manner. However, it is amazing how often this is violated. For example, it is not uncommon to find passwords embedded in application code or to find user roles that are used for authorization decisions embedded in hidden tags in Web pages. The presence of any sensitive data embedded within a Web URL or a Web form makes the site vulnerable to "parameter tampering" or "form tampering," respectively. Along the same lines, Web browser cookies that contain sensitive data should be time-stamped and encrypted. This protects against "cookie poisoning," as well as "cookie snooping."

PRINCIPLE: NEVER STORE SECRETS INSECURELY.

Do not assume that a secret that is embedded in technical artifacts is hard to find. Hackers use special programs that can easily identify passwords in application code or data files. Downloaded Web pages that contain hidden tags that contain sensitive information are the first point of attack. This also extends to variable names, which can often give a clue. A famous example is the presence of a variable named "NSA_KEY" that was discovered in Microsoft Windows in 1999. Microsoft has denied that the NSA has a "key" hidden in Windows for "back-door" access.

> Do not assume that a secret that is embedded in technical artifacts is hard to find.

When sensitive data is no longer needed, erase it in a manner that eliminates all artifacts. The issue of artifact elimination was discussed earlier in Section 7.20.7, "Caches and Artifacts."

9.1.1 Deciding What to Encrypt

Organizations often encrypt sensitive data, even if the data is stored within a secure repository. Encryption provides an additional level of protection and ensures that trusted parties, such as administrators, do not have *inappropriate access* to the data contents.

Encryption creates overhead, however. Most databases that provide encryption provide it on a field-specific basis. For example, Oracle allows a SQL programmer to select an algorithm (for example, AES or DES3) and provide an encryption key to be used to encrypt or decrypt the values of a particular column in a table. Oracle does not (as of this writing) provide encryption key management, so the programmer must make separate provisions for storing and retrieving encryption keys.

A ramification of this approach is that any container-managed persistence facility utilized by an application must be able to support the database's encryption features. At this writing, most do not.

> To use database encryption with container-managed persistence, the container-managed persistence facility must be able to support the database's encryption features.

One of the main drawbacks with encrypting database data is that search fields cannot be encrypted; or if they can be, the performance penalty is very large.

In a server-based application, the main vulnerabilities with regard to backend data are backup tapes and logs because these long-term repositories tend to be relatively vulnerable. A main reason for using encryption is, therefore, to ensure that sensitive data written to backups and logs is protected.

> In a server-based application, the main vulnerabilities with regard to backend data are backup tapes and logs.

It would be desirable if databases provided a feature that encrypts certain columns *when a backup is made*. That would make it unnecessary to encrypt the data in the database itself, which is generally of less value because the database has access controls. Unfortunately, most databases do not have such a feature. For this reason, the best solution is to encrypt backup tapes en-mass as a procedural step after they are made.

In any case, it is important that data encrypted in the database should not be written in the clear to app server logs.

> Data encrypted in the database should not be written in the clear to app server logs.

Every product that deals with sensitive data should undertake a data classification effort in order to decide what data to encrypt in the database, if any. This should include some level of risk analysis to ensure that an appropriate level of effort is expended for the perceived risk.

> Every product that deals with sensitive data should undertake a data classification effort in order to decide what data to encrypt in the database.

If a decision to encrypt certain fields is made, consider using database triggers in order to implement the encryption step for inserts and stored procedures for retrievals. This encapsulates the encryption and decryption operations within the database. The keys can be obtained dynamically from a secure key table that is not included in backups.

Alternatively, encryption can be performed within the application server prior to storage in the database. This approach is less efficient and provides few advantages because the database encryption model is field-level and programmatic anyway.

9.2 Credential Management

Credentials should be treated as high-value secrets and managed through explicitly defined processes and guidelines.

Credentials are often stored insecurely on workstations. A hacker does not need physical access to the workstation in order to get access to credentials that are stored on it. Personal workstations are the easiest computers to hack into because users do not normally follow safe computing practices unless they are under severe pressure to do so, and it is possible to use email to establish a single compromised computer on a network and then use some protocols—for example, RPC—to find other vulnerable personal computers on the local network and insert trojan horse programs on them. Such programs can then potentially provide access to the user's registry and any keystores on their machine. Because such keystores are usually software-based and are protected only by a password—which can be intercepted by the spying program—they are possible to penetrate.

This means that sensitive credentials should not be stored on a relatively insecure machine, even if they are stored within a password-protected keystore. Sensitive credentials should be committed to memory. Credentials that must be stored on a machine should be encrypted or stored in a secure keystore that employs encryption and requires password access, that has sufficient physical security, and that is well-administered.

Highly sensitive credential stores or configurations should be accessed only via a trusted network that is inaccessible from other networks. This is why many security appliances have special administrative ports that are not supposed to be connected to the company LAN.

Some common "best practices" for credential management are summarized in Table 9.1.

Table 9.1 Basic Credential Management Best Practices

Credentials should never be retrievable in clear form or in a form that can be "replayed."
Credentials should never be displayed in clear form.
Users should be allowed to modify their logon credentials.
Re-authenticate whenever the user attempts to modify credentials.
Require credentials to expire. (See the principle "Periodically Replace Secrets," later in this chapter.) Invalidate credentials promptly when they are no longer needed.
Do not re-use identities that were previously in use—either intentionally or unintentionally. It also goes without saying that duplicate identities (existing at the same time) should be prevented.
Disallow null (empty) credentials (passwords).
Do not reveal any information about other credentials as a side effect of authentication or enrollment. For example, do not reveal that a password is disallowed because it is already in use by another user.
Do not divide an authentication process into stages, as that would allow a user to divide an authentication attack into stages.
Secure customization of credential policy should be provided, including (1) required password change at initial logon; (2) refresh of password at regular intervals, and key validity period; (2) password complexity, size, predictability, and re-use rules; (3) encoding and encryption algorithm and strength choices; (4) lockout and alert after *n* attempts; (5) un-lockout period and conditions; number of concurrent sessions per user.
Provide for recovery of encryption keys.
Ensure non-recoverability of signing keys.
Do not use signing keys for encryption, and vice versa.
Distribute securely. (See the principle "Distribute Credentials Securely" later in this chapter.)

PRINCIPLE: EMPLOY SECURE CREDENTIAL PRACTICES.

Apply appropriate timeouts or expirations to all credentials. For example, session credentials should have a validity period that reflects outer envelope of session time of the typical user, and user logon credentials should expire within some period of time judged to be adequate to ensure that they do not become known or "common knowledge" to others. A credential that expires after a period of time is often referred to as a "lease."

Session timeouts based on a period of inactivity should be used to ensure that an unattended session is not vulnerable. Such timeouts are often referred to as "inactive" timeouts.

PRINCIPLE: PERIODICALLY REPLACE SECRETS.

See also the related principle "Provide for Timely Revocation of Privileges" in Section 7.17.6, "Contextual Scope."

Public and private keys used for PKI processes, such as document signing, encryption, and authentication, have different lifecycle management requirements depending on their purpose.[2] Table 9.2 lists the risks with regard to public and private keys, what can be done to mitigate those risks, and the duration over which the risk must be addressed.

Table 9.2 PKI Key Risks and Countermeasures

Key Type	Risks	Countermeasure	Duration of Countermeasure
Encryption public key	Forgery	Validate encryption certificate.	Duration of encryption process (e.g., three days)
Decryption private key	Misplacement over time	Safeguard private key against misplacement.	Lifetime of encrypted artifact (e.g., 30 years)
	Theft and then misuse	Protect secrecy and integrity of key.	
Signing private key	Theft and then misuse	Destroy key after use or after a short expiration period.	Duration of signing process (e.g. three days)

2 PKI key management is discussed in depth in [3].

Key Type	Risks	Countermeasure	Duration of Countermeasure
Signature verification public key[3]	Misplacement over time	Safeguard certificate chain against disposal or modification.	Lifetime of signed artifact (e.g., 30 years)
	Forgery	Validate certificate each time it is used.	
Authentication private key	Theft and then misuse	Protect secrecy and integrity of key.	Duration of expiration period (e.g., six months)
		Invalidate key after a reasonable expiration period.	
Authentication public key	Misplacement over time	Safeguard certificate chain against disposal or modification.	Duration of expiration period (e.g., six months)
	Forgery	Validate certificate each time it is used. Invalidate key after a reasonable expiration period.	

9.2.1 Credential Distribution

Most (but not all) authentication technologies rely on the existence of a secret possessed by the user. The secret is bound to a user identity and is used in an authentication process that proves that the user possesses the secret and therefore represents the identity.

Authentication does not address how the user obtains the secret in the first place or, more generally, how that secret becomes bound to an identity and is distributed to those who need it in order to participate in the authentication process. For example, in order to obtain a digital certificate, the user generates a secret on her computer and submits a "certificate signing request" to a certificate authority ("CA"). The CA is then expected to obtain physical proof that the user is who she says she is (for example, via mailing in a notarized copy of an

3 This also applies to any use for non-repudiation purposes.

identifying paper document), and only then digitally sign the certificate and return it to the user. The certificate can then be used by the user in an authentication process that involves the user's secret, which remains on their computer.

Low-value secrets, such as passwords for many Internet services, are often sent through email, for example, when a user forgets their password. In addition, non-secret data, such as the user's certificate and the certificates of CAs that have validated the user's certificate, are required in order to apply certificate-based authentication processes. Critical objects, such as root CA certificates, must be *distributed and installed in a secure manner* to ensure that they are not compromised, which would make them unreliable for the purposes of authentication and validation of relying (Web site or user) certificates.

The general principle here is to use a secure process for the generation, distribution, and installation (i.e., deployment) of any and all sensitive objects that are needed to perform an authentication process. This generally encompasses user passwords, private keys, and root (CA) certificates.

PRINCIPLE: DISTRIBUTE CREDENTIALS SECURELY.

The sensitivity of the user's functions (i.e., the user's role) should be considered when deciding the appropriate means to distribute credentials, such as passwords, private keys, or certificates. Secure email can be used for enhanced security, but that requires that the user has a personal email certificate already installed. For very sensitive user roles, the user's credentials should be distributed in person or through physically secure means.

Users often forget passwords, and in those cases, it is important to use a secure process for providing the user with a new password or recovering the old one. A common method of authenticating the user automatically for the purpose of restoring a password is to establish an authentication question and answer when the user enrolls, so that if the user forgets their password the question can be presented to them and their answer verified. If the answer is correct, their password can be emailed to them. This approach presumes that they have secure access to their email.

For critical or highly sensitive credentials or pieces of information, such as passwords or account activation credentials for sensitive roles, make sure that an attacker would have to compromise more than one communication pathway in order to succeed.

For example, when providing a new user with account activation credentials, you might send the user *two* separate activation codes: one via email and one via regular mail. The user would then have to access an enrollment Web page and enter both values in order to enable the account.

PRINCIPLE: EMPLOY MULTIPLE INDEPENDENT FACTORS OR CHANNELS.

9.2.2 Alternative Authentication

"Alternative authentication" is an authentication process that is used when the user is not able to use the primary authentication mechanism (for example, because they forgot their password). Alternative authentication data (for example, mother's maiden name) should be treated as highly sensitive and stored in encrypted form. That data should not ever be displayed or transmitted in clear text, nor should it be retrievable by an administrator (i.e., it should be managed in the same manner as logon credentials).

PRINCIPLE: TREAT ALTERNATIVE USER VERIFICATION METHODS AS FORMS OF AUTHENTICATION.

9.3 Summary

This chapter discussed the transport and storage of high-value secrets such as passwords and cryptographic keys. Issues related to the manner and use of storage containers were discussed. Criteria for deciding what kinds of data should be encrypted were presented. Credential management practices were presented, and the problems of key management and distribution in complex business applications was discussed. The concept of alternative authentication was discussed and related to credential management.

The next chapter presents features that are needed for applications to be operated and managed securely. These features must be considered during the design of applications, possibly leading to the addition of derived requirements.

9.4 Exercises

1. A document management application allows a user to flag any of the user's documents as "sensitive," at which point the application encrypts the document using the user's private key. What security principle is violated by this design?
2. A Web application allows users to donate used books to charities online. Users like the service because they can obtain a tax deduction based on the value of the books that they donate. The site requires users to log in using the user's password in order to check their account, print reports of donations, and log the mailing of books. If the user has forgotten their password, they can still log in by providing information that it is presumed that only they would know, such as the name of the book that they donated most recently. What security risks are immediately apparent in this application, and how can they be remedied?
3. An application requires users to log on using a user ID and a password. When a new user joins, the user ID and password are emailed to them using separate emails. What security principle(s) are violated by this approach?
4. In exercise 2, user account data is backed up each day to an offsite storage system. What measures should be taken to protect the data, and which data is particularly at risk?
5. In exercise 1, the user's private key is stored on the user's workstation and is encrypted using a password. What risks exist beside the theft of the password?

Answers and hints for these exercises can be found at `http://www.assuredbydesign.com/haa/`.

Chapter 10

Design Considerations for Secure Operation

10.1 Designing for Secure Deployment

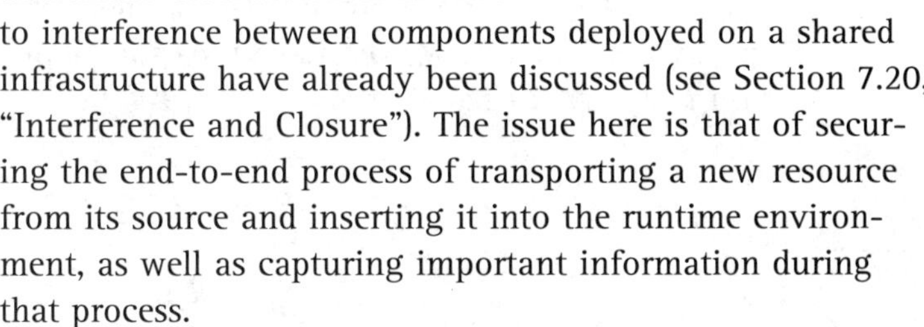

The security implications of deployment are often overlooked and under-estimated. Issues related to interference between components deployed on a shared infrastructure have already been discussed (see Section 7.20, "Interference and Closure"). The issue here is that of securing the end-to-end process of transporting a new resource from its source and inserting it into the runtime environment, as well as capturing important information during that process.

The shortfalls of most computing environments today with regard to deployment are that (1) the deployment process is not automatable without significant development effort; and (2) important security information is not automatically captured or required. For example, information such as who the deployer was, the identity of the source of the application (for example, URL, certificate owner, and so on), and what the configuration is (which should be secured in some manner, such as by ACL or by a MAC[1] or signature[2]) is all relevant from a security perspective. The administrative access rights of a resource are also configured during deployment. Obviously, if the deployment process is not secure, none of this information is trustworthy.

Code signing provided by Java and the Microsoft CLR make identity source verification possible, but these features are not yet widely used, especially in application server environments—hopefully they will become so. It would also be beneficial to automatically verify that the configuration is secure; for example, that the permissions are set appropriately on directories used by the application.

PRINCIPLE: DEPLOY SECURELY.

◆ See the principle "A Trusted Context Should Always Include the Code Context" in Section 7.17.3, "Code Context."

Deployment should be *performed by trusted components.*[3] If an application is obtained with a self-contained deployer, deployment cannot be trustworthy unless the source of the application is highly trusted.♦

If an application is obtained with a self-contained deployer, deployment cannot be trustworthy unless the source of the application is highly trusted.

1 The Unix program md5sum is often used to create a checksum of the application code that can be securely stored and used to later verify that the code has not changed by re-computing it and comparing. A more secure approach is to compute a MAC using an algorithm (for example, "DES-MAC") that also accepts a secret key that is protected independently of the application files.

2 Ref. [1], p. 59. Note that a MAC is similar to a signature, except that a signature is created using public key technology.

3 See [2], the discussion of "life-cycle technical controls," p. 418.

A deployment tool should automatically provide a means for the deployment administrator to configure security policy for the new application right from the start—things such as which directories it should be allowed to access, what network addresses they can access, and so on. This functionality should be built into the operating system and be non-bypassable. This is unfortunately not the way things currently are, and this is why "spyware" has become rampant on Windows systems.

> A deployment tool should automatically provide a means for the deployment administrator to configure security policy for the new application right from the start.

Deployment is normally handled under the umbrella of "system administration." However, *administrators need the help of application builders to create systems that are easily and securely deployable.* For example, an application that is strewn with configuration files enmeshed with the application code, embedded credentials, file paths and URLs, and user group names presents a tremendous problem for deployment. Administrators need to have a concise list of where all these configuration items are, and it must be possible to ensure that they are secure. That is, their file permissions must be set appropriately (according to least privilege), user groups must be set appropriately, critical URL paths must be accessible only by the application and by an administrator, and so on. All this should be documented in one place to ensure that nothing is overlooked.

> Administrators need the cooperation of application builders to create systems that are easily and securely deployable.

For this reason, it is good practice to address deployment as part of a system's high-level design. The deployment design should identify configuration parameters and include annotations of what approach should be used to ensure that those parameters are secure. For example, Figure 10.1 illustrates the use of a class diagram to identify configuration properties, a property file from which they will be obtained, and the intended mechanisms to use to ensure that those properties cannot be compromised.

> It is good practice to identify configuration parameters as part of a system's high-level design.

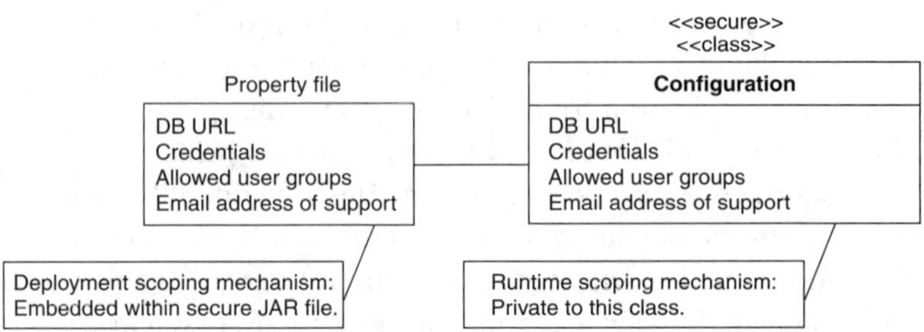

Figure 10.1 Illustration of a design that identifies the mechanisms used to protect the deployment configuration.

The deployment design should also specify how *platform-level configurations should be set that are application-specific or that affect the application.* That is, things such as a system-wide Java classpath (generally inadvisable), process classpath, current working directory, home directory for the user identity under which the application will execute, and so on. These are all potential attack points, so they must not be overlooked. *It is up to the application designer to plan these things out*; it is the deployment administrator's job to assist in this planning, to approve of the final plan and design, and to execute the deployment.

Deployment is increasingly becoming a dynamic process, and other users are increasingly involved. For example, suppose that an organization allows partners to install their own components (such as service stubs) within an infrastructure, such as an application server. These partner-installed pieces might be needed to provide services that are operated by the partners. The responsibility for operating the infrastructure might be shared or delegated so that a single organization does not have to manage all the partner-installed components. For example, the partners who provide components might also provide an automatic update service that keeps the components current. If achievable, this is far more flexible than the monolithic approach of having a single organization manage everything. To make it possible, however, the infrastructure and applications must support secure deployment.

> To make it possible to share or delegate deployment or operation to partners, the infrastructure and applications must support easily-secured deployment.

10.2 Restoration

The application designer, with assistance from the deployment and security administrators, should identify the critical configuration parameters and database checkpoints that should be used if the system needs to be restored after a security breach. Appropriate backups and checkpoints should be performed regularly or continuously as appropriate and maintained in or moved to a separate location. This will help to avoid a "Forced Restart, Forced Re-Install" attack (see Section 5.1.10).

Backups and configuration restoration files should be verifiable via MAC or other means to prove that they have not been tampered with.

PRINCIPLE: PROVIDE FOR SECURE RESTORATION.

Restoration should be as automated as possible because restoration may need to occur in a timely manner and without errors. Any applications developed for the purpose of restoration should be maintained in a secure manner using the same quality control processes as for any sensitive component.

The restoration process should always begin by archiving the current system security configuration in its entirety, using appropriate safeguards for any sensitive archive data. Restoration should proceed only if the current configuration has been archived so that it can be examined later.

Any tools used to restore the system or to respond to a system failure should be secure; otherwise, a compromised tool might be used.

10.3 Designing for Secure Operation

Applications are often to blame in the defeat of infrastructure security mechanisms, and users who install or design their own applications are indeed the bane of security administrators. It is very hard to secure a network if users are allowed to configure their own systems or are allowed to access content on the Internet other than strictly static content.

The desktop computing platforms in use today are especially problematic, and this affects the networks to which they are connected. Today's desktop operating systems are so far from providing the protection that is needed for non-administrative users that the situation is almost hopeless with regard to fully protecting these systems—except in environments that use highly limited desktops such as thin-client workstations. That said, we are all used to living in an imperfect world and managing risk. Nothing is completely secure—including life. In practice, with constant administrative diligence and secure policies, it is possible to maintain a reasonable level of security for general-purpose desktop machines connected to the Internet and reasonable security for the server machines that share those networks. The situation may also improve as desktop operating systems are improved.

> The desktop computing platforms in use today are so far from providing the protection that is needed that the situation is almost hopeless with regard to fully protecting systems!

It is essential to educate users so that they can help to manage the risk inherent in this situation. Users—and especially application designers—should be made to understand the impact that certain practices can have, given the vulnerabilities of today's operating systems. For example, users have been taught not to open attachments in emails from untrusted sources. With continuing education and warnings, users can be taught to know when certain actions might thwart the infrastructure security mechanisms that are in place.

PRINCIPLE: DO NOT THWART INFRASTRUCTURE SECURITY MECHANISMS.

> An application with security holes can make an entire network vulnerable.

Business users who design or install custom applications on server machines need to be especially cognizant of local security policy. Applications with security holes can make an entire network vulnerable, and the high bandwidth and assumption of trust that accompany a server application represent a huge potential for an attack gateway.

If the local environment has policies or systems that provide security features, do not attempt to use those features for anything but their intended purpose. The reason is that different kinds of usage have different usage profiles, and *an application's usage profile is important to security administrators.* For example, do not use a mail server as a system-to-system messaging server unless you have notified the administrator that you are doing that and asked if that would affect their ability to detect anomalies. As another example, do not install any "information services" (including CGI programs, servlets, and so on) that are exposed to the Internet without notifying the network administrator and undertaking the appropriate security analysis. As a final example, do not obfuscate protocol data. A common manifestation of this is the use of client-side scripting to generate protocol (HTTP) parameters, such as URL targets. This has the effect of rendering useless any application proxy filters that are in place.

The core source of danger here is that if you use systems for purposes that are not intended, you might change the normal profile of usage of that system and thereby undermine intrusion detection systems. You might also cause the administrator to turn off traffic filters in order to accommodate your usage, thereby foregoing the added security that such filters can provide. Thus, in the face of rampant misuse of protocols and systems by users, the administrator gives up and turns many security features off.

> The use of client-side scripting to generate protocol (HTTP) parameters, such as URL targets, has the effect of rendering useless any HTML-level proxy filters that are in place.

Protocol tunneling, for example, by piping application protocols through HTTP, is an especially egregious form of this misuse. HTTP was designed as a protocol for the request of static Web data and posting of files and data sets to Web servers. It allows a client to make requests for "resources" (URLs) and receive responses that are normally HTML and are displayed. HTTP's intended usage was for information clients: browsers.

> In the face of rampant misuse of protocols and systems by users, an administrator gives up and turns off many security features.

It was not long after HTTP was developed that people started to use it for other things. The reason is that HTTP became widespread and many organizations configured their firewalls to allow outbound HTTP requests to any destination and inbound HTTP responses. This situation also existed, to some extent, for mail protocols (SMTP and POP) and FTP, but HTTP is far more flexible, so people started using HTTP as a "tunnel" for other protocols. That is, they hid other kinds of traffic inside of HTTP, as the HTTP "content." Administrators allowed it because they had no practical way to stop it, because the risks were not fully understood, and because there were no viable alternatives.

Tunneling presents severe security risks if it is not between trusted endpoints. [3] Because the actual traffic is masked by the tunneling protocol (most commonly HTTP), it cannot easily be examined or filtered by a plain vanilla Web proxy. Instead, a more advanced "application protection proxy" (APP) is required. Few organizations have deployed APPs because they are unsure of the impact on their organization. In the absence of an APP, it is possible for HTTP traffic from a rogue application to expose information about internal systems.

Specialized protocol proxies exist that enable safe firewall traversal without tunneling. For example, an IIOP proxy can translate internal IP addresses into "public" addresses so that public clients cannot learn about the internal network. If IIOP traffic is directly tunneled inside HTTP (without an IIOP proxy), internal IP addresses will likely be embedded in the protocol traffic.

Tunneling should only be permitted between known and trusted destinations, using known and trusted application level protocols.

If tunneling is allowed, it is a good policy to allow it to only known and trusted destinations, using protocols that are known to be secure and not reveal internal application or network details. An administrator that detects unauthorized tunneling should immediately shut it down and contact the users of the application that is performing it.

PRINCIPLE: DO NOT SECRETLY "TUNNEL."

Unfortunately, tunneling is rampant. Many kinds of clients use tunneling automatically, including mail clients, instant messaging clients, and various multi-media clients, such as music players. The destinations of these can usually be enumerated, however, so that they can be explicitly allowed if necessary.

If you are designing an application that uses a protocol that is not supported by the organization's proxy firewall, you should not tunnel the protocol unless you notify the administrator and weigh alternatives. Firewall vendors attempt to support the most commonly used protocols, and it is preferable to send traffic without tunneling if possible. This allows the administrator to monitor, proxy, and filter traffic in an effective manner.

It may seem obvious, but it would be remiss to not mention for completeness sake that physical security of the runtime system is a critical requirement to ensure that the resources that are installed in that environment are secure. This is really a responsibility of the user and administrator, but application designers need to understand this because they often assume that the end-user environment is secure when it is not. This affects the degree to which the application should store secrets in the end-user environment.

The runtime environment must be secure, or all bets are off. This applies to any environment that contains trusted components or information, including both server and client environments. In most systems, some portion will be compromised during the system's lifetime, often as a result of poor physical security. For example, if someone has physical access to a system, they can re-install the operating system without re-formatting the disks and obtain access to the files on it (unless the files are encrypted); or they can install "spyware" or operating system patches to eavesdrop or to enable most of the kinds of attacks discussed previously; or they can copy your credential files or private keys if they know where to look. Physical access removes major obstacles that an attacker would otherwise have to overcome.

PRINCIPLE: RUN SECURELY.

Physical security applies to client-side systems as well, including thin clients that do not store information. In this case, the danger is in assuming that the user will not hack their own system: Never assume that a rogue client will not be able to penetrate a client-side security mechanism. Physical security is a necessity for any form of security: If someone has unrestricted physical access to a computer or its software, it is not trustworthy anymore.[4]

10.4 Provide for Monitoring

Security-related events can be grouped into "abnormal" events and "normal" events. Abnormal events are events that are not expected to occur unless there is a problem. Normal events are events that occur even when there is no problem, but that are significant and can be used to diagnose problems when they do occur.

All abnormal events should be logged, and significant normal events should be logged as well.

PRINCIPLE: LOG SECURITY-RELATED EVENTS.

Examples of important security-related events are listed in Tables 10.1 and 10.2.

Table 10.1 Abnormal Security-Related Events

Authentication attempts and failures.
Authorization failures.

Table 10.2 Normal Security-Related Events

Authentication successes.
Session establishment.
Authorization successes.
Security configuration changes, including role assignment changes or access control list changes, or changes to what is logged.
User security profile changes.
Events or changes that impact authorization rules.
Date and time of creation or update of sensitive data.
User (or complete security context) responsible for any updates to data.

4 See [4] for an interesting approach to centralizing "client-side" resources.

Intrusion detection is based on the interception of abnormal and normal security-related events and interpreting those events according to known attack profiles. Intrusion detection is extremely important because timely awareness of an attack makes all the difference in preventing loss.

Intrusion detection is most effective if it is provided by multiple levels of the system, including the application. Thus, intrusion detection is not purely the job of administrators and generic intrusion detection tools. It should be built into the application.

PRINCIPLE: EMBED INTRUSION DETECTION AT MULTIPLE POINTS.

As an example, an application should fail to run if its security logs are not operating properly, and an alert should then be generated. An application can also discern "normal" user behavior from "abnormal" behavior more accurately than external tools. For example, a banking application can determine if a user is transferring a large portion of their bank account and generate an alert and possibly even freeze the account.

Applications should, therefore, be designed to detect abnormal behavior and generate an alert when it is detected.♦

♦ See Section 4.3, "Think in Terms of Survivability."

For potentially serious threats, *multiple independent means should always be used to contact responders*. This is because the intruder might have disabled the primary means. The intruder might also be relying on slowness of response in order to complete an attack (see Section 5.2.3, "Haste"), so timely notification is of the essence, as is a coordinated reduction in system speed.

PRINCIPLE: MULTIPLE INDEPENDENT MEANS SHOULD BE USED TO CONTACT RESPONDERS.

10.5 Capacity Allocation and Resource Usage Monitoring

A denial of service attack is able to succeed if one or more un-authenticated parties are able to commandeer most of the available real-time capacity of a resource. This is possible because many services accept unauthenticated requests. An authentication service is an example–by definition!

This may appear to be a predicament at first glance, because what defense can possibly exist for this? In fact, there are defenses. Given enough time, engineers can respond to and disable a sustained denial of service attack. The problem is (1) knowing that one is in progress; and (2) preventing the damage that can occur during the attack, especially during the early period before a response is initiated.

The most basic rule to mitigate against a denial of service attack is to devote as little system capacity as is practical to servicing an unauthenticated request. For example, a logon process should be made very efficient and lightweight so that repeated logon attempts cannot be used to cause the system to become over-loaded. It is worth pointing out that newer TCP/IP libraries (specifically, the accept() method) are designed to prevent the allocation of communication resources until the requesting endpoint responds, thereby preventing a common kind of packet-based denial of service attack. Applications should make sure that they make use of available network-level features for preventing network-level denial of service attacks.

> A logon process should be very efficient and lightweight.

PRINCIPLE: ALLOCATE RESOURCE CAPACITY BASED ON TRUST.

There are many strategies for allocating capacity, including priority-based strategies and quota-based strategies. It is generally best to rely on capacity allocation mechanisms that are provided by infrastructure, such as routers for network-level allocation, operating systems for process-level allocation, application servers for application-level allocation, and databases for database user-level allocation. This presents a strong argument for dividing resource access points into classes; for example, using different database connection pools for different classes of user so that they can be dealt with differently in terms of incident response as well as security policy.

In general, all applications and user requests should execute within the constraints of a predefined quota, which may be predefined or be a function of priority, risk, and other factors. This helps to prevent a rogue or malfunctioning application or request from bringing down other applications by draining away system resources, such as by entering an infinite loop, by requesting more and more memory, or by endlessly opening new windows. For a server application, quotas should be adjustable in response to intrustion detection.

> Using different database connection pools for different classes of user allows them to be dealt with differently in terms of incident response as well as security policy.

A dynamic strategy for dealing with denial of service attacks is to allocate less and less capacity to a class of requests if it is determined that those requests have a denial of service profile. Thus, quota and response strategy for a user session or request is a factor of the current threat level for that user and also for the system as a whole. For example, if repeated logon attempts are made, you should start to use cached data to make the authentication decision. Upon continued requests, the application can respond by rejecting future attempts from that IP address until after a "recovery period" after which the IP address is re-admitted. If the user is already logged on but is acting in a suspicious manner, the user's quota should be reduced and their response slowed, and their access rights should be reduced to a harmless level. Of course, if their actions indicate a clear intrusion, they should be immediately shut out at all levels. In all cases, generate an *immediate* alert to the administrator if there is any indication that inappropriate requests are being made or if it appears that a denial of service attack may be beginning.

This points to a third strategy: If a denial of service profile is apparent, begin to push out the handling of the requests that fit the denial of service profile toward the perimeter. In the IP address filtering example, the filtering could be delegated to the border router of the network. This might have to be done manually. Of course, if the attack is sophisticated, advanced networking techniques may be necessary (for example, setting up "shadow" servers for trusted clients), but network configuration strategies are beyond the scope of this book, as the focus here is on application design issues.

In general, you do not want to allow an untrusted user to use a large portion of the system's capacity, and this applies most of all to an unauthenticated user. If you have services that are available to unauthenticated users, such as search services or "trial" services, you should consider deploying these in a separate instance with its own capacity quota managed by the operating system. That way, unauthenticated users will not be able to affect the service level experienced by authenticated users, who presumably constitute a more loyal and trusted user base.

> If you have services that are available to un-authenticated users, consider deploying them in a separate instance.

A balance must be struck between safety and convenience because legitimate users often exhibit behavior that is hard to distinguish from an attack. For example, a user might have forgotten a password and might attempt to log on several times before remembering the correct value. Thus, denial should be graceful and progressive. Unusual behavior should always be reported and an alert generated, but there should be rules that allow some flexibility, for example by restoring a user to good status after an elapsed period. This allows time for an administrator to receive the alert but restores the account to a usable level.

When any system is attacked, all other systems should temporarily convert to a reduced access mode. Any physical emergency should cause equally secure disaster recovery systems to take over, and the primary systems should shut down and enter a high-surveillance condition. This helps to protect against the tactic of attacking a system merely as a diversion, and while responders are diagnosing the attacked system, the real attack is performed—against another system. (See Section 5.2.4, "Reliance on Inadequate Protection.")

> ***PRINCIPLE: WHEN ANY SYSTEM IS ATTACKED, ALL OTHER SYSTEMS SHOULD TEMPORARILY CONVERT TO A HIGHLY SAFE REDUCED ACCESS MODE.***

An application should provide administrators with some tools for responding in a flexible way. For example, if the application automatically throttles requests when a denial of service is detected, the administrator should have the ability to make the throttling more specific by allowing all requests from certain groups of users to be handled and all others to be throttled.

PRINCIPLE: PROVIDE CONVENIENT API FOR INTRUSION RESPONSE.

Applications should ideally provide fine-grained application-level monitoring so that if an administrator is alerted to suspicious activity, they can observe what the suspect user is currently doing from an application perspective, giving much more information. That makes it possible for an administrator to make a better decision about whether further investigation or escalation of alert is needed.

PRINCIPLE: PROVIDE FINE-GRAINED MONITORING.

It is important that application-level monitoring (or any kind of monitoring) not permit an administrator to circumvent application-provided privacy protections that protect sensitive application data. Thus, sensitive data that is normally encrypted when stored should not be viewable by an administrator who is monitoring for a potential security breach.

Application-level monitoring should also provide the administrator with general information about activity, such as which users are currently using the system and what kinds of things they are doing, how much resources they are using, and so on.

10.6 Usability

The user sometimes has to make a decision that affects authorization policy or authentication configuration. This occurs infrequently, and it is highly possible that the user will be somewhat, if not completely, confused. It is well documented that a frustrated user will make a hasty decision in such a decision—the most expeditious decision being to do whatever leads to the quickest solution. This might be the wrong decision.

VITTI: So did you take care of that thing I asked you about?
MANGANO: Yeah, I took care of it.
VITTI: How about that other thing?
MANGANO: I'm waiting for that first thing to come through. I can't move until it does.
...
VITTI: Exactly. (to Ben) Don't repeat any of that to anyone.
BEN: What? The first thing or the second thing?
—from *Analyze This*, screenplay by Peter Tolan, Harold Ramis, and Kenneth Lonergan, July 1998.

It is extremely important that when a user decision is required, the user is given sufficient, clear, concise, and easy-to-understand information to ensure that they truly understand the decision that they are making. Such decisions should be identified and given special attention so that appropriate "help" screens can be designed or other aids to provide the user with the guidance that is needed. Note that if a user is not sure of the actual effect that his decision will have, he will feel frustrated and tend to make the most expeditious decision. Therefore, do not over-simplify information, but instead attempt to present it as clearly and unambiguously as possible. In particular, review the wording of all messages to make sure that the user might not become confused by ambiguous pronouns or poorly structured grammar, such as "Sets group policy for the user to point to it." Programmers are notorious for such ambiguous messages, yet programmers are the ones who know the true consequence of a selection.

PRINCIPLE: MAKE SURE THE USER IS SUFFICIENTLY INFORMED.

In general, follow the guidelines in Table 10.3.

Table 10.3 Guidelines for Instructional Messages

Avoid pronouns if there is *any possibility* of ambiguity.
Be specific; do not assume that the user understands vague references based on the context.
Strictly *adhere* to correct grammar. Poor grammar causes ambiguity.[5]

5 There are many wonderful English grammar resources on the Internet. For example, the Purdue Online Writing Lab's Web site at `http://owl.english.purdue.edu/handouts/grammar/`, and the Connecticut Community College online Guide to Grammar and Writing at `http://webster.commnet.edu/grammar/`. See also Peter Neumann's insightful discussion of eliminating ambiguity in the use of the word "only," online at `http://www.csl.sri.com/neumann/only.html`.

Do not rely on the user's knowledge of grammar. A user who has poor grammar should still understand messages.

Tell the user the consequences of a choice or action.

Tell the user the consequences of *not* making a choice—i.e., of canceling the current action that requires a choice.

Tell the user whether they will be able to reverse a choice later.

Tell the user if a choice or action is potentially unsafe in any way.

Tell the user where they can find more information if they are confused.

If too much information is required and the user might become confused, it means that the system is too complex for the user, and perhaps some functions should be broken up so that the user is not faced with such complex decisions. Regardless, the answer is not to deprive the user of information as that leads to a confused and frustrated user: "I wish this system would tell me what it actually does if I click 'yes'!"

Users should also be kept informed of activity that falls under their purview. This is important for the purpose of alerting the user to the fact that their information has been compromised. For example, in an online application in which the user maintains an account, apprise the user of recent account activity when the user logs on. Alert the user (for example, via a small but noticeable alert message) when sensitive data has been accessed, such as the user's profile or any data that might be used for account holder verification.

PRINCIPLE: INFORM THE USER OF ACTIVITY.

Users should be instructed ahead of time of the means by which they will be contacted in an emergency. This should be done in such a way that they will actually remember. For example, a new user should be made familiar with the organization's domain name, and each time they log on they might be told that all communication will come from that domain.[6] Future contact should then be to alert them that they have a message waiting and to provide them with a location in the organization's domain to retrieve the message. All this is to prevent spoofs of the organization, to avoid so-called "bank examiner" frauds by which the

6 This will not prevent domain name spoofing, however. See "Spoofing" in Section 5.1.12.

user is duped into thinking that a communication is from the organization, instructing the user to do something that exposes their account. (See Section 5.2.5, "Instilling Undeserved Trust.")

PRINCIPLE: EDUCATE USERS OF THE MEANS BY WHICH THEY WILL BE CONTACTED IN AN EMERGENCY.

Of course, users should always be immediately alerted if any illegitimate activity that affects them is detected. This is with the proviso that the alert is guaranteed to be received by the user and not by the intruder. For example, if it is detected that an account is compromised, it is not sufficient (and may be inadvisable) to leave a message for the user when they next log on. Instead, it is preferable to contact them via alternate means—a means that is not modifiable via their account because any information within their account might have been changed by the intruder in order to prevent the user from being notified.

PRINCIPLE: RELIABLY INFORM THE USER OF STATUS.

> Widely available tools make sophisticated attack methods available to unsophisticated hackers.

Users often do not fully appreciate security issues. The reason is that security attacks seem complex, and many users do not realize how simple apparently complex attacks can be to execute using widely available tools. They assume that no one would go to so much trouble when in fact it might be little trouble at all to exploit a user's laxness.

For this reason, it is important that security features be clear and simple to administer and use for both administrators and ordinary users. Security settings should not be buried away and hard to understand. They should be up front and visible so that the user is given an accurate impression of their importance.

PRINCIPLE: DO NOT DESIGN SECURITY-RELATED FEATURES THAT ARE ONEROUS TO USE.

This is sometimes referred to as the principle of "psychological acceptability."[5]

The user should be presented with a clear and consistent set of security concepts that map clearly to the user interface. It is often best if security features are consolidated so that the user can go to one user interface panel to configure security. The effect of each setting should also be clear so that the user does not have to guess what the outcome is of changing a setting. Try to avoid vague aggregate settings such as "high security" and "low security" unless these configurations are going to be reviewed and approved by an administrator, because users will not be able to determine if "low" covers their concerns or if "high" prevents them from being able to do things that they need to do. According to Robert Harris, good directions must include the elements listed in Table 10.4.[7]

Table 10.4 Elements of Good Directions

1. Time. How long will each step take? Examples: "This part of disk preparation requires about ten minutes."
2. Anticipation. What should be happening? What should be expected as the process or journey proceeds? Describe the things for the user to look forward to. Examples: "When connection is made, you will hear a beep."
3. Failure. What event will warn of failure? What remedy should be applied in such a case? Examples: ..."If the page preview reveals too large a space between columns, check your right margin setting in the document, to make sure it is the width of just one column."...

Do not assume that users will be able to fundamentally change the way their organization works in order to be able to implement security technology, even if the technology is very important.

PRINCIPLE: DO NOT ASSUME THAT USERS WILL BE ABLE TO INSTITUTE COMPLEX PROCESSES OR CONTROLS.

This is the mistake that was made with PKI technology. It was assumed that users would be willing to take a top-down approach to privacy and security and that corporate security administrators would be able to take a top-down approach to infrastructure and would have the ability to slowly and

7 Excerpted from a whitepaper by Prof. Robert Harris, "Human-Factor Phenomena in Problem Solving," December 31, 2001. Available online at `http://www.virtualsalt.com/crebok3a.htm`.

methodically draft technology policies, integrate those policies with business policies, and coordinate all this with vendors and partners. What a tall order indeed, especially given the increasingly fast pace and decentralized nature of business.

In general, centralized approaches to technology introduction have difficulty in today's service-focused businesses. If you require centralized or top-down approaches for your technology introduction to be successful, you should make sure that you have the resources and mindshare to see it through.

Sometimes an application's function is inherently complex. In that case, it is counter-productive to minimize the complexity. Instead, a proactive approach should be taken to educate users and to make the function seem normal and necessary. It is the author's opinion that PKI technology has not gained a foothold for end-user applications, such as email, because users were not adequately educated about it.[8] Users saw tabs or buttons such as "Security" in their email programs, and the settings had very limited and confusing explanations. PKI is inherently complex, so the minimalist approach used by email programs did little to educate—in fact, it scared users away because they did not understand what they saw. If instead PKI had been promoted as an aspect of secure email and good tutorials were provided, more users might have learned about it. Thus, it is important that complex functions not be over-simplified or "dumbed down," but instead they should be accompanied by aids that emphasize their value and help the users to relate to and understand them.

Complex functions should be accompanied by aids that emphasize their value and help the users to relate to and understand them.

Processing overhead is another usability factor to consider. The algorithms needed to implement flexible authentication and authorization models can be very complex. If that processing represents a significant fraction of the processing needed to perform a transaction, there is the risk that security features will be blamed for the slowness of the application.

PRINCIPLE: REQUIRE SECURITY FEATURES TO OPERATE EFFICIENTLY AND QUICKLY.

8 I also believe that certificate authorities overcharged for their services while failing to promote those services, stifling adoption by mainstream users. Further, businesses refused to adopt more user-friendly PKI implementations such as PGP.

A common source of overhead is network latency between the "point of enforcement" (where credentials are checked and where an authorization check is made) and where policy and credentials are stored. For this reason, commercial systems rely heavily on caching of these kinds of data, and lots of tuning and testing is needed to design these systems so that they operate efficiently.

An important consideration when designing such caches is the extent to which updates need to be synchronous. See the discussion on "Caching of Authorization Data" in Section 7.21.1.

The basic authorization model is important to consider as well. A complex authorization system may result in more overhead in each access–overhead that needs to be justified by the application's security requirements.

Data consistency and integrity are important usability and confidence factors. Users can become confused when data is out of sync or when a cache is not refreshed immediately after a change. For example, suppose you sign up for a payment processing system that requires that you enter your contact information. After entering this, it asks for your credit card number, and you realize that it requires that your contact information match your credit card billing information, rather than allowing them to be different. You then try to go back in your browser, but the pages have expired, and so in desperation you close the browser and try to sign up again, but this time it will not let you sign up because you have already signed up, but provided incomplete information, and the Web site allowed the incomplete information to be recorded. That indeed would be a poor design, but that is precisely what happened to the author when trying to sign up for a very prominent Internet payment service a few years ago. This kind of behavior will make the user question the integrity of the Web site and makes them mistrust that their information is maintained accurately.

PRINCIPLE: CAREFULLY CONSIDER THE OPERATIONAL EFFECTS OF INCONSISTENCY.

Users who have roles that require them to perform security-sensitive procedures are often pressured to shortcut a procedure in the interest of time and operational efficiency for their company. Unfortunately, requests to skip procedures are a social engineering technique to have procedures relaxed just long enough to do something subversive. (See Section 5.2.2, "Emotional Pressure.") Because it is often unavoidable that some procedures will need to be expedited at some point, it is important that any deviation from a security procedure be recorded and that there is accountability, especially if the request is on short notice. Accountability tends to make people check their sources with more diligence.

Principle: Any Unavoidable Deviations from Security-Sensitive Procedures Should Be Fully Traceable.

In this principle, "traceable" means that procedural deviations should be recorded and all parties should be well known or be very reliably authenticated—more so than usual.

Unclear accountability can be a source of pressure to deviate.

Unclear accountability can be a source of pressure to deviate. For example, if a security procedure must be circumvented in order to expedite approval of a transaction with a new customer, the security administrator deserves to know who is taking responsibility if procedures are circumvented and something goes awry. Otherwise, there will be a tendency to always bow to sales-side pressure, because that is where the power is in most organizations.

Procedures that enroll new users or authenticate new parties should never be skipped unless advance notice is provided.

Procedures that *enroll new users* or *authenticate new parties* should never be skipped unless advance notice is provided or there is very strong alternative evidence that the parties are legitimate and senior management agrees to the deviation from procedure.

10.7 Maintainability

When designing secure software, make sure to compile a list of any known vulnerabilities in any components that you are using. This allows you to design workarounds or avoid features that have known weaknesses and allows you to take steps to prevent those weaknesses from being accessible to users. Of course, any available security patches should be installed.

Principle: Maintain Awareness of Vulnerabilities in Components.

This principle relates to deployment and administration, which is not the subject of this book. However, it also affects design and implementation because much software has weaknesses that can be mitigated if you design in certain safeguards, and it affects testing because security testers should be aware of the kinds of vulnerabilities that have been found in similar products.

10.8 Summary

This chapter focused on application design issues that affect deployment and operation. The limitations of current deployment scenarios were discussed. Responsibility for deployment planning, restoration design, and application features that affect the security of a deployment were discussed. Design practices that tend to subvert these considerations were discussed. The need to an application to provide for monitoring and management was discussed, along with the impact that these concerns have on security and reliability. The importance of usability was related to its affect on assurance. Lastly, maintainability was considered as an important assurance aspect.

The next chapter introduces overarching design patterns and approaches that affect reliability and begins the process of integrating reliability-related design issues with security issues.

10.9 Exercises

1. An application development team designs a new application for their own use. The application must communicate with a server that is outside of the company, using a protocol that is blocked by the company's firewall. In order to circumvent this, the application team "tunnels" the protocol using HTTP, to make it appear to the firewall that the protocol is merely browser traffic. What is wrong with this approach? List at least two alternative approaches that the application team might have used in order to reduce risk.

2. A Web application receives requests from the Internet. The application requires users to sign up to obtain a password, and from that point on they must log on using the password. The application checks the user's password each time a user attempts to log on. To do this, the application must look in a database. Does this approach present a vulnerability with respect to a denial of service attack? What could be done to reduce that vulnerability?
3. A client-server application incorporates intrusion detection at several points. If suspicious user activity is detected, the user is alerted and an operator is alerted via a telecommunications page. List at least two aspects of the approach that are problematic and explain why.
4. A server application has crashed, and operators have discovered that its configuration has become corrupt for unknown reasons. The operators begin the process of reloading the configuration from a staging area copy. What safeguards should be in place to ensure that the reloaded application is uncompromised?

Answers and hints for these exercises can be found at `http://www.assuredbydesign.com/haa/`.

CHAPTER 11

COMPOSITIONAL INTEGRITY

"It has been said: The whole is more than the sum of its parts. It is more correct to say that the whole is something else than the sum of its parts, because summing up is a meaningless procedure, whereas the whole-part relationship is meaningful." –Kurt Koffka, 1935: Principles of Gestalt Psychology, p. 176.

11.1 Composition Concepts

Composition is a core concept for writing reliable and secure software. An object is *composed of* other objects if it *exclusively contains* those objects, in the sense that if the containing object is deleted, moved, or modified, the contained objects are automatically affected as such because they are part of the containing object. The containing object logically owns the objects that are a part of it. A compositional relationship can also be thought of in terms of ownership: The containing object owns the objects that it contains.

In C++, this is a familiar concept because it is possible to define C++ classes that actually *contain* other classes. In contrast, Java does not allow this. Java classes can contain only *references* to other objects. A Java object reference is merely a pointer to another object. Therefore, an instance of the following class *points to*—i.e., references—an Integer object (or it might point to null):

An object is *composed of* other objects if it exclusively contains them.

```
class C
{
        Integer i;
        public C(Integer i) { this.i = i; }
}
```

This method of embedding objects is not composition—it is aggregation. An object aggregates other objects if it references them.[1] Instances of class C do not contain the Integer object—rather, they contain only a reference to the Integer object and, therefore, an instance of C is an aggregation of one Integer object.

Multiple instances of C can contain the same reference. For example:

```
Integer i = new Integer(5);
C ca = new C(i);
C cb = new C(i);
```

In the previous example, ca and cb each reference different objects containing the same instance of i. (Separate references to the same object instance are called "aliases.") This could create a problem if i's value could be changed—i.e., if it were "mutable." (A mutable object is one that can be modified.) The Integer class is immutable—after an Integer instance is created, its value cannot be modified, and it does not reference (point to) anything that can be modified. (The latter allows us to say that it is "deeply immutable.")

If Integer were mutable, ca could modify i's internal value. This might cause problems for cb, especially if cb has already read the int value of i and is assuming that the int value will not

1 Some authors use the term "aggregation" to mean what I am defining as composition. However, the more prevalent use of the terms composition and aggregation are consistent with the definitions here.

change. In order to avoid ambiguities such as this (and consequent difficult-to-diagnose bugs), most of the value object types in package java.lang (i.e., Integer, Long, Double, String, and so on) are defined to be immutable—that is, they have no methods that can modify their value after they are created. (Note that StringBuffer is not immutable because StringBuffer has methods that can modify the contents of a StringBuffer instance.)

Composition implies containership. The term "composable" is a more specialized term that implies retention of properties. (See Section 7.20.1, "Composability," for a definition of composable.)

The "Composite" pattern is a special form of composition.

11.1.1 Related Patterns

The "Composite" pattern is a *special form of composition* in that it requires that all members of the composite implement a *shared interface*. This allows the composite to be manipulated using the same methods that can be used to manipulate the members of the composite. See [1] and [2] for a discussion of the Composite pattern.

Please note that this book often uses the term "composite object." As used here, this term is a general reference to object composition and does not refer specifically to the "Composite" pattern.

The "Decorator" pattern provides a technique for dynamic object extension if the programming language does not support it.[2] Using this pattern, you can embed an object within another object in order to add new methods (or override existing methods) to the first object. Thus, the new object is composed of the first object and adds additional state or methods or both. The new object implements the first object's interface plus additional methods or interfaces. It delegates method calls to the first object and also provides new methods that can be called. For this to work, the first object must extend an abstract class or implement an interface that the new decorator object can extend or implement. For a detailed explanation of this pattern, see [3] and [4].

2 Java has a feature called "dynamic proxy" that serves this purpose. However, it is an SPI and is not directly supported by the language syntax; hence, it is difficult to use.

11.1.2 Value Objects

In the previous example of class "C," if we decide to consider C to represent a *value object class*, we are implicitly saying an instance of C is composed of any objects that it references. That is, any referenced objects are not shared unless they are deeply immutable.

The essential concept of a *value object* is that it is designed to be passed as a "value" and is therefore self-contained. That is, if you follow all of the references that it contains, none of those references are to objects that you did not intend to be part of the "value object." Note that the boundary of a value object is subjective: It depends on what the programmer considers to be part of the composite "value." This is because Java provides "aggregation" rather than "composition," and so programmers have to simulate composition using other means, such as by making objects immutable or merely by not sharing them.

A value object is designed so that it can be safely passed to or returned by methods and safely referenced by other objects. No part of a value object is modifiable unexpectedly by another object. Consider Figure 11.1.

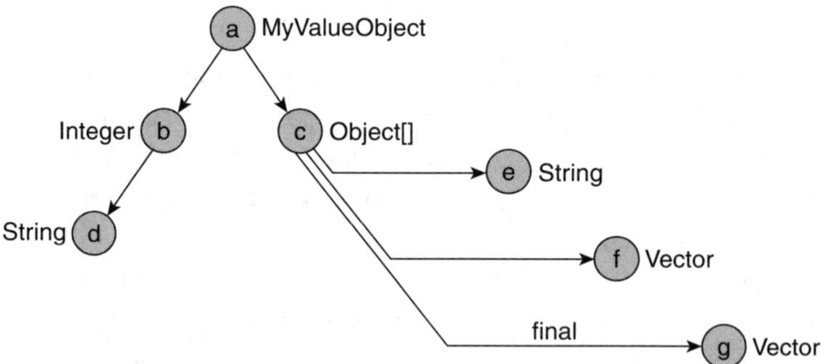

Figure 11.1
Example of a composite object.

In this figure, a programmer could safely treat the entire set of objects { a, b, c, d, e, f, g } as a single value object. That is because these objects do not reference any other objects. However, care must be taken that the vectors f and g do not reference any objects outside of { a...g }.

Could { b, d } be treated as a value object? Yes, because { b, d } do not reference any other objects.

The fact that the reference to g is final does not ensure that { a...g } is a value object. To know, one must know what things g references. If g might reference objects outside of { a...g }, { a...g } cannot safely be treated as a value object.

DESIGN PATTERN: VALUE OBJECT

Related Patterns

The Value Object pattern is widely documented in various forms, for example in [5] and "Transfer Object" in [6]. It is defined as well because of its importance for the reader to understand it.

Context

Object data needs to be exchanged between two different components.

Problem

When an object is transferred by reference from one component to another, there is a risk that each component retains references to (aliases for) the transferred object or objects embedded within or referenced by the transferred object. This can result in the potential for one component to change a value that is being used by the other component by using the aliased references.

Forces

The communicating components may be from different security domains, so there may be concerns related to exposing internal component features.

The communicating components may be written by different programmers, and the unintentional sharing of references to internal structures might introduce bugs.

Solution

Exchange a value object between the two communicating components.

A value object is a *self-contained object graph* that is deeply immutable, and that is held by only one component at a time. Thus, a value object contains no mutable references and no references to mutable objects outside of the graph. Implicit in this is the requirement that all the terminal leaves of the graph represent (1) constant language primitive (indivisible) value types, such as integer, float, and string; (2) arrays or collections of constant primitive value types or other value objects; or (3) references to external value objects that are deeply immutable (i.e., constants).

Because a value object contains no external references except for references to constants, its value or a reference to it can be transferred safely to another component, as if the value object were a primitive value.

A value object should not have aliases.

A value object should not have aliases—that is, its location should be known to only one component at a time. Practically speaking, an alias for a value object must sometimes exist for a short period when the object is created; however, in that case, a maximum of one thread of control should have access to a reference to the value object and no other component.

As an example, if a value object reference is returned by a method to a caller of the method, the component containing the method should not retain a reference to the value object, because it no longer has control of it. This is consistent with the notion of a value object as a "value": a value can be copied, but it does not make sense to have a reference to a value—one can have only a reference to a container for a value.

A value object is merely an object that behaves as if it were a native value: i.e., after you have it, you do not have to worry that its value will change on you.

This is not rocket science. A value object is merely an object that behaves as if it were a native value: i.e., after you have it, you do not have to worry that its value will change on you.

Structure

A value object is represented conceptually in Figure 11.2. Its root begins with the object at the left, and the value objects consist of the composition of all other objects connected via compositional links. These other objects are subordinate to their parent, and the graph of composition relationships is a strict hierarchy. Finally, each object in the composition must be immutable—enforced either through the programming language, through usage policy, or through some other means. The structure is depicted in Figure 11.2.

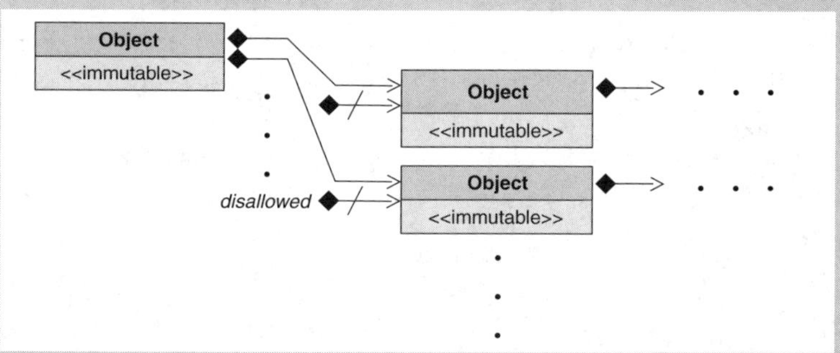

Figure 11.2 Structure.

Consequences

Complex values, consisting of objects, can be exchanged across components without concern that those values will change unexpectedly.

11.1.3 Cloning Risks

A clone operation is an operation that makes a copy of another object. The new copy has the same value as the original, according to the semantics of what is considered to be an identical (equal) value. The semantics of value equality vary from one kind of object (class) to another.

As explained earlier, a value copy should not contain embedded references to the original object's parts unless those parts are immutable. However, parts of an object might be sensitive and inappropriate for copying when the copy is to be *transported outside of the security domain.* In that case, a "safe" copy should be made that is not an identical copy but is functionally equivalent for the purposes of the intended user of the copy.

> Beware when transporting cloned objects outside of the security domain that created them.

As an example, consider an XML document that describes a service for both internal users and external users. Internal users might need to access parts of the document that specify information that is private to the organization, whereas this information needs to be stripped out when the document is sent to external users. Instead of maintaining separate versions of each document, it would be more secure to create a proxy that takes requests for the documents and provides the appropriate version. The proxy would, in effect, clone the internal version of the object, replacing sensitive tags with placeholders or equivalent tags that have values that can be exported to external users.

11.2 Object Allocation and Deallocation

Many programmers believe that the use of languages that provide automated memory reclamation eliminates memory leaks. Automated reclamation does indeed help, but does not completely eliminate leaks. Failure to ensure correct *order of deallocation* can also result in runtime failures or failures at shutdown, possibly corrupting data but at a minimum generating error messages within logs—not the sign of a high-assurance system.

Memory deallocation problems generally occur in two varieties: (1) dynamically allocated objects and (2) static lifetime objects—most commonly singletons. Dynamically allocated objects normally are either created on the thread stack or in the program heap. Static lifetime objects are normally created during the loading and initialization sequence of a library or class file.

11.2.1 Dynamically Allocated Objects

It is a gross misconception, held by many programmers, that languages that provide automated reclamation of allocated objects (i.e., "garbage collection") cannot have memory leaks. Memory leaks in programs written in these languages are indeed less frequent, but can and often do occur. It has been my experience that in programs written in languages with automatic garbage collection, the main sources of memory leaks are:

> It is a gross misconception that languages that provide garbage collection cannot have memory leaks.

1. Failure to nullify unneeded object references contained within long-lifetime objects. Ninety-nine times out of a hundred, the long-lifetime objects are collection objects.
2. Failure to release native resources that must be explicitly deallocated.

The ultimate cause of these two classes of problems is insufficient analysis, specifically a failure to identify which objects own and therefore are responsible for the lifecycle (creation and destruction) of other objects. Thus, let's look at the memory leak problem in terms of an object ownership and object lifecycle.

> The ultimate cause of most memory leaks is a failure to identify which objects own other objects.

When a Java method exits, any stack-based *object references* that were created by the method are deleted, often leaving unreferenced heap objects behind. This allows the garbage collector to subsequently infer that those heap objects are no longer needed, so they will be deleted. By comparison, C++ will actually run the destructors (including one for each supertype as well) of each *stack-based object* when the method that created it returns. In both cases, the effect is usually the same: Objects that should live only for the duration of the method call are reclaimed.

A problem arises if an object is logically composed of multiple child objects. The automated collection mechanism may deallocate the parent object, but not the children. This can occur in both the Java and C++ scenarios, because even in C++, child objects can be allocated separately using heap-allocation methods and can exist on the heap and not the runtime stack. In both languages, a component that deletes an object that it owns is responsible for ensuring that *all child objects that the deleted object owns* are deleted as well, and that all non-ownership references to the deleted objects are also nullified. Otherwise, objects can be left un-reclaimed in the case of Java, or dangling pointers can result in the case of C++.

A component that deletes an object that it owns is responsible for ensuring that all non-ownership references to the deleted object and its child objects are nullified.

Allocation and deallocation are the endpoints of the use of an object, and they should be logically linked in terms of the management of an object by the application. It is, therefore, useful to consider design patterns that enforce that linkage.

The most commonly used pattern for creating objects (besides the constructor pattern) is the Factory pattern [7]. The Factory pattern defines a class whose purpose is to create instances of a particular object type. This layer of abstraction is not always necessary, but it is useful in situations in which a client class must provide another object with a means of making copies of the client, thereby preventing circular compilation dependency between the client and the other object class.

Even though a factory creates objects, it normally does not retain ownership of those objects: Ownership is transferred to the factory client the moment the factory method returns. Thus, deletion of the created object is the responsibility of the client because it is the object's owner. Also, object destruction often occurs at a point far-removed from object creation. In fact, the factory instance might not even be identifiable or directly accessible at that point. This presents a dilemma: Object creation and destruction are logically separated.

Deletion of a factory-created object is the responsibility of the owner of the object—not its creator.

If the object is simple, this is not usually a problem. On the other hand, if the object or one of its child objects contains references to resources that must be deallocated, or if there is the possibility of a growing list or memory leak, or worse—invalid references that might be interpreted as valid—there is justification for using a pattern that ensures consistency across creation and deletion.

Any factory-created instance should be able to identify the factory that created it.

A solution to the factory identification problem is to ensure that any object created by a factory "remembers" what factory created it. Thus, any factory-created instance should include a reference to the factory.[3] If the factory has a destroy(instance) method, the factory can be used to cleanly remove the instance by calling instance.getFactory().destroy(instance). This book calls such a factory a "lifecycle factory" because it reclaims the objects that it creates.

The advantage of this approach is that any resource resolution or allocation that was performed by the factory can be remembered by the factory so that cleanup can be performed appropriately without burdening the application or the object instance itself with knowing how to clean the object up. In addition, the factory can recursively call destroy() on each child object, if there are child objects. This is merely the kind of logic that would appear in a destructor, for languages that have such a feature. Unfortunately, a reliable destructor mechanism is not available in all object-oriented languages.

Even if a lifecycle factory mechanism ensures that all composite child objects are removed, it is the responsibility of the owner of a composite object to initiate deletion and ensure that all non-owning relationships are nullified. A destructor cannot anticipate which clients will use or retain references to an object, so it cannot deal with nullifying inbound references. Such inbound references should be nullified before the object is destroyed, because destruction is the object's endpoint, and the object does not exist after that point.

The object deletion method should be used to reset the primary reference to the object.

When deleting a composite object, non-ownership references should be nullified first, and then finally the ownership reference, of which there should be only one (because an object can have only one owner at any point in time). To ensure that the ownership reference is deleted, it is useful to have the lifecycle factory's destroyInstance() method return a null value if it succeeds, which can be used to reset the primary reference to the object. For example, the following code attempts to delete an object, and the reference to the object is automatically set to null if the deletion succeeds:

3 The reference should be secure when appropriate. For example, if the factory is contained within a secure resource, the reference should merely identify the resource, rather than the internal factory object.

```
// Create a new instance of SomeType...
SomeType instance = someTypeLifecycleFactory.create(...args);
...

// Now time to say goodbye...
try {
instance = (instance.getFactory()).destroy(instance); // returns null
}
catch (CannotDestroy ex) {
...
}
```

This is a lot of trouble to go to for object deallocation. The goal of memory management is to make it as transparent as possible to programmers so that they can worry about their application logic instead of memory housekeeping. Object lifecycle management is justified only for complex objects that are composites or that have complex destruction requirements, such as the management of lists of objects, the closing of resource connections, or the return of objects to a pool. In the last case, the object is not actually destroyed, but is re-initialized so that it can be reused.

DESIGN PATTERN: LIFECYCLE FACTORY

Related Patterns

See also the Factory pattern [8], the Singleton pattern [9], the Manager pattern [10], the Destruction Managed Singleton pattern [11], and the Object Lifetime Manager pattern [12].

Context

An object has complex destruction requirements; for example, (1) the object is variable in size (such as a collection) and could potentially grow indefinitely or very large if deallocation is not performed properly, or (2) the object is a composite and some of its children have complex destruction requirements. The object's concrete type is not known ahead of time, or the factory used to create it is unknown. The object also might change ownership at least once during its lifetime.

Problem

Deallocation is critical to avoid a memory leak because the object can potentially grow to a large size. Deallocation is complex, so it must be encapsulated to make deallocation robust. Normally, deallocation would be performed by the object's owner, but the object might change owners during its lifetime. There is, therefore, no obvious place to encapsulate the deallocation logic.

Forces

Considerations of reliability mandate a robust approach to object deallocation.

Solution

Define a "lifecycle" factory that has methods for performing the destruction of the objects that it creates. For these purposes, a lifecycle factory has create() and destroy(<type>) methods. The create() method creates and returns an instance of the type that the factory produces, on behalf of another component that becomes the owner of the objects that are created. The destroy(<type>) method consumes an object that the factory previously created and returns null. Either method may throw an exception, depending on the kinds of errors that might occur during construction or destruction.

The lifecycle factory also has an initialization method and a termination method to initialize and terminate the operation of the factory, respectively. These may throw exceptions as well. In particular, the terminate() method may throw an exception indicating that the termination did not complete but timed out in some manner. These methods merely start and stop the operation of the factory: *They do not affect the objects created by the factory.* The latter is the responsibility of the owner of those objects.

The objects created by the factory should implement an interface that defines a method for obtaining a reference to the factory. In Figure 11.3, this is depicted by the interface "Manufactured." Thus, any object created by the factory can later provide a reference to the factory when required to do so for the purpose of destroying the object. This reference should be secure; thus, if the factory is protected by a gateway, the reference returned should be a secure proxy. If the factory is protected by a reference monitor, the reference returned should be monitorable for access rights.

It is extremely important that an object be "decommissioned" before it is destroyed. That is, the object's owner should *notify all non-owning users of the object that it will no longer be available, and wait for them to acknowledge it*. This should happen in an application-specific way. For example, it might involve waiting until all transactions involving the object completes or fails; or it might involve synchronously notifying a set of listeners that they should disconnect from the object. Basically, the application must stop using the object, and then—*and only then*—the object's owner can destroy it.

If there is any possibility that a user of the object might not acknowledge notification, this condition must be handled by use of a timer to ensure that the object can never be deallocated because it is being used—causing the thread to hang.♦ Ideally, such a timer should be included in the function of the terminate() method so that the caller does not have to implement it.

It is extremely important that an object be "decommissioned" before it is destroyed.

♦ The issue of timing a blocking call is discussed under the principle "Employ a Timer to Abort Any Resource Call That Could Potentially 'Hang'" in Section 13.11.1, "Resources That Do Not Reliably Timeout," and in Section 12.2.4, "Thread Interruption."

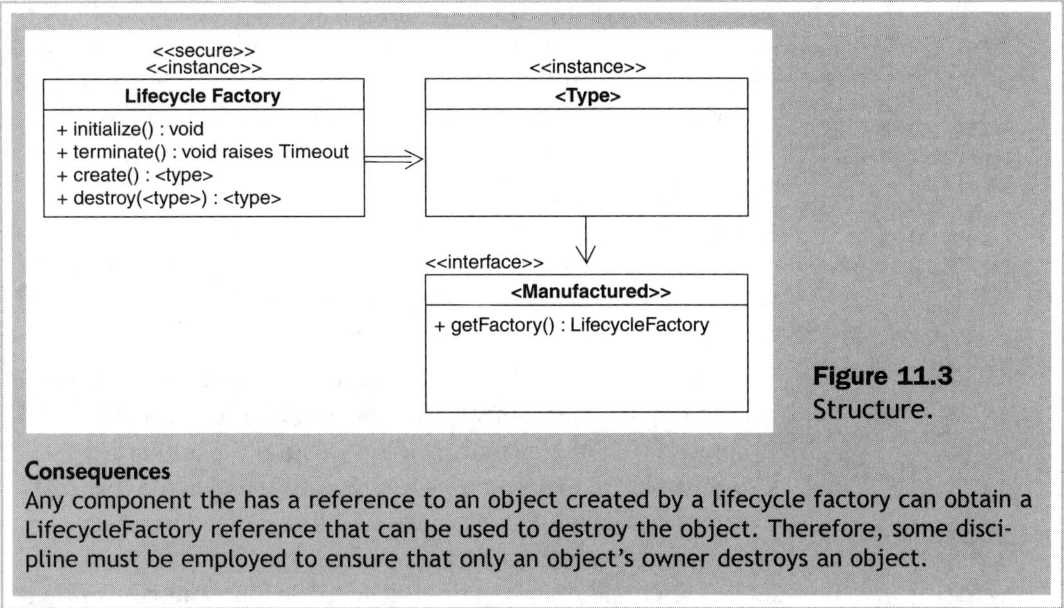

Figure 11.3 Structure.

Consequences
Any component the has a reference to an object created by a lifecycle factory can obtain a LifecycleFactory reference that can be used to destroy the object. Therefore, some discipline must be employed to ensure that only an object's owner destroys an object.

11.2.2 Static Lifetime Objects and Singletons

Static-lifetime objects are those that exist until a program or service terminates and they are cleaned up by the act of termination. Static objects are sometimes created using the Singleton pattern [13], which provides for lazy creation to prevent all static objects from being created during program startup and instead creates them only as soon as they are actually needed.

Static initialization is a powerful mechanism that works fine for most simple applications. It is often inadequate for more complex applications, however. One problem with static initialization, even using a Singleton pattern, is that object destruction is not controlled and not always reliable.[4] Another problem is that an object's destructor—if one exists—does not always have all the information it needs to properly retire the object. A third problem is that if there are bi-directional dependencies across static objects, the order of their destruction is important, and the programmer must take this order into account. A final

4 For example, Java does not guarantee any particular order with regard to the execution of an object's finalize() method, even for objects that are only referenced by static references. See the Java Language Specification, Second Edition, §12.6. Available online at `http://java.sun.com/docs/books/jls/second_edition/html/j.title.doc.html`.

If there are bi-directional dependencies across static objects, the order of their destruction is important, and the programmer must take this order into account.

Static initialization of an object precludes pooling the object.

Static lifetime objects often serve as owning or non-owning containers for other objects that have more limited lifetime.

issue is that reliance on static initialization provided by the language makes it impossible to deploy the component in an environment in which the component is pooled or reused, and static initialization is therefore not performed each time the component must be re-initialized. For example, a Java Enterprise Session Bean is statically initialized only the first time it is loaded, but each client that receives the bean from a pool expects that the bean is freshly initialized. Therefore, static initialization does not work for a Java Session Bean, and initialization methods must be used instead.

Static lifetime objects often serve as owning or non-owning containers for other objects that have more limited lifetime. For example, a window manager might maintain a static process-global structure that contains a reference to each window that exists at any time. If these entries are not properly destroyed (all ownership links traversed and destroyed as well) when windows are closed, the list might grow over time and constitute a memory leak.

Some general requirements that should be considered for the creation and destruction of static lifetime objects are listed in Table 11.1.

Table 11.1 General Requirements for Creation and Destruction of Static Lifetime Objects

They should have single, well-defined points of creation and destruction. This ensures that creation and destruction are performed in a consistent manner throughout an application.
The point of creation and point of destruction should be defined close together; for example, in a single "manager" class. This ensures that creation and destruction strategy are designed together.
The points of creation and destruction should be reliable: (1) Creation should be guaranteed to have occurred if an exception is not thrown, and (2) destruction logic should be guaranteed to be invoked before program termination.
The strategy for creation and destruction should work regardless of how the component is deployed and not rely on language static initialization rules. This enhances reusability if the application is redeployed as a service or pooled object.
The order of destruction should be guaranteed to occur in the reverse order of creation. This provides a deterministic sequence that can be relied upon for the deallocation of resources.

If destruction of a static object fails, the failure should be reported, but an unhandled exception should not be thrown. This enables program termination to complete as cleanly as possible if one particular resource fails to close properly.

The initialization of static objects should not unduly slow program start-up. Lazy instantiation is the most common technique for achieving quick startup, as well as organizing program components so that only those resources that are actually needed at any time are accessed.

Re-initialization after shutdown should be controlled and prevented if necessary or permitted if possible. This ensures that erroneous attempts to re-start something that cannot be re-started are detected and prevented.

Classes should not be required to make their static objects visible to a global manager or to other classes. This allows static objects to have only the visibility that they need without having to make them publicly visible just so that they can be seen by infrastructure components, such as a deallocation manager.

Again, not all applications require all these features. Indeed, many simple applications work fine if all static objects are merely initialized during class loading and destroyed as part of application termination.

The "Delegating Lifecycle Manager" pattern that is presented next addresses all the requirements mentioned in Table 11.1. The pattern defines a static Delegating Lifecycle Manager object, which is referred to here as a "manager" object for short. The manager has responsibility for the startup and shutdown of all the application's components.

As part of an application's startup, it calls startup() on the manager. In response, the manager notifies all subcomponents to start, and those subcomponents in response instantiate or initialize the object factories that they are responsible for.

As part of its shutdown operation, the manager notifies all subcomponents to stop, and in response they notify each of their threads to terminate, and catch and handle any exceptions that might result from early termination. Each subcomponent then utilizes its object factories to deallocate any static lifetime objects that it owns.

This approach retains localized control of object creation and destruction, while providing global coordination.

DESIGN PATTERN: DELEGATING LIFECYCLE MANAGER

Related Patterns

See also the Manager pattern [14], the Destruction Managed Singleton pattern [15], and the Object Lifetime Manager pattern [16].

Context

An application requires multiple static lifetime objects belonging to several different hierarchically nested components. Some of the components have bi-directional or circular references. Further, some components might need to wait for certain processes in other components to complete before they can be destroyed.

Problem

The order of destruction is important for a graceful shutdown of the application. There is, therefore, a need for a coordinating entity that shuts down the various components and then destroys them after they are not being referenced.

Solution

Define a singleton Manager class that has startup() and shutdown() methods. The startup() method should notify all the application's components to start, and those components in response instantiate or initialize the object factories (see the "Lifecycle Factory" pattern discussed in Section 11.2.1, "Dynamically Allocated Objects") for which they are responsible.

The manager's shutdown() method should notify all components to stop. In response, each component should (1) stop all the subcomponents that it owns, (2) nullify its references to other components, (3) cleanly stop all of the threads that it controls, and (4) terminate all its factories. The ordering and specifics of the implementation of these steps depends on the component.

A subcomponent may employ its own lifecycle manager in order to coordinate the shutdown of its own subcomponents. This creates a hierarchy of lifecycle managers, even though the lifecycle managers in such a hierarchy are not directly connected.

The pattern is depicted in Figure 11.4.

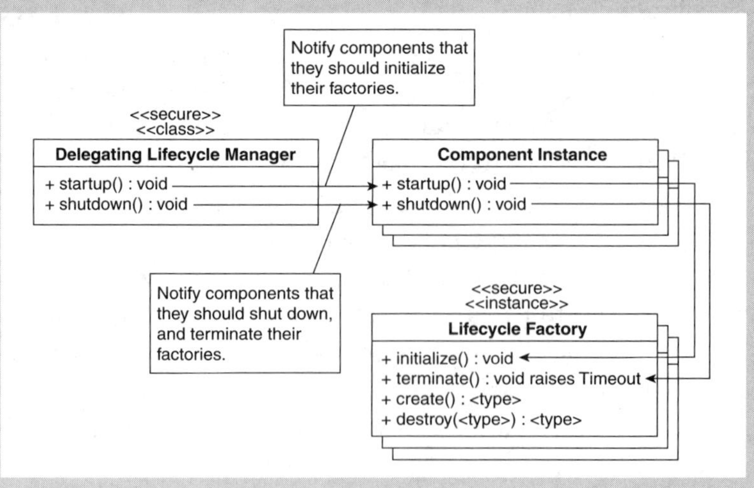

Figure 11.4
Structure.

Consequences
The application can be shut down without any stack traces on the console and can ensure that all resources are closed properly, with dependencies between components removed in a preconceived order. Shutdown of subsystems is decoupled from but coordinated by shutdown of the entire system.

11.3 Component Roles and Contracts

An established concept of object-oriented programming is that an object definition should clearly define what the object is responsible for doing [17]. The object-oriented design methodology known as "responsibility-driven design" [18] requires that every object method should perform only one, well-defined task, and delegate other tasks that it is responsible for. For every logical operation it is, therefore, possible to identify a single method that is responsible for that operation. This approach provides a separation of concerns—an important tenet of aspect-oriented programming—and reduces complexity by factoring separate operations into separate methods.

Unfortunately, in the real world of application programming, object responsibilities are seldom defined in a precise manner. The reason seems to be that designs evolve, and application programmers are too busy to sit back and reflect on object responsibilities as the work progresses, let alone go back and document those responsibilities. Component responsibilities are an extremely important aspect of an application's architecture, so this shortfall has deep consequences in terms of the clarity of the design and the implementation's maintainability, reliability, and security (see Section 7.19, "Domain Integrity").

It is, therefore, extremely important that an application's designers are held responsible for continually thinking through component roles and responsibilities as a design evolves and documenting the decisions that are made as a result. The development methodology should include provisions to ensure that this occurs.

PRINCIPLE: CLEARLY DEFINE THE ROLES AND RESPONSIBILITIES OF EACH COMPONENT.

Some of the aspects of roles and responsibilities that should be considered for a component are listed in Table 11.2.

Table 11.2 Aspects of Roles and Responsibilities That Should Be Considered for a Component

What kinds of errors should be handled?
What kinds of information should be propagated by errors?
On which other modules, packages, or components may the component depend?
What other modules, packages, or components should be able to access the component? How is that access and visibility restricted or enforced?
What functional responsibilities does the component have?
Does the component contain or access sensitive attributes or functions?
What is the expected lifetime of the component when it is used—for example, is it expected to be instantiated statically?
What are the assumptions about the component's invocation context (i.e., the responsibilities of that context); for example, the existence of a transaction, a security context, or environmental properties?
Are there assumptions about prerequisite actions (for example, that security checks have been made or that data validation has been performed before invoking the component)?
What transient or persistent side effects does the component have?
Does the component access monitored or exclusive resources, such as semaphores, database tables, and so on?

The assumed roles and responsibilities of the environment in which the component is instantiated, invoked, deployed, and shared are all important semantics of the component's design, as are the responsibilities of the component to that environment and its roles within the environment.

Along the same lines, the well-established paradigm of "design by contract" [19, 20] requires that an object definition should clearly specify the behavior of the object in terms of the conditions that must hold when an object is accessed and those that must be upheld by the object. Such "pre-" and "post-conditions" are often implemented as tests within an object's methods.

An important aspect of design by contract is ensuring that input arguments are valid. The importance of this has already been discussed in the context of security, under the principles "Employ a Strongly Typed Language and Design Approach for the Interface" and "Validate Anything Received from Untrusted Sources" in Sections 7.13.1, "Type Safety," and 7.17.4, "Validation of Context Data," respectively, and it is equally important for reliability as well.

The validation of inputs must be done in a manner that properly handles any errors that might occur during validation. If an input argument is found to be invalid, the method should throw an exception. However, the validation process itself should not fail. If input validation requires performing operations that might themselves incur an error, those operations should be performed with an error handler. The criteria for what kinds of errors should be handled are discussed later in detail, in Section 18.2.1, "Ensuring That All Situations Are Handled."

> Input validation code should trap any normal or lifecycle errors that might occur during validation.

Any exception raised by the method should accurately report which input argument (or arguments) is (are) problematic, regardless of whether the validation process succeeded or failed.

PRINCIPLE: SAFELY VALIDATE ALL INPUTS TO EACH METHOD.

Input arguments to a method should be typed as specifically as possible. Do not use general-purpose types in order to escape from the type-safety of the programming language. For example, do not use integer codes or string values when it is possible to use an enumeration type instead, and do not use a general object type (for example, "Object" in Java) when it is possible to declare and use an abstract type (for example, a Java interface type) instead. Similarly, do not use arrays or sequences of general purpose types in order to add extensibility to an interface. Instead, it is far preferable to require the array elements to meet type-safe criteria, even if changes mean re-compilation. The use of language-supported "generic" or "template" features to achieve type safety while retaining a generic quality is strongly preferable to using general-purpose types.

> Do not use general-purpose types in order to escape from the type-safety of the programming language.

◆ This is related to the principle "Employ a Strongly Typed Language and Design Approach for the Interface" in Section 7.13.1, except that it emphasizes that the programmer should not subvert the language's type checking by using general purpose types.

PRINCIPLE: USE SPECIFIC ARGUMENT TYPES INSTEAD OF GENERAL-PURPOSE TYPES.◆

Components almost always contain internal state, so many methods of a component might be involved in updating that state. Methods that update internal state should be clearly identified as such, even if the actual updates are performed through delegation.

PRINCIPLE: METHODS THAT UPDATE STATE THAT IS ACCESSIBLE BEYOND THE SCOPE OF THE METHOD CALL SHOULD BE CLEARLY IDENTIFIED AS SUCH.

A component's internal state must be well-protected as part of the security domain of the component. (See Section 7.19.) It is also important that there be clarity with regard to which methods of the component update the component's state. Generally speaking, re-entrant methods do not update internal state. ("Reentrancy" is discussed in Chapter 12, "Concurrency.") Methods whose purpose is to query a component's state should not also update the component's state. Methods that do so are referred to as methods with "side effects." This is a very poor practice and can be a frequent source of unreliability.[5]

11.3.1 External Components or Systems

The published interfaces of critical external components or systems should never be trusted, but should be verified through the use of an automated test suite that validates the components. So-called "third party" components or systems often implement subtle behavior that is not included in published interfaces. Automation of this validation is important so that the external system can be re-validated for each release of the external system.

PRINCIPLE: VALIDATE EXTERNAL COMPONENTS.

5 Meyer has a similar principle, the "Command-Query Separation" principle. See [21], p. 751.

11.4 Summary

Composition is a critically important concept and design issue to comprehend and address within almost every software application, and is an issue that has a large impact on a number of issues related to security and reliability. This chapter provided a foundation with respect to composition that is important for understanding reliability issues for designing correct concurrent applications and reliable object-oriented transactions. Issues related to value objects and cloning were discussed, followed by the important topic of object lifecycle management. Component roles and responsibilities were then related to assurance.

The next chapter introduces the topic of concurrency, not only to discuss it in its own right and its role with regard to assurance, but to lay a foundation for the concept of transactional integrity, which is discussed in subsequent chapters.

11.5 Exercises

1. A sensitive application component exposes an interface that allows any other component to interrogate the sensitive component for a list of resource descriptors. What property should these descriptors have?
2. An application is composed of an application server, application code that runs in the application server, and a database management system. The application code includes a Web application, a transaction layer that accesses the database, a set of client interface utilities, a set of third-party numerical analysis utilities that provide functionality to the application, and a layer that abstracts interaction with the database. The application has a test suite that includes end-to-end integration tests and tests of the database access layer. What additional test set(s) would you recommend?
3. An application requires a complex hierarchical object structure. The nodes in the structure are often moved around. Moving a node from one point in the hierarchy to another logically changes the ownership of the node:

The parent of a node always logically owns the node, and as long as that parent owns a node, the parent is responsible for ensuring that the node's lifecycle is managed. However, the concrete types of the nodes are not predefined—only that they must implement an abstract interface called *Node*. Define methods for the Node interface that would allow a node to manage the lifecycle of its children. Include any additional interfaces in your design that are required.

4. An object graph includes three kinds of objects: (a) Parent, (b) Child, and (c) Data. A Parent object may reference zero or more Child objects. Either a Parent or a Child may reference a single Data object. More than one Parent or Child may reference a single Data object—i.e., Data objects are shared across multiple non-Data objects. None of these objects are considered to contain secret contents: i.e., revealing the contents of a Parent, Child, or Data object to external components is not considered to present a risk. An application component contains several Parent objects, as well as Child and Data objects, in a graph as described. The component provides an method that returns a Parent object. The returned Parent object and any Child objects that it references are always copies of any objects contained within the component. What property should any attached Data object(s) have?

Answers and hints for these exercises can be found at `http://www.assuredbydesign.com/haa/`.

CONCURRENCY

Most server-based applications are multi-user applications. Such applications are inherently more difficult to write than single-user applications because they must deal with the issue of concurrent access: the situation when more than one request is made to read or write a single set of data.

PRINCIPLE: CONCURRENT EXECUTION SHOULD NOT CAUSE APPLICATION PROGRAMS TO MALFUNCTION.[1]

A failure to provide proper coordination for concurrent access can result in malfunction. This is sometimes referred to as a "race condition," although that term is potentially misleading because it is borrowed from the hardware arena in which the issue is actually manifest by a logic race, whereas in software the problem might simply manifest as incorrect results. The terms defined next are more specific and descriptive; for example, "isolation error" or "serialization error."

This book does not attempt to instruct the reader how to design correct concurrent programs. The focus here is on assurance-related issues, and concurrency is a critically important topic with regard to design assurance, and concurrency design errors are a common source of problems in many kinds of business application. This chapter attempts to raise awareness of the things that can go wrong and what can be done to prevent those kinds of problems. For an in-depth treatment of concurrent programming, the reader is referred to [2].

12.1 Review of Fundamentals

In order to understand solutions to the concurrency problem, it is necessary to understand several concepts first. These are isolation, atomicity, serialization, and reentrancy.

ISOLATION

Isolation has to do with the degree to which an operation is affected by or can affect other operations that are performed concurrently. There are two aspects to isolation: (1) whether an operation's internal (intermediate) states or final state are observable by other operations before the operation completes; and (2) whether an operation can observe intermediate states or changes created by other concurrent operations before those operations complete.

1 Quoted directly from [1] as the "First Law of Concurrency Control."

Isolation can have other dimensions to it. For example, it can allow certain kinds of changes to be visible but not others, or it can be comprehensive.

Two operations that are not isolated from each other can *interfere* with each other if they share data and do not coordinate their access to the data.

ATOMICITY

An operation is *atomic* if (1) it is indivisible, such that either the entire operation will complete or no part of it will complete, and if (2) it is executed with complete isolation, such that any internal intermediate states of the operation cannot be observed.

SERIALIZATION

Two operations that are not isolated from each other are *serialized* if they are performed in such a way that they cannot interfere. This can be accomplished by making one operation wait for the other, but other approaches exist as well. Design patterns for achieving this are discussed next.

REENTRANCY

An operation is *reentrant* if it can be invoked repeatedly, each invocation may operate concurrent with respect to the others, and the separate invocations do not interfere.

Reentrancy can be achieved by removing any shared data between the two invocations, or it can be achieved by providing a serialization mechanism. An operation that is reentrant through a serialization mechanism is *guarded reentrant.*

12.1.1 Fundamental Concurrency Coordination Patterns

The patterns that can be used to coordinate concurrent access are diverse. These patterns are not reproduced here. Instead, the patterns that are important to understand the rest of this book are summarized next, and the reader is referred to references [3, 4, 5, 6] for details.

SEMAPHORE

A *semaphore* is a variable whose value can be used to signal other processes. It is often supported by an atomic operation that waits for a variable (the semaphore) to be incremented and then decrements it. The protocol of usage is that when a routine is done with a semaphore, it increments it, thereby signaling other processes that are waiting for it to be incremented. A *mutex* is a binary semaphore. Note that a semaphore is a *cooperative* synchronization mechanism because a semaphore is merely a kind of flag (hence, the name "semaphore") and does not provide any protective barrier around portions of code.

TEST-AND-SET

A *test-and-set* operation atomically tests if a value is false, and if it is, sets it to true and returns the true value; otherwise, it leaves the value unaffected and returns false. A test-and-set operation is different from a semaphore in that it does not wait for a value to change but instead must be invoked by the caller repeatedly. Test-and-set is also a cooperative synchronization mechanism.

ATOMIC QUEUE

A *queue* is a buffer that allows multiple data elements to be added. The sequence in which they are added is maintained: The operation for removing the elements removes them either in the same sequence as they were added ("first-in, first-out") or in the reverse sequence (most recent first).

The primary advantage of a queue for synchronization is that if the operation for adding elements to the queue is atomic, the process that adds to the queue does not have to wait for the queue, because interference cannot occur between the various processes adding to the queue. If the operation for removing elements from the queue is atomic, there can be multiple processes removing elements without interfering. Thus, a fully atomic queue has the effect of fully decoupling "producers" of queue elements from "consumers" of queue elements. The "producer/consumer" design pattern is discussed in Section 12.2.3, "Multithreading Design Patterns."

INTERRUPT

An *interrupt*, "trap," or "signal" causes a processor to stop what it is doing and dispatches the processor to another routine. The interrupt is normally asynchronous with respect to the processor's main operation: that is, it can occur at any time (within a certain granularity). The other routine is often called an "interrupt handler."

Monitor

A *monitor* [7] is essentially a mechanism that *enforces* the semaphore concept. Access to code can be synchronized ("guarded") on the monitor just as access to code can be synchronized on a semaphore. The difference is that when a process holds a monitor (equivalent to having decremented a semaphore), other processes *cannot* access any code that is synchronized on the monitor. Thus, access is based on the *scope of the code that is synchronized.* This is known as "scoped locking" [8]. When languages provide a monitor construct, the monitor is often implemented by the compiler using more primitive constructs.

From "Un autre monde" ("Another World"), 1844.

12.2 Multiprocessing and Multithreading

The term "multiprocessing" is a broad term that refers to the concurrent usage of computing resources. The term multithreading is a much more specific term that applies to computing systems that support "threading." A *thread* is a computing construct that manages a single execution call stack within a program. If a program has multiple threads, the threads are typically allowed to share access to a single static program data space ("global memory"), and that global area often includes a "heap" for allocating and deallocating units of memory. Thus, threads can share data within execution memory and must deal with the issue of concurrent access to that memory.

Most languages and frameworks that provide features for multithreading (such as Java, C#, and the POSIX pthread libraries) give the programmer a powerful tool with which they can shoot themselves. These languages and frameworks do not provide a declarative mechanism for the programmer to instantiate multi-threaded design patterns. Instead, the selection of safe design patterns for using the multithreading primitives is left up to the programmer.

Writing concurrent programs is very difficult and requires care that all conditions are handled. It is, therefore, important that such programs be designed more carefully than single-user programs and that the design follow an accepted multithreading design pattern or one that is shown to be correct through careful analysis before it is implemented.

Thread-based operations that are reentrant or guarded reentrant are referred to as *thread-safe*. Because this term is specific to threading, this book often uses the more general term "reentrant" unless the discussion refers only to multithreading.

12.2.1 Process Coordination

Before operating systems supported threads, the most common way to achieve multiprocessing was by creating multiple program instances—processes. The Unix fork() operation is still widely used to clone a process and launch the clone in such a way that it can tell that it is a clone and, based on that fact, execute different branches of the code. This allows programs to launch multiple processes that perform different tasks concurrently.

Many programs are deployed in a runtime platform that automatically provides for process cloning. For example, Web servers do this whenever a "CGI" program is executed—that is, whenever the Web address specifies a program instead of a static page. The server performs the operations required to launch the target program as a separate process. Many Web sites use scripting languages, such as PERL for CGI programs, so multiple users accessing the site end up executing these PERL programs concurrently. This often leads to concurrency errors if a PERL program does not explicitly ensure that concurrent access to files is serialized—i.e., if the program is not coded to be re-entrant. In the mid-90s, the author made modifications to a popular PERL Web newsgroup program to make it guarded re-entrant. Concurrency problems can also result with Web scripting languages, such as PHP, that execute in the context of the request thread, if proper serialization techniques are not applied to any shared non-transactional resources that are accessed, such as files.

> Concurrency problems can result with Web scripting languages, such as PHP and PERL, if proper serialization techniques are not applied to any files that are accessed.

Process coordination is also important for batch processing. Batch processing is still extremely common in today's corporations. Unfortunately, most programmers who write batch programs are knowledgeable about the business but not about concurrent programming, so it is rare that batch programs are written to provide for reentrancy. As a result, organizations often find out that their batch programs cannot be run concurrently. This leads to a need for a serialization mechanism. A mutex lock provides a good design pattern for this, and a very simple mechanism can be implemented to provide the needed coordination. Sometimes the coordination can even be implemented within a job scheduling system that provides for a trigger capability.

> Organizations often find out that their batch programs cannot be run concurrently.

When designing a mutex mechanism to coordinate business processes, one has the limitation that batch processes cannot easily be made to block on an event. Thus, if a batch program must wait until a resource is available before it can start, it is often better to poll instead.

Design Pattern: Cooperative Process Coordination

Context

Two or more server processes need to share access to one or more non-transactional resources, such as files, or they need to perform long-running transactions such as batch updates. The organization does not have a suitable job scheduling system, or the scheduling requirements change frequently and therefore need to be under programmatic control.

Problem

The processes could be scheduled to avoid conflict, but the schedule often changes or is disrupted, and so unintended conflict between processes results.

Solution

This pattern slightly modifies the mutex pattern in a way that is more practical for implementing lock-based coordination among business processes. The ResumeTask() method takes a boolean Create argument: If Create is true, the method will create the task if the task does not exist or if the task ID argument is null. The Application argument specifies the name of the application that is creating the task. The ResumeTask() method allows an application to verify that a lock created and never released by a prior task is still available and to begin processing as if it were the prior task.

The GetLock() method also takes a Create argument so that if Create is true, it will create a lock if the specified lock does not exist or is null. Note that the API allows for multiple locks, each with a unique ID. The GetLock() method is analogous to a test-and-set operation in that it will fail by raising LockInUse if the specified lock is currently held by a task that is different from the one that is specified in the TaskID argument. This is the only "normal" exception used by this pattern: Other exceptions indicate design errors. The ReleaseLock() method releases the specified lock that is held by the task that currently holds it.

The lock mechanism can most easily be implemented using a database. However, it can also be implemented using a file system via the Unix flock() method or the Java FileChannel.lock() method and by recording the lock scope within the name of each lock file.

Sample Scenarios

Two usage scenarios represent the majority of ways of using this pattern. These are:

1. A process is not yet ready to start but it wants to "reserve" a lock in order to prevent another process from obtaining it, because after the other process starts, it will run for a long time, so the first process will not be able to start on time.
2. A process merely wishes to obtain a lock, perform its work, and then release the lock.

The first scenario divides into two parts: (a) obtaining the lock, and (b) releasing the lock so that the other process can proceed.

The scenarios are shown in Figure 12.1.

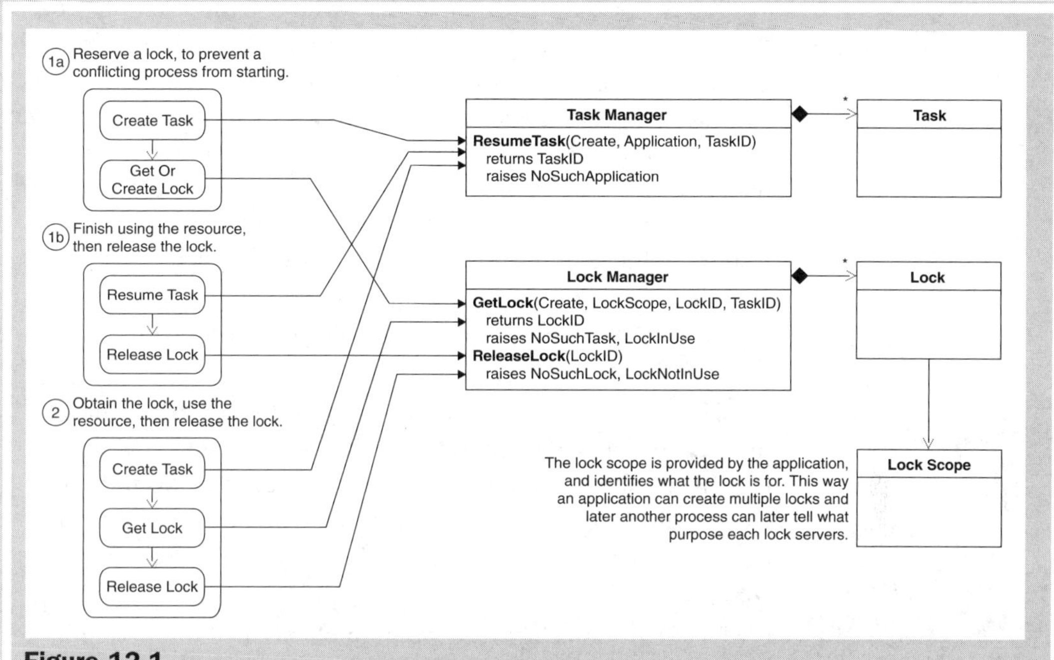

Figure 12.1
Sample scenarios.

Note that when a process requests a lock, it must expect that a LockInUse exception can occur and be prepared to hibernate for a while and then try again to obtain the lock. This "try-until-successful" logic is not shown in Figure 12.1, for the sake of simplicity.

Consequences
Processes can cooperatively coordinate their actions. This helps to automate scheduling in environments in which there are many processes sharing resources, and the organization has not yet settled on a job scheduling system that has sufficient flexibility.

12.2.2 Coordination of Error Response

When responding to an error condition, consider the degree to which the response should include other threads of control, and perhaps even whether it should include the entire application. Just as the separate activities of a multi-process or multi-thread application must be coordinated, the error response must be coordinated.

For example, suppose an application provides a thread pool for the purpose of performing some kind of work in parallel with the main application. Pooled threads that do work on behalf of a main thread are often called "worker threads." If one of these worker threads encounters a fatal error while it is performing its work, its action should be twofold: (1) notify the component on whose behalf it was performing the remote call, and (2) notify the pool manager so that the lost thread resource and any other resources held by that thread can be restored or replaced in the pool (i.e., it is not sufficient to merely throw an exception or write to a log—yet these are the most common responses for in-house inadequately tested applications). Note also that because the error occurs in the context of the worker thread, any exception thrown will not reach the main application thread.

Design worker threads to accept a callback reference to be used for reporting an error.

The most effective approach is often to design the worker threads so that they can accept a callback reference, which is used when there is an error. Thus, when an error occurs, the worker thread can catch the error and the worker thread has a pathway for notifying the rest of the application that something went awry.

Use an "exception firewall" for each application thread.

In general, each thread in an application should contain an impenetrable (to the extent possible) trap for any kind of error condition that might occur, and each such trap should be designed so that it *coordinates its error response with the overall application*, as appropriate.

Principle: Coordinate Error Response Across All Independent Paths of Control.

Error handling design is discussed in detail later in Chapter 18, "Failure Response Design." The discussion here focuses on the need to ensure that handling is coordinated. The author has seen too many designs in which resource pools either grow without bound or run out of resources because the pool's designer did not take the time to consider what actions were needed when an error occurred when using one of the elements in the pool.

A pattern for this kind of callback is shown next.

DESIGN PATTERN: ASYNCHRONOUS ERROR HANDLER

Context

An application thread creates a worker thread to perform some function concurrently. There is no requirement, and therefore no provision, for the worker thread and application thread to rendezvous. However, if an error occurs within the worker thread, the application thread would need to specify what actions should be taken.

Problem

The worker thread is disassociated from the application thread, and there is no way for the worker thread to notify the application thread or receive instructions from it if an error occurs in the worker thread.

Solution

The application thread should provide an error handler as a callback object for the worker thread to invoke when an error occurs. If the worker thread encounters an error, it should (1) close all resources that it opened, (2) release all references that it has (except for those on its stack), and (3) notify the callback of the failure.

The callback error handler should (1) assess the scope of the error, (2) determine an appropriate recovery point for the application as a whole, and (3) restore to that point.

The callback error handler is performed in a different thread from the thread that invoked the service because the service invocation is asynchronous. Therefore, as part of the function of the handler, it could also interrupt the main application thread to force it to deal with the error condition immediately. However, for that to be practical, the main application thread would have to be designed to be interruptible. The ability to be interruptible is discussed in Section 12.2.4, "Thread Interruption."

The activities associated with this pattern are shown in Figure 12.2.

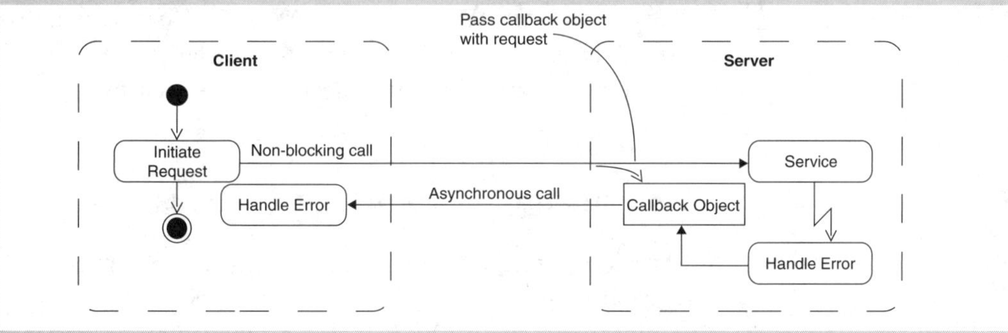

Figure 12.2 Activities.

Consequences

The responsibility for recovery is removed from the worker thread and put where it belongs: in the main application thread, which provides the error handler to the worker thread. Note that even though recovery is defined by the main application thread (because it provides the recovery handler), the actual recovery actions are performed (or at least initiated) by the worker thread because the worker thread calls the handler.

In some applications, it might seem like overkill to burden each kind of worker thread with a callback and to have to write handlers for each kind of callback. If this level of work seems like too much, it probably is an indication that the worker thread approach is an over-engineered design for the application in the first place. For example, many application designs employ worker threads to make remote calls in order to allow the rest of the application to continue while the remote calls are performed. This is a very valid and powerful approach, but it is indeed often overkill, especially for server-to-server applications. In general, remote calls should be performed synchronously whenever possible. This is because synchronous calls ensure an unbroken path for errors that might be returned. In fact, remote call APIs were designed so that they mimic a normal synchronous method call, and to use them to perform asynchronous calls defeats this intent.

Sometimes asynchronous calls are unavoidable. In GUI applications, it is common to use an asynchronous call in order to allow a GUI component thread to resume immediately after an action is initiated. For example, both the Java AWT and Java Swing GUI frameworks will not initiate more than one event at a time on a component: If a component event is being processed, any further events are queued. Asynchronous calls are also common for Web service SOAP calls. However, that is because of the message-oriented nature of Web services, and callback handlers are a standard design for asynchronous Web service calls.

12.2.3 Multithreading Design Patterns

Multithreading design patterns have been studied extensively and there are a great many excellent resources that provide design patterns for multithreading. An exhaustive discussion of multithreading will not be duplicated here. However, we require a summary of the patterns that are most commonly used and important for applications in my experience. The reader is referred to other resources for details and for information on additional patterns [9, 10, 11, 12].

REQUESTER/SERVICER (AKA "PRODUCER/CONSUMER" OR "MANAGER/WORKER")

This design pattern is most commonly referred to as the *producer/consumer* pattern and is also known as the *manager/worker* pattern. This test will refer to it as the "requester/servicer" pattern because that terminology is more consistent with the typical usage of the pattern in multithreading applications.

The pattern consists of a buffer or queue, a set of "requester" (aka "producer" or "manager") processes that add elements to the queue, and a set of "servicer" (aka "consumer" or "worker") processes that remove elements from the queue. The producer processes operate asynchronously with respect to the consumers and the queue. The consumers, on the other hand, *wait* for entries to the queue to be made. Thus, the consumers utilize an operation (such as a monitor wait) that causes them to block until there is data in the queue, whereas the producers put entries into the queue at will. The pattern is depicted in Figure 12.3.

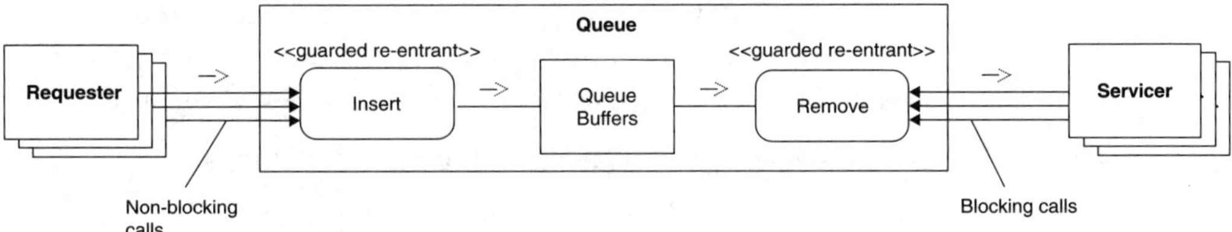

Figure 12.3 Requester/Servicer Pattern, aka "Producer/Consumer" or "Manager/Worker."

There are many variations on the producer/consumer pattern. The basic concept is an old one and has been used for device drivers for decades as a means of decoupling the flow of requests from the service response. A related pattern is the Active Object pattern [13].

PIPELINE

A *pipeline* is a processor assembly line. It consists of a sequence of buffers and processors. A data element cannot be added to the pipeline until all processors in the pipeline are ready for more data. Each processor in the pipeline passes its results to buffer owned by the next processor in the pipeline. The last processor in the sequence outputs the final result.

Pipelines are normally synchronous, in that the processors all perform operations that always take the same amount of time, and the movement of the output of one processor to the buffer of the next downstream processor occurs simultaneously (synchronously) for all processors. The lock-step initiation of processing and data movement is commonly coordinated by a controller or clock component. A synchronous pipeline is depicted in Figure 12.4.

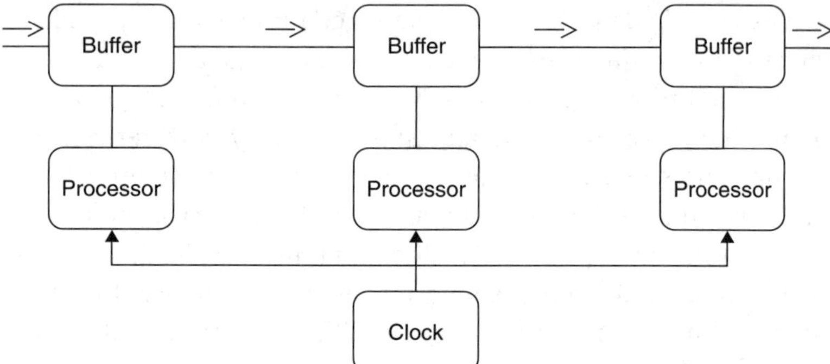

Figure 12.4 Synchronous pipeline.

A non-synchronous pipeline must refuse input until all processors in the pipeline are ready for more input. A non-synchronous pipeline is, therefore, merely a series of queues.

DISCRIMINATING REQUESTER, SPECIALIZED SERVICER

The pattern described here is an important variation on the Requester/Servicer pattern. The essential difference is that *each request specifies a particular servicer.* Think of a real-world example: You arrive at a barber shop and request a particular barber. You are willing to wait (queue up) for the barber that you request: No other barber will do. Further, barbers arrive and leave throughout the day, so the algorithm must accommodate a *varying* number of non-equivalent (specialized) servicers.

This pattern is common in "bridge" applications in which a requester must obtain service from a *particular bridge* in order to access a *particular destination*, such as a peer-to-peer destination.[2] The pattern is explained in detail next.

2 The author used this design pattern in a peer-to-peer application that he developed for an advanced Java course.

DESIGN PATTERN: DISCRIMINATING REQUESTER, SPECIALIZED SERVICER

Context

A variable number of requesters queue for a variable number of *non-substitutable* (specialized) servicers.

Problem

Servicers—and therefore their associated queues—can come and go over time. Requesters need to be able to discover which servicers are available and to be notified when a requested servicer is no longer registered.

Solution

There are two variations of this pattern: the "blocking requester" version, in which requesters request a servicer and then block until that servicer is available, and the "polling requester" version, in which requesters periodically poll until the requested servicer is available. The latter is often more scalable for Internet clients in situations in which there are few service registries compared to the number of clients.

In the blocking requester version, a requester makes a call to a servicer registry to request a particular servicer. The registry returns a reference to a semaphore, on which the requester then makes a blocking call. The requester returns from the blocking call only when the requested servicer becomes available or if an error occurs. If a servicer removed its registration (goes "offline"), any requesters waiting for it will receive a Servicer Unavailable error indicating this condition. Similarly, if a servicer tries to service a requester that is no longer available, the servicer will receive a Requester No Longer Available exception. This pattern is shown in Figure 12.5.[3]

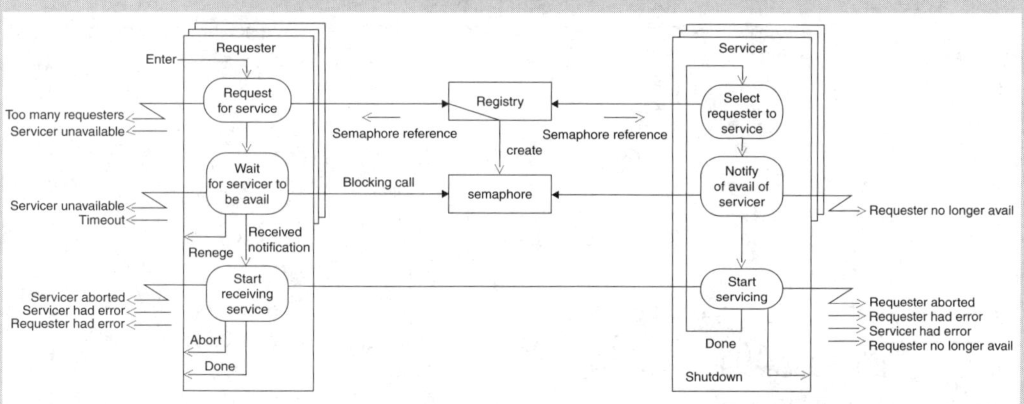

Figure 12.5 Blocking Requester.

The polling requester version of this pattern is very similar, except that the registry does not return a semaphore until the requested servicer is actually available; otherwise, it returns null, in which case the requester waits for a period and then tries again. When a non-null semaphore is finally returned, the requester calls a method on the semaphore to notify it that the requester is ready. This last call might fail if the servicer is no longer available for some reason, and the requester must be ready to respond to this error, either by trying again or by giving up. The pattern (excluding error handling) is shown in Figure 12.6.

3 Compare this pattern with the "Requester Responder" pattern presented in Section 15.1, "Request-Response."

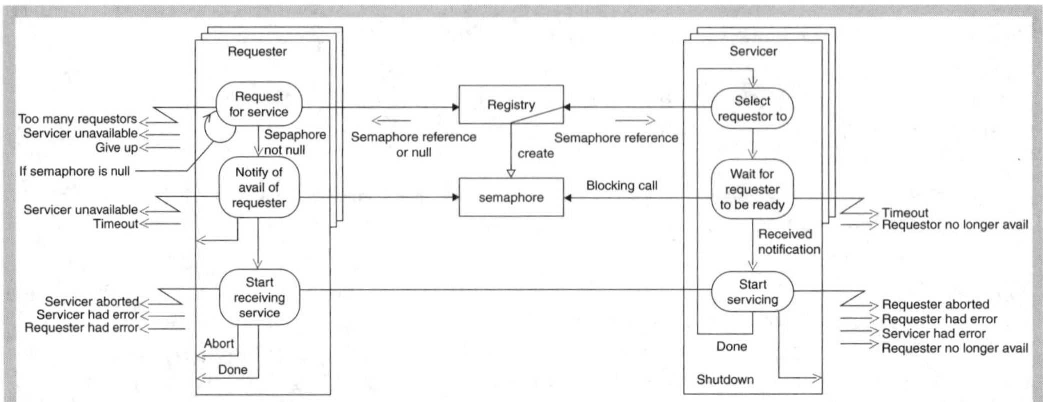

Figure 12.6 Polling Requester.

Instance Structure

Figure 12.7 shows an instance structure for implementing a Requester based on this pattern. Only the Requester instance structure is shown, for the Blocking Requester case, because instance structures for the Servicer and for the Polling Requester case can be derived by analogy.

In the figure, a Requester delegates all the generic behavior required of a Requester to a Requester Helper object.

This pattern assumes that a Requester can make only a single call to Requester Helper at any time. Thus, if multiple concurrent requests are required, each request should have its own Requester Helper. This is enforced by the fact that when a Requester Helper is instantiated, it immediately begins executing.

The Requester contains a Service Handler, and a reference to it is passed when a Requester Helper is created. The Service Handler provides a callback interface for the Requester Helper to use to call the Service Handler. The Service Handler contains the logic to be used to receive service (see the bubble "Start Receiving Service" in the activity diagrams). If the Service Handler is not re-entrant, the Requester must provide a separate Service Handler for each Requester Helper that it creates.

When a Requester Helper is instantiated, the name or ID of the Servicer that is desired is also provided as an argument. The Servicer name or ID uniquely identifies the desired Servicer. If that Servicer is not currently registered, the instantiation will fail with a Servicer Unavailable exception.

In the Blocking Requester variant of this pattern, a timeout parameter is also provided during instantiation. This specifies how long the Requester Helper should wait to obtain the desired Servicer before throwing a Timeout exception.

In the Blocking Requester variant, a Requester instantiates a Requester Helper and then *waits* for a response. If it waits awhile and decides not to wait any longer, it can decide to *renege*, by calling the renege() method on the Requester Helper. This causes the Requester Helper to abort its operation. The renege() method must be called from a separate thread, because the thread that instantiated the Requester Helper is still blocked. Thus, the call to renege() is asynchronous with respect to the waiting (blocked) thread.

The Requester can also abort at any time. If the Servicer has not yet begun to handle the request, this has the same effect as renege(). If the request is being handled, then abort() interrupts the servicing. Both renege() and abort() cause the Requester's blocked thread to return with an exception, indicating a renege or abort. In the Polling Requester variant of this pattern, the renege() operation is not available because the Requester is not waiting and so there is no need to renege.

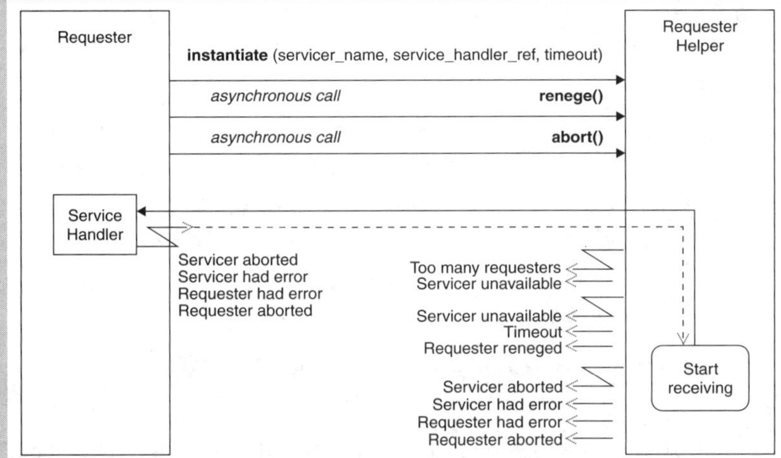

Figure 12.7 Requester instance structure for Blocking Requester variant.

Any exception that occurs within the Service Handler propagates back to the Requester Helper and then causes the blocked thread to return with that exception. If an exception does not occur and servicing completes without error, the instantiation of the Requester Helper completes successfully, and it may then be disposed of because it has completed its work.

Other designs are possible to implement the intent of this pattern.

Consequences

The ability to specify a Servicer and then wait until that Servicer is available or to continue checking if it has become available decouples the process of requesting a Servicer from receiving a connection to a servicer. This is a powerful pattern for gateways that act as a switch or relay to interconnect endpoints. Note that communication is always initiated from the Requester. This pattern, therefore, works well for Requesters that cannot receive inbound communications.

12.2.4 Thread Interruption

Most multithreading APIs provide a method to forcefully terminate a thread. For example, Java has the stop() method. However, calling a method like this can result in unexpected and hard-to-reproduce failures, including corruption of data, if the thread is writing to IO. Therefore, in multithreading applications in which robust operation is a requirement, thread termination must be carefully designed.

Asynchronously aborting a thread can cause hard-to-reproduce failures.

Interruption is desirable in a variety of circumstances that are important to well-designed application programs. First of all, users generally need a way to abort any long-duration action that they initiate. If the abort operation is unreliable or can result in undefined results or inconsistent data, users will not use it, and the abort feature is of no benefit. An alternative to aborting an action is to reverse the action, but if the action takes a long time to complete, it might be important to be able to safely abort it.

Operators may need to safely abort a process as well. The practice of "killing a process" is a poor one, and well-trained operators do not do this unless they have no alternative because the application is not designed to be gracefully stoppable.

Some key challenges in creating a thread processing design that can be interrupted are listed in Table 12.1.

Table 12.1 Design Requirements for Safe Thread Interruption

Interruption should be performed only at well-defined interruption points.
The design must ensure that blocked operations can be interrupted.
The design must protect against race conditions—i.e., unanticipated states due to concurrent access and resulting malfunction.
The design must ensure that all exception conditions caused by interruption are handled and reported where appropriate.
The design must ensure that interruption does not mask or lose exceptions or progress status that should be reported.

It is important to distinguish between an operation that *can* be interrupted and an operation that *should* be interrupted.

When designing an interruptible process, it is important to distinguish between an operation that *can* be interrupted and an operation that *should* be interrupted. For example, in Java, only blocking operations such as IO or waiting for a monitor can be interrupted. When an interruptible action is interrupted, it may have a cleanup action that is to be performed before it exits. The cleanup operation should *not* be interrupted by any subsequent (perhaps accidental or redundant) interrupt call, so provisions must be made to make the cleanup operation uninterruptible, even if it performs operations that can be interrupted. The following design pattern shows an approach for achieving this.

DESIGN PATTERN: INTERRUPTIBLE THREAD

Related Patterns

Also see the Two-Phase Termination pattern in [14].

Uses the "Asynchronous Error Handler" pattern in Section 12.2.2, "Coordination of Error Response."

Context

An application thread needs to be designed so that it can be safely aborted by another thread.

Problem

Interruption must be constrained so that it meets the requirements for safe interruption.

Solution

This design pattern provides for asynchronous thread processing that is interruptible. The application defines a class (ServiceThread) that has one constructor and two public methods. This class encapsulates the behavior that is to be executed by a system thread. Therefore, both of its public methods (start and abort) are invoked by other threads in order to initiate and abort the thread, respectively.

The ServiceThread class's constructor accepts an argument that is a callback object. This callback object is invoked when the thread completes, to notify the client that the thread has finished, and it provides the client with the completion status. The class's start() method can be called only once. It must allocate a system thread, pass it the internal entry point of the ServiceThread's work logic (as shown in Figure 12.8), and then immediately return. The ServiceThread also has an internal method, interrupt(). This method sends a signal to the ServiceThread's thread that it should interrupt what it is doing and pass control to an interrupt handler. This method is used only by the ServiceThread's abort() method and interrupt() is not exposed to other clients of the ServiceThread.

The thread class that is shown in the figure includes embedded logic for the work that is to be done. This logic could be factored out into a separate class in order to generalize the Interruptible Thread pattern.

Any other thread (or even the ServiceThread's thread itself) can abort the thread's work by calling the abort() method on the ServiceThread object. This call merely sets the abort flag in the ServiceThread instance, signals an interrupt to the thread, and then immediately returns.

If the ServiceThread is performing an interruptible operation when it receives an interrupt, it will handle the interrupt by performing any required cleanup, setting the completion status, calling the status listener to notify the client that it has completed, and then terminating. (The status listener plays the role of the "Handle Error" component in the "Asynchronous Error Handler" pattern.) Note that the status listener invocation is performed by the ServiceThread object, so the thread does not actually terminate until this call has finished. There is still the consideration that some processing that is interruptible should not be interrupted. For example, perhaps even though IO can be interrupted, it should not be. This can be prevented by use of forced serialization (see the following paragraphs).

If the ServiceThread is performing an operation *that is not interruptible* when the interrupt occurs, it will not be immediately interrupted. (For example, only blocking API calls in Java such as IO calls or actions that suspend a thread are interruptible.) Therefore, it is necessary for any uninterruptible portion of the work logic to periodically check whether an abort has been requested, by checking the abort flag. If the flag is set, the cleanup sequence is begun, followed by StatusListener notification and then termination. If the work logic does not contain any non-interruptible operations, it is not necessary to periodically check the abort flag, so the portion of the figure in white would not be needed. Any access to the instance variable "abort" must be serialized—i.e., thread-safe. (This is not to be confused with "object serialization.") For example, in Java, this would be achieved by enclosing those accesses in a synchronized block. Further, the cleanup operation should be part of the serialized section to ensure that it is not interrupted. It is important to consider which parts of the interruptible processing *should not be interrupted* and place these portions within a block that is serialized on access to abort.

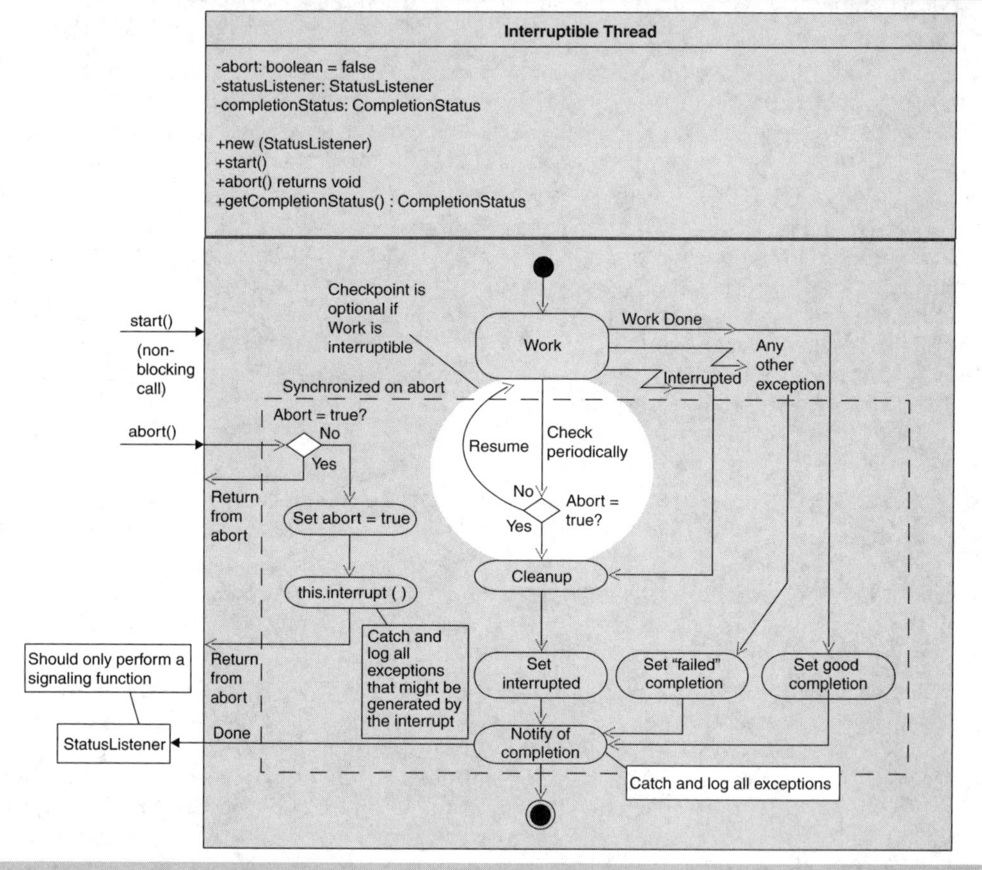

Figure 12.8 Activity structure.

Any errors that occur during processing of the work logic should be trapped and result in an exception that passes control to the cleanup logic. This exception is not shown in the diagram to avoid clutter, because it would merely follow the same path of the Interrupted exception. An error that occurs during the processing of the cleanup logic should also be trapped, but should not result in an exception. Instead, the final completion status should indicate the error.

When the interruptible thread is ready to terminate, its last action is to signal that it is terminating and provide its completion status. *This action should be only a signaling action.* The interruptible thread's termination signal should not be used to synchronously perform work of any kind within the memory space outside of the interruptible thread. To do so is to risk a race condition. Thus, the status listener should merely do something such as notify another thread that is waiting to rendezvous.

If there is a requirement to provide the client with frequent notification of the progress of the thread, rather than only at the thread's completion, this can easily be accommodated by inserting a call to the StatusListener immediately after periodic the test of whether abort has been set. See the "Progress Reporting" design patterns in Section 16.4.5, "Progress Bars."

Structure

The only activities in this pattern that need to be customized for an application are the Work and Cleanup activities. Therefore, these can be factored out by either making them abstract methods or by delegating these activities to external objects. Using the latter approach, an Interruptible Thread concrete class can be defined that takes a Work object and a Cleanup object as constructor arguments.

It would also be desirable to factor out any error reporting and logging performed by the activities of the Interruptible Thread, such as by the this.interrupt() activity. Factoring out error reporting and logging is a normal best practice, however.

Consequences

A thread implemented with this pattern can be safely interrupted by calling its abort() method from another thread.

12.2.5 Designing a Thread Timeout Mechanism

Designing a timeout mechanism for a timed thread requires consideration of the edge conditions of what happens when the timed thread finishes just as the timer is about to issue a timeout interrupt on the timed thread. The approach presented will use the Interruptible Thread pattern provided previously.

Because the Interruptible Thread pattern provides a thread-safe mechanism for interrupting a thread, we can use it for both the timed thread and the timer thread. The general approach is to instantiate a timer thread that implements the Interruptible Thread pattern. The behavior of this thread is merely to wait for a period of time (the timeout period), and when that period has expired to issue an abort() on the timed thread. If the timed thread happens to finish before the timeout elapses, it issues an abort() on the timer thread. Voilá!

DESIGN PATTERN: TIMER THREAD

Related Pattern

See the "Interruptible Thread" pattern in Section 12.2.4.

Context

An application has one or more threads that need to be aborted after a timeout period.

Problem

A reusable solution is needed that can be encapsulated, so that the application design is not burdened with having to implement a timeout mechanism for each aspect of the application that needs to time out.

Solution

In this pattern, there are two thread instances: a Timer Thread that provides the timeout behavior, and a Timed Thread that is the subject of the timeout. The Timed Thread may be any thread that implements the "Interruptible Thread" pattern.

The Timer Thread also implements the Interruptible Thread pattern such that the pattern's Work sub-process performs a Wait and when the Wait is complete it issues an abort() call to the Timed Thread, as shown in Figure 12.9.

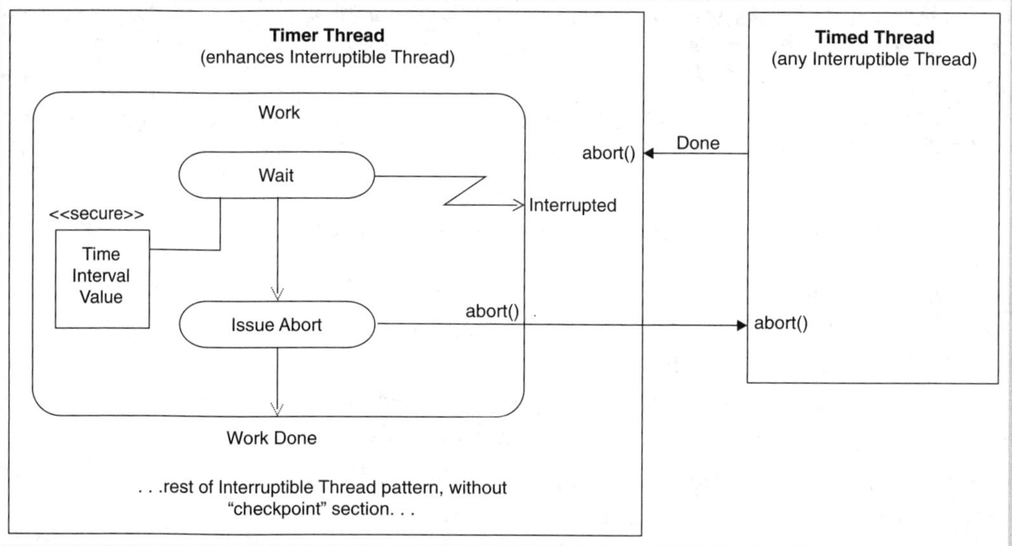

Figure 12.9 Timer activities.

If the Timed Thread completes its operation before the timeout interval, it signals that it is done by calling abort() on the Timer Thread.

Note that the Work sub-process of the Timer Thread does not bother to periodically check to see if it has been aborted, as is provided for in the Interruptible Thread pattern, because an abort() call on the Timer Thread will immediately interrupt its Wait.

Structure

The structural requirements that are presumed for this pattern are that (1) the Timer Thread design must be reusable, and (2) the time interval must be secure so that it cannot be inappropriately modified. The first requirement is easily met because there is no reason to have to customize the Timer Thread class: A general purpose implementation can be defined and reused by simply instantiating it. The second requirement can be met by making the time interval an instantiation argument: It is then as secure as the Timer Thread's runtime instance, and the security of the time interval argument depends on the security of the instantiating context. Note that the Timer's Wait activity depends on a native time service, such as a Java VM System.currentTimeMillis() call, which must be secure for the Timer Thread to be secure.

Consequences

Any thread that will use a Timer Thread to abort after a timeout interval must implement the Interruptible Thread pattern.

12.2.6 Common GUI Concurrency Problems

Designing a correct GUI application is more difficult than most programmers recognize. Most GUI applications today interact with one or more servers. Thus, the GUI must be kept in sync with the server, and this introduces potential concurrency issues.

The Model-View-Controller (MVC) design pattern is the most commonly used design pattern for user interfaces. It specifies the existence of an application model that represents application state, a set of views that represent the display state, and a controller that keeps these in sync. The basic operational paradigm of MVC is that user actions are performed against the model, which then issues model-change events, and the controller ensures that the views are updated in response to these events.

MVC is a simple and very abstract design pattern. Most applications that use it are much more complex in their actual design and the way in which they handle events and update the display. Descriptions of some of the problems that present themselves for the GUI client developer follow.

Lack of Reentrancy

Model changes should be atomic and the code reentrant, or guarded reentrant. In other words, make sure that the model is thread-safe.

THIRD-PARTY GUI MODEL

Most GUI toolkits do not allow a programmer to provide factories for nodes constructed by the GUI.

Often the model is pre-built as a GUI toolkit, allowing for no addition of attributes to the model objects. "Decorating" the pre-built classes is usually not an option because instances are typically constructed by the GUI toolkit. In that case, you might have no choice but to create a parallel model that represents your own model concepts and that is maintained in sync by the model change listeners that you write. This tends to introduce a lot of complexity and the potential for unreliability.

REMOTE MODEL

The *real* model is remote, such as on a server. In a client/server application there are actually two kinds of models—the authoritative server-based model and the local models that exist within the clients—and these must be kept in sync. It is, therefore, beneficial to define a layer that uses some form of concurrency control to keep the local and remote models in sync. See the discussion of Transactional Integrity in Chapter 13, "Transactional Integrity."

DESIGN PATTERN: CLIENT TIER MVC

Context

A GUI client must interact with a remote server to perform transactions against a shared database. The GUI client must also show the state of the relevant portions of the database within the GUI. Asynchronous updates to the database do not need to immediately propagate to the GUI client, but each time the client obtains data from the database, the data retrieved should be fresh. The client might show some of the same data elements redundantly in different portions of its display, for example, in different panels or windows.

Problem

The remote database and GUI client must be kept in sync. Interactions with the remote database can fail due to transaction timeout, transaction conflict, or other conditions. Further, users sometimes click on GUI functions while they are waiting for a function to complete: thus, the GUI's functions (and server's functions) must be re-entrant.

Solution

This pattern elaborates the MVC pattern into a form that is appropriate for typical GUI-based clients that must interact with a remote application server.

The pattern has the usual model and view components. However, it distinguishes between three different model components: the *local model*, the *GUI model*, and the *server model*. These three models must all be kept in sync, and that is the inherent challenge in developing the GUI client of a client-server application.

In this pattern, the action listener receives GUI events, such as when a user clicks a button on the GUI. The action listener then invokes one or more business action handlers to perform the action that the user intends. One must be careful here: The user expects that the action will be completed in full, so the action handler must not attempt to perform more than one action unless it has a way of informing the user of the exact situation if not all actions complete successfully.

The business action handler should first attempt the server actions that are required. In doing this, it may need to access the local model in order to read the current application state. The server request should contain information about the time at which the local model was last updated so that the server can determine if the local data is stale.

Assuming that the server actions complete successfully, the business action handler then invokes any model change listeners that have been linked to it. These change listeners access the GUI API to update the GUI internal model. The GUI then internally (in most GUI toolkits, such as Swing) updates the views that are associated with the GUI model.

Note that the business action handler must be able to respond to these conditions: (1) the server request completes successfully; (2) the request fails because the data presented by the update request is stale; (3) the request times out; (4) the request fails for some other reason. Any failure should result in the handler performing a refresh request to the server in order to obtain new data to use to refresh the display—but without overwriting the data that the user has just entered. This is the Optimistic Concurrency Control design pattern which is discussed in Section 13.3, "Ensuring Consistency Across Transactions," and is also discussed in [15]. The overall interactions are shown in Figure 12.10.

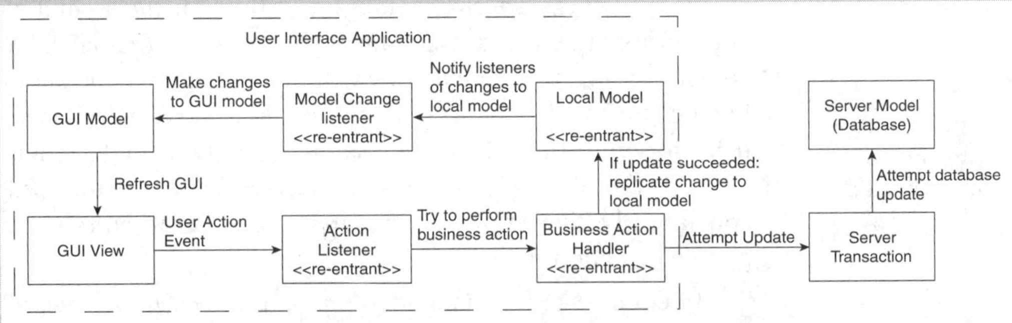

Figure 12.10 Activities of each tier.

So where is the "controller"? You might choose to view the collection of action listeners as a controller. However, rather than try to fit the real-life pattern to the MVC pattern, let's just accept the real-life pattern as it is.

Consequences

This pattern does not provide for asynchronous receipt of database changes. If that is a requirement, the pattern is easily modified by having each GUI client provide the server with a callback handler for propagating asynchronous changes to the client, and modifying each server transaction so that it broadcasts notice of its changes to all clients that have provided a callback.

12.2.7 The Double-Click Problem

Users of GUI applications often erroneously click twice on GUI buttons and hyperlinks. This might be due to accidentally making two clicks, or it might be the result of confusion over whether the GUI expects a single click or a double click. It can also be a result of impatience on the part of the user when a GUI function takes too long; in that case, the extra clicks occur after a substantial period. GUI applications need to take these very common erroneous behaviors into account.

Causes of erroneous extra clicks:

- Accidentally making two clicks.
- Confusion over whether the GUI expects a single click or a double click.
- Impatience on the part of the user.

Different kinds of GUIs handle multiple clicks differently.

Different kinds of GUIs handle multiple clicks differently. For example, GUIs built with the Java Swing toolkit use a single event handling thread, so an extra click that occurs before the first is completely processed will either (1) be treated as a double click (if the clicks are close enough together), or the second click will not execute until the action triggered by the first click has completed: i.e., the second click will be *queued* until the action handler for the first returns. This queuing is very undesirable behavior, unfortunately, if the user wants only a single action to occur. If the GUI toolkit allows multiple clicks to be processed concurrently, the action handlers must be either re-entrant or guarded re-entrant.

In contrast to this, most desktop Web browsers *immediately* process a second click on a hyperlink—even if the first click's action has not yet returned—and the more recent click will *abort any action triggered by the previous click*. Multiple concurrent submit button clicks (in a single window frame) are not possible on most browsers. This is not a problem as long as the actions triggered by a click are robust and transactional and therefore can be aborted without undesirable side effects.

Clicking one-too-many times can be a problem if the action triggered by the extra click might result in costly or inconvenient circumstances, such as a redundant transaction that is hard to reverse. Redundant actions are less of a concern if the action is idempotent. An *idempotent* action is one that can be performed multiple times with the same effect as if it were performed only once. For example, setting a value for a data item that only you have access to is an idempotent operation, because if you perform that operation twice in a row, the effect (for you and for other transactions) is the same as if you had performed it only once.

If the action is idempotent, you only need to ensure that (1) each action is logically complete, and (2) each action is isolated from the other in case they are initiated concurrently. On the client, this generally means using a GUI that processes only one user action at a time, or making the GUI action handlers re-entrant or guarded re-entrant. On the server, it means making the actions transactional.

> If a click's action is not idempotent, the effect of an extraneous click must be detected by the user, and she must be given the ability to reverse the action.

If the action is not idempotent, the effect of the extra click must be *easily detected* by the user, and she must be given the *ability to reverse the action.* For example, if the extra click adds an extra item to a shopping cart, showing the total number of items in the cart will alert them that something is wrong. If they can easily peruse the contents of the cart and delete the extra item, the damage will have been repaired.

Preventing multiple clicks, or equivalently translating multiple clicks that are closely spaced into a single action, is complex. Most GUI toolkits provide the tools needed to do this but do not make it convenient. For example, the Java AWT toolkit provides methods for examining and clearing the event queue, but this is not a type of programming that most GUI programmers are used to performing. Handling the impatient user who clicks redundantly while waiting is also difficult. Some solutions to these problems are shown in Table 12.2.

> Java provides the peekEvent() method to inspect the GUI event queue, and the getNextEvent() method for removing events from the queue. These can be used to remove closely spaced events from the queue.

Table 12.2 Solutions for the Double-Click Problem

#	Solution
1	Fix the GUI to prevent closely spaced clicks: Closely-spaced clicks are collapsed into a single event. Requires a GUI toolkit that exposes an event queue API to the programmer.
2	Ensure that each server action is transactional.
3	Ensure that each server action is uninterruptible when started.
4	Ensure that each server action is apparent and obvious to the user and reversible by the user.
5	Disable GUI functions during intervals when they are unsafe. For example, a GUI action handler can immediately gray out and disable a button until the action handler returns. This is not foolproof: There is a very unlikely narrow window of failure. If server action is asynchronous (i.e., the action handler returns before the server's action is complete), this approach requires a callback from the server or polling the server to know when disabled GUI functions should be re-enabled.
6	Ensure that each GUI action is re-entrant or guarded re-entrant.

These solutions are appropriate in different combinations in different circumstances. For example, if the GUI toolkit queues events, one solution for accidental double clicks would be to add code to remove closely spaced events (solution #1 in Table 12.2), and another solution would be to ensure that if a double click results in two transactions instead of one, the user can see the effect of this and be able to easily remedy it by performing an additional transaction that reverses the redundant one (this is solution #4 in the table), such as by removing an extra erroneous item from a shopping cart.

Various combinations of solutions are listed in Table 12.3. These are grouped according to the GUI's behavior with respect to button click events. Note that a combination of solutions may be called for in order to deal with the separate problems of double clicks and impatient users. In some cases, a single problem type requires multiple strategies; for example, in the case of GUI events that preempt, dealing with double clicks requires either both solutions 2 and 4, or both solutions 3 and 4.

Table 12.3 Applicability of Solutions Based on GUI Behavior

Problem	Solutions					
	1	2	3	4	5	6
GUI events are queued (for example, Java Swing)						
Accidental double clicks or	X					
				X		
Impatient clicks or				X		
					X	
GUI events preempt (most browsers)						
Accidental double clicks or		X		X		
			X	X		
Impatient clicks				X		
GUI events are concurrent						
Accidental extra clicks		X				X
Impatient clicks				X		X

Web applications should also be designed to allow the user to work on multiple pages concurrently. Users often do this to save time. For example, a user might enter information about a purchase on one page while perusing information about products on another page while the purchase page is loading. To make this possible, the application's actions must be re-entrant or guarded re-entrant—even for the same user. That is, access to the session data must be designed for concurrency.

> Web applications should be designed to allow the user to work on multiple pages concurrently.

Multiple page access is a natural result of using a correct client-tier MVC pattern as described earlier, because that pattern ensures serialized access to client data—the "local model" as it is referred to in the pattern. To adapt this pattern to a Web application, do the following: (1) handle incoming HTTP requests with an Action Listener, (2) encapsulate all session data as a Local Model, and (3) render an HTTP response via a GUI Model.

12.2.8 Concurrency Testing and Validation

As for any kind of testing, concurrency testing should be driven by requirements. However, concurrency requirements for an application are not always well-defined. The application's architect often has the job of eliciting service level requirements from users and deriving concurrency requirements from the service level requirements and other assumptions about the application's design and anticipated operation. For example, the following requirement is repeated from Section 2.2.2, "Reliability Categories."

> Up to 200 users can access, use, and enter data via the user interface concurrently, working according to the usage profile developed by the requirements team and included in the appendix to these requirements.

On the face of it, it might seem that in order to test for compliance with this requirement, one merely needs to simulate the actions of 200 users. Indeed, concurrency testing is often done as part of end-to-end "scalability testing." However, while scalability testing should include stressing the ability of the application and infrastructure to manage concurrency, this form of testing is inappropriate as a *primary* means of testing for correct concurrent access.

To limit concurrency testing to an end-to-end level would be woefully inadequate. As with all kinds of requirements, concurrency requirements need to be tested at all levels—not just at an end-to-end level. Unfortunately, in business applications, concurrency requirements are usually specified only at an end-to-end level. The application architect therefore must translate the end-to-end concurrency requirements into a set of derived requirements for each concurrent component in the application.

> The application architect must translate the end-to-end concurrency requirements into a set of derived requirements for each concurrent component in the application.

For example, suppose the application architecture calls for a Web application tier and a transaction processing tier. Each tier should be tested independently for correct concurrent operation.♦ It is the application architect's responsibility to ensure that this principle is satisfied throughout the application, on a system-wide level as well as on a sub-system level, and sometimes even on a unit level for critical concurrent components. This should be approached by reviewing the design of each component and defining derived concurrency requirements that can be tested on a component level and using judgment to decide which components will affect the application's concurrency or have a potential for concurrency errors. In a sense, the concurrency risk of a component should be judged, and testing done in accordance with that risk.

♦ Recall the principle "Concurrent Execution Should Not Cause Application Programs to Malfunction" (presented at the beginning of this chapter), articulated by Jim Gray as the "First Law of Concurrency Control."

Concurrency testing is complex and must have special tests designed for the purpose of verifying correct concurrent operation. This often involves creating special test driver programs that generate many concurrent requests or user sessions and that validate the result of each and every concurrent transaction. Thus, the purpose of concurrency testing is not to discover scalability issues. Rather, it is to *prove that the application's design protects independent operations from interfering with each other.*

Concurrency testing is complex and special tests should be designed for the purpose of verifying correct concurrent operation.

In order to correctly plan and design tests for concurrency, the application architect must consider the various parts of the application that allow for concurrency and design tests that specifically stress those and verify that the application behaves correctly. For example, if an application allows a user to change his address in a database, the concurrency test suite might include a test that generates many concurrent address changes and *verifies that each change is done correctly before another change is allowed to take affect*, as well as verifying that other transactions that read the address never get a value that is incorrect or inconsistent.

A basic level of concurrency testing should be incorporated into the regression test suite for every critical transaction in an application. This is primarily to ensure that maintenance changes do not introduce concurrency problems where none existed before. In addition, the test team should work with the application architect to identify those transactions and request handlers that are complex and that involve multiple resources or perform multiple actions and design concurrency tests specifically to test that they work correctly if multiple users invoke those actions concurrently in different sequences.

The application architect should design additional concurrency tests for those transactions and request handlers that are complex and that involve multiple resources or perform multiple actions.

One of the greatest challenges in creating concurrency tests is establishing the context of each test. The test context is the full context (for example, thread, user identity, process, and so on) of each request or call that is made from the test driver to the component under test. Depending on the nature of the component's interface, some aspects of the context might not be relevant and need not be established. For example, if authentication and authorization are not performed by the interface, it is pointless to set up a security context for each request. Sometimes aspects of the context of the test program are process-specific, so it might be necessary to create each test client as a separate process. Ideally, each can be created as a separate thread.

Ordering of events can sometimes be forced to vary in an abnormal way by overloading a system.

Concurrency testing should consider the implementation of the concurrency control mechanisms. Thus, it is best done as "white box" testing. As an example, if the concurrency mechanism utilizes a queue of a certain size, the test suite should verify correct behavior when the number of entries in the queue is driven beyond the queue size, which is known.

Concurrency tests should undertake to vary the timing of operations, including how frequently they occur and how long they take. Any assumptions that, for example, "operation A always completes before operation B starts" should be stressed, so see if it is possible for such assumptions to be violated and *what happens when they are.* Erroneous assumptions about ordering of events are the source of so-called "TOCTTOU" attacks (see Section 5.1.7, "Exploitation of Non-Atomicity"). Remember that ordering can sometimes be forced to vary in an abnormal way by overloading a system.

Concurrency tests should be performed first in a development environment in order to debug the tests and to discover design flaws that can be uncovered in that environment. The tests should then be repeated in a controlled test environment.

The following design pattern provides an approach for designing a test driver for performing concurrency testing.

Design Pattern: Concurrency Test Driver

Context

An application component's concurrency requirements must be tested.

Problem

Most testing paradigms do not address concurrency.

Forces

A standard pattern is needed for implementing all the concurrency test programs that are required for a project so that they can be executed and managed in a uniform way.

Solution

This pattern presents a basic approach for conducting concurrency tests. It consists of instantiating a test driver program that serves to control or coordinate the actions of the various concurrent tests. The test driver program instantiates a number of independent test client objects. It is these objects that actually interact with the component that is being tested.

Each client object is responsible for establishing the contextual environment that it needs to perform its tests. This contextual environment includes any required test data or configuration, as well as any thread context, security context, or process context that is propagated to the component under test and that might affect the test. After the test context has been established by a client object, the object then executes a series of tests. Each test might require the re-establishment of part of the client's test environment. The activities are shown in Figure 12.11.

Each time a client performs a test, the test's results should be verified. This verification should be performed within the same context as the test client to ensure that it sees the outcome of that client's actions and not the outcome of another client's actions. For example, any locks held by the client object might need to be retained until after verification has occurred.

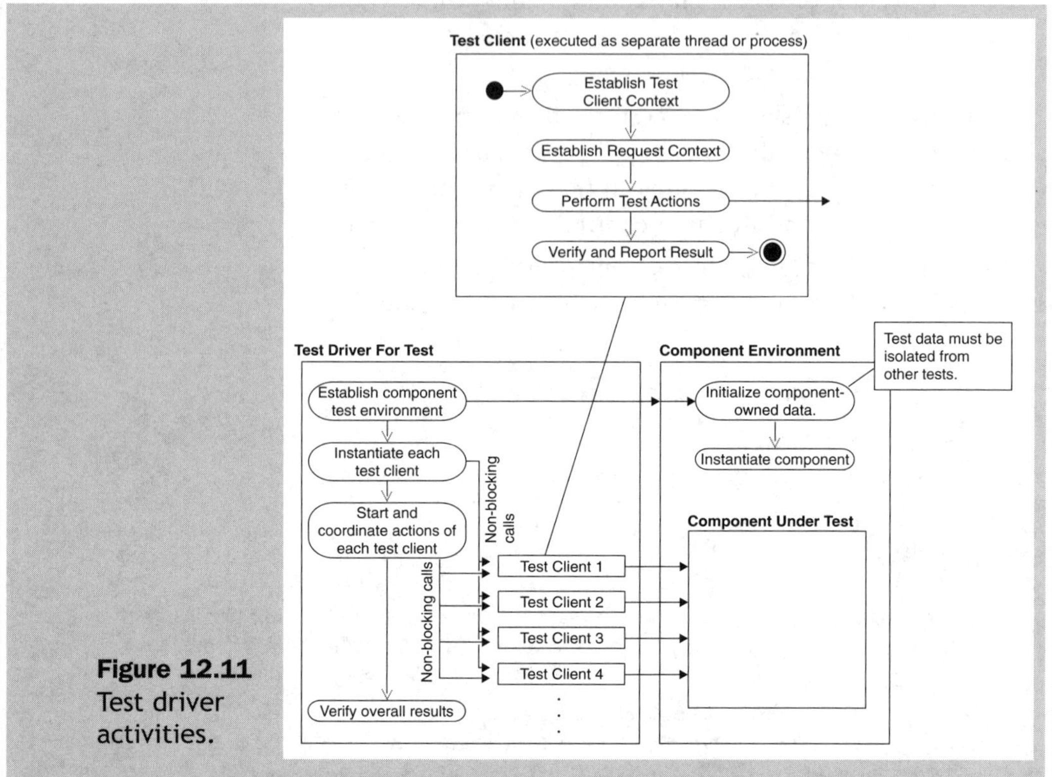

Figure 12.11 Test driver activities.

This pattern does not consider deadlock, which would have the effect of "hanging" a test client object. If deadlock might be possible, each test client object should include a mechanism to time-out a request.

Consequences

Concurrency can be tested in the same manner as other tests by using test drivers that manage their own setup. Concurrency tests tend to require modifications to the components under test in order to facilitate testability. Concurrency tests also tend to require access to the component's execution environment in order to control it; for example, to introduce artificial load or cause specific kinds of failures. Standard practices for ensuring the separation of data sets used for different test suites must also be adhered to.

As an example of the usage of this pattern, consider a Web application that is to be tested. Suppose that the Web application accesses a transactional back end consisting of EJBs, and one of those EJBs has a method called "doAandB." In this application's design, the doAandB() method utilizes an external resource R from a third party that in turn accesses a database. The resource might be, for example, another standalone EJB server. It provides two methods: doA() and doB(). The provider of the resource has alleged that it is transactional, but this must be verified.[4]

The testing team and application architect have wisely decided that the integration of the EJB tier and the external resource should be tested before they are tested in integration with the Web tier. The test setup of the EJB and external resource tiers is shown in Figure 12.12.

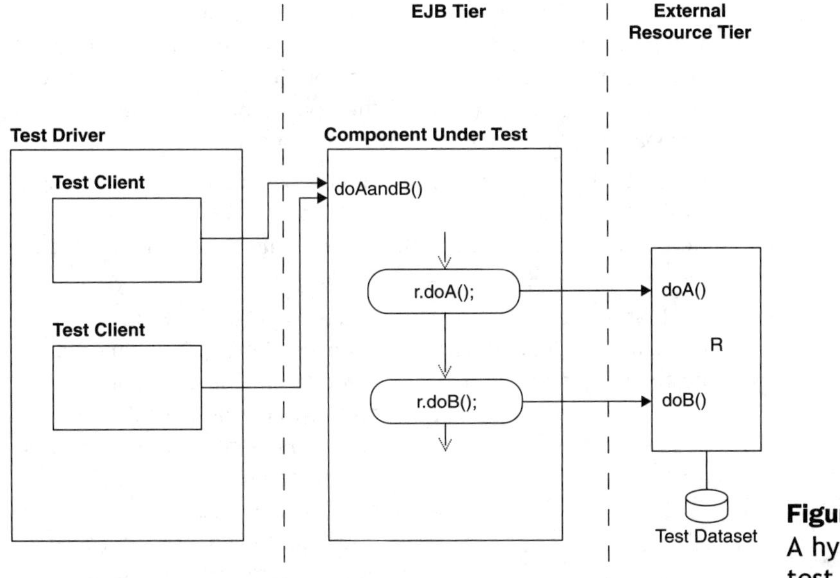

Figure 12.12
A hypothetical test scenario.

Upon consideration of the concurrency requirements for the application, and the design of the application and its tiers, the test objectives shown in Table 12.4 were created by the testing team and the project architect.

Table 12.4 Testing Requirements

#	Objective	Strategy
1	Test that doA() and doB() are properly isolated.	Insert a delay flag into doA(). Invoke doAandB() with the delay flag, and concurrently invoke doAandB() again a short interval after, but without the delay flag. Verify that both complete correctly.

4 The author has encountered situations in which testing proved that a resource was in fact not transactional, despite claims by the vendor that it was.

Table 12.4 Testing Requirements continued

#	Objective	Strategy
2	Test that if doB() fails, doA() is rolled back.	Cause doB() to fail, and verify that doA() did not modify any data.
3	Test that if doAandB() is aborted at various points, the entire transaction is rolled back and has no side effects.	Invoke doAandB(), and stop its thread a short interval later. Verify that either both doA() and doB() completed correctly or neither completed or left any side effects.
4	Test that if doB() runs too long, it times out and the transaction is rolled back and the appropriate error is propagated to the client.	Force doB() to time out by insert ing a delay into it. Verify that a TimeoutException is received by the test client. Verify that doA() has not modified any data.
5	Test that if R is slowed down, a window of potential interference is not introduced.	Greatly overload R by generating a large rate of CRUD transactions. At the same time, run this test suite.
6	Test that if R fails, the connection is cleaned up and the pool is repaired.	Cause doA() to throw an unchecked exception, either by using erroneous data or by delib- erately throwing an unchecked exception. Verify that the resource R is restored to an operational state or replaced and that the resource and connection pools have not grown as a result.

Notice that test #1 requires modifying the code of both the doA() and doAandB() methods. Thus, the design of these methods must be enhanced to make them testable. (See the discussion of "design for testability" in Chapter 3, "Design Specification and Verification.") In order to accommodate this without changing the API used by clients of these methods, a separate non-test version can be created for each method by overriding the method and excluding the test-only arguments. For example:

Version Used for Test #1	Normal Version
doA(boolean delay) { ... }	doA() { doA(false); }
doAandB(boolean delay) { ... }	doAandB() { doA(false); }

The test version of these methods should be made inaccessible to clients during normal operation; for example, by commenting them out before building for deployment.

Test #2 requires the creation or simulation of a failure condition. (This is analogous to "fault injection" for hardware testing.) The required failure condition can be achieved either by building it into the code (design for testability) or by using test data that is known to cause the failure. The latter is a fragile approach because it in effect becomes a requirement of the component: namely, that the particular data causes a particular failure. This brings up an important point: that *any behavior that is embedded within a component for the purpose of testability should be documented as a derived requirement for the component.*

Test #3 requires the use of a mechanism to time the point at which a thread is stopped. The required delay can be achieved *by timing it* or by *keying it to a particular event.* Timing is simpler: for example, a basic timer can be used to delay the point at which the thread is stopped after doAandB() is invoked by the thread. This works fine under test conditions, but will it accurately reflect what might happen if the normal timing of events within the system is skewed, for example, by a denial of service attack? Therefore, when testing sub-components, a more reliable way to test the behavior of components in the presence of delay is to test against *different relative sequences of events*, and to *force those sequences to be deterministic.* For example, there might be different events that occur as a result of the processing of the method doAandB(), and these events can be used to signal the point at which the thread should be stopped. Time-based delay is simpler to implement, however.

> Delay can be inserted by timing it or by keying it to events.

When performing concurrency testing at an *integration level*, it is more appropriate to implement delay using an approach that approximately simulates the expected range of variability of the relative timing of external events and duration of system processes. For example, varying the time between requests and the time to service requests can reveal timing problems in the configuration of server components, such as Web servers and load balancers.

From this example, it is apparent that the test driver serves a critical role, not just for initiating the test client threads, but for coordinating their action. For example, test #3 requires the test driver to start a test client thread that invokes the doAandB() method, and the driver must then wait until the appropriate moment at which to stop that client thread. Thus, the test driver is actually a test program that creates and coordinates multiple smaller concurrent program entities.

The effect of concurrency on scalability must also be tested. For example, transactions that attempt to access the same resources should be performed concurrently to see what impact they have on throughput. This kind of testing is less granular than the kind of testing that is needed for concurrency reliability testing and can be done as part of scalability testing.

12.3 Summary

This chapter presented fundamental principles and patterns for concurrent programming. The reader is expected to be familiar with these ideas, but here their relationship to assurance was emphasized. Process coordination and coordination of error response were discussed, and models for synchronous and asynchronous error handling were presented. Interruption was discussed, along with the error handling problems that must be dealt with, and issues related to timeout. Finally, the design of tests for correct concurrent operation was discussed. This foundation is expanded upon in the next chapter, which discusses concurrency in the context of persistent resources—i.e., databases.

12.4 Exercises

1. A multi-user application incorporates a restart feature that allows the application to restart automatically if it is shut down for any reason. Restart is initiated by a request from a user that is received by a separate

"broker" process that merely waits for user requests. If a user request is received and the application is not running, the broker starts it. Before starting the application, however, the broker checks to see whether a file exists: The existence of this file indicates that the broker, which is multi-threaded, has already begun starting the application. If the file does not exist, the broker starts the application–otherwise, it does not. When the application has been started, the broker deletes the file. What is wrong with this design?

2. An application must act as a single interface for accessing other services. Specifically, it must present a single reentrant method that clients can call. When called, the application must perform a query against each of a configurable number of other services. When all these have returned, the application method must return the result to the waiting client call. However, if a client call is interrupted, the application method must not abort: It must gracefully terminate each service call. Create a design for the application that satisfies these requirements.
3. A client application presents a window-based interface to the user. Various user actions initiate activities that are performed asynchronously. At any time, the user can exit the entire application by closing the main window. Create a design that allows this but provides for graceful termination of any asynchronous activities that are still in progress.
4. A Web application is written in PERL. It allows users to post notes and documents to an online knowledgebase. The action handler operates by opening an XML file containing the current hierarchical structure of the knowledge base, inserting an element to represent the new information, writing the new information to one or more files, and then closing both the XML file and the information files. What is missing from this design?

5. Explain how a semaphore is different from a test-and-set operation.
6. True or false: Programmers should perform concurrency testing in their own development environment. Explain.
7. What are the two aspects of isolation?
8. Explain how guarded-reentrancy is different from reentrancy.

Answers and hints for these exercises can be found at `http://www.assuredbydesign.com/haa/`.

CHAPTER 13

TRANSACTIONAL INTEGRITY

"We must all 'hang together,' or, most assuredly, we shall all hang, separately." –Benjamin Franklin, upon signing the Declaration of Independence

The concept of transactional integrity is the most important and foundational concept of designing any multiuser application that accesses a shared resource, such as a database.

An action performed by an application has *transactional integrity* if it is atomic, isolated, and recoverable. That is, if it is performed all-or-nothing, it is atomic; if it does not interfere with (i.e., see the results of or allow its intermediate results to be seen by) any other transaction in progress until the action is done, it is isolated; and if provisions are made to make the recording of the transaction reliable so that it can be fully recovered if a system failure occurs, it is recoverable. Recoverability is a matter of degree and can never be absolutely 100% reliable.

There are countless references on the subjects of transactional integrity and recoverability—for example, [1, 2, 3]—and the reader is referred to these for a broad treatment that extends beyond issues related to assurance.

> Multiprocessing applications must be designed such that they perform the appropriate collections of work as transactions.

Transactional integrity is important because it provides the programmer with a powerful tool to ensure that an application will work correctly with multiple users. Still it is only a tool, and applications that have concurrency must be designed such that they perform the appropriate collections of work as transactions. From an *application design* perspective, transactional integrity relies on the factors in Table 13.1.

Table 13.1 Factors Contributing to Transactional Integrity

Factor Contributing to Transactional Integrity	Example of Potential Problems
Compositional correctness	Two transactions can each modify a shared object thinking that they have their own copy of the object when, in fact, they do not.
Correct isolation level for each transaction	A transaction's logic can become incorrect if the isolation level is changed, leading to inconsistent data in the database.
Be aware of possible stale data within a transaction	A component can invoke another component, not knowing that the second component updates a table that the first component has read, causing the first component to have stale data—even though the transaction has not completed!
Check for stale data across transactions	An application fetches data in one transaction, modifies the data, and then writes the data to the database in a second transaction—not knowing that the data has been changed in the meantime by another user.

Factor Contributing to Transactional Integrity	Example of Potential Problems
Clear layer rules with regard to database access	A Web tier component uses JDBC to access a database table. However, by doing so, the component bypasses logic in a data access object (DAO) that validates the data that is written to the table.
Clear transaction boundary	A component's designer assumes that two updates occur within a single transaction when they do not, introducing the possibility that data will be updated inconsistently.
Complete error handling	A component does not detect when a SQL exception is due to a database timeout and merely throws an error, leading the client application to believe (incorrectly) that an unrecoverable error occurred instead of merely re-trying the transaction.
Durable and reliable infrastructure	A disk failure occurs, causing the loss of database data. There is no independent transaction log, making it impossible to recover the data.

It should be apparent that transactional integrity is not an automatic result of how a component is deployed or what container it runs in. It is primarily a result of how a component is designed. All these factors are discussed in this chapter.

13.1 Referential Integrity

Transactional inconsistency can arise from merely neglecting to update all the database elements that are required. For example, suppose that there is a cardinality relationship between two element types such that each element (or row) of type B for which the element's P field is not null must have a corresponding parent element (or row) of type A. If a programmer adds an element of type B for which the P field is not null, but forgets to associate it with an A element, the referential integrity of the data will have been violated because a required logical rule has not been maintained. The term *referential integrity* refers to the requirement that all logical relationship rules between database elements are satisfied.

Object-oriented applications are especially prone to intra-transaction inconsistency because of the emphasis on encapsulation of function.

Referential integrity is especially problematic in large corporate environments.

Referential integrity is especially problematic in large corporate environments that use relational databases for applications that span departments and rely on the schema as the integrating element. This approach has been referred to as a "data integration" pattern, because integration occurs via data definitions rather than programmatic APIs or service-message definitions.[4]

In such cases, it is very difficult for a database administrator (DBA) to maintain an understanding of the nuances of the various schema, so DBAs more often than not throw up their hands and leave schema design to application groups and serve mainly as maintainers of schema quality standards. In such a situation, it is almost impossible to maintain referential integrity rules within the database (for those database systems that support embedded referential integrity rules—not all do), so the responsibility for maintaining referential integrity falls to the *applications themselves.* The database's ability to detect integrity violations is then not utilized, and integrity relies on each developer being aware of each and every integrity rule—a *very problematic situation.*

In such an environment, applications become increasingly hard to maintain as the original designers of the applications move on to new assignments and the applications grow in complexity. They soon reach a critical mass where it becomes more cost effective to replace an application than to add new features or fix problems. Such environments are plagued by application glitches and anomalies, the constant need to repair errors every time new features are added, unexpected problems whenever any code is changed, and the need to run the entire test suite whenever any change is made to anything. Such designs also make it impossible to implement granular security policies with regard to who can access data on a row-specific basis.

If referential integrity rules are incompletely specified or poorly maintained, applications that use the database will be plagued by problems.

One way to help prevent this kind of degeneration of the design is to create a layer of "data access objects" (DAOs) around the database. The DAOs provide programmatic encapsulation for the business rules related to data consistency. This appears to defeat the concept of a relational database, which is to provide for easy ad-hoc—as opposed to programmatic—access to data. However, if done properly, it does not. Ad-hoc access is most often done for the purpose of either (1) accounting functions or other functions that must tabulate the data in constantly changing ways or (2) research functions that explore relationships within the data. These functions can be provided via a data warehouse that is created *alongside the primary database*. The DAOs can then be used by programmers to access the primary database. If the DAOs implement all data integrity (consistency) rules, the programmers can be sure that any referential integrity errors or omissions will be detected by the DAO layer.

The disadvantage of this approach is that it separates the data definition (the schema) from the data integrity rules, which are implemented programmatically within the DAOs. It is better than not having any data integrity rules at all, however.

If a separate data warehouse is not in the picture, and ad-hoc queries must be allowed against the primary database, it is important that the schema be maintained in a way that is understandable to users and that meta data descriptions are definitive and kept up to date, even though the primary access is through a DAO layer.

DAO design patterns are available in many sources; for example, [5].

13.2 Transaction Isolation

We have already discussed isolation in the context of multithreading. The same ideas apply to transactions. Isolation refers to the ability of a transaction to see the results of another transaction before the other transaction is complete or before the current transaction is complete. The lack of isolation, or the ability to see "into" another transaction, enables the transactions to interfere with each other. For SQL, there are four standard isolation levels: 0 through 3. These are described in Table 13.2.

Table 13.2 Summary of SQL Isolation Levels

Level	Description
0	Anything can happen.
1	Dirty reads prevented—i.e., data that is read will have been committed by some transaction, although it might later be modified before the current transaction is done.
2	Dirty reads prevented. Non-repeatable reads prevented—i.e., successive queries will contain the same data, although there might be additional records each time.
3	Dirty reads prevented. Non-repeatable reads prevented. Phantom reads prevented—i.e., successive queries will return the same number of records.

In general, the lowest isolation level yields the best performance and concurrency but introduces the risk of incorrect results in a multi-user environment. It is, therefore, very important that isolation level be considered on a transaction-by-transaction basis.

When developing an application, it is best to set the level to the highest level by default to ensure correctness and then lower it level where possible to improve performance. The level assumed for each transaction should be documented in the transaction's source code—not merely in a deployment configuration. Having it documented in the source proves that the issue has been considered by a programmer.[1]

PRINCIPLE: USE MAXIMUM TRANSACTION ISOLATION BY DEFAULT; REDUCE ISOLATION ON A CASE-BY-CASE BASIS, ONLY WHEN ANALYSIS PROVES THAT THE TRANSACTION WILL STILL BE SOUND.

1 Many databases allow the isolation level to be established either administratively or programmatically. For example, Oracle provides the SET TRANSACTION ISOLATION LEVEL <level-name> statement that can be executed by an application program, which can be executed at the start of a transaction. To change the isolation level of an entire session, one can use the ALTER SESSION command to set the transaction isolation level on a session-wide basis. Note that use of these statements in Oracle may require that INITRANS be set high enough to provide sufficient space for storing history.

This ensures that when the application is deployed, it will work under concurrent usage. This assumes that correctness is a higher priority than performance. Higher concurrency can then be achieved through tuning and thoughtfully reducing the isolation level of individual transactions.

Isolation can be achieved by locking or by versioning. With lock-based isolation, separate transactions are kept from interfering by the fact that they must obtain an exclusive lock for any data that they access. With versioning, isolation is achieved by maintaining a separate version of the data for each transaction that needs to access the data concurrently; when the transactions attempt to complete, inconsistencies are reconciled—for example, by aborting and rolling back the later-committing transaction—and the allowed new version becomes the version that is permanently written to the database.[2]

A transaction should be performed by a single thread of execution. If that is not the case, the absence of isolation between the separate transaction threads means that there is no mechanism to serialize access to database data elements, and interference between the separate threads can result.

13.3 Ensuring Consistency Across Transactions

Isolation has to do with preventing interference between separate transactions. Consistency has to do with ensuring that multiple updates make sense when you look at all of them. There are various methodologies for ensuring that the logical consistency—i.e., the referential integrity—of a database is maintained as updates are made to it by separate transactions.

There are two common approaches to preventing this: These are the well-known database access paradigms of *pessimistic concurrency control* and *optimistic concurrency control.* The "pessimistic" approach utilizes the database's locking mechanism to retain control of all data that is used by a session until

---

2 Sybase uses lock-based isolation. Oracle uses version-based isolation and only uses locking if the programmer specifies the Oracle-specific "FOR UPDATE" clause in the SQL.

it is convenient for the client to refresh the data. The "optimistic" approach does not retain control of the data, but at the point at which an update is attempted, it first checks whether the data has changed, and only if it has not does the transaction proceed. Thus, there is the "optimistic" assumption that most of the time it will not have changed.

Either approach can be used when designing the logical transactions to be performed against a database. In fact, it is reasonable to mix and match approaches, depending on the nature of the user process.

When using pessimistic concurrency control, a logical unit of work to be performed by a user is implemented as a single database transaction. Thus, this is a very simplistic approach. This approach is practical only when contention for the resources to be locked is not a concern. This might be the case if the work to be performed is limited in scope and can be performed quickly so that resource locks are not maintained for a long period of time. Contention might also not be an issue if the transaction is performed at a time when there is low contention for the resources. The pessimistic concurrency control pattern is summarized by the following pattern definition.

DESIGN PATTERN: PESSIMISTIC CONCURRENCY CONTROL

Related Patterns

This pattern is the core paradigm for ensuring data integrity in databases, and it is widely documented. (See, for example, the ACID Transaction pattern in [6].)

Context

An application needs to update data in a multi-user database.

Problem

If a user's access has not finished when a second user accesses the same data, interference between the two accesses might result.

Forces

User accesses tend to be short in duration or access resources (for example, table rows) that only that user has an interest in.

Solution

A database provides a resource manager to isolate one transaction from the next, by locking from the moment a user accesses it until the user's transaction completes. Thus, we are assuming that lock-based isolation is being used. This is depicted in Figure 13.1.

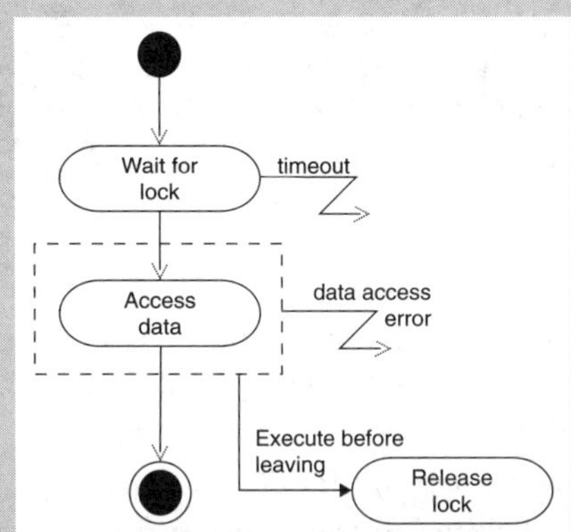

Figure 13.1
Activities.

The lock can either be a read lock or a write lock, depending on whether the access is for read or for write. It can be for any granularity, such as a data row or a database table (as in a relational database), a database page (a physical unit that has no relation to the data model), an application object, or any other unit of data.

A lock indicates that the lock holder has some form of control over access to the data unit to which the lock pertains. Locks can be of different kinds and can have different nuances on different products, but a read lock means that any other database transaction can also obtain a read lock and therefore read the data, but no write locks can be obtained for it. A write lock, on the other hand, is exclusive and means that no other transaction can also have a read lock or write lock.

Different locking policies are effective for different kinds of transactions. There are many other kinds of locks as well. For example, an "intention lock" is a read lock that reserves the exclusive right to upgrade the lock to a write lock before the transaction completes, so other transactions can still read the data but may not obtain a write lock or an intention lock on it. A discussion of the many different kinds of locks is out of the scope of this book, and the reader is referred to [7] for more information.

In the figure, there is one successful termination path and two unsuccessful paths. The first unsuccessful path represents a timeout such that the lock was not obtained after a specified period of time. This kind of error can be caused by a deadlock, or it can simply be caused by a database that is very busy. Differentiating between the two conditions requires the database to execute a deadlock detection algorithm. Some databases perform this automatically, and others do not. In either case, the usual remedy is to try the transaction again, up to a specified number of failed attempts. It is important to recognize that timeout, while unsuccessful, is *normal* when a system is under load and should not be treated as an "error."

The second unsuccessful completion path represents any kind of data access error. This can include timeout as well, but in that case, the timeout is caused by the data access taking too long. A data access error can also occur if there is a error in processing the data access logic (for example, a SQL error), an error performing a stored procedure, a table-full condition, or any other kind of error while performing the data access. All these situations should be differentiated by reading the contents of the access error response, such as the SQL code that is returned.

Note that all completion paths—normal and abnormal—must release the lock if it is held.

Consequences
Locks are held until a transaction completes, successfully or unsuccessfully. Therefore, long duration transactions that use this pattern can have greatly reduced concurrency—the ability of multiple users to access data at the same time.

A major source of inconsistency in poorly designed applications is when clients cache database data and then re-submit it as part of an update without checking whether any of it has changed in the meantime. If the data is checked for changes before the update is applied, you have optimistic concurrency control. Thus, optimistic concurrency control is primarily a client-side strategy, although it often involves some special support on the database side (such as the automatic insertion of timestamps).

Data can be checked for changes either by comparing the data directly to see if it has changed or by having a timestamp field for each unit of data (for example, each table row) and comparing the timestamp whenever a row is updated. Some databases have the ability to automatically maintain a timestamp field, precisely for this purpose. In that case, the client merely has to make sure that it reads the timestamp each time a row is read so that it can read the timestamp value again for comparison purposes when it desires to update the row. The pessimistic concurrency control pattern is summarized next.

DESIGN PATTERN: OPTIMISTIC CONCURRENCY CONTROL

Related Patterns
This pattern is widely used in well-designed database applications and is widely documented; for example, the "Optimistic Offline Lock" in [8], the Optimistic Concurrency pattern in [9], and Optimistic and Timestamp Locking in [10].

Context
An application needs to update data in a multi-user database.

Problem
If a user's access has not finished when a second user accesses the same data, interference between the two accesses might result.

Forces
User accesses tend to be long in duration and access resources (for example, table rows) that other users also have an interest in.

Solution

The basic idea of this pattern is to first read data and then release any locks held on it so that other transactions can have access to it. While the application is computing updates for the data (possibly obtaining input from a human user), time passes. When the proposed updates are finally ready, the same data is *locked for update*—and the original data that was read is compared with the current values in the database. If the values have changed, this indicates that other transactions have modified the data while the updates were being computed, so the original data is now stale, and the updates may be invalid. The updates are, therefore, denied: i.e., the transaction aborts and rolls back, releasing all locks. If, however, the data has not changed in the database, the updates are allowed, and they are written to the database and the update transaction is committed. The activities are shown in Figure 13.2.

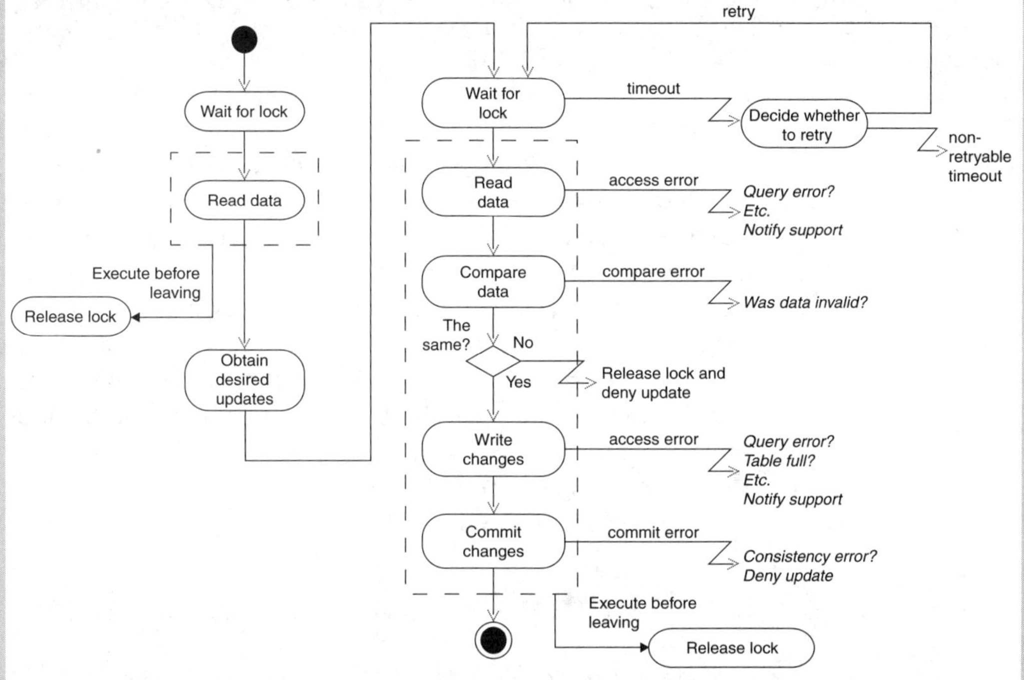

Figure 13.2 Activities.

The comparison can be performed by comparing the data *values*, or it (more commonly) can be based on a timestamp that is written to the database each time data is written. Some optimistic algorithms compare only data elements that are being updated, whereas others also compare any data that was read by the first transaction or perhaps a critical subset of what was read. The latter approach works as long as transactions that only read the data can read slightly stale data without consequences.

Some databases have optimistic techniques built in; in that case, it is possible for a stale data exception to be thrown during the commit, and the update should be denied. This exception should be caught and treated as a normal exception condition—not necessarily an error—because it merely indicates that there was contention for the data.

It is important to ensure that all the possible error conditions are handled. The states represented by the white box are often incompletely provided for, resulting in an application that contains a vulnerability waiting to be discovered. Notice that retry logic has been added to handle a timeout when attempting to obtain the lock. (This could be added to the first lock wait as well, in the left part of the diagram.) An access error most likely is caused by a query syntax error or other program bug, so it should be reported to the user as such and the transaction should not be retried. An error during the data comparison step most likely results from a data format or range error and, ideally, the portion of the data that is failing should be reported to the user.

Consequences

Concurrency is greatly increased because users hold data only for the period required to read it or to update it—they do not hold it while they are performing computations, deciding what the updates should be. However, applications must incorporate logic to deal with the situation in which an update attempt is denied.

Optimistic concurrency control is fundamentally a "cooperative" strategy: Each client must remember to check whether data has changed before it commits any updates. However, the pattern can be built into the data access layer in order to ensure that the check is always performed. In such an implementation, the data access layer's interface records a session-based timestamp value or data item version number that indicates when or which version of the original data was retrieved by the client, and the data access layer checks this against the timestamp or version number of the last update to the data in the database. This approach has been referred to as an "implicit lock" approach by some authors [11].[3]

13.4 Intra-Transaction Consistency

The focus so far has been about consistency across transactions. It is also important to ensure consistency *within* a transaction. For example, suppose that a transaction consists of two program routines. Suppose the first routine reads a record and modifies the value, but does not write the result back to the database because it assumes that the second routine will. Suppose then that the second routine re-reads the value, also modifies it, and then writes it back to the database. The result

3 Oracle provides this as a native feature, called its "serialized" mode. However, Oracle's mechanism only verifies that the data fields that are being updated have not changed—it does not verify that data that has been read during the transaction has not changed. This is often sufficient—but not always.

will be wrong because when the second routine re-read the value, it ignored the change that had been made by the first routine. This might seem like an unlikely goof, but it is in fact very likely if an application consists of many reusable routines. Object-oriented applications are especially prone to this because of the emphasis on encapsulation of function.

The essence of this problem is that data is, in effect, cached by one routine, and then the cache is ignored by another routine. A program variable is a cache, and anytime you read a database value into a variable, you are creating a cache of that database value. Care must then be taken to access only the cache until the cached value is written back to the database, and at that point the cached value should be invalidated. This is basic cache design.

Object-oriented applications are especially prone to intra-transaction inconsistency because of the emphasis on encapsulation of function.

Of course, a database application should not involve building a cache. We need some simple principles to allow programmers to avoid this problem without building complex infrastructure.

One such principle is that if data is retrieved from a database during a transaction, do not maintain more than one copy of that data throughout the entire transaction.

PRINCIPLE: MAINTAIN ONLY ONE COPY OF EACH DATUM WITHIN A TRANSACTION.

This principle ensures that multiple copies of the same data cannot exist. This helps to ensure consistency when data is modified as part of a calculation. It does not completely eliminate the possibility of inconsistency, however, because derived values can exist within a transaction, and care must be taken that if an input to a derived value is changed, the derived value is updated accordingly.

The next principle helps to ensure that if separate parts of a transaction read the same data from a database, and if this data is updated at an intermediate point within the transaction, that any changes to the data are seen by all aspects of the transaction. (This assumes that the transaction isolation characteristics are such that a transaction sees *its own updates* when it *re-reads data* from the database, and this is true for most widely used databases.)

If an application method retrieves data from a database during a transaction and then modifies the data, the method should always immediately write the modified data to the database before exiting or calling any other methods that might read from the database.

PRINCIPLE: WRITE THROUGH PERSISTENT CHANGES BEFORE DATA MIGHT BE RE-READ.

These two principles are sometimes hard to adhere to in an application because it might make sense to wait until several data changes are computed before writing any of them to the database. One solution to this problem is to employ an object-oriented persistence layer that internally maintains a cache. (See the "Identity Map" and "Unit of Work" patterns in [12].) The persistence layer can be used as a facade to save up the actual database writes, and object-level changes can be made at multiple points without worrying about the immediate-write principle.

13.5 Transactions on Composite Objects

The concept of composition discussed earlier is very valuable for designing database transactions for object-oriented applications. A database is a global, persistent, multi-user data structure. When a programmer decides what relational table rows need to be updated by a transaction, the programmer is implicitly deciding what rows and fields are *owned* by an actor in the system at that point in the workflow.

When designing an object-oriented database application, the most natural database paradigm to use is a persistent object model. A persistent object model can be implemented by using a native object database, or it can be mapped to a relational model using a "persistence mapping" tool.[4] A relational mapping can also be designed by hand, using a pattern such as the Data Access Objects (DAO) pattern or Composite Entity pattern. [13]

Regardless, if the persistence model used by programmers is an object model, the programmers will need to think in terms of *transactions on composite objects.*

4 Some popular native object databases include Object Store (`http://objectstore.org`) and db4objects (`http://www.db4objects.com/`).

A *composite object transaction* is a transaction that ensures that each object that is accessed as part of a transaction is retained in the scope of the transaction for the duration of the transaction. (This is not to be confused with the "Composite of Pre-Existing Transactions" pattern discussed in Section 13.7.2, "Combining Pre-Existing Transactions.") This ensures the integrity of the composite objects that are accessed as part of a transaction.

Depending on the isolation level, any updates performed by a transaction can be atomic, and changes can be invisible to other transactions until the update is complete.

Let's consider an application that consists of the processing of a loan application. A loan application contains many data fields that have to be filled in over time. Suppose that much of the data is often not available when the application is created. Therefore, the loan officer must obtain pieces of the data and add them to the application over a period of days, until the application is complete. When it is complete, it is submitted for approval (or rejection).

The set of data that comprises the application represents a composite object: The application's identifying entry (for example, the application number, or key) logically owns all the records that comprise the application data. Further, when the loan is submitted for approval, all this data is logically submitted with the loan identifier as if it were all sent together on a sheet of paper. There is an assumption that the data cannot be altered once submitted or shared with other applications that might alter it.

THE PROBLEM WITH RELATIONAL DATABASES FOR OO APPLICATIONS

- The transport of the data back and forth between a relational database and an application server is tremendously inefficient.
- The relational model is so different from the OO model used by application servers that few programmers are sufficiently well-versed in both to be able to produce well-designed applications.
- Relational access APIs used by OO applications do not provide an extensible persistent view. As a result, the "result set" object that is returned, while technically an object, is useless as a container of data *for processing the data,* and so programmers must copy the data into new objects after each database query.
- In short: The most robust and maintainable model for many, if not most, OO application server applications is a true ("native") object database.

Thus, the transaction that submits the loan for approval is actually a transaction that designates that set of data as "complete" and "ready to be reviewed for approval." It implicitly operates on the entire set of data—not just on the key that identifies the data. Therefore, when designing the transactions that operate on a loan application, it is useful to consider the loan data as a *composite object*, and loan transactions operate on composite objects. This way of looking at the problem gives great clarity to the design and ensures that transactions do not inadvertently update data that is not intended to be shared.

As with any transaction, deadlock can occur in the normal course of operation, and applications must explicitly handle timeout and deadlock. This is discussed further in Section 13.11.2, "Handling Non-Successful But Normal Resource Conditions."

There are many patterns for the lazy loading of object composites (for example, see the "Lazy Load" pattern in [14]), and many persistence products provide this.

13.6 Dealing with Non-Transactional Resources

It is often unavoidable that a transaction must access some resources outside the scope of an application transaction. A typical example is a standard Unix or NFS file system accessed by an application transaction. Another example is an external Web service accessed from an application transaction via HTTP. A third example is an LDAP directory access, accessed from an application transaction via the standard LDAP protocol. In any of these cases, it is not possible to create a true composite transaction because the protocols mentioned do not support transactional cooperation, and products of the types mentioned do not normally provide any kind of transaction management.

If the design calls for embedding a non-transactional resource access within a transactional method, it is extremely important to examine all the failure scenarios and document them as part of the transaction. Further, the transaction's error handler should throw an exception indicating which artifacts remain when the transaction fails and thereby compel clients to handle those cases. For example, if a single transaction accesses both a database and then a file system in that order, and if the transaction then writes three files to the file system but fails when trying to write a fourth, the transaction should not only set itself to roll back, but it should throw an exception, such as "FileWriteException," and attach to the exception a list of the files (for example, as a "data identification" attribute) that were actually written. These files need to be deleted or cleaned up in some manner by the client application, so the client application should be forced to deal with this situations explicitly.♦

◆ This is the principle "Throw Specific Exceptions—Not Generic Ones" that is discussed in Section 18.2.1, "Ensuring That All Situations Are Handled."

PRINCIPLE: DOCUMENT SIDE EFFECTS WITHIN A TRANSACTION.

One effective cleanup strategy is to use the Checkout pattern to reserve access to the affected data until the entire logical transaction is either re-performed successfully or cleaned up.

This entire situation can often be avoided by dividing a transaction up into separate steps that are performed separately by the application. The user can then monitor the progress of each step, and if one fails, not progress to the next. For example, the file writes could be performed as a second application step, with the step's completion status recorded as a workflow state in the database. Thus, the application would be written to not assume that if the database write completed, the file writes completed as well—each would be a separately tracked step. In the design approach, it is important that each step be implemented as a transaction and that the update of the workflow state is performed as part of each transaction.

If a workflow progresses partially through to the end but then must be aborted, "compensating transactions" [15] must be generated to undo those steps that have already been completed, effectively deleting that "job" or "task."[5]

Another solution to the non-transactional resource problem is to replace non-transactional resources with transactional ones. For example, there are transactional file systems, and there are transactional LDAP directories. However, that is often not practical because it typically requires homogeneity with regard to product vendors and the use of non-standard protocols or APIs.

5 This is the motivation behind "compensation handlers" in Business Process Execution Language (BPEL) for Web services, developed by BEA, IBM, Microsoft, SAP, and Siebel.

13.7 Combining Transactions

Resources that are transactional are often referred to as "managed resources" because they are accessed under the purview of a *resource manager*. For example, a database management system includes a resource manager for coordinating access to the files and records controlled by the database. A resource manager provides transaction management, including some level of isolation between transactions, some level of rollback if a transaction fails or is aborted, and some level of recovery if the system fails. The resource manager starts a transaction automatically when a user accesses the resource and commits the transaction when resource access has completed.

Applications sometimes need to take control of the commit of transactions. An application can explicitly command the resource manager to commit a transaction or it can delegate this command to a *transaction manager*. The scenarios that demand these approaches are discussed next.

13.7.1 Kinds of Transaction Composition

A *composite transaction* is a transaction that is created by combining multiple independent transactions into a single transaction.[6] Situations that demand this include:

1. Performing separate actions against a single resource, under a single transaction.
2. Joining transactions against multiple resources into a single transaction.
3. Joining transactions against a single resource into a single transaction.

The first situation is the most common case. It occurs when an application needs to perform more than one access to a resource and requires all these accesses to be treated as one single transaction. In that case, the application tells the resource manager to refrain from committing a transaction after each

6 This term is not standardized. For example, some authors use this term to refer to any transaction that acts on multiple entities as part of a single managed transaction.

access, and when the application has performed all its accesses, it explicitly sends a command to commit. In this situation, the application takes control of the transaction.

The second is also fairly common and occurs when there is more than one resource manager. For example, suppose an application running in an application server uses a database, but also uses a third-party application that is transactional. In this case, there are two resource managers accessed by the primary application: the database and the third-party application. If the primary application needs to perform functions involving both of these resource types, but within a single transaction, it must utilize a distributed transaction involving both resource managers.

To do this, the primary application delegates transaction management to a transaction manager. The transaction manager is often provided by the application platform. For example, EJB platforms provide distributed transaction management. Distributed transaction management utilizes the "XA" distributed transaction protocol and requires the use of so-called "XA drivers."

There are significant overhead and reliability issues when using distributed transactions, and XA drivers often fail to support needed features or have reliability problems. This approach, therefore, should not be used unless it is thoroughly tested ahead of time with the chosen products. However, if done well, the encapsulation provided by aggregating separate resource accesses under a single transaction can greatly simplify a design. The pattern sometimes referred to as Entity Aggregation focuses on this approach. [16]

The third scenario is almost never done intentionally, but it is an important case that must be considered when XA drivers are used to ensure that a certain class of bugs does not arise. If a persistence layer hides the resource accesses, which might involve multiple resources managed by a distributed (for example, XA) transaction manager, it is possible that in some circumstances the *same resource* is accessed *via multiple paths* during the overall transaction. If one access made updates to the database, the question is, will the second access see those updates—even though the transaction has not yet been committed? In a normal transaction, the answer is generally yes, but if the transaction is distributed and the second access occurs via a different path (for example, direct SQL instead of via a stored procedure), or executed from a second application server against the same database, the second access *might not see the updates.* Again, this occurs primarily in the rare circumstance that two parts of a *composite* transaction both access the same database via different paths.

The cause of this kind of inconsistency is that some distributed drivers do not support the full propagation of transaction context across different branches of a composite transaction. This occurs mainly when the branches originate in different application tiers and are not sharing the same driver instance. Distributed transaction drivers that are *tightly coupled* do not have this problem; those that are *loosely coupled* do. The latter is the norm.

To avoid this problem, either avoid composite transactions or ensure that the various transaction branches (paths) do not overlap in terms of the resources that they access.

13.7.2 Combining Pre-Existing Transactions

Composite transactions can often be created by combining multiple previously written transactions into a single transaction by writing a single transaction that invokes both of the previously written transactions. However, this is a bad practice, because (1) the previously written transactions are maintained independently and the global effect of using them within a single transaction must be taken into account, and (2) combining existing transactions violates the principles "Employ a Collaboration Pattern for Intra-Layer Communication" discussed in Section 7.13, "Resource Interface Design," and "A Software Layer Should Define an 'Interface' for Use by Upper Layers Only" discussed in Section 7.19.1, "Layers," because the preexisting transactions represent part of the same layer interface.

It is possible to design transactions from the beginning so that they *could* be aggregated–i.e., so that they could call each other without any problem. This book refers to transactions that belong to a set of transactions that can be called from within a single transaction scope without problems as *composable transactions.*

When designing a composite transaction, the actions of each subordinate transaction must be considered together with the actions of each other subordinate transaction to see if they might conflict. Conflict at this level is unusual but possible and must be checked for. In particular, business rules might actually allow the subordinate transactions to occur together, but the individual transactions might be *designed to exclude each other.* For example, consider a set of pre-existing transactions GiveDiscountA and GiveDisountB that implement separate kinds of discount for a customer deal. Suppose that if GiveDiscountA is performed, GiveDiscountB is not allowed to be performed afterwards. The designers of these transactions, therefore, build logic into the transactions to ensure that after GiveDiscountA is performed, an attempt to perform GiveDiscountB is rejected (i.e., fails and rolls back).

Now suppose that the business decides that both Discount A and Discount B can be granted if they are performed *as part of a single deal.* In order to create a transaction to perform the actions of both GiveDiscountA and GiveDiscountB, a composite transaction cannot be created by simply performing A and B within a single transaction scope. Rather, the exclusivity logic within GiveDiscountA and GiveDiscountB must be removed, or at least re-examined and modified.

Another common source of non-composability is when there is potential collision across *non-transactional* resources, such as system files, non-transactional repositories, non-re-entrant shared libraries, and so on. Non-transactional resources are discussed in Section 13.6, "Dealing with Non-Transactional Resources."

When combining transactions, it is therefore best to perform the combination at the business logic level and create a new transaction representing the combined function. This approach is illustrated by the following pattern.

DESIGN PATTERN: COMPOSITE OF PRE-EXISTING TRANSACTIONS

Context

A transaction must be defined that combines the functions of two or more existing transactions into a single transaction while retaining the pre-existing transactions.

Problem

Blindly combining existing transactions can lead to problems and violates layer separation rules.

Solution

This pattern requires that each transaction is implemented using a "layer interface" (see the "Layer Interface" pattern defined in Section 7.19.1), such that the interface delegates to a lower business logic layer.

The new composite transaction delegates its functionality to a business logic layer component of its own, which in turn accesses pre-existing business logic components. This is depicted in Figure 13.3.

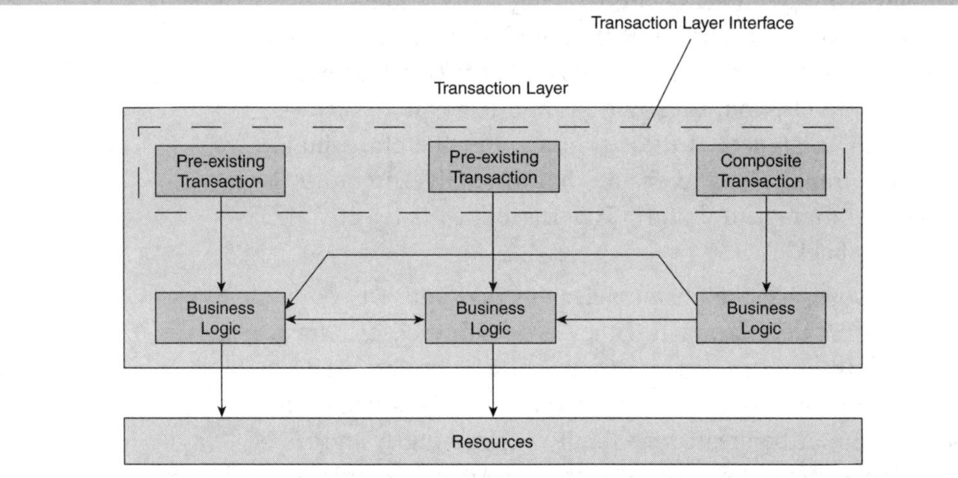

Figure 13.3 Defining a new (composite) transaction based on pre-existing ones.

Note that clients of the transactions interact only with the transaction interface, represented by the dashed line box, whereas the transactions themselves never call this interface: The transaction implementations make only internal calls to non-interface business objects. These internal calls occur within the context of whatever transaction is created when a client call enters at the transaction layer interface.

Consequences

A composite transaction is created, preserving the original transactions, without violating layer access rules.

13.7.3 Transaction Layering

Some applications require specialized processing for certain users or for certain classes of user. This often occurs when an application has a small but powerful minority of users who are able to use their clout to have changes made to the application to accommodate their unique needs. This is not to be confused with the situation in which the application provides for a certain degree of customization for all users, which is referred to as "personalization." Here we are talking about situations in which the application must, in effect, be hacked in order to take account of special requirements for certain users.

This happens a lot in business-to-business applications. As a concrete example, a major business partner or high-volume customer might require that their users interact in a certain manner and be provided with additional information each time they make a request. These custom requirements are specific to a single partner or customer, so they should not necessarily be a basis for changing the core API of the application.

In this situation, one approach is to use the Composite Transaction pattern to add a new transaction by re-factoring the existing transactions and creating a new one. All transactions then share a common set of underlying business logic objects.

Another approach—arguably a better approach in this situation— is to define a "customization layer" *on top of* the core transaction interface layer. This approach is best when the existing transaction facade implements complex functionality that you do not want to disturb but wish to leverage with the new customized transactions. In this approach, the existing transactions are not modified, but a new layer of transactions is added to accommodate the customized functionality. This layer invokes the pre-existing core transaction facade. The new customization layer executes under the same transaction management as the core facade layer, so transactions propagate across the two logical layers. The special client accesses the application via the customized transactions, whereas other users of the application access the application in the normal way. Security policy can be configured to prevent the special user from accessing the application through the "normal" means.

This pattern is defined next.

DESIGN PATTERN: LAYERED TRANSACTION

Context

A specific user or class of users presents unique requirements, which require additional or changed functionality that other users do not need.

Problem

The work required to incorporate these changes into the application is potentially extensive.

Forces

Layering the special requirements on top of the existing application would be easier.

Solution

In this pattern, the customized transactions invoke the existing common facade transactions and, as an upper layer, the customized transactions are never allowed to bypass the core transaction facade. If new business logic objects are needed, additional transactions may be added to the common transaction layer interface, and the customization layer may invoke those new transactions. It is then up to a client dispatching layer to route clients to the appropriate transaction interface—either the original (common) interface or the customization interface. This should not present a risk to the primary transactions because the primary interface's authorization mechanism remains intact. The pattern is shown in Figure 13.4.

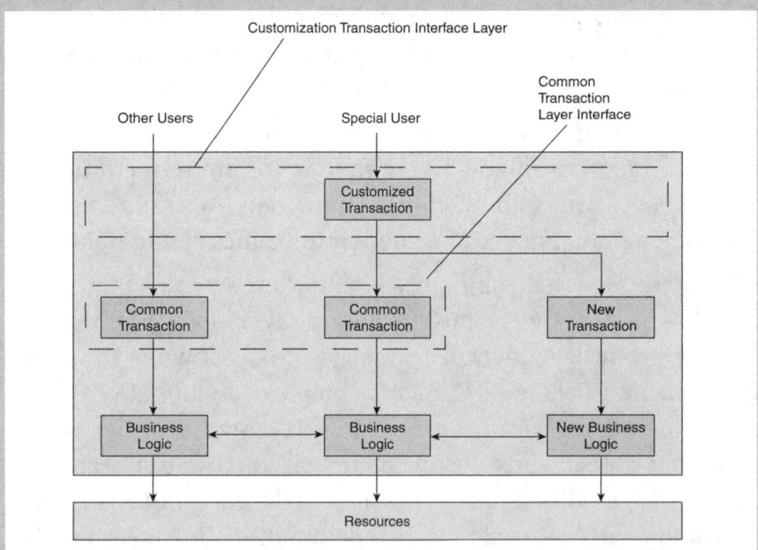

Figure 13.4
Activities.

In order for this approach to work, the common transactions should be composable (see Section 13.7.2), to allow for the case that a customized transaction might need to call multiple existing common transactions. Composability ensures that these transactions can be aggregated into a single transaction.

Consequences

The existing codebase of transactions is unaffected, except to the extent that they might need to be modified to ensure composability. The special user's requirements are satisfied with a minimum of impact.

13.7.4 Transaction Aggregation

It is often the case that a business function requires the action of several existing business transactions, but there may be reasons why the separate transactions cannot be combined into a single transaction. Perhaps they operate on different resources, each with a different resource manager; perhaps the existing transactions are complex or poorly understood and it is not practical to re-engineer them; or perhaps there is not sufficient time to do the re-engineering work. Further, if the transactions are not believed to be composable, it is not wise to merely wrap them in a new transaction as per the Layered Transaction pattern.

In this situation, it may be necessary to create a service entry point for applications to use to invoke the transactions to perform the requested service or function. This book refers to this approach as "transaction aggregation."

The risks in doing this are that changes might occur to resources in between the separate transactions that are performed by the new function (interference); and if one transaction succeeds but the next fails, the business function fails in a manner that is incomplete and that must be cleaned up manually (non-atomicity).

Even if failure or interference is expected to be infrequent, the application designer should think through what might happen if this does occur. Some applications can live with inconsistent data. For example, if a function invokes two separate transactions, and both transactions merely perform queries, the second transaction might return data that is more recent than—and inconsistent with—the first. If these are both shown on the user's display side-by-side, they might appear out-of-sync, but in some applications the user might not care too much in the rare case that this would occur. Whether this is acceptable depends on the application.

Many applications that require functions that perform multiple transactions have this requirement because one of the transactions retrieves a state value of some kind, such as a flag that signals that a certain operation has or has not yet occurred. If the flag indicates that the operation has not yet occurred, the actual business transaction is performed. For example, a business function might first check a manufacturing database to see if an order's status is "shipped," and if not, allow the user to cancel the order in the Sales database. If these two operations—each in a different database—are performed using separate transactions, erroneous order cancellations could occur if an order's status changed immediately after the status is checked.

Again, it would be ideal if these transactions could be performed as a single atomic transaction, but that is not always possible for technical reasons. Because a state flag such as this is often accessed by the user's session for other reasons, it is often necessary to expose the state variable for read access by the user's session. This read must be synchronized so that it is not updated at the same time as it is read because user sessions are often reentrant with respect to user multiple requests.

DESIGN PATTERN: MULTIPLE-TRANSACTION REQUEST

Context
A client function requires the execution of multiple transactions. For one reason or another, it is not practical or possible to integrate those transactions under the scope of a single transaction. An example of this is depicted in Figure 13.5 for the case of two transactions.

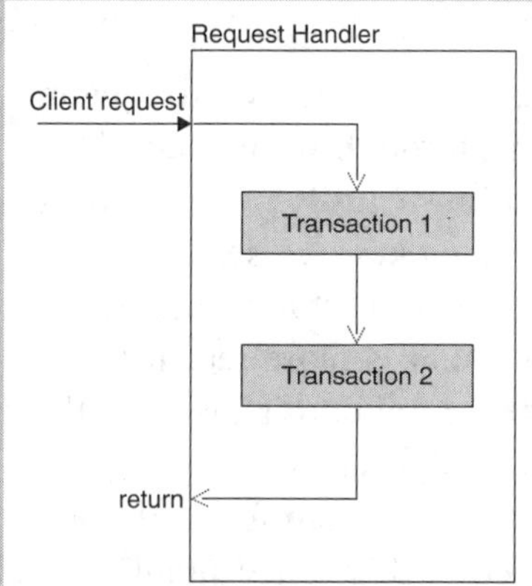

Figure 13.5 Two transactions that must be executed as a single business function.

Problem
The problems inherent in executing multiple transactions as a single function—namely, interference and non-atomicity—must be dealt with.

Solution
In this solution pattern, (1) only the last transaction in the sequence is allowed to perform updates, and (2) it is assumed that the update need not be based on the *very most* recent data from sources read by prior transactions.

In applications of this pattern, it is very common that some of the data that is retrieved from one of the transactions is also cached in a session or internal state object. This pattern, therefore, includes an internal state component that is accessed synchronously (serially) by any clients of the function and by the function itself. Thus, the function is guarded reentrant.

The pattern is illustrated in Figure 13.6. Note that each transaction is bounded by a different shade of gray.

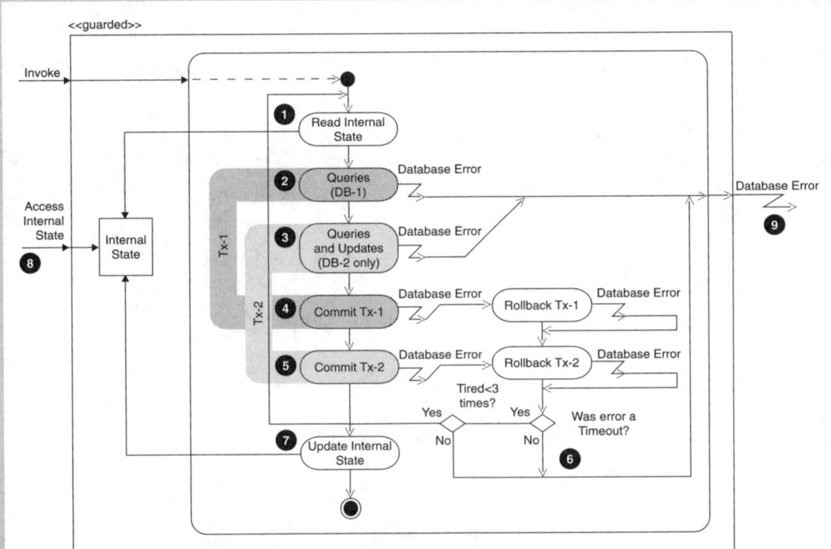

Figure 13.6
Activities.

A client invokes the function through the indicated path "Invoke." The object is guarded, so only one client thread can invoke the object at a time. (This will not prevent other database clients from accessing the data directly.) The first action ❶ is to read the internal state of this guarded object. The internal state can contain anything needed by the function that needs to span invocations; for example, the outcome of the last invocation.

After reading the internal state, the first transaction is executed ❷. This transaction may contain only queries, according to our first assumption. If the transaction does not result in any errors, the second transaction is performed ❸. This transaction may perform updates.

If no errors have occurred during the execution of either transaction, an attempt is made to commit the first transaction ❹. A number of errors can occur at this point. If any kind of error occurs, both transactions should be rolled back as shown in the figure. If the error was anything other than a timeout, the function should be aborted, as shown ❻, and an error thrown ❾. If the error was a timeout, the entire process can be tried again.

Step ❺ indicates the attempt to commit the second transaction. If an error occurs at this point, the second transaction should be rolled back. The first cannot be rolled back because it was already committed at step ❹, but this does not matter because the first transaction is only a read transaction.

If both transactions commit successfully, the internal state should be updated ❼ to reflect the new status of the guarded object. The function is then finished, and it can return.

Note that a client can attempt to access the guarded object at any time to query its status ❽. However, attempts to access the status while the object is performing the function will block. Therefore, the two transactions should not be long-running.

Note that this pattern embeds timeout handling within the pattern. Alternatively, timeout handling can be factored out of the pattern and handled elsewhere within the application that uses the pattern. In that case, a timeout is handled here as an error ❾ and clients can decide whether to retry.

Consequences

This pattern cannot result in artifacts as a result of one transaction succeeding and another failing. That is because only the last transaction performs an update.

It is possible that the second transaction performs its update using slightly stale data obtained during the first transaction. Therefore, there is the possibility of inconsistency. The application should be designed to be tolerant of a small degree of inconsistency between the data read by the first transaction and the data written by the second.

If the first transaction must also perform an update, there is the possibility of artifacts remaining if the second transaction fails at step ❺.

The pattern is easily extended to allow additional read transactions prior to the final update transaction.

13.7.5 Process-Specific Schemas

One of the flaws in the reasoning about relational databases is that a single business data model exists. In reality, large businesses consist of many cooperating divisions, which in turn consist of departments, and so on—requiring a *hierarchy* of processing domains. Each part of the hierarchy has data models that pertain only to its own operations. In addition, many of these models are workflow oriented so that portions of data are inputs to some processes and outputs to others, so their scope is stateful (transient) and not global.

Any hierarchy can always be "flattened" into an equivalent non-hierarchical model, but doing so is unnatural.

A global schema does not accommodate these aspects well. Indeed, any hierarchy can always be "flattened" into an equivalent non-hierarchical model, but doing so is unnatural. Modeling hierarchy and statefulness using a non-hierarchical methodology such as relational tables requires that the workflow states and multiple domains be modeled explicitly as data elements that indicate scope of applicability, and the state and domain data elements are all revealed to all applications, with no encapsulation. It is as if a program were written with "common blocks" reminiscent of Fortran 66.

Some very esteemed relational database experts have even argued that encapsulation is a "red herring," claiming that the term's primary purpose is to define a separation of data from code.[7] Encapsulation is not so much an abstract concept for separating data from code; rather, it allows programmers to separate problems into smaller pieces and *figure out what they can ignore.* The main problem that programmers have when looking at a large relational schema is not knowing what they do not need to know.

The pressure to have a global schema causes many organizations to have tables that are "used by those folks in purchasing" and other tables that are used by "those folks in sales"—all owned by the DBA—with no schema-defined delimiter between the two domains. Because this ends up being unwieldy, organizations often end up having multiple databases for different purposes, interconnected by services or processes that take data from one database and move it to another. This is a reasonable compromise but leads to difficulties if the organization changes and composite transactions need to be written that span more than one database or if overlap is discovered between two databases.

In spite of the prospect of composite transactions, separating workflows into separate databases is often a good solution. This results in a "federated" or service-based architecture for the organization that is often more manageable than trying to fit every process into a single schema. Composite transactions are usually avoidable by separating a transaction into multiple workflow steps and providing "cancellation" workflows.

13.8 Application-Defined Locking and Workflows

In many workflow-oriented applications, portions of data are inputs to some processes and outputs to others, so their scope is limited to the duration of those process steps, and perhaps limited to the artifacts of those steps. For example, consider a process that accepts a loan request as input and outputs an approval status. The approval status pertains only to the loan request version

7 See the article "Encapsulation Is a Red Herring" by C.J. Date, in *Database Programming and Design*, September 1998. Available online at `http://www.dbpd.com/vault/9809date.html`. Date makes some good points regarding the term "encapsulation." However, reliability and programmer productivity are important benefits of encapsulation. Encapsulation allows one to decompose problems in a hierarchical fashion and provides for information hiding, which enables one to achieve greater security and reliability.

input to the approval process: If the loan request is rejected, modified, and then re-submitted to the approval process, the approval (or rejection) applies only to the new version.

In workflow-oriented applications, a user tends to work on an entire set of data as a collection.

In applications such as this, a user tends to work on an entire set of data as a collection—a composite object when viewed from an object-oriented perspective. Work on the collection of data may be long in duration—perhaps hours, days, or even longer. Pessimistic concurrency control is not practical in that case. Optimistic concurrency control is not practical either, because each data object or record would have to have a time stamp and be tracked individually. If the status of the composite object as a whole is represented in the database, it can be queried, and other transactions can decide to prevent other users from accessing the data because it is in a state of flux. This provides an advantage over optimistic concurrency control, which allows other users to access (even modify) data before a user's logical transaction is done.

When data is operated on in aggregations, it is best to track who is working on the data by treating it as a composite object. In terms of the previous loan request example, the entire loan request should be tracked as a unit: When someone needs to modify it, they should be able to "checkout" the entire set of data pertaining to ("owned by") the loan request, and then check it "back in" when done.

The concept of "checkout" is to represent the state of a logical transaction in the application data model itself.

The concept of "checkout" is to represent the state of a logical transaction in the application data model itself. A persistent variable is used to represent the state of a *composite object*. The state can be binary, in which case it is merely a semaphore, and a test-and-set operation can be used to attempt to "check out" the object. The test-and-set operation can be implemented via a database transaction, either using a stored procedure or a transactional object method, such as a session bean method.

It is important to recognize that a checkout lock is cooperative and requires that all transactions first check whether they can set the variable before actually accessing the object, and they must remember to release the lock—i.e., unset the variable—when they are done accessing the object. On the other hand, the cooperative nature can be eliminated by encapsulating all accesses in a layer that enforces the checkout policies.

It is often the case that merely checking out the object is not sufficient, but that it might be necessary to increment the version number of the object after it is modified and "checked in." In that case, the lock variable exists for each version because each version is actually a different composite object. Alternatively, there can be a single lock for only the most recent version, if it is desired that only the most recent version can be modified.

DESIGN PATTERN: COOPERATIVE CHECKOUT

Related Patterns

This pattern is a variation on the Cooperative Process Coordination pattern discussed earlier. It is also described in many sources (for example, see the "Coarse-Grained Lock" pattern in [17]). See also the Versioned Object pattern [18].

Context

Users need to work on collections of data at a time, and the status of each collection needs to be tracked and managed as a unit.

Problem

Databases do not natively provide a model for controlling long-duration access to collections of data.

Solution

This pattern provides an approach to temporarily taking ownership of a composite object for the purpose of updating it. The technique is cooperative in that all applications that access the object must obey the application-level status attribute that is part of the object.

The object may be implemented as a set of database records or persistent objects. Regardless, the object must logically represent a composite object according to the principles of composition discussed earlier in this book.

The basic technique is to maintain an attribute with the object. This attribute can be external to the object or internal. The attribute contains the identity of the current owner of the object. This pattern will refer to this attribute as the CheckoutHolder. Any user whose identity is set as the CheckoutHolder may access the object for update. Other users may not access the object for update, but they may possibly access it for read-only access, depending on the access policies of the application. Refer to Figure 13.7.

The CheckoutHolder attribute represents a lock of sorts, even though it is defined at the application level. However, in spite of this, a database lock must still be obtained to access the composite object (which includes the CheckoutHolder attribute) when the checkout and checkin operations occur. This is to ensure that access to it is serialized with respect to other transactions that compete to set the CheckoutHolder. (In most databases, this lock is obtained transparently as part of the mechanics of starting and completing a transaction.)

The following figures show the activities for Checkout and Checkin operations. A client that wishes to access the composite object must (should) first seek to obtain the CheckoutHolder for exclusive read and update access. After access to the ChecoutHolder is permitted, it reads the value of the holder. If the holder status indicates that the composite is already checked out to another user, an exception is thrown indicating that access is denied. If, on the other hand, the composite object is not already checked out, the holder value is set to the current user. The CheckoutHolder is then released for access by other users.

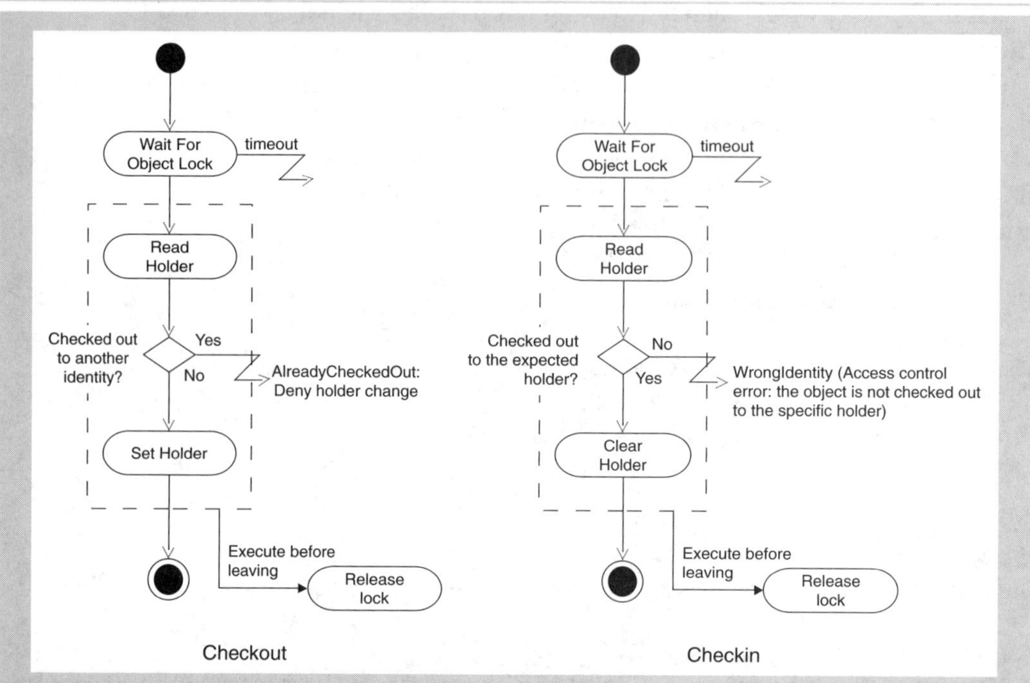

Figure 13.7 Activities for Checkout and Checkin.

The Checkin operation is similar. Checkin can detect that the object that the user wishes to check in has not been checkout to the user (identity/holder), in which case it should raise an exception.

The Checkout and Checkin operations can be defined as an interface that is implemented by a facade that regulates access to the composite object, as shown in Figure 13.8.

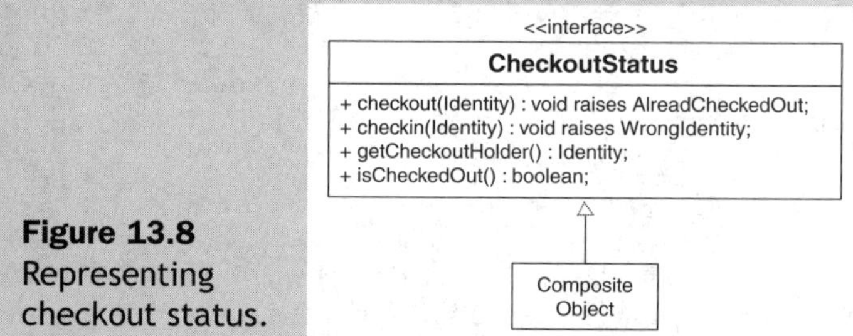

Figure 13.8 Representing checkout status.

Both the Checkout and Checkin operations can have the same kinds of errors that have been described in previous design patterns related to transactional access to database object (specifically access to the CheckoutHolder), but these error conditions have been omitted from the diagrams for simplicity and to focus on what is unique about this pattern.

This pattern is often used with the Versioned Object pattern (see [19]) in order to implement workflows that require users to update a set of objects as a group before allowing others access to the updated set.

Consequences
Entire object compositions can be locked for access, with an isolation policy defined and implemented by the application itself, because adherence to the lock is voluntary and completely under the control of the application.

Object state must be modeled in the database schema as part of the workflow model.

13.9 Layer Access Rules for Transactions

An application should have a clearly demarcated layer that represents the "transactional interface" to its functionality. This layer has the property that its methods are transactional, which is an extremely important functional semantic.

PRINCIPLE: THERE SHOULD BE A CLEAR AND CONSISTENT TRANSACTION BOUNDARY.

This layer is commonly called a "transaction façade." It is the point at which system regression testing should be performed for functional tests, failure tests, and scalability tests. Testing at this layer is not sufficient because client layers must be tested as well, but testing at the transaction layer is most important because it is the functional heart of the system, and a good transaction regression suite results in a very high level of reliability and maintainability.

The design considerations for a transaction facade are so important that they are encapsulated here as a design pattern, described next.

DESIGN PATTERN: TRANSACTION FACADE

Related Patterns
The Transaction Facade pattern is based on the Facade Pattern [20]. (See also the "Transaction Script," "Service Layer," and "Data Transfer Object" patterns in [21]. The J2EE Blueprints recognize a similar pattern, the "Session Façade," but the semantics of that pattern are not very clear. See also the Thread-Safe Interface pattern in [22], which presents an analogous concept for thread serialization.

This pattern builds on the "Authorization as a Precondition" pattern defined in Section 7.21, "Home-Grown Authorization."

Context
An application with multiple layers and tiers provides transactional functionality to higher layers, tiers, or clients.

Problem

In a multi-layer transactional application, it can often be difficult to ascertain whether a method invokes a transaction—unless discipline is exercised in defining the functional roles of each layer. In addition, regression testing is difficult if there is no effective API representing the application's core functionality.

Solution

A transaction facade defines a programmatic API for a transactional application. This API can be used by client layers to access business functions. For this reason, it is normally implemented as a public API layer (for example, it would not be declared to use local EJBs).

Transactionally Managed

Transaction façade objects should be hosted by a transactional container. This container should begin and manage any required transactions used by the object. It should also intercept and manage any implicit context propagated or established by the client request, such as client identity, access rights and roles, and so on. Façade EJBs should be deployed with transaction-type = Container and with trans-attribute = Required.

One Method per Transaction

The transactional nature of a transaction facade is an important part of its functionality and must be taken into account by clients that use it. In particular, clients must recognize that if two façade API calls are performed by the client, and if the second one does not complete for any reason, the first is not automatically undone. Thus, the combination of two transactional operations—each invoked from a client—is not transactional. Therefore, any business functions that require the completion of two or more transaction facade calls and that must be performed as a transactional unit must be cast as a new transaction facade API method. (See also the "Transaction Script" pattern in [23].)

Stateless or Stateful?

Whether a transaction facade should be stateless or stateful depends on the application. However, it is best to create a stateless core, and if any session-oriented layer is required, it can be created on top of the stateless layer. That will lead to more reusability of the facade core.

Statefulness can be useful for maintaining continuity of the work process that the user is trying to perform. However, data that is retrieved via transaction facade API calls should not be cached within the session unless there is a highly robust mechanism for keeping the session cache in sync with the database if any of the cached data is updated by a transaction, or unless the risk of the data being out of sync is acceptable. Data that is often appropriate for a short-lived session includes the user's identity, roles associated with the user, data entered by the user that has not yet been written through to the database, user preferences, and any session-specific calculation data that is not persistent.

Input and Output Types

Parameter and return types for façade methods should be either primitive objects, primitives, value types that are defined globally or in a utility package, value types that are defined by the facade or a subordinate layer, or references to other facades. Input and output types should not be defined in client layers, and objects that are internal to the facade should not be returned. All collection types should be type-safe generics. (See the "Data Transfer Object" pattern.)♦

◆ See also the principle "Use Specific Argument Types Instead of General-Purpose Types" in Section 11.3, "Component Roles and Contracts."

Do Not Cross-Call

(See the Layer Interface pattern discussed in Section 7.19.1.)

Façade methods should not call other façade methods. Façade methods should call Business Layer methods.

Exception Handling

Façade methods should always set the current transaction for rollback when an exception occurs, regardless of the kind of exception.

Exceptions that indicate expected application conditions (for example, an update request that exceeds some kind of application-based limit) should be declared in the throws clause.

Exceptions that indicate transient resource failures (for example, database timeout or inability to obtain a connection) are expected to have been converted by the business layer (called by the façade) from their original type (for example, SQLException) into a *checked application exception* that indicates the kind of failure, such as TimeoutException; such exceptions should be propagated to the client after marking the ransaction for rollback.

A call to a transaction façade method should proceed according to the pattern shown in Figure 13.9.

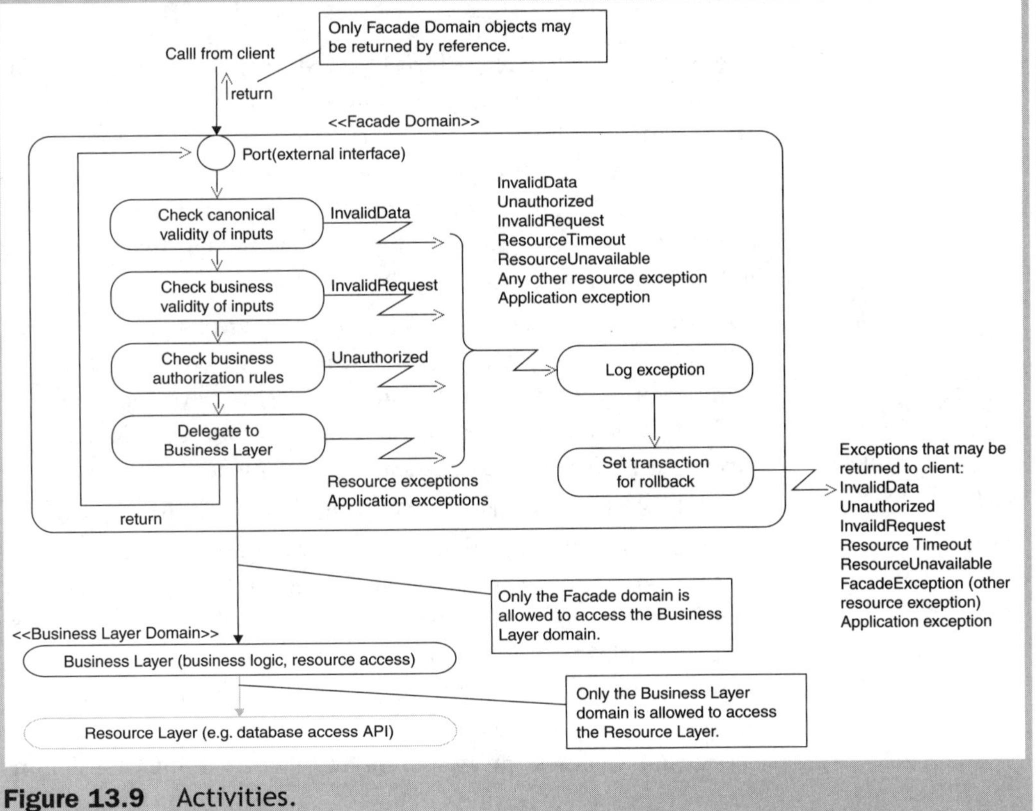

Figure 13.9 Activities.

In Figure 13.9, the "Port" represents the interface that is presented to clients. Internal features of the facade should not be accessible to clients through any other pathway. If the calls are synchronous, values and object references are returned through this interface, as are exception values or objects.

Note that each layer is depicted as a "domain." This is to emphasize that each layer is protected from other access pathways so that it may be accessed only via the intended pathways that are illustrated. See Section 7.18, "Controlling Communication Pathways."

A Resource Layer is shown in the figure for illustration but is not part of this pattern.

Consequences

The application has a well-defined callable "API" that can be regression tested and that has well-defined transactional consistency semantics. This provides a robust foundation on which client tiers can be built.

13.10 Considerations for Business Delegate Patterns

The Business Delegate pattern [24, 25] provides a technique for shielding clients from implementation details and latency characteristics of business services, such as lookup services needed to locate a transaction tier. The intent is that a business delegate can "adapt" a client to a particular business layer or transaction tier, for maximum efficiency, so that the client need not know how to connect to that layer or tier.

From the perspective of a business layer or transaction tier, a business delegate is a client.

From the perspective of a business layer or transaction tier, a business delegate is a client, and it executes outside of the transaction. Therefore, if a business delegate performs any caching, *it must consider all the concerns that have been discussed with regard to caching of data by clients.*

A business delegate can be useful even if it does not perform any caching, and that might be the preferred route in most cases. If an application has to access multiple backend services of different kinds, a business delegate can simplify the process by aggregating the access techniques and present the client with a simple and uniform API; but again, transaction consistency must be considered. If non-transactional resources must be accessed, a business delegate can aggregate the logic of dealing with the failure conditions of those resources and thereby simplify the application.

13.11 Transaction Error Handling

Error handling by transactional methods is often overlooked but is extremely important for application reliability because an application depends on the robustness of its transactions for consistency recoverability. Error handling, therefore, must be explicitly addressed by the design, for each transaction.

Error handling is covered more comprehensively and generically in Chapter 18, "Failure Response Design." This section discusses error handling in the context of transactions.

The error handling design should differentiate those conditions that are normal lifecycle conditions such as timeout, as well as less normal but still anticipated errors, such as resource unavailable due to transient problems. These should be treated separately from unexpected internal errors that represent programming logic flaws.

Consideration should be given to which kinds of errors the transactional container will handle and which will be handled by the application—and by which layer and how.

13.11.1 Resources That Do Not Reliably Timeout

Database transactions that "get stuck" (for example, through deadlock or through procedural SQL loops) will time out, and the driver will throw an exception that the application can catch and interpret. However, some resources do not time out, or the timeout period is too long. For example, a request to an unreachable Web service might not time out until after a minute or more, and that might be too long in some circumstances. Even worse, if the response handler on the other end is in an endless loop, generating an endlessly long response, a timeout would prevent an application crash.

Applications should always consider the timeout period of any resource. If the timeout period is too long, the application should include a timer that aborts the request after a configurable period and that causes the request to throw an exception that is recognizable as a timeout condition.[8] This last part is important because the application must be able to differentiate timeout from other conditions.

Applications should always consider the timeout period of any resource.

8 Meyer refers to this use of a timer as a "watchdog." See [26], p. 1019.

PRINCIPLE: EMPLOY A TIMER TO ABORT ANY RESOURCE CALL THAT COULD POTENTIALLY "HANG."

(This principle is closely related to the more general principle "Time Critical Thread Actions" that is discussed in Section 18.2.3, "Iteration Failures.")

> A timeout exception that is propagated to a client should indicate whether the timeout condition is retryable.

The timeout exception that is eventually propagated to the client application should indicate whether the timeout condition is retry-able. That is, was the transaction aborted atomically?—and is it safe to retry the transaction? For a database transaction, this is generally true, but for non-database resources the exception should indicate so that the application knows how to respond. Handling timeout is discussed more in a later section. Patterns for implementing it include the "Timer Thread" pattern discussed in Section 12.2.5, "Designing a Thread Timeout Mechanism," and the "Progress Reporting to Client Only" pattern discussed in Section 16.4.5, "Progress Bars."

13.11.2 Handling Non-Successful But Normal Resource Conditions

Many kinds of transaction failures are not errors at all, but are normal events. For example, timeout and deadlock are normal events that occur when a system is heavily loaded, so they should not be treated as errors.

Deadlock and timeout are often treated the same by a database. This is because the manifestation of deadlock is that the transaction times out. Determining if deadlock is the cause requires deadlock analysis, and many databases do not run deadlock analysis unless configured to do so. In any case, the response choices are the same: try again, or give up.

> Checking for timeout or deadlock is not always straight-forward.

Checking for timeout or deadlock is not always straightforward, depending on the database API that is being used. Many database APIs (for example, JDBC) allow a failed transaction to return multiple errors at once, requiring that all be checked. For a SQL database, the SQL state code should be checked, which is 40001 for deadlock or timeout.[9]

9 See `http://www.cse.ohio-state.edu/cgi-bin/info/info/mysql,Error-returns` for a listing.

A well-written application should also check for conditions that indicate concurrency problems that may be timing related but manifest themselves as other errors, such as serialization errors. For example, Oracle will generate the exception "ORA-08177: Can't serialize access for this transaction" if a transaction is executing in serializable (full) isolation and cannot commit due to contention for an updated table or row.

If a timeout or another form of contention error occurs, the first response is normally to try the transaction again. However, this should not be done indefinitely, so a maximum number of retries should be configured for the application.

If the choice is to give up rather than try again—either because the maximum number of allowed retries has been exceeded or because there is a technical reason why the transaction should not be retried—an exception should be thrown that expresses the logical outcome: timeout or deadlock (if deadlock is detected). It should not merely be the raw, uninterpreted exception or error that was thrown by the transaction itself. This is because you should not expect higher-level layers to have to scan for SQL codes and the like. However, the exception that is thrown should contain the original exception, in a nested or chained fashion, so as not to lose diagnostic information.

DESIGN PATTERN: HANDLING TRANSACTION TIMEOUT

Context

An application performs SQL transactions.

Problem

SQL transactions can time out, or experience deadlock. This condition is not necessarily an error, and in many applications, a limited number of retry attempts is warranted before returning the timeout condition to the client.

Solution

This pattern provides for retrying a transaction if a timeout occurs. Refer to Figure 13.10.

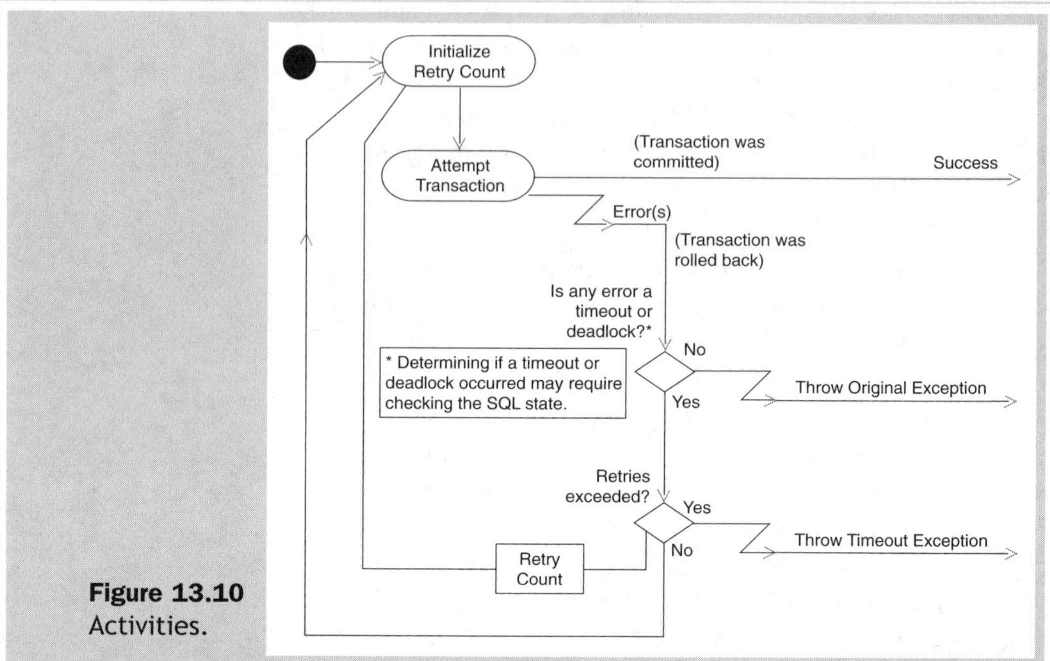

Figure 13.10
Activities.

The figure depicts the operation of a method that encapsulates the transaction retry logic. The method attempts to perform and commit a transaction; if it is successful and committed, the method returns. Otherwise, the error(s) is (are) examined. If there is an error indicating timeout or deadlock, a retry counter is incremented. If the retry count does not exceed a configurable limit (for example, 3), the transaction is automatically retried. If the limit is exceeded, an exception is thrown to the client indicating that the transaction was retried but has nevertheless timed out. The client can elect to invoke the method again or not, but knowing that the transaction already has been retried, the client most likely will not want to retry it. Thus, it is useful if the exception that is thrown indicates that the transaction was already retried; for example, it might be of a type such as "RetriedButTimedOut" or "NonRetryableTimeout" to inform the client that a retry will likely be non-productive.

A Java code sequence for handling timeout according to this pattern can be found on this book's Web site.

Consequences

Retry behavior is encapsulated. Clients that receive an exception indicating that retries have been attempted but nevertheless timed out need not perform a retry, simplifying the client design.

13.12 Transaction Testing and Validation Strategies

The transactions of a multi-user system represent the "API" of the system. Therefore, it is of paramount importance that there be a test suite that thoroughly exercises all transactions. This is not a unit test suite, but a test suite that is designed by testers who have experience testing transactions. The test suite should have both functional and assurance (non-functional) aspects to make sure that incorrectly formed requests or aborted transactions do not result in bad data in the database.

PRINCIPLE: BUILD A REGRESSION TEST SUITE FOR THE APPLICATION'S TRANSACTIONS.

The assurance tests should also include concurrency tests to ensure that the system continues to operate correctly when multiple users try to perform transactions that overlap in terms of data or functionality.[27]

PRINCIPLE: TEST THAT THE APPLICATION WORKS UNDER CONCURRENT ATTEMPTS TO ACCESS THE SAME TRANSACTIONS AND DATA.

Concurrency testing was discussed in detail in Section 12.2.8, "Concurrency Testing and Validation." Here the focus is on applications that use transactional concurrency.

Technical expertise is required to design assurance tests, yet they should not be developed by the technical team alone because they must reflect the application's requirements, and the requirements team must bear responsibility for understanding how all requirements are tested. Thus, the specification and development of assurance tests is a collaborative effort.

Consider again the concurrency requirement from Section 2.2.2, "Reliability Categories":

> Up to 200 users can access, use, and enter data via the user interface concurrently, working according to the usage profile developed by the requirements team and included in the appendix to these requirements.

Such a requirement gives the development team insufficient information because the number of users must be translated into a *transaction rate*. There must also be a calculation of the concurrency of the transactions, and this depends on the profile of usage of the application's functions.

Applications scale based on the transaction rate, not the number of users.

What is needed, therefore, is for the requirements team to develop a set of *usage profiles* (sometimes called "archetypes") that represent anticipated usage: i.e., what functions will be invoked by certain types of users and how often, and how many of those types of users will use the application concurrently. A range of error should be specified for these estimates so that the testing team can test for upper limits.

After a set of usage profiles is defined, the technical team can examine the application design to determine how many transactions of each type will be invoked per second and the kinds of resources that are used by each transaction. This can be used to assess concurrency and transaction rate. From this information, a concurrency and peak load test profile can be designed.

Concurrency calculations should not be a huge analysis effort: Any calculations are bound to be significantly different from reality.

This should not be a huge analysis effort: any calculations are bound to be significantly different from reality. Rather, these calculations should be rough estimates in order to help decide where to focus testing.

Assurance testing should include simulation or creation of all anticipated failure scenarios in order to verify that the application behaves as expected when these kinds of failures actually occur. Again, specifying these kinds of tests requires expertise in both application requirements from the user's perspective as well as technical expertise. The requirements team needs to be responsible for articulating and understanding the failure requirements. For example, merely specifying that the system "should handle all failures of the database" is not sufficient. When asked if failures are handled, programmers will almost invariably say "yes." Rather, the requirements must specify what all stakeholders should experience when a failure occurs; for example, the kind of message or alert that must be dispatched to support, the kind of error message that must be received by the user, and the way in which the database must be recovered,

The requirements team needs to be responsible for articulating and understanding the failure requirements.

if applicable. All these are important requirements for the various parties involved in using and supporting the application, and all must be tested.

PRINCIPLE: TEST ALL CONCEIVABLE FAILURE SCENARIOS.

Simulation or creation of failures is complex and often requires special configurations that must be established within the test environment while the tests are being run. Testing environments are usually scheduled-access environments rather than shared environments because a testing environment must be controlled and often reconfigured during a testing session. Exclusive access to the testing environment is even more important when testing involves failure testing and the special configurations that are required.

13.13 Summary

Clearly defined transactions are the hallmark of a reliable application. For any application that accesses persistent or shared resources, it is not possible to make the application reliable unless the boundary of the application's transactions is explicit and consistent. In this chapter, fundamental concepts related to referential integrity, isolation, and recovery were discussed. Consistency across and within transactions were discussed. The classic models for concurrency control were presented, along with design patterns for implementing them, complete with error handling. Transactions were then discussed from the perspective of object-oriented design and object composition. Issues that arise with non-transactional resources were addressed, and approaches for combining transactions were presented. Application-level approaches were then presented for dealing with usage scenarios that cannot be solved using a transaction approach, including the checkout paradigm. An important pattern was then presented, Transaction Façade, which provides a model for the design of a transaction layer within an application, complete with error handling. Assurance issues were discussed, including timeout, testing, and validation.

The next chapter expands on the concept of a transaction to allow shared data to be distributed and to still be accessed in a reliable and secure manner.

13.14 Exercises

1. Name and explain two fundamentally different ways of achieving isolation.
2. List and explain some types of database access errors that are "normal"—i.e., which can be expected to occur on occasion during the lifetime of a typical application.
3. A Web service application contains a multithreaded request handler to process incoming requests. When the request handler receives a request, it first parses the request message and extracts pertinent data from the request. It then validates the data. Next, it obtains a connection to an LDAP directory and reads information. After the LDAP directory has been read, the handler obtains a connection to a database, performs a read, and then performs an update. It then commits the transaction and releases the database connection. Assuming that all this goes well, a successful return message is then sent to the client. What potential problems do you see with this design?
4. A Web service application uses the business delegate pattern to implement a set of services. Over time, it is discovered that a new service is needed, and that service can be supplied by combining two existing services. What potential problems should be investigated before doing this?
5. An application contains a transaction that invokes a set of "helper" objects to assist in performing the logic of the transaction. Each helper performs database accesses. What potential consistency problems might arise in this design?

6. A Web application provides online access for banking customers to their bank accounts. The application allows customers to view their balance, transaction history, pay bills, and make transfers between all of the accounts that they own. For example, a transfer would debit one account and credit another by the same amount. Some accounts are joint accounts with more than one account owner per account. Thus, for example, a husband at home might access an account and transfer money to another account, while his wife at work accesses the same account to perform the same operation—not knowing that her husband is also doing the transfer at that moment. How should the application be designed to prevent a computational error in this situation?

Answers and hints for these exercises can be found at `http://www.assuredbydesign.com/haa/`.

CHAPTER 14

CACHING AND REPLICATION

14.1 Caching

Caching is a mechanism for keeping frequently used data local to where it is actually used. A cache is a local copy of data, sometimes with provisions for ensuring that the local copy is kept in sync with the primary (authoritative) copy. Cache design patterns have been studied extensively, and there is a tremendous amount written about caching techniques—so much so that it is not even worth trying to cite references here.

Databases and Web servers use caches extensively, although the requirements for these vary greatly. Caching patterns have also been tailored for business application design; for example, there is a good discussion of simple patterns for non-updateable replication as well as updateable replication in [1]. The discussion here focuses on a particular pattern, which is described here as a "Local Database Forward Cache with Synchronous Updates." The author has found this pattern or variations of it to be applicable to many business applications that require replication.[1] This technique has been used in so-called "enterprise service bus" architectures [3] that provide caching of back-end data and utilize a message bus as the mechanism for connecting the local servers and primary server.

Building a cache is complex, and most business applications do not justify the effort required to create a proper cache mechanism from scratch. However, there is a common situation that does justify it and which can be implemented in a relatively simple manner. That is when a remote server (often a mainframe) is the primary source of a large volume of data that must be made available to one or more local application processing environments. In order to avoid constant trips to the main server, the entire set of data from the main server, or portions of it, can be cached in one or more local databases. On a periodic basis, changes to the server data can be distributed to all local databases.

CACHE LOCATIONS

Forward cache—A cache placed close to a client to accelerate client requests.
Reverse cache—A cache placed close to a server to accelerate client requests.

In doing this, there is the risk that data on the server might change before the change is pushed out to the local databases and that obsolete local data might be used as a result. In order to prevent this, the primary database can associate a lifetime with each data element (or with entire groups of elements), such

1 See also the Cache Management pattern in [2]. Can also be found online at http://www.developer.com/design/article.php/630481.

that the data value is guaranteed to be valid until the expiration of the lifetime, when updates are pushed to all local databases or, alternatively, the local databases can request updates.

The guaranteed validity of data for a specified lifetime would have to be a policy that the primary server adheres to, and this is a valid approach in many situations, such as when the data consists of prices that are guaranteed to be valid for a specified period of time.

The primary database can associate a lifetime with each cached data element.

In the event that a data value *must* be changed before its lifetime expires, the central server can push an emergency update to all local servers. Alternatively, the central server can notify all local databases that they should request updates.

The updates to the local databases can be done in a synchronous or asynchronous manner, depending on the stringency of the requirement that all databases reflect the same value. A synchronous push requires first obtaining a global application-level lock on the affected data items and then pushing the update. If updates are done in a synchronous manner, no inconsistency will ever be seen by clients, and the caches and primary server will be "coherent."

Updates to a cache can be done in a synchronous or asynchronous manner.

A cache design of this kind can also be modified to support updates by local applications by allowing an application to request a change to a data value and having the primary server accept or reject the change, much the way optimistic locking works.

To support client-originated updates, a server must accept or reject the update, much the way optimistic locking works.

In designing a caching mechanism, special attention should be paid to security, for a number of reasons. For one thing, the mere replication of data across many systems leaves it much more vulnerable from a security perspective: Each cache server becomes a potential weak link, and the data is therefore no more secure than the least secure server. The added complexity also increases the likelihood of failure, and designing a robust distributed application such as this requires careful design and lots of testing.

Each cache becomes a potential security weak link.

The forward cache approach is presented next as a design pattern. This pattern is often useful in a business setting in which a centralized remote data store (for example, a mainframe) must be accessed with low latency by multiple client systems (such as Web application servers) distributed in different geographic regions.

DESIGN PATTERN: LOCAL DATABASE FORWARD CACHE WITH SYNCHRONOUS UPDATES

Context

One or more application servers access data that is maintained in a primary server that is expensive (in response time or in resource usage cost) to access; yet the application servers must have low latency or economical access.

Much of the data that is accessed is relatively static and changes only at known intervals.

There are also occasions in which an application server must be able to update the data and have the update propagate to the primary server and other application servers.

Problem

Keeping local copies of the data does not provide for the circumstance that data must occasionally be updated outside of its normal schedule, and that some application servers must have the most recent data at all times.

Solution

The pattern uses one or more local databases to act as forward caches. These databases are accessed by local application servers. The application servers access the data via a persistence layer that incorporates the caching strategy. The strategy includes obtaining data refreshes when data is marked as expired and listening for server update instructions ("data pushes," also known as "server-initiated updates" [4] or "server callbacks" [5]) if updates are allowed.

When a local application server wishes to initiate an update, the persistence layer in the application server obtains a lock from the primary server. The lock indicates permission to update the data, and the primary server does not grant the lock until it has invalidated the data in each application server via a callback to each application server.

The main features of this pattern are the following:

1. It is assumed that *most transactions do not involve updates*, so the inefficiency and latency of the locking mechanism is not an important issue.
2. It requires an update transaction to synchronously notify all application server caches before it can complete.
3. Cached data objects have expirations ("time-to-live"): The data is guaranteed to be valid before its expiration unless the primary server pushes an update.
4. The user never perceives any out-of-sync data.

Requirement 2 can be relaxed if occasional inconsistency is tolerable. However, even if cache notification is not synchronous, it should still be performed so that systems are out of sync only briefly (for the time required to receive and process notification).

The topology of this pattern is depicted in Figure 14.1.

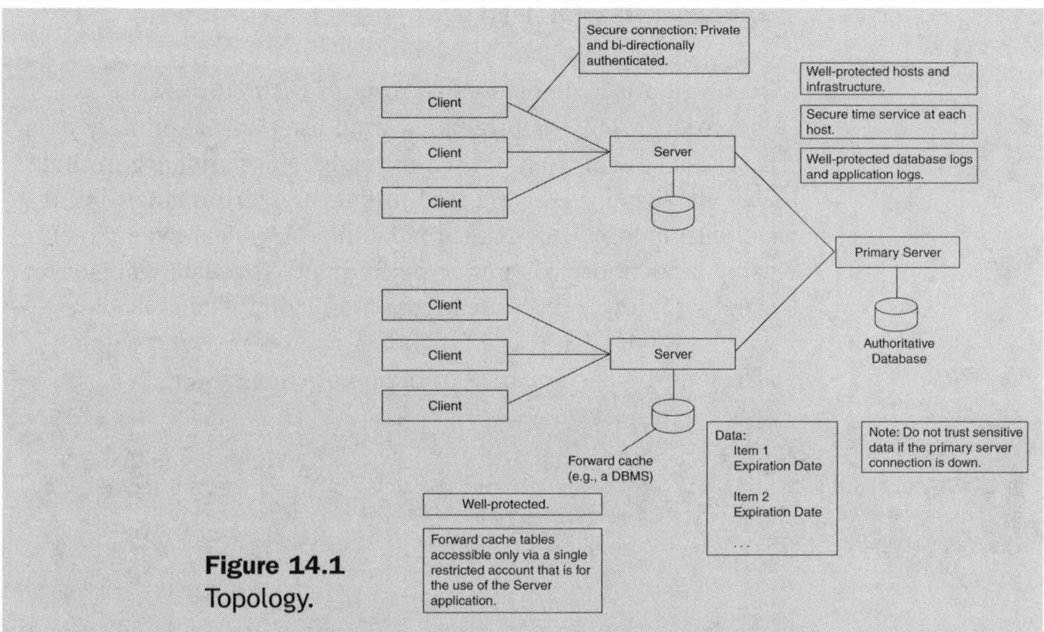

Figure 14.1
Topology.

Security Concerns

The following security issues should be considered when implementing this pattern:

- Application servers should authenticate and authorize each client that accesses sensitive data, even though their clients are local to them.
- Each application server is a potential weak link because it has read access to all of the primary server's data and also because it may initiate updates to that data.
- Application server credentials are a potential vulnerability.
- Delay can cause data to become stale. (See the "Saturation and Delay" and "Exploitation of Non-Atomicity" attacks discussed in Sections 5.1.6 and 5.1.7 respectively.)
- Data pushes or notifications from a server can be potentially interfered with.
- Expiration dates of sensitive data are a potential target of attack.
- Time service or system time for each application server and its database is a potential target of attack.
- Application server logs are potential targets of attack.

Due to the number of risks, this pattern should be used only for relatively non-sensitive data unless very stringent security policies are enforceable at each location.

Consequences

The application designer has control over which data may be temporarily out of sync, and which may not.

The end user perceives a low latency or low cost for accessing the data that is stored in the primary server.

14.2 Replication

Replication is a simpleminded form of caching in which changes can only be originated from users of the primary database. Caching is usually used to increase performance in some way. Replication is often used to increase performance, but it can also be used to enhance reliability. A typical example of using replication to improve performance is a data warehouse: Data is routinely replicated from production databases to a warehouse database where the data can be analyzed without affecting the performance of the production systems.

"Let us save what remains: not by vaults and locks which fence them from the public eye and use in consigning them to the waste of time, but by such a multiplication of copies, as shall place them beyond the reach of accident."
—Thomas Jefferson, 1791.

Replication for achieving reliability is usually handled at an infrastructure level. For example, application servers are often deployed in clusters so that if one system goes down, the others in the cluster pick up its work. Replication is also often used to keep disaster recover systems in a ready state.

Replication can be "active" or "standby." Active replication is real-time, so the replication system can immediately assume the workload. Standby replication is not real-time, so a standby system must be brought online.

14.3 Summary

Application-based caching is a powerful but complex technique and should be used with care and consideration of alternatives. Application designers who decide to use caching should consider all the scenarios that will arise with respect to failure and timing and should also consider the tradeoffs with respect to out-of-sync data. A perfectly synchronized system is not necessary for every application. This chapter discussed caching issues that arise in the design of business applications, and a design pattern that is often useful for application programmers was presented, along with a discussion of its security issues.

The next chapter discusses distributed programming paradigms, and focuses on the failure scenarios that can arise.

14.4 Exercises

1. What term is used to describe a cache and the cache's authoritative data source if the two are never observed by users of either to have different content?
2. A Web application maintains a cache of data that it frequently needs. The authoritative copy of the data is in a database. Is this an example of a forward cache or a reverse cache? Explain.
3. What property of an application does a cache attempt to *reduce*?
4. What is the primary goal of replication, if it is not to increase performance?
5. True or false: A distributed cache can be synchronous. Explain.

Answers and hints for these exercises can be found at `http://www.assuredbydesign.com/haa/`.

CHAPTER 15

DISTRIBUTED SERVICES AND MESSAGING

"My own dear husband. I shall die soon unless I get word from you. All my letters have remained unanswered. Have you even received them?"
–Tess, from Tess of the d'Urbervilles, *by Thomas Hardy, 1891.*

Large organizations typically employ some combination of distributed services and messaging technologies for interconnecting at least some of their internal applications. These services generally fall into one of the following two models:

- **Request-response** (for example, HTTP, EJB, CORBA, SOAP, RPC)
- **Message-based** (for example, Web Service Messaging, EJB Message Bean, CORBA Message Service, "message bus" products)

Note that even request-response protocols utilize messages, and so the mentioned taxonomy can be somewhat confusing. The source of the confusion derives from the distinction between the API used to access the protocol and the underlying nature of the communication used to implement the protocol. For example, while all Internet protocols utilize messages at some level, message-based protocols require the client to interact with the protocol in terms of messages that may or may not receive a response while request-response protocols require the client to interact with the protocol in terms of a request and a response.

15.1 Request-Response

The request-response paradigm requires that every request be followed by a response. In business applications, the response is usually synchronous, so the requester thread normally waits until it is received, but many application protocols allow for the requester to provide a means for asynchronous notification or rendezvous. Still, in a request-response paradigm, each request is followed eventually by a response (by definition)—assuming that no failure event occurs to prevent a response.

Request-response protocols often have APIs that mimic the way that local functions or methods are called, allowing the client to make a remote request in the same manner as a local function or method call. For example, the protocols used by EJBs are accessed using the method-centric API of the EJB being accessed. In contrast, HTTP is a request-response protocol that does not define a standard language-level API, although many HTTP libraries exist.

The request-response paradigm is one of the most fundamental models for computing. It is defined in the following design pattern in order to make reference to it elsewhere in this book without ambiguity. The pattern addresses only the synchronous case.

DESIGN PATTERN: REQUESTER-RESPONDER

Context

An application needs to access a service to obtain information or to initiate a task. The application cannot continue until the service responds, so it must wait for a response.

Problem

In order to provide a request-response API on top of a message-based communication channel, the API must implement the encoding ("marshaling") of the request and response, as well as the dispatching of a request to the corresponding function or method on the receiving end. In the process of performing the marshaling and communication, various errors can occur that would not occur if the function or method were invoked locally. The API and client must accommodate these various error conditions.

Solution

This pattern defines a basic request-response model. In enterprise applications, this pattern is often referred to as a "Client-Server" model.[1]

In this pattern, there are *two* communicating parties: the requester and the responder, using a dedicated bi-directional channel, such as a socket connection, allocated between them. The requester makes requests to the responder, and the responder responds to those requests. The requester's requests can occur at any time, but only one request at a time is issued, and another request is not issued until any pending request has been responded to. In concrete terms, the model applies to a single thread of a requesting client. The responder waits for requests and can handle only one request at a time; thus, the model applies to a single responder thread. If a request is issued and the responder thread is busy or unavailable, or if the communication channel is full, the requester will receive an error response.

Communication between requester and responder occurs via a bi-directional communication channel in which request messages are forwarded to the responder and response messages are forwarded to the requester. Note that this pattern assumes that the communication channel between requester and responder has been allocated. In many HTTP implementations this allocation occurs when a request is received on a server port and a service thread is assigned to handle the request.

Note also that there must be a mechanism built into the request message or communication channel to signal the bounds of a request message so that the responder knows when it has received a complete request; similarly, there must be a way for the requester to know when a complete response message has been received. The requester should make provisions to gracefully and robustly handle all outcomes, including that (1) a response is never sent, and (2) a communication system error is returned. (See Section 13.11.1, "Resources That Do Not Reliably Timeout," and the pattern "Interruptible Thread" in Section 12.2.4, "Thread Interruption.")

After a requester sends a request, the requester waits until the responder has processed the request and responded. After a response has been received, the requester resumes its own work and may at some point send another request. Figure 15.1 illustrates the activities.

1 The term "client-server" is sometimes used to mean specifically the situation in which database accesses are embedded within the server application. In this book, the term is used more generally to refer to any design that utilizes a client and a server.

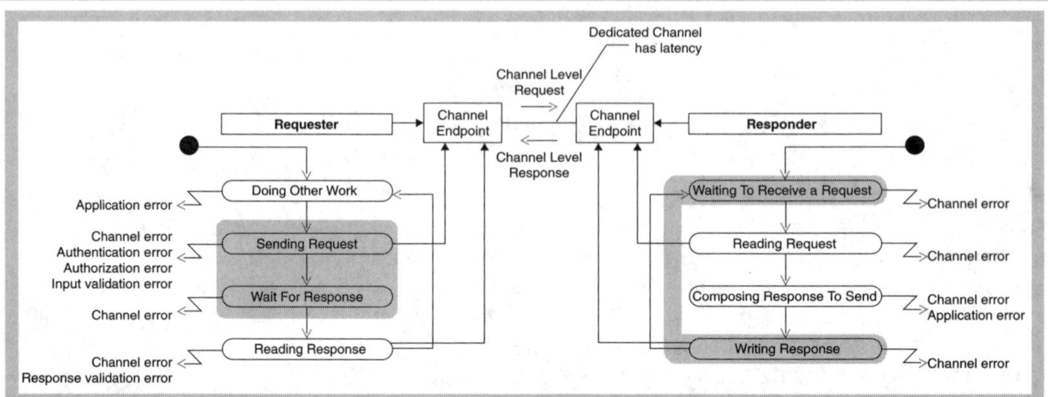

Figure 15.1 Request-Response protocol activities.

In many implementations, the channel endpoints are wrapped by components that provide the requester with a façade API that implements a request-response protocol. For example, HTTP APIs provide this kind of wrapper over the underlying socket connection behavior and HTTP messages to shield the programmer from the details of the HTTP protocol. Such wrapper APIs aggregate the connected portions in gray, as shown in Figure 15.2.

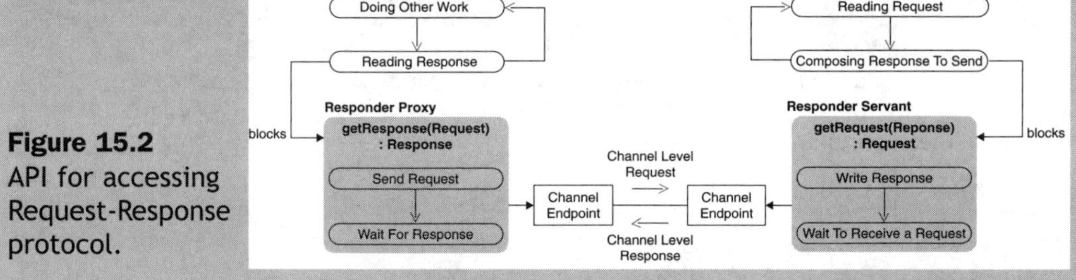

Figure 15.2 API for accessing Request-Response protocol.

Thus, the requester's application logic only has to pass a request via a getResponse (Request) method that blocks until a response has been received, and the responder only has to pass a response via a getRequest(Response) method that blocks until the next request is received. Of course, there are edge conditions to deal with; for example, when the responder first starts and has no message to respond to.

If the API provides a function-like interface with a separate callable function for each kind of request, the pattern is known as a "remote procedure invocation."[2] If the API provides a function-like interface that includes multiple target remote objects, the pattern is known as a "remote method invocation." [2] The use of target objects implies an object-oriented implementation. It also may imply that arguments and return results may be objects, although this is not necessarily the case, or there may be restrictions on the kinds of objects that can be passed between caller and target.

2 For example, see [1]. An overview can be found online at http://www.enterpriseintegrationpatterns.com/EncapsulatedSynchronousIntegration.html.

The error conditions that are shown represent typical general conditions. Conditions such as timeout are wrapped into the error referred to in Figure 15.1 as *channel error*; however, in an implementation of this pattern, the specific conditions should be handled separately.♦

Consequences
Clients have a simple way of interacting with remote services that models the way that local functions are accessed in most programming languages.

◆ See the principle "Careful Design Time Consideration of Error Conditions" in Section 7.15, "Secure Error Handling." Later in Section 18.2.1, "Ensuring That All Situations Are Handled," the principles "Use Checked Exceptions for All Lifecycle Errors" and "Throw Specific Exceptions—Not Generic Ones" are also relevant.

15.1.1 The Unreachable Server

It is often the case that, for one reason or another, a responder (server) is not able to receive requests. For example, a firewall might prevent incoming requests. In effect, any services within the network are unreachable with regard to requests originating from the outside.

For example, most home networks have a firewall that prevents incoming requests of any kind. As a result, so-called "peer-to-peer" (P2P) applications often cannot work without first contacting so-called "super nodes" that are not constrained by a firewall. Those network nodes can receive requests from the Internet, so they are able to serve as hubs for everyone else to use.[3] Thus, these P2P networks are really not peer-to-peer, but rather are a relatively small number of hub-to-hub computer nodes, and everyone else is merely connected to one of those hubs.

In that kind of topology, connecting to a hub connects you to the peer-to-peer network, with the hub acting as your gateway. If someone wants to request a file from you, they make the request via the hub that you are connected to. The hub uses the fact that you are connected to it as a means of forwarding the request to you.

Most home network firewalls can be configured to allow only a limited number of outbound protocols, such as HTTP, POP, SMTP, and so on. Thus, to receive incoming requests via a hub, you have to make a request to the hub using one of the permitted protocols. Your application then waits for a response. The response contains any requests that other users of the

3 The term "hub," as used here, is not to be confused with a packet-level hub.

network have for you. Thus, you make a request to obtain requests. Confusing?

This backwards approach is known as the "blocked registrant" pattern. It is commonly used within commercial "DMZ" portions of a network as a means of safely communicating into the innermost secure network. In this scenario, a gateway service on the perimeter of the inner network makes a request for requests and waits for a response. The public access Web server within the DMZ receives this request and uses it as a channel for getting information from the inner network: When the Web server needs data, it *replies* to the request from the inner network, and its reply contains its actual request.

The blocked registrant pattern is defined next.

DESIGN PATTERN: BLOCKED REGISTRANT

Related Patterns

This pattern utilizes the "Requester-Responder" pattern described in Section 15.1, "Request-Response."

Context

A service needs to receive requests, but it is behind a firewall that prevents requests from reaching the service. Examples of this situation include:

The server is behind a firewall, and inbound connection requests to the server are disallowed.

The server is a callback object within a client, which is behind a firewall, and callbacks to the callback object (which are inbound requests to the client) are disallowed by the client's firewall.

Problem

The firewall cannot be opened for the service, because the service is not judged to be sufficiently secure to be able to properly discriminate different inbound requests.

Solution

The "blocked registrant" design pattern allows connections *from a server* to be used to send requests *to the server*.

In this pattern, a server initiates a connection to a trusted client. The server makes a request to the client, asking it for the next message or next request. The server then waits for clients to respond.

The blocked registrant is essentially a protocol pattern. The blocked registrant implements a higher-level protocol on top of a request-response protocol that allows requests in only one direction. The higher-level protocol effectively reverses the direction of the lower-level protocol, but without introducing additional risk.

This pattern utilizes the "Requester-Responder" pattern to provide the lower-level request-response protocol. (The Requester-Responder pattern is merely the familiar client-server model.) The blocked registrant invokes the lower-level request-response protocol, as shown in Figure 15.3.

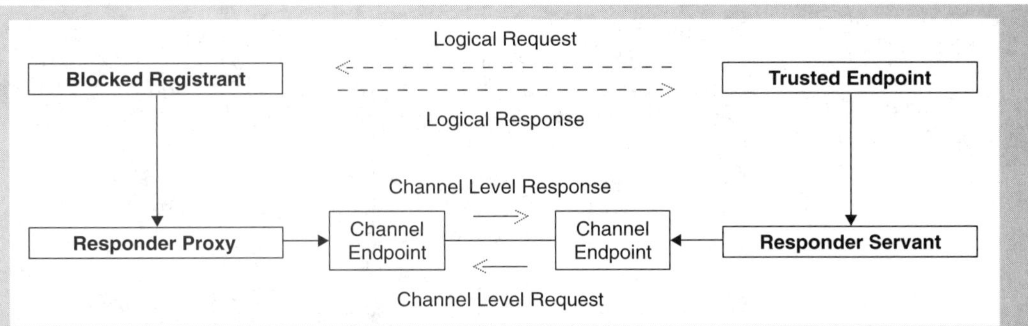

Figure 15.3 Blocked registrant.

The detailed thread state of each component is shown in Figure 15.3. In this diagram, the Blocked Registrant is the server that wants to receive requests from a trusted endpoint client. However, the server is behind a firewall and cannot receive incoming *network* requests. For example, the server (registrant) might actually be a callback object residing within a client workstation. Therefore, the registrant begins by opening a request/response connection to the trusted endpoint and sending a null request, and then waits for a response ❶. To do this, it utilizes a Requester-Responder API that provides a getResponse(Request) method ❷.

Meanwhile, the trusted endpoint is not yet ready to make a request ❸, but at some point it sends a request to the blocked registrant and waits for a response ❹. It does this by invoking the getRequest(Response) method and providing the request as the Response argument ❺.

The registrant receives this request as a response to its getResponse() call, causing the registrant to unblock ❻. The registrant reads the request, prepares a response ❼, and then begins the cycle again ❽ by calling getResponse(Request), providing its response as the Request argument. This causes the trusted endpoint to unblock ❾, read the response, and continue the cycle again on its side ❿.

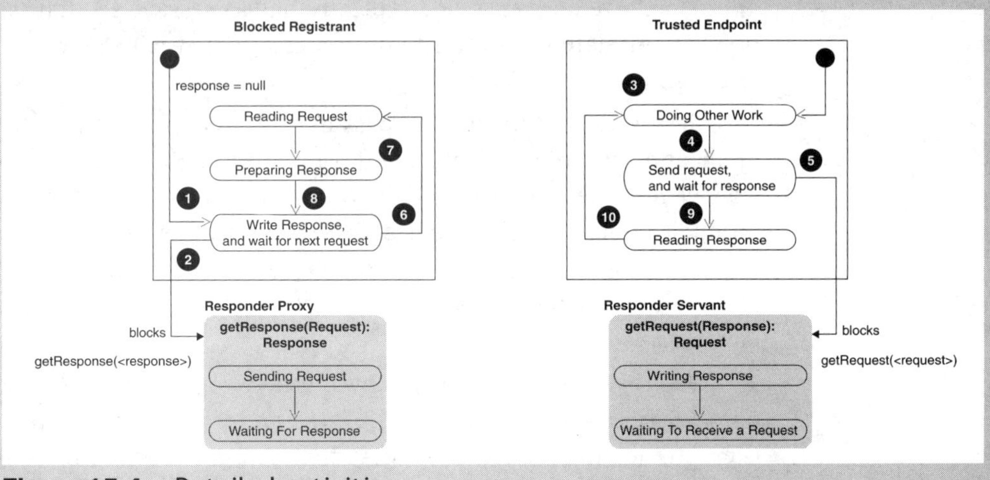

Figure 15.4 Detailed activities.

◆ See the principle "Do Not Secretly 'Tunnel'" in Section 10.3, "Designing for Secure Operation."

Security Concerns
Most implementations of this pattern utilize protocol tunneling in order to pass a request within a protocol response and then to pass a response within a subsequent protocol request. Protocol tunneling is a risky and disruptive practice.◆ However, if authentication on both ends of the connection is sufficient, use of the blocked registrant pattern to tunnel requests and responses can be safer than the alternative of opening a port.

Consequences
Services are able to receive requests from behind a firewall that normally would block those requests. Administrators should be informed of any use of this technique within a managed network.

15.2 Messaging

The message-based paradigm does not presume a response for each message that is sent. A message often signals an event that is responded to by some action, but there is not necessarily an immediate response to the sender of the message. The action that is triggered depends on the workflow.

That said, message-based applications are often implemented with "callbacks" that are message handlers for response messages. This provides an asynchronous request-response model, in which the request does not wait for the response. In this approach, a request message typically has a message ID that is used to correlate it with a response message that is received later on.

Messaging can be used to pass data from application to application in order to implement a planned or *de facto* workflow. When used to pass application data, messaging provides an alternative to using a centralized database. Passing data objects is sometimes easier that designing a consolidated schema that encompasses all the affected applications and data elements.

Web services are actually a hybrid between distributed object services, such as EJB or CORBA, and messaging, because they provide distributed services—often using a remote procedure call API known as SOAP—and also because the message formats are visible to the programmer in the form of service definitions in WSDL or XML schemas. Web services typically form the basis for so-called "service-oriented architectures" that utilize a messaging backbone for interconnecting a broad range of applications via XML. A service-oriented approach can be effective for linking organizations in a technology-neutral (for example, .NET versus J2EE versus WebMethods) way.

The vision articulated by many proponents of message-based infrastructure is that of a service "bus" on which an organization's computational and information services are published and accessed universally by each other [3].

XML provides a rich framework for creating complex messages. One result of this richness has been a return to a kind of file-based processing instead of database processing. However, XML messages ("documents") are structured and adhere to a schema—if designed properly.

One risk in creating a service architecture is that the services will not be implemented in a reliable or transactional manner or that they will be inappropriately aggregated in a non-transactional way.[4] See Section 13.7, "Combining Transactions."

> Before any kind of message backbone is implemented, a process model and information model of the affected parts of the organization should be developed.

Another risk is that the inherent workflow in the invocation of services will be omitted from the design of inter-system messages, causing confusion as to which services can be invoked when and causing the "bus" to degenerate into a *de facto* pipestem system. It is, therefore, critical that before any kind of message backbone is implemented, a core process model and core information model of the affected parts of the organization should be developed.

15.2.1 But Programmers Do Not "Code" In Message Syntaxes

One important fact often overlooked by groups that are new to message-based systems is that a decision must be made as to what point the interface will be standardized: at an API level or

4 Many request handling frameworks are not transactional. This is especially true for most Web Application frameworks. Some Web Service frameworks (for example, BEA WebLogic Integration) provide transaction management as an optional feature.

at a message level. In remote object technologies such as EJB and CORBA, there is no distinction between these two levels because the message format is actually never seen by a programmer. With Web services, interfaces are defined in terms of the message schema. The WSDL message definition looks nice (even though it is prohibitively complex for most programmers to read), but it is of little direct use to a programmer, because ultimately a programmer is more interested in using an API to generate and/or parse a message by using objects and APIs—a task that is performed automatically by EJB and CORBA.

Many message-based technologies provide toolkits to facilitate the parsing and generating of messages, but the point is, do you try to keep the object representation of a message stable, or the message schema stable? The two are related, but not the same. For example, if you define your interface in terms of the message schema (such as by using WSDL), you would then use a tool to generate an API for your programmers to actually use, and any small change to the message schema could potentially have a large impact on the API—so your own programmers as well as external users (for example, partners who must parse your messages) will be unhappy whenever small changes are made to the message format. If, on the other hand, you define an API (for example, as a remote interface) and then use a tool to generate a message schema from the API, any small change to the API could have a far-reaching impact on the generated message schema, and users of the message schema will then be unhappy—*unless they also code to the same API instead of the message format.* A solution that is sometimes offered is to write "mappings" between the message schema and the API, but the efficacy of this approach is questionable because it introduces a great deal of complexity into something that should be very simple: making a remote request.

Message schema pose a potential maintenance nightmare.

Thus, message schema pose a potential maintenance nightmare. It is better to define distributed services by specifying a remote call API (for example, expressed in C# or Java), and use that to generate the actual services layer implementations, but this would tie both ends of the connection to the language in which the API is expressed. A language-neutral approach is to define the remote API of each endpoint, using a language-neutral API specification.

For this reason, many Web services developers specify their interfaces using XML/RPC and distributing sample code—i.e., examples using language bindings and APIs. Others have come up with what they believe are simpler alternatives, including ICE[5] and REST. [4]

Many people have claimed that Web services in fact make things more complex than they should be. [5] The dust has clearly not settled on these issues, and it is best to keep interfaces as simple as possible, unless there is a dominant business driver to do otherwise—one that can afford the expense of the maintenance of these kinds of interfaces.

15.3 Summary

Distributed services enable remotely distributed applications to cooperate but introduce many additional points of failure that must be considered in the design of each application. Situations that are commonly treated as "system failures" must now be dealt with at an application level because the application user might not be in direct contact with the failing system or have a means of ascertaining its status. Distributed applications also must account for simultaneous access to the various components of the total system. This chapter discussed these issues in depth and design patterns for reliable distributed programming were presented, complete with error handling and a discussion of security issues. These factors make the design of distributed applications more complicated, and robust and complete error handling and consideration of failure scenarios is imperative. Finally, the maintainability of distributed interfaces was discussed because poorly maintained interfaces have a tremendous impact on overall reliability.

5 See http://www.zeroc.com/.

15.4 Exercises

1. List and explain two risks in developing a message-based design.
2. A server application has a published message-oriented interface. There are many clients that use the application, each with their own custom-developed client application. The server application is implemented using C++, and its interface and interface definition is automatically generated using a tool. A new version of the application is being developed for release. What is the risk to the clients of the application, and what can the server application developers do to help mitigate that risk?
3. A peer-to-peer (P2P) application utilizes so-called "super nodes" in order to allow bidirectional initiation of interaction with clients that are behind a firewall. What risk does this approach present to the clients, and what security principle does it violate? What can be done to mitigate the risk?

Answers and hints for these exercises can be found at `http://www.assuredbydesign.com/haa/`.

CHAPTER 16

MANAGEABILITY

"How artfully managed! Mrs Stanhope herself could not have done better. So, she can make Lord Delacour do whatever she pleases; and she condescends to make him behave prettily to me, and desires him to bring me peace-offerings of bank-notes." –from BELINDA, *by Maria Edgeworth, 1811*

An application is *manageable* if it has characteristics and provides features that enable it to be effectively and easily managed–i.e., installed, configured, monitored, diagnosed, and upgraded by operators who do not have detailed knowledge of the workings of the application. An application that is not manageable is not a high-assurance application because manageability is required to be assured that a quick and effective response is possible when things go wrong.

A manageable application must be *designed to be manageable.*

It is easy to manage an application when the environment has no other conflicting applications. Designing an application so that it can be monitored, diagnosed quickly when there is a problem, and installed so as not to conflict with other applications in a complex multi-application environment is not simple. There are some guiding principles that can help.

16.1 Deployment and Configuration Processes

Even if an application comes with an administration guide, it is important for the application to verify its configuration before it begins running. This helps the operator have confidence that the application has been installed correctly, especially if changes need to be made and there is not time enough to study the administration guide again.

PRINCIPLE: A MANAGEABLE APPLICATION SHOULD VERIFY THE VALIDITY OF ITS CONFIGURATION.

In order to assist the operator in selecting valid configuration parameter ranges for things such as number of threads, number of log file generations to retain, port numbers to use, and so on, the application should provide hints of what is normal, either in the documentation or in the installation program or package.

PRINCIPLE: A MANAGEABLE APPLICATION SHOULD EXPOSE ITS CONFIGURATION PARAMETER RANGES.

Installation and configuration changes should always be safe. That is, the application should detect if it is overwriting something from a prior installation that might be of value. This helps to ensure that irreversible errors, such as overwriting a log file or initializing an internal database, do not occur unless there is no question that the administrator is aware of those outcomes and intends for them to occur. The installation process should also be idempotent: It should be possible to safely abort it and re-run it and get the same behavior; or if this is not possible, the consequences of aborting at any point should be clearly spelled out so that the application administrator is not stuck wondering, "What will happen if I abort the installation at this point?"

> An application's installation process should detect if something from a prior installation will be overwritten, such as log files or configuration settings.

Another consideration is that there may be environment (for example, operating system) configuration requirements that are important for security; for example, ensuring that the right permissions are used on any paths that reference the application, ensuring that internal passwords are stored securely, and so on. The installation program should verify these things so that the operator does not inadvertently install the application in an insecure manner.

> ***PRINCIPLE: INSTALLATION PROCESS SHOULD BE SAFE: IT SHOULD NOT INADVERTENTLY DESTROY VALUABLE ARTIFACTS OR SILENTLY PERMIT INSECURE SETTINGS.***

To achieve this, applications must be aware of their weaknesses. For example, all sensitive configuration settings and credentials should be explicitly identified in an application design and again in the application's deployment manual. The various user groups or identities for running the application should also be identified, along with the permissions that they need. The deployment administrator should not be left to guess about these things. ♦

◆ See the principle "Deploy Securely" in Section 10.1, "Designing for Secure Deployment," and the discussion of restricted roles for server applications in Section 8.1.4, "Server Roles."

16.2 Avoiding Resource Interference

An application deployment administrator must ensure that there are no conflicts among the various resources used by applications, such as files, databases, ports, and so on.

It is important to make a distinction between "managed resources" and "unmanaged resources." A *managed resource* is a resource whose access is coordinated by a resource manager in order to prevent conflicts. An *unmanaged resource* has no mechanism to prevent conflicts. Managed resources include databases, application server objects and services, and resources provided by a resource container, such as an EJB container.

The best that can often be achieved with unmanaged resources is to list those that are used by each application and cross check them. This can be very tedious and represents a lot of work for an administrator. Therefore, the use of unmanaged resources should be limited to the extent possible.

Managed resources can still be a source of conflict between applications. For example, even though access to a database table is serialized via a transaction manager, processes that use the resources for different purposes, such as creating tables in a temporary database, can conflict, especially if multiple instances of the process are run at the same time. Thus, any "non-global" (for example, departmental) uses for globally visible resources should be listed and cross-checked, even if they are managed resources.

We have seen that *composability* is necessary to be able to assemble separate applications into a system (such as a workflow) and to be sure that if the pieces are secure, that the entire system is as secure as the pieces. Composability, therefore, is a design concept that strives to control the interactions between separate components. One can infer that if a system is composable, it is easy to assemble because there are no hidden interactions between the components.

If you have created a procedure for identifying and cross-checking all unmanaged resources and all non-globally used but globally visible resources, the applications that use those resources are likely to be composable.

PRINCIPLE: A MANAGEABLE APPLICATION SHOULD BE DESIGNED ACCORDING TO COMPOSABILITY PRINCIPLES.

16.3 Application Startup and Shutdown

The processes of application startup and shutdown should be robust. Errors that occur during application initialization are often due to misconfiguration and therefore are potentially easy to repair, but quick repair is possible only if it is immediately apparent what is wrong. Initialization errors are often hard to diagnose because such errors get little attention by programmers. Also, initialization often occurs in portions of code that are executed by an initialization thread and may result in a generic "initialization error" that gives little information. The full error information might be available—but the programmer has to ensure that it is captured and written out and interpreted by the programmer into a form that makes sense to an operator. For example, "null pointer" or IO exception tells little, but "Failure to resolve 'my-app' on port 2000" gives sufficient information to initiate the diagnosis of the problem without having to look at the code.

On shutdown, the stopping of all threads should be coordinated to ensure that no errors result.♦ This applies to abnormal shutdown as well. Nothing is more frustrating to operators than to be presented with an abnormal situation in which applications leave artifacts and files in an inconsistent state, and the operators have to diagnose what to run or do in order to return things to an operational state. This state of affairs is largely due the failure of applications to catch errors and shut down properly when something goes wrong.

> ♦ See the principle "Coordinate Error Response Across All Independent Paths of Control" in Section 12.2.2, "Coordination of Error Response."

> Nothing is more frustrating to operators than to be presented with an abnormal situation in which applications leave artifacts and the operators have to diagnose what to do in order to return things to an operational state.

When an application shuts down abnormally, it should indicate as precisely as possible what the cause of the error was, in terms understandable by the user who will be responding to the error.♦

> ♦ This is discussed further under the principle "Provide Problem Transparency" in Section 18.2.6, "Providing Sufficient Information."

When an operator detects that something is wrong and decides that the application must be shut down, or when the application must be shut down for any reason, there should be mechanisms provided for gracefully stopping the application in such a way that few or no additional errors result, all resources are released (to the extent possible), and all pending updates are committed (see Section 18.2.1, "Ensuring That All Situations Are Handled"); and if any of this fails, the application should report exactly what did not complete and what inconsistencies resulted. (This is discussed further under the principles "Throw Specific Exceptions—Not Generic Ones" and "Use Checked Exceptions for All Lifecycle Errors" in Section 18.2.1.)

Following an abnormal shutdown, operators may need to restore the application to a usable state as quickly as possible—possibly even before the problem that caused the shutdown has been diagnosed. If this is the case, there must be procedures to enable them to do this. This means that the application requirements must define what sorts of checkpoints or recovery mechanisms should exist in order to be able to recover or restore operation.

16.4 Generating Progress and Health Messages

Both users and operators of applications rely on (1) timely and clear indications of correct behavior by an application, and (2) timely and clear indications of incorrect behavior. The latter is often more problematic. For example, if an application takes longer than it normally does and there are no explicit indications of correct operation, valuable time is wasted wondering what the application's status is. This can be very frustrating to all involved.

Monitoring of an application should also include logging, so any event that is generated to notify a user or operators should be logged as well.

16.4.1 Heartbeats

Timely indications of correct behavior are sometimes referred to as a "heartbeat." A *heartbeat* is a message or indication that occurs at frequent and regular intervals to indicate unambiguously that the application is operational. A heartbeat is different from a normal progress event because normal progress events occur at irregular intervals, depending on what the application is doing. A heartbeat is designed to occur frequently—even if the application is idle. The regularity of the heartbeat signal is important in order for its absence to serve as an indication that the application is not in a state of readiness or has failed.

A heartbeat is designed to occur frequently—even if the application is idle.

PRINCIPLE: A MANAGEABLE APPLICATION SHOULD GENERATE CREDIBLE AND MONITORABLE "APPLICATION-IS-OPERATIONAL" EVENTS (I.E., A "HEARTBEAT").

A heartbeat can be implemented by having a separate heartbeat thread or process send requests to the application at regular intervals and, whenever a successful response is received, generate a corresponding heartbeat message that is then sent to heartbeat monitors. The heartbeat thread should input requests at the outermost interface to the application. This is similar to the approach of using an "agent," which is an entirely separate client for the purpose of monitoring. Section 18.3.3, "Use of 'Agent' Clients for Monitoring," discusses agents in more depth.

A heartbeat from an application means that it is "available"—that is, it is able to receive and process a request to completion. *It does not mean that there is nothing wrong with the application*, and monitoring of a heartbeat should be accompanied by monitoring of the application's resource usage. However, it is true that most application failures eventually do lead to a loss of heartbeat, but perhaps after considerable time has passed.

A heartbeat does not replace the need to monitor an application's resource usage.

Any kind of application status event, such as a heartbeat, should be created and delivered securely to whatever monitoring mechanism is being used. This ensures that users and operators have an accurate picture of the application's status.♦

♦ See the principle "Reliably Inform the User of Status" in Section 10.6, "Usability."

DESIGN PATTERN: HEARTBEAT

Related Patterns

This pattern uses the "Interruptible Thread" pattern from Section 12.2.4, "Thread Interruption."

See also the Heartbeat pattern in [1].

Context

The user or operator needs a signal on a continual basis to indicate that a server application is in an operational state.

Problem

The signal should not be tied to specific user requests because the frequency and duration of those requests is somewhat random and therefore cannot be used to continually indicate the health of the application.

Solution

This pattern consists of a "heartbeat thread" that (1) makes a call to the application's service layer, (2) performs some form of simple validation of the return response, (3) signals a successful response (or unsuccessful), (4) waits for a predetermined period, and then repeats this sequence until the application is shut down. The heartbeat thread uses the "Interruptible Thread" pattern. In the "Interruptible Thread" pattern, there is a "Work" sub-process; the heartbeat's logic, as described in the previous four steps, is contained within the Work sub-process. In Figure 16.1, the generated "Heartbeat Signal" contains the result of the response verification.

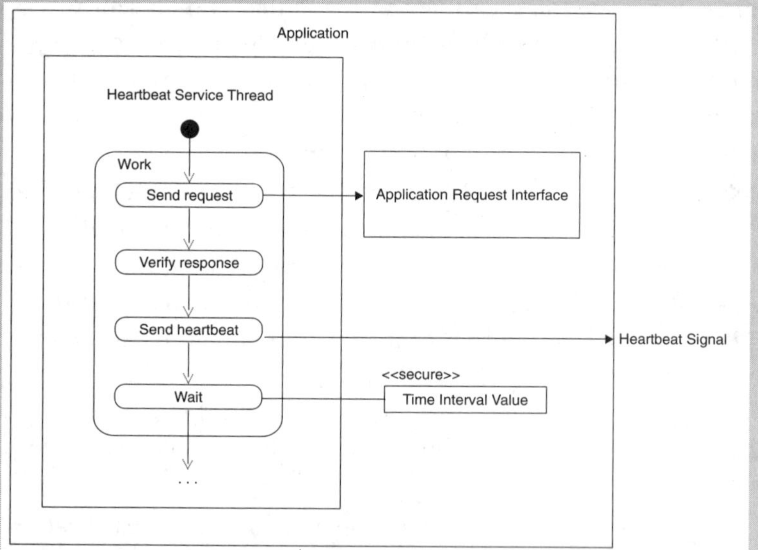

Figure 16.1
Activities.

Consequences

The heartbeat will consume some application resources.

The presence of a heartbeat does not mean that nothing is wrong: it merely means that the application is able to receive and process requests. In order to assess whether the application's processing is *correct*, other events are needed that report on the successful and accurate completion of the application's processing steps.

16.4.2 Progress Events

Heartbeat events do not satisfy a user's need to know what the *progress* of the application is. For this purpose, the application should generate events that correspond to processing milestones. Progress events are important for end users who want to know how far an application has progressed so that they can schedule their work, as well as operators who need to estimate when resources can be released or how far an application has progressed if it needs to be shut down.

The best way to embed progress events into an application is to consistently generate them at the entry and exit of each major processing step. For example, if an application involves many calls to a transaction layer, each transaction layer interface method should generate a "start" event when it is entered and a "finished" event when it completes. If the processing step is long in duration, progress events should be generated at intermediate points within the step. The points at which progress is reported are known as "checkpoints."

The best way to embed progress events into an application is to consistently generate them at the entry and exit of each major processing step.

PRINCIPLE: A MANAGEABLE APPLICATION SHOULD GENERATE MONITORABLE PROGRESS EVENTS AT THE BEGINNING AND END OF AND AT FREQUENT INTERVALS WITHIN EACH SIGNIFICANT PROCESSING STEP.

In an object-oriented application, significant processing steps typically correspond to the significant object methods. Therefore, for an object-oriented application, the previous principle can be recast more simply as follows:

PRINCIPLE: MONITOR ENTRY AND EXIT FROM AND PROGRESS WITHIN TIME-CONSUMING METHODS.

It is important to ensure that each thread generates progress events.

Each thread in each process owned by the application can potentially become hung, so it is important to ensure that each thread generates progress events. This can result in a lot of events, so judgment must be used with regard to where these events are generated to make sure that they do not burden the application. If there are many events of different kinds, the application should contain an embedded monitor of some kind that receives these signals and aggregates them into a coherent assessment of the application's operational status and generates a smaller set of "interpreted" progress messages to send to the user or console.

DESIGN PATTERN: EMBEDDED PROGRESS INTERPRETER

Related Patterns

The design pattern "Condition Logging and Problem Notification"" in Section 18.2.8, "Logging and Notification System Design."

The "Requester/Servicer" pattern in Section 12.2.3, "Multithreading Design Patterns."

The "Timer Thread" pattern in Section 12.2.5, "Designing a Thread Timeout Mechanism."

Context

The user or operator requires feedback indicating the progress of the user's tasks.

Problem

Progress messages can be ambiguous if they are defined in terms that a monitoring tool can understand, and they can be confusing if they are too numerous. This is especially problematic if an error causes a "message storm" in which a very large number of events are generated for essentially the same cause.

Solution

This pattern provides an approach for reducing the number of progress messages generated by an application without sacrificing transparency into the application's operation. The approach is to include a "progress interpreter" into the application's design, which receives all progress messages generated by all threads of the application. These messages are normally generated as a result of a call to a logging mechanisms. (See the design pattern "Condition Logging and Problem Notification.") The progress interpreter analyzes the many messages and generates a smaller number of "summarized messages."

The progress interpreter normally uses a producer-consumer pattern (see Section 12.2.3) so that it does not force each incoming message delivery to wait for the message to be interpreted. In this approach, the "producer" inserts a message into the progress interpreter's queue, and the consumer implements a timed thread pattern (see the "Timer Thread" pattern) to process the entries and forward them to the actual messaging mechanism at regular timed intervals.

The pattern structure is illustrated in Figure 16.2.

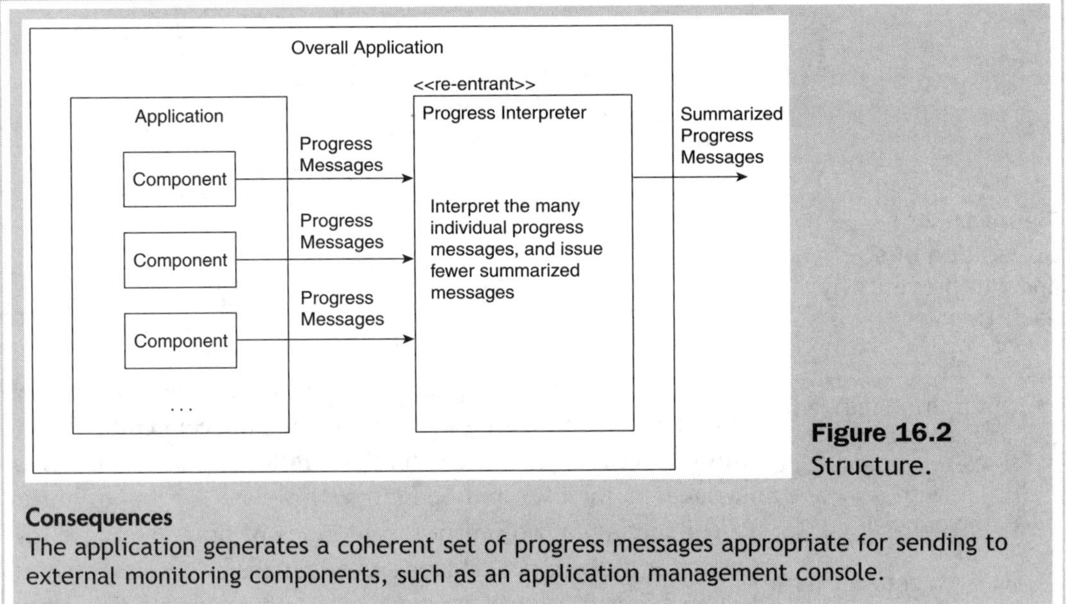

Figure 16.2
Structure.

Consequences
The application generates a coherent set of progress messages appropriate for sending to external monitoring components, such as an application management console.

Progress events should contain contextual information to make it possible to correlate them with user-initiated events. For example, if processing consists of a series of user-initiated updates submitted from a browser, each transaction's "start" and "finish" event could indicate which user request to which it corresponds. (This is discussed further in Section 18.2.5, "Providing Context.")

Each tier of an application should generate progress events. This allows problems to be isolated to the tier that is causing the problem. For example, if an application consists of a messaging tier that makes requests to a transaction tier, each tier might be able to hang, and progress messages (or the lack thereof) would indicate how far the processing of a message had progressed before it "hung." Thus, each entry point method of both the message tier and the transaction tier should generate "start" and "finished" messages, as shown in Figure 16.3.

Each tier of an application should generate progress events.

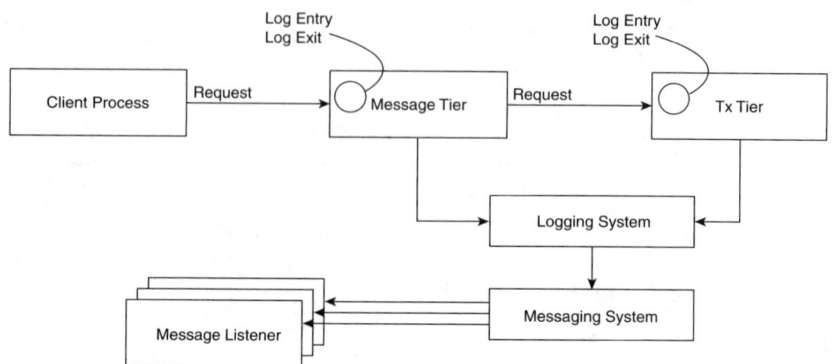

Figure 16.3
Generation of start and finish events by each tier.

◆ This is discussed further in Section 18.2.6, and in particular with regard to the principle "Provide Management 'Aspects' to Exceptions."

In the figure, you might wonder why alert messages are generated by the logging system. This might seem counter-intuitive because not all events that are logged should result in messages to the user and operators. However, it is important to have a single point of entry for all kinds of progress and error events for a given tier. This ensures that there is a single point at which a decision can be made to monitor events of a given kind. Thus, the logging system needs to be "smart" and the event information needs to be of sufficient granularity to enable the logging system to decide which events should be accompanied by notification messages to users and operators.♦

It is important to have a single point of entry for all kinds of progress and error events for a given tier.

16.4.3 Trustworthiness of Status Indication

Abnormal exit from a method should not prevent it from generating an accurate status event or message. In that case, the event should not indicate "finished" but instead should indicate "failed." In languages that support exception handling, this can be enforced by wrapping the method's entire logic within a block (for example, a "try block") that traps an error and signals failure and then allows the error to propagate. The following Java code snippet illustrates this:

```
public class SomeClass
{
    public void doLongMethod(Context context, ...)
    {
        Logger.logEntry(context);
        ...
        boolean status = Failure;  // default
        try
        {
            ...
            status = Success;
        }
        finally { Logger.logExit(context, status); }
    }
}
```

Note that the method in this code snippet logs a context variable at the beginning based on a context argument that is passed in. This example, therefore, assumes that there is explicit context information that would be useful for the user or operator, and this information is captured and reported. For example, the context might include a request ID, the process ID, the key information (for example, an account number) from the user's request, and so on. The nature of the context would depend on the application. The context argument may seem a little unclear at this point, but is discussed further in Section 18.2.5.

16.4.4 Capturing Implicit Context

It is important that implicit (for example, thread-based or request-based) context be captured in a progress event, such as a user identity associated with the current thread or client request.

It is not always simple to design an event generation or logging mechanism that captures thread-based context, because when such a mechanism invokes an API to obtain the current thread context, it must make sure to obtain the context of the *application method*—not its own context. For example, in the previous code snippet, the logExit(...) method might have the following implementation:

```
public void logExit(Context explicitContext)
{
// Get thread context.
StackTraceElement implicitContext = null;
StackTraceElement [] es =
Thread.currentThread().getStackTrace();
if (es.length > 1) implicitContext = es[1];

// Create event.
Event event = new Event(explicitContext, implicitContext);

// Log event.
Logger.log(event); // Log to the secure log.

// Dispatch event to notify operator, user, etc.
Dispatcher.dispatch(event);
}
```

In the previous snippet, the array of stack trace elements (each representing a method call on the current thread's stack) is used to select the *second* element (element 1) from the list: the first element (element 0) corresponds to the current context—*that of the logExit(...) method.* If the code source or module name is being captured as part of the context, it will differ between these two elements.

16.4.5 Progress Bars

Detailed progress events do not normally need to be logged.

In many applications, there are very granular progress events that do not need to be logged but in which the user is very interested. This is because a continuing stream of granular progress events indicates overall progress. A typical example of this is the use of a "progress bar" to display to the user the activity of a user-initiated action on a server. A progress bar works by receiving events from the server that represent some form of progress. The progress bar depicts this graphically. Such detailed events do not normally need to be logged, and the only person interested in them is the end user.

In a progress bar design, there is only one listener for the events generated by the server: the client application. A design pattern for a progress bar is shown next.

DESIGN PATTERN: PROGRESS REPORTING TO CLIENT ONLY

Related Patterns

The "Asynchronous Error Handler" pattern in Section 12.2.2.

The "Interruptible Threat" pattern in Section 12.2.4.

The "Timer Thread" pattern in Section 12.2.5.

Context

A component makes a request to another component (often a remote component) and needs almost continuous feedback on the progress of the request. The first component may also need to be able to cancel the request at any time, or after a timeout period. The request may be synchronous or asynchronous.

Problem

The coordination between the requester and the requestee is complex and must be handled without errors.

Solution

This pattern illustrates the use of a callback to provide continuing notification to a client of the progress of a request made to a service.

In this pattern, the client makes a request to a server and in the process provides a call-back object or handle that the server can use to progressively notify the client of progress, including completion or failure. The client maintains a progress listener for the purpose of receiving these notifications.

The service request can either be asynchronous or synchronous.

The Asynchronous Case

If the call is asynchronous, the request thread does not wait for a request to complete. Calls to the progress handler are made remotely from the server's service thread that is assigned to the request, but in the client they are executed by a remote procedure call service thread. The asynchronous case is shown in Figure 16.4.

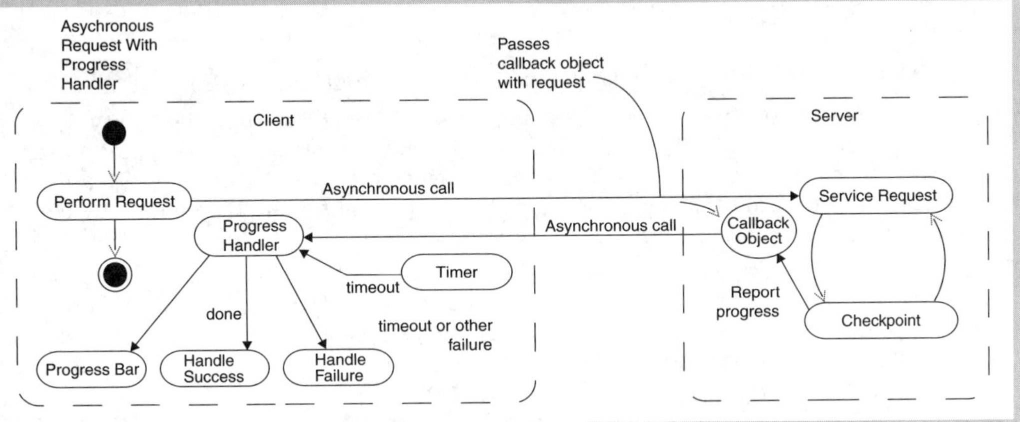

Figure 16.4 Activities for progress reporting of an asynchronous request.

The client can assign a timer thread (see the "Timer Thread" pattern) to watch the progress of the request and initiate a timeout action if too much time passes. In that case, the progress handler must be designed to be interruptible, and its cleanup action should be to cause a "timeout" return value to be returned to the callback object the next time the callback object invokes the progress handler. The callback object should then interrupt the service request and call the progress handler one last time, informing it of the final completion status.

The progress handler can also contain logic to initiate a *remedial action* if a timeout occurs, such as popping up an error message window within the client. Note that any attempt to retry the request should also be asynchronous.

Any client-initiated action to abort the service should also be asynchronous, and processed by the server as a separate request; thus, to provide the ability to abort a service request after it has been made, the service must expose a remote method for aborting a previously-initiated request, based on a unique request ID. This would be useful for the client to be able to terminate a "hung" service request that stops making progress calls.

The Synchronous Case

The synchronous case is shown in Figure 16.5.

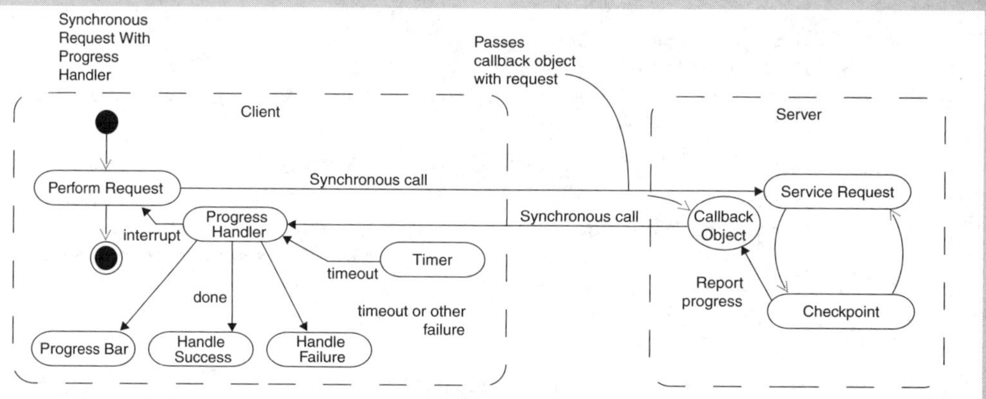

Figure 16.5 Activities for progress reporting of a synchronous request.

If the call to the server is synchronous, the progress handler should have the ability to *interrupt the client's call* in the event that the call times out. Thus, the requester must also be designed to be interruptible. The progress handler does not need to return a time-out indication to the callback object because the service will be terminated directly by the requester interrupting the synchronous remote request.

There also is no need for the service to provide a separate remote method for aborting a hung service request, since the requester can signal an abort merely by terminating the call. This presumes that the service method properly responds to a terminated call, for example by interrupting any worker threads that it has dispatched on behalf of the service request, as per the Asynchronous Error Handler pattern.

Consequences

These patterns are fairly complex, but that is because programming languages do not provide sufficient native support for the various kinds of remote invocation situations that arise. If the patterns are encapsulated into reusable components, they are much easier to instantiate.

In some applications, a server is not capable of making a callback to report progress. Examples of this situation include legacy services that cannot be modified to add this feature, transaction-based interfaces such as mainframes that support only a request-response method of interaction, and server processes that are invoked through process invocation such as shell scripts.

If a service cannot make a callback to a client but intermediate progress events must be recorded, the service can be designed to write progress event records to a database, each keyed on an ID that the client can retrieve and identify as belonging to one of its requests. Thus, the client polls to retrieve status updates related to its work requests.

DESIGN PATTERN: PROGRESS REPORTING OF DISCONNECTED RESOURCE

Related Patterns

The pattern "Progress Reporting to Client Only" in Section 16.4.5, "Progress Bars."

Context

A client invokes a remote service. The client requires progress notification. The service is implemented using a technology that does not conveniently support multithreading or remote calls.

Problem

The approach used in the pattern "Progress Reporting to Client Only" will not work without modification.

Solution

The earlier pattern "Progress Reporting to Client Only" must be modified in such a way that the client polls instead of relying on a callback for progress notification.

The client should create a globally unique request ID and pass it to the service as an argument when it makes a service request. The service's checkpoint step (see Figure 16.6) should write progress records to a database, keyed on the request ID. The client thread that waits on the process can then read the progress log at regular intervals and report progress to the client.

This approach can be used with either synchronous or asynchronous requests, and is shown in the figure.

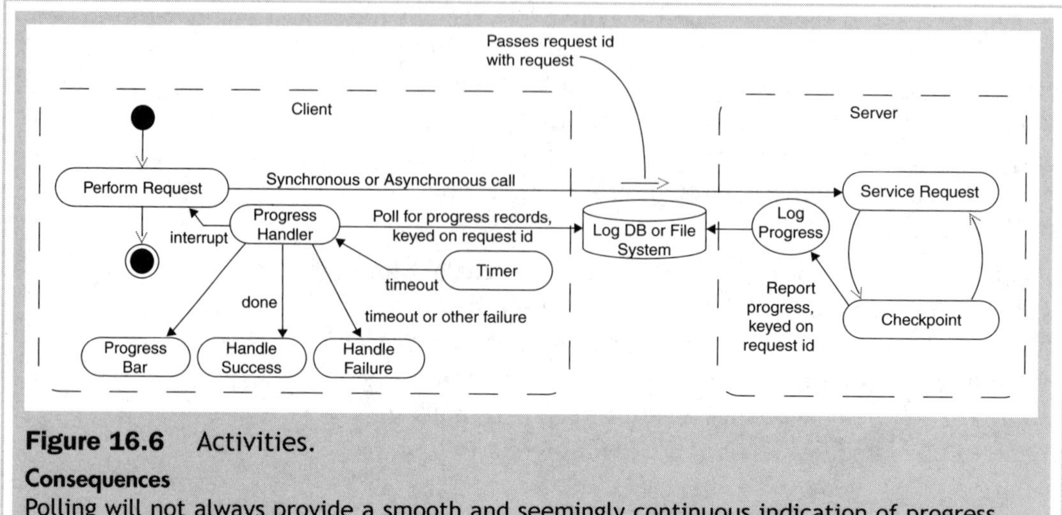

Figure 16.6 Activities.

Consequences

Polling will not always provide a smooth and seemingly continuous indication of progress. The pattern relies on the use of a persistent data store to retain progress events.

In addition to reporting progress, a method should report what resources it acquires and releases. This facilitates monitoring of overall application resource usage and the prediction of resource exhaustion problems through proactive monitoring, as well as postmortem diagnosis when resource-related problems occur.

PRINCIPLE: REPORT RESOURCE USAGE.

There are many out-of-the-box tools available for resource monitoring. Such tools are either based within the platform (for example, the operating system) or are external tools that monitor resources or SNMP events. These tools are valuable, but actively reporting resource usage *within an application* is even more effective. The reason is that the programmer is in the best position to know at any point in a program what resource information is important, and therefore can report exactly those statistics.[2] To facilitate this, an API should be created to make resource usage reporting convenient, and applications should report their resource usage as a component of status events.

16.5 Summary

An application that is not designed with features for administration, monitoring, and graceful startup and shutdown will be expensive and difficult to maintain in a secure and reliable state. Application designers must incorporate such features. If an application will be operated by an operations team that is distinct from the end user, the operations team should be considered to be stakeholders of the same importance as the end user.

This chapter discussed design considerations for reliable application startup and shutdown. Design considerations for monitoring were then discussed, and design patterns for addressing these were presented, including heartbeats and progress events, complete with provisions for error handling. The importance of providing measured information rather than inferred information was discussed.

The next chapter discusses features related to maintaining assurance over time as an application evolves: that is, ensuring that an application retains its security and reliability over time as it is maintained and upgraded.

16.6 Exercises

1. A critical business application logs all of its actions to a log file. The log file—named based on the current date—is created whenever the application starts. What potential problems might occur with regard to the operation and maintenance of this application?
2. A multi-user Java server application provides users with a function that creates an external batch process that is written in a scripting language. The C++ application must notify the user when the external process completes, and provide the completion status. Design an approach for meeting these requirements.
3. An application accepts as input a large set of data items. The application first attempts to purify the data and remove any items that might be problematic. The application then categorizes these data items based on

numerical criteria. The application then passes these categories to an external application server, using an XML message. The external application server will occasionally discover a problem with one or more of the categories, possibly due to incompleteness in the upstream data purification process. The dilemma is, the application server has no way of identifying which original data item is responsible for the problem because the application server only has access to the categories. Design an approach for enabling the application server to correlate errors with the original data that is the cause of the problem.

4. A server application needs to be continuously monitored so that if a problem occurs, operators are notified immediately. The application handles multiple asynchronous user requests. Each request is handed by first parsing the input, validating the input, performing some lengthy computations, and then updating a database. The dilemma is that the lengthy computations are not interruptible except by stopping the thread that is performing them. Design a strategy for adding continuous or near-continuous monitorability for the application and the requests that it handles. The strategy should include the ability to "ping" the application to check the health of each and every request that is being handled. The strategy should provide accurate results that are never misleading.

5. A server application includes a console that allows the application's operators to monitor the status of the application. The console includes indicators to show (a) the current configuration settings, (b) the resource usage (threads, connections), (c) the mode setting of the application (normal mode, diagnostic mode, and so on), and (d) the file path of the log file as entered by the operator. What potential problem(s) do you see with this design?

Answers and hints for these exercises can be found at `http://www.assuredbydesign.com/haa/`.

CHAPTER 17

MAINTAINABILITY

"The four essential principles underlying reliable systems are availability, security, integrity, and maintainability." –Efrim Boritz, Ph.D., FCA, CISA, Ernst & Young Professor of Accounting and Director of the Center for Information System Assurance at the University of Waterloo, Toronto.

The issue of maintainability is often overlooked in an era in which software changes rapidly and is often replaced every few years. However, large organizations especially suffer terribly large but invisible costs due to unmaintainable software, and smaller organizations become dependent on key personnel and cannot afford the cost of changes unless the key people make them, limiting their flexibility.

Maintainability is important for a high-assurance environment because when problems arise, someone needs to fix them. In fact, the very definition of a maintainable system is a system that has a short mean-time-to-repair when something goes wrong, as well as the system's ability to be easily and reliably enhanced to meet evolving needs.

Maintainability is also important for high assurance because when enhancements are made, the programmers must be able to have confidence that their design changes do not have unforeseen impacts—and this is not generally possible if the software is not well documented.

17.1 Documentation

Maintenance documentation takes many forms. These include ancillary artifacts such as design and maintenance documents, and implementation artifacts such as source code, buildscripts, property files, and so on. When using a design-oriented implementation language (see Section 3.2.5, "Design-Oriented Programming"), the design is the implementation, so consistency between design and implementation is not an issue.

> "Draw a flowchart of what you are doing, until you do, you do not fully understand what you are doing. You just have a job." —Dr. W. Edwards Deming

> See also the discussion of ambiguity in error messages in Section 10.6, "Usability."

The most important information for maintainability is almost always excluded, even from "well-documented" systems. That is: *why* each action is performed and *why* each construct exists. Software documentation often has comments that explain *what* is being done, but not *why* it is being done. The "why" is critical to someone who is seeing the application for the first time and is critical for maintainability.

> ***PRINCIPLE: MAINTAINABLE SOFTWARE SHOULD DOCUMENT WHY EACH ACTION IS PERFORMED.***

The documentation of "why" often translates into "how" in terms of how a requirement is met or how a solution strategy is implemented. The key aspect of "how" is its connection to the "requirement" or "solution strategy." Without correlating a "how" to the requirement or the solution, the "how" provides little semantic information. Thus, there should be a *clear link* between requirements or strategies (design decisions) and the "hows" (for example, program structures, algorithms, or policies) that are used in the design. The NCSC guide for documentation for systems undergoing a Trusted Computer Security Evaluation Criteria (TCSEC) evaluation states:

> *"The primary purpose of design documentation is to define and describe the properties of a system. As it relates to the TCSEC, design documentation provides an explanation of how the security policy of a system is translated into a technical solution.... In addition, the design documentation assists the evaluators by providing them with a vehicle by which the completeness and correctness of the implementation can be assessed."*[1]

Design-driven application construction, such as MDA, does not solve all maintainability problems. In particular, the old adage "garbage-in, garbage-out" applies. A system design (including an MDA design) should include not only functional specifications, but specifications for how the system should respond when things go wrong, as well as any other kinds of "non-functional" requirements, such as manageability, security, and performance.

Beyond the requirements level, the actual implementation should document any non-functional behaviors that are important when reusing the system's components. For example, if a program function assumes that it has exclusive use to a particular resource, it should document that so that if the function is reused by another application, the assumption about exclusive use will not be missed. It should also document any assumptions about what other operations have been performed first, the state within a workflow that the function applies to, and so on.

PRINCIPLE: MAINTAINABLE SOFTWARE SHOULD DOCUMENT FUNCTIONAL BEHAVIOR AND REQUIREMENTS AS WELL AS NON-FUNCTIONAL BEHAVIOR AND REQUIREMENTS.

Exceptions are a good example of this. Many languages require checked exceptions to be declared for each method, and this serves to document them. However, if a method can in some circumstances throw an unchecked exception, the compiler will not require it to be declared, so the programmer might be tempted not to document the exception. This means that users of the method will not know that the method can throw that particular exception and makes it hard to write air-tight code for high-assurance applications that must respond to every conditions—even unusual ones.

PRINCIPLE: DOCUMENT ALL EXCEPTION CONDITIONS THAT CAN OCCUR.

17.2 Transparency of Implementation

This book's introduction explained that business rule errors are often the cause of a minority of application failures, possibly because business rules are the main focus of testing. However, catastrophic failures can indeed occur due to business rule errors or business rule obsolescence. In the author's experience, the most common cause is not incorrect implementation, but is when a business rule is embedded within application code and forgotten, so that when real-life business rules change, the embedded rule is not updated or detected by regression testing, resulting in a failure at run time.

It is not possible to completely prevent this situation from ever happening, but it can be made less likely by differentiating between those business rules that are critical and those that are less critical. For example, a business rule in a financial application that computes dollar amounts for all transactions is likely to be more critical than one that handles the workflow for a subset of all transactions. That is, the risk is usually higher when money is involved and when the number of affected transactions or accounts is larger.

If critical business rules are identified, they can then be factored out into a separate portion of the code, such as a separate layer or a rule base. This makes them more transparent to programmers, and possibly even to business analysts. The more visible that business rules are to business analysts, the less likely it will be that the rules become forgotten and obsolete. Thus, business analysts should be able to view, or "audit," the implementation of the most critical business rules that they specified when use cases or user "stories" were written.

PRINCIPLE: CRITICAL BUSINESS RULES SHOULD BE AUDITABLE.♦

◆ Security authorization rules are actually business rules in disguise, so this principle subsumes the principle "Authorization Rules Should Be Auditable" in Section 7.4, "Auditability of Policy Coverage," which is specifically in the context of application resource security.

It almost goes without saying that in order for the implementation of business rules to be transparent, their implementation should be as simple and concise as possible. If the implementation is complex, it will be hard to establish correspondence between the implementation and the real-life business rules and requirements. Thus, some economy should be applied in terms of categorizing business rules as "critical," and the framework used to implement the rules should be easily understandable to business analysts. The rules themselves should also be expressed in a manner that is easily understood by business analysts, rather than in an abstract framework or obscured by complex or poorly documented coding constructs.

PRINCIPLE: MINIMIZE THE NUMBER, SIZE, AND COMPLEXITY OF CRITICAL BUSINESS RULES.

Conciseness and simplicity often imply consolidation–i.e., factoring of common features, logic, or values into a single module to clarify a design and avoid duplication. Avoiding duplication is important in its own right because duplication introduces the possibility that a change will be made in one place but not in another.

PRINCIPLE: AVOID DUPLICATION.♦[1]

◆ This is related to the principle "Avoid Duplication of Access Rules" in Section 7.4.

The components that implement critical business rules should undergo more stringent testing than other components. Most importantly, critical business rules and components should be exercised thoroughly by a regression test suite. This enables them to be re-tested as the application changes over time and as requirements evolve over time.

1 See also the "Single Choice" principle, discussed in [2] on p. 63.

PRINCIPLE: APPLY STRINGENT QUALITY CRITERIA TO CRITICAL BUSINESS COMPONENTS.

Even if an application is thoroughly tested when it is first deployed, it is always possible that over time undetected errors will be introduced as a result of maintenance or real-world business rule changes. Regression testing critical business rules helps to protect against this. However, great assurance is also obtained from having a clear application design. For example, one can be assured that embedded rules do not exist at unknown points only if there is a clear design that separates such rules from the rest of the application and if the maintenance process ensures that the application does not depart from its design. Thus, the existence of a design is important for maintainability as well as reliability over time. In the absence of a verifiable design, extensive testing must be performed to be sure that the application continues to be reliable, because programmers cannot be sure that code changes will not have unintended consequences.

PRINCIPLE: AN APPLICATION THAT HAS NO VERIFIABLE DESIGN MUST BE TESTED MUCH MORE THOROUGHLY IN ORDER TO PROVIDE THE SAME LEVEL OF RELIABILITY.

17.3 Safe Extensions

One of the advantages of object-oriented technology is its extensibility. As we have seen (see Section 7.20, "Interference and Closure"), extensibility exists at odds with the goals of security and to some extent reliability in general.

Existing software languages do not always give us the tools that we need in order to enforce that architectural features that implement closure features or protection domains are maintained and not inadvertently compromised as components are extended or maintained.[2] Thus, programmers must be aware of the ways that they can jeopardize an application's integrity by extending it improperly.

2 Reference [3] documents experience with OS 360 and argues that "The entropy of a system (its unstructuredness) increases with time, unless specific work is executed to maintain or reduce it." Paradoxically, this occurs despite the fact that application "bugs" continue to decrease.

One way in which a component can be compromised is to override methods on which the security or integrity of the component depend. For example, if a component's methods encode preconditions that ensure that the methods are not invoked improperly, these methods need to remain intact. Similarly, postconditions might protect against improper changes of state to an object—perhaps as the result of an attack. It is, therefore, important to ensure that when an object is extended the method pre- and post-conditions remain intact.[3] These conditions protect assumptions that are made by the component and by clients of the component.

PRINCIPLE: DO NOT WEAKEN ANY ASSUMPTIONS MADE BY A SUPERCLASS.

Preconditions can be relaxed when a sub-class overrides a superclass method without endangering the new (overriding) method because the existing clients of the method apparently satisfied the stricter preconditions. However, relaxing preconditions might endanger the existing clients of the method, or the superclass containing the method. For example, the superclass preconditions might have ensured that a condition that would cause an existing method to fail never occurs; if those preconditions are removed, the conditions might then occur.

Relaxing preconditions might also introduce a security vulnerability, particularly if the author of the superclass method introduced the preconditions to ensure that a security weakness was protected against. The author of the superclass method might have assumed that a sub-class would never override the precondition. For this reason, it is useful if preconditions can be scoped and enforced by a language mechanism.♦

◆ See the related security principle "Consider Hierarchical Realms and Inherited Security Policies When Possible" in Section 6.2.2, "Hierarchies of Trust," as well as the principle "Default to the Most Secure (Least Permission) Level" in Section 7.11, "Default Policies."

Another way that an existing component design can be compromised is by weakening security domains that are built into the component. For example, if a component attribute is defined to be private to the component, but an extension to the component redefines it to be publicly accessible, this can create weaknesses in the original component if it is possible to treat (for example, cast) instances of the existing component to the extended component type.[4]

3 In [4]. p. 573. Meyer defines an "Assertion Redeclaration" rule that is similar to this principle.

4 Note that while Java allows a subclass to override the scope of a variable, doing so actually creates a new variable, so that is not an example of this kind of compromise.

17.4 Regression Testing

The term "regression testing" refers to the practice of having a suite of tests that can be run repeatedly. Implicit in this is the assumption that a regression test suite is automated: Tests that must be conducted by human users do not satisfy the goals of regression testing, which are to have a test suite that can be run on short notice, executed quickly, reliably, and with repeatability, and that it imposes sufficiently low overhead so that it can be run often—perhaps daily.

In order to achieve this, it is usually necessary to establish the regression suite from the very beginning of a project. Unit tests created by programmers are an important adjunct to a regression suite but do not satisfy the requirement of ensuring full coverage of the system's external interface with regard to all requirements—both functional and "non-functional."

PRINCIPLE: TESTING OF MAINTAINABLE SOFTWARE SHOULD BE AUTOMATED FROM THE BEGINNING.

◆ This issue was discussed earlier under the principle "A Software Layer Should Define an 'Interface' for Use by Upper Layers Only."

A regression suite should exercise the "API" of the application—the application's external interface.◆

Using stubs to stand in for external resources or lower layers that access resources increases testability and makes it possible for developers to thoroughly exercise tests without conflicting access to a shared resource such as a test database. Such stubs are sometimes referred to as "plugins" [5]. Using stubs during development is important to ensure that full and frequent regression testing is encouraged and is feasible.

PRINCIPLE: MAINTAINABLE SOFTWARE SHOULD EMPLOY STUBS FOR INFRASTRUCTURE THAT IS NOT EASILY DEPLOYED IN THE DEVELOPMENT ENVIRONMENT.

Stubs can be used for routine regression testing, but for system integration testing, actual resources should be used.

17.5 Summary

Reliability and security must be carefully maintained over time; otherwise, an application will inevitably degrade and its reliability and security will suffer, possibly reaching a point of no return, at which point it is more economical to replace the application than to return it to a high-assurance condition. Maintainability is a result of careful design, transparent and accurate documentation, and comprehensive testing processes. This chapter discussed these issues, and presented principles that are important for addressing them.

The next chapter focuses specifically on error handling. Design principles and patterns are presented that enable a designer to enhance the error handling of an application so that errors can be effectively diagnosed and remedied, and the likelihood of non-repeatable errors is reduced. A well-considered approach for error handling enhances maintainability, manageability, and assurance.

17.6 Exercises

1. What things are wrong with the following method definition?

```
/** Calculate the results. Returns the results
 *  for each item in the values list. Calls doInverse for each input item.
 */
public List calculate(List values);
```

2. An application consists of several modules. One provides user interface functionality. Another provides a database interaction layer. A third provides the core application functionality. A fourth provides a set of calculations that are invoked by the core functionality and which represent critical business rules. Based only on this information, how would you order these modules in terms of risk, and for which would you assign the most stringent quality control?

3. An application module contains a class as follows:

```
class ProcessBase {
        protected int a, b = 0;
        protected ProcessBase(int a) { this.a = a; protect(); init(); }
        protected void protect() { assert a > 0; }

        protected void init() { b = 1000/a; }
}
```

Another module in the application contains the following class:

```
class FileBasedProcess extends ProcessBase {
        public FileBasedProcess() { super (1); }
}
```

What potential maintainability problems do you see with this design?

4. An application that is under development by a team of twenty programmers requires access to a security server to provide authentication and authorization. The license for the security server does not permit it to be installed on a developer workstation unless additional fees are paid. The security server provides authentication by intercepting HTTP requests, authenticating the user if necessary, and only forwarding the requests if a successful authentication session exists for the user. The security server provides authorization by allowing the application to query a database and passing the user identity and an identifier that identifies the resource that the user needs to access. In order to reduce licensing costs during development, what approach would you recommend? (Provide a UML-based conceptual design.)

Answers and hints for these exercises can be found at `http://www.assuredbydesign.com/haa/`.

Chapter 18

Failure Response Design

Failure response refers to the manner in which an application and users or operators respond to failures of an application. Failure can be divided into (1) the way that application code deals with error situations, often referred to as "error handling," (2) the facilities available to users and operators to diagnose and respond to errors, often referred to as "monitoring and management" facilities, and (3) the procedures that are used to actually respond. This book does not deal with operational processes, so the focus is on (1) and (2).

Handling a failure boils down to restoring the application state to a suitably stable and correct recovery point, logging the situation when appropriate, and notifying the appropriate people. The devil is in the details: what recovery point to use, which threads or processes are part of that recovery point state and how to get them into that state, what to log, and what people to notify.

The requirements for error handling have already been discussed in various specific contexts, including handling errors from transactions, GUIs, multi-threaded applications, and many other situations. In this chapter, we look more closely at what it means to "handle an error." Error handling is much more than logging an error to a console. Consideration must be given to what kinds of information will make an error useful to the personnel who will be receiving the error message—i.e., to what makes an error message actionable.

Failure response, is an important aspect of an application's design, and should be defined at an architectural level.[1] This ensures that the design addresses failure response in a comprehensive manner that considers the requirements of those stakeholders who will have to respond to a failure when it occurs. It also ensures that design features that address service level requirements take failure scenarios into account.

18.1 Common Failure Response Deficiencies

Error reporting is typically treated casually by programmers and requirements analysts. As a programmer, the author himself has done this: When perhaps too busy trying to implement a requirement (possibly designing the implementation along the way), to stop to think about error handling would get in the way of the creative process. The tendency then is to just skip over error handling and supply an error handler that merely

1 This is discussed in Ferreira [1].

prints to standard output or that throws a runtime exception to compel dealing with it later, and then get on with the real business of writing the rest of the code. Besides, handling errors requires that an error-handling framework has been thought of—and in most business application projects, error handling is added later on when there is time to "clean things up."

This scenario is common, and as a result, application error monitoring is usually addressed in a very inadequate manner, often by having textual messages written haphazardly and with little forethought to the various application platform logs. Such logs are often overwritten by re-starting an application when the logs are needed most—when the application failed and the reason needs to be investigated. The term "monitoring and management" does not even apply to this approach because while it constitutes a limited form of monitoring, it certainly does not represent any rational form of management!

For high-usage or critical applications, inadequate error handling results in very significant costs to a business. Typical inadequacies can be summarized according to the categories in Table 18.1 and have the business impact that is indicated.

Table 18.1 Failure-Response Deficiencies

Inadequacy	Business Impact
Exception data is thrown away: Servers consume exception details and generate generic error messages.	The user does not know the cause of an error when an error occurs, resulting in an inability to react to an error without calling technical support.
Insufficient pinpointing of invalid input: When data validation errors are detected on the server, insufficient information is communicated back to the client to allow the client to pinpoint the error to the erroneous client-side data element.	When data is invalid, the user does not know *what* data is invalid, and therefore does not know what needs to be corrected. The result is an inability to address the error without calling technical support.

Table 18.1 Failure-Response Deficiencies continued

Inadequacy	Business Impact
Timeout not explicitly handled: Transaction timeout is a normal event, but is treated as an internal error—leaving the user not knowing what to do.	Timeouts are normal during peak usage; when timeouts occur, the user receives the same message as if some kind of system failure occurred. The user does not know if data was lost or what happened and wastes time calling technical support when all they need to know is if the transaction can be retried safely.
System failures not interpreted: Many server-side events and conditions that can cause transactions to fail, such as inadequate disk space, are not predicted or interpreted and communicated to parties who can remedy them. Errors are written to logs, but the error information is not evaluated and dispatched to someone who can do something about it.	The lack of failure interpretation by the application and lack of active monitoring results in a myriad of various kinds of failures. Each kind of failure is infrequent, but in the aggregate the system is perceived to be unreliable and unmanageable.
Exception conditions are not handled: For example, resources are not reclaimed.	The application begins to exhibit erratic behavior, and performs worse and worse over time until it is restarted. This results in applications that must be constantly monitored and manually restarted, increasing operational costs and decreasing confidence in the application's integrity.

18.1.1 Effective Monitoring Relies on Effective Error Handling

Error handling and application monitoring and management go hand-in-hand. An application cannot be effectively monitored and managed if it is not designed to generate the information needed to monitor and manage it. We have already discussed the generation of application health messages (a heartbeat) and progress messages. (See Chapter 16, “Manageability.”) When a failure occurs, an application needs to generate monitorable event messages that reliably find their way to a management console, and the messages need to contain sufficient information to allow the person or monitor that is receiving the message to know what to do in response. Thus, error handling patterns within an application must ensure that (a) the right messages are generated, and (b) there are adequate mechanisms (for example, a console) for listening to (monitoring) those messages and interpreting and responding to (managing) them. The generation of error messages is considered in the next section, and the monitoring of those messages is considered in Section 18.3, “Monitoring and Management.”

18.2 Effective Error Handling

When an error occurs within a program thread, the error can be handled by either (1) resolving the problem right then and there or (2) aborting the current routine. No other choice makes sense, because only (1) provides another chance for the routine to succeed.[2] Continuing in the presence of an error is generally not advisable because the routine cannot complete its function.

Trying again is logical only when the error results from asynchronous, variable, or otherwise unknown conditions. For example, if the error represents a timeout, it might make sense to retry the routine again. Previous sections have provided techniques for handling this within the caller (for example, see Section 13.11.2, “Handling Non-Successful But Normal Resource Conditions”), but it can be handled within the callee as well, if the calling mechanism or runtime platform provides a reliable mechanism for restoring the input arguments to their original state and retrying the call as if it had not yet occurred. The disadvantage is that in doing so one loses control over the number of times that a call may be retried.

The most common and robust response to an error within a routine is, therefore, to clean up and throw an exception. Cleanup should involve providing sufficient structured information to the caller so that it can interpret the condition and recover. The types of information to provide are discussed in later sections.

18.2.1 Ensuring That All Situations Are Handled

It is common programming practice in business environments to treat most "abnormal" conditions as "system error" conditions and not expect the user to be able to handle them. Therefore, such errors are not explicitly trapped by the majority of such application programs. Instead, they are allowed to generate internal error messages and cause the program to halt.

This approach may fine for a standalone single-user application. However, in an environment in which business processes often depend on a series of interconnected processes and independent remote resources, or if operation is real-time and errors must be diagnosed quickly and fixed, this approach is very inadequate. Such distributed "high-availability" environments require immediate error diagnosis and repair, so errors must be as transparent as possible and not buried in a multitude of unintelligible logs.

The point has been well expressed by Frank Cohen, author of the widely used open source testing tool "TestMaker":

> *"Design for brittleness.... At every point in your application when resources are touched, handled, or managed, make sure your code can handle the scenario where the resource is not available."*[3]

Figure 18.1 Design for brittleness.

In a high-availability environment, it is best to handle every error condition within the application code.

This forces the programmer to consider things such as (1) what information would be useful for diagnosis of the error, (2) what actually caused the error, (3) whether the error is something that the user might be able to fix (for example, invalid input), something that could be addressed automatically (for example, a transaction retry), or something that requires expert help (for example, an inability to connect to a server), and so on.

In handling an error condition, the programmer must decide whether to attempt to deal with the error immediately (for example, by retrying a transaction or trying again to obtain a connection) or to throw an application exception. When throwing an exception, consideration must be given to what information to incorporate into the exception. Generally, exceptions that contain contextual information are the most useful, as is discussed in Section 18.2.5, "Providing Context."

Many languages, such as Java, C# and C++, have built-in mechanisms to propagate exceptions.[2] These mechanisms allow a programmer to declare that a method throws an exception and, in that case, callers of the method must provide an exception handler. Exception conditions that must be handled are referred to as *checked exceptions*. Thus, there is a way to force callers of the method to deal with certain exceptions.

Consideration also must be given as to the scope of the failure. Does the failure affect the entire application? Or does it merely affect the current thread?◆ Does it affect a certain portion of the input, allowing some processing to continue, or does it affect the entire request? The scope of the failure should be indicated in the exception that is thrown.

◆ See the principle "Coordinate Error Response Across All Independent Paths of Control" in Section 12.2.2, "Coordination of Error Response."

PRINCIPLE: INDICATE FAILURE SCOPE.

A precise indication of failure scope allows an application to salvage some of its work and continue processing, rather than giving up entirely. Again, this is the "incremental" approach rather than the "rocket launch" approach (see Section 4.4, "Think in Terms of Incremental Processing").

Explicit indication of failure scope is necessary only when the scope would otherwise be ambiguous. This is the case when a resource call performs actions on multiple objects and the objects can fail independently or in combinations that are not known to the caller.

2 For an excellent discussion of Microsoft's exception handling framework, see [4].

PRINCIPLE ILLUSTRATION: INDICATION OF FAILURE SCOPE

The scope is the range of the processing context over which the exception applies. For example, if the exception indicates a failure that affects the entire request, the scope would be the request. That is the default assumption if a scope is not specified. If instead the exception indicates a failure that affects a particular subset of accounts that are being processed by the request, the scope is that subset.

The kinds of exception scope that are available determine the degree to which an application can recover when something goes wrong with some of its processing but not all of its processing. For example, if the application is handling a request to update a set of accounts, and it determines that a subset of those accounts is inconsistent, it can return an exception indicating the inconsistency and identifying the affected subset. That way, the entire set of accounts do not have to be reviewed—only the subset—and processing can continue with the accounts that are not inconsistent. This kind of failure resiliency and compartmentalization of incorrect data is important in situations in which there is a processing deadline of some kind.

In the following code snippet, a method debits a monthly processing fee from a set of accounts owned by a single account holder. If something goes wrong when processing one of those accounts, processing does not stop; rather, the account is noted, and when the method completes, an exception is thrown containing a list of problem accounts.

```
void debitMonthlyFees(AccountHolder ah, Set<AccountID> accts)
throws AccountException
{
   Set<Account> disallowedAccts = new Set<Account>();
   Set<Account> overdrawnAccts = new Set<Account>();

   for (Account acct : accts) {
         if (! acct.holder().equals(ah)) {
               disallowedAccts.add(acct);
               continue;
         }

         try {
               acct.debitMonthlyFee();
         }
         catch (OverdraftException ex) {
               overdrawnAccts.add(acct);
               continue;
         }
   }

   if ((disallowedAccts.size() > 0) || (overdrawnAccts.size() > 0)) {
         AccountException ex = new AccountException(
               disallowedAccts, overdrawnAccts);
         throw ex;
   }
}
```

The reason that this approach is valuable is because the caller of the debitMonthlyFees(...) method can discover exactly which accounts are problem accounts and does not need to abort processing: It can continue to process those accounts that are in good standing. This allows time-critical work to continue and narrows the scope of response that is needed by support personnel.

In a high-availability application, it is very advisable to consider which exceptions might *ever occur* in the lifetime of the application. Errors that indicate program bugs do not fall into this category, because these cannot be anticipated; but errors that are the result of a misconfiguration, a resource failure, a timeout, an operator error, or anything else that is considered remotely possible should be handled—or at least considered. Therefore, such "lifecycle" error conditions should result in a checked exception that higher-level application layers are forced to handle. In formal terms, the need to handle lifecycle error conditions results from the need to consider the broader enterprise environment when defining the application's functional domain.

Forcing all lifecycle error conditions to be handled ensures that the programmer has considered all of these situations and has given thought to providing sufficient information within the exception so that the error's cause can be efficiently and quickly diagnosed when it eventually occurs. In a high-availability system, generally anything that *can* happen eventually *will* happen.

PRINCIPLE: USE CHECKED EXCEPTIONS FOR ALL LIFECYCLE ERRORS.

A consequence of this principle is that if a normal lifecycle error manifests itself as an unchecked exception, the code that receives that exception should explicitly catch the unchecked exception and either handle it there or translate it into a checked exception so that higher levels of the application will be forced to explicitly handle it.

DESIGN PATTERN: USING CHECKED EXCEPTIONS FOR ALL LIFECYCLE ERRORS

Related Patterns

See the "Exception Filter" pattern in Section 7.15.2, "Propagation of Unauthorized Information," which deals with the need to prevent sensitive information from being disclosed through exception messages.

Context

A section of code that can raise one or more exceptions. These exceptions might be checked or unchecked.

Problem

Unchecked exceptions often represent lifecycle conditions that should be handled by the application—perhaps by higher layers of the software—so the programmer must ensure that they are actually handled; yet if those exceptions are unchecked, programmers of the higher layers may be unaware of those conditions.

Solution

Let the code section be enclosed in an error trap. The error trap should catch *every kind of exception that can be expected to occur within the contained code during the lifecycle of the application*. Some of these exception types might be "unchecked," in that the programming language does not require that they be handled. However, if they can reasonably be expected to occur—given occasional operator errors, configuration errors, transient network and file system anomalies and so on—they should be caught by the try block and handled.

Checked exceptions can be divided into two categories for our purpose here, which this pattern will refer to as "low-level" and "high-level." The term "low-level" refers to those exceptions that indicate system problems that are not defined by the application processing model. In contrast, high-level exceptions are those that are recognized by the application's high-level design and would be understood by a business analyst. For example, a low-level exception might be "null pointer exception," whereas a high-level exception might be "file system unavailable" or "account is overdrawn." High-level errors often manifest themselves as low-level exceptions and must then either be handled or translated into a high-level exception so that the higher levels of the application can make sense of the situation.♦

◆ This is discussed under the principle "Objects Returned to Higher Layers" in Section 7.19.1, "Layers."

"Low-level" exceptions—indicate system problems that are not defined by the application processing model.

"High-level" exceptions—recognized by the application's high-level design and would be understood by a business analyst.

Figure 18.2 depicts a design pattern for handling unchecked, low-level, and high-level lifecycle exceptions. The try block (which might be implemented as multiple try blocks) catches any lifecycle error. Non-lifecycle errors that represent situations that are considered to be completely impossible (assuming that the code is designed and implemented correctly) are not caught, but all other errors are. For unchecked lifecycle exceptions, control is transferred to an error handler that interprets the condition and its possible causes and transforms the exception into a high-level exception that is then propagated to the caller. In the process, the low-level information is not discarded, but is appended to the new high-level exception (subject to security considerations: see "Filter Sensitive Data from Exceptions" in Section 7.15.2).

Low-level checked exceptions are similarly transformed and then propagated to the caller. High-level exceptions are not transformed because they will make sense to the caller as they are.

This approach does not try to recover from exceptions, but relies on the caller to do that, based on the quality exception information that is returned to the caller.

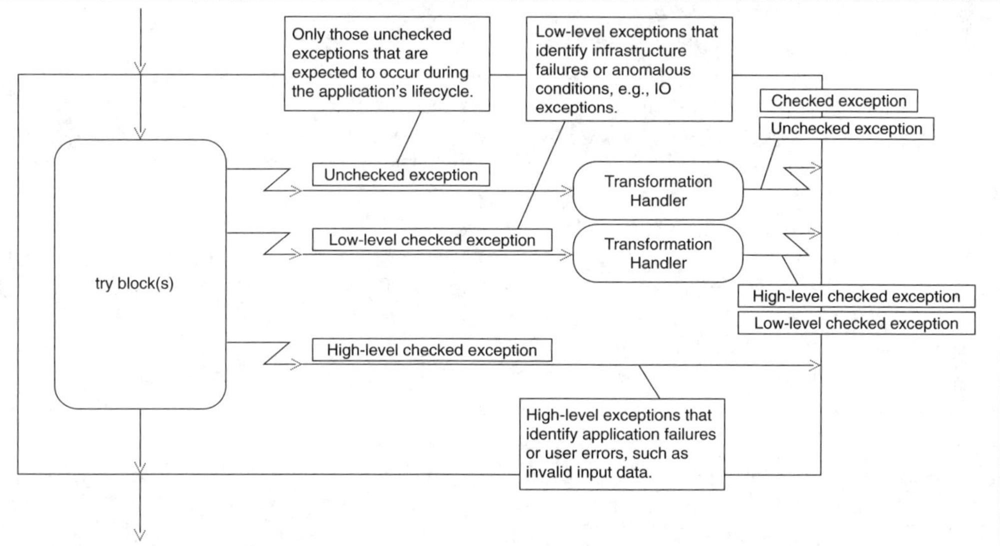

Figure 18.2 Activities.

The following Java code snippet illustrates this approach in action. In this code snippet, the error trap is a set of Java "try blocks." Each of the "catch" clauses of the try block transform an exception according to the principle described here. The "MissingResourceException" is a low-level exception that actually means that the application is misconfigured and that the property "AccountListFileName" was not specified properly when the application was deployed. Thus, this exception is transformed into a new exception, "ConfigurationException," and that exception is documented in the method's header and description. The original exception is preserved, by supplying it as the "cause" argument when constructing the new exception: This preserves the call chain from the point at which the original exception occurred.

```
static final String FilePropName = "AccountListFileName";
String fileName = null;
try {
   ResourceBundle b = ResourceBundle.getBundle(FilePropName);
   fileName = b.getString(FilePropName);
}
catch (MissingResourceException ex) {
   throw new ConfigurationException(FilePropName, ex);
}

File f = null;
try {
   f = new FileInputStream(fileName);
}
catch (FileNotFoundException fnfe) {
   throw new MissingAccountListFile(fnfe);
}
catch (SecurityException se) {
   throw se; // this can never happen if no security manager.
}
```

The second try block catches two exception conditions: "FileNotFoundException" and "SecurityException." The first of these indicates a missing account file, so the exception is replaced by a "MissingAccountListFile" exception that is more meaningful to the caller: This tells the caller exactly what file is missing so that a meaningful error message can be sent to support personnel.

The SecurityException is included for completeness because it can indeed be generated by the code within the try block (based on its documentation), but there is no need to transform it or even respond to it because it is not expected to ever occur within the lifecycle of the application, because it can occur only if there is a security manager installed and the assumption here is that no security manager is installed. If a security manager were installed, the design would have to be reviewed anyway to ensure that security errors were handled properly.

Consequences
Any lifecycle conditions that produce unchecked exceptions are translated into checked exceptions so that they must be handled.

In order to adhere to this principle, it is necessary to be able to ascertain what exceptions can be thrown by a section of code. Because languages such as Java do not require all exceptions to be declared, it is important that methods identify in their documentation what exceptions they can throw that are not declared, or declare them all.♦

◆ See the principle "Document All Exception Conditions That Can Occur" in Section 17.1, "Documentation."

Many home-grown applications treat unset property values as abnormal situations that are not diagnosed and, as a result, the program thread crashes, most likely aborting the program. The operator then has to examine the console to try to ascertain what happened and may find a stack trace and cryptic information about a property, or perhaps a null pointer exception. It would be much better to treat each property retrieval as an operation that might fail and explicitly handle the situation in which the property is not found or has an invalid value. The most useful response is then to generate a console message identifying the missing or invalid property and its value (or lack thereof).

I/O exceptions are often transient. Therefore, they should not always cause a program to abort. For example, in complex environments, file systems are often brought offline temporarily, so a mount might mysteriously disappear for awhile. This might manifest as an IO failure that is hard to reproduce. When an IO failure occurs, it is wise to treat the error as a potentially transient situation. This might mean pausing operation and allowing an operator to respond before stopping the application. Another approach is to retry the operation at intervals for awhile before giving up. If the process is transactional, see the discussion in the pattern "Handling Transaction Timeout" in Section 13.11.2, "Handling Non-Successful But Normal Resource Conditions."

Risky Operations

"Little Deaths" © 2003 Lily Prillinger.

Use a safety net for all risky operations.

Consideration must also be given to non-lifecycle exceptions that are not checked for by the compiler but which could occur. Two prominent types of non-lifecycle unchecked exceptions that can occur are numeric exceptions and cast

◆ See the principle "Coordinate Error Response Across All Independent Paths of Control" in Section 12.2.2, "Coordination of Error Response," as well as "Careful Design-Time Consideration of Error Conditions" in Section 7.15, "Secure Error Handling," and "Securely Transform and Compare Values" in Section 7.13.1, "Type Safety."

exceptions. A type cast exception often represents a programming logic flaw, whereas a value cast exception or numeric overflow (or underflow) might not represent a logical error so much as an oversight with respect to the expected and allowable range of values. (Granted, the value of this distinction is debatable.) Regardless, both of these kinds of exceptions can cause a crash of the thread unless there is an "exception firewall" that catches them and restores the application to a point of stability.♦

Because casting is a common operation in most complex applications, there are opportunities for runtime type or value cast error even in applications written in type-safe languages. Type casts may be safe if your design is compact, reusability and extensibility are limited, and you can ensure that your code will prevent any unexpected types from every occurring. This is a somewhat risky approach, however. In general, if you feel the need to write an assertion that the type is a certain type, it shows that you are not truly sure that a type violation will never occur as your code is reused over time. In that case, mentally think through what the effect of a type error will be: Where will the resulting type violation exception be caught, and how will it be handled? Is it worth converting the type cast exception into a checked exception, to ensure that it is handled?

Consider the following code snippet:

```
import myapp.exceptions.checked.UnexpectedType;
...

        public void myMethod(AbstractType a) throws UnexpectedType
        {
                ConcreteType aa = null;
                try {
                        aa = (ConcreteType) a ;
                }
                catch (ClassCastException cce) {
                        throw new UnexpecteType("Expected 'ConcreteType', found '" +
                                a.getClass().getName() + "'", cce);
                }
                ...
```

The programmer is sure that the type cast will always succeed, because the code is used only within a package written by that programmer, and the programmer is aware of all circumstances in which myMethod(...) is called. However, if the enclosing class is reused, there is a risk that the cast will fail, because the method's interface specifies only AbstractType, so it is reasonable for a programmer to pass any object that implements AbstractType. The exception UnexpectedType is a checked exception, which forces the calling layer to consider what the appropriate recovery should be if the type cast fails.

Numeric value casts and numeric exceptions are often more problematic, and it is harder to ensure that violations will not occur over time as the code is reused. A failure to handle a numeric type conversion error caused the crash of an Ariane 5 rocket, [5] as well as the failure of the $125 million Mars Climate Orbiter mission. [6]

Consider the following example using numeric types:

```
import myapp.exceptions.checked.CalculationException;
...

        public void myOtherMethod(AbstractType a) throws CalculationException
        {
                float a = ...
                float b = ...

                float f;
                try {
                        f = a / b ;
                }
                catch (ArithmeticException ne) {
                        throw new CalculationException(
                                "The 'f' calculation underflowed", ne);
                }
```

In this example, CalculationException should be a checked exception. This forces the application to consider what the appropriate recovery should be if the calculation unexpectedly fails due to the finite range of the computing language's intrinsic types.

PRINCIPLE: SAFELY TRANSFORM AND COMPARE TYPES AND VALUES.

Note the similarity to the security principle "Securely Transform and Compare Values" in Section 7.13.1.

When throwing an exception, it is best to throw an exception that incorporates information in a manner that is encoded or checked by the compiler. An example is when each exception condition is represented by a unique exception type, or by an exception code, that enables the program to eventually be enhanced to handle the condition automatically. It also makes it possible to tabulate the frequency of various kinds of exceptions over time, and failure-mode testing becomes easier as well. Merely expressing the condition informally in an exception message does not make these things possible.

PRINCIPLE: THROW SPECIFIC EXCEPTIONS—NOT GENERIC ONES.

For example, suppose that a persistence layer defines a base exception type called "PersistenceException." Suppose also that the following three failure cases have been identified, all of which need to be trapped by the persistence layer: (1) timeout, (2) database error, and (3) invalid input data. Rather than throwing PersistenceException, each time, it would be better to subclass PersistenceException as shown in Figure 18.3. This allows the caller to detect the different conditions that occur within the callee and enables the client to respond differently for each condition. Notice that all the types are derived from a checked exception type so that the caller is required to handle each case.

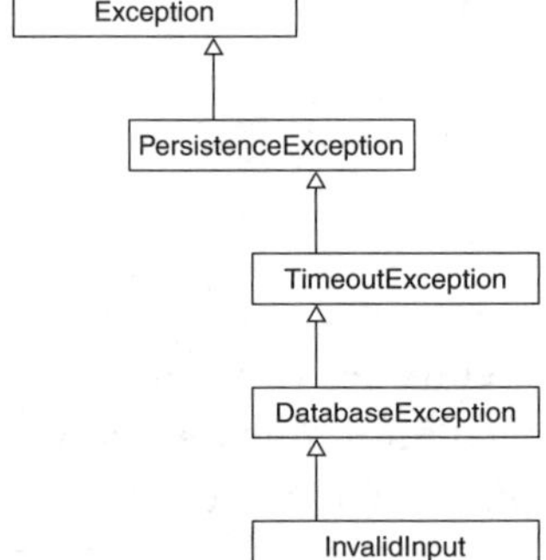

Figure 18.3 Define a concrete exception for each error condition.

Regardless of the actual exception types that a method throws, the method signature should not declare generic exception types in the "throws" or "raises" clause. Instead, declare only specific exceptions (to the extent possible). This is important for interfaces as well, such as remote interfaces, EJB interfaces, Web services (WSDL) definitions, and so on. Generic exception signatures defeat the advantage of having checked exceptions because the programmer is not required to write a handler for each condition—only for the generic condition. Having specific exceptions somewhat locks an interface into a particular implementation, but it allows error conditions to be much more transparent.

18.2.2 Where to Catch and Log

Prevent logging clutter. Do not catch and log exceptions at every level in the software. Instead, catch and log exceptions (any Throwable) only at the "outermost" call point of each tier, or at points at which exceptions are actually handled, although the ability to handle an exception often means that logging is not necessary. This is illustrated in Figure 18.4. Do not log an exception merely when the exception is wrapped with another exception and propagated. Most layers of an application should propagate or wrap exceptions, but not log them redundantly.

PRINCIPLE: *LOG ONLY AT PREDETERMINED LAYER INTERFACES.*

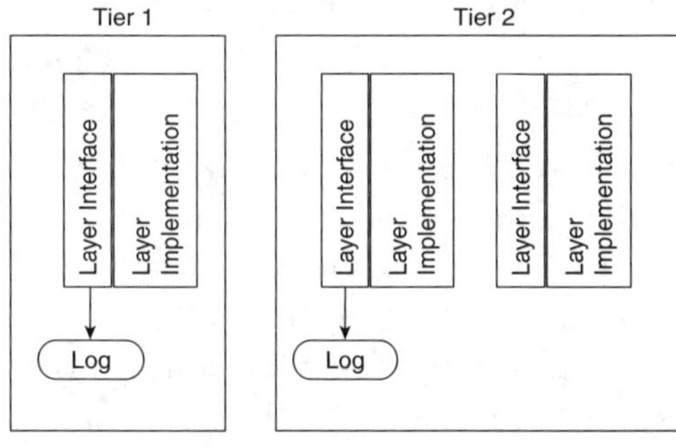

Figure 18.4 Log only at predetermined layer interfaces.

Logging that provides diagnostic (non-exception) information for debugging purposes can be placed anywhere, subject to security considerations. Diagnostic informational logging is not in response to an error but rather provides useful information in case an error occurs later. Such "debug level" logging can be left in the code because it will actually be written to the log by the logger only if the logger is set to be in debug mode. However, in doing so, *the assumption is that debug level logging will never be enabled in a production environment.* If that is possible, then debug-level logging should be written only to a secure logging service according to the logging and exception reporting principles outlined earlier. See, for example, "Filter Sensitive Data from Exceptions" in Section 7.15.2. Consider also the possibility that an intruder might be able to force the system into a debug mode. Thus, do not ever leave in production code statements that write debug information to standard output or to the client.

If debug-level logging might be enabled in production, the debug-level log messages should only be written to a secure log.

Each thread of an application should catch and log exceptions at the outermost layer of the application or application platform, to provide an "exception firewall." *An exception should never be allowed to "crash" a thread.* Application platforms often provide automatic handling of uncaught exceptions, and this is often sufficient. In some platforms, the programmer can define a general-purpose outermost layer by defining a "onException()" method that handled uncaught exceptions.[3] When you write your own handler for uncaught exceptions, pay careful attention to what actions should be taken to restore the application and its resources to a stable and useful state; for example, resources or objects that remain "broken" as a result of the exception should be removed and possibly replaced.

For an EJB, the outermost level of the EJB tier would be the methods declared in the EJB remote interfaces that are provided to clients. Log any checked exception thrown by each remote method that is declared in these interfaces. If the EJB server does not provide a native logging service, provide your own by wrapping the logic of each method in a try block and logging any RuntimeException, Error, or checked exception that is thrown by each method and then re-throwing it. (Do not catch Throwable, because that will cause the explicitly checked exceptions to be hidden.)

For a GUI, the action handlers should perform all their logic inside an error handling block (i.e., in Java, use a try block) and catch and log any kinds of exceptions that could occur that are not explicitly declared; for example, Java RuntimeException and Error. GUI action handlers should also log any checked exception that they catch.

3 For example, BEA WebLogic allows a programmer to define a context_onException() method for catching all unhandled exceptions in a Web service method.

In a multi-threaded application, any operation that blocks should be performed inside an error handling block, either immediately within the method or in an outer method that catches and handles any exception that is thrown as a result of interruption, to ensure that if the operation is interrupted by another thread that any required cleanup will be performed. Refer to Section 12.2.4, "Thread Interruption."

18.2.3 Iteration Failures

The "endless loop" problem has been encountered by every programmer, and the solution in business application settings is usually to review the loop design, correct it as required, and test it sufficiently until the loop performs correctly. Unfortunately, this approach might be insufficient. For example, if a loop's condition depends on external values, or if the logic is complex.

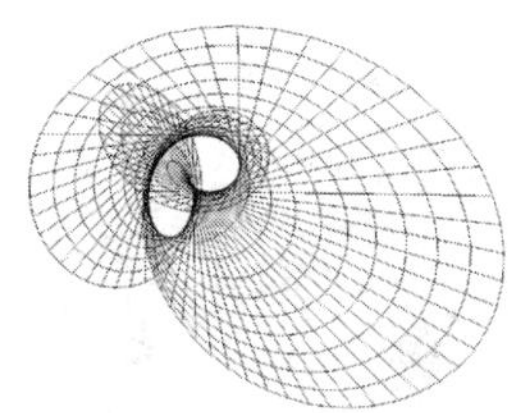

Used with permission Paul Bourke, Astrophysics and Supercomputing Swinburne University of Technology Victoria 3122, Australia

Any kind of iterative action within a program is a potential point at which the program thread might potentially "hang." If the thread implements a resource call, its caller is likely coded to anticipate a possible failure to return within a reasonable amount of time.♦ If the thread is a main thread or is not normally expected to block, there is not likely to be a timer watching its action, so it could hang indefinitely. In this case, there are two approaches: (1) demonstrate the correctness of the design, either through analysis or empirically (i.e., through very thorough testing), or (2) protect the thread from potential failure of the iteration by providing a timer.

♦ See the principle "Employ a Timer to Abort Any Resource Call That Could Potentially 'Hang'" in Section 13.11.1, "Resource That Do Not Reliably Timeout."

In a high-assurance application, it is good practice to have a timer monitor the action of each thread that is not automatically monitored by the runtime infrastructure to ensure that if a thread hangs, the situation is detected and brought to the attention of an operator and provide the operator with the power to terminate the hung thread without terminating the application—if that is possible or appropriate. For example, if a particular application server request thread is hung, the operator should be notified and be able to terminate that request thread, allowing the application server to dispose of the thread and its resources and allocate a new one.

A more serious situation is when a critically important thread hangs. Thus, all critical threads that include iteration or access to resources or asynchronous entities, or that have any potential for hanging due to a programming error, should include a timer and an error handler that is designed to provide for some form of satisfactory recovery if the thread does in fact hang.

PRINCIPLE: TIME CRITICAL THREAD ACTIONS.

PRINCIPLE ILLUSTRATION: THREAD STATUS MONITORING

This example illustrates the use of a timer to time a critical operation that might hang. The operation is not necessarily a resource call: It might be the invocation of a complex algorithm that iterates.

Context: A thread must execute a section of code that might potentially hang.

Forces: The algorithm or operation performed by the code in question is complex or for some reason cannot be shown to be failsafe against hanging. The thread that invokes the algorithm or operation is a critically important thread that cannot be allowed to hang.

Solution Illustration: Consider the following code example (exception handling is omitted for simplicity).

```
// Instantiate completion handler.
completionHandler = new Observer() {
  public void notifyObservers() {
    ...the signaling action to perform when thread completes
    // Nothing: because the client thread is waiting on this
    // thread's destruction.
  }
};

// Instantiate timed object.
thread = new InterruptibleThread(completionHandler) {
  public void run() {
    ...the action to be timed.
  }
}

// Start timed object.
thread.start();

// Wait for timed object to complete.
thread.join(timeout);

// Assume that join timed out.
thread.abort();

// Get completion status.
status = thread.getCompletionStatus();
// One of { completed, failed, interrupted }
```

This example uses the "Interruptible Thread" pattern discussed in Section 12.2.4. In that pattern, there is a "Work" process. That process is implemented in the code above by the "run()" method. The StatusListener is implemented by the "notifyObservers()" method. In this case, the status listener does nothing, because the thread.join(<timeout>) operation serves the same purpose and wakes up the main thread when the interruptible thread has terminated.

The join(timeout) method acts as the timer for the interruptible thread. When the join returns, the interruptible thread has either completed or the join has timed out. In order to handle the second case, the interruptible thread is aborted. This will have no ill effect if the thread has already terminated.

Note that the "Timer Thread" pattern (Section 12.2.5, "Designing a Thread Timeout Mechanism") need not be used for the timer: a simple thread join suffices. This is because the main thread is in effect the timer and does not need to be interruptible.

18.2.4 Robust Error Handling

It is ironic but potentially tragic if an error handler fails. Error handlers must be designed more carefully than normal program logic because they must assume that something is wrong, often without knowing precisely what. Error handlers, therefore, should avoid making resource calls where possible, except for highly monitored and robust resources such as a reliable logging system. If resource access is necessary within an error handler—or any potentially unsafe operation, for that matter—that code should be written to trap any errors that might occur.

It is possible that an error handler might experience some of the same kinds of errors that the application code itself handles, and it is also possible that an error handler might experience additional kinds of errors.

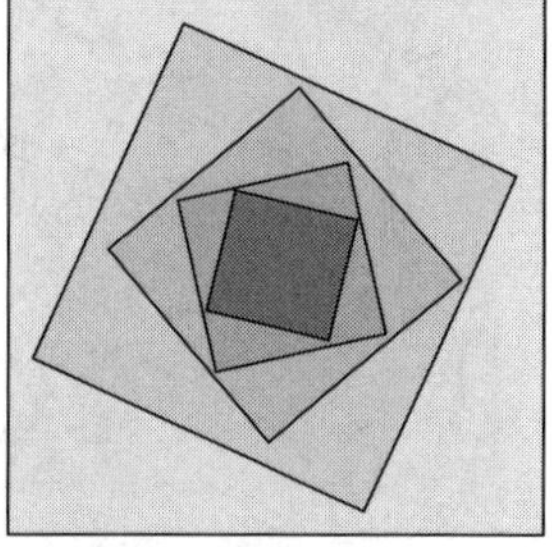

Figure 18.5
Error handlers may need to be nested.

It is necessary is to ensure that the purpose of an error handler is fulfilled: that it reports back the nature of the original error and sufficient contextual information to enable the application operator to ascertain the true source of the problem. Thus, in designing the code for an error handler, lean toward simplicity and avoid making resource calls or accessing any variables that might be invalid. The inputs to any routine should always be validated,◆ so the code of an error handler should avoid referencing any variables that have not been validated. If you must perform a potentially unsafe operation inside

◆ See the principle "Safely Validate All Inputs to Each Method" in Section 11.3, "Component Roles and Contracts."

an error handler, provide an additional (nested) error handler for those calls. In Java terms, this means nesting another try block inside of the try block.

PRINCIPLE: ERROR HANDLERS SHOULD THEMSELVES COMPLETELY TRAP ALL ERRORS THAT MIGHT PREVENT THEM FROM PROPAGATING CONTEXTUAL INFORMATION.

PRINCIPLE ILLUSTRATION: NESTED ERROR HANDLING

This example illustrates the use of nested error handling. In this example, a Java try block contains a set of JDBC (SQL) operations. These operations can throw SQLException. If such an exception is thrown, the transaction is rolled back. However, the rollback might fail, due to a system error. In that case, the caller might need to know that the transaction failed but was not rolled back. This would be especially important if the data modified by the transaction is critical data and the user needs to know immediately if there might be inconsistency.

```
try {
    Connection conn = ...
    conn.setAutoCommit(false);
    Statement stmt = conn.createStatement();
    stmt.execute(sql);
    ...
    conn.commit();
}
catch (SQLException ex) {
    try {
            conn.rollback();
    }
    catch (SQLException ex2) {
            // Caller may need to know that rollback failed.
            throw new CannotRollack(ex2);
    }
}
finally {
    try {
            conn.close();
    }
    catch (SQLException ex) {
            Log.write(ex);
    }
}
```

Note also that the finally block contains a nested try block. This is because an error could occur when closing the connection. However, because at that point the transaction would have been committed or rolled back, the user does not necessarily need to know and so the exception is not propagated. Instead, it is logged: The logging system might alert the operator or support personnel if this kind of error is considered to be severe.

18.2.5 Providing Context

Error messages that appear in a log and that have no context are not very useful. Contextual information, such as who the user was and what they were doing when the error occurred, is invaluable for diagnosing what went wrong. It is, therefore, important to consider ways in which context can be provided when logging errors.

Uncorrelated information is like shredded information.

In a multi-tier application, some aspects of the context can be lost (either purposefully or not) when a request passes from one tier to another. For example, if a Web application that is servicing a user request calls an application server method, the application server method does not know what the user was doing to cause the method call. Yet, that kind of information is valuable when diagnosing problems, and it would be useful if the application server log entries could be correlated with the Web application log entries. This is not always straightforward because these are multi-threaded applications that are servicing multiple user requests simultaneously.

A solution to this dilemma is to design a context mechanism that makes it possible to log what each tier (including the client) was doing when a server-side error occurs. For example, if a Web application creates a unique ID for each request that it services and passes that ID whenever it calls the application server, any application server log entries can include the ID. That enables Web application log entries to be matched up with back end application server log entries.

PRINCIPLE: PROVIDE CONTEXT TO CORRELATE USER ACTIONS WITH SERVER ACTIONS.

A more general solution than passing along a simple request ID is to pass a lightweight context object with every request. Some of the important kinds of contextual information that can be added to such a context object include the client identity, a unique request ID, a session or task ID representing the client's session or overall processing task, a process ID representing the client's process (if there is more than one client process; for example, if the client is a clustered Web application), and various aspects of server context including a unique transaction ID. That is the purpose of the pattern that follows.

DESIGN PATTERN: APPLICATION-BASED PROPAGATION OF CLIENT CONTEXT

Context

A request involves the collaboration of multiple context domains.

Problem

There is no existing provision to propagate context from one context domain to the next, or the context that is propagated is inadequate.

Forces

The benefits of being able to correlate events logged from one context domain with events logged by another context domain.

Solution

This pattern illustrates the passing of client context to a server process to enable the server process to correlate failure events with client events and processing tasks when log entries are written.

In Figure 18.6, a client process makes a request to a server application. The client passes along with the request a context object that contains attributes that uniquely identify the client's user ID, the ID of the client's task (assuming that the client's application supports multiple tasks), a unique ID for the request, and the ID of the client application's process on the client platform. This information should be sufficient to uniquely identify the request. Note that the "task" attribute might not be necessary in all circumstances. Its purpose is to identify a set of client-side activities that are related and that issue one or more requests to a server in order to accomplish a task. For example, a task might be a particular loan application, for a loan approval client application. Any client events that are logged should include the context.

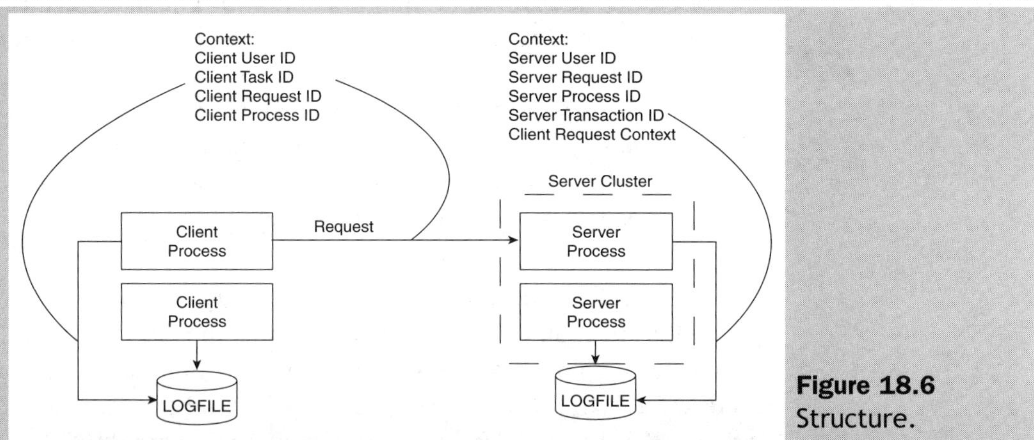

Figure 18.6
Structure.

When the client request arrives at the server, the client request's context is parsed and appended to the context of the server thread that handles the request. Any server events that are logged should include appended client context. This enables incident responders to correlate entries in the client log with entries in the server log.

By way of illustration, the following code shows Java classes that could be defined to represent the client request context and the server-side context. Notice that the server-side context includes all of the information that is in the client request context. Note also that the server has its own values for attributes such as user identity, request ID, and so on, so the client context values need to be unambiguously separated from these.

```
public interface ClientRequestContext
{
   public int getUserId();
   public int getRequestId();
   public int getTaskId();
   public int getProcessId();
}
   public interface ServerContext extends Context
{
   public int getUserId(); // server user identity
   public int getRequestId(); // server request ID
   public int getProcessId(); // server process ID
   public int getTxnId();

   public ClientRequestContext getClientRequestContext();
}
```

In a real application, many server-side context attributes would be available through platform-specific APIs, so it might be unnecessary to store them in application-defined variables. For example, the user ID associated with the server connection is usually available, as is the process ID of the server process.

Consequences

A means must be found to propagate the application-defined context, either as a call argument or through an extension of the call mechanism. (A means of propagation is discussed in the next pattern.)

A side benefit of embedding a context mechanism such as this within a multi-tier application is that it makes it possible to correlate server actions with user actions in real time, thereby enabling the reporting of the status of user requests and tasks. For example, the server would be able to generate a heartbeat message indicating which client tasks are being serviced and what the progress is on each client task.

It was explained earlier in this book (see Section 7.17, "Scope, Session, and Context") that context can be propagated explicitly or implicitly. Implicit context has the benefit that it simplifies the application's API. Most application platforms provide several kinds of context, associated with different context scopes. For example, the Java VM maintains several kinds of implicit context. These include the thread context and the process context. The thread context includes the call stack, the code source (where the executing code came from), and the user's security context. These types of context are automatically propagated along any Java method call and are available to any part of a Java program at any time, via API calls—the programmer does not have to make provisions to pass these aspects of the context.

Most platforms also allow an application to extend the context that is automatically propagated. For example, the POSIX pthread API defines methods for setting and getting "thread local" storage, as does the Java Thread API. Design patterns also exist [for example, 7] for adding thread-specific storage to platforms that do not provide it, as long as it is possible to obtain a unique thread identifier. The following design pattern illustrates how the thread context can be extended in Java in order to create an implicitly propagated context.

DESIGN PATTERN ILLUSTRATION: IMPLICIT CONTEXT AND EXPLICIT CONTEXT

The Java example shown here illustrates (1) the explicit passing of a context object and (2) the use of a context extension mechanism to associate the context with the current thread and thereby cause it to be automatically (implicitly) propagated through all subsequent method calls within the runtime.

Usage Context: When implicit context is desired that goes beyond what is automatically provided by the native runtime context.

Forces: Multi-tier applications often require context to be propagated explicitly, if it is to be propagated at all. Explicitly passing context via arguments from one call to the next is cumbersome, and changes affect many method interfaces. An implicit mechanism circumvents the inconvenience of explicitly passing context as an argument.

In this example, a "ThreadLocal" reference variable is defined within a context class. A Java ThreadLocal reference variable has the property that its value is unique for each thread. Thus, when the reference variable is set, it is set only for the thread that sets it; another thread can also set it, and the value will be different for that thread. This provides a thread-specific context mechanism. In the example, the ThreadLocal reference variable is set at the entry to a server method, causing the context to be propagated along all calls made by the server method. The same method removes the context before it returns.

```
public class ContextImpl implements Context
{
    private static ThreadLocal threadLocal;

    public static void set(Context ctx) throws InvalidContext
     { validate(ctx); threadLocal.set(ctx); }

    public static ContextImpl get() { return threadLocal.get(); }

    public String getUserId()...
    public int getRequestId()...
    public int getTaskId()...
    public int getProcessId()...

    public static final void validate(Context ctx) throws InvalidContext ...
}

public class SomeTierFacade
{
    public void doSomething(Context context, InputMap map, ...)
    throws InvalidContext
    {
        ContextImpl.set(context); // throws InvalidContext

        try
        {
            ...
        }
        finally
        {
```

```
            ContextImpl.set(null);
        }
    }

    protected void validate(Context context) throws InvalidContext ...
}
```

In this code snippet, the method "doSomething()" is part of the exposed interface of a tier, represented by "SomeTierFacade." A client invoking this method must pass a Context object. The doSomething() method first adds this context to the context maintained by a ThreadLocal, by calling ContextImpl.set(Context). This latter method validates the context argument, to make sure that it is valid and is of an implementation type that is allowed.

The main body of doSomething(Context) is performed inside a try block. Any calls made by the code from within this block will carry the context that was set at the beginning of the method. Retrieving the context merely requires a call to ContextImpl.get().

The finally clause of the try block unsets the context that is maintained by the thread local. This ensures that the context does not remain as an artifact of the thread when the doSomething(Context) method returns.

If a call must pass out of the runtime environment and into another, such as when a client calls a remote server, a runtime-provided extension mechanism will not propagate the context out of the runtime, so you must make provisions to propagate your context using the remote protocol. For example, the CORBA IIOP (used by Java EJBs) incorporates an extensible context mechanism, and this mechanism is used by EJBs to add things such as security context and transaction context. Web services APIs also provide for embedding context within requests.

If a suitable context propagation mechanism is not available, the only recourse is to pass context explicitly, via call arguments. These arguments must be added to every method along the call chain.

One consideration when defining an explicit context to propagate is that you must retain awareness of how the context attributes are set, since the context mechanism is highly sensitive code.♦ In contrast, when implicit context is used, it is set via some form of login or authentication mechanism, and it is propagated by infrastructure, so its trustworthiness has presumably already been considered—although perhaps this is a big presumption.

♦ See the principle "Identify and Assess All Context Bindings" in Section 7.17.1, "Identifying Decision Context."

18.2.6 Providing Sufficient Information

The layering principles discussed earlier in this book urge that if an exception is propagated to a higher layer, that it be translated into (i.e., replaced by) an exception type that is appropriate for that layer. For example, if a persistence layer's implementation receives an IO exception from a resource, it should translate that into a more meaningful exception such as "DatabaseConnectionLost" or "FileNotFound" before propagating the exception to a higher layer, such as a transaction facade layer.♦

♦ See the principle "Objects Returned to Higher Layers..." in Section 7.19.1.

However, in replacing the original exception, it is important to retain its information. The easiest way to do this may be to link the old exception to the new one. Java allows this in a simple manner. Most programmers have experienced frustrating internal errors in third-party software components—errors that merely said "Internal error" without indicating the module or the exact condition, which would have enabled the programmer to at least consider possible workarounds. Thus, the stack trace is important. Merely catching all errors may prevent the program from crashing in unexpected ways, but it does not necessarily make the software more user-friendly, as illustrated in Figure 18.7. Diagnostic information must be allowed to propagate.

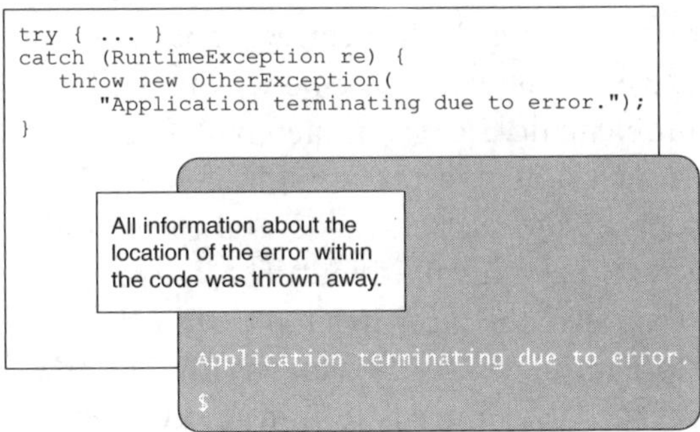

Figure 18.7
Errors are caught, but information about the source is carelessly discarded.

PRINCIPLE: NEVER DISCARD EXCEPTION INFORMATION.

The only situation in which care must be taken is if the low-level exception information reveals too much, from a security perspective. In general, client layers should not be exposed to the internal details of lower layers. See the principles "Do Not Expose Internal Objects or Attributes" in Section 7.13, "Resource Interface Design;" "Filter Sensitive Data from Exceptions" in Section 7.15.2, "Propagation of Unauthorized Information;" and "Securely Log Sensitive Data Rather Than Discard It" in Section 7.15.2.

Besides end users, application support personnel are in the position of having to diagnose and resolve problems that users are having—often in a crisis mode and under great pressure. They therefore appreciate diagnostic information that is informative. The problems that they deal with generally have to do with user errors, program bugs, resource failures, subtle configuration errors, and corrupt data. They need exceptions to specify as much application-related information as is relevant to what the application was doing when the exception occurs. For example, if a particular online order was being processed, the exception should indicate *which* order—down to the database row, and so on. That kind of specific information allows them to narrow the problem quickly. This amounts to making the problem situation as *transparent* as possible so that the cause can be determined with minimal examination.

PRINCIPLE: PROVIDE PROBLEM TRANSPARENCY.

If an error happens that is the result of incorrect input data or corrupt database or file data, the user or responder needs to know *which* data is problematic. However, merely delivering this data back to the user via an exception might be insufficient. For example, suppose the user enters several rows of data on a screen, and two rows have invalid input that is not detectable by the GUI because the error has to do with the relationship of this data to data that is in the database. When the user submits the input, the system needs to inform the user which rows (and perhaps which columns) are invalid. If some of the data is the same from one row to the next, providing the user with the invalid data will not enable them to identify which rows have a problem. Thus, we need a way to identify the actual input elements (for example, rows), but in such a way that the server does not have to know the structure of the input screen.

This leads to the need for a generic mechanism for mapping input elements to elements of a transaction input. If the client passes this mapping along with the transaction and the transaction needs to throw an error, it can use the mapping to pass back to the client a list of the input elements that had a problem. For example, if the client calls the transaction and passes a map of row numbers to transaction input elements, the transaction can return a list of problematic rows—without even knowing that they are rows.

PRINCIPLE: MAP ERRORS TO PROBLEMATIC INPUT.

The problem of mapping client input elements to transaction input elements is a general one and deserves a general solution. The following "Input Map" and "Data Identification" patterns provide an approach to this. The Input Map pattern addressed the client-to-server invocation pathway, whereas the Data Identification pattern addresses the return pathway, which is often simpler in its requirements.

DESIGN PATTERN: INPUT MAP

Context

A client makes requests to a server, providing a large amount of complex data; for example, a collection of some kind.

Problem

If the server returns an error response, it needs to identify which portions of the data are involved in the error; for example, specific elements of a collection. Referring to collection element numbers might be insufficient, for example, if there are multiple collections in the input or if the client-side ordering of the elements might change during the request. In order to compose a response, the server therefore needs a mapping between the client's view and the server's view of the data.

Note: The form of the actual response is addressed in another pattern, "Data Identification," which follows this one.

Solution

This pattern serves to enable a client to logically tag portions of data that the client inputs to a server. Its purpose is to enable the server's response to refer unambiguously to particular elements of the input data, but without requiring the server to understand the client-side meaning of those elements. This is especially useful in a response that must identify which portions of the input are invalid.

This pattern defines a concrete type, InputMap. The InputMap consists of a hashmap of client data keys (tags values), keyed on server data keys. The client key value should uniquely identify an element to the client. For a GUI client, this might be a GUI table row ID or combination or row ID and column ID. The server keys must be unique within the server domain. There can be a many-to-many relationship between client keys and server keys, but there cannot be ambiguity with regard to which client keys correspond to a given server key.

Figure 18.8 depicts an InputMap that might be passed to a server when a server call is made, and Figure 18.9 illustrates the correspondence between the client keys and server keys of the input map.

InputMap

public void putInputElement(<ClientKey>, <ServerKey>);
public Set<ClientKey> getInputElements(<ServerKey>);
public Set<ServerKey> getInputKeys();
public void deleteInputElements(<ClientKey>);

Figure 18.8
An Input map.

A typical use of an input map is as follows:

1. The client (for example, a GUI) invokes a server method and passes an InputMap as an argument.
2. If there is an error, the server throws an exception that contains a list of the client keys (for example, row numbers) that caused the problem. The server does not have to know what the client keys mean, so it is not exposed to the client data model.

GUI Row ID (client key)	Account No. (server key)
4	77442
5	01102
6	80021

Figure 18.9
Illustration of correspondence between client and server keys.

Client data keys should be unique during a client session, so care must be taken that they are not changed; for example, if GUI rows are reordered, added, or deleted. This is especially important if a client is reentrant—for example, if a slow double click might be translated into two clicks.

Client items that do not have a natural unique key (for example, a row number) should be assigned a hidden key that the user does not see.

Avoid using keys whose value might change. For example, a GUI row number might not be stable over time, particularly if rows can be re-ordered, inserted, or deleted. Instead of using a row number to identify a row, assign a row a unique key value that it has for the lifetime of the GUI, or at least for the lifetime of the session with the server.

It might also be that a client key is deleted during the time in which a server request is being processed. This is possible, for example, if the GUI uses an MVC pattern and synchronously displays updates made to a shared model, for example, a database that is accessed by other users. The user's transaction might even have the effect of deleting the key; for example, a row of server data displayed in the GUI. Therefore, it is good practice to always consider the possibility that the information in a client key—or a server key as well—is no longer valid when received. Your code should be resilient to this situation by anticipating it and handling it. The client-side code in the design pattern illustration "Use of Input Map and Data Identification" that follows handles this by checking whether the row still exists before attempting to highlight it. Of course, this check could also be incorporated into the highlightRow() method.

Consequences

The server is decoupled from the client, yet the server is able to reference data elements in the client's model by using the indirection provided by the input map. This makes it possible to return exceptions (or other kinds of return object) that make indirect reference to client-side elements. This simplifies error handling on the client and enables the server to provide very specific feedback to the client about the source of an error.

DESIGN PATTERN: DATA IDENTIFICATION

Related Patterns

Uses "Input Map."

Context

A client has invoked a server method and passes an input map as an argument. The server has a need to identify portions of the client's input.

Problem

If a server-side error occurs, the client will want to know which portions of the input arguments have caused the problem. Referring to the input by value is insufficient because multiple input elements might have the same value. Thus, the server needs a client-independent container for referencing client-side data elements.

Solution

This pattern defines a generic type, DataIdentification, which can be used to return a list of client keys to a client after the client has invoked a server method. A DataIdentification is merely a container for a set of client keys. An example of a DataIdentification is shown in Figure 18.10.

The meaning of the set of keys is defined by the exception that contains it. For example, some exceptions might return a set of keys that represent invalid data inputs, whereas other exceptions might return a set of keys that represent data that was not saved to a database when a transaction failed. The exception definition should document the meaning of a DataIdentification when it is used.

DataIdentification

public void addClientKey(<ClientKey>;
public void addClientKeys(Set<ClientKey>);
public void removeClientKey(<ClientKey>);
public void removeAllClientKeys();
public Set<ClientKey> getClientKeys();

Figure 18.10
A DataIdentification class.

◆ See the principle "Provide Management 'Aspects' to Exceptions" discussed in Section 18.2.6, "Providing Sufficient Information," and exemplified by the design pattern illustration later in this chapter, "Adding Manageability Aspects to the Exception Base Class."

Exceptions that need to identify particular portions of the input should be defined to contain a DataIdentification object. Because this is a global exception handling "aspect" (for example, pertaining to all UserActionable exceptions), a non-aspect-oriented implementation should define it in the exception base class.◆

Figure 18.11 depicts an example of the normal scenario, in which a client makes a server request and passes an input map as part of the request. If an exception is thrown by the server, the server inserts in the exception a DataIdentification that identifies the client elements that are problematic.

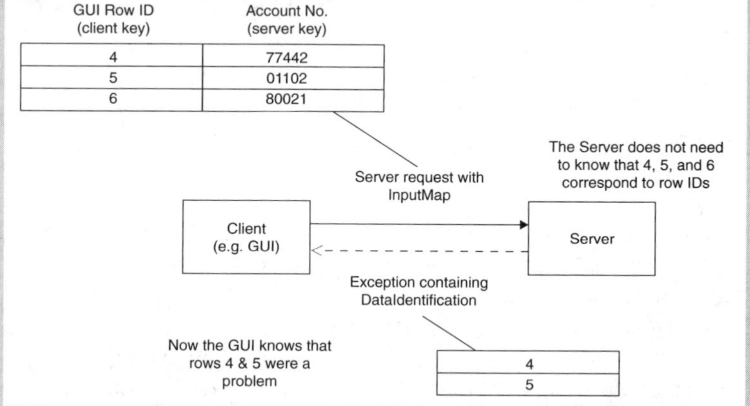

Figure 18.11 Returning an exception containing a DataIdentification.

Consequences

The server is decoupled from the client, yet the server is able to return exceptions (or other kinds of return object) that make indirect reference to client-side elements. This simplifies error handling on the client and enables the server to provide very specific feedback to the client about the source of an error.

DESIGN PATTERN ILLUSTRATION: USE OF INPUT MAP AND DATA IDENTIFICATION

This example illustrates the use of the Input Map and Data Identification patterns. The example consists of a panel in a client GUI application and a remote server application. The client accesses a method doSomething(...) on the server. The doSomething(...) method requires an InputMap as its first argument. The method operates on customer accounts that are stored on the server and displayed in the GUI.

To prepare the input map, the client establishes a unique ID for each account row in the GUI. It then creates an InputMap that maps each account of interest to the corresponding row in the GUI. This map is then passed as an argument, along with the other arguments of the doSomething(...) method.

In this example, the server is an EJB Session Bean, and the method doSomething(...) returns a set of client keys. The example takes advantage of generics to streamline the insulation of the server code from the client code by defining the EJB first as a template and then extending that to create a client-specific EJB.

Client Tier Code

```
public class SomeClientPanel extends SomeGUIBasePanel implementsActionHandler
{
    /**
     * Handle mouse click on the 'Do Something' button.
     */
    public void actionPerformed(ActionEvent event)
    {
        InputMap map = new InputMap() {{
            // Map server keys to row Ids.
            Collection<Row> rows = getRows();
            for (Row row : rows) {
                super.putInputElement(row.getRowID(),
                    new AccountID(row.getAccountNo()));
            }
        }};

        try {
            Set<ClientKey> cks = guiEJB.doSomething(map, ...);

            for ClientKey ck : cks
            {
                    RowID rowId=(RowID)ck;
                    if (! rowExists(rowId)){}...display message
                    else highlightRow(getRow(rowId));
                            // indicates where the user should look.
            }
        }
        catch (InvalidDataException ide) {

        }
    }

    protected boolean rowExists(RowID r) { ... }
    protected void highlightRow(Row r) { ... }
    protected Row getRow(RowID r) { ... }
    protected Collection<Row> getRows() { ... }
}

class RowID implements ClientKey
{
    public RowID() { ...
    public boolean equals(...
}
```

Server Tier Code

```
GUISessionBean extends SomeSessionBean
{
}

public interface ClientKey {}

public class AccountID
{
    public AccountID(int acctNo) {...}
    private int accountNo;
    public int getAccountNo() { return accountNo; }
    public void setAccountNo(int a) { this.accountNo = a; }
}

public abstract class InputMap extends HashMap<AccountID, ClientKey>
{
    public void putInputElement(ClientKey clientKey, AccountID accountID)
    {
        put(accountID, clientKey); }
    public Set<ClientKey> getInputElements(AccountID aid) {...}
    public Set<AccountID> getInputKeys() { return keySet(); }
    public void deleteInputElement(ClientKey ck) { remove(ck); }
}

public class SomeSessionBean
{
    public Set<ClientKey> doSomething(InputMap map, ...)
    throws InvalidDataException
    {
        ...
        try
        {
            return map.getInputElements(skey);
              Note that the server does not have to know that
               the ClientKey is a GUI tab.
        }
        catch (SomeException e)
        {
            ...
            DataIdentification di = new DataIdentification(){...};
            Set<ClientKey> cks = map.getInputElements(sk);
            for (ClientKey ck : cks) {
                di.addClientKey(...identify the problematic data);
            }

            throw
               (new InvalidDataException(msg,e)).setDataIdentification (di);
        }
    }
}
```

> Note in the last line that this implementation utilizes a design for "InvalidDataException" that provides a setter method for setting a DataIdentification object as an attribute. This helps to make the code more compact by allowing the DataIdentification attribute to be set in the same statement that creates the exception.
>
> Notice also that the original exception is not discarded, but is supplied as the "cause" argument to InvalidDataException.
>
> The advantages of this design are:
>
> 1. The bulk of the server code is independent of the client's design (i.e., it does not need to know about client row IDs).
> 2. The server is able to "speak the client's language" when communicating back to it. For example, it can return a set of Row Ids as a result, or return a set of Row Ids within an exception. This allows the client to immediately identify problem data.

INFORMATION NEEDS OF OTHER STAKEHOLDERS

When programmers design exception handling routines, it is often the case that they are primarily considering the functional needs of the end user. However, in a high-availability system, other users and processes have an interest in exception information. Such other users include system operators, application support staff, and so on. These users have different information needs with regard to exceptions, and it is important for the programmer to consider them when designing exceptions and exception handlers.

With regard to the exceptions themselves, the information needs of these other classes of users should be considered. For example, operators will want to know if an exception indicates a resource failure of some kind. The best place to make that determination is often at the point at which the original exception occurs because it is closest to the point of failure and is operating in the same context as the failure. An exception handler is therefore in a position to provide very high quality information to a system operator about *which* resource has failed and exactly *in what manner.*

Unfortunately, it is difficult for a programmer to consider the needs of all of these different actors when designing an exception hierarchy. The programmer is forced to consider ahead of time the collection of user requirements, manageability requirements, and application support requirements. Further, a hierarchical exception model breaks down, because the needs of each of these groups of users produce their own hierarchy to cover the different overlapping error conditions and their information needs. For example, manageability requirements might indicate the need for a manageability base class and several subclasses derived from that to differentiate file system failures, network resource failures, and so on. Yet on top of this, the user requirements might indicate a need to represent a hierarchy of exceptions broken down into categories pertaining to different parts of the application. These two (or more) overlapping hierarchies cannot be accommodated by a single exception hierarchy.

In effect, the needs of users, operators, and application support personnel represent different *aspects* of the overall application requirements. An aspect-oriented programming language can therefore address this situation nicely because it allows the programmer to layer different aspects of functionality into a program without having to consider all those aspects at the same time.

PRINCIPLE: PROVIDE MANAGEMENT "ASPECTS" TO EXCEPTIONS.

If the language is not aspect-oriented, it may be best to create a single exception hierarchy based on the user's needs and then layer requirements for manageability on top of this. The simplest way to do this is to lump all manageability requirements together, put them in a "manageability" exception base class, and then derive all application exceptions from that. This leads to a base class that has attributes that are often unused, but it is often the best compromise solution to ensure that all the required attributes are always available if an exception needs to return information that is important for operators or application support staff in addition to the user. See the following design pattern, "Adding Manageability Aspects to the Exception Base Class."

When designing a manageability base class, consider what error conditions are of primary interest to users, operators, and application support. For example, operators want to know primarily about resource failures or of the need to restart or recover the application according to a predefined procedure. It is, therefore, useful to have a flag in the exception to indicate if the error condition is of a kind that is probably of interest to operators, such as if a connection cannot be established or if a required environment property is not found.

DESIGN PATTERN ILLUSTRATION: ADDING MANAGEABILITY ASPECTS TO THE EXCEPTION BASE CLASS

This illustration, depicted in Figure 18.12, shows how information that is important for application monitoring and management can be added to an exception base class in a generic way. Application exceptions should extend the base class. Not all the attributes of the base class will be used by every exception instance; however, by defining these attributes in the base class, they are universally available for any exception condition. This relieves the programmer from having to consider manageability in the design of each and every exception class.

In situations in which the error results from bad input data, the DataIdentification attribute can be used to identify what portion of the input was problematic. Otherwise, this attribute can be used to identify portions of input data that, for example, were completely processed. The meaning of the attribute depends on the exception subclass.

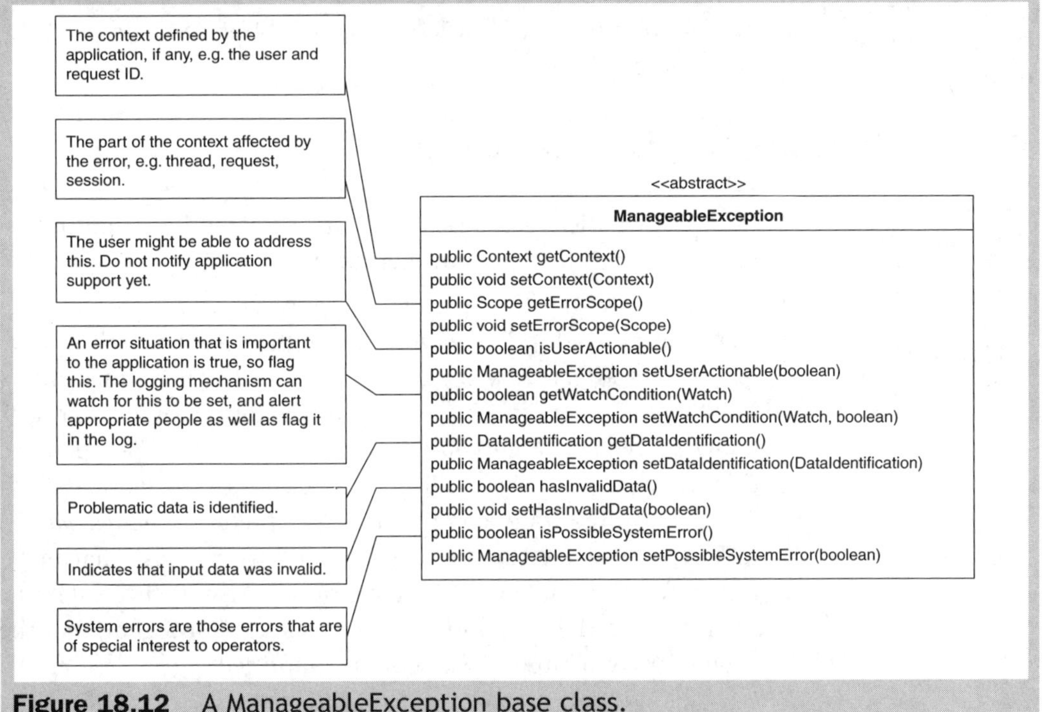

Figure 18.12 A ManageableException base class.

Application support will want to know if the application is behaving correctly, but they will not want to know about user errors that users can correct themselves. However, they might want to know if a data source is corrupt. The programmer is in the best position to encode these determinations in the error handler and set a flag on the exception that is logged indicating that application support might be interested.

Copying diverse groups on notification emails when there is a software problem creates a crisis-like environment.

It is also important to make an effort to prevent support staff from being notified if the error is something that the user can likely correct on their own. Again, the programmer is in the best position to encode such a determination and flag the exception such that the logging mechanism will know that support staff should not be contacted. There are also sometimes business requirements that management be alerted if a problem is not resolved quickly, or if a certain kind of problem arises. It is important to make sure that these groups are not alerted unnecessarily and to automate this determination the exception must clearly differentiate the different kinds of alertable conditions.

Principle: Alert Only Those Who Need to Know.

◆ See the discussion of the principle "Inform the User of Activity" in Section 10.6, "Usability."

If an error indicates a possible security-related intrusion, it is also important that the intruder not be alerted.◆

Simply telling the user the nature of an error is not sufficient. Users need to know what the status of their work is and how it was affected by the error. For example, if a transaction fails, the user needs to know if data was lost. They also need to know *what they should do next:* should they retry the operation—or would that jeopardize the integrity of the database? If an operation partially completed before the error, *which part?* Is the error so severe that the user should stop the task that they are performing, or should they continue? Also, if the system has internally notified support, the users should know that, and they should know if support has not been notified.

The argument is often made that users do not need to know the nature of a system failure because they will be calling support anyway. This is not true. When users do not know the nature of an error, they perceive the system as unreliable. Even if they need to call support to help them fix an error, users feel more confident if they know the *cause of the problem in terms that they can understand.* If users understand an error, there is also a higher chance that they can self-diagnose the problem; for example, if an error message informs them that a server is down, they might wait awhile to see if it comes back up, instead of immediately calling for help.

PRINCIPLE: PROVIDE USER STATUS AND ACTIONABILITY.

Earlier, we discussed why exceptions generated by a particular deployment tier should be handled by a single layer within that tier. However, program statements that log debugging information can appear anywhere that is useful within an application.

For an internal-use-only application, it is often necessary to deploy an application with debug information enabled for quite some time until kinks are worked out, because internal-use applications usually cannot afford the rigorous testing needed to bring the application up to the eventual desired reliability before deployment. However, be cognizant of the security risks in doing this, as discussed earlier (see Section 18.2.2, "Where to Catch and Log"). Debug statements are generally not subject to the same level of design scrutiny as the rest of a program, so it is possible that when debugging is enabled, inappropriate information may be revealed to the user, to operators, and written to the logs. If the user population at initial deployment is small and restricted, the risk in doing this might be acceptable. Debug should never be enabled for an operational system that maintains sensitive information and is used by a large and open user base.

To enable debugging information the runtime platform might have to be configured. For example, a Java virtual machine by default no longer produces line numbers when an exception occurs. This is because the standard configuration is to utilize a "JIT compiler" that strips such information from the runtime image. The JIT may therefore have to be disabled until the application is stable. Software may have to be compiled with debug information enabled as well. For example, when the popular Java build tool "ant" invokes the Java compiler it does not specify that full line number information be included in the generated code, but this can be changed by setting the appropriate switches.

It is important for both the development environment and all pre-production environments to enable full debugging support and for an internal use application, this is valuable for the production environment as well until the application becomes sufficiently reliable. For an externally facing application, the production environment should not have debugging enabled, however, because to do so introduces the possibility of exposing internal information that could compromise the security of the application.

A case can also be made that debug information should be removed from the production runtime image of an externally facing application to be sure that debug information cannot be accessed under any circumstance; however, such a policy requires that the application is sufficiently stable before it is deployed.

PRINCIPLE: BUILD WITH DEBUG INFORMATION, AND DEPLOY INITIALLY WITH DEBUG INFORMATION—SUBJECT TO SECURITY CONCERNS.

18.2.7 Logging and Notification Requirements

◆ See also Section 7.16, "Secure Logging."

Logging seems to be a boring aspect of software design to many and is treated as an afterthought. However, logging is critical for reliability, manageability, and security.◆

The point at which software logs an error or other condition is also identically the ideal point at which notification is often appropriate. For example, when an error occurs and is trapped by a handler and logged, at that point the error should be dispatched to whoever might be interested in that particular kind of error, such as system operators or application support. Therefore, it makes sense to unify the functions of logging and notification. Further, because status reporting is a special kind of notification (notification of "positive" events), it also makes sense to unify the logging and notification functions with status reporting.

There are a great many logging frameworks in use today. However, such frameworks typically provide only the building blocks of a logging and notification system and do not implement the full functionality that is needed. In defining the requirements for a logging and notification system, the following requirements should be considered.

CAPTURE ALL EXCEPTION INFORMATION

The logger interface should have methods that allow the application to directly pass exception objects. All nested or chained exceptions should be logged by the logger, including the stack trace of each nested exception.

The full context of the runtime thread should be captured so that it can be used to determine what the user or system was doing when the error occurred. This includes items such as user identity, transaction ID, or any context attributes that are associated with the thread that experienced the exception (which is presumably the same thread that is invoking the exception handler and, therefore, the logger).

AUTOMATIC LOG LEVEL ESCALATION

If an error is severe, the logging level should be escalated automatically. This should result in debug-level logging being enabled automatically and perhaps later disabled if the error condition goes away.

SATURATION-RESISTANT

An error condition that results in a flood of calls to the logger should not result in the logging mechanism being overwhelmed or in the loss of messages,[4] nor should it result in an endless series of pages, emails, or console alert messages. The logging mechanism must detect a logging flood and respond by progressively throttling the logging response.[5]

INTELLIGENT RESPONSE

Any exception that is not considered to be user-actionable should immediately result in a message (for example, page and email) to application support staff. An exception that is system-related should result in a message to system operators.

If the logging level is not reduced after a configurable period of time, a message (for example, page and email) should be sent to management.

---

4 For example, by the creation of a "runaway" error condition in order to disable the logging system and help to hide or lose messages indicating an intrusion.

5 Some centralized logging systems provide client-side buffering, in case the logging server goes down. However, it is best if the logs are retained persistently in that case.

Capture Status Information

The logging interface should include a logEntry(Context) method, which logs entry to the context that is provided, as well as the name of the method from which logEntry is called. The logging interface should also include a logExit(Context) method, which logs the exit from the context that is provided, as well as the name of the method from which logExit is called. This enables the capture of entry and exit to important application methods for the purpose of status reporting.

Provide Summary Analysis of Log Events

The logging system should provide reports of certain classes of errors, most especially any that are flagged as important "watch" criteria. For example, an application that watches for exceptions that will cause the user to have to stop all work should receive special attention and be flagged as such by the exception handler. These might need to be tabulated and analyzed later for assessing the affect of errors on workers.

Unalterable

It should not be possible for operational staff to delete logs "to make space" or for any normal reason. Logs should not be written over as a result of an application restart or server restart. Logs should be maintained long enough to be able to later analyze the historical causes and frequencies of errors—several months at a minimum.

Unbypassable

It should not be possible for the application to run without the logging system operating normally.

Failure-Proof

Logging methods should internally catch all possible exceptions that might occur *within the logging system* and handle their own recovery and error response. Any logging methods that access external resources (for example, paging systems or other servers) should be protected from hanging, by utilization of a timeout mechanism. A failure of the logging system should be immediately detectable, should halt or slow the application (especially with regard to security-sensitive operations), and generate alerts by directly accessing the core alert mechanisms.

18.2.8 Logging and Notification System Design

The following pattern incorporates all these requirements. The intent is not to design the structure of a logging system, because in most situations a logging system is built on top of an existing tool or log mechanism and so the actual structure will be quite different. The intent, rather, is to illustrate the functionality.

In most custom-developed applications, a logging system is built on top of an existing tool or log mechanism.

DESIGN PATTERN: CONDITION LOGGING AND PROBLEM NOTIFICATION

Related Patterns

This pattern builds on the "Monitored Log Writing System" pattern discussed in Section 7.16.2, "Log Design."

Context

An application requires an intelligent and customizable response to error events.

Problem

Most logging frameworks do not provide any kind of customizable response, but merely log errors.

Solution

The logging design pattern described here provides for intelligent response, as well as automatic log level escalation and saturation resistance. This pattern is conceptual, and many class implementations are possible.

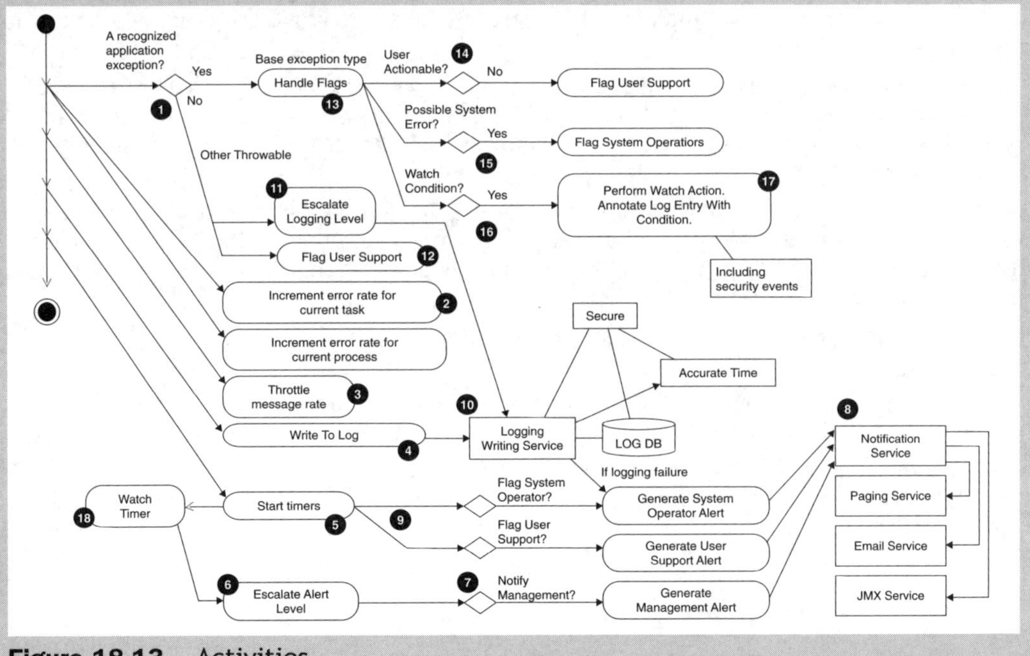

Figure 18.13 Activities.

The five basic steps of this model are: (1) handle watch conditions, including application-defined watches and built-in watches; (2) increment the error rate as appropriate for various execution scopes, including the current user task and current server process; (3) throttle the message rate, if necessary; (4) write through to the log; and (5) generate alerts to support staff and management. Refer to Figure 18.13 as these functions are explained.

Invocation of the exception logging system occurs when part of the application incurs an exception and makes a caller to the logger, passing the exception. At ❶, the exception is compared to the set of application-defined exception base types; if the exception type is recognized, it is handled with precision: Information defined in the base type is extracted ⓭ to determine if the exception meets watch criteria. Watch conditions fall into three categories: (1) user-actionable exceptions ⓮ that should result in a notification to the user or to user support; (2) system-level exceptions ⓯ that should result in a notification for the application operator; and (3) an application-defined watch condition ⓰. The last category includes any security-related exception events that need to be detected and reported.

If the exception is not of a recognized base type, the logging level is escalated ⓫, and user support is notified.

One of the actions ⓱ that a watch can perform is to schedule a watch timer ⓲. A watch timer is a timer that wakes up after a specified period of time and performs a given check; if the check is satisfied, an alert action ❻ is performed. Watch timers are not actually started until the handling of an exception is completed ❺, to ensure that they are timed from that point. In some cases, action is also taken when a watch timer is started.

After watch conditions have been handled, the statistics that are maintained for the error rate are re-computed ❷. The statistics should be maintained for several levels of context, including the user, the task, and any other level of contextual granularity that is provided in the current context.

After the error rate statistics have been re-computed, criteria should be checked to determine if the error rate is too high, and therefore if the application should be throttled ❸. Throttling should be applied when the error rate is such that it is likely to overwhelm the logging system.

After the throttling determination, the log message should be submitted to writing to the actual log database ❿. This should be done by formatting and then writing the log entry ❹. (It is assumed that the log writing system provides queuing so that Step 4 does not wait for the write to complete.)

As the last step, any watch timers that are required are started ❺.

Consequences

Error response logic is consolidated so that there is uniform policy with regard to who should be notified of various kinds of errors, and how they are notified.

The system is resilient to rapidly changing error rates, and the timer feature allows for transient conditions. The watch condition feature provides the application programmers with tremendous flexibility for monitoring for various kinds of error conditions or conditions of concern.

18.2.9 An End-to-End Scenario

This is a design book, not a programming book, but in order to show the intent of the exception handling patterns, it is useful to have an end-to-end example. The example here is not comprehensive and is very simplified. The example is in Java.

The example illustrates two tiers that exist on a server: a "request processing tier" and a "server tier." A "handler layer" on the request processing tier receives requests from end user client programs (for example, Web browsers) and invokes business layer methods to implement workflow logic and process the requests. The business methods in turn delegate to a "tx" layer on the server tier to initiate and manage database transactions. The tx layer delegates the actual database invocations to a "persistence layer" that makes SQL calls. This layout is very typical for Web applications.

When the request processing tier receives a request, it invokes an actionPerformed(...) method to process the request. This method does four things:

1. Establishes implicit context attributes; for example, the user's identity and role. In Java, this might be done using a ThreadLocal object. (See the pattern "Implicit Context and Explicit Context" in Section 18.2.5.)
2. Invokes a business layer method, depending on the nature of the request, passing arguments extracted from the request. The context established in Step 1 is implicitly passed to the business layer. In the Java example, this occurs because the business layer exists within the same Java Virtual Machine as the handler layer.
3. Remove the implicit context that it established in Step 1.
4. Render a response. This might be done inline or by forwarding or delegating to a response generation routine or page.

Steps 1 and 2 must be performed in such a way that no error can prevent Step 3 from being performed; otherwise, the implicit context might remain set to a state that is no longer valid. In the Java example, this is done by wrapping Steps 1 and 2 in a try block and placing Step 3 in the accompanying finally block.

In the example, the catch block catches every possible error that might occur—including error types that the compiler does not require the programmer to catch. This is done to illustrate that error handling must be comprehensive at the outermost level of a tier (see the principles "Use Checked Exceptions for All Lifecycle Errors" and "Log Only at Predetermined Layer Interfaces" in Sections 18.2.1 and 18.2.2, respectively). Otherwise, many kinds of errors that represent unusual but typical lifecycle error conditions, such as IO errors, configuration errors, and so on, will not be detected in a graceful manner. These errors can be re-thrown if the runtime container provides some form of error recovery and logging, but it is important for the programmer to consider each kind of error carefully before simply allowing it to propagate past the outermost level.

Error handling consists of logging the exception and generating a response to the user. The logger should capture the implicit context and include that in its output, subject to security guidelines for the logger. (See Section 7.16.)

The business layer methods follow a pattern that is similar to the one used by the handler layer. In the Java implementation, their logic is performed inside a try block. However, the business layer does not set its own implicit context, so there need not be a finally clause to unset it. The business layer methods merely set up the arguments for the call that they make to the tx layer on the server tier, then make the call, and handle any of the normal kinds of exceptions that might result. Unusual exceptions (in Java, these would be the "unchecked exceptions") are not handled by this layer, but are allowed to propagate to the outermost layer of the tier—i.e., to the handler layer, which catches everything and anything.

Some of the kinds of exceptions that the business layer must catch when it makes calls to the server tier include the failures that any resource can have, including timeout, an IO exception (shown as a "remote exception" in the example), and so on. Exceptions indicating invalid data or other exceptions particular to the kind of resource must also be handled.

When the business layer invokes the server tier, it passes three kinds of things:

1. The implicit context that has been set up by the handler layer.
2. Arguments.
3. A data structure that maps the arguments to key values, as described in the pattern "Input Map" in Section 18.2.6.

The implicit context is passed explicitly because, in the example, there is assumed to be no automatic propagation of the implicit context across the two tiers. Therefore, it is sent as if it were an argument. (See the pattern "Implicit Context and Explicit Context" in Section 18.2.5.)

The layers in the server timer follow a similar pattern. The main differences are that (1) the tx layer must decide when to set the transaction for rollback, depending on the exceptions that occur; and (2) the tx layer must attach attributes to any exceptions that are thrown when such information would be useful to any of the application user–the end user, the operators, or the application support group. The attributes provide important information for the logger to use to decide which application stakeholders need to know about the error. For example, if the error indicates a possible system-wide problem, the exception should be flagged to indicate that system operators need to be informed.♦ Depending on the exception, a data identification object may need to be attached to it to return information that narrows down to cause of the error.

> ♦ See the principle "Provide Management 'Aspects' to Exceptions" in Section 18.2.6.

The overall flow is depicted in Figure 18.14.

This might all seem like a lot of work–and it is. Building a reliable high-availability multi-user application is much more complex than building a normal departmental application.

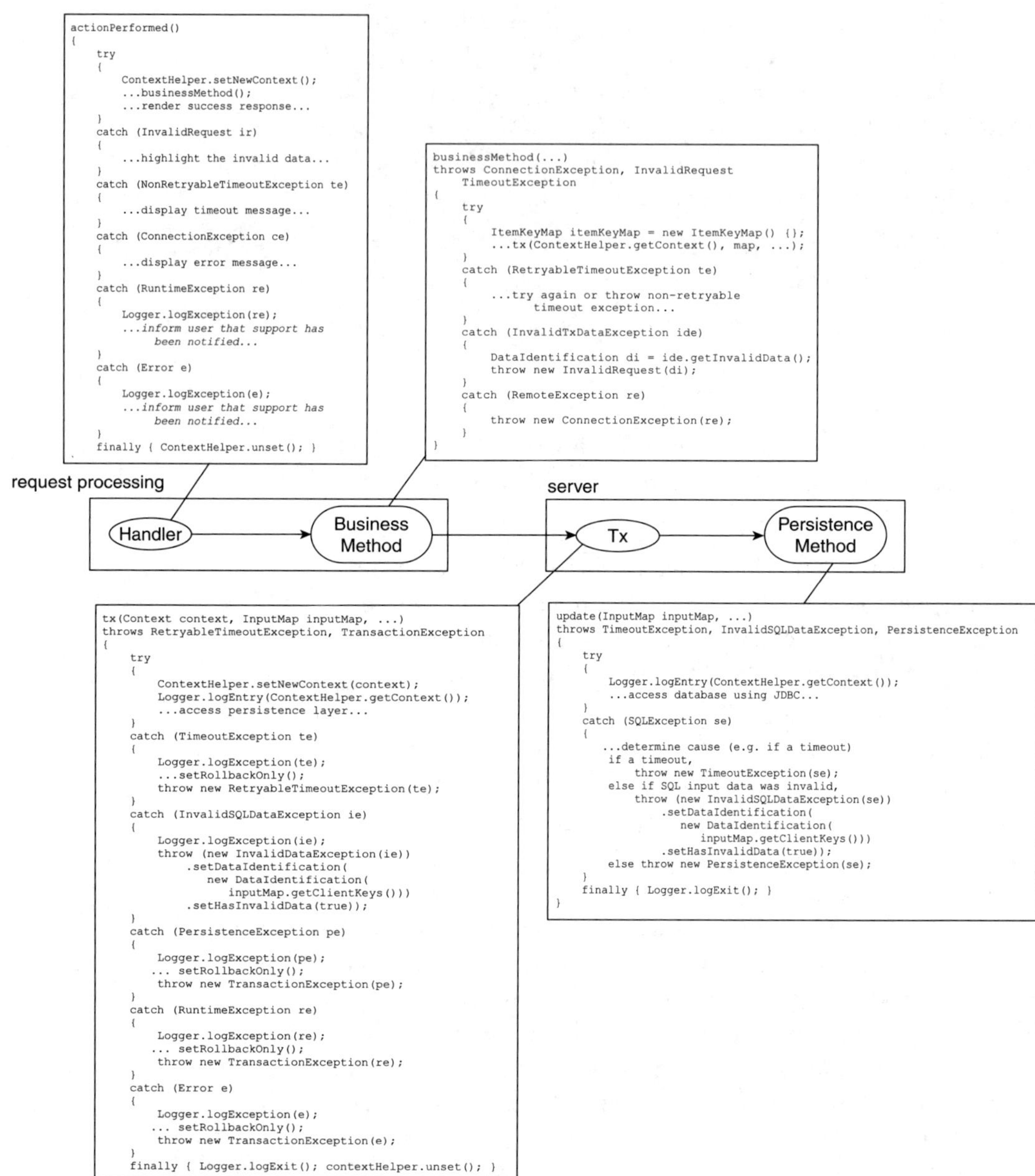

Figure 18.14 Example of end-to-end error handling.

18.3 Monitoring and Management

In terms of failure response, monitoring and management are the other side of the coin with respect to error handling: Monitoring and management are of limited value if the error signals that are generated by applications do not pinpoint the causes of problems, while such error signals are of limited value if there is no means of routing them to the right parties and presenting them in a manner that makes them easy to interpret. This routing and presentation is part of failure monitoring and management.

The routing of error messages or events relies on the degree to which the application encodes the nature of the problem. When the principle "Provide Management 'Aspects' to Exceptions" was presented in Section 18.2.6, an explanation of how this can be done was given. After applications begin to encode the categories of error conditions and their scope within error messages, it is possible to build a routing mechanism into the error logging facility that intelligently alerts only those who should be expected to respond to the error ().◆ The logging design pattern "Condition Logging and Problem Notification" presented in Section 18.2.8, "Logging and Notification System Design," illustrates this through the use of "watches" that check each error that is logged to see if it is of a type that should be reported to a particular party, such as the application operator, the application support group, the business-side management team, the security administrator, and so on.

◆ See the principle "Alert Only Those Who Need to Know" in Section 18.2.6.

Each of these users needs to have a presentation mechanism for these error reports. For application operators, the traditional presentation mechanism is a console that shows the condition of each application that is running. The application support group may require a pager alert in addition to email and a console, and the end user may want access to the application console as well. The security administrator may have a console already for monitoring enterprise-wide security alerts. For other classes of users, email may be sufficient.

When designing any kind of monitoring mechanism, it is critical that the information displayed represents the actual state of the application to the extent possible, and if this is not possible, that the user be made aware that no data is available. Programmers sometimes (without thinking) display values set by the user or operator rather than the actual value that represents the measured configuration. For example, if an application operator sets a console parameter specifying the server address for an application to use, but the application fails to actually utilize that address, and if the console does not display the *actual* address used by the application, there will be no way for the user to know what server the application is actually using.

PRINCIPLE: DISPLAY ACTUAL CONFIGURATION; DO NOT DISPLAY INTENDED CONFIGURATION IN LIEU OF ACTUAL CONFIGURATION.

18.3.1 Operator Consoles

Operator consoles provide operators with a global view of all applications that they are responsible for running. This view consists of the run status of each application, information such as when it started running, any error events generated by the application, the console log of each application, and ideally the resource usage of each application as well. Not all of this information is always available, and that is part of the challenge in designing an application that is "manageable"–i.e., one that can be effectively monitored and run by operators.

Most contemporary operator consoles use messaging protocols designed for monitoring, most notably SNMP. Other protocols are used as well, and many monitoring and management systems use other kinds of messages, such as XML. The messages are received by the console application, correlated with the application, and presented on a display. There is also no reason why an application messaging protocol cannot be used, such as SOAP, provided that the console application is designed to be able to receive and interpret that message type.

The main challenge that application operators have is that most applications are not designed to generate intelligent error messages that the operators can act on.◆

◆ This has been discussed at length under the principle "Provide Problem Transparency" in Section 18.2.6, under "Provide Management 'Aspects' to Exceptions" in Section 18.2.6, under "Provide User Status and Actionability" in Section 18.2.6, and elsewhere.

If an application generates intelligent messages that pinpoint the nature of a problem, these messages can be acted upon by the operator immediately and a support person may not need to be called. For example, if an application runs out of disk space and reports that as a message that identifies what the application was doing when it ran out of space and which file system is out of space, as well as how much disk space the application is currently using, the operator is in a position to assess whether the application needs more space or is using excessive space, possibly due to a program bug.

Consoles always display the run status of the application: that is, the run status of the application process or service. However, this is often insufficient, particularly in multi-threaded applications. A manageable application should report events that unambiguously indicate the application's health.♦ These events need to assess the health of each thread of the application. A model for application events is shown in Figure 18.15. As can be seen in the figure, events are recorded for each request thread.

♦ Discussed under the principle, "A Manageable Application Should Generate Credible and Monitorable 'Application-Is-Operational' Events" in Section 16.4.1, "Heartbeats."

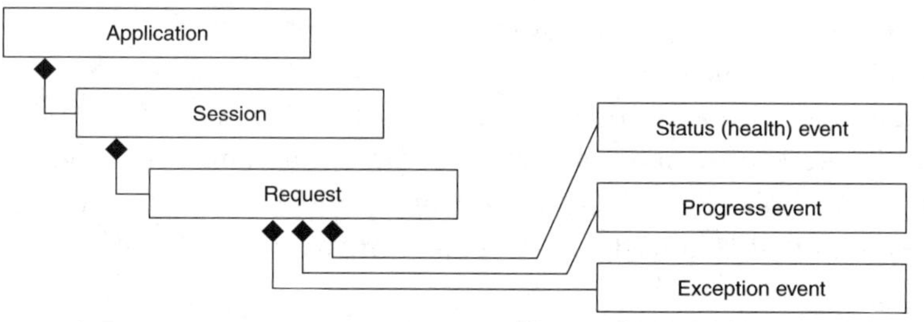

Figure 18.15 Application events should be monitored.

Thread-specific or request-specific information is far more telling than the process status, especially in situations in which the process is "run-away." Statistics, such as thread usage, disk usage, and so on, pertaining to an application are valuable, but these represent an outside view. "Inside views" consisting of intelligent events generated by an application are far more telling and powerful for monitoring, provided that they are organized so that a monitoring console can interpret them and use them.

PRINCIPLE: AN OPERATOR CONSOLE SHOULD MONITOR AND INTERPRET APPLICATION EVENTS, IN ORDER TO ASSESS THE HEALTH OF AN APPLICATION.

A console should not merely be a passive actor, watching for and displaying events and status. It should be *proactive*, providing *active error prevention* rather than merely passive error response. For example, an application should generate configuration events that inform the console how much of each resource it will need, and the console should monitor the resource levels to see if there are enough resources of if the application is beginning to reach its quota or possibly exhaust the resources.

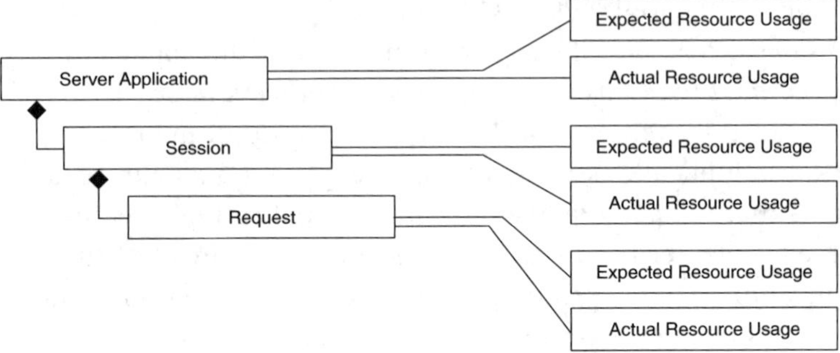

Figure 18.16
Proactively monitor resource usage.

Figure 18.16 shows an approach in which both expected and actual resource usage are tracked. Thus, resource exhaustion should not happen suddenly and by surprise: It should be forecast through active monitoring by the console application. Applications often use resources that are not automatically tracked by the console, so for this to work, applications must generate messages that inform the console of their resource usage.♦

◆ See the principle "Report Resource Usage" in Section 16.4.5, "Progress Bars."

PRINCIPLE: ACTIVELY MONITOR RESOURCE LEVELS TO PREVENT PROBLEMS BEFORE THEY OCCUR.

18.3.2 Application Consoles

An application console provides users and application support personnel with a view of an application's status. This view should interpret and aggregate events in ways that are meaningful to the user and to support personnel. For example, it should incorporate a concept of what the user is trying to accomplish: the user's "task." The task concept has been discussed previously (see Section 13.8, "Application-Defined Locking and Workflows"). To accomplish this, the application console needs to aggregate progress events and infer progress toward the user's task.

An application console can be incorporated into an application's user interface, or it can be a separate application. The latter is necessarily the case for server applications that do not have a user interface *per se*.

Many application servers come with an operator console that provides information on the status of the various applications running on the platform. This type of console is an operator console, not an application console, because it displays system-level information rather than information that is particular to each application. An application console, in contrast, displays events that are unique to the application and tracks the health and progress of the application in a way that is meaningful to end users and application support personnel. Figure 18.17 illustrates a generic model for some of the kinds of status information that interest a user.

PRINCIPLE: AN APPLICATION CONSOLE SHOULD MONITOR AND INTERPRET APPLICATION EVENTS, IN ORDER TO ASSESS THE PROGRESS OF APPLICATION TASKS.

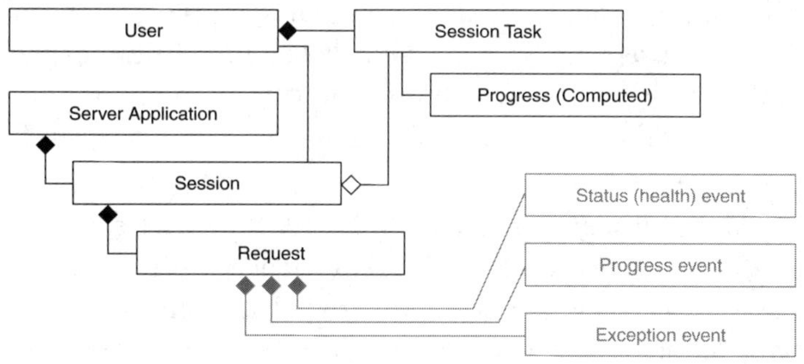

Figure 18.17
The user's view.

This is consistent with the principles of "Inform the User of Activity" and "Reliably Inform the User of Status," discussed in Section 10.6, and "Provide User Status and Actionability" in Section 18.2.6.

An application console should also allow the user and support staff to respond to changes in application status or errors in order to manage the progress of the application. This allows more direct access to the process of restoring an application to an operational status when something goes wrong that requires the joint action of application support staff and operators.

When diagnosing an application problem, it is extremely useful to be able to correlate errors with the user's actions.◆ Thus, if the application is designed to provide sufficient context to enable this correlation, the application console should make use of it and be able to display the association between user

◆ This was discussed under the principle "Provide Context to Correlate User Actions with Server Actions.

actions and any errors that have resulted, across each tier of the application.

18.3.3 Use of "Agent" Clients for Monitoring

Monitoring progress and health events is not always sufficient, particularly if there are parts of the application that do not generate such events. In those cases, it may be more effective to build a simulated client application that monitors the application by generating the same requests that various kinds of real users would. This approach has been used successfully for application monitoring [8] and also for security monitoring [9].

A program that simulates a user for the purpose of application monitoring is a type of software information agent. (See [10] for an overview of software agents.) In this approach, the agent program is designed to simulate the usage profiles of a set of hypothetical users and monitor and evaluate the health of the application response. Any deviations from correct response or from expected responsiveness results in an alert to support staff.

The advantage of this approach over monitoring health messages is that it more closely reports the actual user experience. Health messages can sometimes overlook aspects of the application, so it is possible for appropriate health messages to be generated and yet the users are not able to access the application. An agent is intended to report what real users actually experience.

18.4 Summary

As we have seen, a robust application should have well-placed, consistent, and sufficiently thorough handling of errors that not only considers common errors but also considers any unlikely errors that might occur as a result of system errors or misconfiguration. Features that enable the capture of sufficient error information and context, as well as delivery of that information to the user or operators, are required for a high-assurance application. This information must be precise, useful, and sparing—so that the recipient can quickly identify the source and cause of a problem. In competition with these requirements, error handling must be secure and not reveal internal or sensitive information to inappropriate parties. It is not easy to develop a design that achieves all these requirements.

This chapter presented many design patterns for addressing these issues, including the use of checked exceptions for lifecycle errors, forward propagation of context within an application, contextual error response, and adding manageability concerns to exceptions. A design pattern for incident reporting and logging was presented, with a discussion of the security issues pertaining to it. An end-to-end scenario was presented that serves to illustrate how these things can all be connected together. Finally, issues for the design of application monitoring and management consoles were discussed.

The next chapter examines methodological issues that affect the assurance level of an application under development. No particular methodology is advocated; rather, considerations and universal requirements are stated that apply to any methodology. Some existing methodologies are examined for the same of analysis and clarification of the concepts that are presented.

18.5 Exercises

1. A mission-critical server application connects to several remote resources for information. These remote resources include several databases, a SAN file server, a messaging system, and a set of Web services hosted on an offsite system. In one of the application modules, the following Java code exists:

```
// Get connection.
Connection connection = null;
try {
        connection = webSvcPool.getConnection();
}
catch (IOException ex) {
        throw new RuntimeException("Cannot open connection");
}
```

What is wrong with this code from a manageability perspective? Explain.

2. An application uses several classes of external resources, including a file system, a database connection, and an HTTP server. The monitoring console for the application provides the following information: (a) application error status, (b) number of pooled threads in use, (c) amount of virtual memory in use by the application. What other information would you add to the console in order to prevent problems before they occur?
3. An application console log lists all error and information messages produced by the application. For example, if an error occurs while processing a client request, the error message on the console would read: "ERROR: In module com.abc.financial.core, method computeHedge(): numeric overflow." What kinds of information are missing from this error message to allow a user support expert to effectively diagnose what is wrong?
4. An application contains some computationally intensive methods that predict the market price of certain securities. These calculations must be run on demand for a list of input securities. The calculations are implemented using parallel algorithms on a computing cluster. In some cases, a calculation may experience a runaway error, causing that calculation to run indefinitely. How would you approach the design of the algorithm that dispatches the calculations to the cluster nodes?
5. Consider the following code:

```
public void handleRequest(Request req) {
      try { ... updateAccount(account); }
      catch (AccountException ex) {
            Log.write("Could not handle request: " +
ex.getMessage());
      }
}

public void updateAccount(Account account)  throws
AccountException {
      try { ... updateDatabaseBalance(account,
balance); }
      catch (DBException ex) {
```

```
            Log.write("Database exception for acct. " +
account);
            throw new AccountException(ex, account);
      }
}

public void updateDatabaseBalance(BigDecimal balance)
throws DBException {
      try { ... }
      catch (IOException ex) {
            Log.write("IO exception while accessing
database: " +
                  ex.getMessage());
            throw new DBException(ex);
      }
}
```

What things are wrong with this code, from an error handling perspective?

Answers and hints for these exercises can be found at `http://www.assuredbydesign.com/haa/`.

CHAPTER 19

METHODOLOGICAL CONSIDERATIONS

Many sources [1, 2, 3, 4, 5] have expressed the belief that reliable and secure systems cannot be built unless there is a process that ensures that the end result meets the requirements of security and reliability. The characteristics of reliability and security—or lack thereof—are intrinsic to a system's design and to the process used to produce and maintain the system and cannot be merely added on the way that you would add on a new feature or function.

The Tower of Babel, by Gustave Doré (1832-1883).

Process operates at many levels, for example:

- Organizational and executive level: recognizing risk, making assurance a priority, establishing goals, responsibilities and managerial processes. Developing experience with improved processes. Addresses by standards, such as ISO 9000, CMM, Common Criteria, and so on, as well as approaches promoted by proprietary organizations and experts (for example, [6]).
- Developing the project-level and department-level processes. These address things such as (1) risk assessment, (2) establishing assurance goals, and (3) identifying the tactical tasks to improving implementations, specifying best practices, threat analysis,[1] reliability analysis,[2] improving software development processes,[3] and improving deployment and application operation processes.

This chapter focuses primarily on the second level, which is more tactical and technical.

19.1 Issues and Approaches

Methodologies used in business increasingly focus on short iterations and quick results–i.e., increased "agility" in the response of programmers to requirements [12]. This is because agile methodologies are arguably more responsive and more effective in satisfying business functional needs,[13] as development teams are now expected to respond to new requirements almost immediately as they arise. As a result, development within most organizations increasingly focuses on short-term objectives at the expense of long-term or system-wide objectives, and reliability is increasingly approached in an empirical rather than reductive manner.

1 Established threat analysis methodologies include STRIDE [7] and OCTAVE [8].

2 See for example, [9], [10].

3 Expert-level methodologies include [11].

Unfortunately, while an agile development process may allow teams to respond quickly to changes in business needs, such processes can be deficient if the system needs to be secure or reliable. For example, there is no way to write comprehensive *unit* tests for security or reliability (see Section 3.3, "Defining and Verifying Architectural Rules"), and most agile methodologies rely heavily on unit-level regression testing. Attempts to break into a system can sometimes demonstrate a level of security, but such empirical tests cannot be applied repeatedly in the form of a regression test suite. Further, many widely-used agile processes (such as Extreme Programming ("XP")) deemphasize the need for a formal application design, yet a system that has no consistent software architecture cannot be audited for its security characteristics without reviewing each and every line of code and deriving the as-built architecture, which is not practical, especially given that the review would have to be done each time the system is modified. For these reasons, an organization using an agile methodology must ensure that a full and robust agile process is used, and make provisions for the assurance considerations that are discussed in this chapter. Organizations using other process approaches, such as a "waterfall" approach, must also make provisions for these same considerations, although the challenges in doing so are arguably fewer.

Methodologies that have been developed for designing highly secure and reliable applications (for example, [14] and its derivatives) employ a rigorous process that is appropriate for the most high-value or high-risk applications, such as space vehicle applications and operating systems. Unfortunately the cost, slowness, and specialized expertise requirements of such a rigorous approach have impeded their use for most enterprise applications—even critical ones. Another difficulty is that such methodologies depend on a ground-up secure foundation—yet today's commercial hardware, operating systems, and application platforms, and programming languages do not provide that foundation.

Perhaps this situation will change if the tools and techniques associated with more rigorous approaches can be refined and simplified. Nowadays, enterprise application development must be agile and cost-competitive, yet produce secure and reliable applications—two competing sets of goals. Methodological frameworks, such as [15], do not impose a particular methodology, but identify the things that a methodology must accomplish in order to achieve high assurance.

The challenge with defining an agile methodology that can be used for building a reliable and secure application is then to *design a process that allows the system architects and testers to demonstrate that the system is secure and reliable, but still permit the short iterations and rapid development that has been shown to have great business value.*

Methodologies that provide more formality, such as Rational Unified Process (RUP), treat security as an application requirement and, therefore, do not address security specifically or give security any special status. The project manager is responsible for ensuring that security is adequately incorporated into the system requirements and tracked as such and must work with the system architect to ensure that security testing is adequate and effective.

In designing a software application, it is the architect's task to help the project manager to ensure that all implicit or assumed and explicit security and reliability requirements are captured, and then to help the project manager to fine-tune the development methodology so that it incorporates the processes that will ensure that the requirements are implemented. In doing so, the business requirements are translated into a set of *derived requirements*. For example, a requirement that the application should be maintainable might result in a derived requirement that documentation should match the as-built system. Derived requirements were explained in Section 2.2.3, "Adding Derived Requirements That Affect Reliability."

It is extremely important to consider which derived requirements should be placed in a requirements list and which should be handled by embedding them into the development methodology. For example, a requirement that documentation match the as-built system does not necessarily belong in the requirements list. It can go there, but if it is there, it is subject to scrutiny, and the project manager is then in a position of explaining and justifying every derived requirement. It might be better to adjust the methodology so that there is a process for ensuring that documentation matches the as-built system.

In order to translate the implicit and explicit business requirements into a set of derived requirements, the architect should perform risk and threat analyses and use the principles in this book to augment the system architecture with a set of technical security and reliability requirements. For example, if the business expresses a requirement for "reliable operation," the architect and project manager might agree that this can be translated into the following derived requirement:

- A failure-response test suite must be defined for each sensitive component.

If this very technical derived requirement is placed into the general list of requirements, it will be subject to trade-off analysis with regard to functional requirements, which always have more perceived value, and the project manager will be in the position of explaining how each derived technical requirement maps to articulated or implicit business requirements—often a very difficult task. See Section 2.2, "Writing Reliability Requirements," for more discussion about the challenges of defending technical requirements.

It is the job of the project architect to translate all requirements—those that are articulated and those that are derived—into an application architecture that includes decisions for how the application will be designed and a general map of that design. Architects can use design verification tools (see Chapter 3, "Design Specification and Verification") to verify compliance with architectural decisions, to the extent possible, as well as employ design reviews and code reviews that focus on sensitive components and issues. Design reviews should include review of any analysis models on which the design is based, such as a threat model or reliability model. [16]

Another challenge is that a key concept of building secure and reliable software is to distinguish between those components that have a critical impact on security and reliability and the rest of the code and to apply a more stringent QA or development process for the that part of the codebase.♦ However, it is hard for a project to utilize more than one process. For example, each process might require different methods for tracking task status and level of effort, and the different kinds of measures that are used might need to be reconciled or aggregated to

♦ See the principle "Apply Stringent Quality Criteria to High-Risk Components" in Section 4.1.1, "Security-Related Risk."

estimate total cost. This might be infeasible with certain development process management tools.

Management, therefore, needs to understand the need to manage different kinds of components differently, in order to provide the level of costly QA where it is needed and allow flexibility and less stringency where work can be more relaxed.

Finally, the software development process is only part of the application development process. For example, other processes might include a security threat analysis, a message syntax design effort, a business process design effort, and so on. These kinds of non-code development processes are often managed separately, and appropriately so. However, it is common that efforts that are performed by "experts" are not tracked and managed well. For example, penetration tests that are performed by outside firms are seldom documented and are managed in an ad-hoc manner. This is unacceptable and leaves the organization with no ability to understand what was really done or to compare what was done in one trial with another some time later. Any tests of any kind–including those done by outside groups–should be documented and added to a test suite.

19.2 Universal Methodological Principles

One methodology is not right for all systems. The methodology that is appropriate for a high-reliability real-time system on which lives depend is different than the methodology that is appropriate for a small e-commerce Web site. However, regardless of the methodology that is used for a project, it is possible to enumerate the things that the methodology must accomplish. For example, if an application must be reliable, the development methodology must have processes that ensure that the resulting system meets that requirement.

Some methodologies will attack a reliability requirement upfront as part of design, and others may leave it exclusively for the testing cycle. There are pros and cons of each approach that can be used, and different approaches–different methodologies–are appropriate for different sets of requirements and different kinds of systems. It, therefore, cannot be said that a particular methodology cannot be used to achieve an application's requirements—only that they will be achieved differently, and with a different cost and process, from how they would be if a different methodology were used.

It is possible, however, to say that if certain principles are not adhered to, it will be difficult if not impossible to achieve an assurance-related requirement. For example, it is a certainty that if some form of verification with requirements (such as testing) is not performed, the application will not be reliable with respect to those requirements. Different methodologies impose testing or verification of different kinds and at different points in the development cycle, but all utilize a process that verifies that the implementation meets requirements to achieve a given level of reliability and assurance. It is interesting to note that some methodologies achieve this in very different ways; for example, the "Clean Room" method developed at IBM utilizes functional verification of modules, and no unit testing is performed. [17] Thus, in the Clean Room method, unit-level verification is done, but not via testing.

The prior chapters of this book focused on technical principles related to high-assurance design. The discussion here will focus on the *methodological principles* that are important in order to be able to design and implement a high-assurance software application. These methodological principles apply *regardless of the development methodology that is used*, and the methodology should be adjusted to ensure that these principles are accommodated in a manner that enables the chosen methodology to achieve the application's assurance requirements.

> Methodological principles will not be placed in boxes to differentiate them from technical principles.

Ensure That Someone Competent Is Responsible for the Application Architecture

The application architect is the most experienced project team member from an assurance perspective. This individual (or team) is responsible for working with the project manager, stakeholders, and analysts to develop a comprehensive list of explicit and implicit requirements; deriving technical requirements from those; designing, articulating, and documenting the application architecture; and developing methodological processes that ensure that the architecture is adhered to. The architect should be knowledgeable about the principles and patterns related to high assurance design.

Ensure That All Implied or Assumed Requirements Are Identified

Assurance requirements and critical business requirements must be identified. This requires working with all stakeholders to help them think not only in terms of normal situations but abnormal ones as well. In order for the application to be robust, reliable, and secure, all conceivable lifecycle scenarios must be considered, and the desired application response planned. The process of obtaining these kinds of requirements is discussed in Chapter 2, "Assurance Requirements."

Ensure That Critical Business Rules Are Auditable

The correspondence between critical requirements and implementation must be easily auditable. It is often accepted without argument nowadays that a software implementation departs significantly from its design, and it is commonly accepted with resignation that design documentation is not maintained and therefore cannot be expected to reflect the actual "as-built" design.

This state of affairs may be acceptable for the bulk of the functional logic within business applications. It is *not acceptable* for software that implements security policies or features, however, nor is it acceptable for software that implements important business rules on which the enterprise depends. As an example of the latter, a financial services firm would likely consider an interest rate rule to be a critical business rule, because if the rule fails when business conditions change and earlier assumptions are no longer valid (for example, that rates would never fall below 1.0), severe damage could be done to the firm's reputation as a reliable financial services company. See the principles "Authorization Rules Should Be Auditable" in Section 7.4, "Auditability of Policy Coverages," and "Critical Business Rules Should Be Auditable" in Section 17.2, "Transparency of Implementation."

Regardless of the methodology employed, provisions must be made to factor out the authorization rules that are implemented by the system and to factor out the critical business rules that affect processing results. Provision must be made to document those rules, and in an ideal situation, the business logic code should be generated from that documentation, or it should be verified that all the rules are implemented in a fail-safe manner and according to specification.

The result of doing this is an auditable implementation, such that the implementation has "100%" coverage of the documented business rules. This is the only way that one can be sure that the authorization rules and critical business rules that are mandated by business or legal requirements are, in fact, satisfied. A system that cannot ensure this cannot be said to be secure or reliable even at the most fundamental level, because no one can prove that all rules are fully implemented.

Some methodologies, notably highly iterative methodologies, emphasize the use of unit testing in lieu of design documentation. While this approach has compelling advantages with regard to software features, it falls short when dealing with security and reliability requirements, because many requirements of these kinds are hard to test through unit testing. Further, there is the problem of making sure that the test suite is complete. One cannot present a test suite to business leaders and ask them to check it—one must use a communication mechanism that bridges the business side and the technical side and that implies a document. So-called "stories" do not satisfy this requirement, because there is no guarantee—except the passage of tests—that the implementation of a new "story" (a user requirement) will not change the implementation of another story,. Therefore, the only proof of compliance is the test suite—an artifact that business users and security auditors cannot review and understand and, as explained previously, unit tests cannot be used to prove coverage of all "non-functional" requirements anyway.

Ensure That the Quality-Critical Codebase Is Identified

Good decisions and differentiations must be made regarding where to focus quality effort. The development methodology must provide the criteria for identifying the most sensitive or critical components and define the processes that will be used to verify their implementation, as well as the processes used to verify the implementation of other components; the former should be more stringent. See the principles "Apply Stringent Quality Criteria to High-Risk Components" and "Minimize the Number,

Size, and Complexity of High-Risk Components" in Section 4.1.1 and the principles "Minimize the Number, Size, and Complexity of Critical Business Rules" and "Apply Stringent Quality Criteria to Critical Business Components" in Section 17.2.

Ensure That an Architecture Exists That Explains How the Application Will Meet the Assurance Requirements

There must be an application architecture that provides the *principles, patterns, decisions, and frameworks* that the implementation must follow and shows how they will achieve the assurance requirements.

The mechanisms that interpose and evaluate the authorization rules, as well as the mechanisms that provide inputs (context) to the authorization rules, should be documented in a architecture that can be reviewed and evaluated from a security and reliability perspective.

The existence of a documented architecture provides a means to ensure that:◆

> ◆ See the principle "An Application That Has No Verifiable Design Must Be Tested Much More Thoroughly in Order to Provide the Same Level of Reliability" in Section 17.2 and the principle "A System Cannot Be Said to Be Secure if the Design of the Actual System Cannot Be Articulated" in Chapter 4, "Planning for an Assurable Design."

1. The concepts of the architecture are captured so that developers have an approach to adhere to.
2. The robustness of critical components can be reviewed without having to inspect and make guesses from the implementation.

Ensure the Quality and Faithfulness of Implementation with Respect to the Design

The implementation must be transparent and match design. The development methodology must adequately provide for the verification and enforcement of the *principles, patterns, decisions, and frameworks* that are specified in the design.

Over time, there is a risk that developers will corrupt the design of the security elements or introduce practices that are adverse with respect to assumptions made by security features. The existence of a design provides a basis against which changes to the system can be discussed and evaluated. It also provides a basis against which the as-built system can be compared to determine if the security principles employed by the design have been adhered to, as well as the truthfulness of any assumptions made by the design.

The ramification of this requirement is that the design must be made to stay in sync with the software implementation, at least with regard to components that affect security. That is the only way that the system can be expected to remain secure over time through many maintenance cycles.♦

◆ See the principle "Employ Security Design Patterns That Are Verifiable" in Section 4.2, Designing for Verifiability," and the principle "An Application That Has No Verifiable Design..." in Section 17.2.

Ensure That Architectural Concepts and Decisions Are Documented and Disseminated

Regardless of the software development methodology used, an architecture document *must* be created that addresses the issues of assurance that are important to the organization. That is the only way to be sure that all areas have been thought about. It is best if such a document is a working document so that it serves as a bulletin board of sorts for issues that are addressed during the system design and development and is updated as new issues arise or approaches change. The ideal implementation of such a document is an internal, online, topic-based Web site or knowledge base that is accessible to all architects and developers. Thus, the document can be developed incrementally, which is an approach that is more compatible with agile methodologies—but it must be developed.

The document or Web site should include these separate sections:

- Basic concepts, related to assurance (for example, security and reliability), that are relevant for the project.
- Assurance-related requirements. These are typically based on the derived requirements, as discussed in prior sections.
- Architectural concepts and decisions pertaining to the project application, and explanation of *how they ensure that the assurance requirements are met.* This addresses the important tenet of documentation: "Maintainable Software Should Document Why Each Action Is Performed," discussed in Section 17.1, "Documentation." Include artifacts related to any models that have been developed, such as a trust model, role models, and so on.
- The application's domains of trust, tiers, layers, component types, user roles, and interaction paradigms. This constitutes the application's structural architecture.

- Design patterns to use for each component type. Providing this helps to ensure that the design patterns that are actually used are understood by the architect.

When the author has created such a Web site, it was developed in such a way as to define many independent sections that could be explained independently in short seminars or "brown bag" sessions, as well as allowing the sections to be printable without having to print the entire site. A hyperlinked table of contents was also created that served as a site map.

The site should not be haphazard or too informal, nor should it include "boilerplate" or superfluous content that does not add value. It should not be updateable by anyone; or if it is (such as with wiki sites), the system architects should be able to easily identify, review, and roll back changes. Architectural concepts and mandatory design patterns should be the result of careful decisions that can be changed only by the system architects. At the same time, it is useful to make such a site the core of a project's internal Web site and allow team leads to update those portions that pertain to design details and implementation. In fact, it is a good idea to enlist project technical leads to lead discussions and presentations about the security architecture in order to involve them as directly as possible in the thought leadership process.

All these things are extremely useful to an application support group. Such groups—assuming that they are distinct from the application development team—usually have a very hard time keeping abreast of application changes and long for better documentation. Further, if they are allowed to maintain the application or make emergency changes, they need to be intimately familiar with the application's design patterns and rules so that they do not unintentionally violate a crucial design pattern on which the application's security or reliability depend.

Ensure That Design Is Reviewed by Different Areas of Expertise

Today's technologies are so diverse that even an experienced software architect cannot be expected to have all the qualifications required to verify the design of a complex application. Bring in independent experts who have expertise in the areas of application security and reliability, and use them to help review the design and improve it.

For security threat analysis, it is good practice to perform a risk analysis and threat analysis. Prioritize the identified weaknesses and add them to the list of "bugs," issues, or requirements.

For reliability analysis, make sure that the application support and operations groups have a chance to review the design. Presumably, they have had input to the application requirements, but their experience with real problems and failures is helpful for ensuring that the list of failure scenarios is comprehensive.

ENSURE THAT THERE EXISTS FULL CONFIGURATION MANAGEMENT OF ALL ARTIFACTS

It is impossible to have confidence in a application if there is not certainty with regard to what versions of each file, component, test, or design are actually used at each point in the process. Complete configuration management for all artifacts for each phase of development is therefore a must-have for any high-assurance project or process.

19.3 Analysis of Extreme Programming (XP) for Development of Reliable and Secure Systems

Extreme Programming (XP) is a widely used rapid ("agile") development methodology. XP is a rapidly iterative process that places extreme emphasis on functional features and unit testing and marginalizes or discards many traditional aspects of software development, including detailed use cases, requirements lists, and design artifacts. Extreme programming's strength lies in its proven effectiveness in allowing programmers to work quickly to deliver measurable business value.

XP is a brilliant and revolutionary way of approaching software development. At its essence, XP treats the software development process as a continuous *flow* in which all aspects *occur concurrently*. This is in contrast to earlier approaches that required each aspect of software development to occur in sequence: e.g., requirements gathering would occur prior to design, design would occur prior to implementation, and implementation would occur prior to testing. Such a serial "waterfall" approach prevents a project team from being able to obtain the benefits of downstream feedback until the end of the project.

In contrast, XP creates a continuous feedback loop in which testing occurs continually (daily), and requirements are continually gathered and refined by showing the stakeholders what interim versions of the system looks like throughout the development cycle. This allows the stakeholders to provide interim feedback so that the requirements can be fine-tuned.

For this to succeed for a high-assurance application, it is critical that every aspect of high-assurance development be cast as a continuous process flow. Thus, design cannot be sacrificed, but rather it must be made continual.

Some of XP's features are discussed next in the context of high assurance.

Reliance on Unit Testing

A key concept of XP is that every component that is developed should have a companion unit test. The unit tests serve to define what correct system behavior is.

This is a valuable technique for functional design verification. Unfortunately, many aspects of system behavior are not unit-testable, often because of compositional or temporal behavior. Transactions are a classic example: Transactions have temporal semantics, and those semantics are not easy to specify in a unit test. Security-related concerns also may involve prohibition requirements—making sure that something *cannot* be done—and that is harder to express in a unit test, as explained in Section 3.3.

It is important to be clear that *some* aspects of security are unit-testable. In particular, security *features* are unit testable: For example, testing that a particular authorization rule performs as expected. That is quite different, however, from being able to test that a component is protected by its container. Security relies on the following of best practices that can be checked only by using a combination of design tools, intelligence, knowledge, and rigorous auditing. [18]

It is also not uncommon for organizations that use XP to rely completely on unit testing. This is an incorrect application of the XP methodology. Unit testing cannot catch all errors: Integration testing is required.[4]

The Reduced Role of Design

XP minimizes the role of system design and architecture: A system is built feature-by-feature. Developers are not prevented from considering a big picture, but such a consideration falls outside of the strict XP process. In fact, developers are discouraged from implementing anything that does not add *immediate value*. World-renowned security architecture expert Peter Neumann states that "Questions of how to address architecture in the large seem not to be adequately addressed within Extreme Programming" [19]. Unfortunately, we have seen that architecture is extremely important for security. Some approaches for addressing this within the context of XP are discussed in the next section.

Frequent Uncontrolled Change

The XP development process consists of many small iterations of development work, each lasting a few weeks and focusing on adding a well-defined set of new business value features to the application. An iteration typically begins with a meeting between the technical lead and the development team to discuss and whiteboard the new features. The team then splits up into small groups or pairs and each group implements a set of features.

This works well with a small project in which there is a single technical lead, but when the project is large, there need to be several technical leads, so the initial design meeting becomes several meetings. The tactical nature of this process easily results in a breakdown of communication between the technical leads and the project architect and other stakeholders. An architect often relies on design reviews to achieve architectural conformance, and in XP there is no time for design reviews—by the time they happen, the features have been implemented.

The frequent involvement of stakeholders in the XP development cycle also introduces the risk that requirements will frequently change, rather than merely being added. Chaotic

4 See the frequency analysis of defects detected in various phases of testing in [20], p. 228.

requirements changes can adversely affect the integrity of a design, as designers become frustrated and fail to capture non-functional requirements associated with new or changed features, or partially implemented architectures have to be scrapped, leaving artifacts whose removal "does not add business value." Frequent changes in requirements have a potentially adverse impact on reliability. [21] Preventing this situation requires an experienced XP team.

Lack of Documentation

The XP process does not mandate any form of documentation. Documentation is treated as something that should be inherent in the code, due to the quality of its craftsmanship. Design artifacts are permitted, but can be on scraps of paper, and there is no XP-mandated requirement to preserve these.

As we have discussed, the "whys" of a program's constructs are even more important than the "whats," so design artifacts that document decisions and that map features to design concepts or rules are extremely important for maintainability. (See Chapter 17, "Maintainability.") Documentation is also important to preventing "key person dependencies."

Collective Code Ownership

XP promotes the concept that anyone can work on any module, and that programmers should write code that is so clear that any other programmer can go in and modify it when a new feature needs to be added. This approach has the advantage that code gets looked at by more people, and so there is a high likelihood that it will be improved in the process. The risk is that programmers who are not qualified to work on a module might modify it. As we have seen, sensitive components often need special expertise and familiarity with an application's architecture.♦

> ♦ See the principle "Minimize the Accessibility of Sensitive Components" in Section 4.2.1, "Constraining the Implementation."

Some Good Things for Security and Reliability

On the up side, XP has a positive effect on security and reliability in many ways. For example, it focuses on keeping an implementation simple, because every line of code must add business value. This promotes the principle "Minimize the Number, Size, and Complexity of High-Risk Components" explained in Section 4.1.1.

The use of small teams or pairs to work on code also has the effect of enhancing the correctness of code, because each programmer in a pair uses their own thought process, so the resulting implementation is less likely to miss something important. Unfortunately, few projects that claim to use "XP" actually use pair programming.

19.3.1 Modifications to the Extreme Programming (XP) Paradigm

Organizations that choose a methodology such as XP often benefit greatly from the agility it brings to their IT processes. They, therefore, are not necessarily in a position to adopt a different approach, and arguably should not. Rather, they need guidance on *how to use an agile methodology in a manner to ensure the reliability and security of the applications that they build.*

EXPAND THE "CUSTOMER" CONCEPT TO EACH STAKEHOLDER

XP focuses very heavily on pleasing the customer. As a result, other parties are often forgotten. A high-assurance application has many people who have a stake in the operation, maintenance, and use of the application. These include people in the user community (for example, the managers who requested the application in the first place), the people who will be responsible for operating the application, those who be responsible for maintaining it, those who are responsible for maintaining the environment's security, those who are responsible for affected systems, such as databases, and those who will be responsible for responding to application errors or calls or assistance. All these groups represent stakeholders, and each has requirements that they would like to express. The application cannot be successful unless the needs of all these organizational groups are taken into consideration. Therefore, in the XP view of the world, *these all represent "customers."*

ALLOW FOR ANALYSIS FUNCTIONS THAT ARE NOT TRACKED BY STORY CARDS

Agile processes de-emphasize the need for formal requirements and instead utilize an informal process that involves direct discussions with the stakeholders and the capture of each requirement or feature on an individual "story card." This approach works very well because it streamlines requirements gathering and dispenses with aspects that add no value, such as document formatting and boilerplate.

A difficulty arises, however, if there are goals for the application that require protracted analysis or design. XP provides for prototyping, but not for careful design or the development of standards, frameworks, or architectural changes to the codebase that take months instead of weeks.

It is, therefore, appropriate to selectively "escape from XP" for long-duration tasks that aim to improve an application's architecture. Long-duration architectural improvements, such as adding a new layer to improve security, cannot be divided into discrete additions that individually add business value: The business value is not realized until *all the changes* have been implemented. For these kinds of changes, it is often best to create a separate design branch or activity that works in parallel with the mainstream XP process and keep them in-sync on a regular basis by merging the changes from the main branch (the agile branch) into the non-XP branch; when the non-agile branch is complete and has passed all tests and is fully in sync, it can replace the agile branch.

Include Architect in Each Design Meeting

Because XP treats software development as a nearly continuous "flow," and design is important for a high-assurance application, it follows that design must be treated as a nearly continuous "flow" in order to be compatible with XP.

To achieve this, it is critical that the application's architect be "in the loop" with regard to all design changes, story meetings, coding activities, and participate in all decision-making forums.[5] This is especially critical with XP because in XP, much of the design process is informal and ad-hoc, and it is easy for someone who is responsible for having a global view to get "out of the loop." For this reason, the architect of an agile project must be

5 If sufficiently involved, the architect can serve as a gatekeeper for ensuring that sufficient refactoring is performed and that the implementation of each story satisfies architectural goals. For this to work, however, the architect must have a high degree of credibility with the project manager and business stakeholders so that the urge to put insufficiently refactored implementations into production can be resisted. The informality of this means that successful architectural adherence can become a matter of personalities.

someone who is very personable, somewhat aggressive, and a good collaborator. They must also be somewhat hands-on, because only then will they appreciate the issues that the programmers are having. It is useful for the architect to participate in some—but not too much—pair programming simply for this reason. The architect should also be co-located with the development team—ideally right next to the board on which stories are posted!

The architect should also undertake to involve the project leads in the development of the architecture and to educate them on the architectural concepts so that they become emissaries of a sort and can stand in for the architect, because eventually it becomes impossible for the architect to be present in all decision forums. In order to accomplish this, a good tactic is to make the technical leads and mentors report to the architect, and make them responsible for maintaining the architecture Web site or document.

USE OF "SYSTEMS" ITERATIONS TO INCORPORATE ARCHITECTURAL WORK

For architectural changes that can be accomplished within a single XP iteration (commonly from two to three weeks), it is useful to occasionally dedicate an iteration to "system changes" that do not add functionality, but rather focus on refactoring and making improvements to the architecture and design, in the interest of maintainability, reliability, and security.[6]

EMPLOY CONFIGURATION CONTROL FOR SECURITY-SENSITIVE ELEMENTS (RESOURCE RULES, CONTEXT BINDINGS, AND SO ON). (SEPARATE REPOSITORY, WITH FULL TRACEABILITY.)

For a high-assurance application, the XP concept of "collective code ownership" needs to be tempered to accommodate the need to differentiate a "trusted computing base" from other parts of the application.♦

♦ See the principle "Apply Stringent Quality Criteria to High-Risk Components" in Section 4.1.1.

Because XP relies heavily on in-person intra-team communication, significant challenges can result if a team is distributed geographically. In such a situation, rules must be established that add more formality to communication between separated groups and that restrict ad-hoc access to modules by separated groups.

6 Some development teams utilize the practice of requiring early iterations to focus on "architecturally significant stories" in order to ensure that architectural issues are fleshed out before too much functionality iS built.

RULES ABOUT WHO CAN WORK ON SENSITIVE COMPONENTS, BACKED UP BY ACCESS CONTROL

The collective code ownership paradigm must also be adjusted to allow for restricted access control to sensitive modules.♦

> ◆ See the principle "Minimize the Accessibility of Sensitive Components" in Section 4.2.1.

Most XP software projects utilize a "concurrent" version control system, such as CVS. Such systems often do not provide different levels of access control. In that case, a separate repository may need to be created for sensitive components, with a restricted set of programmers granted access. This means that restricted components would be built using a separate build and release designation, and this is indeed appropriate for sensitive components because they often need to be deployed using a separate security policy.♦

> ◆ See the principle "A Trusted Context Should Always Include the Code Context" in Section 7.17.3, "Code Context."

TRAINING FOR "ASSURANCE-CAPABLE" PROGRAMMERS

It almost goes without saying that if sensitive code must be implemented by more specialized programmers, those programmers must exist on the team. It is regrettable that today's universities do not seem to be producing those kinds of programmers (see the discussion in Section 1.2, "It's the Process"). Moreover, it is incorrect to assume that experienced developers have the required skills: More years of experience in building unreliable applications is no better than fewer.

What is needed are developers who have had to build reliable and secure systems—who have gone through the pain of having to architect and enhance high availability, centrally managed transactional applications throughout several major releases, and who have had to endure security audits. The number of such individuals is too few to go around, so a wise organization will turn such a person into a mentor, instructor, evangelist, and reviewer of designs. This person should be embedded with each project to help the project architect and team leads with the goals of *dissemination of knowledge* to the rest of the programming team through seminars and brown bags and *review of designs.*

EMPLOY EXPERT REVIEWS FOR COMPONENTS REQUIRING VALIDATION. VALIDATION INCLUDES ENSURING THAT THE OVERALL ARCHITECTURE IS PRESERVED AND THAT BEST PRACTICES ARE FOLLOWED.

XP does not utilize design reviews. Instead, design meetings occur on a daily basis among the team members. This is a definite weakness for high-assurance applications because formal design reviews give external experts an opportunity to review a design. Such experts should include representatives from the various aspects of assurance that are of concern, such as security, manageability, and reliability.

In order to remedy this, the architect must learn to act on behalf of those experts by meeting with them on a regular basis to discuss the design and by absorbing and personally incorporating their concerns. This knowledge must also be conveyed to the project team over time, through the daily meetings.

The project architect should also identify the most sensitive layers and components (the "trusted computing base"), and a slightly separate development process should be used for those that includes regular design reviews and more controlled change, as discussed previously. The design reviews should include participation of outside experts. These experts must understand the application architecture prior to reviewing any aspect of the application design so that they are in a position to understand the design choices and approaches. Thus, they should meet with the project architect in advance of any design reviews for sensitive components and be briefed on the architecture.

For Components Requiring Validation, Make Design Artifacts a Business Feature

Because XP does not explicitly mandate documentation, but documentation is very necessary for a high assurance, maintainable application, a simple solution is to make certain design artifacts a "feature" and provide story cards for them. Thus, each enhancement to the application would include a story card for enhancing the documentation; or equivalently, the documentation work can be added to the story card for the new feature. Either approach works. The important thing is that the documentation that is required is agreed to in collaboration with the stakeholders, and is explicitly spelled out in a story.

This again helps to convert design into a continual process. Further, the widespread XP ethos that comments are unnecessary if code is well-written must be dispelled and replaced with a culture that promotes the use of quality code commenting.◆

◆ See Section 17.1, "Documentation."

RECOGNITION THAT ASSURANCE REQUIREMENTS CANNOT BE COMPLETELY TESTED USING FUNCTIONAL UNIT TESTING

XP does not preclude integration testing or other kinds of system-wide testing, but it places a heavy emphasis on unit testing—so much so that developers often get the idea that unit tests are sufficient and they see integration testing as merely running the entire unit test suite and then having users exercise the application—effectively skipping intermediate levels of testing. This is clearly inadequate if done.◆ XP's emphasis on unit testing must be augmented with additional kinds of testing.

◆ See Sections 3.2.2, "Testing," and 3.5, "Levels of Testing."

A testing strategy should include these elements:

1. Assurance function (feature) tests. These are no different from other kinds of feature tests except that they test security-related features. These tests should verify that each authorization rule in the application is correctly implemented, as well as each "feature" that provides security or reliability and that can be tested using an automatically-run test suite.
2. Architectural compliance validation tests or mechanisms, as described in the Chapter 3.
3. Penetration analysis, possibly including one or more actual penetration attempts by an independent party, either with (white-box) or without (black-box) knowledge of the system's internal design. White-box penetration attempts will tell you more about the system's true vulnerability.
4. Failure-response testing.

Do not use an assurance function suite as a replacement for a well-documented authorization rule set; if you do, you will have forgone any mechanism of communicating with the users about authorization requirements.

MAINTAIN CHECKLIST OF "DOS," "DON'TS," AND CONCERNS

Make sure that lessons that are learned during the course of the project are captured. Mistakes that have been made on a project are often made multiple times, so it is worth the effort to capture them.

XP projects often utilize a "wiki" Web site for capturing design-related discussion, notes, and "concerns" (design aspects that are postponed). This can provide a good forum for programmers to post "dos," "don'ts," and concerns of their own. The architect should and technical leads should use a controlled Web site for posting approved architecture, designs, "dos," "don'ts," and concerns.

19.4 Writing Corporate Assurance Guidelines

Many organizations attempt to encode security best practices into a document and have a separate document that mandates standards for the configuration and deployment of high-assurance applications. The idea is that by writing down a set of best standards, they have put the burden on the engineering staff to follow it, and if they do follow it, the organization should be confident that it is protected from application failures. Such guidelines are usually technically focused and not process focused: i.e., they often list general technical rules such as "change passwords every six months," "check for buffer overflows," and "document the job control steps for starting and stopping the application."

This approach to an organization-wide standard for any aspect of assurance has the following shortcomings:

1. The staff is not sure how to incorporate it into the software design or implementation process.
2. The staff does not understand most of it.
3. The staff is often not even aware of its existence, especially new staff.
4. There is often no provision for ensuring that it is followed at a software design level, especially with respect to security.
5. The rules are usually very general in their expression, so it is not clear how to implement them.

6. Different projects need to focus on different aspects of the guidelines, so it is not possible to blindly apply such guidelines: A careful consideration of the software project is needed, along with astute judgment about which principles should be addressed.
7. Any set of guidelines that is complete enough to cover any project that an organization might undertake would be nothing less than a full text on software and infrastructure assurance—and there already are texts on those subjects (such as this one).

Instead of developing a general-purpose technical guidelines document, it is more useful to develop an *organization-wide standard that is process focused.* Such a standard should provide guidance so that each project can develop an architecture and operations documents that are unique to its needs. In order to provide that guidance, a corporate standard should address these issues:

1. When (i.e., how to decide if) a project should develop architecture and operations documents.
2. What elements should be addressed in those documents. (Critical technical design considerations should be enumerated, such as the principles discussed in this book.)
3. Guidelines for determining what aspects are most critical (i.e., risk analysis guidelines).
4. Who should be responsible for those documents.
5. How the project should determine what methodological processes should be employed to ensure compliance.
6. References to assurance methodologies that are endorsed or encouraged.

Such a standard is *much more useful* and is less likely to become obsolete as technology changes. It also allows each project to develop its own guidelines and, in doing so, to *interpret* assurance concepts in terms of the chosen technologies, organization infrastructure, and requirements. Finally, by enumerating technical design considerations (item 2) and requiring the system architect to address each one, the organization is requiring the architect to consider each technical risk area and put their professional judgment in writing—even if it is to say that a particular area is "not applicable."

19.5 Software Releases

The release process itself needs to be documented and highly visible to all developers so that they understand the process. A good approach is to post a top-level diagram of the process on the project internal Web site.

19.5.1 Identifying Release Components

The technical team, project manager, and users must jointly decide which components should be independently released to users. The decision must consider technical issues related to component dependencies, as well as usage issues related to what components need to be upgraded from time to time and what components are shared by other systems that users use.

Each released component should have its own release number. Releases that merely fix bugs and promise full backward compatibility should be identified only by a minor release number. Large and complex systems often fall in between these two endpoints and retain compatibility in some areas but not others; in that case, the decision of whether to apply a minor or major version number is a matter of judgment of the degree of backward compatibility that the project is striving to retain.

The component's release notes should identify (1) all other components (by version) that the system has been tested with for compatibility and (2) all other components (by version) with which compatibility is expected, even if it has not been tested.

19.5.2 Configuration Management of Release Components

The source code of subsystems should not be part of the system-level baseline. Each subsystem should have its own baseline. The system baseline should consist of built releases of its constituent subsystems, along with any code and files that are specific to the system.

If any subsystem of a system is not in the system's CM baseline, it must be added—as a single packaged release object.

If work on a system release requires changes to multiple subcomponents (almost always the case), the CM system will have to be able to let a programmer work on multiple components at once. These changes can be done in the context of a system release, if desired, but there is really no advantage in doing so, because each subcomponent should have its own release. Note that it is not always possible to root all subcomponents under the same CM system hierarchy.

Release management should include approval by the project architect. The architect must evaluate each change from the perspective of (1) compliance with the architecture and architectural goals and (2) compatibility with users of the application, compatibility with other releases, and compliance with released system interfaces. The release manager should maintain awareness of all promised compatibilities and published interfaces, and in general be able to answer the question: "Who would be affected if we make a change to one of our interfaces?"

19.5.3 Building a Release

The output of a release process should be a single clearly identifiable set of artifacts that collectively comprises one and only one version (release number) of a system or component. The build that is used to create the release must be clearly identifiable, but the build number is an internal number for use by the development team and should not be communicated to users. The release is then provided to the various downstream test environments, beginning with the integration test environment.

Building a release typically consists of running a script that extracts a single build of each constituent component, executing a unit test suite, and executing a script that packages the release and places the completed release into a separate release area within the CM system.

There cannot be hard-coded environment values within the codebase. All such values need to be factored out into deployment configuration variables, either via configuration files, environment variables, or templatized values that are elaborated by the deployment process.

In order to ensure consistency of the release process across the various software systems used or developed by an organization, it is useful to have a separate team that specializes in release standards and to embed a member of that team within each project and make them responsible for creating the release build scripts.

The ultimate release manager is the project manager. A prospective release must be approved by the QC function to become an actual release. The release management function is responsible for ensuring that the build is suitable for submitting as a prospective release, based on whether it meets the release objectives and requirements and based on the prospects for passing the QC and test criteria. The release manager is also responsible for ensuring that the CM function and release build processes are complete and that the release process will produce a valid release with artifacts that are under full CM control.

19.5.4 Release Testing

Release testing requires a release to test, tests to run, test data to input to the tests, and a method of validating the results—which often utilizes expected result data. These various tests and data sets are constructed by the persons who are responsible for the particular tests, depending on the level of testing.

Production data should not be used for testing, except as an adjunct to the test suite. This is because production data has unknown coverage: Unless the production data set is examined, the extent to which it tests all application requirements is unknown. Production data also tends to change in a non-repeatable fashion. *Historic* production data can be used if it examined and its coverage is determined. This can be useful to assess assumptions about the quality of data and the legitimacy of the test suite.

Production data should not be used if the data is sensitive in any way; for example, if it contains sensitive data about actual users. Testers are not generally authorized to have access to this kind of data, across the broad scope of the entire set of production data.

PRINCIPLE: DO NOT USE PRODUCTION DATA AS A PRIMARY TEST SUITE.

The only exception is that it is generally advisable to use fairly recent subset of production data at some point to validate the application's test data by showing that the application has passed the test suite and *also* works with production data. The subset of production data to be used should be scrutinized to ensure that the testers can be allowed to have access to it. However, if use of production data uncovers problems, those problems should be identified and the primary test suite augmented rather than continuing to use the production data for tests. Dependence on production data is a liability that imperils a development project by linking it to the production process.

19.5.5 User Acceptance

There should always be an acceptance testing process. For the purposes of reliability and security, this should include some form of "certification test" (see "Certification" in Section 3.2.2) that certifies that the has been able to ensure a given level of stress with acceptable results. The acceptance process should specify the stress testing methods and levels and what degree of success is acceptable.

Having a well-defined user acceptance process is especially important for a high-assurance application because for such an application, the users' expectations are very high in terms of reliability and security, and users need to understand that high assurance does not mean 100% assurance: A failure during acceptance testing does not mean that the application has failed in its assurance goals.

If the application is being developed by an outside vendor, this is even more critical: otherwise, the vendor's work will never be done, because no system can pass continuing tests for reliability and security with no failures of any kind. Therefore, defining what level is acceptable is extremely important unless you want the vendor to be working forever and possibly for free—not the basis for a good relationship.

19.6 Deployment

Deployment is the process of (1) obtaining a packaged release, (2) extracting or moving the release into a target runtime environment, and (3) configuring the release for operation in that environment. *Deployment does not include any release-building activities.* Deployment is done on a fully built release.

Deployment should be done by the owners of the target runtime environment, perhaps with the assistance of a deployment team or technical team. However, it is important that the owners of the environment assume responsibility for the deployment rather than the developers of the release.

Deployment occurs several times during the development process of a system. This is because there are several target runtime environments having to do with various levels of testing. More specifically, when the development team produces a release, the release must be deployed into the integration test environment for testing and then again into any successive test or staging environments before it is finally deployed into the end user's environment. It is important to use the full deployment process for each environment because the deployment and configuration process, configuration files, environment assumptions, and deployment instructions are part of what is being tested—not merely the software code.

19.6.1 Patches

Patches are spot fixes and are changes that are installed without re-deploying an entire release.

Patches are very risky, but are sometimes necessary in order to quickly fix a problem. Patches are often made by an application support group, but can be made and issued by the development team as well. When a patch is issued, it should be followed shortly after by a full release that is fully tested and deployed in the normal ways.

19.7 Summary

A software development methodology has a huge impact on whether assurance requirements can be met. The most carefully-crafted requirements and the most elegant design are inadequate to ensure that the resulting system will be secure and reliable if the development process does not incorporate sufficient control.

Methodologies are cherished by their advocates. While some methodologies are appropriate or more cost-effective for particular domains of use, it is generally true that any methodology can be used to develop an appropriately secure and reliable business application, as long as certain constraints or requirements are placed on the process. This chapter presented constraints and requirements as a set of universal methodological assurance principles to aid in the crafting or adjustment of a software development methodology to ensure that assurance requirements *can* be met. The popular agile methodology known as "XP" was then examined, using these constraints and requirements as a metric to illustrate how assurance concerns can be addressed through an existing methodology that might seem at first glance to be counter to assurance principles. Finally, some miscellaneous issues related to release management are discussed.

This concludes this text.

19.8 Exercises

1. True or false: Agile development projects that develop high-assurance applications do not require an architecture specification effort because design is performed collaboratively and incrementally among programmers and technical leads. Explain.
2. True or false: Agile development projects that build high-assurance applications do not require design documents because the code is the documentation, and any textual documents would be too hard to maintain in sync with the code. Explain.

3. At what point should assurance requirements be defined in an agile project? At what point should compliance with assurance requirements be tested?
4. True or false: As a final check, an application should be tested using actual production data. Explain when, and to what degree this should be done, if at all.
5. True or false: A software release should consist only of deliverable items.
6. Consider the following excerpts from company-wide assurance guidelines:

   ...

   All applications should use 128-bit encryption for SSL.

   ...

   All application development projects should perform regression tests against their transaction tier.

   ...

   What potential problems do you see with these guidelines? How would you rewrite these guideline sections?
7. A deployment plan for a custom-developed application includes the following sections:
   1. Build release
   2. Test release
   3. Copy files to target system
   4. Smoke test

   What is likely to be problematic about this plan?

Answers and hints for these exercises can be found at `http://www.assuredbydesign.com/haa/`.

Chapter 20

Case Study: Transactional Integrity

20.1 Background

A Fortune 100 company had been undertaking the development of a Web-based Java application to be accessed via the Internet, backed by an Oracle database, with several external specialized application servers providing specific services. Application security was provided by Netegrity Siteminder. The system as it existed then is depicted structurally in Figure 20.1.

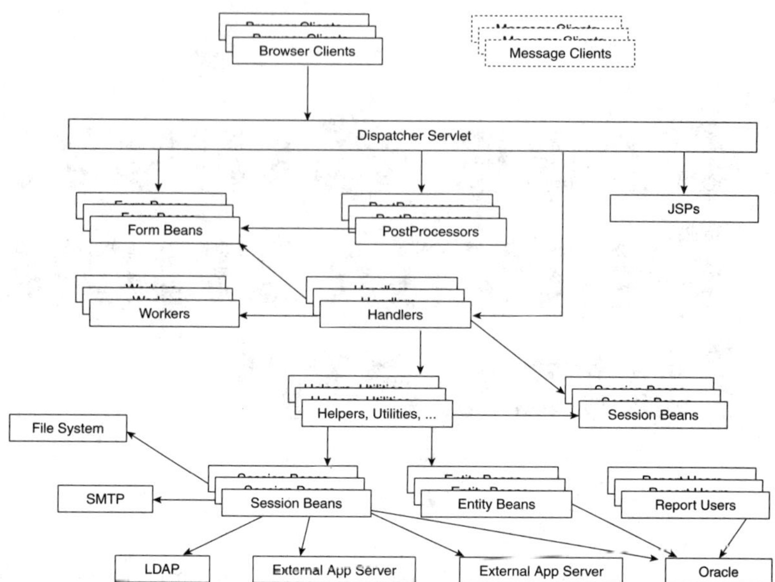

Figure 20.1
The application components.

The application was to be hosted and operated by an ASP. The marketing plan called for a gradual rollout of the application that would initially include a limited user community but eventually open to a broad user community with an anticipated load of thousands of concurrent users. In addition, there would be company-internal report users who would generate reports of the application's activity and user base. The plan at this time was that the report users would access the database directly using reporting tools.

The project's management team reported directly to a corporate vice president directly responsible for the project's success—in effect, a program manager. Under that person, the management team consisted of a marketing manager who was responsible for establishing business requirements, and a highly experienced technical director who oversaw the development work. The marketing manager's team of analysts worked directly with representatives from the business side of the company, as well as with vendors. That group had the most power in the sense that they had a direct relationship with the business side, so they had final say on decisions that were important to them—including technical and process decisions. The technical director also worked with vendors to arrange for resources and services as needed.

The company used an experienced integrator to provide the software engineering staff. That integrator's specialty was in the chosen technology. The software development team's collective experience level was relatively high. Developers averaged more than five years of work experience, and technical leads averaged more than ten. The team included DBAs, three technical leads, and several project managers. Work was divided up along four functional tiers, with each tier reporting to a project manager. There also were managers who were responsible for infrastructure and operations. In all, there were approximately 80 people directly working on the project.

Software development work was approximately one year along, and deployment of basic functionality was planned for a few months' later. The project had been using a RUP-like approach but was about to change to an agile approach.

Despite the experience of the implementation teams, the technical side of the management team had doubts about the robustness of the application and commissioned an independent technical audit of the application's design and implementation in order to discover problems before the application was launched. Therefore, they could not be faulted for the existence of these problems; rather, they should be credited with taking the initiative early to uncover potential problems and dealing with them.

Six weeks were allocated for the audit. The areas to be addressed included:

1. Overall application technical integrity and robustness.
2. Scalability and performance.
3. Application-level security.

The application-level security audit was augmented by another audit performed concurrently by a security technology consulting firm. That firm focused on infrastructure security. The results of its work were combined with the results of the application audit to produce a consolidated security report. Items 1 and 2 were addressed in an application audit results report.

The discussion here includes the results of the audit pertaining to item 1 mentioned previously. Item 2 is not included here because this book does not address scalability and performance, as explained in the Preface. Item 3 is discussed separately in the next case study.

20.2 Analysis Approach

The audit team requested and examined a snapshot of the application code and requested design documents and use cases. The design documents were found to be grossly out of date and were of limited value. The use cases were current, but were primarily of value only for reference on a few occasions because the primary concern of the audit team was technical robustness—not application functionality.

The audit team catalogued the Java packages in the application and identified the functionality of each. Risk areas were identified and tabulated based on the initial cursory examination, and these areas were then explored in depth.

The audit team followed up with questions for staff and for product vendors. Many discussions ensued regarding third-party product interfaces, what kinds of testing had been done, and what the application's functionality was expected to be.

20.3 Problems Found

Examination of the application revealed that the application had severe integrity issues that were pervasive and that had not been revealed in the kind of single-threaded functional testing that had been performed to date. The specific problems found are explained in the following sections.

20.3.1 Resource-Level Interfaces

The problems described in this section pertain to accesses to resources, including third-party or external subsystems.

Calling stateful objects from stateless objects. Stateful session beans in a third-party subsystem were being called from stateless session beans in the main system. (This was simply incorrect design.)

Lack of concurrency control. Concurrency control techniques were not used in situations in which external non-cooperating transactional third-party subsystems were accessed by transactions in the main application. Claims were made by the vendor of one of the third-party subsystems that the interface propagated transactions, when tests indicated otherwise. (See the principle "Validate External Components" in Section 11.3.1, "External Components or Systems.")

Inadequate error handling. Non-robust behavior when errors occurred during an access to an external subsystem, including file artifacts (orphaned files) and corrupt state. (See Section 12.2.4, "Thread Interruption.")

Inappropriate file accesses. EJBs were also being used to write files—which is illegal with respect to the EJB specifications unless it is done via an EJB container mechanism.

Inappropriate LDAP use. Use of LDAP as part of complex multi-resource (database) update transactions. (See Section 13.6, "Dealing with Non-Transactional Resources.") The development team thought that EJB management would provide transactional behavior over this resources.

Lack of recovery design. No procedures for recovery after failure or irregular shutdown had been designed as of yet. (See Section 2.3, "Writing Failure-Response Requirements.")

20.3.2 Web Application Transaction Encapsulation

The Web application code often performed multiple transactions when handling a single user request, with no provision for recovery or cleanup if some of the transactions completed but others did not. For example, the following code snippet (stripped down significantly) was found in a Web application request handler:

```
int orderNumber =
      OrderHelper.getOrder(user, ...);

// Update the order
OrderHelper.updateOrder(user, ...);

// Update the preferences
OrderHelper.updateOrder(user, ...);
```

The highlighted methods themselves perform multiple independent transactions. All this is taking place in a servlet request handler–outside of a transaction. When the transactions were tallied, it turned out that there were a total of *six independent transactional operations performed* when handling the user's single request.

In general, the application exhibited poor layering, with no clear indication of which objects perform transactions and no documented layer responsibility for error handling and recovery.

20.3.3 Multithreading

Utilities written to handle asynchronous functions, such as sending emails, exhibited unnecessary blocking of the application thread rather than using a queue-based design. There were also thread-locking errors, in that an application-defined lock was being checked from non-guarded[1] code.

20.3.4 Failure Testing

The application test suite included absolutely no failure testing. (See the principle "Test All Conceivable Failure Scenarios" in Section 13.12, "Transaction Testing and Validation Strategies.")

20.4 Remediation

The audit results were surprising to the development team and to management. They clearly did not expect that these kinds of problems existed. As a result, a special team was formed to perform remediation planning, consisting of six dedicated software architects and a project manager.

20.4.1 Other Factors

Recall that the audit effort had been initiated by the technical manager. It was an unspoken truth that even though this indicated good judgment on the part of the technical management, the

1 The Java guard mechanism is the *synchronized* keyword.

results could be interpreted in a negative way by the business side of the team. Despite this, the business was made aware that technical improvements needed to be made, but they did not understand the problems or why they happened, nor did they truly believe that there even was a problem. Technical management understood the problems, but was still on the hook for delivering functionality by a certain date. Therefore, development work could not be disrupted, because it would upset the schedule.

To complicate matters, the project was about to make a shift to the use of Extreme Programming (XP). This shift had been initiated by the business side—which had become convinced that it would help them to deliver functionality more quickly.

20.4.2 Actions

The remediation team operated independently from the ongoing application development effort, acting as a sort of "skunk works" for a while. During this time, the remediation team redesigned the core architecture of the application to address the issues identified. Some of the architectural changes included:

- Removal of LDAP as the authoritative source for user group and role data.
- Implementation of a transaction façade for all core application functions, according to the "Transaction Façade" pattern (see Section 13.9, "Layer Access Rules for Transactions").
- Elimination of reliance on transaction cooperation across backend resources.

The remediation team implemented these changes for a small vertical slice of the application, in a separate CVS code branch, which they synched weekly with the development branch. During this time, the project actually made several limited releases to its initial small-scale user community.

When the changes were complete, the remediation team worked with the project technical leads to plan for merging the changes into the main code branch. The merge was executed over a weekend, and the application was tested. There were essentially no problems, and the total lost development team time was two to three days, during which project programmers familiarized themselves with the new design and checked out the changes. The total calendar time for the remediation thus far was approximately six months.

The success of this convinced the business management that the remediation team was credible and would not disrupt the release schedule, and they were given the authority to go forward with implementing the new architecture more broadly and instructing the development teams how to apply the new architecture. An internal Web site was developed that explained the new architecture, and work proceeded to implement the new architecture across the entire application in parallel with ongoing development.

20.5 Reflection

The problems that were uncovered in this study are highly typical for first-release Web-based applications. Indeed, it took only two or three days to identify the problems from prior experience, and the remaining six weeks of the audit were used to document the problems and develop feasible and appropriate recommendations for remediation. It is significant that the problems that were uncovered were systemic and architectural and that an experienced development team had produced them.

CHAPTER 21

CASE STUDY: APPLICATION SECURITY

21.1 Background

This case study presents the results of the application-level security audit of the Web application described in the prior case study in Chapter 20, "Case Study Transactional Integrity."

During the course of the project, the company spun off to an investor the application that was under development, including the intellectual property and entire development effort. The prospective buyer required its own security audit of the product. Therefore, a second independent audit was undertaken, focused only on security. Because the repairs that were underway as a result of the first audit had not been completed, the auditor found essentially the same security problems as before. Fortunately, the work that was underway could be explained and was sufficient to satisfy the buyer on those issues.

In addition, for the second audit, the legal counsel of the investor provided the auditor with a supplementary list of questions regarding the system's treatment of sensitive data from a legal, business, and workflow perspective. The application did not fare so well on these questions (this is discussed next), but these issues were clear cut and fixable by adding application requirements, so the deal was consummated.

Netegrity Siteminder Web Agent provided user authentication using form-based authentication. User identities were stored in an LDAP directory, along with a mapping between users and the roles they could have. Siteminder used this identity repository to authenticate users and then insert the user's authenticated identity into the HTTP request as header values. Siteminder then forwarded the HTTP request to a custom-written login servlet that extracted the HTTP headers and inserted the user's identity into the user's Web application session. The login servlet also obtained the user's permitted roles from the LDAP directory and inserted these into the user's Web application session.

Siteminder also provided URL-based resource protection based on user role and limited the user to one authentication session per browser. The latter prevents two users from logging in (in succession from the same workstation) and having the second session inadvertently inherit the role or capabilities of the first session.

When the user was logged in, the user was able to access Web application features. The Web application code tested the user's role, as well as additional user-specific data, when determining whether a particular action was allowed.

The Web application accessed EJBs, using a fixed set of pre-allocated EJB connection pools. The EJBs in turn accessed an Oracle database and external third-party application servers, again using a fixed set of pre-allocated connection pools.

21.2 Analysis Approach

The application was examined from four perspectives:

1. Application design.
2. Application-level penetration analysis.
3. Completeness and correctness of authorization.
4. Network and infrastructure.

The discussion here focuses on perspectives 1 through 3.

21.3 Problems Found

Examination of the application's design and implementation found that its security level was adequate for a restricted non-malicious user community–but no more. The specific problems found are explained in the following sections.

21.3.1 Defense-in-Depth

Authorization for access to core transactions was based on the perimeter provided by Siteminder, and on rules embedded in Web application request handlers. This made it impossible to reuse authorization rules to protect a message-based interface that was under development in a parallel effort. Thus, the principle "Define Authorization Models Alongside the Resources They Protect" (see Section 7.12, "Association of a Resource and Its Authorization Model") was not adhered to. In addition, it was found that the Siteminder policy rules were incomplete and that some pages could be accessed by users who should not be able to. Denial by default was not configured, violating the principle "Default to the Most Secure (Least Permission) Level" (see Section 7.11, "Default Policies").

21.3.2 Contextual Data

There was no concept of secure session data (see the principle of "Identify and Assess All Context Bindings," described in Section 7.17.1). It took only fifteen minutes of examination to find a security flaw to demonstrate this: the use of a hidden tag within a Web page to identify the user's role.

21.3.4 Data Classification

There was no concept of classification of the data accessed by users (see the principle "Segment Data and Resources According to Risk or Sensitivity" in Chapter 8, "Compartmentalization and Classification." Highly sensitive data about the application's users was stored within the database and accessible to any administrator.

21.3.5 Auditability of Authorization Rules

Authorization rules were spread all over the place, in an ad-hoc manner determined by each individual programmer, violating the principle of "Authorization Rules Should Be Auditable" (see Section 7.4, "Auditability of Policy Coverage"). As a result, no one could say whether all the authorization rules were implemented. An examination of the code revealed that only about 80% of the authorization rules actually were implemented–to everyone's surprise. For example, it was possible for users of certain roles to access–and in some cases modify–several categories of important sensitive information belonging to (and private to) other users of those roles.

When the original audit was performed, the PKI-related features of the application had not yet been developed. By the time of the second audit, they had been. Thus, the second audit uncovered these additional issues related to the use of signed documents:

- Acceptance of signing certificates signed by any CA–or even self-signed.
- Failure to securely map signing signature owner identity against application user identity.
- No verification of signatures when signed documents are accessed.

Further, as part of the second security audit, the legal department provided the auditing team with a supplementary list of questions regarding the system. The questions were designed to uncover gaps in the system's security from a business, legal, and workflow perspective. The audit revealed that almost 50% (31 out of 53) of these questions had negative answers, indicating severe shortfalls in the application's authorization model—at least as implemented. Indeed, *a great many authorization rules were found to be unspecified by use cases.*

21.3.6 Revocation of Permissions

The session-based persistence of a user's role association had the result that a user's permissions endured as long as the user's session endured—even if the user's access was administratively revoked during the session. Thus, there was no way to "shut off" a user who was currently logged on.

21.3.7 Connections to Resources

Some backend resources were connected to without authentication, violating the principle of "Securely Connect to All Resources" (see Section 7.20.4, "Resource Connections").

21.3.8 Credential Management

There were ten classes of credentials in the application and eighteen classes of infrastructure-related or administrative credentials, with no plan for securing these or limiting access to them based on a least-privilege and separation of duties. (See the principle "Employ Secure Credential Practices" in Section 9.2.) Also, user IDs and passwords were being emailed to users—a very vulnerable form of credential distribution.

21.3.9 Logging

The logging system was carelessly designed, with no documented approach with regard to limiting the kinds of information logged or who should have access to the logs. (See the principle "Ensure That Logs Are Secure, Unalterable, and Reliable" in Section 7.16.2, "Log Design.")

21.4 Remediation

The security problems identified by the first audit were addressed by a separate remediation team, consisting of two full-time architects under the same manager as the transactional integrity remediation team. The two remediation teams worked closely together to design and implement changes that overlapped, because many of the problems being addressed by the two teams were related. (Indeed, that is a primary thesis of this book.)

When the second audit occurred, the security improvements had been designed and were being prototyped. The second audit presented a kind of crisis, however, because an important business transaction hinged on whether the issues uncovered could be addressed. In order to quickly respond to the second audit results, approaches were examined that might provide some immediate coverage of the security issues. So-called "application protection proxy" (APP) products were examined, and several of them were selected for in-depth evaluation.

Unfortunately, a hands-on evaluation over a period of several weeks revealed that the APP products would not add much value for this application because they were easily defeated by client-side scripting that dynamically generated URLs and tags in the browser client, and the application made heavy use of this technique. To be able to use the APP products effectively would have required rewriting the entire user interface portion of the application.

The security remediation team, therefore, addressed the identified issues by responding with a written report, identifying the fixes that were underway and how each issue would be addressed. This was sufficient to satisfy the investor.

21.4.1 Actions Taken

The measures taken included:

- A definitive list of all authorization rules was tabulated by the business. All existing rules were removed from the code and re-implemented in an authorization layer, using the "Dynamic Condition Set" design pattern described in Section 7.10, "Dynamic Conditions."

- All transactional business objects were re-implemented using the "Authorization As a Precondition" design pattern described in Section 7.21, "Home-Grown Authorization."
- Credentialed access was implemented for all backend resource connections (see the principle "Securely Connect to All Resources" in Section 7.20.4, "Resource Connections").
- Sensitive data was identified (classified), and database-level encryption was implemented for these columns (see the principle "Segment Data and Resources According to Risk or Sensitivity" in Chapter 8).
- Plans for improved system administration and credential management were developed (see the principle "Enforce Separation of Duties" in Section 8.1.1, "Role Separation").
- Plans for secure logging were developed (see the principle "Securely Log Sensitive Data Rather Than Discard It" in Section 7.15.2, "Propagation of Unauthorized Information").
- An identity propagation mechanism was developed in order to implicitly propagate and present the authenticated user identity to the transactional business objects. (See the patterns "Implicit Context and Explicit Context" in Section 18.2.5, "Providing Context.") This provided a trusted context to the authorization mechanism that had been added to protect these objects. The identity propagation mechanism used advanced features of Siteminder and BEA Weblogic, as well as the Java Authentication and Authorization Service (JAAS) API.
- The message-based subsystem that was under development was able to directly utilize the authorization system and rules by merely providing the user's identity. (See the principle "Avoid Duplication of Access Rules" in Section 7.4.) Because WebMethods was used as the conduit for messages and the messages were in XML, the user identity was obtained from validated portions of the messages.

- Requirements ("stories") were written to address shortfalls in application requirements related to proper use of digital signatures and certificates.

21.5 Reflection

It is significant that the use cases developed for the application fell so far short of the actual security requirements of the application. The implication is that special attention needs to be paid to security requirements or they will be omitted to a significant degree.

It is also significant that many of the security problems were architectural and had to be fixed through a protracted effort. Despite a great deal of thought, no spot-fix approach or "magic bullet" product could be found that would address the issues raised by the audit. It was fortunate that the problems had been identified and fixes begun before the second audit—or the transaction involving the sale of the system might have not completed.

CHAPTER 22

CASE STUDY: MANAGEABILITY

22.1 Background

A Fortune 100 company had developed a complex set of database applications some years before. These applications provided a set of extremely mission-critical business functions that were also time-critical. Initially, the applications worked well, but over time the applications grew in complexity with different parts of the application being maintained by different groups. The applications became increasingly unreliable, and the failures did not seem to fit a consistent pattern and often were undiagnosed.

The failures affected multiple prominent parts of the organization, resulting in lots of finger-pointing and confusion as to what the source of the problem was. As a result, an independent assessment was undertaken to find the cause of the problems. The scope of the assessment included organization structure and responsibility, efficacious use of technology, development and testing processes, configuration management, operational processes, user support processes, and application performance. The discussion here will focus on the use of technology, the development and testing processes, and operational and user support processes.

By the time the assessment was undertaken, the applications included PERL scripts, BASH scripts, Java applications, C++ applications, and CORBA—all accessing Sybases databases and running on shared Solaris E6000 or similar systems.

22.2 Analysis Approach

The assessment began with interviews of managers, followed by interviews of their staff for detailed information. Code snapshots were requested, as were problem reports for the preceding six-month period. A software process flow and data flow was constructed incrementally, and follow-up interviews were conducted to address various technical questions. Eventually, all pertinent artifacts were identified, and most of the requested code modules had been obtained—although not without considerable stonewalling by the technical teams.

It was important to obtain the support of the technical parts of the organization because they would eventually play an important role in remediation, so an effort was made to establish trust by showing a willingness to point out the challenges that they faced in their work while at the same time identifying the problems that they had created.

The final assessment results were documented in a report, with recommendations at both tactical and strategic levels, and meetings were conducted to discuss the results with all of the stakeholders.

22.3 Problems Found

The problems that were found were at all levels. There were major systemic problems that resulted from the organization's structure and division of responsibility, as well as significant process problems and particular staff-related problems–in particular, very substantial key-person dependencies. The technical problems were, of course, a result of these higher-level problems, but the following discussion focuses on the technical and process problems.

22.3.1 Too Much Concentration of Knowledge

A very small group of people who had developed the code knew how things actually worked. This small group was no longer able to support the applications because their success in building the applications caused them to be drafted into other projects that required saving. Most of the maintenance and support team was effectively in the dark due to staff turnover, the lack of design documentation, and the complexity and obscurity of the implementation.

22.3.2 Insufficiently Robust Development Processes for a Mission-Critical System

The processes for configuration management and migration across testing and live environments were highly inadequate. Almost everything was done ad-hoc by technical "gurus," with email as the only traceability mechanism.

22.3.3 Too Much Focus on Productivity at the Expense of Reliability

The business side applied immense pressure to add functionality while expecting high reliability, yet expected that reliability was a natural byproduct of development and did not allocate sufficient resources or priorities to address reliability.

22.3.4 Poorly Defined External Interfaces

The applications relied on large amounts of data from many external systems that were operated by outside companies. The interfaces to these external systems did not have definitive specifications: Specifications were either incomplete, non-existent, or empirically derived.

22.3.5 Many Single Points of Failure

The primary application process was designed as a pipeline, with no failure resiliency built in. If anything went wrong, the entire process had to stop. Restarting from specific checkpoints was possible, but no processing could continue unless all problems were resolved. This was a result of the implementation and not due to the nature of the calculations.

22.3.6 Poor Encapsulation of Function

The code exhibited grossly inadequate encapsulation of business functionality. The use of scripting languages such as PERL exacerbated this problem, making it impossible to have unit tests.

22.3.7 Inability to Perform Effective Problem Diagnosis

Support staff were unable to diagnose problems in an efficient and effective manner due to these factors:

- Inadequate or inappropriate error handling by applications and a failure to save forensic information.
- Meaningless or misleading error messages, such as "connection failure" when the problem was invalid data.
- Massive amounts of data written to logs, with no prior consideration of the organization of this information.
- Every error resulted in a telecommunications page (via a paging gateway) to support staff, with no discrimination regarding what kinds of errors should be reported. Upper management was paged automatically when problems were unresolved after a specified amount of time.

- Application code error handling was grossly inadequate for the kind of application. For example, a connection failure might be transient due to the reboot of a server, but the application would give up. Problems in remote connections resulted in orphaned objects and connection pools that ran out of resources instead of closing bad connections and creating new ones in a robust manner.
- There was no scheme for logging entry and exit from critical routines, so when errors occurred, there was insufficient information available to report where the application was in the process.

22.3.8 Lack of Monitorability

There was no way to monitor the progress of the application, except by scrutinizing intermediate output files and checking for errors.

22.3.9 Unsupported Concurrency

Use of scripting made business logic non-reentrant. Scripts often performed thousands of independent database transactions. Meanwhile, if processing schedules slipped, unintended concurrent access could result from other processes—corrupting data.

22.3.10 Overly Complex Administration

The applications were not designed with operators in mind. Operating them required very complex and interdependent configurations, with no dashboard or tool to provide visibility into the configuration. Given the large number of interoperating applications, errors were inevitable.

22.3.11 Lack of Adequate Regression Testing

There was no automated regression test suite. Testing was performed by running the current day's data and comparing it manually with small sets of calculations done through independent means as well as comparing it with the prior day's data to see if it "looked right." This approach was a byproduct of the application domain (financial services and accounting), which has a tradition of validating data instead of processes.

22.3.12 No Specification of Failure Handling Requirements

There were no requirements documented for how the application should behave when something went wrong, so it was no wonder that there were no provisions in the application for failure resiliency. This was largely a result of the fact that the problem response team was not an authoritative player in the requirements definition process.

22.3.13 Absence of Failure Testing

There was no failure test suite. Failures were viewed as "bugs" and troubleshot, rather than planned for. In a complex environment involving many independent systems and networks, failure resiliency is critical and connection or other component failures cannot be treated as extraordinary by applications.

22.3.14 Inadequate Design or Design Documentation

Design documents were few and far between and out of date.

22.4 Remediation

Organizational changes were recommended and implemented, but the focus here is on the technical problems and software development and maintenance processes. The recommendations and ensuing remediation activities included the following:

1. Migrate logic from PERL and BASH scripts to a programming language supporting encapsulation of function.
2. Design an error handling and reporting strategy using the pattern "Using Checked Exceptions for All Lifecycle Errors" (see Section 18.2.1, "Ensuring That All Situations Are Handled").

3. Design an application context propagation approach and mechanism using the pattern "Application-Based Propagation of Client Context" (see Section 18.2.5, "Providing Context").
4. Design an application event assessment and reporting approach and mechanism using the pattern "Adding Manageability Aspects to the Exception Base Class" (see Section 18.2.6, "Providing Sufficient Information").
5. Design an approach for generating messages at critical processing points to enable monitorability. (See the pattern "Heartbeat" in Section 16.4.1, "Heartbeats," the pattern "Embedded Progress Interpreter" in Section 16.4.2, "Progress Events," and the principle "Log Only at Predetermined Layer Interfaces" in Section 18.2.2, "Where to Catch and Log.")
6. Design an application management and operation console.
7. Establish a regression test suite (see the principle "Build a Regression Test Suite for the Application's Transactions" in Section 13.12, "Transaction Testing and Validation Strategies").
8. Enhance the development process to require a design document (see the principle "Ensure That Architectural Concepts and Decisions Are Documented and Disseminated" in Section 19.2, "Universal Methodological Principles"), and to require that component specifications must include failure response requirements (see the principle "Ensure That All Implied or Assumed Requirements Are Identified" in Section 19.2).
9. Enhance the configuration management processes and formalize the separation of environments (see the principle "Ensure That There Exists Full Configuration Management of All Artifacts" in Section 19.2).
10. Establish a process, including independent design reviews, that includes all stakeholders (see the principle "Ensure That Design Is Reviewed by Different Areas of Expertise" in Section 19.2), including the operational and response teams.

22.5 Reflection

This case study is an excellent example of a situation in which an application that is developed by a small team can degrade over time. It is also an example of the problems faced by support staff in complex environments in which there are many systems that need to be maintained and often restarted, upgraded, or reconfigured. Basically, applications built for small close-knit environments do not scale to larger and more complex environments. Increasing scale needs to include provisions for enhancing the processes as well as enhancing the applications, their resiliency, and their ability to be monitored.

Appendix A

References

Chapter 1

1	Ganssle	*The Art of Designing Embedded Systems*, Jack G. Ganssle. Butterworth-Heinemann, 2000.
2	Cohen	*Java Testing and Design*, Frank Cohen. Prentice Hall, 2004. Available online at `http://www.pushtotest.com/Docs/javatestand design.html`.
3	Meyer	*Object-Oriented Software Construction*, 2nd Edition, Bertrand Meyer. Prentice Hall, 1997.
4	Linden	"Operating System Structures to Support Secure and Reliable Software," Theodore A. Linden. Institute for Computer Sciences and Technology, National Bureau of Standards, Washington D.C. August 1976.
5	Wallace and Ippolito	"A Framework for the Development and Assurance of High Integrity Software," Wallace and Ippolito. December 1994. Available online at `http://hissa.nist.gov/publications/sp223/`.
6	Kirby, Archer, and Heitmeyer	"SCR: A Practical Approach to Building a High and Assurance COMSEC System," Kirby, Archer, Heitmeyer. Presented at ACSAC '99, Phoenix, AZ, December 6-10, 1999. Available online at `http://chacs.nrl.navy.mil/publications/CHACS/1999/1999archer-acsac99.pdf`.
7	National Computer Security Center	Department of Defense Trusted Computer System Evaluation Criteria (TCSEC). National Computer Security Center, December 1985. DOD-5200.28-STD, Orange Book.

8	Boudra	"Report on rules of system composition: Principles of secure system design," P. Boudra, Jr. Technical report, National Security Agency, Information Systems Security Organization, Office of Infosec Systems Engineering, I9 Technical Report 1-93, Library No. S-240, 330, March 1993. For Official Use Only.
9	Saltzer and Schroeder	"The protection of information in computer systems," J.H. Saltzer and M.D. Schroeder. Proceedings of the IEEE, 63(9):1278-1308, September 1975.
10	Ozier	"GASSP: Generally Accepted Systems Security Principles," W. Ozier. Technical report, International Information Security Foundation, June 1997. See `http://web.mit.edu/security/www/gassp1.html`.
11	Neumann	CHATS (Neumann). See `http://www.csl.sri.com/users/neumann/chats4.html`.
12	Levitt, Neumann, and Robinson	"The SRI Hierarchical Development Methodology (HDM) and its Application to the Development of Secure Software," K. Levitt, P. Neumann, and L. Robinson. National Bureau of Standards, Computer Science and Technology. July 1980.
13	OMG	OMG UML Specification. See `http://www.omg.org/uml`.

Chapter 2

1	Musa	*Software Reliability Engineering: More Reliable Software Faster and Cheaper*, 2nd Edition, John D. Musa. ISBN 1-4184-9387-2. Printed on demand. See `http://members.aol.com/JohnDMusa/book.htm`.
2	Weil	"Security breach forces Barclays to temporarily close online bank," News Story by Nancy Weil, IDG News Service, August 01, 2000, published in *Computerworld*. Available online at `http://www.computerworld.com/industrytopics/financial/story/0,10801,47896,00.html`.
3	Haurant	"Online bank suffers security glitch," by Sandra Haurant, November 5, 2004, published in *The Guardian*. Available online at `http://www.guardian.co.uk/Money/onlinebanking/story/0,13813,1344364,00.html`.
4	Howard	*Writing Secure Code*, Michael Howard. Microsoft Press, 2002.
5	BITS	BITS Certification is described at `http://www.bitsinfo.org/fslab.html`.
6	AICPA	American Institute for Certified Public Accountants (AICPA).
7	Common Criteria	Common Criteria is described at `http://www.commoncriteriaportal.org/`. See also `http://csrc.nist.gov/cc`.
8	National Security Agency	National Information Assurance Certification and Accreditation Process (NIACAP). 2000.

9	National Computer Security Center	"Introduction to Certification and Accreditation Concepts," January 1994, NCSC-TG-029. Available online at http://www.radium.ncsc.mil/tpep/library/rainbow/NCSC-TG-029.pdf.
10	National Computer Security Center	"Trusted Product Evaluation Questionnaire," NCSC-TG-019 Version-2, 2 May 1992, National Computer Security Center. Available online at http://www.radium.ncsc.mil/tpep/library/rainbow/NCSC-TG-019.2.html.
11	Musa	*Software Reliability Engineering: More Reliable Software Faster and Cheaper*, 2nd Edition, John D. Musa. ISBN 1-4184-9387-2. Printed on demand. See http://members.aol.com/JohnDMusa/book.htm.
12	Musa	*Software Reliability Engineering: More Reliable Software Faster and Cheaper*, 2nd Edition, John D. Musa. ISBN 1-4184-9387-2. Printed on demand. See http://members.aol.com/JohnDMusa/book.htm.

Chapter 3

1	Bishop	*Computer Security: Art and Science*, Matt Bishop. Boston: Addison-Wesley, 2003.
2	Neumann, Boyer, Feiertag, Levitt, and Robinson	"A Provably Secure Operating System: The System, Its Applications, and Proofs," 2nd Edition (Report CSL-116), P. G. Neumann, R.S. Boyer, R.J. Feiertag, K.N. Levitt, and L. Robinson. Computer Science Laboratory, SRI International, Menlo Park, California, 1980. Available online at http://www.csl.sri.com/neumann/psos/psos80.pdf.
3	Roshandel, Schmerl, Medvicdovic, Garlan, and Zhang	"Understanding Tradeoffs Among Different Architectural Modeling Approaches." R. Roshandel, B. Schmerl, N. Medvidovic, D. Garlan, and D. Zhang. In Proc. 4th Working IEEE/IFIP Conference on Software Architecture, 2004. Available online at: http://www-2.cs.cmu.edu/afs/cs/project/able/ftp/WICSA4-scrover/paper.pdf
4	Dustin	*Effective Software Testing*, Elfriede Dustin. Pearson Education, 2003.
5	National Institute of Standards and Technology	"Software Errors Cost U.S. Economy $59.5 Billion Annually; NIST Assesses Technical Needs of Industry to Improve Software-Testing." NIST press release. See http://www.nist.gov/public_affairs/releases/n02-10.htm.
6	Dustin	*Effective Software Testing*, Elfriede Dustin. Pearson Education, 2003.
7	Parasoft	Parasoft's AEP Methodology. See http://www.parasoft.com/jsp/products/article.jsp?label=what_is_aep.
8	OMG	OMG UML Specification. See http://www.omg.org/uml.
9	Yacoub and Ammar	*Pattern-Oriented Analysis and Design*, Yacoub and Ammar. Addison-Wesley, 2004.
10	Jürjens	"UMLsec: Extending UML for Secure Systems Development," Jan Jürjens. UML 2002, Dresden, September 30-October 4, 2002.

11	Jürjens	Secure Systems Development with UML, Jan Jürjens. Springer-Verlag, 2004.
12	OMG	"UML Profile for Modeling Quality of Service and Fault Tolerance Characteristics and Mechanisms." September 16, 2004. OMG adopted specification. Available online at `http://www.omg.org/cgi-bin/apps/doc?ptc/04-09-01.pdf`.
13	Stavely	Toward Zero-Perfect Programming. Allan Stavely. 1999.
14	Gleick	"A Bug and a Crash" by James Gleick, published in *The New York Times* but available online at `http://www.around.com/ariane.html`.
15	Musa	Software Reliability Engineering: More Reliable Software Faster and Cheaper, 2nd Edition, John D. Musa. ISBN 1-4184-9387-2. Printed on demand. See http://members.aol.com/JohnDMusa/book.htm.
16	Eiffel Software	"Building bug-free O-O software: An introduction to Design by Contract™." See `http://www.eiffel.com/doc/manuals/technology/contract/`.
17	Meyer	*Object-Oriented Software Construction*, 2nd Edition, Bertrand Meyer. Prentice Hall, 1997. (re. design by contract)
18	Leavens, Leino, Poll, Ruby, and Jacobs	"JML: Notations and tools supporting detailed design in Java," Gary T. Leavens, K. Rustan M. Leino, Erik Poll, Clyde Ruby, and Bart Jacobs. In OOPSLA '00 Companion, Minneapolis, Minnesota, pp. 105-106. Copyright ACM, 2000. Also Department of Computer Science, Iowa State University, TR #00-15, August 2000. See `http://www.cs.iastate.edu/~leavens/JML/`.
19	Farias	"Towards a security aspect for Java," Andrés Farías. Thesis, February 4, 2001, Vrije Universiteit Brussels—Belgium, Faculty of Sciences.
20	Eclipse	Eclipse main Web site: `http://www.eclipse.org`.
21	Cantrell	Macker Java static code analysis tool: `http://innig.net/macker/`.
22	Chen and Wagner	"MOPS: An Infrastructure for Examining Security Properties of Software." Hao Chen and David Wagner. University of California at Berkeley, 2002. [re. Defining rules for verification of secure design principles.]
23	Neumann, Boyer, Feiertag, Levitt, and Robinson	"A Provably Secure Operating System: The System, Its Applications, and Proofs," 2nd Edition (Report CSL-116), P.G. Neumann, R.S. Boyer, R.J. Feiertag, K.N. Levitt, and L. Robinson. Computer Science Laboratory, SRI International, Menlo Park, California, 1980. Available online at `http://www.csl.sri.com/neumann/psos/psos80.pdf`.
24	SRI International	The Prototype Verification System (PVS) home page can be found at `http://pvs.csl.sri.com/`.

25	Neumann and Feiertag	"PSOS Revisited," P.G. Neumann and R.J. Feiertag. In Proceedings of the 19th Annual Computer Security Applications Conference (ACSAC 2003), Las Vegas, Nevada, 2003. Available online through `http://www.acsac.org/` or at `http://www.csl.sri.com/users/neumann/psos03.pdf`.
26	Fong	See *Proof Linking: A Modular Verification Architecture for Mobile Code Systems*. PhD Dissertation by Philip W. L. Fong, School of Computing Science, Simon Fraser University, Burnaby, BC, Canada V5A 1S6, January 2004. Available online at `http://www2.cs.uregina.ca/~pwlfong/Pub/dissertation.pdf`.
27	Aldrich, Jonathan	"Using Types to Enforce Architectural Structure," Jonathan Aldrich. PhD Thesis, University of Washington, 2003. See also `http://archjava.fluid.cs.cmu.edu/`.
28	Garlan, Monroe, and Wile	"Acme: Architectural Description of Component-Based Systems," by David Garlan, Robert T. Monroe, and David Wile. In Foundations of Component-Based Systems, Gary T. Leavens and Murali Sitaraman (eds), Cambridge University Press, 2000, pp. 47-68. Available online at `http://www-2.cs.cmu.edu/~able/publications/acme-fcbs/`.
29	Baker and Hsieh	"Maya: Multiple Dispatch Syntax Extension in Java," Jason Baker and Wilson C. Hsieh. In Proceedings of the 2002 Conference on Programming Language Design and Implementation. Berlin, Germany, June 2002. Available online at `http://www.cs.utah.edu/flux/papers/pldi02-maya-base.html`. 172 Advanced Development Methods "Controlled Chaos: Living on the Edge," Advanced Development Methods, Inc. Available online at `http://www.controlchaos.com/ download/Living%20on%20the%20Edge.pdf`.
30	Bahrach and Playford	"The Java Syntactic Extender (JSE)," Jonathan Bachrach and Keith Playford. Presented at OOPSLA-01. See `http://jse.sourceforge.net/`.
31	Tatsubori, Chiba, Killijian, and Itano	"OpenJava: A Class-based Macro System for Java," Michiaki Tatsubori, Shigeru Chiba, Marc-Orivier Killijian, and Kozo Itano. In *Reflection and Software Engineering*, W. Cazzola, R.J. Stroud, and F. Tisato, Eds., LNCS 1826, Springer-Verlag, pp. 119-135, July 2000. See `http://openjava.sourceforge.net/`.
32	TXL	The TXL Language. See `http://www.txl.ca`.
33	Mills	Harlan Mills, "The new math of computer programming," ACM Communications, vol. 18, 1, pp. 43-48, January 1975.
34	Swiderski and Snyder	*Threat Modeling*, Frank Swiderski and Window Snyder. Microsoft, 2004.
35	Cantrell	Macker Java static code analysis tool: `http://innig.net/macker/`.
36	PMD	PMD. See `http://pmd.sourceforge.net/`.

37	Viega, Mutdosch, Felten, and McGraw	Statically Scanning Java Code for Security Vulnerabilities. John Viega, Tom Mutdosch, Gary McGraw, and Edward W. Felten. IEEE Software, September/October 2000 (Vol. 17, No. 5), pp. 68-74.
38	OMG	OMG MDA specifications. See `http://www.omg.org/mda`.
39	Hu and Gill	"Patterns in Flexible Server Application Frameworks," James C. Hu and Christopher D. Gill. PLoP 2000. See `http://jerry.cs.uiuc.edu/~plop/plop2k/proceedings/Hu/Hu.pdf`.
40	Yacoub and Ammar	*Pattern-Oriented Analysis and Design*, Yacoub and Ammar. Addison-Wesley, 2004.
41	Abi-Antoun, Aldrich, Garlan, Schmerl, and Nahas	"Semi-Automated Incremental Synchronization between Conceptual and Implementation Level Architectures," by Marwan Abi-Antoun, Jonathan Aldrich, David Garlan, Bradley Schmerl, and Nagi Nahas. 2005. (Submitted for publication.) Available online at `http://www-2.cs.cmu.edu/afs/cs/project/able/ftp/Submissions/acme-ajava.pdf`.
42	Yacoub and Ammar	*Pattern-Oriented Analysis and Design*, Yacoub and Ammar. Addison-Wesley, 2004.
43	Dustin	*Effective Software Testing*, Elfriede Dustin. Pearson Education, 2003
44	Trowbridge	"Integration Patterns," David Trowbridge, et al. Microsoft, 2004. Available online at `http://msdn.microsoft.com/library/default.asp?url=/library/en-us/dnpag/html/intpatt.asp`.
45	Pettichord	"Design for Testability," by Brett Pettichord. Presented at the Pacific Northwest Software Quality Conference, Portland, Oregon, October 2002. Available online at `http://www.io.com/~wazmo/papers/design_for_testability_PNSQC.pdf`.

Chapter 4

1	Neumann	CHATS (Neumann). See `http://www.csl.sri.com/users/neumann/chats4.html`.
2	Bishop	*Computer Security: Art and Science*, Matt Bishop. Boston: Addison-Wesley, 2003, pp.501.
3	Hughes	Published in *Maintenance Resources Online Magazine*, January 2000. Article available online at `http://www.reliability.com/articles/article32.htm`.
4	Avizienis	"The N-Version Approach to Fault-Tolerant Software," A. Avizienis, *IEEE Transactions on Software Engineering*, Vol. SE—11 (12), pp. 1491-1501, 1985.
5	Vouk, McAllister, and Kim	"An Empirical Evaluation of Consensus Voting and Consensus Recovery Block Reliability in the Presence of Failure Correlation," M.A. Vouk, D.F. McAllister, D.E. Eckhardt, and Kalhee Kim. *Journal of Computer and Software Engineering*, Vol1(4), pp. 367-388, 1993.

6	Microsoft	*Improving Web Application Security: Threats and Countermeasures*, Microsoft Corporation. Chapter 2.
7	Compuware	CompuWare's CARS methodology. See `http://www.compuware.com/library/lm/3671_ENG_HTML.asp`.
8	Swiderski and Snyder	*Threat Modeling*, Frank Swiderski and Window Snyder. Microsoft, 2004.
9	Neumann	CHATS (Neumann). See `http://www.csl.sri.com/users/neumann/chats4.html`.
10	National Computer Security Center	Department of Defense Trusted Computer System Evaluation Criteria (TCSEC). National Computer Security Center, December 1985. DOD-5200.28-STD, Orange Book.
11	Yacoub and Ammar	"A Methodology for Architectural-Level Reliability Risk Analysis," Sherif M. Yacoub and Hany H. Ammar. IEEE Transactions on Software Engineering, 2001.
12	Wang, Hassan, Abdelmoez, Goseva-Popstojanova, and Ammar	"Architectural Level Risk Assessment Tool Based on UML Specifications," Wang, Hassan, Abdelmoez, Goseva-Popstojanova, and Ammar. Proceedings, icse 2003. Available online at `http://csdl2.computer.org/comp/proceedings/icse/2003/1877/00/18770808.pdf`.
13	Moore and Ellison	"Trustworthy Refinement Through Intrusion-Aware Design," Andrew Moore and Robert Ellision. Carnegie Mellon University Technical Report CMU/SEI-2003-TR-002. March 2003. Available online at `http://www.sei.cmu.edu/pub/documents/03.reports/pdf/03tr002.pdf`.
14	Richardson	From *Prospects for Inexpensive Space Transportation*, by R.C. Richardson. Presented at SPS'91 1991. Available online at `http://www.spacefuturejournal.com/archive/prospects_for_inexpensive_space_transportation.shtml`.

Chapter 5

1	Greene	From "Chapter One: Kevin Mitnick's story" by Thomas Greene, in *The Register*, 13 January 2003. Available online at `http://www.theregister.co.uk/2003/01/13/chapter_one_kevin_mitnicks_story/`.
2	Bisbey and Hollingworth	"Protection Analysis: Final Report," Richard Bisbey and Dennis Hollingworth, Information Sciences Institute, University of Southern California, May 1978. [An original taxonomy.]
3	Hoglund and McGraw	*Exploiting Software*, Greg Hoglund and Gary McGraw. Pearson Education, 2004.
4	Abbott	R. P. Abbott et al., "Security Analysis and Enhancements of Computer Operating Systems," Report NBSIR 76-1041, Institute for Computer Science and Technology, National Bureau of Standards, 1976.

5	Aslam	"A Taxonomy of Security Faults in the Unix Operating System," T. Aslam. Thesis, Purdue University, 1995. Available online at `ftp://ftp.cerias.purdue.edu/pub/papers/taimur-aslam/aslam-taxonomy-msthesis.ps.Z`.
6	Bisbey and Hollingsworth	"Protection Analysis Project Final Report," R. Bisbey and D. Hollingsworth, Information Sciences Institute, University of Southern California, Marina Del Rey, CA, 1978.
7	Bishop	M. Bishop, "A Taxonomy of UNIX System and Network Vulnerabilities," Technical Report CSE-95-10, Purdue University, May 1995. Available online at `http://downloads.securityfocus.com/library/ucd-ecs-95-10.pdf`.
8	Du and Mathur	"Categorization of Software Errors that Led to Security Breaches," Wenliang Du and Aditya P. Mathur. In Proceeding of the 21st National Information Systems Security Conference (NISSC'98), Crystal City, VA, 1998.
9	Jiwnani and Zelkowitz	"Maintaining Software with a Security Perspective," Kanta Jiwnani and Marvin Zelkowitz. Available online at `http://www.cs.umd.edu/~kanta/icsm2002.pdf`.
10	Landwehr, Bull, McDermott, and Choi	"A Taxonomy of Computer Program Security Flaws, with Examples," C.E. Landwehr, A.R. Bull, J.P. McDermott, and W.S. Choi. Naval Research Laboratory, 1994. Available online at `http://chacs.nrl.navy.mil/publications/CHACS/1994/1994landwehr-acmcs.pdf`.
11	Marick	"A survey of software fault surveys," Brian Marick. Technical Report UIUCDCS-R-90-1651, University of Illinois at Urbana-Champaign, December 1990. Available online at `http://web.mit.edu/afs/dev.mit.edu/software/gct/docs/fault.ps`.
12	Spafford	"Common System Vulnerabilities," Eugene H. Spafford. Proceedings of the Workshop on Future Directions in Computer Misuse and Anomaly Detection, pp. 34-37, 1992.
13	National Computer Security Center	"A Guide to Understanding Covert Channel Analysis of Trusted Systems," National Computer Security Center, November 1993. Available online at `http://www.radium.ncsc.mil/tpep/library/rainbow/NCSC-TG-030.pdf`.
14	Syverson	"A Taxonomy of Replay Attacks," Paul Syverson, Naval Research Laboratory. Available online at `http://chacs.nrl.navy.mil/publications/CHACS/1994/1994syverson-foundations.pdf`.
15	Jiwnani and Zelkowitz	"Maintaining Software with a Security Perspective," Kanta Jiwnani and Marvin Zelkowitz. Available online at `http://www.cs.umd.edu/~kanta/icsm2002.pdf`.
16	ibid.	

17	Felten, Balfanz, Dean, and Wallach	"Web Spoofing: An Internet Con Game," Felten, Balfanz, Dean, and Wallach. Technical Report 540-96 (revised February 1997), Department of Computer Science, Princeton University. Available online at `http://www.cs.princeton.edu/sip/pub/spoofing.pdf`.
18	Jiwnani and Zelkowitz	"Maintaining Software with a Security Perspective," Kanta Jiwnani and Marvin Zelkowitz. Available online at `http://www.cs.umd.edu/~kanta/icsm2002.pdf`.
19	Ford and Baum	*Secure Electronic Commerce*, Ford and Baum. Prentice Hall PTR; 2nd Edition (December, 2000).
20	ibid.	
21	Bishop	*Computer Security: Art and Science*, Matt Bishop. Boston: Addison-Wesley, 2003.
22	Karger	"Limiting the Damage Potential of Discretionary Trojan Horses," Paul A. Karger. Proceedings of the 1987 Symposium on Security and Privacy, IEEE Computer Society, Oakland, California, April 1987, pp. 32-37.
23	Markoff and Bergman	"Internet Attack Called Broad and Long Lasting by Investigators" by John Markoff and Lowell Bergman, *The New York Times*, May 10, 2005.
24	Landwehr, Bull, McDermott, and Choi	"A Taxonomy of Computer Program Security Flaws, with Examples," C.E. Landwehr, A.R. Bull, J.P. McDermott, and W.S. Choi. Naval Research Laboratory, 1994. Available online at `http://chacs.nrl.navy.mil/publications/CHACS/1994/1994landwehr-acmcs.pdf`.
25		"Jail for 'Robin Hoods' who cost Microsoft millions," *The New York Times*, May 7, 2005.

Chapter 6

1	Gambetta	*Trust: Making and Breaking Cooperative Relations*, Gambetta, D (Reprint ed.). Basil Blackwell: Oxford, 1990.
2	Abdul-Rahman	"The PGP Trust Model," Alfarez Abdul-Rahman. Department of Computer Science, University College, London. Available online at `http://www.cs.ucl.ac.uk/staff/F.AbdulRahman/docs/pgptrust.html`.
3	Abdul-Rahman and Hailes	"A Distributed Trust Model," Alfarez Abdul-Rahman and Stephen Hailes. Department of Computer Science, University College, London. Available online at `http://www.cs.ucl.ac.uk/staff/F.AbdulRahman/docs/hicss33.ps`.
4	Douceur	"The Sybil Attack," John R. Douceur. Lecture Notes In Computer Science; Vol. 2429: 2002. Available online at `http://www.cs.rice.edu/Conferences/IPTPS02/101.pdf`.

5	Ford and Baum	*Secure Electronic Commerce*, Ford and Baum. Prentice Hall PTR; 2nd Edition (December, 2000).
6	Soloman and Flores	*Building Trust: In Business, Politics, Relationships, and Life*, Robert C. Solomon and Fernando Flores. Oxford University Press, 2001.
7	Wang and Vassileva	"Trust and Reputation Model in Peer-to-Peer Networks," Yao Wang and Julita Vassileva. University of Saskatchewan. Available online at http://www.cs.usask.ca/grads/yaw181/publications/120_wang_y.pdf.
8	Grandison and Sloman	"Specifying and Analysing Trust for Internet Applications," Tyrone Grandison and Morris Sloman. Department of Computing, Imperial College. Presented at 2nd IFIP Conference on e-Commerce, e-Business, e-Government, I3e2002, Lisbon, Portugal, October 2002. Available online at http://www.doc.ic.ac.uk/~mss/Papers/I3e2002.pdf.
9	Abdul-Rahman and Hailes	"Supporting Trust in Virtual Communities," Alfarez Abdul-Rahman and Stephen Hailes. University College, London. Available online at http://www.cs.ucl.ac.uk/staff/F.AbdulRahman/docs/hicss33.pdf.
10	Yang, Brown, Newmarch, and Lewis	"A Trusted W3 Model: Transitivity of Trust in a Heterogeneous Web Environment," Yang, Brown, Newmarch, and Lewis. Presented at AusWeb99. Available online at http://ausweb.scu.edu.au/aw99/papers/yang/paper.html.
11	Isode	"Directory Based Trust—A New Model for E-Commerce," Isode. Whitepaper (http://www.isode.com). Available online at http://www.isode.com/whitepapers/ic-6110.html.
12	Abdul-Rahman and Hailes	"A Distributed Trust Model," Alfarez Abdul-Rahman and Stephen Hailes. Department of Computer Science, University College, London. Available online at http://www.cs.ucl.ac.uk/staff/F.AbdulRahman/docs/hicss33.ps.
13	Abdul-Rahman	"The PGP Trust Model," Alfarez Abdul-Rahman. Department of Computer Science, University College, London. Available online at http://www.cs.ucl.ac.uk/staff/F.AbdulRahman/docs/pgptrust.html.
14	Chen and Yeager	"Poblano: A Distributed Trust Model for Peer-to-Peer Networks," Rita Chen and William Yeager, Sun Microsystems. Available online at http://www.jxta.org/docs/trust.pdf.
15	Khambatti, Dasgupta, and Ryu	"A Role-Based Trust Model for Peer-to-Peer Communities and Dynamic Coalitions," Mujtaba Khambatti, Partha Dasgupta, and Kyung Dong Ryu. Available online at http://www.public.asu.edu/~mujtaba/Articles%20and%20Papers/khambattim_communities.pdf.

16	Popescue, Crispo, Tanenbaum, and Zeeman	"Expressing Security Policies for Distributed Objects Applications," Bogdan C. Popescu, Bruno Crispo, Andrew S. Tanenbaum, and Maas Zeeman. Presented at the 11th Cambridge International Workshop on Security Protocols, April 2003. Available online at `http://www.cs.vu.nl/~bpopescu/papers/sec_prot03/sec_prot03.pdf`.
17	Clifford	"Networking in The Solar Trust Model: Determining Optimal Trust Paths in a Decentralized Trust Network," Michael Clifford, The Aerospace Corporation. Presented at the Annual Computer Security Applications Conference, 2002. Available online at `http://www.acsac.org/2002/papers/9.pdf`.
18	Blume and Appel	"Hierarchical Modularity," Matthias Blume and Andrew Appel. To appear in ACM Transactions on Programming Languages and Systems, 1999. Available online at `http://people.cs.uchicago.edu/~blume/papers/cm-TOPLAS.ps.gz`.

Chapter 7

1	Lampson	"Computer Security in the Real World," Butler Lampson. Presented at the Annual Computer Security and Applications Conference in 2001.
2	Lampson	"A Note on the Confinement Problem," Butler W. Lampson. Xerox Palo Alto Research Center. This note originally appeared in *Communications of the ACM*, Vol. 16, No. 10. Available online at `http://www.cis.upenn.edu/~KeyKOS/Confinement.html`.
3	Bishop	*Computer Security: Art and Science*, Matt Bishop. Boston: Addison-Wesley, 2003.
4	Parnas	"On the criteria to be used in decomposing systems into modules," D.L. Parnas. Communications of the Association of Computing Machinery, December 1972.
5	Anderson	"Computer Security Technology Planning Study," James P. Anderson. ESD-TR-73-51, ESD/AFSC, Hanscom AFB, Bedford, MA 01731 (October 1972) [NTIS AD-758 206]. Available online at `http://csrc.nist.gov/publications/history/ande72.pdf`.
6	Welch and Stroud	"Using Reflection as a Mechanism for Enforcing Security Policies in Mobile Code," Ian Welch and Robert J. Stroud. Available online at `http://citeseer.ist.psu.edu/cache/papers/cs/20224/http:zSzzSzwww.cs.ncl.ac.ukzSzresearchzSztrszSzpaperszSz705.pdf/welch00using.pdf`.
7	Anderson	"Computer Security Technology Planning Study," James P. Anderson. ESD-TR-73-51, ESD/AFSC, Hanscom AFB, Bedford, MA 01731 (October 1972) [NTIS AD-758 206]. Available online at `http://csrc.nist.gov/publications/history/ande72.pdf`.

8	Goldstein	"The Gateway Security Model in the Java Commerce Client," Theodore Goldstein, Chief Java Commerce Officer, Sun Microsystems Laboratories, JavaSoft. Available online at `http://java.sun.com/products/commerce/docs/whitepapers/security/gateway.pdf`.
9	Dennis and Van Horn	"Programming Semantics for Multiprogrammed Computations," Dennis and Van Horn. MIT, 1963. See `http://www.lcs.mit.edu/publications/pubs/pdf/MIT-LCS-TR-023.pdf`.
10	Balfanz, Dean, and Felten	"Extensible Security Architectures for Java," Wallach, Balfanz, Dean, and Felten. Princeton, published at the 16th Symposium on Operating Systems Principles (Saint-Malo, France), October 1997. Available online at `http://www.cs.princeton.edu/sip/pub/sosp97`. pdf.
11	Daley and Neumann	"A General-Purpose File System for Secondary Storage," R.C. Daley and P.G. Neumann. AFIPS Conference Proceedings, Fall Joint Computer Conference, Spartan Books, November 1965, 213-229. Available online at `http://www.multicians.org/fjcc4.html`.
12	Sun	The Java 2 Platform Security Architecture. Available online at `http://java.sun.com/j2se/1.5.0/docs/guide/security/spec/security-spec.doc.html`.
13	Vassilis Prevelakis and Diomidis Spinellis	"Sandboxing Applications," Vassilis Prevelakis and Diomidis Spinellis. Presented at FreeNIX'01. Available online at `http://www.prevelakis.net/FreeNIX01/sandbox32final.html`.
14	NIST	Role-Based Access Control, a NIST effort. See `http://csrc.nist.gov/ rbac/`.
15	Karger	"Limiting the Damage Potential of Discretionary Trojan Horses," Paul A. Karger. Proceedings of the 1987 Symposium on Security and Privacy, IEEE Computer Society, Oakland, California, April 1987, pp. 32-37.
16	Bhimani	"PKI: Be Careful What You Wish For," Anish Bhimani. *Information Security*, May 2000. Available online at `http://www.infosecuritymag.com/articles/may00/cover.shtml`.
17	Black Hat	"Java and Virtual Machine Security Vulnerabilities and Their Exploitation Techniques." LSD-PlaNet, Poland, Black Hat Briefings, Singapore, Oct. 3-4, 2002.
18	Sindre and Opdahl	"Templates for Misuse Case Description," Guttorm Sindre and Andreas L. Opdahl. Presented at the Seventh International Workshop on Requirements Engineering: Foundation for Software Quality, June 4-5, 2001, Interlaken, Switzerland. Available online at `http://www.ifi.uib.no/conf/refsq2001/papers/p25.pdf`.
19	Neumann	CHATS (Neumann). See `http://www.csl.sri.com/users/neumann/chats4.html`.

20	Lilien	"Developing Pervasive Trust Paradigm for Authentication and Authorization," presentation by Dr. Leszek Lilien, Center for Education and Research in Information Assurance and Security (CERIAS), and Department of Computer Sciences, Purdue University, October 2003. Available online at `http://www.cs.purdue.edu/homes/llilien/perv_trust.pdf`.
21	Neumann	CHATS (Neumann). See `http://www.csl.sri.com/users/neumann/chats4.html`.
22	Neumann, Boyer, Feiertag, Levitt, and Robinson	"A Provably Secure Operating System: The System, Its Applications, and Proofs," 2nd Edition (Report CSL-116), P. G. Neumann, R.S. Boyer, R.J. Feiertag, K.N. Levitt, and L. Robinson. Computer Science Laboratory, SRI International, Menlo Park, California, 1980. Available online at `http://www.csl.sri.com/neumann/psos/psos80.pdf`.
23	Neumann	CHATS (Neumann). See `http://www.csl.sri.com/users/neumann/chats4.html`.
24	Ford and Baum	*Secure Electronic Commerce*, Ford and Baum. Prentice Hall PTR; 2nd edition (December, 2000).
25	Saltzer and Schroeder	"The protection of information in computer systems," J.H. Saltzer and M.D. Schroeder. Proceedings of the IEEE, 63(9):1278-1308, September 1975.
26	Common Criteria	Common Criteria is described at `http://www.commoncriteria-portal.org/`. See also `http://csrc.nist.gov/cc`.
27	Boudra	"Report on rules of system composition: Principles of secure system design," P. Boudra, Jr. Technical report, National Security Agency, Information Systems Security Organization, Office of Infosec Systems Engineering, I9 Technical Report 1-93, Library No. S-240, 330, March 1993. For Official Use Only.
28	Howard	*Writing Secure Code*, Michael Howard. Microsoft Press, 2002.
29	Howard, Pincus, and Wing	"Measuring Relative Attack Services," M. Howard, J. Pincus, and J.M. Wing. Proceedings of Workshop on Advanced Developments in Software and Systems Security, Taipai, December 2003.
30	Saltzer and Schroeder	"The protection of information in computer systems," J.H. Saltzer and M.D. Schroeder. Proceedings of the IEEE, 63(9):1278-1308, September 1975.
31	Neumann	CHATS (Neumann). See `http://www.csl.sri.com/users/neumann/chats4.html`.
32	Howard	*Writing Secure Code*, Michael Howard. Microsoft Press, 2002.
33	Karger and Schell	"Thirty Years Later: Lessons from the Multics Security Evaluation," Paul Karger and Roger Schell. Paper presented at the 18th Annual Computer Security Applications Conference, December 9-13, 2002. Available online at `http://www.acsac.org/2002/papers/classic-multics.pdf`.

34	Howard	*Writing Secure Code*, Michael Howard. Microsoft Press, 2002.
35	Stross	"Whoops! We Seem to Have Misplaced Your Identity," May 8, 2005, *The New York Times*, by Randall Stross.
36	Sun	Security Code Guidelines, by Sun Microsystems. Available online at `http://www.java.sun.com/security/seccodeguide.html`.
37	Ford and Baum	*Secure Electronic Commerce*, Ford and Baum. Prentice Hall PTR; 2nd Edition (December, 2000).
38	Neumann	CHATS (Neumann). See `http://www.csl.sri.com/users/neumann/chats4.html`.
39	National Computer Security Center	Department of Defense Trusted Computer System Evaluation Criteria (TCSEC). National Computer Security Center, December 1985. DOD-5200.28-STD, Orange Book.
40	Farias	"A security aspect for Java," Andrés Farias. Master thesis. Ecole des Mines de Nantes. September 1999.
41	Ford and Baum	*Secure Electronic Commerce*, Ford and Baum. Prentice Hall PTR; 2nd Edition (December, 2000).
42	Howard	*Writing Secure Code*, Michael Howard. Microsoft Press, 2002.
43	Karger	"Limiting the Damage Potential of Discretionary Trojan Horses," Paul A. Karger. Proceedings of the 1987 Symposium on Security and Privacy, IEEE Computer Society, Oakland, California, April 1987, pp. 32-37.
44	Howard	*Writing Secure Code*, Michael Howard. Microsoft Press, 2002.
45	ibid.	
46	Swiderski and Snyder	*Threat Modeling*, Frank Swiderski and Window Snyder. Microsoft, 2004.
47	Pietrek	"A Crash Course on the Depths of Win32™ Structured Exception Handling," Matt Pietrek. *Microsoft Systems Journal*, January 1997. Available online at `http://www.microsoft.com/msj/0197/exception/exception.aspx`.
48	Chen, Wagner, and Dean	"Setuid Demystified," Hao Chen, David Wagner, and Drew Dean. Presented at the 11th USENIX Security Symposium, 2002. Available online at `http://www.cs.berkeley.edu/~daw/papers/setuid-usenix02.pdf`.
49	Howard	*Writing Secure Code*, Michael Howard. Microsoft Press, 2002.
50	Hoglund and McGraw	*Exploiting Software*, Greg Hoglund and Gary McGraw. Pearson Education, 2004.
51	Sun	Security Code Guidelines, by Sun Microsystems. Available online at `http://www.java.sun.com/security/seccodeguide.html`.
52	Yacoub and Ammar	*Pattern-Oriented Analysis and Design*, Yacoub and Ammar. Addison-Wesley, 2004.

53	VHDL	http://www.vhdl.org/.
54	Grand, Mark	*Patterns in Java* (Volumes 1 and 2), Mark Grand. John Wiley & Sons, 1998. See http://www.mindspring.com/~mgrand/.
55	Bauer, Appel, and Felten	"Mechanisms for Secure Modular Programming in Java," Bauer, Appel, and Felten. Princeton. TR-603-99. July 1999. Available online at http://ncstrl.cs.princeton.edu/expand.php3?id=TR-603-99.
56	Aldrich, Jonathan	"Using Types to Enforce Architectural Structure," Jonathan Aldrich. PhD Thesis, University of Washington, 2003. See also http://archjava.fluid.cs.cmu.edu/.
57	ibid.	
58	Neumann	CHATS (Neumann). See http://www.csl.sri.com/users/neumann/chats4.html.
59	Neumann, Boyer, Feiertag, Levitt, and Robinson	"A Provably Secure Operating System: The System, Its Applications, and Proofs," 2nd Edition (Report CSL-116), P. G. Neumann, R.S. Boyer, R.J. Feiertag, K.N. Levitt, and L. Robinson. Computer Science Laboratory, SRI International, Menlo Park, California, 1980. Available online at http://www.csl.sri.com/neumann/psos/psos80.pdf.
60	Fowler	*Patterns of Enterprise Application Architecture*, Martin Fowler. Addison-Wesley Professional, November 2002. For Martin's pattern catalog, see http://www.martinfowler.com/eaaCatalog.
61	Neumann, Boyer, Feiertag, Levitt, and Robinson	"A Provably Secure Operating System: The System, Its Applications, and Proofs," 2nd Edition (Report CSL-116), P. G. Neumann, R.S. Boyer, R.J. Feiertag, K.N. Levitt, and L. Robinson. Computer Science Laboratory, SRI International, Menlo Park, California, 1980. Available online at http://www.csl.sri.com/neumann/psos/psos80.pdf.
62	National Computer Security Center	"The Computer Security Contribution to the Composition Discussion," C TECHNICAL REPORT 32-92, June 1992. Available online at http://www.radium.ncsc.mil/tpep/library/rainbow/C-TR-32-92.pdf.
63	Grand, Mark	*Patterns in Java* (Volumes 1 and 2), Mark Grand. John Wiley & Sons, 1998. See http://www.mindspring.com/~mgrand/.
64	Brodsky, Farkas, and Jajodia	"Secure Databases: Constraints, Inference Channels and Monitoring Disclosures," Brodsky, Farkas, and Jajodia. IEEE Transactions on Knowledge and Data Engineering archive Volume 12, Issue 6 (November 2000). Available online at http://portal.acm.org/citation.cfm?id=628099.
65	Bhimani	"PKI: Be Careful What You Wish For," Anish Bhimani. *Information Security*, May 2000. Available online at http://www.infosecuritymag.com/articles/may00/cover.shtml.

66	Sun	"Permissions in the Java 2 Standard Edition Development Kit (JDK)." Available online at http://java.sun.com/j2se/1.5.0/docs/guide/security/permissions.html.
67	Microsoft	Microsoft Developer Network. See http://msdn.microsoft.com.
68	Gamma, Helm, Johnson, and Vlissides	*Design Patterns*, Erich Gamma, Richard Helm, Ralph Johnson, and John Vlissides. Addison-Wesley Professional, January 1995. See http://hillside.net/patterns/DPBook/DPBook.html.
69	Bauer, Appel, and Felten	"Mechanisms for Secure Modular Programming in Java," Bauer, Appel, and Felten. Princeton. TR-603-99. July 1999. Available online at http://ncstrl.cs.princeton.edu/expand.php3?id=TR-603-99.
70	Howard	*Writing Secure Code*, Michael Howard. Microsoft Press, 2002.
71	Swiderski and Snyder	*Threat Modeling*, Frank Swiderski and Window Snyder. Microsoft, 2004.
72	Hoglund and McGraw	*Exploiting Software*, Greg Hoglund and Gary McGraw. Pearson Education, 2004.
73	Sewell and Vitek	"Secure Composition of Untrusted Code: Wrappers and Causality Types," Peter Sewell and Jan Vitek. PCSFW: Proceedings of The 13th Computer Security Foundations Workshop, 2000. Available online at http://citeseer.ist.psu.edu/rd/0%2C322079%2C1%2C0.25%2CDownload/http://citeseer.ist.psu.edu/cache/papers/cs/15654/http:zSzzSzwww.cs.purdue.eduzSzhomeszSzjvzSzpubzSzcsfw00.pdf/sewell00-secure.pdf.
74	Sewell and Vitek	"Secure Composition Of Insecure Components," Peter Sewell and Jan Vitek. Proceedings of the 12th IEEE Computer Security Foundations Workshop (CSFW-12), Mordano, Italy, June 1999. Available online at http://citeseer.ist.psu.edu/rd/8123637%2C145966%2C1%2C0.25%2CDownload/http://citeseer.ist.psu.edu/cache/papers/cs/4695/http:zSzzSzcui.unige.chzSzOSGzSzpeoplezSzjvitekzSzPublicationszSzsl.pdf/sewell99secure.pdf.
75	Howard	*Writing Secure Code*, Michael Howard. Microsoft Press, 2002.
76	National Computer Security Center	"A Guide To Understanding Covert Channel Analysis Of Trusted Systems," National Computer Security Center, November 1993. Available online at http://www.radium.ncsc.mil/tpep/library/rainbow/NCSC-TG-030.pdf.
77	Sun	Security Code Guidelines, by Sun Microsystems. Available online at http://www.java.sun.com/security/seccodeguide.html.
78	Karger and Schell	"Thirty Years Later: Lessons from the Multics Security Evaluation," Paul Karger and Roger Schell. Paper presented at the 18th Annual Computer Security Applications Conference, December 9-13, 2002. Available online at http://www.acsac.org/2002/papers/classic-multics.pdf.

Chapter 8

1	Bell and La Padula	"Secure Computer System: Unified Exposition and Multics Interpretation," Bell and La Padula. MITRE technical report #2997, March 1976. Available online at `http://seclab.cs.ucdavis.edu/projects/history/papers/bell76.pdf`.
2	Golm, Felser, Wawersich, and Kleinöder	"A Java Operating System as the Foundation of a Secure Network Operating System," Michael Golm, Meik Felser, Christian Wawersich, and Jürgen Kleinöder. Department of Computer Sciences 4, Distributed Systems and Operating Systems. August 2002.
3	Whitmore, Bensoussan, Green, Hunt, Robziar, and Stern	"Design for MULTICS Security Enhancements," J. Whitmore, A. Bensoussan, P. Green, D. Hunt, A. Robziar, and J. Stern. ESD-TR-74-176, ESD/AFSC, Hanscom AFB, Bedford, MA 01731 (December 1973). Available online at `http://csrc.nist.gov/publications/history/whit74.pdf`.
4	Karger and Schell	"Thirty Years Later: Lessons from the Multics Security Evaluation," Paul Karger and Roger Schell. Paper presented at the 18th Annual Computer Security Applications Conference, December 9-13, 2002. Available online at `http://www.acsac.org/2002/papers/classic-multics.pdf`.
5	Schwartz	"The Insecurity of Computer Security," John Schwartz. *The New York Times*, December 1, 2002.
6	Thurrot	"AOL Employee Sells 93 Million Email Addresses," Paul Thurrott. *Windows IT Pro*, June 24, 2004. See `http://www.winnetmag.com/Article/ArticleID/43079/43079.html`.
7		"Call centre theft may bust India's BPO boom," rediff.com, April 08, 2005. Available online at `http://www.rediff.com/money/2005/apr/08bpo.htm`.
8	Kuhn	"Mutual Exclusion of Roles as a Means of Implementing Separation of Duty in Role-Based Access Control Systems," D. Richard Kuhn. National Institute of Standards and Technology, Gaithersburg, Maryland 20899. `http://hissa.ncsl.nist.gov/rbac/rickwkshp2.ps`
9	National Computer Security Center	"Guide to Understanding Trusted Facility Management," National Computer Security Center. June 1989. NCSC-TG-015. Available online at http://www.radium.ncsc.mil/tpep/library/rainbow/NCSC-TG-015.pdf.
10	Bishop	*Computer Security: Art and Science*, Matt Bishop. Boston: Addison-Wesley, 2003.

Chapter 9

1	Poulsen	"Hacker breaches T-Mobile systems, reads US Secret Service email," by Kevin Poulsen, SecurityFocus. Published in The Register, 12th January 2005. Available online at `http://www.theregister.co.uk/2005/01/12/hacker_penetrates_t-mobile/`.
2	Howard	*Writing Secure Code*, Michael Howard. Microsoft Press, 2002.
3	Ford and Baum	*Secure Electronic Commerce*, Ford and Baum. Prentice Hall PTR; 2nd Edition (December, 2000).

Chapter 10

1	Howard	*Writing Secure Code*, Michael Howard. Microsoft Press, 2002.
2	Ford and Baum	*Secure Electronic Commerce*, Ford and Baum. Prentice Hall PTR; 2nd Edition (December, 2000).
3	Howard	*Writing Secure Code*, Michael Howard. Microsoft Press, 2002.
4	Sirer, Grimm, Gregory, and Bershad	"Design and Implementation of a Distributed Virtual Machine for Networked Computers," Gün Sirer, Grimm, Gregory, and Bershad. University of Washington, Department of Computer Science and Engineering. Presented at the 17th ACM Symposium on Operating System Principles (SOSP'99). Published as Operating Systems Review 34(5):202-216, December 1999. Available online at `http://www.cs.cornell.edu/People/egs/kimera/papers/kimera-sosp99.pdf`.
5	Saltzer and Schroeder	"The protection of information in computer systems," J.H. Saltzer and M.D. Schroeder. Proceedings of the IEEE, 63(9):1278-1308, September 1975.

Chapter 11

1	Gamma, Helm, Johnson, and Vlissides	*Design Patterns*, Erich Gamma, Richard Helm, Ralph Johnson, and John Vlissides. Addison-Wesley Professional, January 1995. See `http://hillside.net/patterns/DPBook/DPBook.html`.
2	Nikander, Pekka	Pekka Nikander's GOF pattern diagrams: `http://www.tml.hut.fi/~pnr/Tik-76.278/gof/html/`.
3	Gamma, Helm, Johnson, and Vlissides	*Design Patterns*, Erich Gamma, Richard Helm, Ralph Johnson, and John Vlissides. Addison-Wesley Professional, 1995. See `http://hillside.net/patterns/DPBook/DPBook.html`.
4	Nikander, Pekka	Pekka Nikander's GOF pattern diagrams: `http://www.tml.hut.fi/~pnr/Tik-76.278/gof/html/`.

5	Fowler	*Patterns of Enterprise Application Architecture*, Martin Fowler. Addison-Wesley Professional, November 2002. For Martin's pattern catalog, see `http://www.martinfowler.com/eaaCatalog`.
6	Sun	"Core J2EE Patterns: Best Practices and Design Strategies." See `http://java.sun.com/blueprints/corej2eepatterns`.
7	Gamma, Helm, Johnson, and Vlissides	*Design Patterns*, Erich Gamma, Richard Helm, Ralph Johnson, and John Vlissides. Addison-Wesley Professional, January 1995. See `http://hillside.net/patterns/DPBook/DPBook.html`.
8	ibid.	
9	ibid.	
10	ibid.	
11	Gabrilovich	"Destruction-Managed Singleton: A Compound Pattern for Reliable Deallocation of Singletons," Evgeniy Gabrilovich. *C++ Report*, ADTmag.com (originally from JOOP). See `http://www.adtmag.com/joop/crarticle.asp?ID=325`.
12	Levine, Gill, and Schmidt	"Object Lifetime Manager—A Complementary Pattern for Controlling Object Creation and Destruction," D.L. Levine, C.D. Gill, and D.C. Schmidt. *C++ Report*, vol. 12, Jan. 2000.
13	Gamma, Helm, Johnson, and Vlissides	*Design Patterns*, Erich Gamma, Richard Helm, Ralph Johnson, and John Vlissides. Addison-Wesley Professional, January 1995. See `http://hillside.net/patterns/DPBook/DPBook.html`.
14	ibid.	
15	Gabrilovich	"Destruction-Managed Singleton: A Compound Pattern for Reliable Deallocation of Singletons," Evgeniy Gabrilovich. *C++ Report*, ADTmag.com (originally from JOOP). See `http://www.adtmag.com/joop/crarticle.asp?ID=325`.
16	Levine, Gill, and Schmidt	"Object Lifetime Manager—A Complementary Pattern for Controlling Object Creation and Destruction," D.L. Levine, C.D. Gill, and D.C. Schmidt. *C++ Report*, vol. 12, Jan. 2000.
17	Wirfs-Brock	*Designing Object-Oriented Software*, Rebecca Wirfs-Brock et al. Prentice Hall, 1990.
18	Wirfs-Brock and McKean	*Object Design: Roles, Responsibilities, and Collaborations*, Wirfs-Brock and McKean. Addison-Wesley, 2002.
19	Eiffel Software	"Building bug-free O-O software: An introduction to Design by Contract™." See `http://www.eiffel.com/doc/manuals/technology/contract/`.
20	Meyer	*Object-Oriented Software Construction*, 2nd Edition, Bertrand Meyer. Prentice Hall, 1997. (re. design by contract)
21	ibid.	

Chapter 12

1	Gray and Reuter	*Transaction Processing: Concepts and Techniques*, Jim Gray and Andreas Reuter. Morgan Kaufmann Publishers, Inc., 1993. See also `http://www.research.microsoft.com/~gray/WICS_99_TP/`.
2	Lea	"Concurrent Programming in Java," Doug Lea. 2000. See `http://gee.cs.oswego.edu/dl/cpj/`.
3	Grand, Mark	*Patterns in Java* (Volumes 1 and 2), Mark Grand. John Wiley & Sons, 1998. See `http://www.mindspring.com/~mgrand/`.
4	Silberschatz, Galvin, and Gagne	*Operating System Concepts with Java*. John Wiley and Sons, 2004.
5	Lea	"Concurrent Programming in Java," Doug Lea. 2000. See `http://gee.cs.oswego.edu/dl/cpj/`.
6	Gordon College	Gordon College CS322 Web site. See `http://www.cs.gordon.edu/courses/cs322/lectures/concurrency5.html`.
7	Schmidt	"Monitor Object: An Object Behavioral Pattern for Concurrent Programming," Douglas C. Schmidt. Department of Computer Science, Washington University, St. Louis. See `http://www.cs.wustl.edu/~schmidt/PDF/monitor.pdf`.
8	Douglas C. Schmidt	"Strategized Locking, Thread-safe Decorator, and Scoped Locking: Patterns and Idioms for Simplifying Multi-threaded C++ Components." C++ Report, SIGS, Vol. 11, No. 9, September, 1999.
9	Laurence Livermore National Labs	Laurence Livermore National Labs Posix Threads Programming online tutorial. See `http://www.llnl.gov/computing/tutorials/workshops/workshop/pthreads/MAIN.html`.
10	Lea	"Concurrent Programming in Java," Doug Lea. 2000. See `http://gee.cs.oswego.edu/dl/cpj/`.
11	Lea	Doug Lea's concurrency utilities. Threads, JSR 166: Concurrency Utilities (`http://www.jcp.org/en/jsr/detail?id=166`). Now package java.util.concurrent.
12	Schmidt	"Patterns for Concurrent, Parallel, and Distributed Systems (Web page)," Douglas C. Schmidt. Department of Computer Science, Washington University, St. Louis. See `http://www.cs.wustl.edu/~schmidt/patterns-ace.html`.
13	Lavender and Schmidt	"Active Object: An Object Behavioral Pattern for Concurrent Programming," R. Greg Lavender and Douglas C. Schmidt. See `http://www.cs.wustl.edu/~schmidt/PDF/Act-Obj.pdf`.
14	Grand, Mark	*Patterns in Java* (Volumes 1 and 2), Mark Grand. John Wiley & Sons, 1998. See `http://www.mindspring.com/~mgrand/`.
15	Grand, Mark	*Java Enterprise Design Patterns*, Mark Grand. John Wiley & Sons, 2001. See `http://www.mindspring.com/~mgrand/`.

Chapter 13

1 Gray and Reuter — *Transaction Processing: Concepts and Techniques*, Jim Gray and Andreas Reuter. Morgan Kaufmann Publishers, Inc., 1993. See also `http://www.research.microsoft.com/~gray/WICS_99_TP/`.

2 OMG — OMG CORBA Transaction Service (OTS) specification. See `http://www.omg.org/technology/documents/formal/transaction_service.htm`.

3 Sun — Java Transaction Service (JTS). See `http://java.sun.com/products/ jts/`.

4 Trowbridge — "Integration Patterns," David Trowbridge, et al. Microsoft, 2004. Available online at `http://msdn.microsoft.com/library/default.asp?url=/library/en-us/dnpag/html/intpatt.asp`.

5 Sun — "Core J2EE Patterns: Best Practices and Design Strategies." See `http://java.sun.com/blueprints/corej2eepatterns`.

6 Grand, Mark — *Java Enterprise Design Patterns*, Mark Grand. John Wiley & Sons, 2001. See `http://www.mindspring.com/~mgrand/`.

7 Gray and Reuter — *Transaction Processing: Concepts and Techniques*, Jim Gray and Andreas Reuter. Morgan Kaufmann Publishers, Inc., 1993. See also `http://www.research.microsoft.com/~gray/WICS_99_TP/`.

8 Fowler — *Patterns of Enterprise Application Architecture*, Martin Fowler. Addison-Wesley Professional, November 2002. For Martin's pattern catalog, see `http://www.martinfowler.com/eaaCatalog`.

9 Grand, Mark — *Java Enterprise Design Patterns*, Mark Grand. John Wiley & Sons, 2001. See `http://www.mindspring.com/~mgrand/`.

10 Gray and Reuter — *Transaction Processing: Concepts and Techniques*, Jim Gray and Andreas Reuter. Morgan Kaufmann Publishers, Inc., 1993. See also `http://www.research.microsoft.com/~gray/WICS_99_TP/`.

11 Fowler — *Patterns of Enterprise Application Architecture*, Martin Fowler. Addison-Wesley Professional, November 2002. For Martin's pattern catalog, see `http://www.martinfowler.com/eaaCatalog`

12 ibid.

13 Sun — "Core J2EE Patterns: Best Practices and Design Strategies." See `http://java.sun.com/blueprints/corej2eepatterns`.

14 Fowler — *Patterns of Enterprise Application Architecture*, Martin Fowler. Addison-Wesley Professional, November 2002. For Martin's pattern catalog, see `http://www.martinfowler.com/eaaCatalog`.

15 Trowbridge — "Integration Patterns," David Trowbridge, et al. Microsoft, 2004. Available online at `http://msdn.microsoft.com/library/default.asp?url=/ library/en-us/dnpag/html/intpatt.asp`.

16 ibid.

17	Fowler	*Patterns of Enterprise Application Architecture*, Martin Fowler. Addison-Wesley Professional, November 2002. For Martin's pattern catalog, see `http://www.martinfowler.com/eaaCatalog`.
18	Grand, Mark	*Java Enterprise Design Patterns*, Mark Grand. John Wiley & Sons, 2001. See `http://www.mindspring.com/~mgrand/`.
19	ibid.	
20	Gamma, Helm, Johnson, and Vlissides	*Design Patterns*. Addison Wesley Professional, January 1995. See `http://hillside.net/patterns/DPBook/DPBook.html`.
21	Fowler	*Patterns of Enterprise Application Architecture*, Martin Fowler. Addison-Wesley Professional, November 2002. For Martin's pattern catalog, see `http://www.martinfowler.com/eaaCatalog`.
22	Schmidt, Douglas C.	"Strategized Locking, Thread-safe Decorator, and Scoped Locking: Patterns and Idioms for Simplifying Multi-threaded C++ Components." C++ Report, SIGS, Vol. 11, No. 9, September, 1999.
23	Fowler	*Patterns of Enterprise Application Architecture*, Martin Fowler. Addison-Wesley Professional, November 2002. For Martin's pattern catalog, see `http://www.martinfowler.com/eaaCatalog`.
24	Sun	Sun Java Blueprints. Available online at `http://java.sun.com/blueprints/patterns/catalog.html`.
25	Sun	Sun Core J2EE Blueprints. Available online at `http://java.sun.com/blueprints/corej2eepatterns/Patterns/`.
26	Meyer	*Object-Oriented Software Construction*, 2nd Edition, Bertrand Meyer. Prentice Hall, 1997. (re. design by contract)
27	Dustin	*Effective Software Testing*, Elfriede Dustin. Pearson Education, 2003.

Chapter 14

1	Teale	"Data Patterns," Philip Teale, et al. Microsoft, 2003. Available online at `http://msdn.microsoft.com/architecture/patterns/default.aspx? pull=/library/en-us/dnpatterns/html/dp.asp`.
2	Grand, Mark	*Patterns in Java* (Volumes 1 and 2), Mark Grand. John Wiley & Sons, 1998. See `http://www.mindspring.com/~mgrand/`.
3	Chappel	*Enterprise Service Bus*, David Chappell. O'Reilly, 2004.
4		`http://www.cse.ogi.edu/class/cse515/lectures/DistributedFS.pdf`.
5		`http://www.scs.cs.nyu.edu/V22.0480-005/notes/l16.pdf`.

Chapter 15

1	Hohpe and Woolf	Enterprise Integration Patterns: Designing, Building, and Deploying Messaging Solutions, Hohpe and Woolf. Addison-Wesley, 2004.
2	OMG	Object Management Group (OMG) CORBA™/IIOP™ Specification, available online at `http://www.omg.org/technology/documents/formal/corba_iiop.htm`.
3	Chappel	*Enterprise Service Bus*, David Chappell. O'Reilly, 2004.
4	Fielding	"Architectural Styles and the Design of Network-based Software Architectures," Dissertation, Roy Thomas Fielding. University of California, Irvine, 2000. Available online at `http://www.ics.uci.edu/~fielding/pubs/dissertation/top.htm`.
5		"Trying to make Web services make sense," c|Net News.com, June 22, 2004. Available online at `http://news.com.com/Trying+to+make+Web+services+make+sense/2100-7345_3-5242747.html?tag=nefd.lede`.

Chapter 16

1	Grand, Mark	*Java Enterprise Design Patterns*, Mark Grand. John Wiley & Sons, 2001. See `http://www.mindspring.com/~mgrand/`.
2	Cohen	*Java Testing and Design*, Frank Cohen. Pearson Education, 2004. ISBN: 0131421891. See `http://www.pushtotest.com/Docs/javatestanddesign.html`.

Chapter 17

1	National Computer Security Center	"A Guide to Understanding Design Documentation in Trusted Systems," 6 October 1988. Available online at `http://www.radium.ncsc.mil/tpep/library/rainbow/NCSC-TG-007.pdf`.
2	Meyer	*Object-Oriented Software Construction*, 2nd Edition, Bertrand Meyer. Prentice Hall, 1997. (re. design by contract)
3	Belady and Lehman	"A model of large program development," Belady and Lehman. *IBM Systems Journal*, 1976, vol. 15, no. 3., pp. 225 ff. Available online at `http://www.research.ibm.com/journal/sj/153/ibmsj1503E.pdf`.
4	Meyer	*Object-Oriented Software Construction*, 2nd Edition, Bertrand Meyer. Prentice Hall, 1997. (re. design by contract)
5	Fowler	*Patterns of Enterprise Application Architecture*, Martin Fowler. Addison-Wesley Professional, November 2002. For Martin's pattern catalog, see `http://www.martinfowler.com/eaaCatalog`.

Chapter 18

1	Ferreira	"Explicit Representation of Exception Handling in the Development of Dependable Component Based Systems," Ferreira, Rubira, and de Lemos. Sixth IEEE International Symposium on High Assurance Systems Engineering, 2001.
2	Meyer	*Object-Oriented Software Construction*, 2nd Edition, Bertrand Meyer. Prentice Hall, 1997. (re. design by contract)
3	Cohen	*Java Testing and Design*, Frank Cohen. Pearson Education, 2004. ISBN: 0131421891. See `http://www.pushtotest.com/Docs/javatestanddesign.html`.
4	Pietrek	"A Crash Course on the Depths of Win32™ Structured Exception Handling,"Matt Pietrek. *Microsoft Systems Journal*, January 1997. Available online at `http://www.microsoft.com/msj/0197/exception/exception.aspx`.
5	Gleick	"A Bug and a Crash" by James Gleick, published in *The New York Times* but available online at `http://www.around.com/ariane.html`.
6		See for example "NASA: Human error caused loss of Mars orbiter orbiter," CNN.com, November 10, 1999, at `http://www.cnn.com/TECH/space/9911/10/orbiter.03/`.
7	Schmidt	"Thread-Specific Storage for C/C++: An Object Behavioral Pattern for Accessing Per-Thread State Efficiently," Douglas C. Schmidt, Nat Pryce, and Timothy H. Harrison. Published in the 4th annual Pattern Languages of Programming conference held in Allerton Park, Illinois, September 1997. See `http://www.cs.wustl.edu/~schmidt/PDF/TSS-pattern.pdf`.
8	Cohen	*Java Testing and Design*, Frank Cohen. Pearson Education, 2004. ISBN: 0131421891. See `http://www.pushtotest.com/Docs/javatestanddesign.html`.
9	Karygiannis	"Network Security Testing Using Mobile Agents," T. Karygiannis. National Institute of Standards and Technology. See `http://csrc.nist.gov/mobilesecurity/Publications/Agents_PAAM98.pdf`.
10	Nwana	"Software Agents: An Overview," Hyacinth S. Nwana. Intelligent Systems Research, Advanced Applications & Technology Department, BT Laboratories, Martlesham Heath, Ipswich, Suffolk, IP5 7RE, U.K. Published in *Knowledge Engineering Review*, Vol. 11, No 3, pp.1-40, September 1996, Cambridge University Press. See `http://www.sce.carleton.ca/netmanage/docs/AgentsOverview/ao.html`.

Chapter 19

1	Musa	*Software Reliability Engineering: More Reliable Software Faster and Cheaper*, 2nd Edition, John D. Musa. ISBN 1-4184-9387-2. Printed on demand. See `http://members.aol.com/JohnDMusa/book.htm`.
2	Howard	*Writing Secure Code*, Michael Howard. Microsoft Press, 2002.
3	Neumann	CHATS (Neumann). See `http://www.csl.sri.com/users/neumann/chats4.html`.
4	Viega and McGraw	Viega and McGraw. *Building Secure Software*. Addison-Wesley Professional, September 2001.
5	Anderson	*Security Engineering: A Guide to Building Dependable Distributed Systems*, Ross J. Anderson.
6	Viega	"Why Application Security Is The New Business Imperative—and How to Achieve It." Whitepaper by John Viega, Secure Software. Available online at `http://www.securesoftware.com/resources/whitepapers/appsec.pdf`.
7	Microsoft	*Improving Web Application Security: Threats and Countermeasures*, Microsoft Corporation. Chapter 2.
8	CERT	OCTAVE. See `http://www.cert.org/octave/`.
9	Dolbec and Shepard	"A Component Based Software Reliability Model," Jean Dolbec, Terry Shepard. 1995. See `http://citeseer.ist.psu.edu/dolbec95component.html`.
10	Musa, Iannino, and Okumoto	*Software Reliability: Measurement, Prediction, Application*, J.D. Musa, A. Iannino and K. Okumoto. McGraw-Hill, 1987.
11	Levitt, Neumann, and Robinson	"The SRI Hierarchical Development Methodology (HDM) and its Application to the Development of Secure Software," K. Levitt, P. Neumann and L. Robinson. National Bureau of Standards, Computer Science and Technology. July 1980.
12	Agile Manifesto	Agile Software Development home page, `http://agilemanifesto.org/`.
13		"The Agile Journey: Adopting XP in a Large Financial Services Organization," Proceedings, XP2005. Available online at `http://www.digitalfocus.com/research/`.
14	Levitt, Neumann, and Robinson	"The SRI Hierarchical Development Methodology (HDM) and its Application to the Development of Secure Software," K. Levitt, P. Neumann, and L. Robinson. National Bureau of Standards, Computer Science and Technology. July 1980.
15	Wallace and Ippolito	"A Framework for the Development and Assurance of High Integrity Software," Wallace and Ippolito. December 1994. Available online at `http://hissa.nist.gov/publications/sp223/`.

16	Swiderski and Snyder	*Threat Modeling*, Frank Swiderski and Window Snyder. Microsoft, 2004.
17	Stavely	Stavely, Allan. Toward Zero-Defect Programming, 1999,
18	Neumann	CHATS (Neumann). See `http://www.csl.sri.com/users/neumann/chats4.html`.
19	Musa	*Software Reliability Engineering: More Reliable Software Faster and Cheaper*, 2nd Edition, John D. Musa. ISBN 1-4184-9387-2. Printed on demand. See `http://members.aol.com/JohnDMusa/book.htm`.
20	Neumann	CHATS (Neumann). See `http://www.csl.sri.com/users/neumann/chats4.html`.
21	Musa	*Software Reliability Engineering: More Reliable Software Faster and Cheaper*, 2nd Edition, John D. Musa. ISBN 1-4184-9387-2. Printed on demand. See `http://members.aol.com/JohnDMusa/book.htm`.

APPENDIX B

FAILURE RESPONSE CONDITIONS AND REQUIREMENTS

This table provides a starting point from which you can write your own list of failure-response requirements. This list is generic, with a slant toward J2EE applications, and should be customized to be specific to the kind of system that you have.

Sample Failure-Response Requirements

Condition or Event	Requirements
A resource call does not return within a reasonable period of time. Examples: • A call to a persistence layer takes longer than it should. • Session bean call does not return within a reasonable period of time.	• The *caller* should timeout and throw an exception indicating a timeout condition. The exception should indicate whether the call can be safely interrupted. • A user interface layer intercepting the timeout exception should give the user the option of interrupting the call. • If the user interrupts the call, an interruption exception should be thrown. That exception should indicate whether the operation completed as a whole or what portions of it completed and whether the operation or any portion of it may be tried again safely. • A client layer intercepting an interruption exception should be able to ascertain whether any portion of the call can be safely retried. If the retry state is uncertain, a user interface client should instruct the user what to do in order to ascertain whether to retry or how to respond to the problem.

Sample Failure-Response Requirements (continued)

Condition or Event	Requirements
A resource request times out. Examples: • A JDBC statement for which a QueryTimeout has been set times out and throws a SQLException. • A Web service request times out.	• A layer intercepting a timeout exception should translate the condition to one that makes sense in the context of the layer. For example, a SQLException containing a timeout code might be translated into a "TimeoutException." • A client layer intercepting a timeout exception should be able to ascertain whether any portion of the call can be safely retried. If the retry state is uncertain, a user interface client should instruct the user what to do in order to ascertain whether to retry or how to respond to the problem.
Resource conflict, in which two or more users attempt to access a resource in a manner that causes one or both requests to fail (not time out). Examples: • Attempts by two different processes to obtain the same file lock. • An attempt by a user to perform an update using data is stale, causing the application to detect that the user update is in conflict with an earlier update (i.e., the "optimistic locking" paradigm). • Attempts by two users to perform operations that are only allowed to be performed by one user at a time, based on application rules.	• The exception that is thrown should indicate which data is affected by the conflict. • A client layer intercepting a resource conflict exception should be able to ascertain whether any portion of the call can be safely retried. If the retry state is uncertain, a user interface client should instruct the user what to do in order to ascertain whether to retry or how to respond to the problem.
Data not yet available, due to delays. Examples: • Required file-based inputs from an external source have not yet arrived. • A precursor process has not yet completed.	• A client layer intercepting this condition should be able to ascertain unambiguously what to do and when or if the request should be retried. If the retry state is uncertain, a user interface client should instruct the user what to do in order to ascertain whether to retry or how to respond to the problem.

Condition or Event	**Requirements**
Long-duration runs or requests. Examples: • A server is run for a long time without being shut down. • A transaction takes a long period of time to complete; for example, more than two hours.	• A client or server should not run out of any kind of resource (memory, threads, connections, etc.) when it is run for a long time without being shut down. • If there is a maximum transaction time, the exception returned to the caller should indicate that the cause of the failure is that the maximum time was exceeded.
Server operating system runs out of a type of resource that it provides. Examples: • TCP ports. • Socket/file descriptors. • Threads. • File system space (including for log files). • Virtual memory.	• Technical support should be notified automatically. To the extent possible, no database data should become corrupt or inconsistent as a result of the failure. • The exception that is returned to the caller should specify the *specific condition (for example, which server resource could not be connected to)* and the *completion status of any transactions that were in progress on the caller's behalf, and any inconsistencies that might have resulted.* • Any exception that is logged should include the full context of the error, including the stack trace, the user identity, and a request or task identity for the purpose of correlating log events across different environments. • A GUI-level client should instruct the user to wait until a message is received indicating that the resource is available again. • When the system becomes usable again, users should receive a message instructing them with what operations they should re-perform. • When the server becomes usable again (perhaps because it was rebooted), clients should not have to be restarted, and should resume working normally.
Server-based resource runs out of a type of resource that it requires. Examples: • Database table space (especially temporary tables). • Java memory. (Note: this is less likely with Java 1.5.) • Java threads.	• Same as previous.

Sample Failure-Response Requirements (continued)

Condition or Event	Requirements
An attempt to establish a connection to or otherwise obtain a resource fails. Examples: • An EJBHome.create() call fails. • A URL.openConnection() call fails. • A DNS call fails. • An attempt to establish a database connection fails. • A file system mount temporarily "disappears" because a machine or router is rebooted. • A remote machine is being rebooted or was shut down. • A utility such as a task management system, a queuing system, or a file transport system is unavailable.	• Same as previous.
A resource connection fails unexpectedly. Examples: • A socket connection times out due to inactivity. • A socket connection times out due to a blocking operation taking longer than the value set for SocketOptions.SO_TIMEOUT. • The other end of a connection is reset. • A remote machine is being rebooted or was shut down.	• Same as previous.
An attempt to locate (resolve) a resource fails. • A host name is not found. • A JNDI lookup of an EJBHome fails. • A database table is not found because it is not in the user's schema.	• Same as previous.

Condition or Event	Requirements
An attempt to locate a name resolution service fails. • A DNS server cannot be found. • An EJB JNDI provider cannot be found. • An RMI Registry cannot be found. • A Web service UDDI registry cannot be found.	• Same as previous.
There is a software version, message version, or protocol version mismatch between two ends of a remote connection or session. Examples: • A class mismatch exception when making or receiving an EJB or RMI call. • An XML message or Web Service invocation fails a schema or DTD validation (at either endpoint).	• Same as above.
There is a protocol usage or internal error of some kind that is not immediately identifiable as a version incompatibility. Examples: • Java serialization error in an RMI or EJB call. • A semantic error within a Web Service message, such that the message is ill-formed based on usage rules that are not encoded in the schema, or no schema is being used. • An unrecognized tag is posted to a servlet.	• Same as previous.

Sample Failure-Response Requirements (continued)

Condition or Event	Requirements
An internal error in a server-based application occurs when making a remote call to the application. Examples: • A Java Web Service throws a RuntimeException or Error. • An EJB call throws a RuntimeException or Error.	• Same as previous.
Any of the above errors, in the context of their occurrence within a server accessed indirectly via the primary server. Examples: • Any of the above kinds of failurc, within a backend application server that is used by the main application server.	• Same as previous.
Application restarts and machine restarts.	• Log files should be preserved across restarts and not be lost or overwritten.
An attempt to authenticate to a resource or to obtain authorization to access the resource fails. Examples: • An attempt to invoke an EJB method fails with an authorization exception. • An attempt to update a database table fails with an authorization exception. • An attempt to access a file fails due to lack of the required access permission.	• All exception information should be logged in a secure manner, and the exception should then be replaced with a generic exception indicating an authentication or authorization failure, as appropriate.
Input validation error.	• Any exception that is returned to the caller should indicate the specific input items that were problematic. If the caller is a user interface, the specific problematic items should be visually indicated. • The intended transaction should not occur.

Condition or Event	Requirements
Deployment of new release of a component. Examples: • A new version of an EJB is deployed, along with an updated client JAR file containing updated remote interfaces. The EJB is used by clients in different parts of the organization. • A new version of a Web Service is deployed, with an updated WSDL definition. The service is used by other applications within the organization and also by applications hosted by partners and customers. • A new version of an embedded Java component, such as a new version of JUnit, is included in a build that is then deployed.	• All deployments of the full system release should be tested for backward compatibility with all supported component versions.

LIST OF DESIGN PRINCIPLES, BY CHAPTER

Name	§	Page
A Trusted Context Should Include a Proven Identity	7.17.2	209
A Trusted Context Should Always Include the Code Context	7.17.3	209
Validate Anything Received from Untrusted Sources	7.17.4	213
Set Session and Credential Scope Appropriately	7.17.6	215
Provide for Timely Revocation of Privileges	7.17.6	216
Propagate Context Accurately or Pessimistically	7.17.7	217
Require Every Execution Context to Have Permission	7.17.8	218
Define Privileged Context Boundaries	7.17.9	219
Tightly Encapsulate Privileged Operations	7.17.10	223
Package Resources of Equal Trust and Equal Capability Requirements Together	7.17.11	225
Do Not Intermix Business Logic with infrastructure or Other Non-Business Logic, Unless the Separation Is Simple and Clear	7.19	231
Application-Specific Dependencies Should Flow Only Toward the Business Model	7.19.1	232
Layers Should Not Be Bypassed	7.19.1	233
Objects Passed to Lower Layers Should Be Expressed in the Types Defined in Those Layers	7.19.1	233
Objects Returned to Higher Layers May Be Translated by Each Layer into Types That Are Meaningful in That Layer	7.19.1	234
A Software Layer Should Define an "Interface" for Use by Upper Layers Only	7.19.1	235
Transfer of Information from One Domain to Another Should Always Be Through an Interface That Considers the Trustworthiness and Authorization of Each Domain	7.19.2	236
Specify Closure	7.20	237
Implement Closure	7.20	237
Clearly Delineate Which Components Share Internal Dependencies	7.20.2	242
Tightly Control Access to Resource References	7.20.3	243
Tightly Scope All Resources	7.20.3	244
Securely Connect to All Resources	7.20.4	244
Prefer to Initiate Connections from a Point of Trust	7.20.4	245
Do Not Make Blind Callbacks	7.20.4	247
Prefer Stateful Protocols	7.20.4	247
Rely on Secure Scoping Mechanisms	7.20.5	248
Securely Identify All Resources	7.20.5	248

Name	§	Page
Canonicalize All Security-Sensitive Names	7.20.5	250
Prefer Static Resource Paths	7.20.5	252
Secure Non-Run-Time Resources	7.20.5	253
Secure Configuration Data	7.20.5	254
Secure Administrative Resources	7.20.5	254
Secure Native Resources	7.20.6	255
Encapsulate Native Resource Access	7.20.6	256
Secure All Caches	7.20.7	256
Erase Sensitive Data Immediately After Use	7.20.7	257
Dispose of Sensitive Data Securely	7.20.7	257
Provide Secure Locations for Failure Artifacts	7.20.7	258
Authorization Should Be a Precondition for Execution of Any and All Business Logic Within a Function or Method	7.21	260
Compartmentalization and Classification		
Segment Data and Resources According to Risk or Sensitivity	8	269
Compartmentalize Roles	8.1.1	274
Enforce Separation of Duties	8.1.1	274
Roles That Grant Access Rights Must Have Those Same Rights	8.1.1	275
Ensure That Traceability Functions Such as Logging and Monitoring Are Independent of Other Application Operation Functions	8.1.1	275
If Two Roles Are Required to Be Independent, Their Communication Channels Should Also Be Independent	8.1.2	276
For Sensitive Operations, Enforce One Action at a Time	8.1.3	277
Delay the Effect of Sensitive Operations	8.1.3	277
Implement Single Sign-On Sparingly	8.1.3	277
Prefer to Employ Different Credentials for Each Role	8.1.3	278
Create Unique Roles or User Identities for Each Server Application, with Only the Permissions That Are Required	8.1.4	278
Provide a Server's Execution Role or User Identity with Exclusive Access to the Resources That the Server Owns	8.1.4	279
Compartmentalize Server Connections	8.1.4	279
Transport and Storage of Secrets		
Transport Sensitive Data Securely	9	282
Do Not Store Unsecured Data in a Secure Location	9	283
Never Store Secrets Insecurely	9	284
Employ Secure Credential Practices	9.2	288

Name	§	Page
Periodically Replace Secrets	9.2	288
Distribute Credentials Securely	9.2.1	290
Employ Multiple Independent Factors or Channels	9.2.1	291
Treat Alternative User Verification Methods as Forms of Authentication	9.2.2	291
Design Considerations for Secure Operation		
Deploy Securely	10.1	294
Provide for Secure Restoration	10.2	297
Do Not Thwart Infrastructure Security Mechanisms	10.3	298
Do Not Secretly "Tunnel"	10.3	300
Run Securely	10.3	301
Log Security-Related Events	10.4	302
Embed Intrusion Detection at Multiple Points	10.4	303
Multiple Independent Means Should Be Used to Contact Responders	10.4	303
Allocate Resource Capacity Based On Trust	10.5	304
When Any System Is Attacked, All Other Systems Should Temporarily Convert to a Highly Safe Reduced Access Mode	10.5	306
Provide Convenient API for Intrusion Response	10.5	307
Provide Fine-Grained Monitoring	10.5	307
Make Sure the User Is Sufficiently Informed	10.6	308
Inform the User of Activity	10.6	309
Educate Users of the Means by Which They Will Be Contacted in an Emergency	10.6	310
Reliably Inform the User of Status	10.6	310
Do Not Design Security-Related Features That Are Onerous to Use	10.6	310
Do Not Assume That Users Will Be Able to Institute Complex Processes or Controls	10.6	311
Require Security Features to Operate Efficiently and Quickly	10.6	312
Carefully Consider the Operational Effects of Inconsistency	10.6	313
Any Unavoidable Deviations from Security-Sensitive Procedures Should Be Fully Traceable	10.6	314
Maintain Awareness of Vulnerabilities in Components	10.7	314
Compositional Integrity		
Clearly Define the Roles and Responsibilities of Each Component	11.3	333
Safely Validate All Inputs to Each Method	11.3	335
Use Specific Argument Types Instead of General-Purpose Types	11.3	336

Name	§	Page
Maintainability		
Maintainable Software Should Document Why Each Action Is Performed	17.1	466
Maintainable Software Should Document Functional Behavior and Requirements as Well as Non-Functional Behavior and Requirements	17.1	467
Document All Exception Conditions That Can Occur	17.1	468
Apply Stringent Quality Criteria to Critical Business Components	17.2	469
See the related security principle, #87.		
Avoid Duplication	17.2	469
See the related security principle, #15.		
Critical Business Rules Should Be Auditable	17.2	469
See the related security principle, #12.		
Minimize the Number, Size, and Complexity of Critical Business Rules	17.2	470
See the related security principle, #111.		
An Application That Has No Verifiable Design Must Be Tested Much More Thoroughly in Order to Provide the Same Level of Reliability	17.2	470
Do Not Weaken Any Assumptions Made by a Superclass	17.3	471
Testing of Maintainable Software Should Be Automated from the Beginning	17.4	472
Maintainable Software Should Employ Stubs for Infrastructure That Is Not Easily Deployed in the Development Environment	17.4	472
Failure Response Design		
Indicate Failure Scope	18.2.1	481
Use Checked Exceptions for All Lifecycle Errors	18.2.1	483
Safely Transform and Compare Types and Values	18.2.1	489
Throw Specific Exceptions—Not Generic Ones	18.2.1	490
Log Only at Predetermined Layer interfaces	18.2.2	491
Time Critical Thread Actions	18.2.3	494
Error Handlers Should Themselves Completely Trap All Errors That Might Prevent Them from Propagating Contextual Information	18.2.4	496
Provide Context to Correlate User Actions with Server Actions	18.2.5	497
Never Discard Exception Information	18.2.6	503
Provide Problem Transparency	18.2.6	504
Map Errors to Problematic Input	18.2.6	505
Provide Management "Aspects" to Exceptions	18.2.6	512
Alert Only Those Who Need to Know	18.2.6	514
Provide User Status and Actionability	18.2.6	515

Name	§	Page
Build with Debug Information, and Deploy Initially with Debug Information—Subject to Security Concerns	18.2.6	516
Display Actual Configuration; Do Not Display Intended Configuration in Lieu of Actual Configuration	18.3	526
An Operator Console Should Monitor and Interpret Application Events, In Order to Assess the Health of an Application	18.3.1	527
Actively Monitor Resource Levels to Prevent Problems Before They Occur	18.3.1	528
An Application Console Should Monitor and interpret Application Events in Order to Assess the Progress of Application Tasks	18.3.2	529
Methodological Considerations		
Ensure That Someone Competent Is Responsible for the Application Architecture	19.2	541
Ensure That All Implied or Assumed Requirements Are Identified	19.2	542
Ensure That Critical Business Rules Are Auditable	19.2	542
Ensure That the Quality-Critical Codebase Is Identified	19.2	543
Ensure That an Architecture Exists That Explains How the Application Will Meet the Assurance Requirements	19.2	544
Ensure the Quality and Faithfulness of Implementation with Respect to the Design	19.2	544
Ensure That Architectural Concepts and Decisions Are Documented and Disseminated	19.2	545
Ensure That Design Is Reviewed by Different Areas of Expertise	19.2	546
Ensure That There Exists Full Configuration Management of All Artifacts	19.2	547
Do Not Use Production Data as a Primary Test Suite	19.5.4	562

APPENDIX D

LIST OF DESIGN PATTERNS, ALPHABETICAL

Name	Category	§	Page
Adding Manageability Aspects to the Exception Base Class	reliability	18.2.6	513
Application-Based Propagation of Client Context	reliability	18.2.5	498
Approval-Based Trust	security	6.1.1	126
Asynchronous Error Handler	reliability	12.2.2	349
Authorization as a Precondition	security	7.21	261
Blocked Registrant	reliability	15.1.1	438
Cooperative Checkout	reliability	13.8	409
Client Tier MVC	reliability	12.2.6	362
Closure of Reusable Components	security	7.20.2	240
Component and Port	security	7.18.1	229
Composite of Pre-Existing Transactions	reliability	13.7.2	400
Concurrency Test Driver	reliability	12.2.8	371
Condition Logging and Problem Notification	reliability	18.2.8	519
Cooperative Process Coordination	reliability	12.2.1	346
Data Identification	reliability	18.2.6	507
Delegating Lifecycle Manager	reliability	11.2.2	332
Discriminating Requester, Specialized Servicer	reliability	12.2.3	353
Dynamic Condition Set	security	7.10	171
Embedded Progress Interpreter	reliability	16.4.2	454

Name	Category	§	Page
Exception Filter	security	7.15.2	189
Extensible Role and Derived Role	security	8.1.1	271
Handling Transaction Timeout	reliability	13.11.2	417
Heartbeat	reliability	16.4.1	452
Implicit Context and Explicit Context	reliability	18.2.5	501
Input Map	reliability	18.2.6	505
Interruptible Thread	reliability	12.2.4	357
Layer Interface	security	7.19.1	235
Layered Transaction	reliability	13.7.3	402
Lifecycle Factory	reliability	11.2.1	327
Local Database Forward Cache with Synchronous Updates	reliability	14.1	428
Monitored Log Writing System	security	7.16.2	198
Multiple-Transaction Request	reliability	13.7.4	404
Optimistic Concurrency Control	reliability	13.3	388
Parameterized Permissions	security	7.8	166
Pessimistic Concurrency Control	reliability	13.3	386
Privileged Context Boundary	security	7.17.9	219
Progress Reporting of Disconnected Resource	reliability	16.4.5	461
Progress Reporting to Client Only	reliability	16.4.5	459
Reference Monitor	security	7.1.1	139
Requester-Responder	reliability	15.1	435
Resource Proxy Gateway	security	7.1.2	140
Role-Based Permissions	security	7.1.6	145
Timer Thread	reliability	12.2.5	360
Transaction Facade	reliability	13.9	411
Using Checked Exceptions for All Lifecycle Errors	reliability	18.2.1	484
Value Object	reliability	11.1.2	321

APPENDIX F

LIST OF ATTACK PATTERNS, BY SECTION

#	Name	§	Page
Related:	**Non-repudiation.**		
17.	Exploit of Incomplete Validation	5.1.17	105
Related:	**Buffer overflow.**		
18.	Exploit of Incomplete Authentication or Authorization	5.1.18	105
19.	Exploit of Exposure of Internal State	5.1.19	105
20.	Exploit of Residual Artifacts	5.1.20	106
Related:	**"Dumpster-diving" or "trashing."**		
21.	Embedded Attack	5.1.21	106
Related:	**Planting. Trojan Horse. Time bomb. Logic bomb.**		
22.	Pattern Matching and Brute Force Guessing	5.1.22	108
Related:	**Exhaustive search.**		
23.	Namespace Attack	5.1.23	108
24.	Weak Link as Gateway	5.1.24	108
25.	Trusted Resource Attack	5.1.25	109
26.	Scope Attack	5.1.26	110
Related:	**Domain errors.**		
	Social Engineering		
27.	Physical Theft	5.2.1	111
28.	Emotional Pressure	5.2.2	112
29.	Haste	5.2.3	113
30.	Reliance on Inadequate Protection	5.2.4	114
31.	Instilling Undeserved Trust	5.2.5	116
32.	Breaking Prior Trust	5.2.6	117
33.	Trusted Resource Attack	5.2.7	118

Index

Symbols

A

B

E

F

G

H

J

K

L

M

X-Y-Z